Lecture Notes
in Business Information Processing   **263**

More information about this series at http://www.springer.com/series/7911

Witold Abramowicz · Rainer Alt
Bogdan Franczyk (Eds.)

Business Information Systems Workshops

BIS 2016 International Workshops
Leipzig, Germany, July 6–8, 2016
Revised Papers

 Springer

Editors
Witold Abramowicz
Poznań University of Economics
   and Business
Poznan
Poland

Rainer Alt
Leipzig University
Leipzig
Germany

Bogdan Franczyk
Leipzig University
Leipzig
Germany

ISSN 1865-1348   ISSN 1865-1356 (electronic)
Lecture Notes in Business Information Processing
ISBN 978-3-319-52463-4   ISBN 978-3-319-52464-1 (eBook)
DOI 10.1007/978-3-319-52464-1

Library of Congress Control Number: 2016963648

Printed on acid-free paper

This Springer imprint is published by Springer Nature
The registered company is Springer International Publishing AG
The registered company address is: Gewerbestrasse 11, 6330 Cham, Switzerland

Preface

During each edition of the BIS Conference we make efforts to provide an opportunity for discussion about up-to-date topics from the area of information systems research. However, there are many topics that deserve particular attention. Thus a number of workshops are co-located with the BIS Conference. Workshops give researchers the possibility to share preliminary ideas and initial experimental results and to discuss research hypotheses from a specific area of interest. BIS Workshops are an ideal place to present research ideas to a well-focused audience.

Six workshops took place during the 19th BIS conference. We were proud to host well-known workshops such as AKTB (eighth edition) and BITA (seventh edition) as well as some fairly new initiatives like DeBASE, iCRM, INCLuDE, and IDEA (second edition). Each workshop focused on a different topic: knowledge-based business information systems (AKTB), challenges and current state of business and IT alignment (BITA), big data ecosystems (DeBASE), innovative aspects of social CRM (iCRM), digital enterprises (IDEA), and integrative analysis and computation (INCLuDE).

Additionally, BIS hosted a Doctoral Consortium. It was organized in a workshop formula, thus the best papers from this event are included in the book. Moreover, all authors had the possibility to discuss their work with a designated mentor.

The workshop authors had the chance to present their results and ideas in front of a well-focused audience; thus the discussion of the scholarly work that was presented constructive and provided the authors with new perspectives and directions for further research. Based on the feedback received, authors had the opportunity to edit the workshop articles for the current publication.

The volume opens with a paper prepared by one of the BIS keynote speakers: Dr. Sebastian Kiebusch.

We would like to express our thanks to everyone who made the BIS 2016 workshops successful. First of all, our workshop chairs, members of the workshop Program Committees, authors of submitted papers, invited speakers, and finally all workshop participants. We cordially invite you to visit the BIS website at http://bis.kie.ue.poznan.pl/ and to join us at future BIS conferences.

July 2016

Witold Abramowicz
Rainer Alt
Bogdan Franczyk

Conference Organization

BIS 2016 was co-organized by the Poznań, University of Economics and Business, Department of Information Systems, and Leipzig University, Information Systems Institute.

Conference General Chairs

Witold Abramowicz   Poznań, University of Economics and Business, Poland
Rainer Alt   Leipzig University, Germany
Bogdan Franczyk   Leipzig University, Germany

BIS Organizing Committee

Christian Franck   Leipzig University, Germany
Barbara Gołębiewska   Poznań University of Economic and Business, Poland
Karen Heyden (Co-chair)   Leipzig University, Germany
Elżbieta Lewańska   Poznań University of Economics and Business, Poland
  (Co-chair)
Włodzimierz Lewoniewski   Poznań University of Economics and Business, Poland
Bartosz Perkowski   Poznań University of Economics and Business, Poland
Wilfried Röder (Co-chair)   Leipzig University, Germany
Milena Stróżyna   Poznań University of Economics and Business, Poland

AKTB 2016 Workshop Chairs' Message

The 8th Workshop on Applications of Knowledge-Based Technologies in Business (AKTB 2016) has become a traditional and integral unit of the BIS conference. This year it discovered Leipzig as a new inspirational location of knowledge exchange continuing the previous successful series of AKTB workshops held in Poznan, Berlin, Vilnius, and Larnaca.

The AKTB 2016 workshop pursued its specific goal of discussing innovative computational solutions validated by experimental research and based on in-depth knowledge of business domains. The application aspect enriches the broad topic area of business information systems pursued by the BIS 2016 conference. The smart data issue highlighted by BIS 2016 set a challenge to researchers and practitioners as well as market analysts for utilizing all types of data available for enterprise decisions. We invited research papers analyzing advanced services for information systems users and proposing innovative solutions for smart business and process modelling.

There were 14 submissions to AKTB 2016. Each research paper was evaluated by three or four independent Program Committee members. The seven highest ranked articles and one invited paper were selected for presentation during the conference. The accepted articles represent research works of 21 authors from 11 institutions located in seven countries.

After the conference, the authors prepared improved versions of their articles by taking into account new insights and remarks that emerged during the discussions of the presentations in the workshop sessions. The revised versions of the articles passed a second stage of reviewing before being included in the conference proceedings.

During the reviewing process, the articles were evaluated by 22 researchers with internationally recognized competence in diverse knowledge areas. The reviews included an in-depth analysis of the submissions and valuable notes for the authors. The high standards followed by the reviewers enabled us to ensure the high quality of the workshop event, excellent presentations, intensive scientific discussions, and added value to the workshop proceedings.

We would like to express our gratitude for the success of AKTB 2016 to all the authors of submitted papers, the members of the Program Committee, the Department of Informatics of Vilnius University (Lithuania), and the Department of Information Systems of the Poznan University of Economics (Poland). We would also like to acknowledge the outstanding efforts of the Organizing Committee for hosting the 19th International BIS Conference.

July 2016

Virgilijus Sakalauskas
Dalia Kriksciuniene

Organization

Chairs

Dalia Kriksciuniene   Vilnius University, Lithuania
Virgilijus Sakalauskas   Vilnius University, Lithuania

Program Committee

Lia Bassa	Foundation for Information Society, Hungary
Tânia Bueno	Instituto de Governo Eletrônico, Brazil
Dumitru Dan Burdescu	Universitatea din Craiova, Romania
Mario Hernandez	University of Las Palmas de Gran Canaria, Spain
Daning Hu	University of Zurich, Switzerland
Ferenc Kiss	Foundation for Information Society, Hungary
Irene Krebs	University of Technology Cottbus, Germany
Dalia Kriksciuniene	Vilnius University, Lithuania
Audrius Lopata	Vilnius University, Lithuania
Saulius Masteika	Vilnius University, Lithuania
Dhrupad Mathur	SPJCM, United Arab Emirates
Elpiniki I. Papageorgiou	Technological Educational Institute of Central Greece
Laima Papreckiene	Kaunas Technological University, Lithuania
Justyna Patalas-Maliszewska	University of Zielona Góra, Poland
Tomas Pitner	Masaryk University, Czech Republik
Jose Raul Romero	University of Córdoba, Spain
Vytautas Rudzionis	Vilnius University, Lithuania
Virgilijus Sakalauskas	Vilnius University, Lithuania
Darijus Strasunskas	NTNU, Norway
María Dolores Suárez	SIANI, Spain
Margaret Tan	Nanyang Technological University, Singapore
Sebastián Ventura	Cordoba University, Spain
Leonard Walletzky	Masaryk University, Czech Republik
Danuta Zakrzewska	Technical University Lodz, Poland

BITA 2016 Workshop Chairs' Message

A contemporary challenge for enterprises is to keep up with the pace of changing business demands imposed on them in different ways. There is today an obvious demand for continuous improvement and alignment in enterprises, but unfortunately many organizations do not have the proper instruments (methods, tools, patterns, best practices etc.) to achieve this. Enterprise modeling, enterprise architecture, and business process management are three areas belonging to traditions where the mission is to improve business practice and business and IT alignment (BITA). BITA is often manifested through the transition of taking an enterprise from one state (AS-IS) into another improved state (TO-BE), i.e., a transformation of the enterprise and its supporting IT into something that is regarded as better. A challenge with BITA is to move beyond a narrow focus on one tradition or technology. There is a need to be aware of and able to deal with a number of dimensions of the enterprise architecture and their relations in order to create alignment. Examples of such dimensions are: organizational structures, strategies, business models, work practices, processes, and IS/IT structures. Among the concepts that deserve special attention in this context is enterprise architecture management (EAM). An effective EAM aligns IT investments with overall business priorities, determines who makes the IT decisions, and assigns accountability for the outcomes. IT governance is also a dimension that traditionally has had a strong impact on BITA. There are ordinarily three governance mechanisms that an enterprise needs to have in place: (1) decision-making structures, (2) alignment process, and (3) formal communications.

This workshop aimed to bring together people who have an interest in BITA. We invited researchers and practitioners from both industry and academia to submit original results of their completed or ongoing projects. We encouraged a broad understanding of the possible approaches to and solutions for BITA, including EAM and IT governance subjects. Specific focus was on practices of business and IT alignment, i.e., we encouraged submission of case studies and experiences papers.

The workshop received 12 submissions, and the Program Committee selected six for presentation at the workshop.

We thank all the members of the Program Committee, the authors, and the local organizers for their efforts and support.

July 2016

Ulf Seigerroth
Kurt Sandkuhl
Julia Kaidalova

Organization

Chairs

Julia Kaidalova	Jönköping University, Sweden
Kurt Sandkuhl	University of Rostock, Germany
Ulf Seigerroth	Jönköping University, Sweden

Program Committee

Jānis Grabis	Riga Technical University, Latvia
Stjin Hoppenbrouwers	HAN University of Applied Sciences, The Netherlands
Christina Keller	Jönköping University, Sweden
Marite Kirikova	Riga Technical University, Latvia
John Krogstie	Norwegian University of Science and Technology, Norway
Birger Lantow	University of Rostock, Germany
Andreas Opdahl	University of Bergen, Norway
Oscar Pastor	Polytechnical University of Valencia, Spain
Anne Persson	University of Skövde, Sweden
Erik Proper	Public Research Centre Henri Tudor, Luxemburg
Andrea Resmini	Jönköping University, Sweden
Nikolay Shilov	SPIIRAS, Russia
Alexander Smirnov	SPIIRAS, Russia
Janis Stirna	Stockholm University, Sweden
Vladimir Tarasov	Jönköping University, Sweden

DeBASE 2016 Workshop Chairs' Message

The notion of big data and its application in driving organizational decision-making has attracted enormous attention over the past few years. As the term itself indicates, big data refers to large volumes of data generated and made available online and in digital media ecosystems. Associated with the notion of big data are aspects such as the diversity of data, the frequency by which they are updated, and the speed at which they grow. Companies are realizing that the data they own and the way they use them can differentiate them from competition, and even provide them with a competitive edge. Thus, today's companies try to collect and process as much data as possible. Big data and business analytics are also challenging existing modes of business and well-established companies. The need to harness the potential of rapidly expanding data volume, velocity, and variety has seen a significant evolution of techniques and technologies for data storage, analysis, and visualization. Yet, there is limited understanding of how organizations need to change to embrace these technological innovations and the business shifts they entail. As big data tools and applications spread, they will inevitably change long-standing ideas about decision-making, management practices, and most importantly competitive strategy formulation. But as with any major change, the challenge of becoming a big-data-driven enterprise can be enormous. Nevertheless, it is a transition that executives need to navigate through, with limited empirical knowledge to guide their decisions.

The purpose of the Workshop on Big Data and Business Analytics Ecosystems was to shed some light on how big data and business analytics tools are reshaping contemporary companies. All of the articles present different facets of how companies can leverage the potential of big data in order to improve their performance and gain a competitive edge. The paper entitled "Do You Write What You Are in Business Communications? Deriving Psychometrics from Enterprise Social Networks" explores the discriminability of psychometrics derived from an automated linguistic analysis within a business setting. With a focus on the sociotechnical aspects of big-data, the paper "A Framework for Describing Big Data Projects" analyzes case studies and identifies challenges linked to these newly defined project characteristics. On a more strategic level, the paper "Social Media and Analytics for Competitive Performance: A Conceptual Research Framework" emphasizes the multiple aspects that should be considered when implementing social media analytics for a sustained competitive advantage, through a theoretically grounded framework. Finally, the paper "Sequential Anomaly Detection Techniques in Business Processes" deals with the issue of analyzing data that stem from business processes and comparing different techniques in terms of their effectiveness.

July 2016

Patrick Mikalef
Ilias O. Pappas
Michail N. Giannakos
John Krogstie
George Lekakos

Organization

Chairs

Michail N. Giannakos   Norwegian University of Science and Technology (NTNU), Norway

John Krogstie   Norwegian University of Science and Technology (NTNU), Norway

George Lekakos   Athens University of Economic and Business, Greece

Patrick Mikalef   Norwegian University of Science and Technology (NTNU), Norway

Ilias O. Pappas   Norwegian University of Science and Technology (NTNU), Norway

Program Committee

Pekka Abrahamsson   Norwegian University of Science and Technology (NTNU), Norway

Damianos Chanjiantoniou   Athens University of Economics and Business, Greece

Remko Helms   Utrecht University, The Netherlands

Letizia Jaccheri   Norwegian University of Science and Technology (NTNU), Norway

Björn Johansson   Lund University, Sweden

Dimitris Karlis   Athens University of Economics and Business, Greece

Nikolaos Korfiatis   University of East Anglia, UK

Panos E. Kourouthanassis   Ionian University, Greece

Benjamin Müller   University of Groningen, The Netherlands

Adamantia Pateli   Ionian University, Greece

Demetrios Sampson   Curtin University, Australia

Frantisek Sudzina   Aalborg University, Denmark

Rogier van de Wetering   Open University of the Netherlands, The Netherlands

Johan Versendaal   HU University of Applied Sciences Utrecht, The Netherlands

iCRM 2016 Workshop Chairs' Message

Businesses are increasingly using social media as interaction channels with their customers. This holds valuable potential: First, interactions are directly between the customer and the company (representative) and, second, interactions may occur in real-time and via mobile devices independent of specific locations. The value is largely determined by not misusing the direct contact for bontransparent data collection and by linking social media activities to business processes, in particular marketing, sales, and service. Integrated social customer relationship management (social CRM) refers to a comprehensive approach that recognizes that integration is not only necessary between the world of social media external to companies and the world of CRM within companies, but also that an aligned perspective on strategies, processes, and information systems is necessary (Alt and Reinhold 2012)[1].

In view of the large volume of data in social media, a variety of information systems based on Web and text mining techniques for identifying relevant social media postings and for extracting basic information (e.g., number of likes, occurrence of keywords in postings, identification of simple sentiments) have become available. However, these tools are insufficient to identify more complex patterns, for example, semantic relationships between actors, profiles, and postings from large, dispersed, and unstructured databases. Advanced techniques, such as semantic business intelligence (SBI; e.g., semantic enrichment and disambiguation of social media data, data warehouses based on the Semantic Web, semantic interoperability) or computational intelligence (CI; e.g. artificial neural networks, Bayesian models, fuzzy systems and evolutionary computing), promise improvements in knowledge discovery and may also enable new usage scenarios (e.g., impact simulation, network analysis, topic development, trend prediction) in domains such as tourism, banking, energy, public sector, publishing, health, logistics, or education.

The First International Workshop on Intelligent Data Analysis in Integrated Social CRM (iCRM 2016) shed some light on the current research efforts targeting the development of innovative tools and methods. It comprised a collection of five papers. First, the paper "Social CRM: Biggest Challenges to Make it Work in the Real World" illustrates some of the CRM processes that may be enriched with data from the social web, and also the challenges that arise on the systems level. Second, the paper "Emotions in Online Reviews to Better Understand Customers' Brand Perception" presents an approach on how companies can assess the emotions that are connected with their brands. Third, the research-in-progress paper "Performance Evaluation of Sentiment Analysis Methods for Brazilian Portuguese", however, indicates that available methods for text analysis need still to be improved and that social CRM managers should currently combine human with machine intelligence for accurate results. The fourth paper titled "Social Media Analytics Using BI and Social Media Tools – Differences and Implication" presents research in progress on how the

---

[1] Alt, R., Reinhold, O., Social Customer Relationship Management (Social CRM) – Application and Technology, in: Business & Information Systems Engineering 4(2012)5, pp. 287–291.

available social media analytic tools and business intelligence tools may be used for social CRM. Finally, the paper "Assessment of Business Benefits for the Operation of a Smart City Energy Management Platform" provides a different perspective on the integration of actors via a smart platform and presents an approach on how business benefits may be identified and measured.

Clearly, the workshop was a community effort and the contribution of all authors as well as Program Committee members is highly appreciated.

July 2016

Rainer Alt
Olaf Reinhold

Organization

Chairs

Rainer Alt   Universität Leipzig, Germany
Olaf Reinhold   Universität Leipzig, Germany

Program Committee

Emílio Arruda   FUMEC University and University of Amazon, Brazil
Sören Auer   University of Bonn, Germany
Nino Carvalho   Fundacao Getulio Vargas and Universidade do Porto, Brazil
Marco Cristo   Federal University of Amazonas, Brazil
Harry Cruz   Social CRM Research Center, Germany
Renato Fileto   Federal University of Santa Catarina, Brazil
Marcia Fontes   University of Amazon and Federal University of Pará, Brazil
Antonio Fernando Lavareda Jacob Jr.   State University of Maranhão and Federal University of Pará, Brazil
Fábio Lobato   Federal University of Pará and Federal University of Western Pará, Brazil
Axel Ngonga   University of Leipzig, Germany
Ádamo Santana   Federal University of Pará, Brazil
Sandra Turchi   Digitalents and Escola Superior de Propaganda e Marketing, Brazil
Matthias Wittwer   University of Leipzig, Germany
Hans Dieter Zimmermann   FHS St. Gallen University of Applied Sciences, Switzerland

IDEA 2016 Workshop Chairs' Message

Digitization is the use of digital technologies for creating innovative digital business models and transforming existing business models and processes. Information is captured and processed without human intervention using digital means. Digitization creates profound changes in the economy and society. Digitization has both business and technological perspectives. Digital business models and processes are essential for many companies to achieve their strategic goals.

Digitization impacts the product, the customer, and the value-creation perspective (Schmidt et al. 2015)[2]. Digitized products are dynamic; their functionality can be extended on the fly by using external services. They are capable of reflecting on their own status and thus morph the selling of physical assets to services. Digitization changes the relationships with the customer significantly. Personal interaction is replaced by self-service and proactive action. The customer interacts with the enterprise using a multitude of implicit touch points provided by the Internet of Things. Digitization fosters new models of value creation such as service-dominant logic (Vargo and Lusch 2004)[3]. Value is also created by platform and network effects.

The goal of the workshop was to identify challenges from digitization for enterprises and organizations and to advance digital enterprise engineering and architecture to cope with these challenges. The workshop allowed us to identify and develop concepts and methods that assist in the engineering and the management of digital enterprise architectures and the software systems supporting them.

To achieve the goals of the workshop, the following research themes were pursued:

- Methods for the design and management of digital enterprises
- Alignment of the enterprise goals and strategies with the digital enterprise architecture
- Digital strategy and governance
- Architectural patterns for value-co-creation, dynamic and servitized products
- Service in digital enterprises
- Business process management in digital enterprises
- Advanced analytics for the support of digital enterprises
- Self-service and automation in digital enterprises
- Customer journeys and relationship management in digital enterprises
- Internet of Things and digital enterprises
- Impact of digitization on society and economy
- Security in digital architectures

---

[2] Schmidt, R., Zimmermann, A., Möhring, M., Nurcan, S., Keller, B., Bär, F.: Digitization - Perspectives for Conceptualization. In: Celesti, A. and Leitner, P. (eds.) Advances in Service-Oriented and Cloud Computing. pp. 263–275. Springer International Publishing, Taormina, Italy (2015).

[3] Vargo, S.L., Lusch, R.F.: Evolving to a new dominant logic for marketing. J. Mark. 68, 1–17 (2004).

We wish to thank all the authors who submitted papers to IDEA 2016 for having shared their work with us, as well as the members of the IDEA 2016 Program Committee, who made a remarkable effort in reviewing the submissions. We also thank the organizers of BIS 2016 for their help with the organization of the event.

July 2016

Selmin Nurcan
Rainer Schmidt
Alfred Zimmermann

Organization

Chairs

Selmin Nurcan	University of Paris 1 Panthéon-Sorbonne, France
Rainer Schmidt	Munich University of Applied Sciences, Germany
Alfred Zimmermann	Reutlingen University, Germany

Program Committee

Said Assar	Institut Mines-Telecom, France
Lars Brehm	Munich University of Applied Science, Germany
Eman El-Sheikh	University of West Florida, USA
Bogdan Franczyk	University of Leipzig, Germany
Robert Hirschfeld	Hasso-Plattner-Institut, Germany
Peter Mandl	Munich University of Applied Sciences, Germany
Michael Möhring	Munich University of Applied Science, Germany
Selmin Nurcan	Université de Paris 1 Panthéon – Sorbonne, France
Gunther Piller	University of Applied Sciences Mainz, Germany
Manfred Reichert	University of Ulm, Germany
Kurt Sandkuhl	University of Rostock, Germany
Rainer Schmidt	Munich University of Applied Sciences, Germany
Christian Schweda	LeanIT42 GmbH, Germany
Samira Si-Said Cherfi	CEDRIC – Conservatoire National des Arts et Métiers, France
Frank Termer	Bitkom e. V., Germany
Gottfried Vossen	ERCIS Münster, Germany
Norman Wilde	University of West Florida, USA
Alfred Zimmermann	Reutlingen University, Germany

INCLuDE 2016 Workshop Chairs' Message

For some time, the improvements in information technologies (IT) have been used in the context of biomedical and ecological systems with the goal of realizing a healthy as well as economically efficient environment. Owing to increased miniaturization and decreased costs of hardware, data are emerging from manifold sources, such as sensors, smart devices, business information systems, or social networks. However, this complex and dynamic flow of data requires advanced methods for extracting, handling, and analyzing meaningful information from the data. While the data generating systems can also be investigated separately, an important aspect is their continuous interaction in larger ecosystems. New paradigms of thought are needed to understand, design, and optimize these high-dimensional, spatio-temporally interacting systems and processes. The content as well as the influence of these relationships is only partly investigated and poses many challenges for innovative concepts, methodologies, models, and IT architectures to use "life data."

The workshop INCLuDE provides the opportunity for interdisciplinary discussions of problems and potential solutions as well as for enabling cooperation among researchers in the fascinating new world of complex life data-determined ecosystems. Among the relevant scientific disciplines are information systems, data science, environmental science, computer science, mathematics, medicine, psychology, philosophy, and business administration. The proceedings of the INCLuDE workshop comprise a total of five papers from teams of various researchers from the disciplines mentioned above. These research-in-progress as well as research contributions focused on the modelling of complex life and ecological processes as well as on various aspects around the integration of complex multimodal and multiscale data. The first paper by Aleithe et al. discusses approaches for IT infrastructures and architectures suitable for the real-time pattern recognition of dynamical biomedical network patterns. The second paper by Schima et al. presents an integrated data model that helps to monitor environmental processes, while the third paper authored by Müller et al. proposes an architecture for big data and cross-domain integration. The integration aspect was also addressed in the paper of Kirsten et al., who explored the perspective of integrating health and environmental data. Finally, Reinhold et al. present an analysis of various solutions to model the customer or patient context, which is a key element for enabling customer or patient orientation.

Overall, the INCLuDE workshop established a valuable platform for presenting and exchanging expert knowledge from various disciplines. We are looking forward to future interdisciplinary research that is necessary to develop promising technologies for exploring, optimizing, and designing complex life data ecosystems.

July 2016

Galina Ivanova
Rainer Alt
Bogdan Franczyk

Organization

Chairs

Rainer Alt	Universität Leipzig, Germany
Peter Dietrich	Helmholtz Center for Environmental Research, Leipzig and Environmental Eberhard Karls University Tübingen, Germany
Bogdan Franczyk	Universität Leipzig, Germany
Galina Ivanova	Universität Leipzig, Germany
Markus Löffler	Leipzig University, Germany

Program Committee

Rainer Alt	Leipzig University, Germany
Jörn Altmann	College of Engineering Seoul National University, South Korea
Peter Dietrich	Helmholtz Center for Environmental Research and Eberhard Karls University Tübingen, Germany
Bogdan Franczyk	Leipzig University, Germany and Wroclaw University of Economics, Poland
Ulrich Hegerl	Leipzig University and German Depression Foundation, Germany
Galina Ivanova	Leipzig University, Germany
Wieland Kiess	Leipzig University, Germany
Stefan Kirn	University of Hohenheim, Germany
Toralf Kirsten	Leipzig University, Germany
Ryszard Kowalczyk	Swinburne University of Technology, Australia
Markus Löffler	Leipzig University, Germany
Tobias Mettler	University of St. Gallen, Switzerland
Hubert Österle	University of St. Gallen, Switzerland
Reinhold Orglmeister	Technische Universität Berlin, Germany
Tilmann Sander-Thömmes	Physikalisch-Technische Bundesanstalt, Germany

Doctoral Consortium Chair's Message

The Doctoral Consortium on Business Information Systems provided a forum where PhD students can share their work and interact with their peers as wells as senior scholars to receive valuable feedback on their work. By creating a collegial and friendly atmosphere, the objective of the consortium was to support PhD students in the effective design, implementation, and communication of their research. In particular, each student was assigned a mentor who provided in-depth private feedback. In addition, the consortium offered opportunities for networking and, through the proceedings, publishing early results. The consortium was open to PhD students from areas concerned with the development, implementation, and application of business information systems, based on innovative ideas and computational intelligence methods. The consortium was not restricted to particular research methods and considered conceptual, theoretical, and empirical research as well as novel applications.

All submissions received were peer reviewed by members of the international Program Committee. In total, we received 17 submissions from four countries. Based on the review reports, we accepted seven dissertation proposals for presentation in the plenary sessions, which amounts to an acceptance rate of 41.2%. Based on the feedback received from the reviews and the consortium, authors submitted revised papers, which then underwent a second round of review. All seven revised papers were accepted for publication in the proceedings at hand.

While the set of dissertation proposals covers a broad range of topics, it is noteworthy that each proposal belongs to design science research in business information systems. Each proposal is concerned with solving an important organizational problem by developing and evaluating a novel IT artifact. Behind this background, the discussions during the consortium focused on research methodology, including problem identification, analysis of prior research/theory, artifact specification, selection of appropriate evaluation methods to demonstrate that the planned artifact will be useful for solving the addressed problem, and communication of research.

July 2016   Jörg Leukel

Organization

Chair

Jörg Leukel   University of Hohenheim, Germany

Program Committee

Witold Abramowicz   Poznań University of Economics and Business, Poland
Rainer Alt   University of Leipzig, Germany
Ricardo Buettner   FOM University of Applied Sciences, Germany
Bogdan Franczyk   University of Leipzig, Germany
Paul Karaenke   Technical University of Munich, Germany
Stefan Kirn   University of Hohenheim, Germany
Karol Kozak   Fraunhofer IWS, Germany
Andre Ludwig   Kühne Logistics University, Germany
Marcus Mueller   University of Hohenheim, Germany
Henk G. Sol   University of Groningen and Delft University
                                 of Technology, The Netherlands
Rainer Unland   University of Duisburg-Essen, Germany

Contents

Keynote Speech

Governmental IT – Challenges in a Federal State Setup
and Possible Solutions... 3
  Sebastian Kiebusch

AKTB Workshop

Exploring the Influence of the Use of an ERP System on Strategy
Development in German and Polish Manufacturing Enterprises:
An Empirical Investigation....................................... 13
  Justyna Patalas-Maliszewska and Irene Krebs

Visual Language and Ontology Based Analysis: Using OWL
for Relation Discovery and Query in 4EM........................ 23
  Birger Lantow, Kurt Sandkuhl, and Michael Fellmann

Targeting Advertising Scenarios for e-Shops Surfers............. 36
  Dalia Kriksciuniene and Virgilijus Sakalauskas

A Proposal of an Academic Library Management System Based
on an RDF Repository... 44
  Loredana Mocean, Vasile Paul Bresfelean, and Mara Hajdu Macelaru

The Paradigm of Relatedness.................................... 57
  László Grad-Gyenge and Peter Filzmoser

Enterprise Model Based UML Interaction Overview Model
Generation Process... 69
  Audrius Lopata, Ilona Veitaite, and Neringa Zemaityte

Speaker Authentication System Based on Voice Biometrics
and Speech Recognition... 79
  Laurynas Dovydaitis, Tomas Rasymas, and Vytautas Rudžionis

Decision Support System for Foreign Exchange Markets........... 85
  Róbert Magyar, František Babič, and Ján Paralič

BITA Workshop

Visual Analytics in Enterprise Architecture Management: A Systematic
Literature Review.. 99
  Dierk Jugel, Kurt Sandkuhl, and Alfred Zimmermann

Modeling Alignment as a Higher Order Nomological Framework   111
    Rogier van de Wetering

Multi-touch Table or Plastic Wall? Design of a Study for the Comparison
of Media in Modeling   123
    Anne Gutschmidt, Kurt Sandkuhl, and Ulrike Borchardt

The Communicative Nature of Information Systems Integration as an
Enabler for Business IT Alignment   136
    Iyad Zikra

From Products to Product-Service Systems: Business and Information
System Changes   148
    Alexander Smirnov, Nikolay Shilov, Andreas Oroszi, Mario Sinko,
    and Thorsten Krebs

Information Quality Framework for the Design and Validation of Data
Flow Within Business Processes - Position Paper   158
    Michael Vaknin and Agata Filipowska

DeBASE Workshop

Do You Write What You Are in Business Communications?
Deriving Psychometrics from Enterprise Social Networks.   171
    Janine Viol Hacker, Alexander Piazza, and Trevor Kelley

A Framework for Describing Big Data Projects   183
    Jeffrey Saltz, Ivan Shamshurin, and Colin Connors

Sequential Anomaly Detection Techniques in Business Processes   196
    Christian Linn and Dirk Werth

Social Media and Analytics for Competitive Performance:
A Conceptual Research Framework   209
    Ilias O. Pappas, Patrick Mikalef, Michail N. Giannakos, John Krogstie,
    and George Lekakos

iCRM Workshop

Social CRM: Biggest Challenges to Make it Work in the Real World   221
    Fábio Lobato, Márcia Pinheiro, Antonio Jacob Jr., Olaf Reinhold,
    and Ádamo Santana

Emotions in Online Reviews to Better Understand Customers'
Brand Perception.   233
    Armin Felbermayr

Performance Evaluation of Sentiment Analysis Methods
for Brazilian Portuguese.................................... 245
    Douglas Cirqueira, Antonio Jacob Jr., Fábio Lobato,
    Adamo Lima de Santana, and Márcia Pinheiro

Social Media Analytics Using Business Intelligence and Social Media
Tools – Differences and Implications.......................... 252
    Matthias Wittwer, Olaf Reinhold, Rainer Alt, Finn Jessen,
    and Richard Stüber

Assessment of Business Benefits for the Operation of a Smart City
Energy Management Platform................................. 260
    Stefan Reichert and Jens Strüker

IDEA Workshop

A Meta-Framework for Efficacious Adaptive Enterprise Architectures...... 273
    Rogier van de Wetering and Rik Bos

Multi-perspective Digitization Architecture for the Internet of Things 289
    Alfred Zimmermann, Rainer Schmidt, Kurt Sandkuhl, Dierk Jugel,
    Justus Bogner, and Michael Möhring

Data-Centered Platforms in Tourism: Advantages and Challenges
for Digital Enterprise Architecture........................... 299
    Barbara Keller, Michael Möhring, Martina Toni, Laura Di Pietro,
    and Rainer Schmidt

Applying the Research on Product-Service Systems to Smart
and Connected Products.................................... 311
    Lars Brehm and Barbara Klein

INCLuDE Workshop

An Architectural Model for High Performance Pattern Matching
in Linked Historical Data.................................. 323
    Michael Aleithe, Ulrich Hegerl, and Galina Ivanova

Research in Progress: Implementation of an Integrated Data Model
for an Improved Monitoring of Environmental Processes 332
    Robert Schima, Tobias Goblirsch, Christoph Salbach, Bogdan Franczyk,
    Michael Aleithe, Jan Bumberger, and Peter Dietrich

Exploring Context from the Consumer Perspective: Insights from eBusiness
and Health Care 340
    Olaf Reinhold, Matthias Wittwer, Rainer Alt, Toralf Kirsten,
    and Wieland Kiess

Research in Progress on Integrating Health and Environmental Data
in Epidemiological Studies.. 347
  Toralf Kirsten, Jan Bumberger, Galina Ivanova, Peter Dietrich,
  Christoph Engel, Markus Loeffler, and Wieland Kiess

Doctoral Consortium

Decision Support Enhancement for Player Substitution in Football:
A Design Science Approach...................................... 357
  Pavlina Kröckel

A Bayesian Network Approach to Assessing the Risk and Reliability
of Maritime Transport 367
  Milena Stróżyna

Development of an Information System Architecture for Online
Surgery Scheduling... 379
  Norman Spangenberg

Towards Automatic Business Networks Identification 389
  Elżbieta Lewańska

Classification of Data Analysis Tasks for Production Environments........ 399
  Sebastian Eckert and Jan Fabian Ehmke

Toward a Configuration Model for User-Oriented Representations
of Analytical Services 408
  Christian Hrach

Improving the Quality of Art Market Data Using Linked Open Data
and Machine Learning... 418
  Dominik Filipiak and Agata Filipowska

Author Index 429

Keynote Speech

Governmental IT – Challenges in a Federal State Setup and Possible Solutions

Sebastian Kiebusch(✉)

Saxon IT Services, Riesaer Str. 7, 01129 Dresden, Germany
Sebastian.Kiebusch@sid.sachsen.de

Abstract. The Saxon IT Services (Staatsbetrieb Sächsische Informatik Dienste - SID) is a public agency and provides IT solutions in a federal organized state. Therefore some restrictions apply. For example, decreasing numbers of employees and an increasing average of age can lead to organizational problems in the long run. This paper gives a short overview on how to respond to new customer requirements from a public agency perspective.

Keywords: Federal state government · Information technology · Data security · Demography · Research · Consolidation

1 Introduction

Germany as a federation is constituted of 16 federal states. The competencies and responsibilities between the federal government and the state governments are defined by law. In their sphere of competence all states are free to create own rules and principles. This includes decisions about the IT infrastructure. Governmental IT is always linked to very specific public service processes. Highly differentiated types of services require an extensive level of know-how to design and maintain the underlying infrastructure and software packages. Since 2008 the Saxon IT Services (Staatsbetrieb Sächsische Informatik Dienste - SID) is the main IT Service Provider for the public administration on the state level in the Free State of Saxony. For ministries and a variety of customers the SID serves as a competent partner for all kinds of IT solutions. Today public agencies are often facing budget constraints as well as decreasing numbers of available employees for an increasing amount of tasks to fulfill. To meet these challenges, the SID has developed a strategy and is now examining the results of the incorporated measures. Section 2 of this paper gives a short outline about the status quo. Section 3 provides an overview about the actions being made to stay competitive in a changing market environment. Section 4 summarizes the lessons learned.

2 Challenges in a Federal State Setup

Status Quo. The Saxon State Ministry Of The Interior is performing the **supervisory control** over the SID as a public institution of Saxony.

W. Abramowicz et al. (Eds.): BIS 2016 Workshops, LNBIP 263, pp. 3–9, 2017.
DOI: 10.1007/978-3-319-52464-1_1

The SID at a glance:

- around 400 employees
- total revenue of 64 Mio. Euro per year
- 4 sites
- 3 data centers at the sites in Dresden, Kamenz and Lichtenwalde

The key working areas of the SID are [8]:

- Development, Implementation, Operation and Maintenance of IT procedures
- Central IT Procurement
- IT Consulting
- Specific IT Security Concepts

Today three data centers are used to provide the different services for the customers. More than 900 square meters combined are available to house the necessary IT systems. Figure 1 shows some of the services hosted by the different data centers.

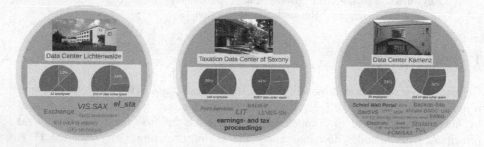

Fig. 1. SID Data centers in Saxony and their main hosting functions

Over the past years SID has developed a rich portfolio of E-Government-Applications. These so called "Basiskomponenten (BaK)" (base components) are individual applications that can be used and integrated by the SID customers. These BaK are for example:

- BaK OpenData - handling of OpenData,
- BaK ZV - processing of online payments;
- BaK ESV - electronic signature and encryption,
- BaK zCMS - central content management system;
- BaK Suchmaschine- search engine

Challenges in the Public Service Sector. Some restrictions cannot be influenced by the SID itself: (1) The fixed structure regarding sites and data centers, (2) A limited flexibility regarding the extent of the workforce and (3) A rigid salary system.

Restriction 1: Fixed Structures

The organization of the SID as a government agency, as it is today, does not allow for flexible adjustments in the structure: Since the foundation in 2008 the SID operates with 4 sites. Changes are only possible with a political consent of the government. Every change process is timely and several different parties are involved. This can cause phases of high uncertainty for the management level in a public agency.

Restriction 2: Limited Capacities in the Workforce

To understand this second restriction a short explanation about the setup of the SID might be helpful. The amount of available full time equivalents is given in 2-year periods and is financially secured at the beginning of each accounting period. During the year a strictly limited number of new staff can only be hired as so called project employees. The costs for these additional employees will then be paid by one or more customers. From a service provider perspective this system is clearly not desirable, because of the very high response time to new customer requirements. Especially in times of high workloads and increasing customer orders it is difficult to have the right amount of workforce in the different teams. Making this situation even more complicated, the SID is forced to reduce the amount of full time equivalents over time due to political decisions to cut costs.

As a serious side effect, the average age of employees is higher than in any other public IT agency at the federal state level in Germany. A comparison to these other public agencies is shown in Fig. 2.

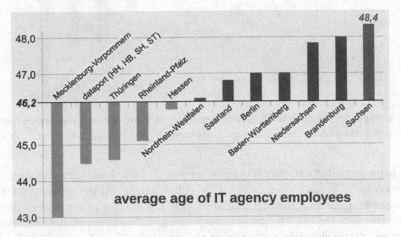

Fig. 2. Average age of IT agency employees, showing Saxony on the right side of the diagram with the highest average age

As you can see, there are significant differences between Mecklenburg-Vorpommern (the bar on the left side) and Saxony (the bar on the right side of the diagram). The goal of having a variety in age in the teams is hard to achieve although it is vital [2, 7] since the demographic change should not be underestimated. The knowledge distribution between young and unexperienced employees and older ones with more experience is an essential factor in securing a continuous service operation [3, 9]. Unfortunately, a planned and accompanied knowledge transfer is not established yet in a formal way. Academic research in business sciences often reveals the potential of a well-designed knowledge management system for the success of a company [4, 5]. This is clearly a field to improve in the public service sector. We will have a second look on this in Sect. 3.

Restriction 3: Rigid Salary System

The average gross income at the SID is the lowest compared to the rest of the German public IT agencies. The salary system in the public service sector is mostly orientated on particular job specifications and job descriptions. Every job description corresponds to a level in the public service salary system depending on needed qualification and tasks to perform by the employee. The differences in average gross income among public service IT institutions in Germany is shown in Fig. 3.

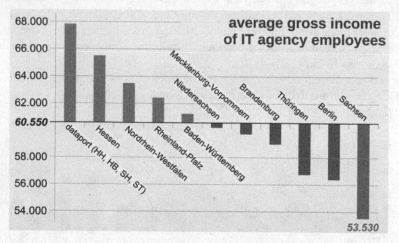

Fig. 3. Average gross income of IT agency employees in Euro, showing Saxony on the right side of the diagram with the lowest average gross income

It is to mention, that monetary incentives for potential employees are very small. The competition for new employees between the public sector and the private sector and between public agencies across the federal states is not in favor of the eastern states of Germany (see also Fig. 3). The possible consequences should not be ignored: Having the right people for the right tasks becomes more and more difficult. Either because important employees are leaving the agency or new employees cannot be found.

Section 3 is going to present some ways, how the SID is handling the given limitations from Sect. 2.

3   How to Stay Competitive as a Public Agency

The SID is going to change over the next years in order to adapt to new customer requirements. The restrictions presented in Sect. 2 are being addressed along this transformation process.

Structure. The consolidation of IT is one of the biggest challenges right now. Beside the 4 main SID sites there are more than 140 further - mostly small - IT sites of state administration. The long-term goal is to concentrate these distributed sites at two redundant locations that comprise a central data center as well as a backup data center making the overall controlling and maintenance much more efficient. Figure 4 represents the intended vision of a new IT organization for the federal state government of Saxony.

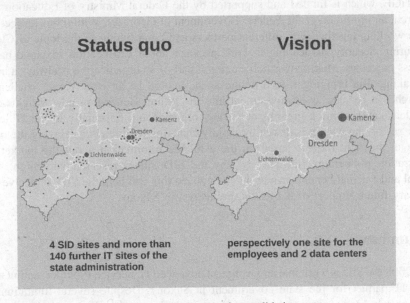

Fig. 4. The process of consolidation

Consolidation helps to make the whole system more robust and cost-efficient. Applying IT-security concepts and measures for a small number of data centers becomes easier and reliable compared to a situation with more than hundred different sites. Once a solid organizational structure is in place, optimization and adaption can follow.

Workforce and Payment. As we have described, decisions about personnel and payment are very limited in public agencies like the SID. Two factors become more and more important: first, keeping the skilled employees in the agency and second, keeping the knowledge [10, 11]. Instruments like project work and job rotation can be used to keep employees motivated [1]. New challenges are often perceived as an integral component in the work life [6]. The SID is cooperating with the Dresden University of Technology to find out more about possible ways to maintain knowledge in a public agency. Through this partnership between an academic institution and a public service institution a few basic findings evolved very quickly: (A) Knowledge management can be an important source for efficiency and innovation and (B) Knowledge management should be implemented much more than it is right now. Furthermore, the SID will position itself as an innovator to get the attention of customers and potential employees. For example, a service called SiDaS (Secure Data Exchange for Saxony) has been established to act as a Dropbox-like alternative for public agencies. Now it is possible for employees to share and exchange documents across different institutions, making the processes easier but still secure. An implemented end-to-end encryption for transport as well as an optional encrypted storage on the servers provides a high level of confidentiality and data security.

Complementing to consolidation and innovation, the SID will also follow the path of research. Beginning in 2014 the SID became a partner in a research project called PREsTiGE, which is funded and supported by the Federal Ministry of Education and Research, an institution of the Federal Government of Germany. Within this project the SID is working together with different partners and contributing to the topic of Cloud Computing Security by leading a work package about certification in cloud-based business processes. Making research a cultural part of an organization is always a huge undertaking. But bringing it to a public agency could be an even bigger challenge. Research can be seen as an investment into the future. Generating new insights and new ideas can become a great asset for any organization. Especially in the IT technology sector, innovation is driven by rapidly changing requirements. Having the right answer at the right time is based on the available information about the market an organization is operating in. That is why the SID values research very high. The internal and external benefits can be significant and this will help the SID to receive the necessary future support of the leading ministries in Saxony.

4 Summary

Since 2008 the SID is a reliable and technical advanced IT Service Provider, acting as a strong IT partner for the state government in Saxony. Despite several limitations a public agency has to incorporate into its strategic decisions, the SID is adapting to new challenges. By following the route of consolidation, innovation and research the SID is corresponding to the high demands the customers have. Some changes are well on their way like the process of consolidation. Others are in a very early research phase like a coherent companywide knowledge management. Being a public agency does not mean, that best practices from business management could not be applied. To the contrary the public service sector should make intensive use of academic findings. Small changes in the processes can lead to higher efficiency, higher motivation for employees and higher customer satisfaction. But these potential changes have to be uncovered first. Hence openness is needed. Connecting to partners in other agencies and getting involved in research projects are first steps to a network of mutual learning. A public agency may be bound to external conditions as shown in Sect. 2. But as long as an organization is willing to learn and improve, every challenge is a chance to grow. This is true for private businesses as well as for a public IT agency.

References

1. Deller, J., et al.: Personalmanagement im demografischen Wandel. Ein Handbuch für den Veränderungsprozess mit Toolbox Demografiemanagement und Altersstrukturanalyse. Springer, Heidelberg (2008)
2. Herrmann, N.: Erfolgspotential älterer Mitarbeiter. Den demografischen Wandel souverän meistern. Carl Hanser Verlag, München (2008)
3. Lehner, M., Gerner, M., Müller, C.: Transfer von Expertenwissen. Ein Leitfaden für Kleinunternehmen. Wissenschaftlicher verlag, Berlin (2005)
4. Mangliers, S.: Strategische Wissensmanagementkompetenz von Unternehmen. Cuvillier Verlag, Göttingen (2009)
5. Mertins, K., Seidel, H.: Wissensmanagement im Mittelstand: Grundlagen, Lösungen, Praxisbeispiele. Springer, Heidelberg (2009)
6. Mohr, H., Wodok, A.: Erfolg mit der Generation 50plus. Ein Leitfaden für kleine und mittlere Betriebe. Deutscher Instituts-Verlag GmbH, Köln (2006)
7. Möller, H., Laschalt, M.: Der ältere Arbeitnehmer – ein vernachlässigtes Subjekt in der Personalentwicklung. Der demographische Wandel und seine Herausforderungen für eine zeitgemäße Mitarbeiterführung. In: Möller, H. (ed.) Beratung in einer ratlosen Arbeitswelt. Vandenhoeck & Ruprecht GmbH & Co. KG, Göttingen (2010)
8. Staatsbetrieb Sächsische Informatik Dienste: Geschäftsbericht 2014. Dresden (2015)
9. Tenckhoff, J.: Alter(n) und Altersakzeptanz in Unternehmen. In: Brauer, K., Clemens, W. (eds.) Zu alt? "Ageism" und Altersdiskriminierung auf Arbeitsmärkten, pp. 231–250. Wiesbaden: VS Verlag für Sozialwissenschaften (2010)
10. Voelpel, S., Leibold, M., Früchtenicht, J.-D.: Herausforderung 50 plus: Konzepte zum Management der Aging Workforce: Die Antwort auf das demographische Dilemma. Wiley-VCH-Verlag GmbH & Co KGaA, Erlangen (2007)
11. Zölch, M., et al.: Fit für den demografischen Wandel? Ergebnisse, Instrumente, Ansätze guter Praxis. Haupt Verlag, Bern (2009)

AKTB Workshop

Exploring the Influence of the Use of an ERP System on Strategy Development in German and Polish Manufacturing Enterprises: An Empirical Investigation

Justyna Patalas-Maliszewska[1](✉) and Irene Krebs[2]

[1] University of Zielona Góra, Zielona Góra, Poland
J.Patalas@iizp.uz.zgora.pl
[2] Brandenburg University of Technology Cottbus-Senftenberg,
Cottbus, Germany
krebs@b-tu.de

Abstract. This article aims to explore the effects of the use of an ERP system in a manufacturing company on strategy development as described by defined factors. The work is based on a survey and data obtained from 62 Polish manufacturing enterprises from the Lubuskie region, and from 23 German manufacturing enterprises from the Brandenburg region, in which the companies were categorised as either "construction" or "automotive" – a total of 85 manufacturing enterprises. Special attention was placed on the description of understanding the usage of an ERP system within a company. Nevertheless, relatively little information has been published that focuses on the post-implementation stages of ERP usage in a manufacturing company. In particular, this study pays attention to the likely consequences and results of the use of defined functionalities of an ERP system by employees. This is followed by a discussion of the results of the empirical studies and of key supporting literature. The summary indicates potential directions for further work.

Keywords: ERP system · Strategy development · Manufacturing enterprises in poland and in germany

1 Introduction

Many manufacturing companies invest in implementing ERP systems and, naturally, expect positive benefits to the firm. According to Al-Mashari (2001) [1], an ERP system is software which integrates information and processes within an organization. Many authors have researched critical success factors (CSF's) in the ERP implementation process [3, 6, 11]. However, we can observe a gap in the research on

This work was supported in part by the project: "Assessing the relationship between business strategy and knowledge transfer in German Manufacturing Enterprises" by the German Academic Exchange Service (DAAD), Bonn, Germany, Nr: 235585.

© Springer International Publishing AG 2017
W. Abramowicz et al. (Eds.): BIS 2016 Workshops, LNBIP 263, pp. 13–22, 2017.
DOI: 10.1007/978-3-319-52464-1_2

post-implementation ERP usage [5, 9]. Gable et al. [7] stated that organizational impact can define an ERP's success. Moreover, DeLone and McLean (2004) [2] observed that in the context of an ERP system, service quality, which includes the uses of the system and intentions of use, is the most significant factor of ERP success.

So, it is very important to adequately understand ERP usage. Based on the definition of Hsieh and Wang [10], this study focuses on ERP use by employees in a company. This is understood as the work by an employee in a defined module of the ERP system. The work must consist of at least 6 h per day, and be related to the department of the company in which the employee works, especially: (1) Production, (2) Customer Relationship Management (CRM), (3) Supply Chain Management (SCM), (4) E-Commerce. Our previous research, conducted in Polish manufacturing companies in the construction and automotive industries, showed that 52% of respondents were able to identify effects which directly resulted from ERP implementation within the company; usually only in the form of processes, which are carried out by the workers using the ERP system.

The analysis in this study also shows the relationships between the ERP system in the defined four areas of employee activity and also the four departments in manufacturing companies, along with factors describing strategy development. In accordance with Porter [20], in this study the following objectives in a company are defined in the context of strategy development (objectives that should be achieved by strategy realization), namely: (1) improving the competencies of staff, (2) increasing sales results, (3) improving process efficiency, (4) improving access to data and information, (5) increasing customer satisfaction, (6) increasing the number of new products and/or services, and (7) improving process quality. The proposed research model (which was based on data gathered from 62 Polish manufacturing companies from the Lubuskie region; and from 23 German manufacturing companies from the Brandenburg region) can enable management staff to analyze the progress of strategy realization over time as measured in the effects of the use of an ERP system.

Also, using survey data from Polish and German manufacturing companies, this study discusses the use of defined functionalities of ERP systems and how they affect the strategy realization processes in the cross-border cooperative region of Lubuskie/Poland-Brandenburg/Germany, in an approach that is expected to contribute to both academics and practitioners.

The remainder of this paper is organized as follows. A number of related works are briefly introduced in the following section. Section 3 presents an overview of the design of a research model and a hypothesis. Section 4 elaborates the research details and a structural model is presented. Closing remarks and a summary are then outlined in the last section.

2 Theoretical Framework and Research Model

Nwankpa and Roumanii (2014) [16] stated that the use of an ERP system can be understood as the exploitation of this system by employees to perform their tasks. Moreover, Nwankpa (2015) [15] pointed out that ERP usage is a consequence of a worker's competence in identifying and applying information technology. Therefore, in this paper, and in accordance with Hsieh and Wang [10] and Moon [14] the use of an ERP system in a manufacturing company is defined as the work by a worker in a defined module of an ERP system: (1) Production, (2) Customer Relationship Management (CRM), (3) Supply Chain Management (SCM) and (4) E-Commerce. Also, the worker must use the functionality of the ERP system that relates to the department of the company in which he/she works, and the time must amount to at least 6 h per day.

A strategy in a company is typically described in a strategic document and is the configuration of a company's resources within a changing environment to achieve an advantage for the firm [12]. According to Johnson and Scholes [12] and our previous research [18–20], the implementation of a business strategy will be completed when a set of defined results is achieved. Moreover, based on previous research [17] this success is defined as the stage at which expected results in companies have been at least 70% achieved after a period of time of five years after the adoption of a strategic

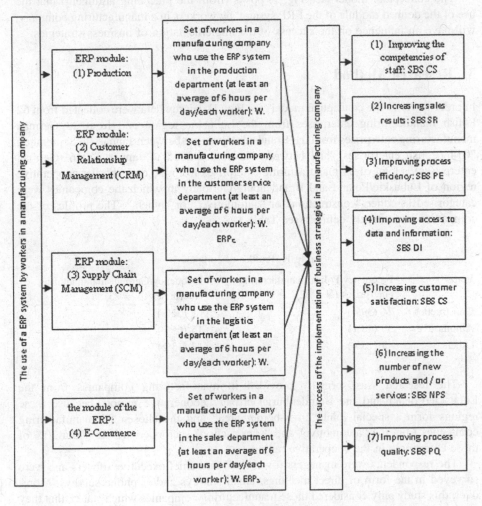

Fig. 1. A conceptual model

document. Therefore, the following factors describing the success of the implementation of business strategies in manufacturing companies are formulated: (1) improving the competencies of staff: SBS CS, (2) increasing sales results: SBS SR, (3) improving process efficiency: SBS PE, (4) improving access to data and information: SBS DI, (5) increasing customer satisfaction: SBS CT, (6) increasing the number of new products and/or services: SBS NPS, and (7) improving process quality: SBS PQ.

Kaplan and Norton [13] stated that relationships in a company exist between financial, customer and internal business processes; and learning and growth opportunities. Ehie and Madsen [4] pointed out that the effect of the use of an ERP system is a form of top management support, so we agree that the use of an ERP by employees in a firm should contribute to the effects of business strategy realization.

According to the results of the literature study, the following research model is defined (Fig. 1):

The conceptual model (see Fig. 1) posits (from the preceding argument) that the use of the defined module of the ERP system, by workers in a manufacturing company, will have an influence on the success of the implementation of business strategies.

3 Research Method

In order to verify the conceptual model (see Fig. 1), survey data were collected from 62 Polish manufacturing enterprises from the Lubuskie region and from 23 German manufacturing enterprises from the Brandenburg region between January to September, 2014 (Polish enterprises), and between November 2015 to January 2016 (German enterprises), a total of 85 manufacturing enterprises from the cross-border cooperative region of Lubuskie/Poland and Brandenburg/Germany in which the companies were categorised as either "construction" or "automotive", or "others". The profiles of the companies were strictly defined (see Table 1):

Table 1. Profiles of companies

Items	Frequency/Polish manufacturing enterprises (N = 62)	Frequency/German manufacturing enterprises (N = 23)
Construction	24 (39%)	5 (22%)
Automotive	30 (48%)	15 (65%)
Others	8 (13%)	3 (13%)

The research was specially provided in manufacturing companies from the Lubuskie/Poland and the Brandenburg/Germany cooperative region, because these regions form a special joint "cross-border area" and the chosen 85 manufacturing companies from the "automotive" and "construction" sectors contribute about 20% of those enterprises in the cooperative region.

The respondents were managers (over 80%) and chief executive officers and were surveyed in the form of direct meetings, email surveys and/or phone surveys. Moreover, this study only considered those manufacturing companies which stated, that they have implemented an ERP system and that their workers use this system to help carry out their work activities.

The list of factors for the description of the use of the defined modules of ERP systems in Polish and German companies was based on feedback surveys and its sources are listed here:

The use of the defined module of the ERP system: the degree to which there is a statement of the use by workers of the defined module of the ERP system of at least an average of 6 h per day/each worker.

- WERP-factor1: I know that, in my organization, the use of the defined module in the ERP system is not very important for the achievement of strategic goals.
- WERP-factor2: I know that, in my organization, the use of the defined module in the ERP system is not important for the achievement of strategic goals.
- WERP-factor3: I know that, in my organization, the use of the defined module in the ERP system is marginally important for the achievement of strategic goals.
- WERP-factor4: I know that, in my organization, the use of the defined module in the ERP system is important for the achievement of strategic goals.
- WERP-factor5: I know that, in my organization, the use of the defined module in the ERP system is very important for the achievement of strategic goals.

Factors that describe the success of the implementation of business strategies in Polish and in a German manufacturing companies were based on feedback surveys and their sources are listed here:

The factors that describe the success of the implementation of business strategies in manufacturing companies: The degree to which the results from the realization of a business strategy in a company has been at least 70% achieved after a period of time of five years from the adoption of the strategy [17].

- SBS-factor1: I do not know that my work activities influence the success of the implementation of business strategies in my company.
- SBS-factor2: I know only a little that my work activities influence the success of the implementation of business strategies in my company.
- SBS-factor3: I know marginally that my work activities influence the success of the implementation of business strategies in my company.
- SBS-factor4: I know well that my work activities influence the success of the implementation of business strategies in my company.
- SBS-factor5: I know very well that my work activities influence the success of the implementation of business strategies in my company.

The surveys used for testing the research model (see Fig. 1) were developed by a five-point defining scale.

4 Research Results

The research model (see Fig. 1) was explored using a correlation approach with Statistica ver. 10.0. The data were carefully examined with respect to linearity, equality of variance and normality. No significant deviations were detected. Table 2 presents descriptive correlations for the main variables.

Table 2. Research results

Construct/Item: WERP-factor1/WERP-factor2/WERP-factor3/WERP-factor4/WERP-factor5 SBS-factor1/SBS-factor2/SBS-factor3/SBS-factor4/SBS-factor5	Correlation	r2	t	p
Polish manufacturing companies: Wi ERP$_P$/SBS CS	0.1368	0.0187	1.0694	0.2892
German manufacturing companies: Wi ERP$_P$/SBS CS	0.1111	0.0124	0.5125	0.6137
Polish manufacturing companies: Wi ERP$_P$/SBS SR	0.2929	0.0858	2.3730	0.0209
German manufacturing companies: Wi ERP$_P$/SBS SR	0.1331	0.0177	0.6153	0.5450
Polish manufacturing companies: Wi ERP$_P$/SBS PE	0.0693	0.0048	0.5381	0.5925
German manufacturing companies: Wi ERP$_P$/SBS PE	−0.2732	0.0746	−1.3013	0.2072
Polish manufacturing companies: Wi ERP$_P$/SBS DI	0.3359	0.1128	2.7619	0.0076
German manufacturing companies: Wi ERP$_P$/SBS DI	−0.2416	0.0584	−1.1412	0.2666
Polish manufacturing companies: Wi ERP$_P$/SBS CT	0.2594	0.0673	2.0808	0.0417
German manufacturing companies: Wi ERP$_P$/SBS CT	0.2875	0.0827	1.3756	0.1835
Polish manufacturing companies: Wi ERP$_P$/SBS NPS	0.3769	0.1421	3.1523	0.0025
German manufacturing companies: Wi ERP$_P$/SBS NPS	0.1476	0.0218	0.6837	0.5017
Polish manufacturing companies: Wi ERP$_P$/SBS PQ	0.2815	0.0793	2.2727	0.0266
German manufacturing companies: Wi ERP$_P$/SBS PQ	−0.0694	0.0048	−0.3187	0.7531
Polish manufacturing companies: Wi ERP$_C$/SBS CS	0.2866	0.0821	2.3171	0.0239
German manufacturing companies: Wi ERP$_C$/SBS CS	0.2061	0.0425	0.9654	0.3453
Polish manufacturing companies: Wi ERP$_C$/SBS SR	0.4144	0.1717	3.5266	0.0008
German manufacturing companies: Wi ERP$_C$/SBS SR	0.1078	0.0116	0.4967	0.6246
Polish manufacturing companies: Wi ERP$_C$/SBS PE	0.3526	0.1243	2.9185	0.0049
German manufacturing companies: Wi ERP$_C$/SBS PE	0.5190	0.2694	2.7826	0.0112
Polish manufacturing companies: Wi ERP$_C$/SBS DI	0.4248	0.1805	3.6350	0.0006
German manufacturing companies: Wi ERP$_C$/SBS DI	0.3615	0.1307	1.7770	0.0901
Polish manufacturing companies: Wi ERP$_C$/SBS CT	0.2182	0.0476	1.7317	0.0885
German manufacturing companies: Wi ERP$_C$/SBS CT	0.0484	0.0023	0.2220	0.8265
Polish manufacturing companies: Wi ERP$_C$/SBS NPS	0.1277	0.0163	0.9973	0.3226
German manufacturing companies: Wi ERP$_C$/SBS NPS	0.1884	0.0355	0.8792	0.3893
Polish manufacturing companies: Wi ERP$_C$/SBS PQ	0.2972	0.0883	2.4114	0.0190
German manufacturing companies: Wi ERP$_C$/SBS PQ	0.4704	0.2213	2.4429	0.0235
Polish manufacturing companies: Wi ERP$_L$/SBS CS	0.1968	0.0387	1.5546	0.1253
German manufacturing companies: Wi ERP$_L$/SBS CS	0.1881	0.0354	0.8777	0.3900
Polish manufacturing companies: Wi ERP$_L$/SBS SR	0.0966	0.0093	0.7515	0.4553
German manufacturing companies: Wi ERP$_L$/SBS SR	0.0881	0.0078	0.4053	0.6893
Polish manufacturing companies: Wi ERP$_L$/SBS PE	0.3692	0.1363	3.0772	0.0031
German manufacturing companies: Wi ERP$_L$/SBS PE	−0.1135	0.0129	−0.5235	0.6061
Polish manufacturing companies: Wi ERP$_L$/SBS DI	0.1611	0.0259	1.2643	0.2110
German manufacturing companies: Wi ERP$_L$/SBS DI	−0.2336	0.0546	−1.1008	0.2834
Polish manufacturing companies: Wi ERP$_L$/SBS CT	0.0018	0.0000	0.0137	0.9891
German manufacturing companies: Wi ERP$_L$/SBS CT	0.1486	0.0221	0.6886	0.4986

(continued)

Table 2. (*continued*)

Construct/Item: WERP-factor1/WERP-factor2/WERP-factor3/WERP-factor4/WERP-factor5 SBS-factor1/SBS-factor2/SBS-factor3/SBS-factor4/SBS-factor5	Correlation	r2	t	p
Polish manufacturing companies: Wi ERP$_L$/SBS NPS	0.3611	0.1304	2.9996	0.0039
German manufacturing companies: Wi ERP$_L$/SBS NPS	0.0131	0.0002	0.0600	0.9527
Polish manufacturing companies: Wi ERP$_L$/SBS PQ	0.3907	0.1527	3.2877	0.0017
German manufacturing companies: Wi ERP$_L$/SBS PQ	0.0378	0.0014	0.1733	0.8641
Polish manufacturing companies: Wi ERP$_S$/SBS CS	0.0622	0.0039	0.4824	0.6312
German manufacturing companies: Wi ERP$_S$/SBS CS	0.1653	0.0273	0.7679	0.4511
Polish manufacturing companies: Wi ERP$_S$/SBS SR	0.0321	0.0010	0.2485	0.8046
German manufacturing companies: Wi ERP$_S$/SBS SR	–0.0698	0.0049	–0.3208	0.7515
Polish manufacturing companies: Wi ERP$_S$/SBS PE	–0.0616	0.0038	–0.4778	0.6345
German manufacturing companies: Wi ERP$_S$/SBS PE	–0.1356	0.0184	–0.6274	0.5372
Polish manufacturing companies: Wi ERP$_S$/SBS DI	0.0279	0.0008	0.2165	0.8294
German manufacturing companies: Wi ERP$_S$/SBS DI	–0.3362	0.1130	–1.6358	0.1168
Polish manufacturing companies: Wi ERP$_S$/SBS CT	–0.1045	0.0109	–0.8138	0.4190
German manufacturing companies: Wi ERP$_S$/SBS CT	0.1239	0.0154	0.5724	0.5732
Polish manufacturing companies: Wi ERP$_S$/SBS NPS	0.1422	0.0202	1.1126	0.2703
German manufacturing companies: Wi ERP$_S$/SBS NPS	–0.0074	0.0001	–0.0339	0.9733
Polish manufacturing companies: Wi ERP$_S$/SBS PQ	0.2997	0.0898	2.4330	0.0180
German manufacturing companies: Wi ERP$_S$/SBS PQ	–0.0704	0.0050	–0.3236	0.7494

In our research results we can match the relationships between the use of an ERP system by workers and the success of the implementation of business strategies in manufacturing companies in German and in Polish companies. In Polish manufacturing companies we can observe many significant relationships between the use of an ERP system by workers and the success of the implementation of business strategies those manufacturing companies:

- workers in a manufacturing company who use an ERP system in the production department (at least an average of 6 h per day/each worker) can positively influence the improvement of access to data and information within a company (corr = 0.3359) and also the increase in the number of new products and/or services (corr = 0.3769).
- workers who use an ERP system in the customer service department can positively influence the increase in sales results (corr = 0.4144) and also the improvement of process efficiency (corr = 0.3526) and the improvement of access to data and information (0.4248).
- workers who use an ERP system in the logistics department can positively influence the improvement of process efficiency (corr = 0.3692) and also the increase in the number of new products and/or services (corr = 0.3611) and the improvement of process quality (corr = 0.3907).

According to our research results, we can also state that workers in Polish manufacturing companies who use the ERP system: module e-commerce in the sales department (at least an average of 6 h per day/each worker) have a negative influence on the improvement of process efficiency (corr = –0.0616) and also a negative influence on the increase in customer satisfaction (corr = –0.1045).

It is a surprising result, perhaps it due to the fact that this is a new module in the ERP system and users need still to improve their skills to fully use its functionality. However, this assumption requires further research and verification.

In German companies, the interaction of the use of the module of the ERP system: CRM by workers in the customer service department makes a significant contribution to an increase in process efficiency: SBS PE (corr = 0.5191) and also to an increase in process quality SBS PQ (corr = 0.4704). Unfortunately, other relationships between the use of the ERP system and the success of the implementation of business strategies in manufacturing companies are not expressed in German manufacturing companies. However, we can also find negative relationships (but also not so significant) between the use of the ERP system by workers in a manufacturing company and the factors describing the success of the implementation of business strategies. This is especially evident with workers who use the ERP system: module e-commerce in the sales department, as they may decrease sales results (corr = –0.0698), process efficiency (corr = –0.1356), access to data and information (corr = –0.3362, the number of new products and/or services (corr = –0.0074), process quality (corr = –0.0704).

We received similar research results from both German and Polish manufacturing enterprises (based on research results from Polish and German companies in a special joint cross-border region of Lubuskie/Poland and Brandenburg/Germany). So, the findings determine our further research in manufacturing enterprises from the cross-border cooperation region to explain this negative interaction.

Also similar research results were received for the positive relationship between workers in a manufacturing company who use the ERP system: module CRM in the customer service department (at least an average of 6 h per day/each worker) who can have a positive influence on the improvement of process efficiency (corr = 0.3526). This finding corresponds with the statement of Ghalayini, Noble and Crowe [8], that the use of an ERP system within a company can facilitate the evaluation of organizational performance at the strategic level.

Our research model was developed and tested. It was evident that the use of an ERP system can play an important role in the success of the implementation of business strategies in manufacturing companies in German and in Polish companies (based on a total of 85 manufacturing enterprises from the cross-border cooperation region which exists between Poland and Germany).

5 Conclusions

The results of our research demonstrate the positive influence of workers in a manufacturing company, who use the ERP system: module CRM in the customer service department (at least an average of 6 h per day/each worker), on the improvement of process efficiency. This was evident in Polish and in German manufacturing companies, based on a total of 85 manufacturing enterprises from the cross-border cooperative region of Lubuskie/Poland and Brandenburg/Germany in which the companies were categorised as either "construction" or "automotive". Unfortunately, on the other hand, a negative effect is also present in relationships between the use of the ERP system: module e-commerce by workers from the sales department and an improvement in process efficiency. Therefore, it would be useful to provide research to identify a practical exploitation of this finding.

Furthermore, the research results indicate, in accordance with the views of Kaplan and Norton [13], Ehie and Madsen [4], that the use of an ERP system: especially with the CRM module may influence the success of the implementation of business strategies in German and Polish manufacturing companies. The research is focused on those manufacturing companies which have implemented an ERP system and that their workers use this system to help carry out their work activities.

This may possibly be a good recommendation for an area of further cooperation between Polish and German manufacturing companies in the cross-border cooperation region which exists between Poland and Germany regarding the field of post-implementation ERP usage in a manufacturing company.

References

1. Al-Mashari, M.: Process orientation through enterprise resource planning (ERP): a review of critical issues. Knowl. Proc. Manag. **8**(3), 175–185 (2001)
2. DeLone, W., McLean, E.: Measuring e-commerce success: applying the DeLone & McLean Information systems success model. Int. J. Electron. Commer. **9**(4), 9–30 (2004)
3. Dezdar, S., Sulaiman, A.: Successful enterprise resource planning implementation: taxonomy of critical factors. Ind. Manag. Data Syst. **109**(8), 1037–1052 (2009)
4. Ehie, I.K., Madsen, M.: Identifying critical issues in enterprise resource planning (ERP) implementation. Comput. Ind. Eng. **56**, 545–557 (2005)
5. Esteves, J., Bohorquez, V.: An updated ERP systems annotated bibliography: 2001–2005. Commun. Assoc. Inf. Syst. **19**, 386–446 (2007)
6. Finney, S., Corbett, C.: ERP implementation: a compilation and analysis of critical success factors. Bus. Proc. Manag. J. **13**(3), 329–347 (2007)
7. Gable, G., Sedera, D., Chan, T.: Re-conceptualizing information system success: the IS-impact measurement model. J. Assoc. Inf. Syst. **9**(7), 1–32 (2008)
8. Ghalayini, A.M., Noble, J.S., Crowe, T.C.: An integrated dynamic performance measurement system for improving manufacturing competitiveness. Int. J. Prod. Econ. **48**(3), 207–225 (1997)
9. Grabski, S., Leech, S., Schmidt, P.: A review of ERP research: a future agenda for accounting information systems. J. Inf. Syst. **25**(1), 37–78 (2011)
10. Hsieh, J., Wang, W.: Explaining employees' extended use of complex information systems. Eur. J. Inf. Syst. **16**(3), 216–227 (2007)
11. Huang, Z.: A compilation research of ERP implementation critical success factors. Inf. Syst. **9**(1), 507–512 (2010)
12. Johnson, G., Scholes, K.: Exploring Corporate Strategy. Pearson Education, Prentice-Hall, Harlow (2002)
13. Kaplan, R.S., Norton, D.P.: The balanced scorecard-measures that drive performance. Harvard Bus. Rev. **70**, 71–79 (1992)
14. Moon, Y.: Enterprise resource planning (ERP): a review of the literature. Int. J. Manag. Enterp. Devel. **4**(3), 235–264 (2007)
15. Nwankpa, J.K.: ERP system usage and benefit: a model of antecedents and outcomes. Comput. Human Behav. **45**, 335–344 (2015)

16. Nwankpa, J., Roumani, Y.: Understanding the link between organizational learning capability and ERP system usage: An empirical examination. Comput. Hum. Behav. **33**, 224–234 (2014)

17. Patalas-Maliszewska, J.: Assessing the relationship between business strategy and knowledge acquisition in Polish Manufacturing Enterprises. Manag. Econ. **16**(2), 137–148 (2015)

18. Patalas-Maliszewska, J.: Knowledge Worker Management: Value Assessment, Methods, and Application Tools. Springer, Heidelberg (2013)

19. Patalas-Maliszewska, J., Krebs, I.: Decision support model based on the GMDH method for implementing business strategies in Polish manufacturing enterprises (DS-BSI). In: 20th International Conference on Methods and Models in Automation and Robotics - MMAR 2015 (2015)

20. Patalas-Maliszewska, J., Krebs, I.: Model of innovation transfer is small and medium enterprises (SME). In: Advances in Production Engineering APE 2010: Proceedings of the 5th International Conference, Warsaw University of Technology, Faculty of Production Engineering (2010)

Visual Language and Ontology Based Analysis: Using OWL for Relation Discovery and Query in 4EM

Birger Lantow[✉], Kurt Sandkuhl, and Michael Fellmann

Chair of Business Information Systems, University of Rostock,
18051 Rostock, Germany
birger.lantow@uni-rostock.de

Abstract. Usually, enterprise models consider different aspects and include different abstraction levels of enterprises. It is hence challenging to integrate these models and to maintain their consistency. In the light of these challenges, ontologies seem to be relevant to complement enterprise models since they are intended to support communication, computational inference, consistency checking, querying, and the organization of knowledge. In our contribution, we demonstrate that Enterprise modelling can benefit from these characteristics. In order to check feasibility and pertinence of ontology-based Enterprise Models, we selected the goal modelling part and its relations to actors and resources from the "For Enterprise Modelling" (4EM) method. In more detail, this paper provides (1) a formal OWL representation of the 4EM Goals meta-model; (2) a discussion of goal relations regarding transitivity and domain specific inference; (3) a formalization of the discussed inference rules; and (4) an analysis of an exemplary goals model instance. This paper extends earlier work on the topic by the introduction of inter-model relations, a discussion of formalization alternatives, and a comparison of query results with and without ontology-based reasoning.

Keywords: 4EM · OWL · Enterprise architecture · Enterprise modelling · Goal modelling · SWRL · SPARQL · Enterprise model analysis · Meta-Modelling

1 Introduction

In general terms, enterprise modelling is addressing the systematic analysis and modelling of processes, organization structures, products, IT-systems or other perspectives relevant for the modelling purpose [16]. Usually, enterprise models consider different enterprise aspects and include different abstraction levels induced by refinements of, e.g., processes into sub-processes or goals into sub-goals. Ontologies are content theories about the sorts of objects, properties of objects and relations between objects possible in a specified knowledge domain [5]. The application of ontologies as conceptual bases that can clarify relations within and between different abstraction levels in enterprise models is believed to be helpful [13, 18]. Ontologies have shown their usability for this type of tasks. They provide a way of knowledge representation,

© Springer International Publishing AG 2017
W. Abramowicz et al. (Eds.): BIS 2016 Workshops, LNBIP 263, pp. 23–35, 2017.
DOI: 10.1007/978-3-319-52464-1_3

which is widely used today for intelligent analysis of knowledge. As a consequence of this, ontologies will also have the power to clarify the relations between focal areas and the constructs within a focal area [9]. Furthermore, ontologies provide means for consistency checking, discovery of new facts, and query by computational inference [4] in general and especially in the domain of Enterprise Modelling (e.g. [1–3]).

This paper investigates the use of ontologies for formalizing enterprise modelling languages and enriching their semantics. The focus in this context is on visual languages which have the advantage to be better understandable by non-experts in enterprises. From the existing EM methods, the "For Enterprise Modelling (4EM)" [14] has been selected for checking feasibility and pertinence of our approach because the 4EM-meta-model has not yet been formalized, but is publically available. Thus, the community that uses 4EM can benefit by the explication of the domain knowledge held in the meta-model and by the support of computational inference provided by ontology use and construction.

4EM uses six interrelated sub-models which complement each other and capture different views of the enterprise, i.e. each of the sub-models represents some aspect of the enterprise: (1) *Goals Model*, (2) *Business Rule Model*, (3) *Concepts Model* (4) *Business Process Model* (5) *Actors and Resources Model*, and (6) *Technical Components Model*. Out of these, the Goals Model and its relations to the Actors and Resources Model have been selected for presentation in this paper. Goal modelling in conjunction with enterprise models as such is an established topic [10].

However, if these models become large and complex, visual analysis and construction of models is error prone. Existing relations may be overlooked. For example, when a sub-goal is in a conflict or underlies some constraints. These circumstances are not visible at top-level. Furthermore, inherent inconsistencies like supporting top-level goals having conflicting sub-goals need attention. Organizational responsibility for a sub-goal also means responsibility for achieving the corresponding top-goal. Ontology-based reasoning provides a tool to address these representative exemplary problems. The following general requirements for the ontology and ontology-based reasoning are set:

RQ1. All model instances that comply with the 4EM meta-model can be represented.
RQ2. Implicit relations between model elements can be discovered automatically.
RQ3. Analysis of the model content on different abstraction levels is supported.

If these requirements are fulfilled in the domain of discourse, feasibility and pertinence of the approach are assumed. The structure of this paper follows this idea. In Sect. 2, the 4EM meta-model is analysed and formalized in OWL 2 (RQ1). Section 3 investigates the discovery of implicit relations (RQ2) using transitive properties in conjunction with domain knowledge and rules. Section 4 shows that RQ3 is fulfilled by formalizing analysis questions as SPARQL-Queries. Furthermore, an additional validation is provided by instantiating an example model. Section 5 summarizes and concludes our work. This paper extends earlier work [12] by the introduction of inter-model relations, a discussion of formalization alternatives, and a comparison of query results with and without ontology-based reasoning.

2   Ontology Construction

In the following, the ontological representation of the 4EM Goals meta-model will be constructed according to the 4EM method description in [14, pp. 87–101]. Up to now, there is no common view on goal modelling although some ontologies contain goal conceptualizations such as the Enterprise Ontology [17], DEMO [6] or the DIO ontology [3] from ArchiMate's meta-model. However, none of these ontologies provides the concepts and relations required to both capture goal hierarchies and their relations to other perspectives of enterprise modelling such as the Actors and Resource Model in 4EM. Hence in this section, we devise a specific goals meta-model explicitly geared towards 4EM. First, the taxonomy of goals model component types (classes) is constructed (Sect. 2.1). In a second step, the construction of binary, n-ary, and inter-model relation types follows (Sects. 2.2, 2.3 and 2.4). Relation transitivity is discussed separately in Sect. 3 because it is not specified in [14]. Protégé is used as ontology editor. Thus, the formalisation of the introduced concepts has been done by modelling them in Protégé. For reasons of brevity disjoint class axiom are not discussed. However, disjointness can be assumed for most of the concepts if they are not connected by specialization/generalization.

2.1   Component Types

The model component types are represented as classes in OWL. All goals model component types are specializations of the abstract class GM_ModellingCompo-nent. The Goal class represents goals or objectives respectively. The 4EM method describes *priority* and *criticality* as optional attributes for goals. These have not been considered in the meta-model so far. This is left open for future work. Problems symbolize environmental circumstances that hinder the achievement of goals. Problems can be described more specifically as *weaknesses* (internal factors) and *threats* (external factors. Problems are represented in OWL with the Problem class and its sub-classes Threat and Weakness. A *cause* expresses explanations or reasons for problems (Cause class). Apart from causes, constraints (Constraint class) express business restrictions, laws or external policies that affect components of the goals model. The last component type are opportunities (Opportunity class) symbolizing resources supporting the achievement of certain goals.

Component types of the *Actors* and *Resources Model* are subsumed under the abstract class ARM_ModellingComponent. Component types of the ARM and ontology classes respectively are Individual, OrganizationalUnit, Resource, and Role whereby Individual is a predefined symbol in Protégé. Therefore, individuals meaning natural persons in 4EM terminology are subsumed under the 4EM_Indi-vidual class. The class hierarchy of the ontology is shown in Fig. 1.

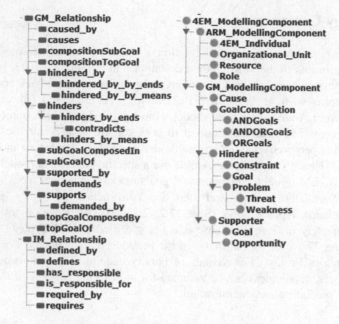

Fig. 1. Object property and class hierarchy of the 4EM goals meta-model

2.2 Goals Model Binary Relation Types

Relation types are represented as object properties in OWL. Object properties are directed binary relations. The usage of object properties can be further described and constrained by defining a *domain* and *range*. The domain class defines all instances that an object property can be applied to. The range class defines all instances that an object property can point at. Further semantics can be added to object properties by defining characteristics like transitivity, symmetry, reflexivity and relations to other object properties, including specialization/generalization as well as cardinality constraints such as minimum or maximum occurrence numbers on individuals.

The 4EM goals model describes four binary relation types. First, the supports-relation shows that fulfilling one goal also supports the achievement of another. Furthermore, the relation is used to relate opportunities to goals. The contradicts-relation in contrast shows that the achievement of one goal is in conflict with another. This relation is considered to be *symmetric*. Hence, if goal A contradicts goal B, goal B contradicts goal A as well. The hinders-relation is less strict. It can be used between goals model components to show negative influences. This relation is not considered symmetric but can also be used to link goals. The contradicts–relation can be assumed as a specialization of hinders (see Fig. 1). However, semantics of hinders can be further detailed according to the 4EM method (see [14, p. 100]). A so called *ends conflict* occurs when the goals' objectives are contradictory. A *means conflict* occurs when goals require the use of the same resources. Thus, the specializations hinders_by_ends and hinders_by_means are sub-properties of hinders. Consequently, contradicts is further specified as a sub-property of

Table 1. Goals model object properties

Object property	Domain	Range	Inverse	Characteristics
supports	Supporter	Goal	supported_by	Transitive
contradicts	Goal	Goal	–	Symmetric
hinders	Hinderer	Goal	hindered_by	–
causes	Cause	Problem	caused_by	–

hinders_by_ends. A symmetry is assumed for the latter. The last binary relation is the causes-relation. It is used to link *causes* to *problems*.

Experience from the field of Ontology Engineering shows that inverse relations should be included in an ontology in order to fully specify concept relations. For example, a problem can be linked to one of its causes by a caused_by-relation. These inverse relations are automatically added to instances by OWL reasoning if defined in the meta-model. Table 1 shows the specification of the introduced binary relations.

Two additional abstract classes have been added. Supporter for goal model element types that can support the achievement of a goal (sub-classes Goal and Opportunity) and Hinderer for element types that can have a negative influence on the achievement of a goal (sub-classes Goal, Problem, and Constraint). The supports-relation is considered to be transitive. Hence, if A supports B and B supports C, A also supports C. Similar assumptions cannot be made for the other binary relations.

2.3 Goals Model N-ary Relation Types

N-ary relations define different semantics of goal decomposition in the 4EM goals model. The AND-relation decomposes a top-goal into a set of sub-goals that have to be fulfilled each in order to achieve the top-goal. The OR-relation defines a set of sub-goals where it is sufficient to fulfil one of the alternatives. Finally, the AND/OR-relation needs a combination of some of the sub-goals to be fulfilled. N-ary relations are not directly supported in OWL. Logical Ontology Design Patterns can be used in order to model cases where the ontology language does not provide appropriate constructs [8]. The catalogue of the NeON-projects provides the n-ary relation pattern for modelling such relation types in OWL [7]. A class for the relation type is created and appropriate object properties are associated. For goal modelling, the class GoalComposition is used to represent the decomposition of goals. The respective sub-classes are ANDGoals, ORGoals, and ANDORGoals. Accordingly, object properties have been defined. They are shown in Table 2. According to the 4EM method, goal composition structures are special cases of the supports-relation. Therefore, the chain of composition object properties can be defined as a sub-property of supports (subGoalComposedIn o compositionTopGoal SubProp-ertyOf supports). Figure 1 shows the complete OWL class and object property hierarchies that are used to represent the 4EM goals meta-model.

Table 2. Object properties for decomposition

Object property	Domain	Range	Inverse
compositionTopGoal	GoalComposition	Goal	topGoalComposedBy
compositionSubGoal	GoalComposition	Goal	subGoalComposedIn

Table 3. Inter-model object properties

Object property	Domain	Range	Inverse
defines	ARMComponent	Goal	defined_by
is_responsible_for	ARMComponent	Goal	has_responsible
requires	Goal	ARMComponent	required_by

2.4 Inter-Model Relation Types

Three relation types between Goals *Model* and *Actors* and *Resources Model* elements can be identified in the 4EM meta-model: defines, responsible_for, and requires (see also Table 3). defines is the relation between a Role or an Organizational_Unit and a Goal that it defines. This relation type allows to pinpoint the originator of the goal. is_responsible_for on the other hand connects *roles* or *organizational units* with the goals whose achievement lies in their responsibility. The requires-relation links *goals* to the *resources* that need to be employed for their achievement. ARM components are not further specified here, for more a detailed reference see [14].

3 Transitivity and Rules

After modelling the 4EM goals meta-model, the possibility of formal statements regarding transitivity of goal properties is investigated. In a first step, a systematic analysis of possible property propagations between goals is performed (Sect. 3.1). In a second step, the formalization of transitivity and rules is discussed (Sect. 3.2).

3.1 Transitivity and Inference Rules for Goal Properties

With reference to the meta-model, we focus on relations between model components. These are represented as object properties in OWL 2. Attributes which are represented as data properties in OWL 2 are not considered.

It is straightforward to assume that the properties of sub-elements in a partonomy aggregate at the top-elements. In this sense, all goals that are sub-goals of an AND-composition are required in order to achieve the top-goal. Thus, all relations defined for the sub-goals are also true for the top-goals. This holds also for decompositions of the sub-goals. In consequence, a demands relation between top- and sub-goals is defined, which is transitive. Thus, the demands relation semantically expresses that the sub-goal must be achieved in order to achieve the top-goal. Additionally, all relations of sub-goals are assigned to the top-goals.

Looking at OR-compositions and ANDOR-compositions, it can be assumed that the achievement of a certain sub-goal supports the achievement of the top-goal but is not required. Achieving a sub-goal increases the probability of achieving the top-goal. Thus, there are optional parts. Propagation of sub-goal relations to the top-goal is not straightforward. However, it can be concluded that OR-compositions and ANDOR-compositions define supports relations between sub-goals and top-goals. Generally, relations are propagated from sub-goals to top-goals in supports and demanded_by hierarchies (going-up). Conclusions regarding relations for sub-goals going-down in these hierarchies cannot be made. For a further analysis of transitivity, the special semantics of GM relations need to be considered.

Having a supports-relation, the influence of the sub-goal on the achievement of other goals besides the top-goal is not propagated to the top-goal. In this case, there is clearly *no* transitivity for hinders-, supports-, and demanded_by-relations. Influence on the achievement of the sub-goal however also influences the achievement of the top goal. If the sub-goal is hindered_by something this also hinders the top-goal and if the sub-goal is supported_by something it also supports the top-goal. contradicts and demands are specializations of hinders and supports. These relations are translated to their generalization for the top-goal.

Transitivity via goal conflicts is not considered. For example, if goal B hinders goal A and goal B is hindered by goal C no assumption can be made that goal C supports goal A (double negation). Furthermore, goals are desired future states. Conflicts between goals need to be solved by a decision in favour of one of the goals or by relating the degree of goal fulfilment. The focus is on the goal conflict but not on relating the context of one goal to the other.

causes as the last GM relation to be considered only directly relates Causes and Problems and is not subject to transitivity concerns.

Table 4 shows the derived transitivity rules. In addition to transitivity, further rules can be defined that allow to infer properties of model elements. In the 4EM Goals Model, the hinders_by_means relation can be inferred if two goals require the same resource. We assume, that only restricted resources are considered in enterprise models. A conflict by means is only likely to occur, when both goals are not connected in a part-of relation in an AND-composition.

3.2   Formalization

After clarifying which object property propagation semantics and further rules should be supported, a formalization of these semantics is required. Generally, there are three possibilities to add such object property related semantics for inference mechanisms:

1. **OWL-axiom-based reasoning.** Object property axioms provide means to infer object property assertions based on existing object property assertions.
2. **SWRL-rule-based reasoning.** New facts are inferred based on a test of freely defined OWL statements against the ontology. A rule consists of a *body* and a *head*. If the body of a rule is true based on the available knowledge, the head is concluded to be true as well and a new fact can be added to the ontology.

Table 4. Object property transitivity by goal-to-goal relations

	Supports	demanded by
hindered by	hindered by	hindered by
supported by	supported by	supported by
contradicts	hindered by	contradicts
AND composed by	supported by	AND composed by
OR composed by	supported by	supported by
AND/OR composed by	supported by	supported by
Hinders	–	hinders
Supports	–	supports
contradicts	–	contradicts
defined by	–	defined by
has responsible	–	has responsible
Requires	–	requires

3. SPARQL-based construction of new facts. Based on the RDF- or graph-serialization of OWL, SPARQL can be used to query for patterns in the ontology and to use the query result for the construction of new facts.

OWL-axiom- and SWRL rule-based reasoning provides the benefits of DL-safe, forward chaining reasoning by standard OWL reasoners with guaranteed complexity and decidability. However, this implies restricted expressiveness and the OWL inherent Open World Assumption (OWA). Thus, discovery of new relations can generally not be based on the absence of certain facts unless the latter are explicitly denied in the ontology. Furthermore, not all current implementations such as *Hermit* or Protégé do support reasoning based on OWL axioms that use property chains. For example, OWL axioms cannot be used to model `hinders` transitivity along `supports` relations nor the property chain defined in Sect. 2. SWRL rules are supporting this because of their higher expressiveness. However, SWRL rules do not allow the negation of property assertion in the rule body as well.

The use of SPARQL queries provides Closed World Assumption (CWA)-like behaviour in supporting a weak form of negation, Negation as Failure (NAF). However, forward chaining is not supported in SPARQL. Further, implications of newly added facts are not derived. Adding forward chaining would result in issues regarding complexity and termination.

In the case of goal modelling, transitivity and basic rules can be expressed using OWL axioms and SWRL rules. Some of the OWL axioms have already been defined during ontology construction in Sect. 2. SWRL is needed in order to model that goal compositions are a collection of support relations (see Sect. 2):

```
GoalComposition(?Comp), compositionSubGoal(?Comp, ?SubGoal),
compositionTopGoal(?Comp, ?TopGoal) -> supports(?SubGoal, ?TopGoal)
```

For the special case of an AND-composition we have a collection of demanded_by-relations:

```
ANDGoals(?ANDComp), compositionSubGoal(?ANDComp, ?SubGoal),
compositionTopGoal(?ANDComp, ?TopGoal) -> demanded_by(?SubGoal,
?TopGoal)
```

Table 5. OWL/SWRL formalization of object property inference rules

supports	
hindered by	hindered_by_by_ends(?SubGoal, ?c), supports(?SubGoal, ?TopGoal) -> hindered_by_by_ends(?TopGoal, ?c) hindered_by_by_means(?SubGoal, ?c), supports(?SubGoal, ?TopGoal) -> hindered_by_by_means(?TopGoal, ?c)
supported by	supports is defined transitive
Contradicts	contradicts(?h, ?SubGoal), supports(?SubGoal, ?TopGoal) -> hindered_by_ends(?TopGoal, ?h)
AND/OR/ ANDOR composed	supports is defined transitive
demanded by	
hindered by	demanded_by subProperty supports
supported by	demanded_by subProperty of supports
contradicts	contradicts(?c, ?SubGoal), demanded_by(?SubGoal, ?TopGoal) -> contradicts(?c, ?TopGoal)
AND composed by	ANDGoals(?ANDSubComp),ANDGoals(?ANDComp),compositionSubGoal (?ANDSubComp, ?SubSubGoal), compositionTopGoal(?ANDSubComp, ?SubGoal), compositionSubGoal(?ANDComp, ?SubGoal), compositionTopGoal(?ANDComp, ?TopGoal) -> compositionSubGoal(?ANDComp, ?SubSubGoal))
OR composed by	demanded_by subProperty of supports
AND/OR composed by	supports is defined transitive
hinders	demanded_by(?SubGoal, ?TopGoal), hinders(?SubGoal, ?c) -> hinders(?TopGoal, ?c)
supports	demanded_by subProperty of supports, supports is defined transitive
contradicts	contradicts is defined symmetric
defined by	defined_by(?SubGoal, ?c), demanded_by(?SubGoal, ?TopGoal) -> defined_by(?TopGoal, ?c)
has responsible	demanded_by(?SubGoal, ?TopGoal), has_responsible(?SubGoal, ?c) -> has_responsible(?TopGoal, ?c)
requires	demanded_by(?SubGoal, ?TopGoal), requires(?SubGoal, ?c) -> requires(?TopGoal, ?c)

Table 5 shows the formalization of the transitivity rules discussed in Sect. 3.1. The rows contain the relation type and the corresponding rule for transitive propagation each. This is done in the first part for transitivity via supports relations. The second part of the table considers demanded_by relations.

The rule regarding hinders_by_means-relations has to be formulated as a SPARQL-statement because of the included negation:

```
CONSTRUCT {?goal1 gm:hinders_by_means ?goal2}
{?resource gm:required_by ?goal1;gm:required_by ?goal2. OPTIONAL
{{?goal1 ?relation ?goal2. FILTER(?relation =
gm:demanded_by)}UNION{?goal1 ?relation ?goal2. FILTER(?relation =
gm:demands)}}. FILTER (!bound(?relation) && ?goal1 != ?goal2)}
```

Interpreting this SPARQL statement as a rule, the rule body matches pairs of goal instances that are not connected by a partonomy-relation, that not resemble the same goal, and that require the same resource. The body of the rule adds the hinders_by_means relation between matching goals.

Forward chaining is not considered here. The added relation hinders_by_means does not lead to new requires und new partonomy-relations by inference. Thus, no additional facts are added or inferred by rule application that match the rule body.

An ontology containing the instances of the example from Sect. 4 can be found here: http://win.informatik.unirostock.de/fileadmin/win/Downloads/onto/4EM_GM_ARM.owl

4   Exemplary Model and Model Analysis

In order to assess the applicability of the ontology to 4EM Goals models and the benefits of OWL-reasoning, we have adopted the exemplary A4Y case from [11] with slight modifications to add complexity and to simulate a less systematic modelling. The hinders-relation between goal 2 and 3 has been removed in favour of a sub-goal (goal 10) of goal 2 hindering goal 3. Goal 10 has been split into 2 goals (9 and 10). The CAM-System has been introduced as a required resource and at last, the blacksmith is modelled as responsible role for goal 2.

It was possible to instantiate the complete model using the ontology, to add inference-based facts using the Hermit 1.3.8 reasoner and to check consistency successfully. Additionally, the complete context is constructed automatically for a goal. All hindering and supporting influences are assigned to the goals for detailed analysis. This includes the consequences of the discovered conflict by means between goal 2.2 and goal 4.

This is an additional proof for RQ1 and RQ2. RQ3 is addressed by queries to the model instance. In ontology engineering, so called *Competency Questions* (CQ) are used for the specification of queries that should be supported by an ontology [11]. We formulated typical CQ in the domain of goal modelling and also including inter-model relations. Furthermore, different abstraction levels are considered. Analysis is based on

SPARQL-queries (cf. Sect. 3.2). G1_Increase_profits_15_percent and G2_Increase_ sales_with_promotions are used as examples and can be replaced by arbitrary goals:

CQ1:   Which goals are related to a certain goal?

```
SELECT ?goal WHERE { ?goal a gm:Goal; gm:GM_Relationship
                gm:G1_Increase_profits_15_percent.}
```

CQ2:   Which goals are in conflict with a certain goal?

```
SELECT ?goal WHERE { ?goal a gm:Goal; gm:hinders
gm:G1_Increase_profits_15_percent.}
```

CQ3:   Which goals are in conflict with a certain goal regarding objectives?

```
SELECT ?goal WHERE { ?goal a gm:Goal; gm:hinders_by_ends
gm:G1_Increase_profits_15_percent.}
```

CQ4:   What resources are required for the achievement of a certain goal?

```
SELECT ?resource WHERE { ?resource gm:required_by
gm:G2_Increase_sales_with_promotions}
```

CQ5:   What sub-goals have to be achieved in order to achieve a goal?

```
SELECT ?goal WHERE {?goal gm:demanded_by
gm:G2_Increase_sales_with_promotions}
```

CQ6:   What top-level goals can be identified?

```
SELECT ?goal1 {?goal1 gm:supported_by ?goal2. OPTIONAL {?goal1
gm:supports ?goal3}. FILTER (!bound(?goal3))}
```

CQ7:   Which goals share inherent conflicting and supporting relations?

```
SELECT ?goal WHERE { ?goal rdf:type gm:Goal; gm:hinders
gm:G1_Increase_profits_15_percent; gm:supports
gm:G1_Increase_profits_15_percent.}
```

For evaluation of the approach, query results based on the original model and query results after reasoning and rule application (RQ2, Sect. 1) are compared. The first column contains the number of the CQ and the analysed goal if applicable. The results without reasoning in column 2 are derived from relations that are directly connected with the analysed goal in the visual model. Indirect relations are not considered. The third row shows the result based on OWL 2 and SPARQL reasoning. Goals G1 and G2 have been chosen as an example for this paper because the model intentionally contains relations for discovery regarding G1 and G2. The result shows that OWL reasoning adds relevant knowledge to the model. For all CQ (except for question 6), the answers are more comprehensive in comparison (Table 6).

Table 6. Query results for competency questions

CQ/Goal	Results without reasoning	Results with reasoning
1/G1	G2, G3	G2.2, G4.2, G3.2, G2.1, G6.2, G5, G3.1, G6, G3.3, G10, G4, G4.3, G4.1, G3, G9, G12, G2.3, G11, G13, G2, G6.1
2/G1	–	G10, G2.1, G3, G2, G2.2, G4
3/G1	–	G10
4/G2	–	Cam_System
5/G2	G2.1, G2.2, G2.3	G2.1, G2.2, G2.3, G9, G10
6/-	G1	G1
7/G1	–	G10, G2.1, G3, G2.2, G4

5   Summary and Outlook

Based on the example of 4EM goal modelling, this paper investigated the possibility to transform meta-models of existing enterprise modelling languages into ontologies. The purpose of this transformation was to further specify the relations between focal areas and the constructs within a focal area, to discover new relations and to provide comprehensive model analysis. Additionally, logical consistency checking and integration mechanisms are provided by the use of ontologies. However, these aspects have not been investigated in this paper.

Our work showed that the developed ontology is applicable and the implemented reasoning provides support for analysis of the goal model. In comparison to the situation without the application of semantic technologies, more relations have been discovered in a model instance and the modelling vocabulary has been enhanced by adding new concepts during ontology construction. The steps undertaken in order to provide the required functionality based on semantic technologies can be roughly generalized to (1) meta-model-based ontology construction including components/class construction, binary and n-ary relations construction, (2) identification of transitivity and rules and (3) formalization of transitivity and rules. Additionally, the way of formalizing transitivity for partonomies can be generalized as a rule pattern rela-tion_x(?a,?b), relation_y(?a,?c) - > relation_x(?c,?b)

Future work will have to investigate whether the proposed steps are sufficient for enabling semantic support for Enterprise Modelling and whether more rule patterns can be identified. The inclusion of the other 4EM sub-models and of other enterprise modelling languages is planned. Additionally, the benefits of consistency checking and integration support should be investigated. Further open issues requiring research are problems due to OWL's Open World Assumption and the lack of possibilities to express negation in rules (we used SPARQL as a workaround), how to integrate forward chaining or OWL additions such as [15].

References

1. Antunes, G., Bakhshandeh, M., Mayer, R., Borbinha, J., Caetano, A.: Using ontologies for enterprise architecture integration and analysis. Complex Syst. Inf. Model. Q. 1, 1–23 (2014)
2. Antunes, G., Caetano, A., Bakhshandeh, M., Mayer, R., Borbinha, J.: Using ontologies for enterprise architecture model alignment. In: Proceedings of BITA 2013, Poznan, Poland (2013)
3. Bakhshandeh, M., Antunes, G., Mayer, R., Borbinha, J., Caetano, A.: A modular ontology for the enterprise architecture domain. In: 17th IEEE International Proceedings of EDOCW 2013, pp. 5–12, 9–13 September 2013
4. Bürger, T., Simperl, E.: Measuring the benefits of ontologies. In: Meersman, R., Tari, Z., Herrero, P. (eds.) OTM 2008. LNCS, vol. 5333, pp. 584–594. Springer, Heidelberg (2008). doi:10.1007/978-3-540-88875-8_82
5. Chandrasekaran, B., Josephson, J.R., Benjamins, V.R.: What are ontologies and why do we need them? IEEE Intell. Syst. 14(1), 20–26 (1999)
6. Dietz, J.: Enterprise Ontology: Theory and Methodology. Springer, Heidelberg (2006)
7. EU-FP7 funded IP NeON: http://www.neon-project.org
8. Gangemi, A., Presutti, V.: Ontology design patterns. In: Staab, S., Studer, R. (eds.) Handbook on Ontologies. International Handbooks on Information Systems, pp. 221–243. Springer, Heidelberg (2009). 2nd edn.
9. Kaczmarek, T., Seigerroth, U., Shilov, N.: Multi-layered enterprise modeling and its challenges in business and IT alignment. In: Proceedings of ICEIS 2012, Wroclaw, Poland, pp. 257–260 (2012)
10. Kavakli, V., Loucopoulos, P.: Goal-driven business process analysis application in electricity deregulation. Inf. Syst. 24(3), 187–207 (1999)
11. Noy, N.F., McGuinness, D.L.: Ontology development 101: a guide to creating your first ontology (2001)
12. Lantow, B., Sandkuhl, K.: From visual language to ontology representation: using owl for transitivity analysis in 4EM. In: Proceedings of Short and Doctoral Consortium Papers, PoEM 2015, Valencia, Spain, pp. 51–60 (2015)
13. Sandkuhl, K., Smirnov, A., Shilov, N., Koç, H.: Ontology-driven enterprise modelling in practice: experiences from industrial cases. In: Persson, A., Stirna, J. (eds.) CAiSE 2015. LNBIP, vol. 215, pp. 209–220. Springer, Heidelberg (2015). doi:10.1007/978-3-319-19243-7_21
14. Sandkuhl, K., Stirna, J., Persson, A., Wißotzki, M.: Enterprise Modeling: Tackling Business Challenges with the 4EM Method. The Enterprise Engineering Series. Springer, Heidelberg (2014). ISBN 978-3662437247
15. Sengupta, K., Krisnadhi, A.A., Hitzler, P.: Local closed world semantics: grounded circumscription for OWL. In: Aroyo, L., Welty, C., Alani, H., Taylor, J., Bernstein, A., Kagal, L., Noy, N., Blomqvist, E. (eds.) ISWC 2011. LNCS, vol. 7031, pp. 617–632. Springer, Heidelberg (2011). doi:10.1007/978-3-642-25073-6_39
16. Vernadat, F.B.: Enterprise Modelling and Integration. Chapman & Hall, London (1996)
17. Uschold, M., King, M., Moralee, S., Zorgios, Y.: The enterprise ontology. knowl. Eng. Rev. 13(01), 31–89 (1998)
18. Fellmann, M., Thomas, O., Dollmann, T.: Management of model relations using semantic wikis. In: Proceedings of the 43rd HICSS Conference, Koloa, Kauai, Hawaii, USA. IEEE Computer Society Press (2010)

Targeting Advertising Scenarios
for e-Shops Surfers

Dalia Kriksciuniene and Virgilijus Sakalauskas[✉]

Department of Informatics, Vilnius University,
Universiteto Str.3, Vilnius, Lithuania
{dalia.kriksciuniene,
virgilijus.sakalauskas}@khf.vu.lt

Abstract. Buying goods in e-shops turns to be a very attractive activity for internet surfers. The shopping behaviour of online customers holds attention not only of e-shop businesses, but also the researchers analysing perspectives of online marketing. The most serious consideration is given to discovery of consumer interest patterns, visualization of customer online shopping behaviour or evaluation of advertising campaigns with the goal to attract more e-shop visitors and to grow sales. Unfortunately, selection of the most potentially promising customers draws less attention in the research works. The paper proposes new method of selecting the best e-shop clients for which we can offer the personalized advertising campaign. This study demonstrates how by using only e-shop clickstream data we can identify the potential buyers, select the best suitable advertising campaign and increase the e-shop sales level. The research is based on real clickstream data of two e-shops.

Keywords: Advertising scenarios · Clickstream data · e-shops surfers · Online marketing · e-commerce

1 Introduction

Using e-shops for searching and purchase is a pervasive process, constantly increasing in its purchase volume and number of visitors. The sales value of e-commerce retailers has reached \$294 billion, and expected to reach \$414 by 2018. In 2015 the average spending of \$1,700/person is calculated out of purchases made by 200 million digital shoppers (NChanel.com, 2016, [1]).

The cases of huge online e-shops (Amazon, eBay, www.Booking.com) show that they already receive more than one million visitors per day, which creates dramatic challenges for e-commerce enterprises in the areas of increasing sales, attracting new customers, exploring and measuring customers interest patterns, identifying potential buyers and offering the most attractive service package to them. The source for making these types of decisions is e-shop online clickstream data.

The article proposes algorithm which could enable to measure consumers engagement for making a purchase, and calculate the customer ratings based on the e-shop surfing data. The algorithm can be further applied for assigning cost-effective personalized advertising campaign.

© Springer International Publishing AG 2017
W. Abramowicz et al. (Eds.): BIS 2016 Workshops, LNBIP 263, pp. 36–43, 2017.
DOI: 10.1007/978-3-319-52464-1_4

The scientific works admit the challenges of measuring level of customer engagement. In general this measurement should reflect how the customers like the target items [2–4]. However no exact measurement is proposed for this purpose. The described methods include visualization of online shopping behaviour [5], evaluating time spent on each item page [6, 7], exploring browsing patterns for detecting most perspective online shoppers [8, 9].

The behaviour pattern detection methods are based on customer segmentation, where the grouping is made according to particular characteristics. For this purpose [10] uses the frequency of purchase and statistical methods, [11] prefer soft-clustering based on demographic and other customer data. The clusters of internet surfers were detected by applying self-organising maps [12, 13]. The prediction of customer behaviour is explored by K-means algorithm and its various modifications [2, 14].

The distinct feature of the algorithm proposed in this article is the dynamic evaluation of compound customer index, which could take into account activeness of the e-shop surfer, expedience in choosing items and time spend for exploring them. We aim to use the standard e-commerce clickstream data file in order to get this information. The calculated customer index intends to predict client intension to make a purchase at online shop. It provides quantitative variable for assigning the intensity and value of personalized advertising campaign in order to encourage customer to take the best purchase decision.

The paper consists of two main parts. In Sect. 2 we describe the proposed algorithm for evaluating the behaviour e-shop customers by introducing Custom Merit (CM) index and propose method for selecting perspective customer group for assigning advertising campaign. The Sect. 3 experimentally tests the designed algorithm by applying clickstream data from 2 different e-shops, shaping different customer behaviour patterns. The research results of setting different algorithm parameters and its efficiency are presented.

2 The Method of Selecting Most Perspective Customers for Targeted Advertising

In this article the proposed strategy for targeting advertising scenarios for e-shops surfers is based on extended analysis of the visitors and calculation of accumulated activeness indicator by using clickstream data. Clickstream data includes a list of all the pages viewed by a visitor, presented in the order the pages were viewed. Usually visitor clickstreams also have the fields of visit durations, timestamp, search terms, ISPs, countries, browsers, computer etc.

The data set used for the research includes the basic information of the clickstream database (Fig. 1), which is called Tracks DB (TDB). The data includes customer ID (CID), visited Webpage address (URL) and Date and Time of page visit (usually in Unix format). The detailed information about product is stored in a separate file, here called Product DB–PDB (Fig. 1). This information is available if the customer clicks the link of selected product item and it contains price, current discounts, and detailed description.

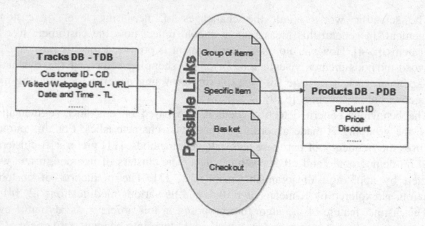

Fig. 1. Example of clickstream data and possible links list

The proposed method is designed on assumption that usage of particular links show different level of customer readiness to purchase. The visits to the general webpage of the e-shop can indicate some curiosity of the customer, which has stronger expression in case of using links of detailed item description. This level can characterize customers' wish to analyse and compare product features or prices among different suppliers. Even putting the items to shopping basket does not necessarily indicate purchase act, as about 20% of basket items are abandoned without payment. In general, the level of interest of e-shop surfers can be assigned to 4 types, as expressed by their access to clickstream webpage links:

- the pages representing group of Items;
- link to Specific Item;
- link allowing transfer of selected item to the basket;
- link to purchase of the basket content.

Each type of link provides more information about product and leads to its purchase.

The most valuable customers can be characterized by their frequency of visits, the purchases performed at the e-shop, and their total value. The value of the customer is assumed to increase if the spending value at the e-shop is increasing.

The above described link-based patterns can be expressed by weights. The total indicator characterizing dynamics of customer engagement in e-shop surfing is designed as accumulated value, consisting of inputs measured for all types of weighted links. Only the customers who have sufficient value of cumulative index can be assigned the advertising campaign.

If the weights of visited possible links are denoted as w_1, w_2, w_3 and w_4 (Fig. 2), the cumulative value, further nominated as Customer Merit (CM) index will be equal to total weighted sum of visited links. All types of adjustments, based on observing and mining customer information can be included, such as setting minimum time spent at the link webpage. If the customer has spent only few seconds his awareness of

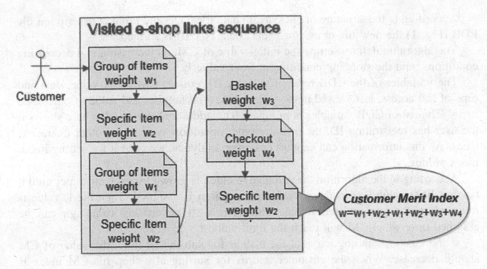

Fig. 2. Example of one customer e-shop browsing session

presented information at the link is not sufficient, and the visited link will not be included to the index.

In Fig. 2 we can see an example of one customer e-shop browsing session, which was completed by making purchase of specific Item and switching to preview of another product. After each visited link the CM index is recalculated and verified if it has reached the limit value. The customers with CM index above the limit are assigned advertising campaign, and their CM index is set to the initial value. If not - the CM index value is further updated according to tracking customer activities.

The initial CM can obtain various values. The default initial CM is 0, but it can be increased for some merits, e.g. the customers who have registered to e-shop, agreed to receive the promotion info or other interactions enabling to increase their initial CM.

The selection of values of weights w_1, w_2, w_3 and w_4 is not constant. It was researched that the values of weights have to be adjusted for each e-shop, and should be regularly recalculated within time periods (monthly) or after events which had significant effect for the turnover of the e-shop.

The weight evaluation for e-shop links can be performed by various methods of processing tracking data (file Tracks DB). The intelligent computational methods were explored for this purpose, such as artificial neural networks, analytical hierarchical process, expert and decision support systems or statistical analysis. In this research the weights were assigned using statistical stream data analysis in a way (1) that total weight sum was equal to 1:

$$w_1 + w_2 + w_3 + w_4 = 1 \qquad (1)$$

The algorithm of computing CM index and assignment of personalized advertising campaign is further presented.

According to the structure of clickstream data file TDB and product description file PDB (Fig. 1) the new file of customer data base (CDB) is formed.

The algorithm defines setting the initial value of CM, its increasing and decreasing conditions, and the stopping condition at limit value L.

The variables of the CDB reflect Customer ID, current CM index value, date and time of last access, last viewed items with prices, total number and value of purchased items. The list of CDB variables is in Fig. 3. The additional information here shows if the user has registration ID, the browser type, operation system and other characteristics. As this information can support customer analytics, we used it for setting initial index values.

According to the algorithm the cumulative index is grown for each customer until it reaches limit value L, and the advertising campaign is assigned. Then the L value is returned to the personalized initial value. The next advertising campaign can be assigned only when CM will reach the limit value L.

If the customer is not active at the e-shop for substantial time, the value of CM should decrease. When the customer returns for surfing at e-shop his CM index is decreased by 1% for each day with no activity.

The entire procedure of the CM computing algorithm is in Fig. 3.

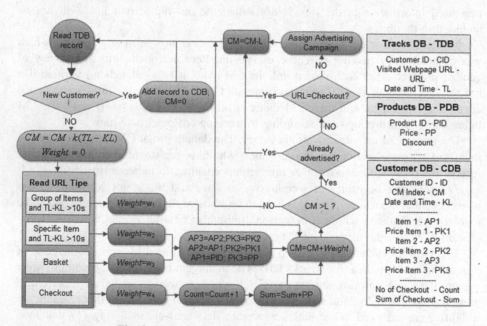

Fig. 3. Advertising campaign assignment algorithm

In Fig. 3 the coefficient k is used to decrease CM index value. If $k = 0.01$, then CM is reduced by 1% for each day since last visit.

If the customer makes a new visit, but his CM > L and the advertising campaign has been already assigned, the new campaign is not provided, and the CM value is decreased by L. The advertising campaign is also not assigned if the customer has just made checkout.

The following chapter presents analysis of applying the proposed algorithm for experimental data. The amount of advertising campaigns assigned to the customers in each particular e-shop and size of the target group of e-shop surfers is adjusted according to the dynamics of their CM index.

3 Experimental Validation of Surfers' Targeting of Advertising Campaign Algorithm

The effect of targeted advertising is difficult to define due to numerous influence factors. However each e-shop set their advertising budgets based on the available historical information or consultant advice. There are no doubts that the effect is positive, e.g. the study report of NAI (2010) [15], found that behaviorally-targeted advertising is more than twice as effective at converting users who click on the ads into buyers (6.8% conversion vs. 2.8% for run-of-network ads), and that behavioral advertising accounted for approximately 18% of advertising revenue. We explore the experimental data of two e-shops (marked as A and B) operating in Lithuania. Number of visitors per day in A is about 50, and in B-about 20 thousand. The daily number of items in clickstream data is correspondingly 460 and 110 thousand. The experimental research aims to reveal the differences in defining weights which form the CM index values and the sizes of target customer groups selected for advertising campaigns.

The differences among statistical characteristics of e-shops A and B are in Table 1.

Table 1. Some statistical characteristics of e-shops A and B

e-Shop	$\frac{Link}{Customer}$	$\frac{Item}{Customer}$	$\frac{Basket}{Customer}$	$\frac{Checkout}{Customer}$	$\frac{Time, min}{Customer}$	$\frac{Time, min}{Link}$
A	10.46	2.81	0.17	0.04	7.07	0.68
B	5.88	2.08	0.09	0.03	3.86	0.66

Index $\frac{Link}{Customer}$ shows that average number of links visited by customer is 10.46 at the e-shop A, and 5.88 links at B.

The number of visited pages containing description of Items is equal to 2.81 (at A) and 2.08 (at B). On average only 17% customers from A, and 9% from B put their selected Items into Basket. The percent of customers making purchases in e-shops A and B is correspondingly 4% and 3%. The time spent by customers in site A is almost twice as long as in B, although the average time spent for particular link is very similar for both e-shops.

According to the Table 1 we can state, that the e-shop A has almost 2 times more customers than B, and duration of time the surfers spend in site A is twice longer as well. The percent of customers who buy is very similar at both e-shops, but the customers of site A use the basket for their purchase twice more often, and the number of items per basket is 1, 35 times bigger.

The procedure of Fig. 3 was applied for computing weights for visited links by customers of both e-shops. The results are in Table 2.

Table 2. Weights for all types of visited links in e-shops A and B

e-Shop	Group of items	Specific item	Basket	Checkout
A	0,02389	0,06984	0,28426	0,62201
B	0,06840	0,12885	0,29769	0,50506

In e-shop B the bigger weight is assigned for visiting link Group of Items, Specific item and Putting in basket. But the visitors of A are assigned bigger weight for the completed purchase due its lower ratio to total number of purchases.

The size of target group of customers selected for advertising campaigns is calculated for both shops. The results of applying the proposed algorithm (Fig. 3) showed that the size of target groups is similar for both e-shops. The results are in Table 3.

Table 3. The share of selected customers for targeted advertising in relation to L

L=	0.8	0.85	0.9	1.0
A	47.3%	41.5%	36.2%	23.7%
B	46.8%	41.7%	35.9%	22.1%

By changing CM limit value L we can optimize number of target customers and intensity of personalizes advertising campaign. In Table 3 the average percent of target customers selected for assigning them advertising campaign is explored for four values of L: 0.8, 0.85, 0.9 and 1. Some differences are observed among the different e-shops A and B.

The expert analysis for defining CM limit value L for each e-shop could increase efficiency of advertising expenses. Same applies to the duration, intensity and content of the advertising campaign.

4   Conclusions

The research revealed that majority of e-commerce sites meet challenge of selecting the customers who need assistance and encouragement for making their buying decisions at the online shops.

The article presents algorithm for calculating Customer Merit index, which enables estimation of the customer value from his clickstream data and to decide the need of assistance. In most cases the assistance takes the form of special personalized advertising campaign which reflects the customer interest scope.

As the e-commerce websites have agile and migratory structure, broad variety of customers and goods, the proposed method of dynamic customer ranking enables to recalculate the weights of evaluation factors and get the adjusted Customer Merit values which comports to the changes of trading situation. Introduction of the Limit Customer Merit Index parameter allows modifying the cluster of customers which were assigned the advertising campaign. This feature is very important for meeting changes of the advertising budget, advertising modes and campaign formats.

The experimental testing of the proposed method was performed for the use case of two online shops which differ by their parameters (size, number of customers, assortment of goods, etc.). The results of empirical research confirm the stability of the method.

References

1. NChanel.com: https://www.nchannel.com/blog/retail-data-ecommerce-statistics/
2. Su, Q., Chen, L.: A method for discovering clusters of e-commerce interest patterns using click-stream data. Electron. Commer. Res. Appl. **14**, 1–13 (2015)
3. Zhao, X., Niu, Z., Chen, W.: Interest before liking: two-step recommendation approaches. Knowl. Based Syst. **48**, 46–56 (2013)
4. Cleger-Tamayo, S., Fernández-Luna, J.M., Huete, J.F.: Top-N news recommendations in digital newspapers. Knowl. Based Syst. **27**, 180–189 (2012)
5. Pragarauskaite, J., Dzemyda, G.: Visual decisions in the analysis of customer online shopping behaviour. Nonlinear Anal. Model. Control **17**(3), 355–368 (2012)
6. Rathipriya, R., Thangavel, D.K.: A fuzzy co-clustering approach for clickstream data pattern. Glob. J. Comput. Sci. Technol. **10** (6), 11–16 (2010)
7. Zheng, L., Cui, S., Yue, D., et al.: User interest modeling based on browsing behavior. In: 2010 3rd International Conference on Advanced Computer Theory and Engineering (ICACTE), vol. 5, pp. V5-455–V5-458. IEEE (2010)
8. Chiang, R.D., Wang, Y.H., Chu, H.C.: Prediction of members' return visit rates using a time factor. Electron. Commer. Res. Appl. **12**(5), 362–371 (2013)
9. Ganesh, J., Reynolds, K.E., Luckett, M., Pomirleanu, N.: Online shopper motivations, and e-store attributes: an examination of online patronage behavior and hopper typologies. J. Retail. **86**, 106–115 (2010)
10. Chen, Y., Kuo, M., Wu, S., Tang, K.: Discovering recency, frequency, and monetary (RFM) sequential patterns from customer's purchasing data. Electron. Commer. Res. Appl. **8** (5), 241–251 (2009)
11. Wu, R.S., Chou, P.H.: Customer segmentation of multiple category data in ecommerce using a soft-clustering approach. Electron. Commer. Res. Appl. **10**(3), 331–341 (2011)
12. Kurasova, O.: Visual analysis of multidimensional data using self-organizing maps (SOM). Ph.D. dissertation, Institute of Mathematics and Informatics, Vilnius (2005)
13. Kriksciuniene, D., Pitner, T., Sakalauskas, V.: Tracking customer portrait by unsupervised classification techniques. Transform. Bus. Econ. **11**(3), 167–189 (2012)
14. Voges, K.E., Pope, N., Brown, M.R.: Cluster analysis of marketing data examining on-line shopping orientation: a comparison of k-means and rough clustering approaches. In: Heuristics and Optimization for Knowledge Discovery, pp. 207–224 (2002)
15. NAI: Study finds behaviorally-targeted ads more than twice as valuable, twice as effective as non-targeted online ads (2010). https://www.networkadvertising.org/pdfs/NAI_Beales_Release.pdf

A Proposal of an Academic Library Management System Based on an RDF Repository

Loredana Mocean[1]($\boxtimes$), Vasile Paul Bresfelean[1],
and Mara Hajdu Macelaru[2]

[1] Faculty of Economics and Business Administration, Babes-Bolyai University,
Teodor Mihali Str. 58-60, 400591 Cluj-Napoca, Romania
{loredana.mocean,paul.bresfelean}@econ.ubbcluj.ro
[2] North University Baia Mare, Baia Mare, Romania
macelaru.mara@gmail.com

Abstract. The application of Semantic Web technologies has the potential to overcome the limitations of classic WWW architectures and can be used to build Web portals with enhanced semantic interoperability. This paper proposes an innovative approach to implement e-learning portals components using state of the art Semantic Web technologies. We propose a new architecture in which a number of components are to be described and modeled using the Linked Data technological space built around RDF [24]. Creating and incorporating a virtual library based on RDF allows the combination of semantic links between resources, with the possibility of extending these semantics. At the application level, there will be entities capable of processing information in an intelligent manner and capable of reasoning, thus offering complex services like data search, resources retrieval, monitoring applications' activities or information filtering for both machines and people.

Keywords: Semantic Web · RDF · Database · Academic portal requirements · Virtual library

1 Introduction

In recent years portals development has been driven by the fact that organizations must provide the user with information and Web-based services in a required format and also extension opportunities. This is an important challenge, principally because most organizations, including universities, have rarely organized the information in a different format than the one imposed by legacy data storage practices (e.g., relational databases). A new and exciting aspect of Web management offered by portals is based on the idea of creating data and content models based on RDF-based learning objects and learning processes [1]. The evolved interfaces of most recent years could have a possible approach based on RDF, a framework meant to process metadata but also to interconnect it and to enable advanced interoperability. Therefore, we believe that online education based on RDF-driven portals is a highly relevant opportunity [2, 17, 18].

© Springer International Publishing AG 2017
W. Abramowicz et al. (Eds.): BIS 2016 Workshops, LNBIP 263, pp. 44–56, 2017.
DOI: 10.1007/978-3-319-52464-1_5

The aim of our study is to build a new architecture based on advanced interfaces using RDF [23]. We chose not to convert an existing database [20] but to substitute it with one based on an RDF graph repository [21] that is open to connectivity with other resources developed for an academic management portal. Starting with these premises, in Sect. 2 we present the existing characteristics and concepts of a classic portal, a research literature study and the main educational portals in Romania. Section 3 includes a summary of a comprehensive case study on Babes-Bolyai University's implemented portals, from their development to their higher levels, such as the logical level. These models can be examples for a future RDF specification that we intend to address. Section 4 describes the extended system architecture for an e-learning portal to which we aim to develop a Virtual Library, designed for plugging in different applications with semantic tools for the portal. Furthermore, in the same Sect. 4 we describe the RDF schema design of our new database and some insights regarding an early-stage implementation. At this level, we have the possibility to specify simple ontologies in order to define a hierarchical description of concepts and properties. The paper ends with a Conclusion section.

2 Problem Statement and Background

The recent development of Web technologies has led to the integration of multiple applications with semantic interoperability enabled by technologies proposed by the Semantic Web community (e.g. RDF and SPARQL). Among the advantages of this integration we mention: ease of federation, unified security model, collaboration features, localization, platform independence as well as the possibility of distributing RDF graphs across an enterprise or link them to enterprise partners' repositories.

2.1 State of the Art

Several articles describe RDF portals specification, technologies, architecture, and their novelties compared to other similar portals from a technological/algorithm point of view and/or from a functionality point of view. The portals were already implemented, their development process was finalized, and therefore the comparison with other existing portals is more accurate. Paper [3] introduces a functional representation of RDF graphs, while in [4] the authors propose an effective and scalable solution for search depth-determining problem of keyword query on a RDF data set. Keyword query on RDF data is an effective choice as there is no need to have knowledge about the data schema or a formal query language such as SPARQL. The article also compares two RDF management systems, one is their proposed system and the other one is Jena used to evaluate performance and usability. Another article [5] shows that the current e-learning standards and techniques are limited and proposes the use of RDF for mechanisms representation.

Paper [6] proposes an important query type over a large RDF graph. The article is inspired by the fact that the standard SPARQL query over RDF data requires query initiators to have a good domain knowledge of the data. This means that SPARQL queries over RDF data are not flexible and it is difficult to generate queries without knowing the domain.

In [7] the authors provided a precise theoretical framework for faceted search in the context of RDF-based knowledge graphs enhanced with OWL 2 ontologies. The framework allows to identify well-defined fragments of SPARQL that can be captured using faceted search as a query paradigm, and establish the computational complexity of answering such queries. Paper [8] investigates and finally explores the perspectives and steps for a seamless and meaningful databases integration into Semantic Web. In paper [9] the authors describe in what manner the RDF graphs are modeled using Jena, and compare how Semantic Web concepts can be designed and modeled using the two APIs. It also gives information about which API should be used in the development of the Semantic Based Web Applications for better performance. Other authors [10] propose a semantic search and a navigation method for semantic visualization based on a twofold procedure: querying and navigation. The former uses interrelations between concepts as opposed to the traditional keyword search that focuses just on resources.

Based on the state of the art research we choose to implement our application using RDF due to its flexibility, and that it can represent the triple nature in many ways and while being able to fit in our with particular application. At the same time, a major advantage to the RDF approach is the data query. In RDF all we have to do is store the triple nature of the specification, then look for triples that match complex patterns involving multiple entities which may require complex table joins in a relational database.

2.2   Education Portals in Romania

Higher education institutions have always described themselves as being communities: communities of students or educational communities. A harmonious mix of strategies based on campus and Internet relations could be a powerful and successful resolution. Implementing and integrating a portal within an institution are more related to changing the relationship management approach methods than to replacing the software and hardware equipment. In order to succeed, universities must predominantly invest in information technologies, business practices, institutional policies and last but not least human factors (culture, organization).

In Romania, portals have become a tool widely used in everyday activity. Some of the best known portals are presented in Table 1. According to trafic.ro, the most visited education portals sorted by number of visitors are the following: www.didactic.ro (the teacher modern portal - news, lessons, tests, textbooks, etc.), portal.edu.ro (SEI Educational portal - eLearning, computerization forum, teachers tenure), e-referate.ro, www.calificativ.ro (essays, games, quizzes, questions and answers, homework assistance, baccalaureate) www.ro-en.ro (Romanian-English, English-Romanian Dictionaries with collaborative features, lessons and games), www.studentie.ro (college admission, essays, scholarships and summer schools), www.e-scoala.ro (games and essays, music, horoscope, library, foreign language counseling).

Table 1. Best known portals in Romania

Website	Features	Description
www.edu.ro	The portal of Ministry of Nat. Education	Presents official information and documents
http://portal.edu.ro	Program initiated by the Min. of National Ed. and Sc. Research Program in 2001	Sustains the teaching/learning process in pre-university education with state of the art technologies
www.e-scoala.ro	Online School	Offers a database with useful free resources to students, pupils, and teacher; an open platform, anyone can contribute.
www.didactic.ro	Educational portal	Contains teaching materials specific to pre-university education. Materials are grouped into sections.
http://alegetidrumul.edu.ro	Vocational and technical education developing program	Offers the young students the possibility to get a job qualification while still in school and then get a paid job.
www.tvet.ro	National Centre for the development of vocational and technical education CNDIPT	Continues the reform of vocational and technical education (CIPT) that began with assistance from European Union assistance.
www.eos.ro	EOS Foundation Romania	Educational resources in information technology.
www.ise.ro	Institute of Education Sciences	Actively contributes to educational innovation through expertise, training, studies and research.
http://escoala.edu.ro	Virtual laboratories	Physics, Chemistry, Biology experiments
http://scoala.discovery.ro	Discovery school	Project by Discovery Networks, the company that owns channels Discovery Channel, Animal Planet and Discovery Science, in collaboration with the Romanian Ministry of National Education and Scientific Research
www.academiaonline.ro	e-learning platform	Offers free or paid courses in various fields
www.elearnacademy.ro	e-learning platform	Consultancy and training for e-learning

2.3 Research Challenge

All the websites and portals presented before are built in a traditional manner. However, the scientific, technological, economic and social implications of the Semantic

Web are substantial. Resources can be described in a machine-interpretable manner and vocabularies can be defined in a standardized way with terms provided by RDF Schema [11]. RDF Schema (RDFS) provides a terminology for building axioms that define classes, instances and properties using the RDF syntax, as well as class hierarchies, property hierarchies, property domains and ranges or annotations. In view of that, we plan to create and implement a new e-learning portal where we could utilize RDF and contextual applications for data management. Some major challenges of such a portal would be the related to content availability for e-learning, evolving ontologies, scalability, multilanguage, visualization in order to reduce information overload. This paper presents the case of the Babes-Bolyai University academic portal, its requirements, and describes a proposed approach and design decisions for a supporting resource management system based on RDF graphs, which will be exemplified for the Virtual Library component of the portal.

3 Case Study: Portals Implemented Within Babes-Bolyai University

In this section we describe several IT modules and technical applications from our institution, principally for a future development. Within Babes-Bolyai University (BBU) of Cluj-Napoca the systems' modules, IT applications, websites, e-Learning portals etc. can be divided into several categories presented in the following subsections.

3.1 Systems and Applications Developed In-House

The BBU Department of Information Technology and Communications has developed during the recent years a number of applications so as to improve facilities offered to students, teachers and employees. These are grouped into three major systems.

AcademicInfo (http://dtic.ubbcluj.ro/academicinfo/) models the school records processes for secretaries, on-line grades for the exams, provides access to school records and evaluation information for both teachers and students, and generates synthetic information and relevant reports for the education processes. We highlight here some of its features: choosing optional courses for the whole university, detailing the educational activities (different levels of education, modules for lifelong and continuous learning, specific study plans), multilingual support, tax integration between faculties and the economic administration, students' requirements, courses evaluation.

ManageAsist (http://dtic.ubbcluj.ro/manageasist/) is an integrated system used by the administrative management of the university, intended to model and integrate its specific activities and provide assistance facilities for different managerial levels. The system has a number of core features, including: distributed access, integrated database, modeling the organizational chart and the information flows between departments, specific procedures and processing, statements and reports on various levels, security granularity and access rights etc. (Fig. 1).

Research management (http://dtic.ubbcluj.ro/managementul-cercetarii/) is an integrated online information system for research management in the university. It

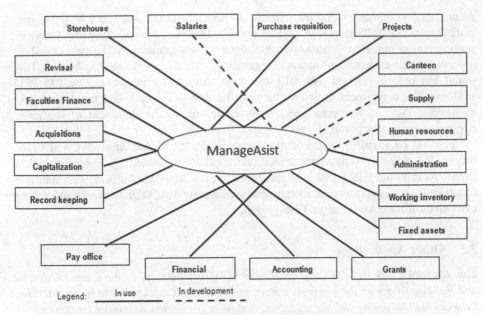

Fig. 1. ManageAsist structure in the present day (http://dtic.ubbcluj.ro/manageasist/)

plays an important role in quantitative analysis by providing summaries for research and artistic results.

The structure of Research management application consists of three sections (according to http://dtic.ubbcluj.ro/managementul-cercetarii/):

- Web access for departments' and units' managers (reports, syntheses for departments and units)
- Web access for University's and faculties' managers (reports, syntheses for faculties and university)
- Web access for professors, researches and PhD candidates (input for their activities and individual reports).

3.2   eLearning Portals

In this subsection we concisely describe some relevant portals from BBU, all based on traditional web technologies. **ID-FR Portal** (https://portal.portalid.ubbcluj.ro) was initiated in 2010 after an investment of over one million Euro acquired with European Union funding.

Business Information Systems (BIS) department's portal (http://bis.econ. ubbcluj.ro/moodle/) from the Faculty of Economics and Business Administration (FSEGA) is based on the Moodle (Modular Object-Oriented Dynamic Learning Environment) platform, an e-Learning Open Source which can be downloaded free, used, modified and even distributed under the terms of the GNU GPL - General public license. Some of the advantages of the Moodle platform comprise the ability to expand, to encompass a wide range of features and to adapt to various courses, requirements, methods of examination. Students from BIS specializations and other FSEGA specializations take full advantage of this portal's features; among those we mention: posting course materials, laboratories, bibliography, assignments, assessment based on diverse models of tests and quizzes, organizing virtual groups, messaging etc. This portal has been developed with BIS own funds and was implemented by BIS PhD students. The department preferred this solution due to the ease and rapidity of customization that can be performed by any professor, to the detriment of the more expensive university portal.

FSPAC e-Learning portal of the Faculty of Political, Administrative and Communication Sciences (http://fspac.ubbcluj.ro/moodle/) supported by European Union funds. Akin to the BIS portal it is also based on the Moodle platform, with multiple functionalities to support educational processes for its own ODL students and for its extensions from other cities in Transylvania.

3.3 Other Applications

The **Alumni UBB** website (http://alumni.ubbcluj.ro/) belongs to the Career, Alumni and Relationship with the Business community Center. It is intended to be an interface between the university and its graduates, and its main goal is to build a community of alumni based on communication and adapted to alumni's and faculties' necessities.

UBBstudJobs portal (http://job.stud.ubbcluj.ro/) belongs to the CCARMA center (developed on the CMS platform Joomla! / Job Board), and aims to be an online recruitment platform that brings together job offers, traineeships and internships for students and graduates. Through this platform, employers can post job vacancies, traineeships, internships and students /graduates can apply for them by uploading their Curriculum Vitae, a letter of intent or can recommend a particular job further on to their friends through social networks etc. It is a very good idea but the portal needs updates and continuous upkeep.

In 2014 the Center for Information Systems of the Direction of Information Technology and Communications launched the **online payment service** (https://plati.ubbcluj.ro).

Faculties' and departments' own websites - in most cases being implemented and maintained by their own staff. For example, we present the **website of the Faculty of Economics and Business Administration FSEGA** (https://econ.ubbcluj.ro/) which includes information and announcements about courses and labs, timetable, infrastructure, education and scientific events and meetings, internships, career opportunities etc. It contains important hyperlinks to other websites belonging to FSEGA's own departments, entities and centers (Lingua Center, Counseling and Vocational Guidance Center FSEGA etc.) and also to students organizations' websites.

FSEGA Online platform is a project started in 2013 and is still being upgraded in order to become an IT tool to support students, teaching and management staff. Therefore, there are a number of features related to teaching staff's curriculum vitae and general information, FSEGA on-line archive, links to the e-learning portals and other BBU portals (AcademicInfo).

4 Proposal of an RDF-Based Virtual Library

4.1 General Architecture

In line with the implemented systems in BBU, we attempt to create a new one, based on Web 3.0 technologies. With the new proposed architecture, we aspire the following for our academic portal: to be a central access point for a wide range of information and activities; to be specifically designed to ensure an efficient user interface for multiple customizable devices; to apply a set of tools and APIs in order to design and develop components based on the new semantic web; to develop standard mechanisms for integrating other basic applications for Web and post interesting information. Our

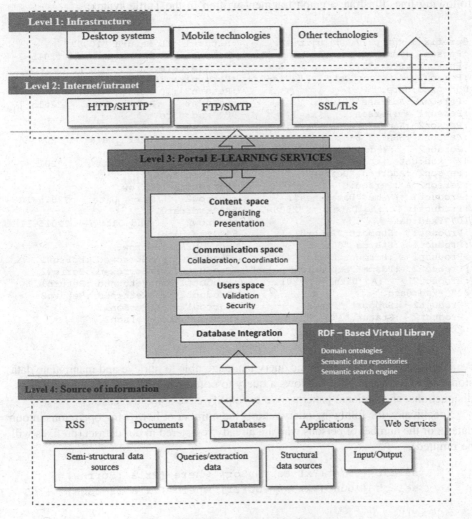

Fig. 2. The proposed portal architecture

contribution is to integrate a virtual library based on the RDF - Schema, a new solution for Web applications with a significant impact on users' community (see Fig. 2).

4.2   Design Details

Our database structure of the virtual library puts forward an innovative approach, being based on RDF and RDF schema for data management purposes. The application data will be stored, processed and queried by using Linked Data technologies [22], while the data model is based on RDF (Fig. 3 shows a graph representation for the Virtual Library database). This opens the potential to use queries that integrate information from the virtual library graph with information relevant to some other module (e.g., library data with student data). We also used Sesame as storage technology [14]. The following lines illustrate a graph fragment written in the Turtle syntax:

```
@prefix : <http://ubbcluj.ro#>.         :Return1 :ID_Return "1000".
:Person1 :Name "Steven Alexander".      :Return1    :Return_Date    "2015-7-
:Person1 :SSN  "190".                   8"^^xsd:date.
:Person1    :RecordDate    "2014-03-    :Return1 a :Return.
05"^^xsd:date.                          :Return2 :ID_Return "1001".
:Person1 :Address "Cluj".               :Return2    :Return_Date    "2015-7-
:Person1 a :Person.                     9"^^xsd:date.
:Person2 :Name "Abraham David".         :Return2 a :Return.
:Person2 :SSN  "188".                   :Borrow1    :Start_Date    "2015-6-
:Person2    :RecordDate    "2014-17-    10"^^xsd:date.
4"^^xsd:date.                           :Borrow1    :End_Date    "2015-7-
:Person2 :Address "Dej".                10"^^xsd:date.
:Person2 a :Person.                     :Borrow1 a :Borrow.
:Product1 :PName "Databases".           :Borrow2    :Start_Date    "2015-10-
:Product1    :Aq_Date    "2009-11-      5"^^xsd:date.
10"^^xsd:date .                         :Borrow2    :End_Date    "2015-11-
:Product1 :Support "Paper".             5"^^xsd:date.
:Product1 :Status "0".                  :Borrow2 a :Borrow.
:Product1 a :Product.                   :Product1 :wasBorrowed :Borrow1.
:Product2 :PName "WebDesign".           :Product2 :wasBorrowed :Borrow2.
:Product2    :Aq_Date    "2011-12-      :Product1 :wasReturned :Return1.
22"^^xsd:date.                          :Product2 :wasReturned :Return2.
:Product2 :Support "Paper".             :Borrow1 :to :Person1.
:Product2 :Status "1".                  :Borrow2 :to :Person2.
:Product2 a :Product.
```

We use the SPARQL semantic query language able to retrieve and manipulate data stored in RDF format [13]. It allows a query to comprise triple patterns, conjunctions, disjunctions, and optional patterns. We exemplify here some use cases.

Specifically, the following query returns the number of borrowing operations in our dataset or the number of persons who are already registered in our dataset (prefixes will be omitted).

```
select (count(?x) as ?NuBor) where {?x a :Borrow}
select (count(?x) as ?NuPer) where {?x a :Person}
```

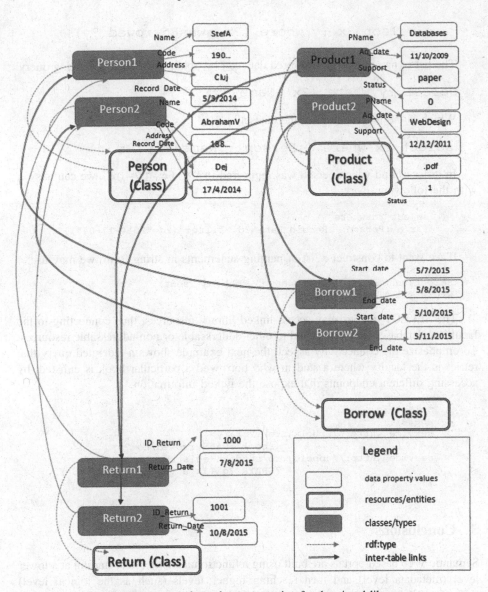

Fig. 3. The proposed graph representation for the virtual library

Another example lists all the persons from the dataset with their name and their personal code.

```
select ?y where {?x a :Person; :Name ?y; :SSN ?z}
```

The list of all borrowed objects can be obtained with the next query:

```
select ?x ?y where {?x :wasBorrowed ?y}
```

The list of names existing in stored data can be obtained with the following query:

```
select ?y where {?x :Name ?y}
```

Which is the first name from the dataset?

```
select ?x where {:Person1 :Name ?x}
```

In order to find which person was registered in "2014-17-04", we can answer with the following query:

```
select ?d where
{?x a :Person; :Record_Date ?d  filter (?d="2014-17-04")}
```

If we want to construct a list of naming statements in string form, we may use:

```
select(concat(?t,"has the name",?b)) as ?sent)
where {?x :SSN ?t; :Name ?b}
```

The SELECT queries may access linked library resources, thus connecting to the faculties' databases, to e-books and to other addressable or non-addressable resources. To emphasize the connectivity aspect, the next example shows a federated query that retrieves the faculty where a student who borrowed a particular book is enlisted, by accessing different endpoints that expose the linked information:

```
select ?g
where {
service <http://ubbcluj.ro/library>
                         {?book :wasBorrowed/to ?x}
service <http://ubbcluj.ro/studentRegistry
                         {GRAPH ?g {?x a :BachelorStudent}}
}
```

5 Conclusions

Semantic Web based portals are built using a functional architecture, starting at a lower level (metadata level) and then reaching higher levels (such as the logical level) ([15, 16, 19]). Languages available on each of these levels can meet the requirements of different types of applications. Direct mapping from relational data to RDF [17] and the metadata level provides the general framework for expressing simple semantic assertions. The model offered in this article consists of RDF specifications and can be used by languages that are positioned on the higher levels. The schema level offers the opportunity of specifying simple ontologies in order to define a hierarchical description of concepts and properties. The logical level will introduce some more complicated ontology languages capable of modeling sophisticated ontologies. These languages are based on the schema level, while the theoretical framework is assigned by description logics which can be expressed with terms from OWL [25] and RDF Schema.

The virtual library based on the RDF Schema is designed for easily retrieving instance data from a potential organization-wide knowledge base. Due to the continuous growing volume of information that overloads the new portals, it may be difficult to automate the intelligent data retrieval. The architecture model and the components proposed for implementation are intended to enable intelligent retrieval of information that can be connected across data sources relevant for an academic portal.

As future research directions we indicate here the aim of enriching such a repository with reasoning capabilities and also to evaluate query performance in comparison to the existing portal based on relational databases.

Acknowledgement. The present research was supported by the PNII-RU-TE-2014-4-2640 UEFISCDI grant "eTrajectory – students' professional trajectory".

References

1. Buchmann, R.A., Szekely, A., Pulcher, D.: Temporary belief sets management in adaptive training systems. In: Abramowicz, W., Maciaszek, L., Węcel, K. (eds.) BIS 2011. LNBIP, vol. 97, pp. 99–110. Springer, Heidelberg (2011). doi:10.1007/978-3-642-25370-6_10
2. Reynolds, D., Shabajee, P., Cayzer, S.: Semantic Information Portals (2016). http://www2004.wwwconference.org/docs/2p290.pdf
3. Gayo, J., Jeuring, J., Rodríguez, J.M.Á.: Inductive representations of RDF graphs. Sci. Comput. Program. **95**(2014), 135–146 (2014)
4. Bae, M., Kang, S., et al.: Semantic similarity method for keyword query system on RDF. Neurocomputing **146**(2014), 264–275 (2014)
5. Sancho, P., Martínez, I., Fernández-Manjón, B.: Semantic web technologies applied to e-learning. J. Univers. Comput. Sci. **11**(9), 1470 (2005)
6. Kisung, K., Bongki, M., Hyoung-Joo, K.: RG-index: an RDF graph index for efficient SPARQL query processing. Expert Syst. Appl. **41**, 4596–4607 (2014)
7. Xiang, L., De Hoyos, E., Chebotko, A., Bin, F., Reilly, K.: k-nearest keyword search in RDF graphs. Web Semant. Sci. Serv. Agents World Wide Web **22**, 40–56 (2013)
8. Spanos, D.E., Stavrou, P.S., Mitrou, P.: Bringing relational databases into the semantic web: a survey. Semant. Web 1–41 (2016). IOS Press
9. Arenas, M., Graub, B.C., Kharlamov, E., Marciuška, S., Zheleznyakov, D.: Faceted search over RDF-based knowledge graphs. Web Semant. Sci. Serv. Agents World Wide Web **37–38**, 55 (2015)
10. Wang, D., Zou, L., Zhao, D.: Top-k queries on RDF graphs. Inf. Sci. **316**, 201–217 (2015)
11. Kumar, A.P., Kumar, A., Vipin, K.N.: Architecting and designing of semantic web based application using the JENA and PROTÉGÉ – a comprehensive study. Int. J. Comput. Sci. Inf. Technol. **2**(3), 1279 (2011)
12. Myungjin, L., Wooju, K., Hong, J.S., Park, S.: Semantic association-based search and visualization method on the semantic web portal. Int. J. Comput. Netw. Commun. (IJCNC) **2**(1), January 2010
13. SPARQL Query Language for RDF (2016). https://www.w3.org/TR/2006/WD-rdf-sparql-query-20061004/
14. Sesame official site (2016). http://rdf4j.org/

15. Benjamins, R., Contreras, J., Corcho, O., Gómez-Pérez, A.: Six challenges for the semantic web. In: Proceedings of the First International Semantic Web Conference, SWC2002, Cerdena, Italia (2002). ISBN 978-3-540-43760-4
16. Relational Databases on the Semantic Web (2016). https://www.w3.org/DesignIssues/RDB-RDF.html
17. A Direct Mapping of Relational Data to RDF, https://www.w3.org/TR/rdb-direct-mapping/
18. D2RQ Accessing Relational Databases as Virtual RDF Graphs (2016). http://d2rq.org/
19. Fayed, G., Sameh, D., Ahmad, H., Jihad, M., et al.: e-learning model based on semantic web technology. Int. J. Comput. Inf. Sci. **4**, 63 (2006)
20. Changtao, Q., Wolfgang, N., Schinzel, N.: Integrating schema-specific native XML repositories into a RDF-based e-learning P2P network. Proc. Int. Conf. Dublin Core Metadata e-Communities (2002)
21. De Virgilio, R., Maccioni, A., Torlone, R.: Converting Relational to Graph Databases (2016). http://www.inf.uniroma3.it/ ~ torlone/pubs/grades2014.pdf
22. Heath, T., Bizer, T.C.: Linked Data: Evolving the Web into a Global Data Space (2016). http://linkeddatabook.com/editions/1.0/
23. Turtle - Terse RDF Triple Language (2016). https://www.w3.org/TeamSubmission/turtle/
24. RDF (2016). https://www.w3.org/RDF/
25. OWL (2016). https://www.w3.org/2001/sw/wiki/OWL

The Paradigm of Relatedness

László Grad-Gyenge[1]([✉]) and Peter Filzmoser[2]([✉])

[1] Creo Group, Budapest, Hungary
laszlo.grad-gyenge@creo.hu
[2] TU Vienna, Vienna, Austria
peter.filzmoser@tuwien.ac.at

Abstract. This paper introduces the paradigm of relatedness, the generalization of the paradigm of user interest. Relatedness is typically interpreted in a graph based information representation environment, where the content-based and collaborative information is treated at the same abstraction level. To demonstrate the effectiveness of the paradigm, various graph based recommendation methods are evaluated on standard datasets, as MovieLens and MovieTweetings. In our experiment, we focus on the information sparse environment and measure coverage, precision, recall and nDCG on top-N recommendation lists. The primary conclusion of our work is that the paradigm of relatedness is a promising direction as the evaluation results show a significant increase in the recommendation quality of the method implementing the paradigm.

Keywords: Paradigm of relatedness · Paradigm of user interaction · Knowledge graph · Spreading activation · Recommendation spreading · Graph recommender

1 Introduction

The formula of the traditional collaborative filtering method is built around the known rating values. The essence of the method is to aggregate the user ratings on the specified item to calculate a rating estimation. Generalizing the traditional method, matrix factorization, a prominent class of recommendation techniques, derive the recommendations by finding the latent factors of the user feedback. These techniques focus on the information found in the either explicit or implicit user interest on items, thus the mentioned methods are inherently based on the paradigm of user interest. Next to matrix factorization methods, graph based recommendation techniques are also a promising direction. Compared to matrix factorization methods, graph based techniques have the potential (i) to involve transitivity into the recommendation process, (ii) to generalize the relations between the entities and (iii) to operate with heterogeneous information sources.

Grad-Gyenge et al. [7] introduce the knowledge graph, an information representation method. The involved graph based technique generalizes the concept of information source, thus the method is capable to model heterogeneous information. As the knowledge graph represents the information necessary to conduct

© Springer International Publishing AG 2017
W. Abramowicz et al. (Eds.): BIS 2016 Workshops, LNBIP 263, pp. 57–68, 2017.
DOI: 10.1007/978-3-319-52464-1_6

collaborative filtering, content-based filtering and partly knowledge based recommendations at the same generalization level, the methods operating on the graph generalize the paradigm of user interest to relatedness. As it is illustrated in more details in Sect. 3, relatedness can mean, for example (i) a social relation between two users, (ii) a user interest on an item or (iii) a common attribute value of two items. The examples show that relatedness can mean any connection or association between the entities of the recommendation scenario. An important property of relatedness is the transitivity, i.e. a friend of a friend bought an item or the user bought a similar item. Our expectation for a calculation method is to assign a higher rank to those items, which are topographically close and to those which are related in multiple ways to the user in question.

In their paper, Grad-Gyenge et al. define recommendation spreading, which method can be treated as the generalization of collaborative filtering for the graph based case. Although recommendation spreading conducts its calculation on the knowledge graph, the method strongly relies on the rating relation between the users and items. In other words, recommendation spreading is constrained by the paradigm of user interest. In our paper, spreading activation, a well-known method operating on semantic networks is evaluated. As the method does not model the user interest as a distinguished relation, it can be treated as the demonstration of operating with relatedness instead of user interest. The evaluation results show a significant increase in the recommendation quality.

Section 2 gives insight into related research conducted. Section 3 contains how the information is represented in the knowledge graph. Section 4 provides an overview on the datasets and discusses the representation of the information. Section 5 describes the recommendation methods. Section 6 contains the evaluation method. The evaluation results can be found in the Sect. 7. Section 8 concludes the paper.

2   Related Work

First of all, we would like to mention recommendation techniques based on various information sources, in order to show how the relatedness can be interpreted in a concrete recommendation scenario. To demonstrate the capabilities of graph based techniques, social network based approaches are mentioned, as the graph based representation is typical in the case of social networks. Then spreading activation based techniques are presented. In most cases, the approach is used to enhance the recommendation method with semantic functionality, as the technique is typically used in conjunction with ontologies.

Konstas et al. [18] extend the basic collaborative filtering technique with tags to recommend music tracks. They conduct a random walk on a tripartite graph of users, items and tags. Their method is based on collaborative filtering and can be treated as a step in the direction of the generalization of user interest. The relatedness can be interpreted between the different combinations of user, item and tag pairs. Hidasi et al. [12] involve the context information into the recommendation process. Their representation method is a tensor, which is a possible alternative to the graph based representation. We would like to mention here that the interpretation of relatedness is not trivial in a tensor environment because the interpretation of the transitivity is atypical in the user interest paradigm.

The social network has been found to be a useful information source to calculate recommendations from [8–10]. Social relations are typically represented in a graph. The concrete cases of social relations can be treated as relatedness between the users. The involvement of trust networks into the recommendation process was popular in the years of 2004–2006 [16, 19, 23]. Trust is also interpreted as a social relationship and is modelled as an asymmetric relation between the users. Next to contact lists, tags, groups favourites, opinions, Kazienko et al. [17] calculate the recommendations also from the social network. Their work illustrate several cases of relatedness between the entities of the recommendation process.

Blanco-Fernandez et al. [2] focus on content based recommendation and present a spreading activation based technique. Hussein et al. [14] introduce SPREADR to close the gap between context-awareness and self-adaptation. Gao et al. [6] propose a method incorporating user interests and domain knowledge in an ontology. Codina et al. [3] define a reasoning method to estimate user ratings on items. The item score is calculated as the weighted average of related concepts. Troussov et al. [22] define a tag aware recommendation technique and investigate the decay and spreading parameters of spreading activation methods. Alvarez et al. [1] introduce ONTOSPREAD, a sophisticated, spreading activation technique in the scope of medical systems. Jiang et al. present an ontology based user model [15] and a spreading activation based recommendation technique.

3   Representation

As described by Grad-Gyenge et al. [7], similarly to the representation method of ontologies, the information is stored in a heterogeneous undirected graph. Nodes represent the entities playing role in the recommendation process, edges represent the relations between the entities. A generalized practice is used to represent user and item attributes. For each attribute, a new node is inserted in the graph and is bound to the corresponding user or item with an edge of respective type. In this case, users sharing a common attribute value are connected with a path of length 2.

The information is represented in a labeled, weighted, restricted multigraph as introduced in [7].

$$\mathcal{K} = (N, E, T_N, T_E, t_N, t_E, r).$$

N is the set of nodes, $E \subseteq \{\{u, v\} | u \in N \wedge v \in N\}$ is the set of undirected edges in the graph. T_N and T_E denote the set of node types and edge types, respectively. Function $t_N \subset N \times T_N$ and function $t_E \subset E \times T_E$ assigns a node type to each node and edge type to edge respectively. The function $r \subset E_r \times \mathbf{R}, E_r = \{e | e \in E, t_E(e) = \mathtt{ItemRating}\}$ assigns rating values to the edges of type rating. The graph is restricted to one edge of a type between a specific pair of nodes.

4   Datasets

4.1   MovieLens

The MovieLens datasets are published by GroupLens [11]. The MovieLens 1M dataset is used as this is the richest one in user and item attributes among the published MovieLens datasets. The dataset contains users with attributes, items (movies) with attributes and ratings data. The user attributes are gender, age, occupation and U.S. ZIP code. Each user attribute corresponds to one node in the graph, except ZIP codes. In the case of the ZIP code, only the first digit is used, as it encodes the geographical region in the U.S. Item attributes are also represented with nodes, introducing a graph node for each attribute value. The item attributes are year of publishing and genre. One movie can have multiple genres meaning that a node representing a movie can have multiple neighbour nodes representing a genre. The dataset contains 6040 users, 3883 movies and 1000209 ratings. Ratings are time-stamped. A rating represents a user preference on a movie on the $[1, 5]$ scale. In our experiment, the rating value is normalized to the $[0, 1]$ scale by dividing it by 5.

Table 1. Count of graph entities by type in the MovieLens dataset

(a) Count of Node Types

Node type	Count
Person	6 040
AgeCategory	7
Gender	2
Occupation	21
ZipCodeRegion	10
Item	3 883
Genre	18
YearOfPublishing	81

(b) Count of Relation Types

Edge type	Count
PersonAgeCategory	6 040
PersonGender	6 040
PersonOccupation	6 040
PersonZipCodeRegion	6 040
ItemGenre	6 408
ItemYearOfPublishing	3 883
ItemRating	1 000 209

Table 1a summarizes the node types and counts. Nodes of type `Person` represent the users in the system. Nodes of type `Item` represent items (movies) contained in the dataset. Nodes of type `AgeCategory` represent age categories like `25-34`. Nodes of type `Gender` represent gender like `female` and `male`. Nodes of type `Occupation` represent occupations like `scientist`. Nodes of type `ZipCodeRegion` represent the U.S. region encoded in the first digit of the ZIP code, for instance `1`. Nodes of type `Genre` represent movie genres like `drama`. Nodes of type `YearOfPublishing` represent the year when a movie was published, for instance `1997`.

Table 1b presents the edge types and counts used to represent the MovieLens dataset in the knowledge graph. Edge types `PersonAgeCategory`, `PersonGender`, `PersonOccupation` and `PersonZipCodeRegion` represent that the specific person has the specific person attribute value. Edges types of

`ItemGenre` and `ItemYearOfPublishing` represent that the specific item has the specific item attribute value. Edges of type `ItemRating` represent a true rating (with the rating value assigned by r to the edge) for the specific user on the specific item.

4.2 MovieTweetings

The MovieTweetings dataset [4] is extracted from Twitter data, containing rating values from well structured tweets. In our experiment, the MovieTweetings 200 K variant is used. The dataset contains users, items (movies) with attributes and ratings data. The item attributes present in the dataset are year of publishing and genre. Similarly to the MovieLens dataset, a movie can have multiple genres. The dataset contains 25011 users, 14732 items and, as the name of the dataset indicates, 200000 rating values. Rating values have a time-stamp. A rating represents a user preference on a movie on the $[0, 10]$ scale. In our experiment, the rating value is normalized to the $[0, 1]$ scale by dividing it by 10. In our experiment, only the ratings having a value greater than 0 are involved, as these ratings encode user ratings on items.

Table 2. Count of graph entities by type in the MovieTweetings dataset

<table>
<tr><td colspan="2">(a) Count of Node Types</td><td colspan="2">(b) Count of Relation Types</td></tr>
<tr><td>Node type</td><td>Count</td><td>Edge type</td><td>Count</td></tr>
<tr><td>Person</td><td>25 011</td><td>ItemGenre</td><td>34 975</td></tr>
<tr><td>Item</td><td>14 732</td><td>ItemYearOfPublishing</td><td>14 732</td></tr>
<tr><td>Genre</td><td>26</td><td>ItemRating</td><td>200 000</td></tr>
<tr><td>YearOfPublishing</td><td>108</td><td></td><td></td></tr>
</table>

Table 2a summarizes the node types and counts. Nodes of type `Person` represent the users in the system. Nodes of type `Item` represent items (movies) contained in the dataset. Nodes of type `Genre` represent movie genres like `drama`. Nodes of type `YearOfPublishing` represent the year when a movie was published, for instance `1997`.

Table 2b presents the edge types and counts used to represent the MovieTweetings dataset in the knowledge graph. Edges types of `ItemGenre` and `ItemYearOfPublishing` represent that the specific item has the specific item attribute value. Edges of type `ItemRating` represent a true rating (with the rating value as edge attribute) for the specific user on the specific item.

5   Methods

Three recommendation methods are defined in the experiment. Collaborative filtering acts as the benchmark method of spreading activation and recommendation spreading.

5.1   Collaborative Filtering

Collaborative filtering [21] is a well-known method in the field of recommender systems. In our experiment, the method is utilized to generate rating estimations of users on items. To provide a rating estimation for user u on item i, collaborative filtering uses the following formula

$$\hat{r}_{u,i} = \bar{r}_u + \frac{\sum_{e \in E_r, \{v,i\}=e, v \neq i, u \neq v} (r(e) - \bar{r}_v) s_{u,v}}{\sum_{e \in E_r, \{v,i\}=e, v \neq i, u \neq v} s_{u,v}},$$

where $\hat{r}_{u,i}$ is the estimated rating value for user u on item i. Notation $\bar{r}_u$ stands for the average of the already issued ratings by user u, $u \in N_P$. The function r is defined in Sect. 3. The similarity between user u and user v is calculated with Pearson correlation on the common rated items, as

$$s_{u,v} = \frac{\sum_{i \in C_{u,v}, e \in E_r, e=\{u,i\}, f \in E_r, f=\{v,i\}} (r(e) - \bar{r}_u)(r(f) - \bar{r}_v)}{\sqrt{\sum_{i \in C_{u,v}, e \in E_r, e=\{u,i\}} (r(e) - \bar{r}_u)^2} \sqrt{\sum_{i \in C_{u,v}, f \in E_r, f=\{v,i\}} (r(f) - \bar{r}_v)^2}}.$$

5.2   Spreading Activation

Spreading activation [20] is a well-known method in the field of ontologies, associative networks, semantic networks and RDF knowledge bases [13]. In our experiment, spreading activation is utilized to calculate activation scores for nodes representing items to recommend on a knowledge base introduced in Sect. 3. The method runs an iteration until a certain **step limit** (c) is reached.

In each iteration step, spreading activation calculates the activation of each node in the knowledge graph. The activation function is denoted as $a_{(i)} \subset N \times \mathbf{R}$, where i is the iteration step. In the initial step of the iteration, the activations are set to 0 except for n_s, $a_{(0)}(n_s) = 1$, where n_s denotes the source node, which is the node representing the user to generate recommendations for.

In each iteration step, the activation of the nodes is recalculated. For each node, a part of the activation is kept at the node and another part of the activation is distributed to its neighbours. The former amount is controlled by the **activation relax** parameter (r_a), the latter amount is determined by the **spreading relax** parameter (r_s). The activation in the next iteration step is determined by the following formula

$$a_{(i+1)}(n) = r_a a_{(i)}(n) + r_s \sum_{m \in M_n} \frac{a_{(i)}(m)}{z_m},$$

where $n \in N$, $i > 0$, M_n denotes the neighbour nodes of n, $M_n = \{m | \{m,n\} \in E\}$, z_m denotes the count of neighbours of m, $z_m = |\{p | \{m,p\} \in E\}|$. This way the outgoing activation of each node is distributed along all neighbour nodes equally. To calculate the activation scores, an iteration is performed until the specified **step limit** is reached.

5.3 Recommendation Spreading

Recommendation spreading is involved to estimate rating values of users on items as introduced by Grad-Gyenge et al. [7]. The method is based on spreading activation, running the same iteration as defined in Sect. 5.2. During the iteration, the activation flown through each rating edge is summarized as

$$A_e = \sum_{i \in [0, s-1], m \in e, m \in N_P} r_s \frac{a_{(i)}(m)}{z_m},$$

where e is an edge representing a rating, $e \in E_r$, N_P is the set of nodes representing persons, $N_P = \{n | n \in N, t_N(n) = \texttt{Person}\}$. Similarly to collaborative filtering, to estimate the rating values for an item, recommendation spreading uses a weighted average of rating values as

$$\cdot \; \hat{r}_{u,i} = \bar{r}_u + \frac{\sum_{e \in E_r, \{v,i\} = e, v \neq i, u \neq v} (r(e) - \bar{r}_v) A_e}{\sum_{e \in E_r, \{v,i\} = e, v \neq i, u \neq v} A_e}.$$

5.4 Recommendation Lists

As in this experiment we are interested in the quality of the top n recommended items, the described methods are utilized to generate recommendation lists. The recommendation lists are the sorted list of the items by the estimated user preference in descending order. This way the item with the highest estimated preference is the first item in the recommendation list. In the case of collaborative filtering and recommendation spreading, the user preference is the estimated rating value. In the case of spreading activation, the user preference is the activation of the node representing the item. Nodes with no rating estimation or activation are not included in the recommendation list.

6 Evaluation

6.1 Method Configurations

In the case of spreading activation and recommendation spreading, different step limit settings are evaluated, while keeping the spreading parameters at a constant value. As our preliminary evaluation results show, these calculation methods are not sensitive to the various r_a and r_s settings, hence both r_a and r_s are set to 0.5. In the rest of the paper, the following abbreviations are used to identify the method configurations.

- CF – collaborative filtering
- SA_n – Activation spreading with step limit n
- RS_n – Recommendation spreading with step limit n

6.2   Evaluation Measures

During the evaluation process, coverage, precision, recall and nDCG are measured on the top 10 items. If the method in question is not able to generate at least 10 recommendations, the recommendation case is treated as a non-coverage case and no evaluation measure is recorded. To calculate precision and recall, the items having a true rating value greater or equal than 0.8 are treated relevant.

6.3   Evaluation Method

To evaluate the methods, an iteration is conducted through the true ratings in time-stamp order until the specified `evaluation step limit` is reached. Each evaluation step consists of the following tasks.

1. The next rating (user, item, rating value) is taken from the dataset.
2. A recommendation list is generated for the user by the evaluated method.
3. Evaluation measures are logged.
4. The true rating is added to the knowledge base as a new edge of type `ItemRating`.

Before starting to evaluate a method, all the edges of type `ItemRating` are eliminated from the knowledge base. The knowledge base is filled with edges of type `ItemRating` during the evaluation process.

7   Results

The method configurations described in Sect. 6.1 are evaluated on the MovieLens and on the MovieTweetings dataset. The datasets are represented in the knowledge base as described in Sect. 3 and are evaluated with the evaluation method described in Sect. 6.3. The `evaluation step limit` in both the case of the MovieLens dataset and the MovieTweetings dataset is set to 10000. A portion of the rating data is used for evaluation because we are interested in the information sparse case.

Table 3 summarizes the evaluation measures of the evaluated methods on the top 10 results after the last evaluation step on both the MovieLens and the MovieTweetings dataset. Column `Method` contains the method configuration as described in Sect. 6.1. Column `Coverage` contains the number of cases the method configuration is able to deliver at least 10 recommendations. Columns `nDCG`, `Precision` and `Recall` present the mean of nDCG, mean of precision and mean of recall of the specific method, respectively.

Looking at the evaluation results, the $RS_{[4,8]}$ notation is introduced to stand for the subset of RS_n where $n \in [4,8]$, as unlike RS_3, the method configurations in this group show a very similar performance. At first, the performance of the method configurations is compared, then the measures are analysed over the datasets.

Table 3. Evaluation results on the MovieLens and on the MovieTweetings dataset

Dataset	MovieLens				MovieTweetings			
Method	Coverage	nDCG	Precision	Recall	Coverage	nDCG	Precision	Recall
SA_3	9998	0.916	**0.674**	**0.073**	6204	**0.937**	0.431	0.158
SA_4	9998	0.916	**0.674**	**0.073**	6204	**0.937**	0.431	0.158
SA_5	**9999**	**0.917**	0.672	**0.073**	6204	0.935	0.434	0.158
SA_6	**9999**	**0.917**	0.667	**0.073**	6204	0.934	0.435	0.159
SA_7	**9999**	0.914	0.661	0.072	6204	0.932	**0.437**	**0.16**
SA_8	**9999**	0.908	0.655	0.072	6204	0.931	**0.437**	**0.16**
RS_3	9980	0.293	0.148	0.009	4823	0.299	0.109	0.036
RS_4	9990	0.292	0.146	0.009	6200	0.056	0.016	0.004
RS_5	9990	0.291	0.144	0.009	6200	0.054	0.015	0.004
RS_6	9990	0.291	0.142	0.009	6202	0.052	0.014	0.004
RS_7	9990	0.29	0.141	0.009	6202	0.051	0.014	0.003
RS_8	9990	0.29	0.140	0.009	6202	0.05	0.014	0.003
CF	9669	0.27	0.055	0.003	4248	0.128	0.03	0.009

7.1   The Comparison of the Methods

Regarding to the coverage, the SA_n delivers the best result, as this method is constrained the less to reach an item node. The CF has the lowest coverage, as this method has the most constraints on the properties of the path between the user and the items to recommend. To be more exact, the path is restricted to edges of type ItemRating and to the exact length 3. The RS_n has a bit lower coverage than SA_n. In this case, the type of the last edge of the path should be ItemRating. In the case of the MovieTweetings dataset, the RS_3 is an exception, as the coverage of the RS_3 is closer to the coverage of the CF than to the coverage of the $RS_{[4,8]}$. The low coverage can be explained by the lack of user attribute values in the dataset.

In the case of the MovieLens dataset, regarding nDCG, precision and recall, the SA_n shows the highest performance. The next is the RS_n and the CF delivers the worst results. The difference between the RS_n and the CF is not remarkable. In the case of the MovieTweetings dataset, regarding to nDCG, precision and recall, the SA_n delivers the highest performance. Comparing to the MovieLens dataset, only the RS_3 shows better measures than the CF. The $RS_{[4,8]}$ performs the worst. This phenomena can be explained by the similarity between the RS_3 and the CF, as both methods operate with paths of length 3. The difference is that RS_3 is less constrained to the type of the edges. The poor performance of the $RS_{[4,8]}$ can be explained by the lack of user attributes.

7.2 The Comparison of the Datasets

The more visible difference between the MovieLens and MovieTweetings dataset is the presence and absence of the user attributes. The less visible difference is the structure of the true rating values. Taking a look at the true ratings of the MovieLens dataset, the ratings in some cases are grouped by the issuer.

Comparing the evaluation results over the datasets, a significant decrease is visible in the coverage for all the method classes. In the case of spreading based methods, the difference can be explained by the lack of user attributes. As the CF and the RS_3 strongly relies on user-item interactions, the reason for the additional decrease of the coverage of these methods can probably be found in the structure of the true ratings data. Investigating nDCG, the SA_n and the RS_3 shows a stable performance while the quality of the $RS_{[4,8]}$ and the CF decreases. The precision decreases for all the methods. Interestingly, the recall increases for most of the methods, as the SA_n, the RS_3 and the CF.

8 Conclusion

The representation method of the knowledge base is explained in Sect. 3. The calculation techniques as collaborative filtering, recommendation spreading and spreading activation are described in Sect. 5. The methods are evaluated on the MovieLens and the MovieTweetings datasets, as described in Sect. 4. Section 6.3 presents the evaluation method focusing on top list measures.

The evaluation results show that spreading activation delivers significantly higher quality recommendations than collaborative filtering and recommendation spreading does regarding to evaluation measures coverage, precision, recall and nDCG. The most important property of spreading activation is that the method does not treat the rating relation distinguished. In other words, unlike collaborative filtering and recommendation spreading, spreading activation is based on the paradigm of relatedness. The performance of spreading activation demonstrates that the paradigm of relatedness is a promising principle and should be further investigated.

The evaluation results let us draw a conclusion related to the application scope of collaborative filtering and recommendation spreading. While recommendation spreading also involves user and item attributes into the recommendation process, collaborative filtering is based only on user-item interaction. The evaluation on the datasets demonstrates that the presence of additional information to user-item interaction can slightly influence the recommendation quality of these methods. However, the absence of the additional information (user attributes) can be compensated with the fine-tuning of the method parameters in the specific case of the RS_3 on the MovieTweetings dataset.

In our future work we are interested in defining novel calculation algorithms based on node kernels on graphs, in order to develop mathematically established methods, such as node kernels investigated by Fouss et al. [5]. We would also like to investigate the potential of the paradigm of relatedness on the domain of the social recommendations.

References

1. Alvarez, M., Polo, L., Abella, P., Jimenez, W., Labra, J.E.: Application of the spreading activation technique for recommending concepts of well-known ontologies in medical systems (2011)
2. Blanco-Fernández, Y., Nores, M.L., Gil-Solla, A., Cabrer, M.R., Arias, J.J.P.: Exploring synergies between content-based filtering and spreading activation techniques in knowledge-based recommender systems. Inf. Sci. **181**(21), 4823–4846 (2011)
3. Codina, V., Ceccaroni, L.: Taking advantage of semantics in recommendation systems. In: Alquézar, R., Moreno, A., Aguilar-Martin, J. (eds.) CCIA, vol. 210, Frontiers in Artificial Intelligence and Applications, pp. 163–172. IOS Press (2010)
4. Dooms, S., De Pessemier, T., Martens, L.: MovieTweetings: a movie rating dataset collected from Twitter. In: Workshop on Crowdsourcing and Human Computation for Recommender Systems, CrowdRec at RecSys 2013 (2013)
5. Fouss, F., Yen, L., Pirotte, A., Saerens, M.: An experimental investigation of graph kernels on a collaborative recommendation task. In: Proceedings of the 6th IEEE International Conference on Data Mining (ICDM 2006), 18–22 December 2006, Hong Kong, China, pp. 863–868. IEEE Computer Society (2006)
6. Gao, Q., Yan, J., Liu, M.: A semantic approach to recommendation system based on user ontology and spreading activation model. In: Cao, J., Li, M., Weng, C., Xiang, Y., Wang, X., Tang, H., Hong, F., Liu, H., Wang, Y. (eds.) NPC Workshops, pp. 488–492. IEEE Computer Society (2008)
7. Grad-Gyenge, L., Filzmoser, P., Werthner, H.: Recommendations on a knowledge graph. In: 1st International Workshop on Machine Learning Methods for Recommender Systems, MLRec 2015, pp. 13–20 (2015)
8. Gu, H., Gartrell, M., Zhang, L., Lv, Q., Grunwald, D.: AnchorMF: towards effective event context identification. In: Proceedings of the 22nd ACM International Conference on Conference on Information & Knowledge Management, CIKM 2013, pp. 629–638, New York, NY, USA. ACM (2013)
9. Guy, I., Zwerdling, N., Carmel, D., Ronen, I., Uziel, E., Yogev, S., Ofek-Koifman, S.: Personalized recommendation of social software items based on social relations. In: Bergman, L.D., Tuzhilin, A., Burke, R.D., Felfernig, A., Schmidt-Thieme, L. (eds.) RecSys, pp. 53–60. ACM (2009)
10. He, J.: A social network-based recommender system. Ph.D. thesis, Los Angeles, CA, USA, AAI3437557 (2010)
11. Herlocker, J.L., Konstan, J.A., Borchers, A., Riedl, J.: An algorithmic framework for performing collaborative filtering. In: Proceedings of the 22nd Annual International ACM SIGIR Conference on Research and Development in Information Retrieval, SIGIR 1999, pp. 230–237, New York, NY, USA. ACM (1999)
12. Hidasi, B., Tikk, D.: Fast ALS-based tensor factorization for context-aware recommendation from implicit feedback. In: Flach, P.A., Bie, T., Cristianini, N. (eds.) ECML PKDD 2012. LNCS (LNAI), vol. 7524, pp. 67–82. Springer, Heidelberg (2012). doi:10.1007/978-3-642-33486-3_5
13. Hochmeister, M.: Spreading expertise scores in overlay learner models. In: Helfert, M., Martins, M.J., Cordeiro, J. (eds.) CSEDU, vol. 1, pp. 175–180. SciTePress (2012)
14. Hussein, T., Westheide, D., Ziegler, J.: Context-adaptation based on ontologies and spreading activation. In: Workshop Proceedings of Lernen - Wissen - Adaption, Halle, LWA 2007, pp. 361–366, September 2007

15. Jiang, X., Tan, A.-H.: Learning and inferencing in user ontology for personalized semantic web search. Inf. Sci. **179**(16), 2794–2808 (2009)

16. Jøsang, A., Marsh, S., Pope, S.: Exploring different types of trust propagation. In: Stølen, K., Winsborough, W.H., Martinelli, F., Massacci, F. (eds.) iTrust 2006. LNCS, vol. 3986, pp. 179–192. Springer, Heidelberg (2006). doi:10.1007/11755593_14

17. Kazienko, P., Musial, K., Kajdanowicz, T.: Multidimensional social network in the social recommender system. Trans. Sys. Man Cyber. Part A **41**(4), 746–759 (2011)

18. Konstas, I., Stathopoulos, V., Jose, J.M.: On social networks and collaborative recommendation. In: Proceedings of the 32nd International ACM SIGIR Conference on Research and Development in Information Retrieval, SIGIR 2009, pp. 195–202, New York, NY, USA. ACM (2009)

19. Massa, P., Avesani, P.: Trust-aware collaborative filtering for recommender systems. In: Meersman, R., Tari, Z. (eds.) OTM 2004. LNCS, vol. 3290, pp. 492–508. Springer, Heidelberg (2004). doi:10.1007/978-3-540-30468-5_31

20. Quillian, M.R.: Semantic memory. In: Minsky, M. (ed.) Semantic Information Processing, pp. 227–270. MIT Press, Cambridge (1968)

21. Resnick, P., Iacovou, N., Suchak, M., Bergstrom, P., Riedl, J.: GroupLens: an open architecture for collaborative filtering of netnews. In: Proceedings of the 1994 ACM Conference on Computer Supported Cooperative Work, CSCW 1994, pp. 175–186, New York, NY, USA. ACM (1994)

22. Troussov, A., Parra, D., Brusilovsky, P.: Spreading activation approach to tag-aware recommenders: modeling similarity on multidimensional networks, pp. 57–62 (2009)

23. Ziegler, C.-N., Lausen, G.: Propagation models for trust and distrust in social networks. Inf. Syst. Front. **7**(4–5), 337–358 (2005)

Enterprise Model Based UML Interaction Overview Model Generation Process

Audrius Lopata, Ilona Veitaite[(✉)], and Neringa Zemaityte

Department of Informatics, Kaunas Faculty of Humanities,
Vilnius University, Muitines g. 8, 44280 Kaunas, Lithuania
{Audrius.Lopata, Ilona.Veitaite,
Neringa.Zemaityte}@khf.vu.lt

Abstract. The main scope of the research is to analyse Unified Modelling Language (UML) models generation process from Enterprise Model (EM) in Information Systems (IS) development process by using knowledge-based subsystem. The knowledge-based subsystem is proposed as an additional computer aided software engineering (CASE) tool component to avoid IS development process based on empirics. For comprehensible perception there is also presented relation between EM and ontologies and its use in generation process.

As the result of this part of research transformation algorithms are presented and described. These algorithms are capable of whole UML models elements generation from Enterprise Model. Example of UML Interaction Overview model generation illustrates full process.

Keywords: Enterprise Modelling · Ontology · Knowledge-based · CASE · IS engineering · UML · Interaction Overview model

1 Introduction

In a modern world software development and software applications are becoming more complex and demanding. Developers, analysts, engineers, researchers are creating and seeking for new techniques and procedures to streamline software engineering processes to ensure shorter development time and reduce costs by re-using different components. The development of software systems is a complex activity which may imply the participation of people and machines (distributed or not). Therefore, different stakeholders, heterogeneity and new software features make software development a heavily knowledge-based process [1, 11].

In modern day enterprise engineering, it is paramount that Enterprise Models are grounded in a well-defined, agreed-upon Enterprise Architecture that captures the essentials of the business, IT, and its evolution. Enterprise architectures typically contain different views (e.g. Business, Information, Process, Application, Technical) on the enterprise that are developed by distinct stakeholders with a different background and knowledge of the business. Consequently, the developed Enterprise Models that populate these views are hard to integrate. A possible solution for this integration problem is using a shared terminology during the development of these different views [2].

W. Abramowicz et al. (Eds.): BIS 2016 Workshops, LNBIP 263, pp. 69–78, 2017.
DOI: 10.1007/978-3-319-52464-1_7

Such explicit formal representations, often materialized in the form of ontology – in a business context called an enterprise-specific ontology – provide a myriad of advantages. Ontologies are shared views of domains. They provide conceptualizations that are agreed upon by participants in collaborative action and decision making. The explicit existence of such shared perspectives makes it possible for both people and programs to collaborate by ensuring that everybody makes the same distinctions and uses the same terms with the same meaning [18]. On an intra-organizational level, they ensure model re-usability, compatibility and interoperability, and form an excellent basis for enterprise-supporting IT tools, such as Enterprise Resource Planning (ERP) systems, business intelligence (BI) tools or information systems (IS), for which they serve as common terminology. On an inter-organizational level, they facilitate interoperability, cooperation and integration by allowing formal mappings between, and alignment of separately developed Enterprise Models [12].

2   Enterprise Modelling and Ontologies Relation

An Enterprise Model is a computational representation of the structure, activities, processes, information, resources, people, behaviour, goals and constraints of a business, government, or other enterprise. It can be both descriptive and definitional - spanning what is and what should be. The role of an Enterprise Model is to achieve model-driven enterprise design, analysis and operation [6, 18]. Enterprise Modelling is an activity where an integrated and commonly shared model of an enterprise is created [7, 12, 28]. The resulting Enterprise Model comprises several sub-models, each representing one specific aspect of the enterprise, and each modelled using an appropriate modelling language for the task at hand. For example, the Enterprise Model may contain processes modelled in BPMN, data modelled in ER and goals modelled in n*. The Enterprise Model is thus developed by several enterprise engineers, and aggregates all information about the enterprise. As a result, Enterprise Models without homogenized underlying vocabulary suffer interoperability and integration problems [12, 25]. An Enterprise Model can be developed for single or more different purposes. Few Enterprise Modelling formal purposes are presented [3, 20, 22]:

1. To capitalize enterprise knowledge and know how.
2. To illustrate relations and dependencies within the enterprise and with other enterprises, to achieve better control and management over all aspects.
3. To provide support to business process re-engineering.
4. To get a common and complete understanding of the enterprise.
5. To improve information management across organizational and application system boundaries and provide a common means for communication throughout the organization. Rationalize and secure information flows.
6. To provide operative support for daily work at all levels in the enterprise from top to bottom.
7. To control, co-ordinate and monitor some parts of the enterprise.
8. To provide support for decision making.
9. To provide support the design of new parts of the enterprise.
10. To simulate processes.

Ontology is a discipline rooted in philosophy and formal logic, introduced by the Artificial Intelligence community in the 1980s to describe real world concepts that are independent of specific applications. Over the past two decades, knowledge representation methodologies and technologies have subsequently been used in other branches of computing where there is a need to represent and share contextual knowledge independently of applications [22, 23].

Ontology engineering is a filiation of knowledge engineering that studies the methods and methodologies for building ontologies. In the domain of enterprise architecture, ontology is an outline or a schema used to structure objects, their attributes and relationships in a consistent manner. As in Enterprise Modelling, ontology can be composed of other ontologies. The purpose of ontologies in Enterprise Modelling is to formalize and establish the shared understanding, reuse, assimilation and dissemination of information across all organizations and departments within an enterprise. Also, an ontology enables integration of the various functions and processes which take place in an enterprise [10].

Using ontologies in Enterprise Modelling offers several advantages. Ontologies ensure clarity, consistency, and structure to a model. They promote efficient model definition and analysis. Generic enterprise ontologies allow for reusability and automation of components. A common ontology allows to ensure shared understanding, clearer communication, and more effective coordination among the various divisions of an enterprise. These lead to more efficient production and flexibility within the enterprise [24].

3 Transformation Algorithm

The computerized IS engineering specific methods are developed based on common requirements, which systematize the selected methodology. Computerized knowledge-based IS engineering project management basis is CASE system knowledge-based subsystem. CASE system's knowledge-based subsystem's core component is knowledge base, which essential elements are enterprise meta–model specification and Enterprise Model for certain problem domain [4, 8, 24]. Knowledge-based subsystem is one more active participant of IS engineering process beside analyst, whose purpose is to verify results of IS life cycle phases [5, 9].

Knowledge-based CASE systems holding substantial components, which organize knowledge: knowledge-based subsystem's knowledge base, which essential elements are enterprise meta–model specification and Enterprise Model for certain problem domain [7, 13, 16]. Figure 1 presents knowledge-based subsystem connection to the Enterprise Model and Enterprise Meta–Model inside CASE tool presented as Sequence diagram.

Information system design methods indicate the continuance of systems engineering actions, i.e. how, in what order and what UML models to use in the design process and how to fulfil the process. Association between UML models and EM is realized through the transformation algorithms and presented in Fig. 2 [14, 15].

Enterprise Model as organization's knowledge repository enables generate UML models with the help of transformation algorithms. Enterprise meta-model holds

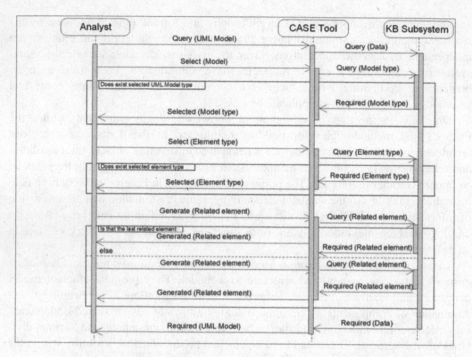

Fig. 1. Knowledge-based subsystem connection to the Enterprise Model and Enterprise Meta–Model inside CASE tool presented as Sequence diagram

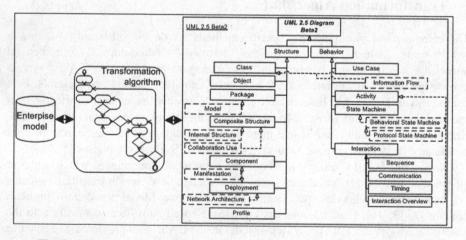

Fig. 2. UML models generation by using the transformation algorithm [21, 27]

essential elements of business modelling methodologies and techniques, which ensures a proper UML models generation process [17, 19].

Presently, used CASE system's Enterprise Models constitution is not verified by formalized criteria. Enterprise Models have been formed in compliance with the notations. However, their composition has not been proved by the characteristics of the specific domain area [26, 27].

In IS engineering all design models are fulfilled on the basis of the empirical expert experience. Experts, who participate in the IS development process, do not gain enough knowledge, and process implementation in requirements analysis and specification phases can take a too long time. Enterprise meta–model contains essential elements of business modelling methodologies and techniques, which insures a suitable UML diagrams generation process [26, 27].

Figure 3 presents top level transformation algorithm for Enterprise meta–model based UML models generating process. Main steps for generating process are identifying and selecting UML model for generating process, identifying starting elements for the selected UML model and selecting all related elements, reflecting Enterprise Model elements to UML model elements and generating the selected UML model [21, 26, 27].

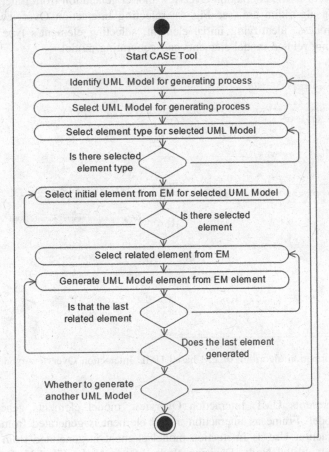

Fig. 3. Transformation algorithm of EM based UML model generation process

4 UML Interaction Overview Model Transformation

UML Interaction Overview diagram determines interactions through a variant of activity diagrams in a manner that maintains overview of the control flow. Interaction Overview model concentrate on the overview of the flow of control where the nodes are interactions or interaction uses. The lifelines and the messages do not perform at this overview level. UML Interaction Overview model combines elements from activity and interaction diagrams [21]:

- the following elements of the activity diagrams could be used on the Interaction Overview diagrams: initial node, flow final node, activity final node, decision node, merge node, fork node, join node;
- the following elements of the interaction diagrams could be used on the Interaction Overview diagrams: interaction, interaction use, duration constraint, time constraint.

Main steps of UML Interaction Overview model generation from Enterprise Model transformation algorithm are (see Fig. 4): selecting Interaction Overview model for generating process, identifying initial element, selecting element's type for chosen model, selecting related model elements and generating model.

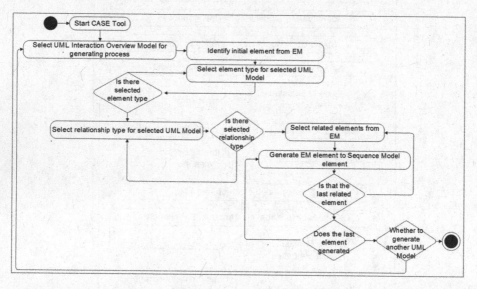

Fig. 4. Transformation algorithm of EM based UML Interaction Overview model generation process

Table 1 presents UML Interaction Overview model elements generated from Enterprise Model. Frame as Interaction model element is generated from EM Actor element, Interaction Use as Interaction model element is generated from EM Information Activity, Initial Node, Decision Node, Merge Node, Final Node as Activity model elements are generated from EM Business Rules elements and Decision Guard as Activity model element is generated from EM Information Flow element.

Table 1. EM and Online service ordering UML Interaction Overview model elements

EM		UML Interaction Overview model						
		Frame (Interaction model element)	Interaction use (Interaction model element)	Initial node (Activity model element)	Decision node (Activity model element)	Merge node (Activity model element)	Final node (Activity model element)	Decision guard (Activity model element)
Actor		+						
Event								
Process	Material input							
	Material output							
Function	Business rules			+	+	+	+	
	Information flow							+
	Information activity		+					

Figure 5 presents an example of UML Interaction Overview model. The necessary elements through transformation algorithms were received from CASE tool's knowledge-based subsystem's Enterprise Model, where all knowledge of subject area is stored. In this figure it is clearly seen all necessary UML Interaction Overview model elements generated from Enterprise Model.

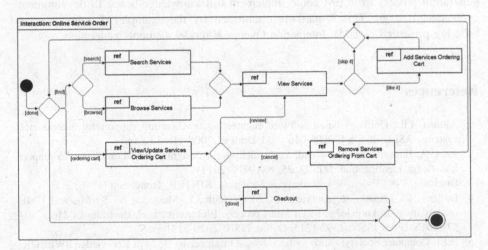

Fig. 5. UML Interaction Overview model example: online service order

5 Conclusions

Computer aided IS engineering is based on empiric and IS development life cycle stages are fulfilled on the basis of the expert's experience. A large part of the CASE tools design models are generated only partially, and complete realization is possible only non-automatic and with experts participation. Today IS engineering should be based on knowledge. In this way, knowledge-based IS engineering computerized IS development activities are executed using the subject area knowledge, which is stored in the knowledge base of CASE tool repository.

In order to decrease the influence of empirical factors on IS development process, the decision was made to use knowledge-based IS engineering approach. The main advantage of this approach is the possibility to validate specified data stored in EM against formal criteria, in that way decreasing the possible issues and ensuring more effective IS development process compared to classical IS development methods.

Using ontologies in Enterprise Modelling offers several advantages. Ontologies ensure clarity, consistency, and structure to a model. They promote efficient model definition and analysis. Generic enterprise ontologies allow for reusability of and automation of components. Because ontologies are schemes or outlines, the use of ontologies does not insure proper Enterprise Model definition and analysis. Ontologies are limited by how they are defined and fulfilled. Ontology not always includes ability to cover all of the aspects of what is being modelled.

The paper deals with the generation process of UML models from EM options. Every element of UML model can be generated from the EM using CASE Tool knowledge base's subsystem and transformation algorithms. Method of UML model generation process from EM could implement full knowledge-based IS development cycle design stage. This is partially established by the example of online service ordering presented as UML Interaction Overview model elements generation.

References

1. Alonso, J.B.: Ontology-based software engineering, engineering support for autonomous systems. ASLab-ICEA-R-2006-016 v 0.1 Draft of 2006-11-15 (2006)
2. Bera, P., Burton-Jones, A., Wand, Y.: Guidelines for designing visual ontologies to support knowledge identification. MIS Q. **35**, 883–908 (2011)
3. Brathaug, T.A., Evjen, T.Å.: Enterprise Modeling. SINTEF, Trondheim (1996)
4. Butleris, R., Lopata, A., Ambraziunas, M., Veitaite, I., Masteika, S.: SysML and UML models usage in knowledge based MDA process. Elektronika ir elektrotechnika **21**(2), 50–57 (2015). Print ISSN: 1392-1215, Online ISSN: 2029-5731
5. IEEE Computer Society: Guide to the Software Engineering Body of Knowledge SWEBOK. Version 3.0. Paperback ISBN-13: 978-0-7695-5166-1 (2014)
6. Gudas, S.: enterprise knowledge modelling: domains and aspects. Technological and economic development of economy. Baltic J. Sustain. **15**, 281–293 (2009)

7. Gudas, S.: Architecture of knowledge-based enterprise management systems: a control view. In: Proceedings of the 13th World Multiconference on Systemics, Cybernetics and Informatics (WMSCI 2009), 10–13 July 2009, Orlando, Florida, USA, vol. III, pp. 161–266 (2009). ISBN-10: 1-9934272-61-2 (vol. III). ISBN-13: 978-1-9934272-61-9 (vol. III)

8. Gudas, S.: Informacijos sistemų inzinerijos teorijos pagrindai. Vilniaus universiteto leidykla (2012). ISBN 978-609-459-075-7

9. Gudas, S., Lopata, A.: Meta-model based development of use case model for business function. Information Technology and Control, vol. 36, no. 3 (2007). ISSN 1392 – 124X 2007

10. Fadel, G., Fox, M., Gruninger, M.: A generic enterprise resource ontology. In: Proceedings of the 3rd Workshop on Enabling Technologies: Infrastructure for Collaborative Enterprises, pp. 117–128 (1994)

11. Force, S.E.T.: Ontology driven architectures and potential uses of the semantic web in systems and software engineering (2001)

12. Gailly, F., Casteleyn, S., Alkhaldi, N.: On the symbiosis between enterprise modelling and ontology engineering. In: Ng, W., Storey, V.C., Trujillo, J.C. (eds.) ER 2013. LNCS, vol. 8217, pp. 487–494. Springer, Heidelberg (2013). doi:10.1007/978-3-642-41924-9_42

13. Lopata, A.: Veiklos modeliu grindziamas kompiuterizuotas funkcinių vartotojo reikalavimų specifikavimo metodas, Disertacija (2004)

14. Lopata, A., Veitaite, I., Gudas, S., Butleris, R.: CASE tool component – knowledge-based subsystem. UML diagrams generation process. Transformations Bus. Econ. 13, no. 2B(32B), pp. 676–696 (2014). ISSN: 1648 - 4460

15. Lopata, A., Veitaite, I.: UML diagrams generation process by using knowledge-based subsystem. In: Abramowicz, W. (ed.) BIS 2013. LNBIP, vol. 160, pp. 53–60. Springer, Heidelberg (2013). doi:10.1007/978-3-642-41687-3_7

16. Lopata, A., Ambraziunas, M., Gudas, S., Butleris, R.: The main principles of knowledge-based information systems engineering. Electron. Electr. Eng. 11, no. 1(25), 99–102 (2012). ISSN 2029-5731

17. Lopata, A., Ambraziunas, M., Gudas, S.: Knowledge based MDA requirements specification and validation technique. Transformations Bus. Econ. 11, no. 1(25), pp. 248–261 (2012). ISSN 1648-4460

18. Fox, M.S., Barbuceanu, M., Gruninger, M., Lin, J.: An Organization Ontology for Enterprise Modelling. MIT Press, Cambridge, pp. 131–152 (1998). ISBN:0-262-66108-X

19. Morkevicius, A., Gudas, S.: Enterprise knowledge based software requirements elicitation. Inf. Technol. Control 40(3), 181–190 (2011). ISSN 1392 – 124X

20. Khan, N.A.: Transformation of enterprise model to enterprise ontology. Master Thesis, Jonkoping, Sweden (2011)

21. OMG UML: Unified Modelling Language version 2.5. Unified Modelling (2012). http://www.omg.org/spec/UML/2.5/Beta2/

22. OMG ODM: OMG Formal Versions of Ontology Definition Metamodel (2014). http://www.omg.org/spec/ODM/1.1

23. Ostie, J.K.: An introduction to enterprise modeling and simulation (1996)

24. Perjons, E.: Model-driven process design. Aligning value networks, enterprise goals, services and IT systems. Department of Computer and Systems Sciences, Stockholm University, Sweden by US-AB, Stockholm (2011). ISBN 978-91-7447-249-3

25. Stirna, J., Persson, A., Sandkuhl, K.: Participative enterprise modeling: experiences and recommendations. In: Krogstie, J., Opdahl, A., Sindre, G. (eds.) CAiSE 2007. LNCS, vol. 4495, pp. 546–560. Springer, Heidelberg (2007). doi:10.1007/978-3-540-72988-4_38

26. Veitaite, I., Lopata, A.: Additional knowledge based MOF architecture layer for UML models generation process. In: Abramowicz, W. (ed.) BIS 2015. LNBIP, vol. 228, pp. 56–63. Springer, Heidelberg (2015). doi:10.1007/978-3-319-26762-3_6
27. Veitaitė, I., Ambraziūnas, M., Lopata, A.: Enterprise model and ISO standards based information system's development process. In: Abramowicz, W., Kokkinaki, A. (eds.) BIS 2014. LNBIP, vol. 183, pp. 73–79. Springer, Heidelberg (2014). doi:10.1007/978-3-319-11460-6_7
28. Vernadat, F.: UEML: towards a unified Enterprise Modelling language. Int. J. Prod. Res. **40**, 4309–4321 (2002)

Speaker Authentication System Based on Voice Biometrics and Speech Recognition

Laurynas Dovydaitis[✉], Tomas Rasymas[✉],
and Vytautas Rudžionis[✉]

Kaunas Faculty of Humanities, Vilnius University,
Muitinės str. 8, Kaunas, Lithuania
{laurynas.dovydaitis,tomas.rasymas,
vytautas.rudzionis}@khf.vu.lt

Abstract. In this paper we are analyzing possibility to authenticate speaker by using user voice biometrics and speech recognition. Process of authentication is simple: user says his personal ID number, then system makes prediction of users' identity and compares it to claimed ID. If these two parameters are equal system makes a positive decision. Using proposed algorithms we managed to achieve 70.45% accuracy for system, with identification module accuracy of 100% and recognition module accuracy of 70.45%.

Keywords: Voice biometrics · Speech recognition · Hybrid system

1 Introduction

The most common way to protect users' information is by using password. This method requires user to remember his password for extended period of time. More over user usually has more than one account, which means that he has to remember more than one password. There are cases when passwords are forgotten or hacked. One of the solutions for this inconvenience is Biometric Identification Systems. These systems use biometric characteristics of an individual that is unique to users and different from everyone else. In this research we focus on an implementation of speech recognition system as gateway for security access control in order to authorization for restricted services, such as phone banking system, voice mail or access to database services. In order to login to such system user has to say his personal ID number. Personal ID number consists of eleven digits and it is unique in this systems' context. When voice stream is analyzed, it identifies user by his voice features. Second step is to recognize speech of personal ID that was said. If these two parameters belong to same person, system grants access for resources. For user authentication we use Hidden Markov Models and for speech recognition we are using hybrid approach by combining Lithuanian, German, French and English recognizers. For the latter part hybrid recognition is achieved by using several different speech recognizers, maximizing the hope that at least one of the recognizers will give the correct result and it will be possible to detect the correct answer.

© Springer International Publishing AG 2017
W. Abramowicz et al. (Eds.): BIS 2016 Workshops, LNBIP 263, pp. 79–84, 2017.
DOI: 10.1007/978-3-319-52464-1_8

2   Prototype Architecture

Proposed authentication system architecture consists of two main parts: identification of speaker and recognition of speaker ID. Block diagram for this system is displayed in Fig. 1.

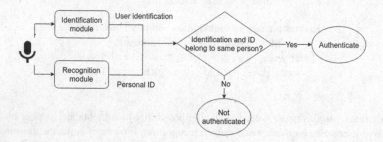

Fig. 1. Block diagram of system architecture.

Speech signal from microphone is passed to both modules in parallel. Identification module analyzes user voice and makes prediction of user identity. Recognition module tries to recognize user personal ID. When both processes are complete system has two parameters: users' identity and users' personal ID. If these two parameters belong to the user, he gets authenticated.

2.1   Identification Module

The Identification module in this system uses HTK[1] - The Hidden Markov Model Toolkit. Using this toolkit we build Hidden Markov models (HMM) for each enrolled speaker.

Identification module has 3 separate steps:

- Speaker model creation for each enrolled speaker
- Unknown (sample) speaker model creation for given sample
- Result comparison

These steps are outlined in Fig. 2.

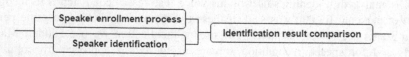

Fig. 2. Identification model blocks

---

[1] http://htk.eng.cam.ac.uk/.

Details of a speaker enrollment module are detailed in Fig. 3. As a primary identification module feed, toolkit extracts speaker voice features. 39 dimensional Mel frequency cepstral coefficients (MFCC) [7] are used for HMM.

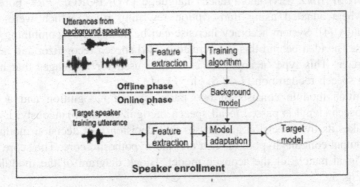

Fig. 3. Speaker enrollment process diagram [8]

No additional preprocessing is made and original utterance is analyzed in HTK toolkit. Full number samples are used feature extraction. In order to create HMM model, number of determined hidden states needs to be setup before the model creation. Identification module uses 60 hidden states. This number was determined after initial experimental work with the sample data. Identification module detailed process is outlined in Fig. 4.

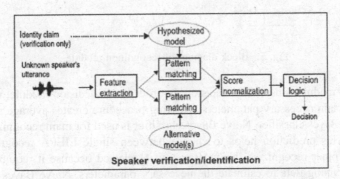

Fig. 4. Speaker identification process diagram [8]

Using previously shown configuration creates a model for unknown speakers' utterance. By comparing sample claim with existing data, decision for the speaker identity is made. Identity is chosen from speaker database. Recognition score is forwarded to next module for further analysis.

2.2 Recognition Module

Recognition module uses one native Lithuania language recognizer LIEPA[2] and few adapted foreign recognizers: Germany[3] language (VOXFORGE_DE), English[4] language (CMUSPHINX_EN) and French[5] language (VOXFORGE_FR). Foreign recognizers where adapted using transcription rewriting rules, which were obtained experimentally [4]. System accuracy increase can be achieved by combining different recognizers. The idea behind this is to create hybrid speech recognizer and adapt it to other language. This type of approach is usually used for languages that have less research in speech recognition [1–3, 5, 6].

Recognition module consists of two parts: speech recognition and a decision making. Speech signal is passed to all speech recognizers simultaneously. Every recognizer makes its own decision and passes that decision to a decision module. As a result, all output contains hypothesis text and the hypothesis score. The score is based on audio signal match for the acoustic model. Block diagram of the module is displayed in Fig. 5.

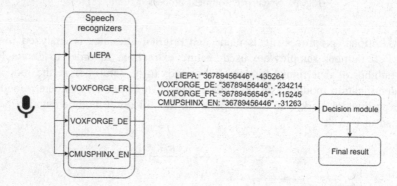

Fig. 5. Block diagram of recognition module.

Decision module is used final decision. In order to use decision module, we have to train it, to obtain necessary parameters. Training procedure creates average matrix and trains Naïve Bayes classifier. Naïve Bayes classifier is used for main recognizer LIEPA prediction. This prediction helps to choose between single LIEPA recognizer or to combine all other recognizers. Naïve Bayes was selected because it requires a small amount of training data to estimate the necessary parameters. Naive Bayes classifiers can be extremely fast compared to more sophisticated methods. For Naïve Bayes training we are using LIEPA best hypothesis score.

---

[2] https://github.com/liepa-project.

[3] https://sourceforge.net/projects/cmusphinx/files/Acoustic%20and%20Language%20Models/German%20Voxforge/.

[4] https://sourceforge.net/projects/cmusphinx/files/Acoustic%20and%20Language%20Models/US%20English%20Generic%20Acoustic%20Model/.

[5] https://sourceforge.net/projects/cmusphinx/files/Acoustic%20and%20Language%20Models/French/.

If Naïve Bayes classifier returns LIEPA result as correct we terminate the process. Else, if LIEPA is wrong we have to combine output of foreign recognizers. In this case to achieve correct result we need to combine recognizes using average matrix. Average matrix is calculated by splitting each recognizer by each users' ID into single digits and calculating every digit for accurate recognition sum. Then this sum is divided by total number of examples. Example of average matrix generation is displayed in Fig. 6.

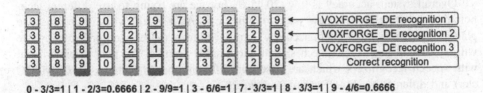

0 - 3/3=1 | 1 - 2/3=0.6666 | 2 - 9/9=1 | 3 - 6/6=1 | 7 - 3/3=1 | 8 - 3/3=1 | 9 - 4/6=0.6666

Fig. 6. Averages matrix generation example.

As we can see in the example above, third digit is 9. Two times it was recognized as 8, so in final average calculation we have 4 correct and 2 incorrect recognitions. This way number 9 accuracy is 4/6 = 0.6666. Calculated average matrix of all digits and recognizers is displayed in Table 1.

Table 1. Generated averages matrix.

	0	1	2	3	4	5	6	7	8	9
LIEPA	0.84	0.96	0.91	0.95	0.92	0.86	0.96	0.86	0.95	0.88
VOXFORGE_FR	0.72	0.28	0.54	0.69	0.75	0.65	0.6	0.68	0.68	0.71
VOXFORGE_DE	0.39	0.56	0.73	0.64	0.42	0.38	0.62	0.53	0.5	0.58
CMUSPHINX_EN	0.43	0.83	0.82	0.67	0.59	0.61	0.77	0.74	0.84	0.71

When we need to combine results using average matrix we sum accuracy of every recognizer for every digit at same position. The digit with highest sum value is selected as correct choice. Using this combination method, we increased system overall recognition accuracy by 2.67%, compared to single recognizer LIEPA 67.78%.

3 Experimental Evaluation

Main speech corpora, containing 11 personal ID numbers was used. Speech corpus used in the experiments was gathered from 11 people (4 female and 7 male). Each of these speakers pronounced their personal ID for 20 times in a single session. 12 recordings of single user were used for training, 8 for testing.

We achieved 70.45% total accuracy. Identification module produced 100% accuracy, while recognition module only 70.45%. Overall system accuracy depended on accuracy of recognition module.

4 Conclusions and Further Work

Results of our experiments showed that such system can be used for user authentication. The identification module performance should be tested on larger database set. Although during the experiments we saw that this identification accuracy achieved only if signals without noise. We'll need to adjust algorithms and try them in different environments.

Overall system accuracy is low (70.45%), but we are trying to use different technologies and searching for new ways to improve it. As it is still work in progress we plan to increase overall system accuracy. In order to increase recognition accuracy, we will try to split users' ID speech stream into smaller chunks. We plan to experiment with speech recognizers which are based on different speech features (LPC, MFCC etc.) and different machine learning techniques.

References

1. Rasymas, T., Rudžionis, V.: Lithuanian digits recognition by using hybrid approach by combining Lithuanian google recognizer and some foreign language recognizers. In: Dregvaite, G., Damasevicius, R. (eds.) ICIST 2015. CCIS, vol. 538, pp. 449–459. Springer, Heidelberg (2015). doi:10.1007/978-3-319-24770-0_38
2. Rasymas, T., Rudžionis, V.: Evaluation of methods to combine different speech recognizers. In: Proceedings of the Federated Conference on Computer Science and Information Systems, vol. 5, pp. 1043–1047 (2015). doi:10.15439/2015F62
3. Rudžionis, V., Ratkevičius, K., Rudžionis, A., Raškinis, G., Maskeliunas, R.: Recognition of voice commands using hybrid approach. In: Skersys, T., Butleris, R., Butkiene, R. (eds.) ICIST 2013. CCIS, vol. 403, pp. 249–260. Springer, Heidelberg (2013). doi:10.1007/978-3-642-41947-8_21
4. Kasparaitis, P.: Transcribing of the Lithuanian text using formal rules. Informatica 10(4), 367–376 (1999)
5. Schultz, T., Waibel, A.: Language-independent and language-adaptive acoustic modeling for speech recognition. Speech Commun. 35(1), 31–52 (2001)
6. Meneido, H., Neto, J.: Combination of acoustic models in continuous speech recognition hybrid systems. In: Proceedings of the International Conference in Spoken Language Processing, vol. 9, pp. 1000–1029 (2000)
7. Dovydaitis, L., Rudžionis, V.: Asmens balso panaudojimas autentikavimui, Informacinės technologijos 2015. 20-oji tarpuniversitetinė magistrantų ir doktorantų konferencija, pp. 147–151 (2015). ISSN 2029-249X
8. Kinnunen, T., Li, H.: An overview of text-independent speaker recognition: from features to supervectors. Speech Commun. 52, 12–40 (2009)

Decision Support System for Foreign Exchange Markets

Róbert Magyar, František Babič[(⊠)], and Ján Paralič

Department of Cybernetics and Artificial Intelligence,
Faculty of Electrical Engineering and Informatics,
Technical University of Košice, Letná 9/B, 042 00 Košice, Slovakia
{robert.magyar, frantisek.babic, jan.paralic}@tuke.sk

Abstract. Selection of the right decision strategy is a crucial factor to success in the foreign exchange market. This article presents an innovative approach how to support related decision steps by means of suitable data mining methods applied on collected data from the market. The motivation is a trading under the best conditions, i.e. with the highest chance to be successful. To meet this requirement, we designed and implemented a decision support system (DSS) for trading on the foreign exchange market which uses a possibility to speculate on this market and in line with extracted rules, economic news and outputs of the technical analysis recommend the future trading direction. We extracted the rules from the historical Forex data with the C5.0 and CART algorithms for decision trees generation. The best achieved accuracy was 56.03% that is typical for this type of data. We used the best rules to design a dynamic trading strategy, which we experimentally verified as profitable.

Keywords: Forex · Data mining · Decision support system · Technical analysis

1 Introduction

Foreign Exchange (FOREX) refers to the foreign exchange market in which the foreign currencies of the world are traded and where an exchange rate is formed as a single price, which enables the transfer of funds from one currency to another [7]. It is the largest and liquid market in the world. The advantage of this market is the possibility to trade twenty-four hours a day, except Saturday and Sunday. The main function of this market is the exchange of the money from one currency to another for investing, travel, international trade, etc. The importance of this market represents a number of states having different national currencies and they need to trade with each other.

The motivation for the presented experiments included two factors: to enable a better understanding of the behaviour of the foreign exchange market and a possible usability of the designed system in real business cases with the aim to make a profit through trading on the Forex market. It is important to state that the profit was not a primary goal of our work but it represents one of the specified main success criteria.

In general, the main reason for working with the Forex data is a prediction of their future development. The right prediction represents a major advantage for the

© Springer International Publishing AG 2017
W. Abramowicz et al. (Eds.): BIS 2016 Workshops, LNBIP 263, pp. 85–96, 2017.
DOI: 10.1007/978-3-319-52464-1_9

participants of the market trading. In this case several approaches how to define the right strategies are used, but the problem of the strategies that are based on technical analysis is that they do not specify under what conditions should be deployed the relevant strategy. The result, in this case, is a high turnover of the prediction's accuracy of the future development caused by the changing conditions not underpinned by the strategy. This fact motivated us to design our own strategy, whose main requirement was to determine which currency is globally strong or is globally weak and use the chosen strategy on a currency pair created from the strong and weak currency. The result is a trading on the financial markets under the best conditions, i.e. with the highest chance to be successful.

To meet this requirement, we designed and implemented a decision support system (DSS) for trading on the foreign exchange market which uses a possibility to speculate on this market and in line with extracted rules, economic news and outputs of the technical analysis recommend the future trading direction. The rules extracted from the historical Forex data by means of suitable data mining methods represent one main aspect of the proposed DSS. This extraction is the crucial part of the whole recommendation process in combination with the selected methods of the technical analysis. Our goal was not to generate a model with the highest accuracy but to extract the rules that really appear on the market. Besides the main tasks described above, the data mining should help to answer a question: what is a probability of the situation that the negative economic news will affect negatively the whole market, and on the other hand, the positive economic news will have a positive impact. In addition, if including the fundamental news and technical analysis into decision process will have a significant positive impact.

We think that it is important to find out whether a determination of the global power of the currency creates an opportunity for trading in terms of its future development. The aim of this work is to verify a hypothesis that in this market we can determine the direction of currency's movement based on the movement of the related currency pair containing this currency. We derived a statement whether the currency is strong, weak or has a neutral development from all relevant currency pairs. Therefore, the idea for proposed experiments is first to abstract actual trend from the price, determine the strength of the currency and make the prediction for the future development. The success criterion will be at least 55% accuracy of the generated model to determine the currency's strength. All experiments were realised based on the major world currencies that are the Euro, US dollar, British pound, Australian dollar, New Zealand dollar, Japanese yen, Canadian dollar and Swiss franc [1]. We took this decision due to their high liquidity compared to other currencies and relatively low fees.

The article contains the four main parts. The first introduces the trading on the forex markets and our motivation to design a DSS to support this trading. The second describes the proposed DSS and realised experiments in accordance with the CRISP-DM methodology [17]. The third one is devoted to the evaluation of the obtained rules with the aim to confirm or decline the specified hypothesis and to meet the specified objectives and criteria. The last one concludes the article with the proposed directions of the future work.

1.1 Related Works

Fredrik Larsen in his work [10] proposed an automatic stock market trading based on the technical analysis. This system focused on a monitoring of the development of 24 stocks. It works with data from 1970 to 1998 and the whole system consists of 26 agents. Each agent represents one of the indicators or a related price formation from the technical analysis. The author used several methods of artificial intelligence and machine learning such as the neural networks to determine the purchase or sale, and decision trees ID3 and J48 available within a supporting tool Weka. Each agent works alone and produces a signal evaluated by a weight. These weights are optimised by a genetic algorithm and based on specified formula they are counted together to determine the future direction of the prediction. The result is a system in which each agent has its own accuracy and this factor determines the strength of his voting rights. The users cannot use the proposed system for real trading because its experimental evaluation with the real data was not successful. In addition, it does not take into account the business parameters as Stop Loss, Take Profit and economic fundamental news.

Peachavanish in his work [14] proposed a method using cluster analysis to identify a group of stocks that has the best trends and momentum characteristics at a given time. The author realized his experiments on five-year historical price data of stocks listed on the Stock Exchange of Thailand. In order to compare price trend and momentum of the different stocks, he calculated some technical indicators for the long term trend and for the short term trend too. Since, the nature of technical indicators used in the proposed method lag behind prices, it took some time for the selection process to recover and outperform the market in the long run.

A collective of authors [5] proposed a FOREX trading expert system based on some new technical analysis indicators and a new approach to the rule-based evidential reasoning. The authors design this approach to solve an issue that the traditional fuzzy logic rules lose important information when dealing with the intersecting fuzzy classes. The limitation is that this system selects the stocks for the trading based on historical data, indicators of the technical analysis and proposed trading rules and not considered some other important inputs as a political policy, macroeconomics, etc. [13].

In the work of Lai et al. [9] a web-based DSS using neural networks for FOREX trading is described. This system consists of two main modules: neural network and DSS available on-line. The neural network generated a model used for the prediction of the future development of the major currency pairs. The proposed DSS module used the generated model to recommend the possible directions for the user by specified rules. The authors did not mention the concrete accuracy of their system, but the DSS module contained following four types of rules. The first type determines the trading strategy in a very simple way, i.e. If prediction > current price THEN buy. The second type selects cases created by the first group of rules in line with the fact that the buy or sell recommendation will be not applied if the difference between the actual and predicted price is very low. The third type of rules determines the likelihood of a profit when buying or selling. The fourth type of rules is taking into account the risk of trading.

The authors in [6] describe a similar approach using the neural networks. At first, they proposed ten criteria calculate from the stock financial statements report to use for the fundamental analysis. Next, they applied a multi-layer perceptron on the five-year historical stock dataset to classify the good return stocks, i.e. those likely to win the market in the future. In addition, the authors analysed the short historical prices of the good return stocks by using technical factors to identify the buying or selling signal in the decision support process. The performance of the proposed approach was evaluated by the real information about the stock prices. The average returns of the ports following the system suggestions continuous increased.

Three students described in their work [11] a trading system based on testing of the simple well-known strategies of the technical analysis. These strategies consist of the indicators such as moving averages, Bollinger Bands, Keltner Channel, Commodity Channel Index, Volume Oscillator and Volume Ratio. The authors implemented the whole system through a TradeStation platform using a programming language called EasyLanguage based on predefined indicators. They proposed the four strategies using the indicators listed above and tested them with the aim to evaluate their's performance. In the next step, the authors selected the best two strategies to create the trading system. In addition, they optimised the system with a sample of data from two previous months and tested for the next month. The most powerful strategy based on Commodity Channel Index and Volume Oscillator reached 72.73% accuracy with eight profitable and three losing trades.

Based on realised research we can state that many of them use the indicators and technical analysis to create the decision rules. In recent years, a fundamental analysis is gaining an importance to improve the percentage of the recommendations. These systems mainly consist of an integrated set of modules including a voting system for final prediction of the future development for the related currency pair. At first, these systems test and verify the accuracy of the prediction and further build a recommendation on this prediction to buy or to sell. Many of the existing systems do not provide information about their structure because of the trade secret and a protection of the intellectual property. The overall aim is to design a method or a combination of the suitable methods to provide a decision support system with the highest possible profit and the lowest risk.

2   DSS Design and Creation

The core of the proposed system consists of the knowledge obtained through suitable data mining methods represented by the decision rules describing frequented events in the market. The Fig. 1 visualises a process how was the proposed DSS constructed.

In addition, we extended a set of basic rules with the outputs of the fundamental and technical analysis. The first one was represented by a set of fundamental news for whose we can predict their impact on the market with the higher accuracy and the second one contained well-known indicators as moving averages and Bollinger Bands [2]. We used the resulting knowledge to create the trading platform further used for the testing and evaluation of the input knowledge with the aim to ensure a competitive advantage. We performed many experiments with different values of the parameters. We stored a result of each experiment and evaluated if the related rules are still valid. If the recommendation is successful, the weight of the rule increases. Otherwise, a constant number

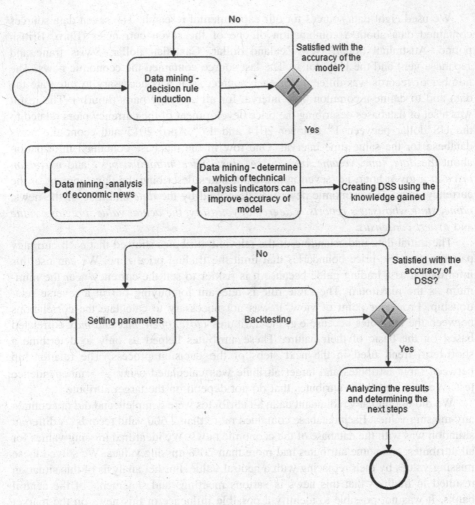

Fig. 1. Simple visualisation of the creation process of the proposed system

reduces the weight. The system works with two types of the external inputs. The first is the market price of a currency pair that is constantly changing and the second one contains the fundamental messages published at certain times on certain days of the month.

2.1 Rules Extraction Using CRISP-DM Methodology

In the text below, we specified that the success criterion would be at least 55% accuracy of the prediction for the future direction based on the strength of the related currency. In addition, it will be important to confirm that the currency's strength has inertia and a determination of this global factor at a given hour creates a positive impact.

We used eight data sources for our experimental research. The seven data sources contained data about a combination of one of the seven currencies (Euro, British pound, Australian dollar, New Zealand dollar, Canadian dollar, Swiss franc and Japanese yen) and the U.S. dollar. The last source contained the economic news. The number of records was different for each source, so it was necessary to integrate the data and to define a common time interval for all currency pairs (hourly). The result was a set of databases describing the price development of the currency pairs related to the US dollar between 1st October 2014 and 17th April 2015 and economic news database for the same time interval. One row in the database contained information about the *date*, *time*, *volume*, *open price*, *close price*, *minimum price* and *maximum price* in a given hour, i.e. seven numeric attributes describing the development of the currency pairs. The economic news was described by the *date* and *time* of the news, *name, state who issues reports*, a *degree of volatility, the actual value, previous value* and *expert consensus*.

The initial data understanding of the relevant attributes showed that each currency pair has concrete price boundaries that limit the trading price zone. We can use this information as a trading guide because it is riskier to sell the currency near the minimum as the maximum. The same rule is relevant for buying but in a reverse relationship. From our point of view, it was not necessary to calculate the correlations between the attributes because e.g. the attributes *close, open, mix* and *max* correlated based on the basic of their nature. These attributes helped us only to determine a short-term trend used in the next steps of the decision process. The relationship between input attributes and target attribute was calculated using χ^2 - independence test. We removed those attributes that do not depend on the target attribute.

We did not find any redundant data; all attributes were complete and did not contain any missing values. Each database contained more than 2 600 valid records. A different situation was with the database of the economic news. We identified missing values for all attributes, e.g. some attributes had more than 20% missing values. We solved these missing values by their replacing with a neutral value. Further analysis of this situation resulted in findings that this news is various meetings and statements of the central banks. It was not possible to identify a possible influence of this news on the market because they evoke an irregular volatility in the market lasting for only a few hours. In addition, we smoothed the noise and removed the outliers. In the processing phase, we created twenty-one new attributes, e.g. *strength/weakness* attribute to label a weakening or strengthening of the currency pair or minimal price range that smooth a noise in the cases when opening and closing prices were too close.

Modelling phase included an application of the selected algorithms on the processed data. We selected following methods CART [3] and C5.0 [16]. The C5.0 generates a decision model based on the trees or rules set, it is faster that C4.5, requires a less memory, generates smaller decision trees and has a greater ability to process classes that have very low representation in the training data [8]. The Classification And Regression Trees (CART) implementation is very similar to C4.5, but this algorithm constructs the tree based on a numerical splitting criterion recursively applied to the data. Resulting binary trees are more sparing with data and detect more patterns/rules/structures before too little data are left for learning [12].

In addition, we divided the processed data into two sets: 80% for training and 20% for testing based on the previous experiences. We realised a number of experiments to find the model with the best accuracy. The C5.0 model obtained the best accuracy 56.03% within a boosting set up to the value 10. The best models showed that a strict reduction of the input attributes makes the prediction worse, but the newly created attributes improve the accuracy.

Finally, we extracted 236 rules categorised into four groups:

- The rules describing the loss trade (80 rules).
- The rules describing the indecision of the U.S. dollar (55 rules).
- The rules describing the weakening of the U.S. dollar (59 rules).
- The rules describing the strengthening of the U.S. dollar (69 rules).

The first two categories do not add values for the proposed DSS because we need to have the rules describing a tendency of the US dollar to continue with the current trend. Therefore, we selected the best twenty rules from the third and fourth category based on their accuracy.

In addition, we followed the U.S. economic reports published by the US Department of Labor or the U.S. Federal Reserve System (FED) annualised during the period between 2nd February 2014 and 31st December 2015. We found out within realised experiments that about 60% of the time was the real development of the currency equal to the expected consequences of the published economic news. However, the highest expected impact had only the news published by the FED, i.e. if the FED statement about an interest rate was oriented to weakening the U.S. dollar; the market reacted in the same way with the probability near the 100%. In addition, we were able to predict the influence of the following factors such as the unemployment rate, the durable good orders and ISM (Institute for Supply Management) services sector with the accuracy higher than 70%.

After testing, we concluded that fundamental analysis would not improve the system in any way and that it would create the possibility to higher drawdowns. We would change our decision if we find a larger set of news with a better precision. However, chosen technical analysis indicators improved overall precision of the system by 7%, so we decided to apply them in the final version.

We can state that we met the specified success criteria with the best-achieved accuracy 56.03% that is typical for this type of data [4, 15]. The system's ability to recommend the right decision strongly depends on the ratio between risk and profit and not so much on the particular accuracy. We will discuss this statement discussed in the next section.

2.2 Decision-Making Process Proposal

We proposed the decision-making process as an iterative service in the completely trading platform (see Fig. 2). An each change in the price executes this process. It starts with a determination of the input parameters. After these parameters are set up, the DSS switches to sleeping mode during awaits for an external factor. If this factor occurs, the

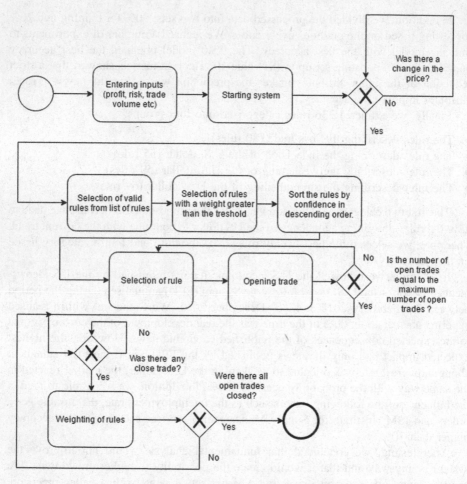

Fig. 2. Visualization of the decision-making process

DSS identifies a list of the valid rules, selects those whose weight is higher that specified boundary and sorts the rules by confidence in descending order.

For each rule in the sorted list, the DSS opens iteratively a new trade and the number of these open trades limits the relevant parameter. The system analyses a result of each closed trade and a new weight for the relevant rule is determined. During testing, we used 0.5 as a value of an initial weight of the rules, 0.1 as the boundary and similarly value 0.1 for an incremental or decremental change of the rule's weight. It is important to say that closing of the trade is an event, which may not occur in every iteration.

3 Evaluation

At first, it is important to explain that the number of open trades has a direct impact on the number of monitored rules. If the DSS reaches a maximal number of the allowed open trades, a next trade will be not open even a valid rule will exist. The particular trades are not limited by their duration, but by their expected profit and risk. This was the reason why we selected only the top 10 buying and selling rules.

The following tables contain a list of profit rules with similarly specified weights: boundary 0.1, initial weight 0.5, incremental and decremental change 0.1, a maximal number of open trades 1 and a volume of the trade as 0.1 lot. We used in all experiments an account with 1:200 leverage.

The optimisation was realised with data represented the currency pair EUR/USD between 1st July 2015 and 31st October 2015. After this optimisation, the initial set of rules from the first group (see Table 1) was reduced (rules 2, 6 and 10 were omitted, because they generated a loss). It means that the decision process did not include this type of rules and the rules with a low frequency of their validity (no. 5, 8 and 9). The rule no. 3 had a high drawdown, so we also eliminated it from the decision-making process.

Table 1. The profit rules from the category describing the strengthening of the U.S. dollar.

Rule	Risk (pip)	Target profit (pip)	Drawdown (EUR)	Max. number of the open trades	Overall profit (EUR)
1	350	90	251.44	6	478.21
7	10	350	127.18	7	256.60
9	240	240	168.17	1	219.39
3	260	330	624.22	5	124.92
4	340	10	208.12	14	120.53
5	10	50	0	1	45.28
8	320	10	12.49	1	9.02

We eliminated also the rule no. 7 from the second group of rules (see Table 2), because it was generally lossy even after optimisation of the parameters. The rule no. 8 is the best one in this group because it has a higher frequency of its validity, above-average earnings, a reasonable ratio between the target profit and the risk, and a relatively low drawdown. In the next step, we eliminated the rule no. 9 too due to its low frequency and low profit compared compared to other rules.

The result represents a list of the profitable rules that have a standard drawdown and a sufficient frequency. The realised testing and optimisation showed that we cannot label all rules as profit and an effective selection can improve the overall accuracy.

All described operations resulted in a modified set of rules. Table 3 shows a performance of the optimised DSS before and after the modification of the rules selection process on the currency pair EUR/USD between 1st November 2015 and 22nd February 2016.

Table 2. The profit rules from the category describing the weakening of the U.S. dollar.

Rule	Risk (pip)	Target profit (pip)	Drawdown (EUR)	Max. number of the open trades	Overall Profit (EUR)
8	20	330	181.93	19	927.47
5	230	280	352.37	5	474.93
3	230	160	346.46	7	458.02
10	280	160	139.14	3	417.43
1	310	160	367.16	6	394.38
6	170	160	349.73	13	351.63
2	120	280	347.69	10	311.00
4	330	10	236.59	20	165.66
9	130	230	139.83	2	73.91

Table 3. The obtained results before and after the rules modification.

	Initial rules selection	Modified rules selection
Gross profit (€)	896.61	572.95
Total net profit (€)	361.17	276.66
Number of positions	62	71
Maximal drawdown (%)	1.47	0.92
Profit position (%)	14.52	88.73
Successive wins	1	7
Successive loss	6	1
Risk (pip)	10	40
Expected profit (pip)	100	10

The previous rules provided a greater total net profit, but the usage of these rules has a disadvantage in a low profit position 14.52%. This system strongly depends on a few highly profitable trades. Since the aim of our work is to design a reliable system, more suitable is the system containing modified rules with 88.73% accuracy.

In order to describe the overall performance of the proposed DSS, it is necessary to divide the investigated time interval into smaller parts, specifically into sixteen weeks. This evaluation provides information about a consistency of the system performance and a distribution of the frequencies.

We can see in Table 4 that trades frequency in the particular weeks ranges from two to eight, except the Christmas period. We can label the eleven weeks as profitable. It can be stated that proposed DSS was successful even in the 6th week in which the system recommended only 40% right trades. A difference between total net profit in Table 3 and a sum of the all total net profits in Table 4 is caused by the trades that were opened at the end of the week and finished at the beginning of the following week.

Table 4. DSS performance evaluation for 16 weeks.

Week	Total net profit (€)	All positions	Profitable positions (%)
01.11–08.11	30.09	5	80
09.11–15.11	−09.47	4	75
16.11–22.11	−17.77	8	75
23.11–29.11	27.68	3	100
30.11–06.12	17.54	7	85.71
07.12–13.12	−56.12	5	40
14.12–20.12	63.31	7	100
21.12–27.12	0	0	–
28.12–03.01	08.90	6	83.33
04.01–10.01	27.53	3	100
11.01–17.01	36.73	4	100
18.01–24.01	−18.18	3	66.67
25.01–31.01	48.15	6	100
01.02–07.02	54.37	6	100
08.02–14.02	17.76	2	100
15.02–22.02	26.93	3	100

4   Conclusion

The aim of this work was to design a new approach how to use data mining approaches to improve decision support process for trading on the forex market. For this purpose, we propose to use the decision rules extracted from the historical data representing various trades on the forex market. These rules take into account different aspects of the macro analysis and microanalysis of the related currency. The rules represented a basis of the proposed decision support system, which was necessary to optimise to ensure its long profitability through continuous rules' adaptation based on weights changes in accordance with their performance. At the beginning, we specified the hypothesis that in this market we can determine the direction of currency's movement based on the movement of the related currency pair containing this currency. The obtained results confirm this hypothesis, i.e. it is important to determine the global currency direction, i.e. to determine if the currency is globally strong or weak against other major currencies and this knowledge has a positive influence on the prediction of the currency development. People, who want to trade on the forex market, can use this system not only as a recommender, but it is possible also to use it as an automatic trading system without human intervention.

We see our future work in several directions, e.g. it will be possible to extend the list of indicators resulting in more complex rules or to change used classification method. We selected the decision trees because of their simple understandability and readability.

Acknowledgments. The work presented in this paper was partially supported by the Slovak Grant Agency of the Ministry of Education and Academy of Science of the Slovak Republic under grant No. 1/0493/16 and by the Cultural and Educational Grant Agency of the Slovak Republic under grant No. 025TUKE-4/2015.

References

1. Bank of international settlements: Trennial Central Bank Survey (2013)
2. Bollinger, J.A.: Bollinger on Bollinger Bands, 1st edn. McGraw-Hill Education, New York (2001)
3. Breiman, L., Friedman, J.H., Olshen, R., Stone, C.J.: Classification and Regression Tree. Chapman & Hall/CRC Press, Boca Raton (1984)
4. Castiglione, F.: Forecasting price increments using an artificial neural network. Complex Dyn. Econ. 3(1), 45–56 (2001)
5. Dymova, L., Sevastjanov, P., Kaczmarek, K.: A Forex trading expert system based on a new approach to the rule-base evidential reasoning. Expert Syst. Appl. 51(C), 1–13 (2016)
6. Eiamkanitchat, N., Moontui, T.: Decision support for the stocks trading using MLP and data mining techniques. In: Kim, K.J., Joukov, N. (eds.) Information Science and Applications (ICISA) 2016. LNEE, vol. 376, pp. 1223–1233. Springer, Heidelberg (2016). doi:10.1007/978-981-10-0557-2_116
7. Kathy, L.: Day Trading and Swing Trading the Currency Market, 2nd edn. Wiley, New Jersey (2009)
8. Kuhn, M., Johnson, K.: Applied Predictive Modeling. Springer-Verlag, New York (2013)
9. Lai, K.,K., Yu, L., Wang, S.: A neural network and web-based decision support system for Forex forecasting and trading. In: Shi, Y., Xu, W., Chen, Z. (eds.) CASDMKM 2004. LNCS (LNAI), vol. 3327, pp. 243–253. Springer, Heidelberg (2005). doi:10.1007/978-3-540-30537-8_27
10. Larsen, F.: Automatic stock market trading based on Technical Analysis. Master thesis (2006)
11. Mehta, J.R., Menghini, M.D., Sarafconn, D.A.: Automated foreign exchange trading system. An Interactive Qualifying Project Report (2011)
12. Patil, N., Rekha, L., Vidya, C.: Comparison of C5.0 & CART classification algorithms using pruning technique. Int. J. Eng. Res. Technol. (IJERT) 1(4), 1–5 (2012)
13. Pham, H.V., Cao, T., Nakaoka, I., Cooper, E.W., Kamei, K.: A proposal of hybrid Kansei-som model for stock market investment. Int. J. Innov. Comput. Inf. Control 7(5), 2863–2880 (2011)
14. Peachavanish, R.: Stock selection and trading based on cluster analysis of trend and momentum indicators. In: Proceedings of the International MultiConference of Engineers and Computer Scientists 2016, vol. 1, IMECS 2016, Hong Kong, pp. 317–321 (2016)
15. Peramunetilleke, D., Wong, R.K.: Currency exchange rate forecasting from news headlines. In: Proceedings of the 13th Australasian Database Conference, pp. 131–139, Australia (2002)
16. Quinlan, J.R.: C4.5: Programs for Machine Learning. Morgan Kaufmann Publishers Inc., San Francisco (1993)
17. Wirth, R., Hipp, J.: CRISP-DM: towards a standard process model for data mining. In: Proceedings of the Fourth International Conference on the Practical Application of Knowledge Discovery and Data Mining, pp. 29–39 (2000)

BITA Workshop

Visual Analytics in Enterprise Architecture Management: A Systematic Literature Review

Dierk Jugel[1,2(✉)], Kurt Sandkuhl[1], and Alfred Zimmermann[2]

[1] Rostock University, Rostock, Germany
{dierk.jugel,kurt.sandkuhl}@uni-rostock.de
[2] Reutlingen University, Reutlingen, Germany
alfred.zimmermann@reutlingen-university.de

Abstract. In times of dynamic markets, enterprises have to be agile to be able to quickly react to market influences. Due to the increasing digitization of products, the enterprise IT often is affected when business models change. Enterprise Architecture Management (EAM) targets a holistic view of the enterprise' IT and their relations to the business. However, Enterprise Architectures (EA) are complex structures consisting of many layers, artifacts and relationships between them. Thus, analyzing EA is a very complex task for stakeholders. Visualizations are common vehicles to support analysis. However, in practice visualization capabilities lack flexibility and interactivity. A solution to improve the support of stakeholders in analyzing EAs might be the application of visual analytics. Starting from a systematic literature review, this article investigates the features of visual analytics relevant for the context of EAM.

Keywords: EAM · Literature review · Visual analysis · Decision support

1 Introduction

In times of dynamic markets, enterprises in many industrial and service sectors have to be able to quickly adapt to changing market conditions or customer demands. In particular changes in the business models have several impacts on the enterprise architecture (EA) [1] including business processes, business units, information systems, and IT infrastructure. These architectural elements have manifold relations to each other which makes the EA a highly complex structure. Enterprise Architecture Management (EAM) is a method to support stakeholders in adaptation and transformation processes. Based on an up-to-date description of the enterprise model [2] and current EA, analyses are performed to understand adaptation needs and implications.

In practice, stakeholders commonly use visualization techniques and tools to analyze the EA. These visualizations, i.e. purpose-oriented or stakeholder-centered views on the EA, are usually created using EAM tools. However, as described in [3, 4], these tool-created views often are report-like, i.e. static with respect to the displayed information. As static visualizations do not sufficiently support interaction mechanisms for a detailed analysis of an EA, it is very time-consuming for stakeholders to work out relevant characteristics. From the perspective of business and IT-alignment [5], enterprise architecture can serve as planning and road-mapping support for the

W. Abramowicz et al. (Eds.): BIS 2016 Workshops, LNBIP 263, pp. 99–110, 2017.
DOI: 10.1007/978-3-319-52464-1_10

implementation of business requirements in appropriate IT-solutions. Improvement of visualization and analysis functions for EA models is expected to help stakeholder groups from both, business and IT, to identify relevant change needs in the EA and to improve understanding between each other.

In earlier work, we investigated this improvement potential of analysis and visualization features in EAM by using different techniques, such as cockpits [6], embedded real-time information in EA models [7] or decision modeling [8]. One research direction resulting from this work was to investigate the use of approaches from the field of visual computing. Besides different visualization techniques developed in this field, our attention was specifically attracted by the field of visual analytics (VA). According to [9] "Visual Analytics is the science of analytical reasoning facilitated by interactive visual interfaces". Visual analytics techniques for example can be applied to synthesize information and "derive insights from massive, dynamic, ambiguous, and often conflicting data". The authors of [7] define the following focus areas of Visual Analytics: Analytical reasoning techniques, visual representations and interaction techniques, data representations and "techniques to support production, presentation, and dissemination of the results of an analysis to communicate information in the appropriate context to a variety of audiences". Keim et al. [10] describe that in VA, algorithmic analyses performed by a tool are semi-automatically and interactively applied to the subject of analysis under consideration.

The aim of this paper is twofold: (1) to investigate which work already has been performed on using VA in EAM, and (2) to identify the most relevant lines of VA work for EAM.

With respect to the first aim, concepts of visual analytics seem not to have been applied in research: a recent survey on the state-of-the-art of visual EAM conducted by Roth et al. [4] does not identify any related concept in today's EAM tools. In order to widen and deepen this state-of-the-art work, we perform a systematic literature review (SLR) which has the main purpose to identify existing approaches targeting visual analytics in the context of EAM. For the second aim, we take the perspective of the well-accepted "scalability challenges" in visual analytics and discuss to what extent they are relevant and have to be addressed in EAM. The scalability challenges are considered as defining the roadmap for future VA research which makes them an interesting aspect for our investigation. The main contributions of this paper are a systematic account of visual analytics work in EAM and the discussion of relevance of scalability challenges in EAM.

Section 2 presents the approach of the systematic literature review including the process of paper identification, data collection and analysis. Section 3 addresses the relevant areas of VA for EAM by discussing the scalability challenges. In Sect. 4 we summarize the results.

2 Systematic Literature Review

This section addresses the question, which work on visual analytics in EAM has already be performed in scientific research. The section describes the research approach used, the data collection and the findings.

2.1 Research Approach

As a means to systematically identify the existing research about visual analytics in the field of EAM, we performed a SLR according to the guidelines of Kitchenham [11]. According to these guidelines, the SLR is a structured and comprehensive review process with the aim to "identify gaps in current research", provide "background in order to appropriately position new research activities" and collect all "existing evidence concerning a treatment or technology" [11]. Kitchenham [11] suggests six steps, which we document in the following and which guide the inner structure of the section.

Firstly, according to [11], we develop research questions (RQ) to be answered by the SLR:

RQ1: How much activity has there been in the field of Visual Analytics in EAM?
RQ2: What research topics are being investigated?
RQ3: Who is active in the research area?
RQ4: What approaches concerning Visual Analytics in the field of EAM are there?
RQ5: How are the VA scalability challenges in the context of EAM discussed in literature?

The research questions one to three deal with general issues to provide an overview about who addresses the research topic of applying visual analytics to EAM and in which context the topic is discussed. Research questions four and five focus on the application of visual analytics to EAM in detail. Whereas the goal of RQ4 is to identify literature that describes an application of visual analytics to EAM, the goal of RQ5 is to examine how the scalability challenges introduced in Sect. 3 are discussed in the context of EAM. Such discussions might be an indicator whether there is a demand for applying certain aspects of visual analytics to EAM or not.

2.2 Identification of Papers

In this section, we describe the process of paper identification. Firstly, literature sources have to be determined, which defines the overall search space. Subsequently, we describe the search process itself. For a better overview, at the end we give a summary about the search process for a better understanding.

2.2.1 Literature Sources

Before the search process can be performed, the literature sources to be taken into account have to be defined. We decided to examine the following five repositories that include important journals and conferences in the context of computer science and business information systems:

ACM digital library[1], AIS electronic library (AISeL)[2], IEEE Xplore[3], Science-Direct[4], and SpringerLink[5]. This decision is based on the assumption that all work on visual analytics in EAM should reach one of these major outlets.

The Association for Computer Machinery (ACM) hosts conferences that are relevant to our research topic, like the conference on "Computer Supported Cooperative Work" (CSCW). The Association for Information Systems (AIS) hosts important and high ranked international conferences in the area of business informatics like "International Conference on Information Systems" (ICIS). AIS also is publisher of numerous high ranked journals like "Management in Information Systems Quarterly" (MISQ).

SpringerLink includes all papers and books published by Springer. This repository also includes important international conferences and journals in the area of business informatics like "Conference on Advanced Information Systems Engineering" (CAiSE) and the working conference on "Practice of Enterprise Modeling" (PoEM). IEEE Xplore Digital Library includes high ranked international conferences and journals like "Enterprise Distributed Object Conference" (EDOC), which are important sources in EA research. ScienceDirect is a repository that includes more than 200 journals in the field of computer science like "Information Systems".

2.2.2   Search Process

In this section we describe further steps of Kitchenham's review process. The next step to do is so-called "population" [11]. In this step the search string is developed. Afterwards the step "paper selection" is done by a manual selection of papers found by applying the search string on the literature sources defined in Sect. 2.2.1.

The Population. The aim of the SLR is to get an overview about Visual Analytics approaches in the field of EAM. To answer RQ5 we also added the scalability challenges to get an overview about papers that discuss these challenges in the field of EAM. The initial search string we developed is the following:

> ("visual analytics" **OR** "information scalability" **OR** "software scalability" **OR** "visual scalability" **OR** "display scalability" **OR** "human scalability" **OR** "scalability challenge")
> **AND**
> ("enterprise architecture")

We applied this search string to the full text papers and all fields of the literature sources. Due to the fact that the research topic is relatively new and we do not expect many papers, we want to get all papers published in journals, conference proceedings and books from the past by the year 2015. We do not limit the publishing date, because sometimes it takes a while until proceedings of conferences are published in a repository. It may happen that proceedings of a conference hosted in 2015 are

---

[1] http://dl.acm.org.

[2] http://aisel.aisnet.org.

[3] http://ieeexplore.ieee.org/Xplore/home.jsp.

[4] http://www.sciencedirect.com.

[5] http://link.springer.com.

published in 2016. In case we find papers of journals or conferences of 2016 we manually sort them out.

After performing the search, we only found 31 papers. Therefore, we refined the search string by adding synonyms for both "visual analytics" and "enterprise architecture" to increase the number of publications to get a better overview about current research. As a synonym for visual analytics we choose "visual analysis". Heer and Shneiderman define visual analysis as an "iterative process of view creation, exploration, and refinement" [12]. In other words, visual analysis targets analyzing something by using (interactive) visualizations. Using this definition, visual analytics can be interpreted as a concretization of visual analysis. Visual Analytics and Visual Analysis paradigms are not the same. However, probably there are papers describing visual analytics mechanisms, but name it visual analysis. As a synonym for "enterprise architecture" we choose "enterprise model" because enterprise models also contain the elements (e.g. business processes and applications) that are part of an enterprise architecture. The refined search string we used for performing the SLR looks like the following:

("visual analytics" OR "visual analysis" OR "information scalability" OR "software scalability" OR "visual scalability" OR "display scalability" OR "human scalability" OR "scalability challenge")

AND

("enterprise architecture" OR "enterprise model")

We performed this search at June, 9th 2016 and found 70 papers (ACM: 0, AISeL: 6, IEEE Xplore: 20, ScienceDirect: 9, SpringerLink: 35). We also applied the refined search string to the full text papers and all fields of the literature sources without limiting the publishing date. With this search result at hand, relevant papers that are suitable to answer the research questions have to be filtered by reading the papers' abstracts.

2.2.3 Paper Selection

In this step all abstracts of the 70 papers have to be read to select relevant papers for answering the research questions. For selecting relevant papers, we defined criteria. For us a paper is relevant if the authors describe an approach or a method to enable visually analyzing an enterprise architecture or an enterprise model. Thereby, the authors have to describe mechanisms like combining automated analyses and visualizations that outrun visual analysis approaches towards visual analytics. Moreover, the central part of the paper has to contain such an approach. Papers, in which the authors only mention that visual analysis or visual analytics may help for specific issues are not relevant for us. In addition, papers are relevant if the authors discuss scalability challenges in the field of analyzing enterprise architectures or enterprise models.

Before we read the abstracts, we excluded all found items, which are no papers. We filtered out 10 items, because they are table of contents, abstracts of books and so on. Afterwards we read the abstracts of 60 remained papers and identified only 7 relevant ones according to our criteria. In case of unclear situations, we read the full text to decide whether a paper is relevant or not.

2.2.4   Summary of the Search Process

We started with the population. In first step we applied an initial search string on the previously defined literature sources – the repositories ACM digital library, AISeL, IEEE Xplore, ScienceDirect and SpringerLink. However, only 31 papers are found. Therefore, we refined the search string by adding synonyms to cover a broader field of research papers. By applying the refined search string, we found 70 papers. These papers are the starting point for the identification of relevant papers. We defined criteria to determine which papers are relevant to answer our research questions. Before we started to identify relevant papers, we excluded all found items, which are no papers, because e.g. they are table of contents or abstracts of books. 60 papers were left over. After reading the abstracts we identified only 7 relevant papers, which we analyze in detail in Sect. 4.

2.3   Analysis of Data and Interpretation

In this section, we answer the research questions of Sect. 2.1 by using collected data of relevant papers identified in Sect. 2.2.3. RQ1 to RQ3 deal with general information about research topics, used research approaches, who is active and how much activity in the investigated field of research there is. RQ4 concerns the presented approaches of the papers itself. To answer this question, we give a short summary of each approach to get an overview about the current situation in research. RQ5 targets the papers that discuss scalability challenges in EAM.

RQ1: How much activity is in the field of Visual Analytics in EAM?

We found only 7 papers, which deal with visual analytics in EAM. Before we started this SLR we did not expect many papers, because experience from own practice shows that tools in EAM to a large extent offer only conventional reporting features and no visual analytics possibilities. Tool surveys and case studies like [3, 4] confirm this assumption, which do not cover visual analytics capabilities. The authors of [13] performed a research study investigating visual analytics capabilities of the EAM tools. As a result, in some cases first approaches concerning modern and interactive techniques for visual analysis exist. However, the visual capabilities of EAM tools mostly are limited on static visualizations without interaction possibilities. All these information indicates that visual analytics is a very innovative field of research in the domain of EAM.

Figure 1 illustrates the respective number of relevant papers by literature repository and year of publication. Only AISeL, IEEE Xplore and SpringerLink contain relevant papers. When we go in detail we see that 4 papers are workshop papers and 3 conference papers. The oldest paper we found was published in 2012. This situation also indicates that this field of research is relatively new and there is much research in progress. The Enterprise Distributed Object Conference (EDOC) is the conference with the most paper (3 workshop papers). There are no relevant papers in ACM digital library and ScienceDirect. ACM digital library only contains premium conferences. Therefore, this situation is not surprising, because the most papers are work in progress, which cannot be published in journals and it is very difficult to publish them in high ranked conferences. The situation of ScienceDirect is quite similar. This repository only contains journals.

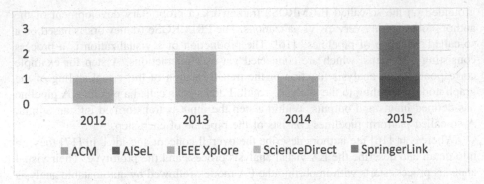

Fig. 1. Research activity by year

RQ2: What research topics are being investigated?

While reading the relevant papers, it appears that most of all address analyzing enterprise architectures [14–18]. However, the way how an EA is analyzed differs. Roth et al. address the topic of a business user-friendly configuration of visualizations [18]. An approach to analyze enterprise application landscapes and related monitoring data is presented by Fittkau et al. [14]. Visual analysis of EAs is focused in [15–17]. Naseer et al. present a tool to build up a data-centric EA by using semantic techniques to integrate different data sources and to make them accessible and analyzable [19]. The integration of different enterprise models by using visual techniques is also the focus of [20].

RQ3: Who is active in the research area?

The 7 papers are written by 13 authors. 4 papers are written by the same co-authors named David Naranjo, Mario Sánchez and Jorge Villalobos [15–17, 20]. All the papers describe the same approach in different stages of progress and focusing. Two papers are written by authors of the Technical University of Munich in Germany [14, 18]. Another one is written by Fujitsu Laboratories Europe [19]. Only one paper is written by a cooperation between Technical University of Munich and Kiel University [14]. All other papers are written by one institution. Summarizing it seems to be that research groups of the Universidad de Los Andes and Technical University of Munich are the only ones, which research in this field for years.

This situation is surprising, because the impact of this topic on practice is very high. An explanation for that could be that this topic is very practice-oriented, which maybe is more suitable for applied research than for fundamental research projects.

RQ4: What approaches concerning Visual Analytics in the field of EAM are there?

We identified 6 papers discussing visual analytics in the field of EAM. There are 3 papers, which describe the same approach in different stages of progress. In [16] the authors present an idea of visual EA analysis. The aim is to develop a metamodel-independent platform that is flexible and configurable. Based on this platform the authors want to combine automated analysis functions, which are composable, with visualizing the analysis' results. The combination of automated analyses and visualizing their results is a first step towards visual analytics. The platform is grounded on the so-called PRIMROSe framework, a proprietary development of the authors focusing on overview visualizations. The PRIMROSe framework is based on a so-called "pipeline of pipelines" [16]. The production of a visualization is a process consisting of 5 steps, which are connected via user interactions. A step for example corresponds to an analysis function or the transformation of the visual styling of the graph nodes according to the analysis' result. Each step is called a pipeline. A pipeline has defined inputs and outputs. Within a step the input is transformed into an output. A so-called platform pipelines consists of the pipeline of each step.

Whereas in [16] the authors describe the overall concept and idea, in [17] they go into detail and describe the EA visual analysis process and the prototype. Their visual analysis process starts with importing the EA model, followed by automatable analysis functions. Afterwards the analysis' results have to be visualized for stakeholders. Now stakeholders create hypotheses based on the information they can see. To ensure hypothesis, stakeholders interact with the systems by e.g. triggering further analyses or to filter information. As a result, a new visualization will be created, which leads to new information for the stakeholder. Now the stakeholder can decide what is to do next. The stakeholder is also able to communicate analysis results. Another use case of visual EA analysis is described by Naranjo et al. in [20]. In this paper they use PRIMROSe to integrate different enterprise models in a visual way. They use visualizations to connect same elements of different models. The authors present a tool named Sigourney based on PRIMROSe to do this integration.

Roth et al. present in [18] an approach of a business user-friendly configuration of visualizations. For this purpose the authors introduce a meta-information model, that includes technical information demands of abstract viewpoints and the information offer of an EA model. The technical information demand of an abstract viewpoint depends on the type of the visualization. For instance, a matrix diagram requires a concept of an EA model for the cells, and related concepts for x- and y-axis. The information offer of an EA model includes concepts and their properties and relations. In addition, the authors develop a structural pattern matching algorithm to bind visualizations and bindings. For non-technical users the authors provide a configuration wizard.

Fittkau et al. present an approach to visually analyze enterprise application landscapes and related monitoring data, like CPU workload [14]. The authors emphasize the importance of combining data about enterprise application landscapes with related real-time monitoring data to increase data quality of application landscape documentations and to take better decisions about the landscape. They demonstrate how to link several data sources using a tool called "ExplorViz" that provides interactive 2d and 3d visualizations on different levels of abstraction in real-time.

Naseer et al. describe in [19] an advance to build-up a data-centric EA. In companies there are many structured and unstructured information. The authors consider their tool as a visual analytics tool, because the tool provides interactive functions and visualizations to visualize analysis results.

RQ5: How are the VA scalability challenges in the context of EAM discussed in literature?

There are two papers that indirectly discuss scalability challenges. Naranjo et al. develop an evaluation framework to assess EA visual analysis capabilities of EAM and general visualization tools. For the framework, the authors identify 14 requirements important for visually analyzing enterprise models. The requirements "Keep the context (KC)" and "Focus of Interest (FI)" for us are especially of interest. Naranjo et al. argue that enterprise models can be very large and stakeholders often have problems to find one's way. Therefore, they propose mechanisms "for encoding large models without losing the big picture" (requirement KC) [15]. In addition, stakeholders have to be able to dynamically choose the focus of interest. That implies that elements, which are especially of interest have to be highlighted whereas less important elements also have to be present, but in another way (requirement FI). The authors do not explicitly mention visual analytics' scalability challenges, but the requirements KC and FI reveal problems concerning the adaption of data to the audience (information scalability) and effectively display massive data sets (visual scalability).

Roth et al. [18] point out dynamic information demands of stakeholders in EAM. However, the configuration of visualizations mostly is not trivial and often only can be done by experts. This leads to long-time configuration processes, which hinders ad-hoc analysis of stakeholders. The issue addressed by Roth et al. also targets information scalability.

3   Visual Analytics in EAM

The SLR discussed in Sect. 2 confirmed that nearly no work was done on visual analytics in EAM. Thus, we addressed our second aim to identify relevant areas from VA for the field of EAM. As guiding structure for discussing what parts of VA could be relevant for EAM, we selected the scalability challenges of VA. The five scalability challenges, which visual analytics should address, are information scalability, visual scalability, display scalability, human scalability, and software scalability (see below). In VA the five scalability challenges are considered as cornerstones in the roadmap of future VA research, which from our perspective motivates its use for investigating the relevance for EAM.

One of the motivations for performing the systematic literature analysis was to identify existing work and potentials of visual analytics in EAM. Since not much work was identified in the intersection of both subject areas "visual analytics" and "EAM" (see Sect. 2), this combination either is not relevant for EAM or there is room for additional research. Due to our impression that EAM tools still can be improved (see Sect. 1) our conjecture is that there is unexplored potential. Thus, we decided to analyze relevance of visual analytics in more detail and to base this analysis on the scalability challenges identified in this field. Scalability challenges initially were meant to identify future research directions for visual analytics but also can be seen as representing dimensions of functions in this discipline.

Visual analytics is expected to be in particular useful when large amounts of data have to be managed, analyzed and visualized. Especially large enterprises with an EA containing thousands of elements have the problem to handle large amounts of data. Five scalability challenges were identified, which visual analytics should be address: information scalability, visual scalability, display scalability, human scalability, and software scalability [9].

Information scalability describes "the capability to extract data from massive data streams", to cope with quick change rates of information and to adapt information to the audience [9]. This scalability challenge clearly exists in EAM. As soon as EAM is linked to operational data reflecting the current status of EA elements, like application instances, process instances or technical systems, extracts from real-time data are required which have to meet the needs of decision makers. This also indicates the need to scale the information to the audience – in EAM many stakeholders in different roles are involved (see [21]). Therefore, it is important to provide information, which the stakeholder is able to interpret.

Visual scalability includes interaction techniques with visual representations and ability to effectively display massive data set, i.e. either a large amount of data elements or dimensions [9], for example by using appropriate visual metaphors. This can also be important for EAM cases if several thousands of application or systems instances are active in an enterprise, but does not have the same priority as information scalability.

Display scalability addresses the issue of different display resolution, sizes and other form factors [9] which, for example, require display scale-independent interaction techniques. In most enterprises, there are many different display types in use starting from conventional desktop computers to tables, smartphones and large screens in meeting rooms. Although EAM traditionally is done in desk work and meeting rooms, there are more and more tasks assigned to mobile users. Visual analytics functions available on different display forms probably would be well-received by EAM stakeholders.

Human scalability addresses the fact that analysis activities are not always done by single persons but by groups of people in different numbers. In such a collaborative setting, the different participants still need to have different tasks and problems they need to focus on. Such situations are quite typical for EAM scenarios as many roles are involved in analysis and decision making processes regarding enterprise architectures, i.e. human scalability seems to be very relevant to EAM.

The software scalability, which is described as the capability to "interactively manipulate large data sets" and addresses algorithms and approaches for scalable software [9]. In principle, scalable software systems for the management of enterprise architecture data are also important for EAM. However, in our opinion that aspect is not of highest priority since existing EAM tools seems to scale in an acceptable way.

Williams et al. investigate in [22] impacts on decision making by doing visual analytics. Traditionally reports or visualizations are created by experts that provides it to users like managers, enterprise architects and so on. Thus, visual analytics provides interactive functions to analyze data in an ad hoc manner, studying, analysis and decision making become an iterative process. The authors write about self-service analysis for decision makers and managers and "visual decision making" [22]. However, this has organizational impacts. The target group of visual analytics are decision makers and managers. Nevertheless, these stakeholders do not have expert knowledge about the information, because currently they get their packaged reports from experts. The stakeholders "only" have to interpret the data they see on the reports. Studying and analyzing the data require fundamental knowledge about the data, their structure and coherences.

Based on the above discussion, our conclusion is that all scalability challenges from visual analytics are to some extent relevant for EAM, i.e. visual analytics functionality of future EAM tools should observe these challenges and implement appropriate features. Thus, the challenges can be used as general requirements when designing future functionalities of EAM tools. Of highest importance are from our perspective information scalability and human scalability.

4 Summary and Future Work

Using a systematic literature analysis, we investigated the state of research on visual analytics in EAM. One of the analysis purposes was to explore, to what extent visual analytics techniques were applied in EAM research and what improvement potentials exist. The literature analysis showed that only a few papers and approaches address visual analytics in EAM, but these papers do not address the scalability challenges.

Furthermore, we discussed the scalability challenges from visual analytics and their relevance for EAM. From our perspective information scalability and human scalability are of highest importance for implementation in EAM tools.

We are planning to use the different scalability dimensions for analysis of established EAM tools in order to identify improvement potentials. As a precondition, the scalability challenges need to be operationalized in a catalogue of more concrete functionalities which indicate their support in the tool and which support the possibility of differentiation between tools. Furthermore, we plan to use the same operationalization for investigating EAM stakeholder opinion about the need for respective functions. Both views, i.e. the extent of existing features in tools and the requirements from user side, are expected to help in setting priorities for tool improvement.

References

1. Ahlemann, F., Stettiner, E., Messerschmidt, M., Legner, C.: Strategic Enterprise Architecture Management: Challenges, Best Practices, and Future Developments (Management for Professionals). Springer, Heidelberg (2012)
2. Sandkuhl, K., Stirna, J., Persson, A., Wißotzki, M.: Enterprise Modeling: Tackling Business Challenges with the 4EM Method. Springer, Heidelberg (2014)
3. Matthes, F., Buckl, S., Leitel, J., Schweda, C.M.: Enterprise architecture management tool survey 2008, München (2008)
4. Roth, S., Zec, M., Matthes, F.: Enterprise architecture visualization tool survey 2014, München (2014)
5. Seigerroth, U.: Enterprise modeling and enterprise architecture. Int. J. IT Bus. Alignment Gov. 2, 16–34 (2011)
6. Jugel, D., Schweda, C.M.: Interactive functions of a cockpit for enterprise architecture planning. In: 2014 IEEE 18th International Enterprise Distributed Object Computing Conference Workshops and Demonstrations, pp. 33–40 (2014)
7. Christiner, F., Lantow, B., Sandkuhl, K., Wißotzki, M.: Multi-dimensional visualization in enterprise modeling. In: Business Information Systems, Vilnius, pp. 139–152 (2012)

8. Jugel, D., Kehrer, S., Schweda, C.M., Zimmermann, A.: A decision-making case for collaborative enterprise architecture engineering. In: Lecture Notes in Informatics (LNI) - Informatik 2015, pp. 865–879. Gesellschaft für Informatik (GI) (2015)
9. Thomas, J.J., Cook, K.A.: Illuminating the path: the research and development agenda for visual analytics (2005)
10. Keim, D., Andrienko, G., Fekete, J.-D., Görg, C., Kohlhammer, J., Melançon, G.: Visual analytics: definition, process, and challenges. In: Kerren, A., Stasko, John, T., Fekete, J.-D., North, C. (eds.) Information Visualization. LNCS, vol. 4950, pp. 154–175. Springer, Heidelberg (2008). doi:10.1007/978-3-540-70956-5_7
11. Kitchenham, B.: Procedures for performing systematic reviews, Keele, UK (2004)
12. Heer, J., Shneiderman, B.: Interactive dynamics for visual analysis. Queue **10**, 30 (2012)
13. Jugel, D., Schweda, C.M., Zimmermann, A., Läufer, S.: Tool capability in visual EAM analytics. Complex Syst. Inf. Model. Q. **2**, 46–55 (2015). doi:10.7250/csimq.2015-2.04
14. Fittkau, F., Roth, S., Hasselbring, W.: Explorviz : visual runtime behavior analysis of enterprise application. In: ECIS 2015 Completed Research Papers (2015)
15. Naranjo, D., Sanchez, M., Villalobos, J.: Visual analysis of enterprise models. In: 2012 IEEE 16th International Enterprise Distributed Object Computing Conference Workshops, pp. 19–28 (2012)
16. Naranjo, D., Sanchez, M., Villalobos, J.: Towards a unified and modular approach for visual analysis of enterprise models. In: 2014 IEEE 18th International Enterprise Distributed Object Computing Conference Workshops and Demonstrations, pp. 77–86. IEEE (2014)
17. Naranjo, D., Sánchez, M., Villalobos, J.: PRIMROSe: a graph-based approach for enterprise architecture analysis. In: Cordeiro, J., Hammoudi, S., Maciaszek, L., Camp, O., Filipe, J. (eds.) ICEIS 2014. LNBIP, vol. 227, pp. 434–452. Springer, Heidelberg (2015). doi:10.1007/978-3-319-22348-3_24
18. Roth, S., Hauder, M., Zec, M., Utz, A., Matthes, F.: Empowering business users to analyze enterprise architectures: structural model matching to configure visualizations. In: 2013 17th IEEE International Enterprise Distributed Object Computing Conference Workshops, pp. 352–360. IEEE (2013)
19. Naseer, A., Laera, L., Matsutsuka, T.: Enterprise BigGraph. In: Proceedings of the Annual Hawaii International Conference on System Sciences, pp. 1005–1014 (2013)
20. Naranjo, D., Sánchez, M., Villalobos, J.: The devil in the details: fine-grained enterprise model weaving. In: Persson, A., Stirna, J. (eds.) CAiSE 2015. LNBIP, vol. 215, pp. 233–244. Springer, Heidelberg (2015). doi:10.1007/978-3-319-19243-7_23
21. Wißotzki, M., Köpp, C., Stelzer, P.: Rollenkonzepte im enterprise architecture management. In: Zimmermann, A., Rossmann, A. (eds.) Digital Enterprise Computing (DEC 2015). Lecture Notes in Informatics (LNI), vol. P-244, pp. 127–138. Gesellschaft für Informatik, Böblingen (2015)
22. Williams, B.G., Boland, R.J., Lyytinen, K.: Shaping problems, not decisions: when decision makers leverage visual analytics. In: Twenty-First Americas Conference on Information Systems (AMCIS 2015), pp. 1–15. Association for Information Systems (AIS), Puerto Rico (2015)

Modeling Alignment as a Higher Order Nomological Framework

Rogier van de Wetering[✉]

Open University of the Netherlands,
Valkenburgerweg 177, 6419 AT Heerlen, The Netherlands
rogier.vandewetering@ou.nl

Abstract. Achieving Business/IT-alignment (BITA) and pursuing intended goals within organizations seems an intricate and poorly examined process. We argue that without proper theories concerning BITA, the 'mapping' of theoretical constructs onto empirical phenomena, is ambiguous. In this paper we synthesize a higher order nomological framework for BITA with a considerable degree of complexity, coherence and causality. We aim to extend and generalize previous work on BITA within the healthcare domain, drawing on principles of complexity science. Our framework explains how BITA is related to firm performance. Using this knowledge, organizations can define improvement activities that can be executed along five organizational dimensions that best meets a organizations' current and future needs; done simultaneously and hence by an integrated management perspective. This work contributes to academia by using a modeling approach that overcomes acknowledged limitations of existing approaches. Doing so, the outcomes of this study also offer many opportunities for future research.

Keywords: Business/IT-alignment · Complexity science · Structural Equation Modeling (SEM) · Nomological framework · Firm performance

1 An Acknowledged Omission in Scientific Literature

Business/IT-alignment (hereinafter referred to as BITA) has been a major concern for executives and IT practitioners for decades and refers to applying IS/IT in an appropriate and timely way, in harmony (i.e. complementarity between activities) with business strategies, goals and needs [1] and remains an enduring challenge for firms worldwide [2]. Current literature points out that BITA remains a top priority for business and IT executives [3]. However, strong theoretical foundations of BITA have not been developed or tested extensively [4].

Following both recognized work and more recent studies [4–7], we argue that achieving BITA and pursuing intended goals and objectives within organizations seems an intricate and poorly examined process and lacks convincing theoretical grounds. Little scientific knowledge is available about the underlying theoretical mechanisms that govern firm performance (i.e. explanandum, and hereinafter referred to as performance) and how BITA contributes to this as an antecedent.

© Springer International Publishing AG 2017
W. Abramowicz et al. (Eds.): BIS 2016 Workshops, LNBIP 263, pp. 111–122, 2017.
DOI: 10.1007/978-3-319-52464-1_11

Over the past decade, the MIS community increased attention towards the adaptive and co-evolutionary nature of IS/IT [8] and dynamic, multi-faceted, and non-deterministic processes to align IS/IT in constantly-changing business environments [9]. This evolutionistic and dynamic approach has its roots in nonlinear science such as physics, biology, bio-chemistry and economy and has a profound impact on management, strategy, organization and IS/IT studies. A number of authors have stated that the science of complexity and complex adaptive systems (CAS) can be considered a valuable instrument to cope with organizational and IS/IT changes in non-linear turbulent environments [10–12].

We employ the basic thought that in order to truly understand the nature of BITA, you will need a 'holistic' and 'complex' theoretical framework that fits the diversity of organizational components and interactions among the many agents that are involved in organizations. To turn this claim and perspective into a framework, a systematic agenda is required, linking theory development with mathematical or computational model development.

Therefore, the main objective of this paper is to develop an integrative nomological framework to model, on the one hand, BITA, and, on the other hand, its foundational relationship with performance. This does imply that performance is defined as having multifactorial impacts and benefits, consistent with many studies investigating IS/IT and performance [13, 14]. Doing so, we build upon and generalize work done by Van de Wetering and Batenburg [7, 15, 16] that developed a holistic approach towards alignment and maturity of IS/IT in clinical practice that extends acknowledged limitations of the resources-based view of the firm [9].

However, they did not explicitly provide theoretical mechanisms of the holistic and complex framework that fits the diversity of organizational components and interactions involved with BITA. Neither did they elaborate extensively and discuss the outcomes their results in terms of modeling BITA as the interdependency of underlying organizational dimensions represented by a higher-order construct.

The current approach is similar to those in [4, 17] although our objective, approach and focus is different. Defining BITA through the use of a nomological framework occurs for instance also in Chan [17]. This work elaborates extensively on a multitude of factors that affect BITA. Also, current work by Gerow et al. [4] evaluate whether indirect relationships exist between BITA and firm performance. They do so, offering a more nuanced configuration of performance constructs and focus in their model on causal relationships between the various forms and types of BITA. Various other alternative approaches for modeling BITA are available in extant literature. While these contributions are valuable, they do not provide a comprehensive foundation to operationalize theorized constructs, relations and outline the internal logic among the various dimensions of BITA. Conceptual models, relationships and links between constructs often described can be seen to be special cases of a more general higher-order statistical nomological framework, which will be the main focus of this paper.

Hence, in this paper we address the following research questions:

RQ1: What is the role complexity science in understanding the emergent nature of IS/IT in organizations and the dynamics of BITA in particular?

RQ2: How can BITA and its relationship with performance be modelled as a parsimonious nomological framework that serves both theory and practice by capturing the complex entanglement of BITA within organizations? And finally, RQ3: How can this framework subsequently be operationalized using a statistical scheme that maps conceptual constructs onto empirical phenomena?

The remainder of this paper is outlined as follows. First, principle concepts are reviewed. Subsequently, we outline our method, the applied multistep approach and propose a nomological framework containing higher-order – i.e. the hierarchical component model – latent constructs within the context of simultaneous equation systems. In the last section of the paper, main findings are presented and discussed, inherent limitations of the current study are identified and future research opportunities are outlined.

2 Overview of Principle Concepts

2.1 IS/IT Maturity

The concept of IS/IT maturity and adoption goes back to the early 1950s [18, 19]. The idea was proposed of considering different evolutionary levels or business transformations of IS/IT, and what can be expected from each, outlining in that way a number evolutionary steps that organization should follow. Since then, various maturity models have been developed to plan and assess the evolution of IS/IT in organizations. Within the field of information systems, Nolan and Gibson [20] are considered the founders of the stage-based maturity perspective. They proposed a six-stage (initially four) model representing the level of IS/IT expense for an organization in relation to the stages of increasing the sophistication and maturity of IS/IT. This stage-based concept has been further extended and applied to organizations by many others [19, 21].

In general, IS/IT maturity models provide insight into the structure of elements that represent process effectiveness of IS/IT in organizations. They also allow organizations to define roadmaps on how to get from one level of maturity and evolve to the next [21].

2.2 Business/IT-Alignment

Strategic alignment has been a major concern for executives and IT practitioners for decades and refers to applying IS/IT in an appropriate and timely way, in harmony with business strategies, goals and needs [1]. Achieving BITA comes with various performance gains, including market growth, cost control, financial performance, increased outflow of innovation, and augmented reputation [22, 23]. Within this field the classic Strategic Alignment Model (SAM) [24] is undoubtedly the most cited concept and has also been extended by others [1, 25]. SAM implies that a systematic process is required to govern continuous alignment between business and IS/IT domains, i.e. to achieve 'strategic fit' as well as 'functional integration.' The model does, however, have its limitations. The SAM (as well as other extensions of the model) are also not able to monitor or measure maturity and/or performance, and relations in the model are not operationalized or clearly defined [26]. This was improved by Scheper [26], who extended the SAM by combining it with the MIT 90s model [27] and defining various organizational dimensions. In contrast to the SAM, Scheper also defined levels of incremental maturity for each of the five dimensions. Next, he claims that alignment can be measured by comparing the maturity levels of all five dimensions at the same time. His alignment principle is based on the idea that organizations can mature each single domain, but only equalization among all dimensions (i.e., alignment) will significantly improve organizations' performances.

Scheper's framework has been applied in various fields including Customer Relationship Management, e-procurement, supply chain management and health IS/IT-alignment [15, 28–30].

2.3   Complexity Science and Complex Adaptive Systems

The field of Complex Adaptive Systems (CAS) [8, 10, 31] and complexity science has its roots in evolutionary biology, physics and mathematics. It is based on the fundamental logical properties of the behavior of non-linear and network feedback systems, no matter where they are found [11]. CAS are considered collections of individual agents with the freedom to act in ways that are not always totally predictable (non-linear), and whose actions are interconnected so that one agent's actions change the contexts for other agents. CAS theories presume that the adaptation of systems to their environments emerge from the adaptive efforts of individual agents that attempt to improve their own payoffs [12]. Commonly referred examples include financial markets, weather systems, human immune system, colonies of termites and organizations.

Various authors have stated that the science of complexity can be considered a valuable instrument to cope with organizational and IS/IT changes in non-linear turbulent environments [8, 10–12]. Both complexity science and CAS are applicable to the field of information systems in that IS/IT act like CAS.

3   Toward a Nomological Framework for BITA

For this study an incremental development process was employed following the initial stages of the design science research methodology approach [32]. In this approach, knowledge is produced by constructing and evaluating artifacts which are subsequently used as input for a better awareness of the problem [33]. Doing so, the current study pays considerable attention to link the articulation of the theoretical position with existing baseline and empirical work. This study focuses on designing a generalized nomological framework (the artifact) to statistically model BITA and its foundational relationship with performance. To ensure quality and validity of the framework, we followed analytical design evaluation methods, guidelines and a systematic process [32, 33]. Figure 1 provides an overview of the four interrelated process steps that were conducted, within the scope of this study, using a process-deliverable diagram (PDD) [34]. A PDD is a meta-modeling technique based on UML activity and class

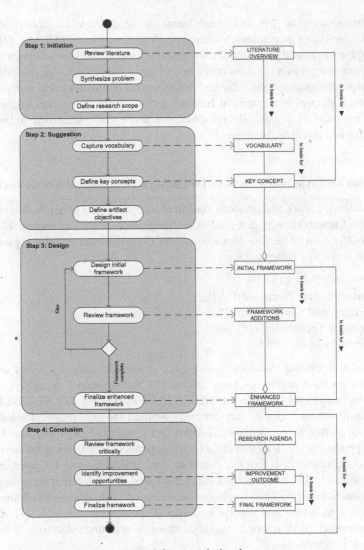

Fig. 1. Nomological framework development process

diagrams. Within such a model, the activities and processes are modeled on the left-hand side and deliverables on the right-hand side (see Fig. 1). In this diagram we have included only the main (simplified) deliverables.

During the *initial step* we did an extensive literature review concerning the research topic and synthesized the 'problem'. Based on this review and the researcher's own field experience, the research field vocabulary was subsequently captured, initial concepts were synthesized and designed (i.e. *step 2*). Additionally, we defined what the artifact should accomplish. Hence, (1) we acknowledged that it is import to define and explain the rationale underlying the functional form of the artifact, i.e. the nomological framework (including dependent and independent variables) [35] and (2) devote attention to the nature and direction of relationships between the various constructs [36]. Taking these concepts as a basis, an initial nomological framework was designed – *step three* – which subsequently was enhanced and extended based on critical reflections and comparisons with previous empirical baseline work. *Step 4* is the conclusion. In this final step we once more critically reviewed the framework, identified improvement opportunities and possible future work.

3.1 A Multistep Approach Toward Designing a Nomological Framework

Based on extensive work and previous statistical analyses [7], a generalized conceptual nomological framework was designed combining three central elements: (1) BITA, (2) maturity (for each of the five dimensions) and (3) performance as the explanandum. For each of these five dimensions,

(1) Strategy and Policy (S&P),
(2) Organization and Processes (O&P),
(3) Monitoring and Control (M&C),
(4) Information Technology (IT) and
(5) People and Culture (P&C),

modelled as independent variables (constructs), distinctive maturity levels and associated indicators have previously been defined [7]. Subsequently, distinctive maturity levels can be successively labeled for O&P3, O&P4 and O&P5; IT3, IT4 and IT5; and so on. Maturity levels 1 and 2 – are currently omitted for pure practical reasons.

Next, we formalize performance, following the same steps, logic and balanced evaluation perspective [37], as a multifactorial (dependent) construct to be measured in terms of a complementary I. External construct (i.e. subdivided into I. Customer and II. Financial) and an II. Internal construct (i.e. subdivided into I. Internal processes and II. Organizational capacity). This is also in accordance with studies evaluating IS/IT performance from a rich and diverse understanding of outcomes [13, 14]. The performance construct, as developed, enables a more diverse understanding of outcomes from various perspectives.

Hence, we apply a multistep approach using path modeling to hierarchically construct latent variables for all latent constructs of our nomological framework. With regard to the independent part of the framework, we model:

1. The first-order exogenous constructs as represented the different maturity levels (labeled SP3–SP5, OP3–OP5, MC3–MC5, IT3–IT5, PC3–PC5) and relate each of them to their respective manifest variables: SP3: MV_1 & MV_2; SP4: MV_3 & MV_4; SP5: MV_5 & MV_6; OP3: MV_7 & MV_8; IT4: MV_{21} & MV_{22}; etc.;
2. The second-order construct as the five organizational dimensions, constructed by relating the blocks of the underlying first-order latent constructs (i.e. step 1);

3. The third-order construct, labeled as BITA, as related to the underlying second-order constructs (i.e. step 2).

With regard to the dependent part of the nomological framework (i.e. performance), we model:

4. First-order exogenous constructs and relate them to their respective manifest variables as defined (Customer: MV_{31} & MV_{32}; Financial: MV_{33} & MV_{34}; Internal processes: MV_{35} & MV_{36}; Organizational capacity: MV_{37}, MV_{38});
5. The second-order constructs (External construct and Internal construct), as related to the block of the underlying first-order latent constructs (see step 4);
6. The third-order construct, labeled as Performance, as related to the underlying second-order constructs (i.e. step 5).

Thus, we develop a nomological framework that combines three concepts:
(1) BITA, describing the interdependency and synergetic mechanisms of five underlying organizational dimensions (i.e., independent constructs), (2) maturity, defined as the level of incremental maturity for each of the five dimensions; thus a classification according to a stage of development, and finally (3) performance as the multifactorial impacts and benefits (i.e. dependent constructs) to be measured in terms of a complementary external construct and an internal construct.

3.2 Operationalizing Using the Structural Equation Modeling Notation

BITA as part of the nomological framework is modeled as a third-order latent construct, whereas the second-order constructs represent the organizational dimensions to be co-aligned and the first-order constructs represent the IS/IT maturity levels. This type of modeling is statistically appropriately captured by a pattern of covariation, which coincides with the concept of (co-)alignment [38].

Our framework follows the central concept of internal logic among the various dimensions, since it is in accordance with the theories of complexity science and CAS outlined previously. Our framework is a more parsimonious presentation of the underlying factors gleaning interdependency of complex constructs [39]. The co-alignment as covariation approach is, therefore, preferred over other common alignment schemes (e.g. leveling, gestalt, moderator, mediator, etc.) since the operationalization of their optimal profiles – with numerical scores along a set of underlying areas of resource allocations – is difficult [38].

The operationalization of our nomological framework can be performed most accurately using Structural Equation Modeling, SEM [40]. SEM (or 'causal modeling') is a second generation data analysis family of statistical models that seeks to explain complex relationships among multiple observable and latent constructs in models. The application of SEM fits a mode of integrative thinking about theory construction, measurement problems and data analysis. It enables stating the theory more exactly, testing the theory more precisely and yielding a more thorough modeling/understanding of empirical data about complex phenomena and relationships [41]. In interconnecting the principle concepts of our framework, i.e. BITA, maturity and performance (see previous section), we propose a reflective construct model (molecular, principal factor model, common latent construct), through which the manifest variables are affected by the latent variables (in contrast to the formative constructs) [42]. Our factor model, i.e. higher order reflective construct model, is specified as an alternative to a mode in which latent constructs are modelled using patterns of correlations.

Within PLS, higher-order constructs can be constructed using repeated indicators (i.e. the hierarchical component model) [42]. That is, all indicators of the first-order constructs are reassigned to the second-order construct, as second-order models are a special type of PLS path modeling that use manifest variables twice for model estimation. The same patterns are applicable to subsequent higher-order constructs. A prerequisite for this model approach is that all manifest variables of the first-order and higher-order constructs should be reflective [36].

Figure 2 portrays our nomological framework using the SEM notation. It captures the theorized relationships between the maturity levels (i.e. first-order construct), organizational dimensions (i.e. second-order construct) and BITA (i.e. third-order construct), on the one hand, and its impact on performance (i.e. third-order construct), on the other hand. The framework fits the diversity of organizational components and interactions among the many agents involved in turbulent environments. This is in accordance with the complexity science lens.

4 Discussion and Conclusion

This study demonstrates that that BITA can be represented, in the context of a higher order nomological framework, as the interdependency of five underlying organizational dimensions, each containing maturity levels that in their turn can be represented by manifest variables, i.e. measurable indicators. Likewise, performance follows this parsimonious concept and can be represented by a higher-order construct.

Also, we presented how the three imperative theoretical concepts of BITA, maturity and performance coincide with covariation (or co-alignment) using higher-order latent structures as an operationalized statistical scheme within SEM. Doing so, we acknowledged the importance of the rationale underlying the functional form of constructs (dependent and independent constructs) [35] and devote attention to the nature and direction of relationships between the various constructs [36].

We employed a systematic agenda linking theory development with a computational model, thereby overcoming the acknowledged limitations of existing approaches. The adoption of complexity science – and specifically CAS – as both a theoretical and practical lens opens up a whole new vista of perspectives, approaches and techniques.

Following the frameworks' logic, organizations can define improvement activities – with accompanying investments – that can be executed along the five organizational dimensions that best meets an organizations' current and future needs; done simultaneously and hence by an integrated management perspective. Hence, a set of measurements can then be defined which are organized into projects that take into account the risks involved, investment costs, critical success factors and benefits. In the course of the execution of all improvement activities, the level of alignment between the five

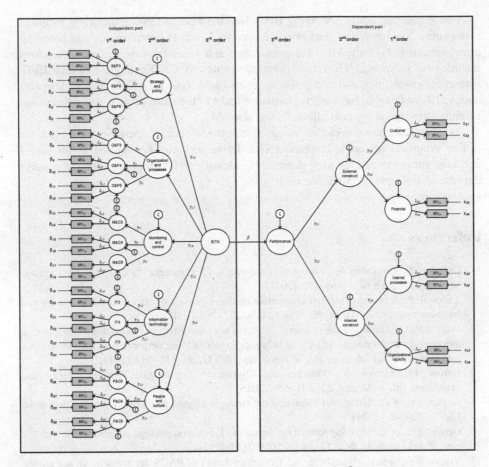

Fig. 2. Theoretical SEM notation for the nomological framework (δ_i/ε_i = measurement errors, ζ = disturbance terms for higher-order constructs, λ_i = first-order factor loadings, γ_i = factor loading coefficients for higher-order constructs, β = estimated value for the path relationship in the structural model)

organizational dimensions should monitored in managing similarities, overlap and synergy between the improvement projects.

The current study has several limitations. Obviously, empirically applying our nomological framework is needed to further enhance and validate it. Yet, we have undertaken considerable efforts to ensure that we synthesized a framework for BITA with a considerable degree of complexity, coherence and causality. Comparing results across industries, countries and distinct groups might also contribute to the generalizability of our findings. Next, critical readers might argue that we did not explicitly address the mediating and/or moderating impact of environmental dynamics and e.g. collaborative network organizations (CNO's) in the context of our framework. Albeit, we argued that the co-alignment approach in the context of this study is the preferred operationalization scheme.

Future research could also apply BITA into the field of CNO's including business ecosystems, long-term and goal-oriented networks, virtual communities and breeding environments [43]. Following this perspective and field, relevant research questions include the following 'How can partners within an CNO's align different IS/IT resources, capabilities and competences to enable I. co-creation, II. business evolvability, III. sustainable business performance and IV. the management and governance of multi-direction alignment effects?', see also [44].

To conclude, the developed nomological framework is therefore designed for further empirical research. In practice, our framework can be applied as an useful checklist for organizations to systematically identify BITA improvement areas using the central concepts of our framework.

References

1. Luftman, J., Kempaiah, R.: An update on business-IT alignment: "a line" has been drawn. MIS Q. Executive 6(3), 165–177 (2007)
2. Tallon, P.P.: A process-oriented perspective on the alignment of information technology and business strategy. J. Manag. Inf. Syst. 24(3), 227–268 (2007)
3. Wu, S.P.-J., Straub, D.W., Liang, T.-P.: How information technology governance mechanisms and strategic alignment influence organizational performance: insights from a matched survey of business and IT managers. MIS Q. 39, 497–518 (2014)
4. Gerow, J.E., Grover, V., Thatcher, S.: Alignment's nomological network: theory and evaluation. Inf. & Manag. 53, 541–553 (2016)
5. Avison, D., et al.: Using and validating the strategic alignment model. J. Strateg. Inf. Syst. 13(3), 223–246 (2004)
6. Gerow, J.E., et al.: Looking toward the future of IT-business strategic alignment through the past: a meta-analysis. MIS Q. 38(4), 1059–1085 (2014)
7. Van de Wetering, R., Batenburg, R.: Towards a theory of PACS deployment: an integrative PACS maturity framework. J. Digit. Imaging 27(3), 337–350 (2014)
8. Benbya, H., McKelvey, B.: Using coevolutionary and complexity theories to improve IS alignment: a multi-level approach. J. Inf. Technol. 21(4), 284–298 (2006)
9. Teece, D.J., Pisano, G., Shuen, A.: Dynamic capabilities and strategic management. Strateg. Manag. J. 18(7), 509–533 (1997)
10. Dooley, K.: A complex adaptive systems model of organization change. Nonlinear Dyn. Psychol. Life Sci. 1(1), 69–97 (1997)
11. Stacey, R.: The science of complexity: an alternative perspective for strategic change processes. Strateg. Manag. J. 16(6), 477–495 (1995)
12. Anderson, P.: Complexity theory and organization science. Organ. Sci. 10(3), 216–232 (1999)
13. Hitt, L.M., Brynjolfsson, E.: Productivity, business profitability, and consumer surplus: three different measures of information technology value. MIS Q. 20, 121–142 (1996)
14. Kohli, R., Devaraj, S.: Measuring information technology payoff: a meta-analysis of structural variables in firm-level empirical research. Inf. Syst. Res. 14(2), 127–145 (2003)
15. Van de Wetering, R., et al.: A situational alignment framework for PACS. J. Digit. Imaging 24(6), 979–992 (2011)

16. Van de Wetering, R., Batenburg, R., Lederman, R.: Evolutionistic or revolutionary paths? a PACS maturity model for strategic situational planning. Int. J. Comput. Assist. Radiol. Surg. 5(4), 401–409 (2010)
17. Chan, Y.E., Sabherwal, R., Thatcher, J.B.: Antecedents and outcomes of strategic IS alignment: an empirical investigation. IEEE Trans. Eng. Manag. 51(3), 27–47 (2006)
18. Somogyi, E.K., Galliers, R.D.: From data processing to strategic information systems: a historical perspective. In: Somogyi, E.K., Galliers, R.D.E. (eds.) Towards Strategic Information Systems, pp. 5–25. Abacus Press, Cambridge (1987)
19. Ward, J., Peppard, J.: Strategic Planning for Information Systems, 3rd edn. Wiley, Chichester (2002)
20. Gibson, C.F., Nolan, R.L.: Managing the four stages of EDP growth. Harvard Bus. Rev. 52(1), 76–88 (1974)
21. Galliers, R.D., Sutherland, A.R.: Information systems management and strategy formulation: the 'stages of growth' model revisited. J. Inf. Syst. 1(2), 89–114 (1991)
22. Chan, Y.E., Reich, B.H.: IT alignment: what have we learned? J. Inf. Technol. 22(4), 297–315 (2007)
23. Kearns, G.S., Lederer, A.L.: A resource-based view of strategic IT alignment: how knowledge sharing creates competitive advantage. Decis. Sci. 34(1), 1–29 (2003)
24. Henderson, J.C., Venkatraman, N.: Strategic alignment: leveraging information technology for transforming organisations. IBM Syst. J. 32(1), 4–16 (1993)
25. Chan, Y., Reich, B.: IT alignment: an annotated bibliography. J. Inf. Technol. 22(4), 316–396 (2007)
26. Scheper, W.J.: Business IT Alignment: Solution for the Productivity Paradox (in Dutch). Deloitte & Touche, The Netherlands (2002)
27. Scott Morton, M.S.: The Corporation of the 1990s: Information Technology and Organizational Transformation. Oxford Press, London (1991)
28. Batenburg, R.S., Versendaal, J.M.: Business alignment in the CRM domain: predicting CRM performance. In: Leino, T., Saarinen, T., Klein, S. (eds.) Proceedings of the 12th European conference on Information Systems. Turku School of Economics and Business Administration, Turku (2004)
29. Mikalef, P., et al.: Business alignment in the procurement domain: a study of antecedents and determinants of supply chain performance. Int. J. Inf. Syst. Proj. Manag. 2(1), 43–59 (2014)
30. Mikalef, P., et al.: Investigating the impact of procurement alignment on supply chain management performance. Procedia Technol. 9, 310–319 (2013)
31. Benbya, H., McKelvey, B.: Toward a complexity theory of information systems development. Inf. Technol. People 19(1), 12–34 (2006)
32. Peffers, K., et al.: A design science research methodology for information systems research. J. Manag. Inf. Syst. 24(3), 45–77 (2007)
33. Hevner, A.R., et al.: Design science in information systems research. MIS Q. 28(1), 75–105 (2004)
34. Van de Weerd, I., Brinkkemper, S.: Meta-modeling for situational analysis and design methods. In: Syed, M.R., Syed, S.N. (eds.) Handbook of Research on Modern Systems Analysis and Design Technologies and Applications, pp. 38–58. Idea Group, Hershey (2008)
35. Bagozzi, R.: Expectancy-value attitude models: an analysis of critical theoretical issues. Int. J. Res. Mark. 2(1), 43–60 (1985)
36. Jarvis, C., MacKenzie, S., Podsakoff, P.: A critical review of construct indicators and measurement model misspecification in marketing and consumer research. J. Consum. Res. 30(2), 199–218 (2003)

37. Kaplan, R.S., Norton, D.P.: Alignment: Using the Balanced Scorecard to Create Corporate Synergies. Harvard Business Press, Boston (2006)
38. Venkatraman, N.: The concept of fit in strategy research: towards verbal and statistical correspondence. Acad. Manag. Rev. 14(3), 423–444 (1989)
39. Morel, B., Ramanujam, R.: Through the looking glass of complexity: the dynamics of organizations as adaptive and evolving systems. Organ. Sci. 10(3), 278–293 (1999)
40. Jöreskog, K.: Structural analysis of covariance and correlation matrices. Psychometrika 43(4), 443–477 (1978)
41. Hughes, M., Price, R., Marrs, D.: Linking theory construction and theory testing: models with multiple indicators of latent variables. Acad. Manag. Rev. 11(1), 128–144 (1986)
42. Wetzels, M., Odekerken-Schröder, G., Van Oppen, C.: Using PLS path modeling for assessing hierarchical construct models: guidelines and empirical illustration. MIS Q. 33(1), 177–195 (2009)
43. Camarinha-Matos, L.M., et al.: Collaborative networked organizations–Concepts and practice in manufacturing enterprises. Comput. Ind. Eng. 57(1), 46–60 (2009)
44. Coltman, T., et al.: Strategic IT alignment: twenty-five years on. J. Inf. Technol. 30(2), 91–100 (2015)

Multi-touch Table or Plastic Wall? Design of a Study for the Comparison of Media in Modeling

Anne Gutschmidt[1(✉)], Kurt Sandkuhl[1,2], and Ulrike Borchardt[1]

[1] Chair of Business Information Systems, University of Rostock,
Albert-Einstein-Str. 22, 18059 Rostock, Germany
{anne.gutschmidt,kurt.sandkuhl,
ulrike.borchardt}@uni-rostock.de
[2] ITMO University, Kronverkskiy pr. 49, 197101 St. Petersburg, Russia

Abstract. An important aspect of participatory enterprise modeling is the work in a group. However, does the collaboration of the group members change depending on which medium is used to generate the models? Are there for example differences in the group's behavior when working with a plastic wall, similar to a whiteboard, or with a multi-touch table? Based on the state of research and theoretical foundations of group work as well as previous research, relevant research issues are raised and an experimental design will be described in order to examine possible differences in the group work depending on the medium. Relevant aspects will be forms of cooperation, i.e. verbal and non-verbal contributions of the participants, but also territorial behavior and group performance.

Keywords: Multi-touch-table · Plastic wall · Enterprise modeling · Intermedia comparison

1 Introduction

When an enterprise is faced with changes such as new products, new IT-systems, new competitors or new legal regulations, it is important to know the enterprise as a whole with all its processes, structures and dependencies. In this regard, business process modeling and enterprise modeling provide important tools. They can visualize the as-is state of an organization and they often provide the only means of revealing causes for problems and potentials for changes at all [30]. To draw maximum benefits from modeling, it is useful to include the persons concerned in the modeling process, i.e., persons in charge of individual departments and IT managers. Participative modeling follows exactly this approach. It ensures that people actually concerned actively participate in model development and the models, as a result, achieve higher acceptance. To support the domain experts of the enterprise in modeling, persons providing expertise in the modeling language are invited as moderators (so-called facilitators) to lead the discussion and to document the results in digital form [28]. Thus, the group work is an essential aspect of process and enterprise modeling.

W. Abramowicz et al. (Eds.): BIS 2016 Workshops, LNBIP 263, pp. 123–135, 2017.
DOI: 10.1007/978-3-319-52464-1_12

In a participative modeling session, very different tools can be used. [30] describe the use of plastic walls as an appropriate way to motivate the persons involved to active participation. Usually, the plastic wall is attached to a wall where it can be written on and colored cards can be added, similar to a whiteboard. However, using the plastic wall requires the moderators not only to lead the discussion but also to take care that all group members follow the notation rules of the modeling language used. Finally, moderators transfer the results into digital form. Therefore, it would be preferable to use a modeling tool facilitating the observation of notation rules as well as the documentation of the results without losing the participative character of the modeling session. Multi-touch tables, also called tabletops, enable several users to interact simultaneously with a software by touching the surface [16]. Therefore, they could be used as an alternative tool to the plastic wall for participative modeling. Since this is a computer-aided tool, a development environment can be provided for modeling which facilitates the application of the modeling language. Above this, the models can be stored digitally already during the session.

This leads to the question to what extent a multi-touch table in its use for modeling differs from the traditional plastic wall. An empirical study shall clarify the differences between both tools in participative modeling. Particular emphasis is placed on which differences the media cause in the group work and if the specific way how the tools are used for the group work differs.

The goal of this article is the design of an experiment, which allows the comparison between multi-touch table and plastic wall in collaborative modeling. Because group work is the central issue of the study, the corresponding state of research as well as related theories are briefly described in Sect. 2. Concerning multi-touch-table usage, several studies have been conducted. Section 3 shows, however, that these studies are usually either exploratory or, even more often, of a descriptive kind. Studies with an experimental design comparing multi-touch tables with media such as paper or PCs, do not yet provide a satisfactory picture of the group work with tabletops. On the one hand, they do not provide a sufficient basis to draw conclusions for the comparison with a plastic wall, and on the other hand, they show partially contradictory results. After presenting the theories and the state of research, concrete research questions to be answered through the study will be deduced. In Sect. 4, the research design of the study will be introduced.

2 Group Work

Participative modeling is a classical group work in which domain experts and methodology experts work on a shared task. In the literature, different features may be found to characterize groups. A group is referred to as three or more persons interacting directly and over a longer period of time. According to [20], group phenomena actually emerge only from a number of at least three persons. Within the group, different roles evolve over time, such as the role of the leader or the specialist. In order to know how to behave in their working with others, common standards, values and goals have to be determined. The group members typically perceive and present themselves as belonging together to the outer world [13, 25, 32].

Group work can lead to numerous advantages, especially when tasks are too complex to be solved by a single person. However, in many cases it was shown that the performance of a group can be lower than the performance obtained by its members separately. Thus, the actual performance deviates from the potential performance in such a way that a loss in performance occurs due to group processes. This depends, amongst others, on the kind of the task the group is working on [13]. According to [29], tasks can be distinguished by their possibility to be split among the members, whether quantity or quality is aimed at and in what way the group members contribute to the overall result. Gains and losses by group processes result from motivation, individual skills and coordination [10]. Social facilitation and social compensation are examples of process gains in the area of motivation [32]. In social facilitation, the mere presence of others makes a person work harder than being alone. We talk of social compensation when a stronger member of the group tries to counterbalance performance deficits [10, 32]. Thus, if some members of a modeling session could contribute less due to a possible lack of knowledge, another member with a higher expertise would work even harder than working on this task only by himself in order to compensate the deficits of his colleagues.

However, process losses can also occur due to a lower motivation of the group members. So-called social loafing occurs when group members perform less than working alone because they cannot see their own contribution to the overall solution [10, 15, 32]. If the individual input is made visible for the group members, motivation will rise again. This can even lead to the so-called Köhler effect [14], a form of social facilitation, where a group member works harder to avoid being responsible for a lower group performance [10]. If colors have not yet been assigned a certain meaning in the notation of a modeling language, the contributions of individual group members could remain identifiable by the colors of their cards or pens they use.

If group members deliberately perform less believing that they have only little influence on the result of the group work, it is called free-riding effect [10, 13]. A participant of a modeling session should not get the feeling that his contributing or not to a solution is irrelevant. This could happen in a modeling session, for example, when modeling is done at the computer with only one mouse and one keyboard, as in a study of [24]. The authors found that oral and physical contribution in the sense of inputs were distributed significantly unevenly among the group members using a laptop only compared to the use of a multi-touch table.

Process losses and gains in the area of individual proficiency can result, for instance, from cognitive limitation and cognitive stimulation respectively [10, 13]. In enterprise modeling, ideas and knowledge are partly collected in the style of brain storming according to [21]. On the one hand, the statements of one group member can direct the others towards a certain topic and thus limit their range of thoughts. On the other hand, these statements can inspire new ideas, which they would possibly not have produced otherwise [10].

Process losses can also occur due to difficulties in coordination. During brainstorming, for example, group members have to let one another speak out before they can present their own ideas. Empirical studies have shown several times that actually fewer ideas were produced during brainstorming than when group members recorded their idea by themselves [18]. Process gains in the area of coordination could not be stated so far [10].

3   Multi-touch Table as a Tool in Group Work

Because of their direct and natural handling and their very good visualization options, multi-touch tables are introduced in many different areas, e.g. as teaching tool [22], in medicine [17], and in architecture [19]. The size of the medium and innovations with regard to data input [16] enable several persons to operate the user interface simultaneously. Therefore, they are especially useful for tasks concerning collaborative designs and modeling. There are some studies describing how public places are designed using a multi-touch table [19, 24] or how software is developed by several persons drawing UML diagrams [5]. They have also been approved for tasks implying more generally creativity and the collecting of ideas as used in brain storming [4, 26].

In this section, previous findings concerning territorial behavior and awareness (Sect. 3.1), behavior in cooperation (Sect. 3.2) and performance (Sect. 3.3) are presented.

3.1   Territorial Behavior and Awareness

In a study with students being asked to assemble pieces of a poem like a puzzle, [23] put the focus on the size of tabletops. They found out that even larger groups in their study would not profit from a larger table. The test persons using the larger table were neither faster nor did the size of the table influence the division of labor or the subjective evaluation by these persons. The authors partially explain this by the setting up of territories on the table. [23] always observed three kinds of territories for the users: one area within reach of the respective user only, one area within reach of the respective users as well as for all the other users, and one area in reach of the other users only. [27] describe a similar territorial behavior mentioning a personal area that no other user has access to without being asked, one area accessible by the entire group and another area accessible for the respective user and their neighbors. The latter serves primarily to store work objects temporarily. Both [23, 27] concluded that the sense of responsibility for objects decreases with a growing distance between them and the users. Therefore, a larger table may lead to a larger area of the table that no user feels responsible for.

Nevertheless, a multi-touch table that is big enough for the users to set up their private spaces offers certain advantages. [9, p. 107] emphasize the importance of awareness defining it as "an understanding of the activities of others, which provides a context for your own activity." In order to coordinate the group work, it is essential for everybody to know who is doing what and why. A private space on the multi-touch table enables the user to try things apart from the group whereas the other group members still can have a look over his shoulder. In this way, the group members are kept informed about the activities and can possibly ask questions to their neighbors or provide help [27].

An outsourcing to external devices like tablets or other mobile devices may seem obvious. The results of a study from [8] suggest, however, that a group is most encouraged to cooperate when using a tabletop exclusively. [27] also dissuade from establishing fixed areas on a multi-touch table observing that the territories continuously change. There are also design approaches, which provide for special features of the user interface to ensure awareness (see [11], for example). Plastic walls, on the contrary, offer only limited possibilities. The setting up and the dynamic change of territories on the plastic wall seem rather unlikely, since changes and corrections are more complicated. [22] showed that children preferred tabletops to paper for solving tasks, because mistakes could be corrected more easily. Similar results can be found in studies from [3] comparing paper and multi-touch table for developing UML diagrams and in interviews by [24] on using tabletops, beside other tools, for designing a park. Thus, tabletops seem to offer an advantage through their flexibility. In sum, awareness is an important aspect for the coordination among the group members and thus for the entire collaboration. It might be supported by offering areas on the work surface where individuals may try out designs or models on their own, but which are still visible to the other group members.

3.2 Behavior in Collaboration

In studies dedicated to the collaboration at multi-touch tables, the authors are primarily interested in how close the cooperation of the group member is, whether the persons work in parallel and if the contributions are evenly distributed. These contributions mainly refer to oral contributions, gestures or interactions with the user surface to work on the task. With their experiments, [4] showed that less oral contributions and gestures were produced during a brainstorming task using a tabletop than those using a table covered with paper, even though the authors provided software with attractive features for the multi-touch table. Flipcharts, however, scored lower than tabletops. [4] concluded from their study that the arrangement of the work surface essentially influenced the collaboration, whereas the attractiveness of the tabletop with its features provided were rather distracting. [3] also compared in first place the use of paper and pen with multi-touch tables and concluded that the test persons spent a larger proportion of time working together closely. In contrast, the group members using paper spent a larger proportion of time working on their own. In another study, [6] compared the use of PC and multi-touch table. They examined how evenly the contributions in the form of inputs to generate UML state diagrams were distributed in a two-person team. The contributions were significantly more balanced at the tabletop. Moreover, they stated that the collaboration was closer at the multi-touch table and that at the PC, it was more likely that one person was working while the other person was only watching. [24] came to a similar result in experimentally comparing laptop, tabletop, and tabletop connected with boards and tangible objects by which one can additionally interact with the tabletop. The authors focused on interactions with the user interface as well as oral contributions. Tabletops, especially in connection with tangible objects, seem to foster collaboration and obviously make it easier to invite other users to participate.

The authors noticed that persons participating less by oral contributions did compensate this by more pointing and gesticulating when using a more tangible interface. However, this could be an advantage of the plastic wall, because the persons operate with objects like colored cards and can thus draw attention to themselves. In sum, most studies existing on the subject compare multi-touch tables with paper media or PCs.

Plastic wall could turn out more flexible, however, since it allows small corrections and the media seems more tangible by using of additional auxiliary tools such as cards.

3.3   Performance

Some of the above-mentioned studies comparing multi-touch tables with other media also investigated possible differences in group performance. Regarding the performance, the authors were mostly interested in how much time a group needed to tackle a problem, as well as the quality of the solution. [2] reports that test persons needed more time to elaborate UML state diagrams using a tabletop than using the PC. According to the author, this is due to the more difficult input of text using a touch keyboard, since the test persons performed twice as fast with a common PC keyboard. On the other hand, the quality of the solutions was significantly higher at the multi-touch table, as measured by two software experts on a scale of ten. [4] did not find any differences in the amount of ideas produced in the group when either using flipcharts and tables covered with paper or multi-touch tables for brainstorming tasks. However, the authors also evaluated the categorization of the ideas produced in the group with the paper table obtaining the best results.

While [12] did not try to compare multi-touch tables and other media, they still found out that the quality of a solution for an analysis task was higher at the tabletop when the group worked more closely together.

4   Research Questions and Method

4.1   Research Questions

The previous sections showed that empirical investigations regarding multi-touch tables were mostly of a descriptive or exploratory kind. Experimental studies in this area allow predictions regarding the comparison of plastic wall and multi-touch tables only to a small extent. The tasks assigned to the test persons were not always exactly comparable with the issues of enterprise modeling, even though some elements, such as brainstorming, can be recognized. Above this, often groups of only two persons were examined in the studies, e.g. in [5, 8, 12]. According to [20], though, group phenomena emerge only at a number of at least three persons. Furthermore, some of the empirical findings are contradictory. Moreover, the plastic wall is not quite comparable to the media which were contrasted with multi-touch tables in the studies presented.

Since the previous results in collaborative modeling at multi-touch tables have to be considered still insufficient, we suggest an exploratory study in order to generate hypotheses on differences in the use of multi-touch tables and plastic walls. To further define the investigated area, concrete research questions have to be elaborated. As mentioned before, the main issue of the study is collaboration, whereas it is of interest how well and how closely the group members work together. Previous studies considered how evenly the contributions were distributed among the participants. To get indications for possible process losses such as coordination losses or motivation losses, subjective individual contribution should also be scrutinized. However, it would be particularly interesting to find out if and how the relevant medium is used for collaboration: E.g., do group members gesticulate with cards, or do they move objects on the multi-touch table to illustrate their ideas? Hence, the first research question arises with the following subquestions:

1. Is there a difference in participative enterprise modeling between multi-touch table and plastic wall in group collaboration?

(a) Are there differences in the actual distribution of the contributions?
(b) Are there differences in the distribution of the contributions as perceived by the group members?
(c) Are there differences in the use of the media for the collaboration?
(d) Are there differences in the motivation of the group members depending on the medium?
(e) Are there differences in the coordination of the group members depending on the medium?

It is important for the collaboration that the group members are informed about what the others are working on at the moment. In this context, we use the term awareness. Whether the group members feel informed, however, can be best assessed by asking them. For this reason, subjectively perceived awareness will be of prior interest. But how do the group members notice what the others are currently working on? Our study will also deal with this question. To this end, the notion of personal working areas that are nevertheless recognizable to the others could be probably helpful. This could also be interesting for future investigations, since motivational aspects could play a role here. If one group member realizes, what, and above all, *that* others contribute to the solution, it is possible that this group member wants to avoid "lagging behind". The group member could also realize the weaknesses of the others and try to support them in the sense of social compensation. Activities in one's own working area could also contribute to social facilitation, i.e., the own performance is rising because it is visible for the others. This cannot be explained completely by the first study, yet it could provide first indications. For this reason, both awareness and the setting up of territories will be explored with the following research questions:

2. Are there differences in participative enterprise modeling between multi-touch table and plastic wall regarding the setting up of territories?
3. Are there differences in participative enterprise modeling between multi-touch table and plastic wall in the perceived awareness of the persons in relation to the other group members?
4. What kind of information is important to the group members to stay informed about their colleagues when using plastic wall and multi-touch table, respectively?

As mentioned, multi-touch tables have been compared to media such as PCs, paper tables and flipcharts so far. Paper tables and flipcharts are only partly comparable to a plastic wall. As with flipcharts, additional cards can be used. The orientation of the work surface is similar as well, although at the plastic wall, corrections are possible – although not as easy and as fast as on the multi-touch table. Therefore, it is not exactly predictable how multi-touch table and plastic wall will differ regarding their performance operationalized through speed and quality. This results in the last research questions:

5. Are there differences in participatory enterprise modeling between multi-touch table and plastic wall regarding the group performance?

   (a) Are there differences in the task duration?
   (b) Are there differences in the quality of the solution?

4.2   Method

As mentioned in the previous section, an exploratory study is suggested for the empirical comparison of multi-touch table and plastic wall. This means that at first no hypotheses will be formulated, since previous empirical findings and theories did not provide sufficient knowledge. The study rather aims at exploring the research area and, if possible, setting up hypotheses which have to be tested in future explanatory studies [7].

Sample and Procedure. For the study, a group size of three persons is chosen since group phenomena emerge only from a number of at least three persons [20]. In practice, usually more persons concerned should be involved in the enterprise modeling [30]. However, the size of the multi-touch table available for the study is a limiting factor since everybody should find enough space at the table.

As test persons, students of Business Informatics and Computer Science familiar with the modeling language 4EM are to be recruited. The first goal is to provide a homogeneous sample to minimize influences that could possibly emerge from sample properties. Nevertheless, the test persons should the target group as well as possible. We chose an experimental design: The experimental design is the only possibility to prove causal relationships [7]. An independent variable will be manipulated in order to measure its effects on one or more dependent variables. In order to measure the effects of the modeling tool (independent variable) on dependent variables such as the performance (measured by speed and quality) or the collaboration, the modeling tool itself will be manipulated in the first place: modeling tasks are carried out either with the plastic wall or the multi-touch table. After the randomized selection of the work tool, the group is asked to solve a task from the area of goal-oriented modeling and problem-oriented modeling. To motivate the test persons, it is announced that their results have to be officially presented afterwards. We suggest a repeated measurement design where the groups are supposed to work at two different dates on one task respectively. In case the same group works on two tasks, learning effects are probable. In order to minimize this influence, the order of the employed media will be randomized for each group, i.e., it will be randomly decided whether a group will use the plastic wall first and then the tabletop or vice versa.

For measuring the dependent variables, it is necessary to employ several survey instruments. These are behavioral observations on the one hand and the survey with semi-structured interviews as well as questionnaires on the other hand. Table 1 shows all dependent variables in summary arranged according to the research questions and how they are to be gathered.

Table 1. Overview of the dependent variables and how they are measured arranged according to the corresponding research questions.

Dependent variable	Data collection method
1. (a) Contributions (type, distribution etc.)	Observation
1. (b) Perceived contribution	Questionnaire
1. (c) Media usage for the contributions	Observation
1. (d) Motivation	Questionnaire
1. (e) Coordination	Questionnaire, interview
2. Territorial behavior	Observation
3. Awareness	Questionnaire, interview
4. Awareness-indications	Interview
5. (a) Task duration	Time measurement
5. (b) Quality of the solution	Evaluation by means of Experts Criteria

Observation as Method of Data Collection. As mentioned above, we intend to apply several methods to collect data. However, here, we will concentrate on presenting how we plan to implement the data collection by means of observation, because it appears to be the most important method of exploring the collaboration in the group working either with a plastic wall or a multi-touch table. In similar studies (e.g. [4, 5, 12]), the authors observed their tests persons with video cameras to investigate details of their collaboration. Usually, more than one observer is needed in order to raise the reliability, i.e., the measuring accuracy [7, 20]. This means that several observers have to be recruited. These persons have to undergo an intensive observation training first. With the help of video recording, the procedure can be significantly simplified, since the observers can watch the recordings independently from one another and as often as necessary.

Scientific, structured observations are made using an observation scheme [7, 20]. While [5, 12] were coding the observed behavior according to a scheme by [31], which was set up in an inductive way by the researchers, it is recommendable to employ a more established observation scheme for group work like the interaction process analysis by [1]. It divides actions into 12 categories, such as "agrees" and "asks for opinion." Finally, an observation scheme can be used to determine how often a certain kind of behavior occurred on group level or personal level.

It is interesting to learn whether the individual actions of the participants are concrete contributions to the solution, whether they are verbal or non-verbal and from whom exactly they originate. In this way, the balance among the members' contributions can be analyzed. Furthermore, the way in which the respective medium is used for these actions can be analyzed. Specific ways of usage can thus be determined which may be transferred from plastic wall to tabletop, or completely new ways of usage at the tabletop may be observed.

In order to capture the possible set up of territories on the work surface, a procedure following [27] will be chosen. For the observation, the work surface will be divided into several fields by a (virtual) grid. Using the video material, it will be analyzed in which section and how often the single test persons work – measured by the frequency of the interactions with the user interface. This should show whether personal areas emerge where a particular test person works primarily.

4.3   Lab Environment

The experiments will be performed in the "enterprise modeling observatory" at Rostock University. This lab consists of various enterprise modeling tools and a lab room equipped with cameras and recording tools for observing modelers, decision makers and other enterprise stakeholders in using tools, modeling languages, notations and software systems. The purpose of this lab is to contribute to a better understanding what kind of role distribution in modeling teams, notations or modeling languages, human computer interaction and software functionality supports what kind of enterprise architecture management task in the best way. All modeling phases from initial modeling on plastic to modeling with specialized enterprise modeling software are supported for teams of up to six persons. Most relevant equipment of the observatory for the planned experiment is:

Table 2. Equipment in the modeling lab and supported modeling phases

Phase	Equipm.		
	Established industrial tools	Tools with innovation potential	Documentation and analysis tools
Scoping and goal modeling	Whiteboard, moderator's case	SmartBoard, Mobile Modeling	Video recording
Initial conceptual modeling	Whiteboard, moderator's case	SmartBoard Tabletop	Video recording, tracking software
Conceptual modeling	Modeling tools (Troux, 4EM)	SmartBoard Tabletop Mobile Modeling	Video recording, software for usability testing
Model verification and analysis	Whiteboard + Modeling on paper; modeling tool + beamer or SmartBoard	Digital Pen Touch Table Mobile Modeling	Video recording, Software for usability testing
Development of operational models	Workflow-Tool (Troux, ARIS)		Software for usability testing
Model maintenance and evolution	Workflow Tool + Software development environment	Digital Pen Mobile Modeling	Software for usability testing

- Two 56" multi-touch tables (Tacton and 3M)
- Plastic wall, whiteboards and smartboard for participatory modeling
- Enterprise modeling environments (Troux Architect, 4EM, Sparx)
- Cameras and microphones for video and audio recording in the room
- Software MaxQDA for qualitative content analysis and TechSmith Morae for usability/tracking analysis

Table 2 summarizes the equipment and supported modeling phases in the room.

5 Summary and Future Work

The paper investigated the background for conducting an experiment that compares the use of plastic walls and multi-touch tables during participatory modeling. Based on theoretical background, we derived an experimental design, which was presented in large parts. The actual experiments still have to be performed which is planned for autumn 2016.

Our long-term objective is to develop a theory of collaborative modeling with multi-touch tables. This will require a larger number of experiments, where factors possibly affecting collaborative modeling will be systematically manipulated similar to the procedure in grounded theory using theoretical sampling [7]. We are especially interested in how group members' contributions can be made visible for others and how this will influence motivation.

Acknowledgment. The research was supported by the state of Mecklenburg-Western Pomerania with funds from the European Union (EFRE) in the project "Integrated Environment for Enterprise and Knowledge Modeling". Part of this work was financially supported by Government of Russian Federation, Grant 074-U01. The authors thank Peggy Sterling for her work on translating former German parts of the text and language check.

References

1. Bales, R.F.: Interaction Process Analysis: A Method for the Study of a Small Group. The University of Chicago Press, Chicago (1950)
2. Basheri, M.: Multi-touch table for enhancing collaboration during software Design. Ph.D. thesis, Durham University (2013)
3. Basheri, M., Burd, L.: Exploring the significance of multi-touch tables in enhancing collaborative software design using UML. In: Frontiers in Education Conference (FIE), pp. 1–5 (2012)
4. Buisine, S., Besacier, G., Aoussat, A., Vernier, F.: How do interactive tabletop systems influence collaboration? Comput. Hum. Behav. **28**(1), 49–59 (2012)
5. Basheri, M., Burd, L.: Baghaei, N.: Collaborative software design using multi-touch tables. In: Engineering Education (ICEED), pp. 1–5, December 2012
6. Basheri, M., Burd, L., Baghaei, N.: A multi-touch interface for enhancing collaborative UML diagramming. In: Proceedings of the 24th Australian Computer-Human Interaction Conference (OzCHI 2012), pp. 30–33. ACM, New York (2012)

7. Bortz, J., Döring, N.: Forschungsmethoden und Evaluation - für Human- und Sozialwissenschaftler: Limitierte Sonderausgabe. Wiesbaden 4. überarb. Aufl. Springer, Heidelberg (2006)
8. Bachl, S., Tomitsch, M., Kappel, K., Grechenig, T.: The effects of personal displays and transfer techniques on collaboration strategies in multi-touch based multi-display environments. In: Campos, P., Graham, N., Jorge, J., Nunes, N., Palanque, P., Winckler, M. (eds.) INTERACT 2011. LNCS, vol. 6948, pp. 373–390. Springer, Heidelberg (2011). doi:10. 1007/978-3-642-23765-2_26
9. Dourish, P., Bellotti, V.: Awareness and coordination in shared workspaces. In: Proceedings of the 1992 ACM Conference on Computer- supported Cooperative Work (CSCW 1992), pp. 107–114. ACM, New York (1992)
10. Drewes, S., Schultze, S., Schulz-Hardt, S.: Sozialpsychologie – Interaktion und Gruppe, Kap. Leistung in Gruppen, pp. 221–244. Hogrefe Verlag, Göttingen (2011)
11. Isenberg, P., Fisher, D.: Collaborative brushing and linking for co-located visual analytics of document collections. Comput. Graph. Forum 28(3), 1031–1038 (2009)
12. Isenberg, P.; Fisher, D.; Morris, M.R.; Inkpen, K.; Czerwinski, M.: An exploratory study of co-located collaborative visual analytics around a tabletop display. In: Visual Analytics Science and Technology (VAST), pp. 179–186 (2010)
13. Jonas, K., Stroebe, W., Hewstone, M.: Sozialpsychologie. Springer-Lehrbuch. Springer, Heidelberg (2014)
14. Kerr, N.L., Messé, L.A., Park, E.S., Sambolec, E.J.: Identifiability, performance feedback and the Köhler effect. Group Process. Intergroup Relations 8(4), 375–390 (2005)
15. Karau, S.J., Williams, K.D.: Social loafing: a meta-analytic review and theoretical integration. J. Pers. Soc. Psychol. 65(4), 681–706 (1993)
16. Laufs, U., Ruff, C.: Aufbau von Multi-Touch-Systemen: Multi-Touch. In: Schlegel, T. (Hrsg.) Multi-Touch. Xpert.press, pp. 145–152. Springer, Heidelberg (2013)
17. Lundström, C., Rydell, T., Forsell, C., Persson, A., Ynnerman, A.: Multitouch table system for medical visualization: application to orthopedic surgery planning. IEEE Trans. Vis. Comput. Graph. 17(12), 1775–1784 (2011)
18. Lamm, H., Trommsdorff, G.: Group versus individual performance on tasks requiring ideational proficiency (brainstorming): A review. Eur. J. Soc. Psychol. 3(4), 361–388 (1973)
19. Maquil, V.; Psik, T.; Wagner, I.; Wagner, M.: Expressive interactions - supporting collaboration in urban design. In: Proceedings of the 2007 International ACM Conference on Supporting Group Work (GROUP 2007), pp. 69–78. ACM, New York (2007)
20. Nerdinger, F.W.: Grundlagen des Verhaltens in Organisationen. Organisation und Führung, Kohlhammer (2012)
21. Osborn, A.F.: Applied Imagination; Principles and Procedures of Creative Problem-Solving. Scribner, New York (1963)
22. Piper, A.M., Hollan, J.D.: Tabletop displays for small group study: affordances of paper and digital materials. In: Proceedings of the SIGCHI Conference on Human Factors in Computing Systems (CHI 2009), pp. 1227–1236. ACM, New York (2009)
23. Ryall, K., Forlines, C., Shen, C., Ringel Morris, M.: Exploring the effects of group size and table size on interactions with tabletop shared-display groupware. In: Proceedings of the 2004 ACM Conference on Computer Supported Cooperative Work (CSCW 2004), pp. 284–293. ACM, New York (2004)
24. Rogers, Y., Lim, Y., Hazlewood, W.R., Marshall, P.: Equal opportunities: do shareable interfaces promote more group participation than single user displays? Hum. Comput. Interact. 24(1–2), 79–116 (2009)
25. Sader, M.: Psychologie der Gruppe. Grundlagentexte Psychologie. Juventa-Verlag (1991)

26. Schmitt, L., Buisine, S., Chaboissier, J., Aoussat, A., Vernier, F.: Dynamic tabletop interfaces for increasing creativity. Comput. Hum. Behav. **28**(5), 1892–1901 (2012)
27. Scott, S.D., Carpendale, S.: Theory of tabletop territoriality. In: Müller-Tomfelde, C. (ed.) Tabletops - Horizontal Interactive Displays. Human-Computer Interaction Series, pp. 357–385. Springer, London (2010)
28. Stirna, J., Persson, A., Sandkuhl, K.: Participative enterprise modeling: experiences and recommendations. In: Krogstie, J., Opdahl, A., Sindre, G. (eds.) CAiSE 2007. LNCS, vol. 4495, pp. 546–560. Springer, Heidelberg (2007). doi:10.1007/978-3-540-72988-4_38
29. Steiner, I.D.: Models for inferring relationships between group size and potential group productivity. Behav. Sci. **11**(4), 273–283 (1966)
30. Sandkuhl, K., Stirna, J., Persson, A., Wißotzki, M.: Enterprise Modeling: Tackling Business Challenges with the 4EM Method. Xpert.press. Springer, Heidelberg (2014)
31. Tang, A., Tory, M., Po, B., Neumann, P., Carpendale, S.: Collaborative coupling over tabletop displays. In: Proceedings of the SIGCHI Conference on Human Factors in Computing Systems (CHI 2006), pp. 1181–1190. ACM, New York (2006)
32. von Rosenstiel, L., Nerdinger, F.W.: Grundlagen der Organisationspsychologie: Basiswissen und Anwendungshinweise. Schäffer-Poeschel (2011)

The Communicative Nature of Information Systems Integration as an Enabler for Business IT Alignment

Iyad Zikra$^{(\boxtimes)}$

Department of Computer and Systems Sciences (DSV),
Stockholm University, Stockholm, Sweden
iyad@dsv.su.se

Abstract. Patterns of systems integration strive to accommodate the diversity of business ecosystems, including novel Web- and cloud-based services. In this paper, we apply the principles of the language/action paradigm (LAP) to develop a decentralized integration pattern that supports dynamic integration of services. A model is proposed for designing the interacting systems as active and independent entities that seek to communicate with each other. Two modes are enabled in the communication model: an indirect mode, where systems interact via business processes; and a direct mode, where systems directly interface with each other, following four categories. The communication perspective of the proposed integration pattern contributes to realizing the vision of a marketplace for cloud services. It supports a more flexible alternative to centralized integration patterns. The communication model builds on the improved alignment between system design models and the overall organizational design offered by the unifying meta-model for enterprise modeling.

Keywords: Communication model · Systems integration · Business IT alignment · Integration patterns · Meta-Model

1 Introduction

Enabling Information Systems (IS) to interact automatically with each other is an attractive value offering that organizations usually rely on. Patterns of systems integration describe the technologies employed for integration and the topology of the integration architecture [15]. They evolve to accommodate the diversity of data and services associated with novel business ecosystems. Recent advances in network-based systems (e.g. Web services, RESTful services, cloud computing) and in agile development methods have broadened the diversity and flexibility of data and service provisioning. Existing integration patterns are becoming strained by the constant and rapid evolution of functionality and connectivity [9]. The autonomy and ubiquity of service provisioning associated with cloud computing is contributing to the popularity of cloud-based services. The vision of cloud computing is to establish a marketplace for offering, discovering, and consuming services dynamically to accommodate constantly changing needs [5]. Integration patterns need to be able to sustain the increasing

W. Abramowicz et al. (Eds.): BIS 2016 Workshops, LNBIP 263, pp. 136–147, 2017.
DOI: 10.1007/978-3-319-52464-1_13

volume and heterogeneity of data and the needed dynamic service selection and switching [18].

An efficient approach to business oriented IS design and development is essential for achieving higher performance in, and deeper insights into, product and service delivery. Service oriented designs can enrich the organizational environment [12]. Information systems, including those composed of integrated subsystems, must be aligned with and motivated by the organizational goals. The necessary contextual knowledge that defines and binds the elements of the enterprise architecture are captured using goals [17]. Relying on an overview of the organization can simplify the complexity of the relationships between the business and IS capabilities. Such a view can represent the essential elements of business, information, application, and technology components [16]. Enriching the enterprise design with Model-Driven Development (MDD) principles [2] facilitates the development of supporting IS and guarantees a better fit between the IS and organizational goals [27].

Integration solutions must be considered within the larger context of organizational design. After all, the purpose of integration is to capitalize on the value of the combined use of the systems being integrated [3]. A suitable integration pattern supplies the mechanisms for efficiently connecting systems and reduces the overhead introduced by direct connections between individual systems or manual integration work. Furthermore, expressing the integration of cloud-based services as part of the organizational design can improve the alignment between the organizational goals and the integration solution.

The purpose of this paper is to propose an integration pattern that recognizes the communicative nature of systems integration. We rely on principles of the language/action paradigm [26] to develop a decentralized pattern that is flexible enough to support the dynamic integration of Web- and cloud-based services. The pattern describes a model that maintains a communication perspective of the integrated systems. Rather than passively being integrated, the systems independently establish the necessary communication channels and actively seek to communicate with one other. The stages of a conversation between two systems are outlined as part of the proposed integration pattern.

Direct connections between systems are more efficient, since they eliminate the overhead of managing the interaction via a central point. However, such patterns are usually avoided due to scalability issues; the complexity of point-to-point integration patterns increases exponentially with the number of integrated systems. We argue in this paper that approaching integration as a communication problem can help in reducing the complexity of point-to-point patterns.

The remainder of the paper is structured as follows. Section 2 provides a brief historical account of the evolution systems integration patterns. Section 3 illustrates the notions of communication perspective that influenced the design of the proposed communication model. Section 4 introduces the Information Systems Communication Model as part of the unifying meta-model for enterprise modeling: the Communication View and the four categories of systems conversations are described. Finally, concluding remarks and future research opportunities are presented in Sect. 5.

2   Overview of Systems Integration

The increased diversity of data sources and available services, especially on the Web, have influenced the relationship between organizational goals and the IS that are utilized to achieve these goals. Increased attention is being paid to the role that systems integration plays in supporting communication amongst organizational actors and in facilitating collaborative knowledge and value creation in the organization [18].

Early forms of systems integration can be traced back to socket programming [22]. A socket is a communication point with a specific, identifiable address on a network, offering the basic function of direct data communication. The structure and purpose of the data has to be shared beforehand between the integrated systems. The simplicity of sockets enables them to provide the underlying communication mechanism for most integration patterns that appeared later.

Remote Procedure Call (RPC) offers the additional ability of sharing functionality across applications following the client/server architecture [4]. The client system calls a function on the server system similarly to how a local function call is performed. RPC allows a limited level of modularity and loose coupling. The notion of service interface is rooted in the definition of function interface in RPC.

The Object Request Broker (ORB) technology [19] introduced encapsulation into the domain of distributed computing and systems integration. With ORB, objects and their associated functionality are shared across applications. ORB hides the location of the distributed object from the systems using it, effectively making the client and server indistinguishable. Two well-known ORB technologies are the Common Object Resource Broker Architecture (CORBA) [19] and Java's Remote Method Invocation (RMI) [20]. CORBA introduced a platform-independent Interface Definition Language (IDL) that abstracts from the specific implementation platforms of the integrated systems. Commercial products that support ORB technologies are called application servers.

Message-Oriented Middleware (MOM) [7] technologies use message queues to enable asynchronous communication, thereby enhancing loose coupling between the integrated systems. MOMs support message routing, persistence, and a centralized publish/subscribe communication pattern.

Web services evolved to support platform-independent integration of heterogeneous systems. A public interface describes the Web service's functionality, and the business logic behind it is hidden from the system using the service. Web services usually implement a combination of XML-based technologies: XML Schema [24] to describe and transport the service parameters; SOAP [23] as the communication protocol between the service and the consuming system; and UDDI [13] as the registry technology for publishing and finding Web service interface descriptions.

The integration technologies described above (except for MOMs) only support point-to-point integration. They all require low-level intervention by the integration designer. More importantly, none of them address the heterogeneity of systems in a satisfactory manner [9]. The Enterprise Service Bus (ESB) integration pattern was developed as a centralized solution to address this problem. ESB utilizes many of the technologies discussed above (such as distributed objects, message queues, routing, etc.) to offer integration capabilities while maintaining a central point to which all systems are connected. ESB off-loads the problem of heterogeneity by offering data and protocol translation for each of the integrated systems. ESB-based solutions are scalable since they are able to maintain the number of connections at the level of the number of integrated systems.

In recent years, RESTful services have been gaining in popularity as a simpler and more lightweight alternative to XML-based Web services [21]. RESTful services utilize the architecture of the Web: the triad of transfer protocol, media types, and resources (i.e. URIs). However, integrating RESTful services introduces new challenges. Systems need to know the syntax and semantics of communicating with the service beforehand. Furthermore, the wide range of ESB capabilities adds an overhead that is incompatible with the lightweight RESTful services.

Cloud computing is an emerging technology that supports flexibility in service provisioning in order to meet variable usage styles, variable pricing, and minimum maintenance and operational costs [5]. Cloud computing represents a shift in management attitude towards the utilization of existing technologies to capitalize on the combined added value [1, 5]. However, the details of what constitutes "cloud computing" are still hotly debated [6]. The rise in the popularity of cloud computing is also affected by the increasing reliance on RESTful services [6]. The vision of cloud computing is to elevate computing to become a basic social utility, where services are selected and composed freely to generate more value [5].

3 The Communication Perspective

Communication analysis is a useful tool for modeling the interaction between users of Information Systems (IS) [11]. It emerged out of the fields of Language/Action Paradigm (LAP) [25], Communicative Action Paradigm (CAP) [8], and Communication Theory [14]. Communication is one of the primary dimensions of human cooperative activity in information systems design [26]. It involves three layers of abstraction [26]:

- Syntax, i.e. grammar, describes the patterns for ordering and combining communication tokens (e.g. words in natural language) to construct sentences and conversations.
- Semantics of communication describe the relationships between communication tokens and a space of possible interpretations (i.e. meaning).
- Pragmatics is applied to interpretations to identify the anticipated response that the sender expects from the receiver in a conversation. The context within which the communication occurs guides the choice of the intended interpretation.

Conversation is the minimum unit of communication. It is defined as "a coordinated sequence of acts that can be interpreted as having linguistic meaning" [26]. The CAP extends the scope of conversations to cover all types of communication, not only that which involves natural language [8]. Five categories of conversation are identified by [26]: Conversation for action; conversation for clarification; conversation for possibilities; conversation for orientation; and the larger web of conversations that establishes a common background context to enable correct interpretation of conversation messages.

The language/action perspective complements the information/data perspective that usually affects domain models [25]. In systems integration, the information/data perspective translates into data structures and transformation rules. The language/action perspective can be used to describe the interaction between the communicating parties.

The research in [8] explores the communicative act paradigm as an effective perspective for designing information systems. Adopting this perspective enables system designers to identify the elementary components, their actions, and their added value in order to construct composite functions and behavior.

4   Information Systems Communication Model

In this section, the details of the proposed communication model are illustrated. The unifying meta-model for enterprise modeling, which was first proposed in [28], is briefly presented, because it provides the formal definition of the modeling components that comprise the communication model. What these components are and how they capture the communication between integrated systems is then discussed. The stages of conversations between systems, which describe the semantics of the proposed integration pattern, are finally outlined.

4.1   The Unifying Meta-model for Enterprise Modeling

The unifying meta-model is designed to support a platform for capturing enterprise models and eliciting supporting IS design models, thereby providing a holistic view of the organization [28]. Complementary views constitute the unifying meta-model (Fig. 1) and are conjointly transformed into a functioning and complete system implementation following MDD principles. The meta-model is organized into primary views that capture specific perspectives of the organization (namely: goals, concepts, business processes, business rules, systems, and information systems architecture). Composite views cut across the primary views and offer customized and more elaborate representations of the organization.

In addition to the *intra-model relationships*, which link components within a single primary view, the unifying meta-model relies on *inter-model relationships (IMRs)* to connect modeling components from different primary views together. IMRs account for the inherent connections that exist between the primary views of the organization, thereby enabling the holistic view. Furthermore, IMRs facilitate traceability across the views.

4.2   The Communication View

The *Communication View (CommV)*, illustrated in detail in Fig. 2, is proposed in this paper as a composite view that groups together the modeling components that are involved in describing communication between systems. It cuts across other primary

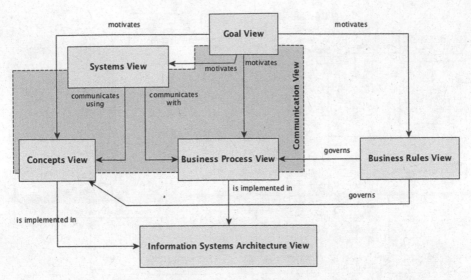

Fig. 1. Overview of the Unifying meta-model for Enterprise Modeling, highlighting the Communication View.

views to describe how systems communicate with each other. Being part of the unifying meta-model, CommV describes the relationships that systems have to other organizational design components.

System is a modeling component that represents systems that interact, communicate, and coexist in the business ecosystem. It represents the top-level element in an envisioned taxonomy of systems. The specific type of a system affects the selection of the appropriate transformation rules that are applied to generate the integration solution, following MDD principles. Modeling systems as part of the CommV, and within the larger scope of the organizational design, enables the switching of systems (e.g. selecting a different cloud-based service from within the business ecosystem) based on the changing needs as described by the organizational goals. Customized transformation rules can be then applied to generate the integration solution.

CommV enables describing two modes of communication between systems:

Indirect communication mode: A system çan *provide* concepts that are consumed by a business process. It can conversely *require* as input concepts that are produced a business process. In this case, the business process is of relevance to the organization and is also represented in the enterprise model. The details of the process can be described by an instance of the business process view. Since no restriction is set on the number of different systems that can provide/require concepts to/from a given process, the systems are able to indirectly communicate with each other. They are effectively integrated. In the indirect communication mode, concepts that are exchanged between systems and processes represent the communication tokens in a conversation. This mode corresponds to the centralized integration pattern usually associated with ESBs.

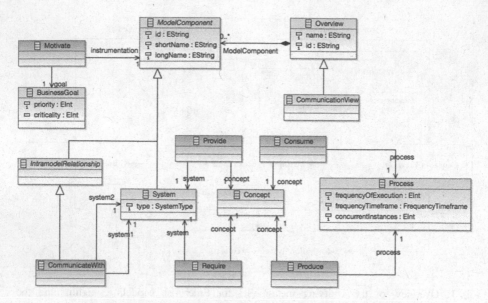

Fig. 2. The meta-model of the Communication View (CommV).

Direct communication mode: A system can communicate directly with another system, which is captured in CommV by the *CommunicateWith* intra-model relationship. This relationship emphasizes the point-to-point nature of the communication: it allows the connection of only two systems at a time. The semantics of the CommunicateWith relationship are derived from notions of CAP to describe how systems communicate according to the proposed integration pattern. They are discussed in the following subsection. The CommV is able to capture the motivation for establishing a communication channel between two systems, relative to the organizational goals. This is highlighted by the *Motivate* IMR being part of the CommV. In the unifying meta-model, Business goals are able to motivate any modeling components. This is highlighted in the specific case of CommV by revealing the hierarchy between ModelingComponent and System.

4.3   Categories of Communication in Systems Conversations

The conversation categories formulated by [26] and listed in Sect. 3 were intended to describe the interaction between computers and their human users. This paper extends the notion of conversation to include communication between integrated systems. Unlike people, systems need to be able to interpret the communication in order to deduce the appropriate response. The semantics can be described as part of supporting methods for establishing and conducting a conversation. This paper takes the first step of identifying the syntax and formulating the communication framework. Figure 3 illustrates the stages of the conversation from the perspective of the broadcasting system. Figure 4 illustrates the stages of the conversation from the perspective of the data/service provider.

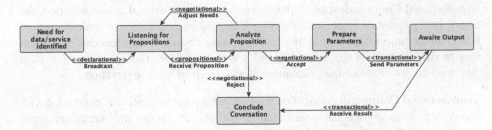

Fig. 3. Stages of a conversation between two systems – broadcasting system's view.

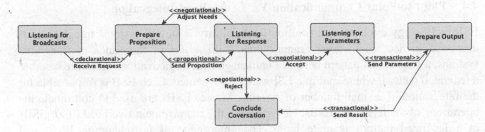

Fig. 4. Stages of a conversation between two systems – provider system's view.

When it comes to computer systems design, what matters is the structure of the interactions between the computer systems. The internal representation of knowledge within each system, just as with the thought patterns of individuals involved in traditional communication [26], is irrelevant. Integration by its nature is external to all systems being integrated, and must be studied as such. The conversation between systems is the action of integration.

To this end, communication between systems can be classified in four categories, which govern the syntax of communication. Those categories are:

Declarational Communication: a system that requires a certain piece of data or a service can use declarational communication to broadcast its need. Listening systems that receive the request and are able to react and provide the required data or service can then respond to the broadcasting system. This is the opposite of what is traditionally found in the Service Oriented Architecture [10], where a service is published and made available for consumers to find. Declarational communication highlights the fact that the broadcasting system is the party actively initiating the conversation.

Propositional Communication: a system that receives a declarational communication and is able to fulfill it can respond with a propositional communication. The responding system may be able to fulfill all or part of the request. It may even offer an alternative service or piece of data that is semantically compatible. The flexibility required in the envisioned service marketplace [5] necessitates that systems are able to negotiate alternative propositions and choose the most appropriate one, rather than being confined to predefined service descriptions.

Negotiational Communication: Upon receiving the propositional communication, the broadcasting system's response falls in the category of negotiational communication. Based on the proposition sent by the data or service provider, the broadcasting system may modify its original request and resend it to the provider. The broadcasting system may also accept or reject the proposition at any point in the conversation.

Transactional Communication: If the negotiational communication is concluded with acceptance, transactional communication is initiated to submit any necessary input parameters to the data or service provider and to retrieve the output.

4.4   Point-to-Point Communication Vs. Centralized Integration

ESB technology evolved as a solution to scalability issues in systems integration, as discussed in Sect. 2. In large organizations, with scales of thousands of integrated systems, a single ESB pattern becomes unmanageable. Organizations therefore resort to a federated pattern, where multiple ESBs are implemented. Each ESB is responsible for the integration of a small number of systems. Master ESBs are used to coordinate the operations of the federated ESBs. Nevertheless, the management overhead of all ESBs in a federated pattern is quite large. The emergence of fast-changing Web- and cloud-based applications and services is challenging the dominant integration patterns.

Contrary to patterns with a single point of integration, a point-to-point integration pattern minimizes the overhead of integrating multiple systems. Adopting a communication perspective isolates each two systems and enables complexity to be evaluated from the perspective of each system individually. Complexity, measured by the number of connections that each system has to other systems, is therefore reduced.

Concretely, given N integrated systems, point-to-point integration patterns have N* (N − 1)/2 connections. A centralized pattern reduces the number of connections to N, since each system requires a single connection to the central solution. However, adopting the communication perspective can potentially reduce the number of connections to (N/2) − 1; the number of connections that each system has ranges from

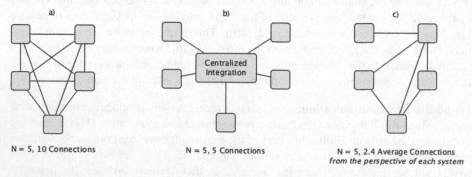

N = 5, 10 Connections   N = 5, 5 Connections   N = 5, 2.4 Average Connections
                                                                   from the perspective of each system

Fig. 5. Comparison of complexity associated with different integration patterns. (a) point-to-point integration; (b) centralized integration; (c) point-to-point communication from the perspective of each system. N represents the number of integrated systems.

1 to N − 1, and the total complexity is the average of the individual complexities. Figure 5 summarizes the comparison of complexity associated with each integration pattern.

Applying the communication perspective to centralized integration using ESB may appear to be more advantageous. Each system in the integrated solution will have only 1 connection to the central integration point. However, the practical complexity of managing the ESB, in terms of adapting the data structures and communication patterns of each system, limits the ability of adopting the communication perspective in this case. A substantial effort is still required for the central management of the solution. Considering a decentralized pattern, the direct connection between each two interacting systems is the only overhead that remains, and the additional overhead that ESB implies is eliminated.

5 Conclusion

Existing system integration patters are unable to keep up with the fast growing diversity and heterogeneity of Web- and cloud-based services. This paper proposes an integration model that adopts a communication perspective. The model that facilitates this decentralized approach enables viewing systems as participants in pair-wise conversations. The communication model is positioned in the larger perspective of organizational design. The unifying meta-model for enterprise modeling provides the underlying modeling concepts necessary to describe systems, the communication between systems, and the motivation for integrating the systems relative to organizational goals. The Communication View, or CommV, was describes in Sect. 4 as a tool for designing the interaction between systems. It allows two modes of communication between systems: an indirect mode, where systems communicate with each other via modeled business processes; and a direct mode captured using the CommunicateWith relationship.

The syntax of direct communication is governed by four categories. The stages for conducting a conversation using the communication categories were outlined from the point of view of the broadcasting system and the provider system. The communication perspective enables the reduction of the number of connections between integrated systems, compared with the alternative centralized systems integration pattern.

The proposed communication model is a step in the direction of establishing a framework for creating service marketplaces. The vision is to enable to dynamic identification, selection, and switching of cloud-based services.

Designing the CommV as part of the unifying meta-model enables relating the integrated systems to other components of the organizational design, thereby improving alignment between organizational goals and the integration solution.

Following MDD principles, we are currently developing transformation rules to generate an integration solution that implements the designed communication model. The focus of the implementation is cloud-based services, and transformation rules are being adapted to generate the concrete conversation tokens that belong to the four communication categories proposed in Sect. 4.3. A prototype tool implementation for designing CommV models and generating cloud-based integration solutions is planned.

Furthermore, the envisioned taxonomy of systems will facilitate the integration of different types of systems, by enabling the selection of corresponding transformation rules that are customized for each system type.

References

1. Armbrust, M., Fox, A., Griffith, R., Joseph, A.D., Katz, R., Konwinski, A., Lee, G., Patterson, D., Rabkin, A., Stoica, I., Zaharia, M.: A view of cloud computing. Commun. ACM **53**(4), 50–58 (2010)
2. Atkinson, C., Kühne, T.: Model-driven development: a metamodeling foundation. IEEE Softw. **20**(5), 36–41 (2003)
3. Bhatt, G.D.: An empirical examination of the effects of information systems integration on business process improvement. Intl. J. Oper. Product. Manage. **20**(11), 1331–1359 (2000)
4. Birrell, A.D., Nelson, B.J.: Implementing remote procedure calls. ACM Trans. Comput. Syst. **2**(1), 39–59 (1984)
5. Buyya, R., Yeo, C.S., Venugopal, S., Broberg, J., Brandic, I.: Cloud computing and emerging IT platforms: vision, hype, and reality for delivering computing as the 5th utility. Future Generation Comput. Syst. **25**(6), 599–616 (2009)
6. Creeger, M.: CTO roundtable: cloud computing. Queue Distrib. Comput. **7**(5), 1–17 (2009)
7. Curry, E.: Message-oriented Middleware. In: Mhamoud, Q.H. (eds.) Middleware for Communications, pp. 1–28. John Wiley & Sons, Ltd. (2004)
8. Dietz, J.L.G., Goldkuhl, G., Lind, M., van Reijswoud, V.E.: The communicative action paradigm for business modelling – a research agenda. In: Seigerroth, U. (ed.) Proceedings of the 3rd International Workshop on Language/Action Perspective (LAP 1998), Jönköping International Business School (1998)
9. Dillon, T., Wu, C., Change, E.: Cloud computing: issues and challenges. In: 24th IEEE International Conference on Advanced Information Networking and Applications, p. 27–33 (2010)
10. Erl, T.: Service-oriented Architecture: Concepts, Technology, and Design. Pearson Education India (2005)
11. España, S., González, A., Pastor, Ó.: Communication analysis: a requirements engineering method for information systems. In: Eck, P., Gordijn, J., Wieringa, R. (eds.) CAiSE 2009. LNCS, vol. 5565, pp. 530–545. Springer, Heidelberg (2009). doi:10.1007/978-3-642-02144-2_41
12. Estrada, H., Morales-Ramírez, I., Martínez, A. Pastor, O.: From business services to web services: an MDA approach. In: Castro, J., Franch, X., Mylopoulos, J., Yu, E. (eds.) Proceedings of the 4th International i* Workshop, CEUR-WS, vol. 586, pp. 31–35 (2010)
13. Graham, S., Davis, D., Simeonov, S., Daniels, G., Brittenham, P., Nakamura, Y., Fremantle, P., Koenig, D., Zentner, C.: Building Web Services with Java: Making Sense of XML, SOAP, WSDL, and UDDI. SAMS Publishing, Indianapolis (2004)
14. Habermas, J., McCarthy, T.: The theory of communicative action, vol. 1. In: Reason and the Rationalization of Society. Beacon Press (1985)
15. Hasselbring, W.: Information system integration. Commun. ACM **43**(6), 32–38 (2000)
16. Kaisler, S.H., Armour, F., Valivullah, M.: Enterprise architecting: critical problems. In: Proceedings of the 38th Annual Hawaii International Conference on System Sciences (HICSS 2005), vol. 08. IEEE Computer Society, Washington, DC (2005)

17. van Lamsweerde, A.: Goal models as architectural knowledge. In: Avgeriou, P., Lago, P., Kruchten, P. (eds.) Proceedings of the 3rd International Workshop on Sharing and Reusing Architectural Knowledge, SHARK 2008, pp. 1–2. ACM, Leipzig (2008)
18. Meimaris, M., Vafopoulos, M.: Knowledge-based semantification of business communications in ERP environments. In: Haller, A., Huang, G., Huang, Z., Paik, H.-y., Sheng, Q.Z. (eds.) WISE 2011-2012. LNCS, vol. 7652, pp. 159–172. Springer, Heidelberg (2013). doi:10.1007/978-3-642-38333-5_17
19. OMG: Object Management Group. Common Object Resource Broker Architecture (CORBA). http://www.omg.org/spec/CORBA/. Accessed on 25 Nov 2015
20. Pitt, E., McNiff, K.: Java.rmi: The Remote Method Invocation Guide. Addison-Wesley Longman Publishing Co., Inc. (2001)
21. Richardson, L., Ruby, S.: RESTful Web Services. O'Reilly Media, Inc. (2008)
22. Stevens, W.R., Fenner, B., Rudoff, A.M.: UNIX Network Programming, vol. 1. Addison-Wesley Professional (2004)
23. W3C. SOAP Version 1.2 Part 1: Messaging Framework (Second Edition). http://www.w3.org/TR/soap12/. Accessed on 25 Nov 2015
24. W3C. W3C XML Schema Definition Language (XSD) 1.1 Part 1: Structures. http://www.w3.org/TR/xmlschema11-1/. Accessed on 25 Nov 2015
25. Winograd, T., Flores, F.: Understanding Computers and Cognition, Reissue edition. Addison-Wesley (1987)
26. Winograd, T.: A language/action perspective on the design of cooperative work. In: Greif, I. (ed.) Computer-Supported Cooperative Work: A Book of Readings, pp. 623–653. Morgan-Kaufmann, San Mateo, California (1988)
27. Zikra, I., Stirna, J., Zdravkovic, J.: Analyzing the integration between requirements and models in model driven development. In: Halpin, T., Nurcan, S., Krogstie, J., Soffer, P., Proper, E., Schmidt, R., Bider, I. (eds.) BPMDS/EMMSAD -2011. LNBIP, vol. 81, pp. 342–356. Springer, Heidelberg (2011). doi:10.1007/978-3-642-21759-3_25
28. Zikra, I., Stirna, J., Zdravkovic, J.: Bringing enterprise modeling closer to model-driven development. In: Johannesson, P., Krogstie, J., Opdahl, Andreas, L. (eds.) PoEM 2011. LNBIP, vol. 92, pp. 268–282. Springer, Heidelberg (2011). doi:10.1007/978-3-642-24849-8_20

From Products to Product-Service Systems: Business and Information System Changes

Alexander Smirnov[1,2], Nikolay Shilov[1,2(✉)], Andreas Oroszi[3],
Mario Sinko[3], and Thorsten Krebs[4]

[1] SPIIRAS, 14 Line 39, 199178 St. Petersburg, Russia
{smir,nick}@iias.spb.su
[2] ITMO University, Kronverkskiy pr. 49, 197101 St. Petersburg, Russia
[3] Festo AG & Co., Ruiter Straße 82, 73734 Esslingen, Germany
{oro,sni}@de.festo.com
[4] encoway GmbH, Buschhöhe 2, 28357 Bremen, Germany
krebs@encoway.de

Abstract. Due to increasing competition in globalized markets companies are forced to search for new business models to get a competitive advantage. One of the trends is to shift from selling products to offering product-service systems. However, such shift requires significant changes in the business processes and related information systems. The paper is based on the analysis and modification of the information management processes related to Product Service Systems (PSS). It investigates the problem of PSS engineering information management in a customer-oriented way. Implementing such an application-system view addresses the problem of designing the customer view on PSS selection, configuration and usage. Though the research results are based on the analysis of one company, the presented work can give significant input to achieve benefits for component manufacturers that tend to become system vendors in general.

Keywords: Product-service systems · Customer-oriented application view · Information systems · System architect

1 Introduction

Modern global saturated and commoditized markets force companies to implement new production and marketing paradigms [1, 2]. The markets are shrinking and companies see service provision as a new path towards profits and growth. Automation equipment production is not an exception. The carried out analysis of the business and information management processes related to an automation equipment producer shows that instead of offering separate products, the company now tends to offer complex products (which may consist of several other products), whole integrated systems and also software units using different services [3, 4]. Product-Service Systems (PSS) assume orientation on combination of products and services (often supporting the products) instead of focusing only on products. This paradigm fits well automation equipment producers, for which tight relationships with customers are of high importance (with possibilities to get valuable equipment usage statistics, analyse use

W. Abramowicz et al. (Eds.): BIS 2016 Workshops, LNBIP 263, pp. 148–157, 2017.
DOI: 10.1007/978-3-319-52464-1_14

cases, get feedback, etc.). A good way to create new customer value is to provide the customer with PSS configuration possibilities. Both physical and software components are not used individually but in a greater context at the customer's site (integrating product, system, and service data as well as their valid combinations).

The paper is based on the analysis and modification of the information management processes related to PSS configuration and engineering at the automation equipment producer Festo AG & Co KG. It produces pneumatic and electronic automation equipment and products for various process industries and has more than 300 000 customers in 176 countries supported by more than 52 companies worldwide with more than 250 branch offices and authorized agencies in further 36 countries. For companies with wide assortments of products (more than 30 000–40 000 products of approx. 700 types, with various configuration possibilities) ranging from simple products to complex systems (Fig. 1), it is very important to ensure that customers can easily navigate among them to define needed services.

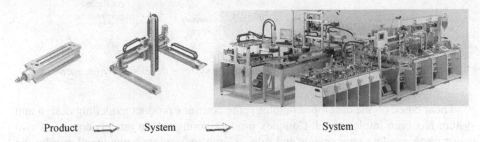

Product ⟹ System ⟹ System

Fig. 1. Assortment range: from simple products to complex systems.

1.1 Background

The overall summary of the background research is shown in Fig. 2. One of the first projects of the considered company related to this problem was launched in 2010 [5]. It was aimed at modification of work and information flows related to configuration of product combinations.

The business process reorganization started with setting up a product ontology originally aimed at product codification (order code scheme) [6]. The resulting ontology consists of more than 1000 classes organized into a four level taxonomy, which is based on the VDMA (Verband Deutscher Maschinen- und Anlagenbau/Mechanical Engineering Industry Association) classification [7]. Taxonomical relationships support inheritance that makes it possible to define more common attributes for higher level classes and inherit them for lower level subclasses. The same taxonomy is now used in the company's PDM (Product Data Management) and ERP (Enterprise Resource Planning) systems. For each product family (class) a set of properties (attributes) is defined, and for each property, its possible values and their codes are defined as well. The lexicon of properties is ontology-wide, and as a result, the values can be reused for different product families. This is a key enabler for modular product structures achieved by the ability to compare product components and their descriptions.

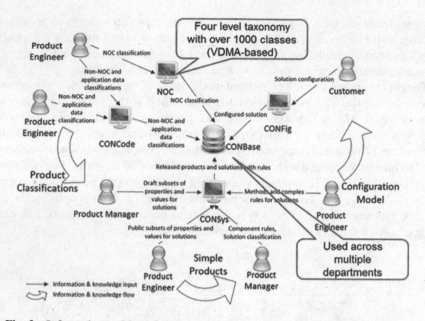

Fig. 2. Information and knowledge management systems developed by the moment.

Then, based on the developed ontology, the complex product modelling design and system has been implemented. Complex product configuration models consist of two major parts: product components and rules. Complex product components can be the following: simple products, other complex products, and application data. The set of characteristics of the complex product is a union of characteristics of its components. The rules of the complex products are union of the rules of its components plus extra rules. Application data is an auxiliary component, which is used for introduction of some additional characteristics and requirements to the product (for example, operating temperatures, certification, electrical connection, etc.). They affect availability and compatibility of certain components and features via defined rules.

Based on the configuration model the process of complex product or solution configuration in accordance with given requirements can be automated. A pilot research project aimed at developing a product configuration tool (called CONFig) was aimed at testing this possibility. The tool supported the configuration process in terms used within the company (company's knowledge level). In reality, the customers are used to operate different terminology (customer level), which doesn't correspond one-to-one to that used within the company. Besides, customers from different industries can also operate different terms. As a result, there is a need to create configuration tools that can map customers' requirements to those used in the company taking into account the context (customer's industry segment, history of customer's orders, etc.).

Although some significant results have been achieved in the area of complex product and system configuration, still a lot has to been done to support the whole life cycle of this type of products. We see the most apparent open issues in this context not in the run-time, i.e. configuration and order creation applications, but in the build-time, i.e. setting up and maintaining the required product master data, configuration rules, and application data, and so on. This is one of the goals of the future research.

1.2 Paper's Goal

The paper investigates the problem of PSS engineering information management in a customer-oriented way and the way it has been solved. Implementing such an application-system view addresses the problem of designing the customer view on PSS selection, configuration and usage (defining user experience, "talking in a customer-understandable language"). The customer should not be aware of distinctions between system types (built-to-stock, built-to-order, engineered-to-order, etc.). To the customer, the sales process should always "feel" the same.

In this paper, we share our vision of required improvements in business processes and information systems at the considered company related to life cycle management for product and system configurations. Though the research results are based on the analysis of one company, the presented work can give significant input to achieve benefits for component manufacturers that tend to become system vendors in general.

The remaining part of the paper is structured as follows: Sect. 2 presents the developed approach to the problem being solved. Section 3 lists the main findings of the carried out research. Some summarizing remarks are presented in the Conclusion.

2 Approach

2.1 Research Approach Used

The used gap analysis methodology was implemented through the following steps. First, the analysis of the current organisation of the information management was carried out. Then, the expert estimation of the company benchmark was done. Based on this, the comparison of the present and future business process and information management organisation was done resulting in creating corresponding process matrixes. This has made it possible to identify major gaps between the present and the future business organization, analyse these and define strategies to overcome these gaps.

Research efforts in the area of information management show that information and knowledge needs of a particular employee depend on his/her tasks and responsibilities. Different stages of the product lifecycle management processes in the company are associated with different roles like product managers, sales personnel and even customers. The representatives of different roles have different needs when interacting with an application like a PSS configurator. A product manager, for example, knows about the products and is able to configure by deciding on technical facts. A customer, on the other hand, may not know about the technical details of the company's products or even what kind of product he/she may use to solve his/her application problem. This is the reason why technical product details should be hidden from the customer under the application layer.

2.2 Application View

The complex PSS view comes from the application side. After defining of the application area, configuration rules and constraints to the product are defined. They are followed by characteristics and product structure definition. Finally, the apps (software applications) enriching the product functionality or improving its reliability and maintenance are defined. The same applies to the sales stage.

As a result, implementing such application-constraints-system view addresses the problem of designing the customer view on product selection, configuration and processing (defining user experience, "talking in a customer-understandable language") [8].

As it was already mentioned, based on the different complexity level, the company's products can be classified as simple discrete components, configurable products or system configurations. Of course, the selection and configuration of these different types needs to be addressed accordingly. But the customer should not be aware of this distinction. To the customer, the sales process should always "feel" the same.

The different stages of the PLM process in the company are associated with different roles like product managers, sales personnel or even customers. The representatives of different roles have different needs when interacting with an application like a product configurator. A product manager, for example, knows about the products and is able to configure by deciding on technical facts. A customer, on the other hand, may not know about the technical details of the company's products or even what kind of product he may use to solve his application problem. This is the reason why technical product details should be hidden under the application layer. In addition, the selection of the right product for solving the application problem can be based on a mapping between the application layer and a (hidden) technical product layer. In the optimal case a customer does not notice whether (s)he is selecting a discrete product, configuring a complex system, and so on.

As a result, the overall concept of customer-centric view on the products has been formulated as shown in Fig. 3. It includes the introduced above new role of "System architect" responsible for the holistic view to the system and its configuration, description of its functionality and applications, and designing a customer view to it.

2.3 Changes in Information Systems

The changing requirements on business processes also induce changing requirements on information systems.

In today's world most companies do product specification with word documents or similar approaches. These documents are handed over to construction. Construction hands over other data, e.g. technical characteristics via PDM systems or CAD files, to manufacturing, and so on. At the time a sales channel is set up for the new product, the initial data from product specification is lost. Thus, a new requirement for effectively setting up sales configurators and after-sales support is a continuous database. Knowledge about the product's application domain should be formally acquired already in the early phases of new product development. In this case the data is available whenever needed in later steps of the product lifecycle process.

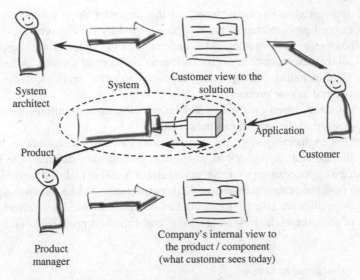

Fig. 3. The shift from the product view to the system view.

Typically the new product development process is structured in several milestones, such as design approval, technical approval or sales approval. During the entire life cycle, different roles work on product-centered data: product managers, engineers, controllers, marketing, sales personnel, and so on. Thus, either the relevant product data needs to be handed over – and potentially transformed – from a phase of the life cycle to later phases, or there is a single information system with which all the different roles carry out their daily work; every role on their specific view on a portion of the product data. In both cases, one of the major benefits for all concerned roles would be a seamless integration of all product life cycle phases within a comprehensive workflow.

A product modelling environment must be capable of designing modular product architecture. This means that using such an environment, it must be possible to reuse single product models in the scope of system configurations and assign product or system models to application knowledge. This requires the definition of well-formed product model interfaces to allow for modularity. Such interfaces enable a black-box approach, in which all products or modules implementing this interface can be chosen for the complex product/system; i.e. they become interchangeable.

Last but not least, it is also important to support multi-user activities on the different parts of product, system and application models without losing track of changes and implication that such changes have.

2.4   Pilot Case Study Implementing the Developed Approach

The developed approach has been verified on a pilot case for the Control cabinet product. This is a complex product consisting of a large number of different control elements, some of which are also complex products. Due to variety of components its functionality is significantly defined by the software control system. Control cabinets are usually configured individually based on the customer requirements since their configurations are tightly related to the equipment used by the customer.

Before the change, the customer had to order a large bill of materials in order to get the control cabinet. Now, with a holistic view to the control cabinet as to a single complex product including corresponding apps and software services, it can be configured and ordered as one product.

At the first stage, based on the demand history, the main requirements and components are defined at the market evaluation stage.

Then, at the engineering stage the components, baseline configurations based on branch specific applications as well as possible constraints are defined. The result of this is a source data for creating a cabinet configurator tool that makes it possible for the customers to configure cabinets based on their requirements online. At this stage, such specific characteristics are taken into account as components used, characteristics and capabilities of the cabinet, as well as resulting lead time and price (Fig. 4).

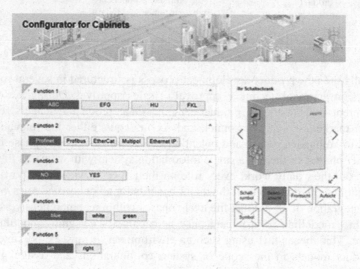

Fig. 4. Control cabinet configurator: an interface example.

Based on the customer-defined configuration the engineering data is generated in an automatic (in certain cases – semi-automatic) way, which is used for the production stage. As a result, the centralized production of cabinets is based on the automatically generated engineering file (Fig. 5).

The product maintenance is also significantly simplified due to the system-based view. All the data about this product (not only separated components) is available and can be used for modification of its configuration on customer's demand.

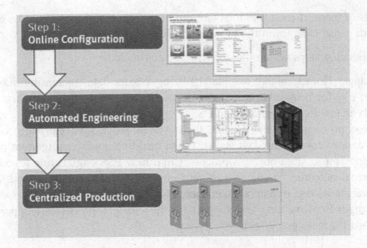

Fig. 5. Control cabinet: from online configuration to production.

3 Findings

As it was mentioned earlier, the result of the carried out gap analysis are strategies aimed at overcoming identified gaps:

1. Designing customer view on product selection, configuration and processing.
   There are different types of users, like product managers, sales personnel or customers. These users have different needs when interacting with an application like a product configurator. The customer view and the company's internal view describe two contrary views addressing the intersection between the company's product diversity and the customer's individuality with a common goal: being able to guide a customer in selecting and configuring the right system for his/her application problem. At first sight, diversity and individuality seem to have a lot in common, but the goal behind each is rather distinct. It is important to analyse the customer's context (especially for offering services): system usage, customer's industry, who does the maintenance, country-specific regulations, etc.

2. Increasing system modularity/reusability in the context of product combinations and systems.
   The structure of product combinations and systems needs to modularized. Comparable modules have the key ability to be used in multiple configuration contexts. This concerns not only products and components, but also product combinations and whole PSSs assuming building a multilevel PSS engineering model. Thus, a general PSS model architecture needs to be set up.

3. From business processes to IT or vice versa?
   Though it is reasonably considered that the changes of business processes are the driver to changes in the corresponding IT systems, the experience has shown that it is not always the case. Having defined a general strategy, the company can try to implement some pilot particular IT solutions to support existing business processes

or parts of them. If such solutions turn out to be successful they could be extended and will cause changes in the business processes.

More detailed steps within the above strategies include:

1. (IT change) Homogenizing and standardizing master data (increasing master data quality; e.g. for being able to compare components, which are necessary to build partially defined combinations and PSSs).
2. (Business process change) Aligning the business processes (improving interoperability and avoiding redundant tasks). When building a new configurator platform, it is important to align business processes like new PSS engineering together with the desired outcome. Doing so can help improving interoperability and avoiding redundant tasks e.g. in data maintenance.
3. (IT change) Implementing tool support for the changed processes (supporting the improved business processes).

4 Conclusions

The paper presents results of the ongoing shift from separate product and component to integrated PSS offering. In particular, it is concentrated on improving user experience in configuring and ordering for configurable PSS. The core idea is the change from the convenient for the company view of the products to the customer-friendly view from the system application perspective, which required an introduction of a new PLM role of "System architect". The developed business process and supporting information systems made it possible to implement the scenario of the automated production of the customer-configured control cabinet.

The presented work is an ongoing joint research, which is still in an intermediary step of implementation. So far a pilot case for the control cabinet product has been implemented for selected customers. The future work will include achieving automated production of other customer-configured PSS. The research is based on the company Festo AG&Co KG, however, the results can give significant input to achieve benefits for component manufacturers that tend to become system vendors in general.

Acknowledgment. The research was supported partly by projects funded by grants # 14-07-00378, # 15-07-08092 of the Russian Foundation for Basic Research and Program I.5 of the Russian Academy of Sciences. This work was also partially financially supported by Government of Russian Federation, Grant 074-U01.

References

1. Zhang, M.-R., Yang, C.-C., Ho, S.-Y., Chang, C.H.: A study on enterprise under globalization competition knowledge management and creation overhead construction. J. Interdisciplinary Math. **17**(5–6), 423–433 (2014)

2. Erdener, K., Hassan, S.: Globalization of Consumer Markets: Structures and Strategies. Routledge (2014)
3. Ceschin, F.: Product-service system innovation: a promising approach to sustainability. In: Sustainable Product-Service Systems, pp. 17–40. Springer International Publishing (2014)
4. Wallin, J., Parida, V., Isaksson, O.: Understanding product-service system innovation capabilities development for manufacturing companies. J. Manufacturing Technol. Manage. **26**(5), 763–787 (2015)
5. Smirnov, A., Shilov, N., Kashevnik, A., Jung, T., Sinko, M., Oroszi, A.: Ontology-driven product configuration: industrial use case. In: Proceedings of International Conference on Knowledge Management and Information Sharing (KMIS 2011), pp. 38–47 (2011)
6. Oroszi, A., Jung, T., Smirnov, A., Shilov, N., Kashevnik, A.: Ontology-driven codification for discrete and modular products. Int. J. Product Develop. **8**(2), 162–177 (2009)
7. VDMA, German Engineering Federation (2014). http://www.vdma.org/en_GB/
8. Smirnov, A., Kashevnik, A., Shilov, N., Oroszi, A., Sinko, M., Krebs, T.: Changing business information systems for innovative configuration processes. In: Matulevičius, R., Maggi, F. M., Küngas, P. (eds.) Joint Proceedings of the BIR 2015 Workshops and Doctoral Consortium Co-located with 14th International Conference on Perspectives in Business Informatics Research (BIR 2015), CEUR, vol. 1420, pp. 62–73 (2015)

Information Quality Framework for the Design and Validation of Data Flow Within Business Processes - Position Paper

Michael Vaknin[✉] and Agata Filipowska

Department of Information Systems,
Faculty of Informatics and Electronic Economy,
Poznan University of Economics and Business, Poznan, Poland
miki.vaknin@gmail.com,
agata.filipowska@kie.ue.poznan.pl

Abstract. Poor data quality may be a cause for problems in organizational processes. There are numerous methods to assess and improve quality of data within information systems, however they often do not address the original source of these problems. This paper presents a conceptual solution for dealing with the data quality issue within information systems. It focuses on analysis of business processes being a source of requirements for information systems design and development. This analysis benefits information quality requirements, in order to improve data quality within systems emerging from these requirements.

Keywords: Data/information quality · Business process modeling · IS/IT alignment · IS/IT design · Data quality dimensions

1 Introduction

1.1 Research Motivation

Nowadays, organizations face numerous challenges in efficiently and effectively executing their business processes, and therefore require strong Information Systems (IS) - business alignment [29, 49]. To sustain their position in the market, these organisations need to find ways to better manage and adapt their business processes in response to changes, trends and developments in the business environment [9, 42, 45].

Business processes produce and use data and information and are based on information flow [12]. A process refers to a sequence of activities, which are performed in coordination in an organizational and technical environment [53]. These activities jointly realize a business goal, reflected by data items in a process representation [41]. "Many business processes leave their 'footprints' in transactional information systems" [2, p. 198]. Such processes, in practice, can suffer from quality aspects such as a poor level of data quality along their activities or in communication between processes. Therefore, the correctness, effectiveness, and efficiency of the business processes supported by information systems are becoming vital to the organization [3]. There is an evident need to incorporate data quality considerations into the whole data cycle,

© Springer International Publishing AG 2017
W. Abramowicz et al. (Eds.): BIS 2016 Workshops, LNBIP 263, pp. 158–168, 2017.
DOI: 10.1007/978-3-319-52464-1_15

encompassing managerial/governance as well as technical aspects [4, 37]. While the need for the alignment of business processes and their support systems has been emphasized and discussed, there is still a great need for systematic approaches and tools with regards to data quality [27, 29, 57].

1.2 Problem Description

Recent studies [8, 19, 31, 32, 35, 43] show that many information systems projects were "challenged" or "failed" in the combination of budget and/or schedule overruns and/or for not meeting user requirements. Even when these projects are completed, many meet no more than a mere shadow of their original specification requirements [43].

A substantial part of system development failures can be attributed to problems that arise during system analysis. Hence, understanding and improving system analysis and design are central to the research mission of the Information Systems (IS) discipline [26]. Other empirical studies [21, 30–32, 43] show that more than half of the errors which occur during system development are a result of inaccurate or incomplete requirements. In addition, unclear or poor requirements and errors in specifications are critical factors and the most common cause of failure in system development projects [22, 35].

Data is a critical asset in every organization [18, 36]. The quality of the data affects the quality of decisions [6, 15, 33, 55]. Data quality (DQ) refers to the quality of the content of information systems and the degree to which a set of characteristics of data fulfills the requirements, and is viewed as "fitness for use" by information consumers [7, 24, 44, 50–52, 57]. Based on this definition, Wang and Strong [52] defined a set of dimensions of data quality from the consumer's point of view via a systematic multistage survey study. Prior to this research, data quality had been characterized by attributes identified via intuition and unsystematically selected by individual researchers [57].

Data quality directly affects the effectiveness and efficiency of business processes and also plays a major role in customer and user satisfaction [12]. Data quality improvement often requires changes in processes and organizational behaviors [57], and problems with the quality of this data can have catastrophic consequences [33, 54]. Poor data quality is a primary reason for 40% of all business initiatives failing to achieve their targeted benefits [16]. In fact, many research reports show that huge amounts of resources and money are spent in organisations due to poor data quality, or in order to improve data quality [17, 24]. Furthermore, as more business processes become automated, data quality becomes the rate-limiting factor for overall process quality.

Generally, the idea of integrating data quality issues into business process models as such is not new. Different approaches and measures have been developed over the years to deal with information quality assessment needs, but the notion of information quality within process modeling and IS design methods has received relatively little attention [4, 33]. This research will concentrate on the linkage between two topics - information quality and business processes modeling, since there is still a great need for methods and models dealing with quality of information flow in business processes [29, 57].

We will focus on the importance of information quality dimensions for the successful execution of business processes. We aim to investigate and analyze the business process design and validation methods using information quality requirements, and develop a conceptual model and a tool for business process analysts, designers and practitioners, which combine data quality requirements and business process design, to check and validate business processes in order to achieve the defined process goals.

To the best of our knowledge, these two issues have not been sufficiently discussed yet, and there is a lack of systematic approaches, models and tools with regards to data quality. Therefore, the following analysis is considered a novelty.

The structure of this paper is as follows: In the next section we provide an overview of previous related work. Section 3 presents the solution proposal. In Sect. 4 we present the case study and address the research challenges. Finally, we offer our conclusions and a summary.

2 Related Work

In the past two decades many researchers have addressed different aspects of the problem of data quality from various perspectives. Xu et al. [56] developed a framework for identifying data quality issues in implementing ERP systems. Other researchers (e.g. [13, 14, 39]) investigated the impact of data quality on the performance of organizational units (including individuals), evaluated the costs and benefits of data quality initiatives, and assessed the impact of data quality on operations and decision making.

DeLone and McLean [10, 11] present models for evaluating the success of implementation of information systems, models in which information quality is one of the central dimensions. They reviewed the existing definitions of IS success and their corresponding measures, and classified them into six major categories.

Other researchers [20, 34, 51] claim that there exists an analogy between quality issues in product or service manufacturing and those in information manufacturing. They suggest assessing the information quality from the product or service quality perspective, using methods and techniques like total data quality management (TDQM) based on a total quality management (TQM) approach. These perspectives are limited, since they do not focus on process requirements and the design stage, and none of them links data quality to defined soft goals for implementation and their achievement by the process.

An example of this analogy, however in a different form, is suggested by Wand and Wang [50] in terms of process design. They argue that similarly to the way the quality of a product depends on the process by which the product is designed and produced, the quality of data depends on the design and production processes involved in generating the data. They emphasize that to design for better quality, it is necessary to first understand what quality means and how it is measured. Sun et al. [46], and later Sun and Zhao [45], emphasized the importance of data-flow perspective in the workflow analysis. They argue that given a correct process sequence, errors can still occur during workflow execution due to incorrect data-flow specifications, and that no formal methodologies are available for systematically discovering data-flow errors in a workflow model. They present a data-flow perspective for detecting data-flow anomalies based on concepts of data dependencies within processes.

Another approach to cope with this issue is to improve, redevelop, and revise the data quality perspective of affected business processes, since major business processes are supported, controlled and/or monitored by information systems as mentioned above. For example, Lee et al. [25] investigated data quality improvement initiatives in a large manufacturing firm, which iteratively adapted technical data integrity rules in response to changing business processes and requirements. Cao and Zhu [5] investigated inevitable data quality problems resulting from the tight coupling effects and the complexity of Enterprise Resource Planning (ERP) systems in their case study in China. The findings show that organizations that have successfully implemented ERP can still experience certain data quality problems and the efficient operation of ERP systems largely depends on the data quality. They identified major data quality problems in data production, storage and maintenance, and utilization processes. The researchers also analyzed the causes of these data quality problems by linking them to certain characteristics of ERP systems within an organizational context.

Glowalla and Sunyaev [17] examined the application of process-driven data quality management (PDDQM) techniques (such as Workflow and DFD) based on literature review. They provided two options to integrate data quality into existing process models: within-model integration and across-model integration. Within-model integration allows to enhance existing process models with data quality information by integrating data quality checks. Across-model integration provides a new process model with an information product-centric perspective, linking it to existing models. Furthermore, the researchers also examined the integration approaches' impact on the models' complexity and patterns for complexity reduction [17].

The existing literature on business process design and validation shows a need of methods and models for dealing with quality of information flow in business processes. Existing design methods in business process management remain a manual and experiential effort, and result in inefficiency in design tasks and potential errors in workflow models [45]. The focus of the research (e.g. [38, 46, 48]) has been on combining data flow with activity flow, i.e. data-aware process design, and it has been investigated already to some extent, but avoids design time errors [6, 40]. Furthermore, since the research is concerned with the process design and validation activities meant to reflect the requirements from information systems as represented in the real world, a framework is required in order to describe the design and validation activities in terms of information quality within organizational processes, and to overcome these two main shortcomings.

3 Solution Proposal

Business process design is based on a set of requirements which are collected and analyzed by professional process analysts. Business process models could be used often to make the process explicit as-is. However, a gap is created between the requirements process to-be and the as-is process. To overcome this gap and to acquire an optimal fit between the designed process and its planned outputs, and finally to achieve its soundness, there is a great need for a structured modeling approach to lead and direct the practitioners.

As a consequence of poor design, a process can fail and reach one or more undesired results as outcomes. Furthermore, process design without taking quality considerations into account is probably expected to fail as discussed above. These poor outcomes are a result of low level of strictness about DQ dimensions, since there is a dependency between data values in the process. Moreover, the data flow in processes and along their activities is the basis for data requirement representing in IS stage. Hence, if we want to ensure that the IS works properly and presents desired data values in high quality, we have to check data item values before recording them to IS to ensure DQ.

We built a conceptual model to summarize the terms and constructs discussed using the UML class diagram (Fig. 1):

Business Process refers to a set of activities. Process specifies which steps are required and in what order they should be executed. It is also known as: routing definition, procedure, workflow script [1], e.g. purchase order, tax declarations and insurance claims process. In general, business process includes cases (also named 'process instance' or 'job') which are handled and need to be processed by following the process definition, e.g. a customer order, a job application, etc. Each case has a unique identity. The Activity (also named 'task', 'operation', 'action', 'step', 'process element', or 'work-item') is a logical unit of work, e.g. typing a letter, stamping a document and checking personal data [1]. Activity contains one or more of the data

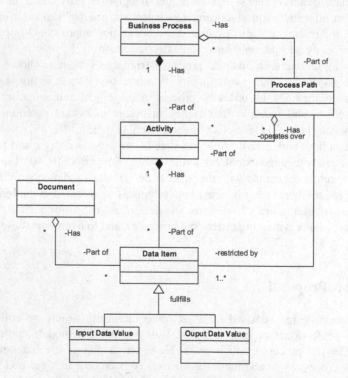

Fig. 1. The conceptual model. Source: own study

items. A process path is one possible trajectory or route that includes a sequence of activities in order, from the initial activity to the final activity, which have dependencies between them. In fact, trajectory in a business process describes the sequence of data items by the dependence between data values.

Data Item is a data element or a character in a document that consists of values, which is represented as a field in a database. Data Value is a raw data in data item, i.e. collection of characters, and can be given any text, numeric, date or Boolean value, etc. Any data value can be an input for an activity or an output of an activity. A document is a general name for any collection of data items (e.g. forms, applications, certificates, enquiry etc.). Similar to the idea of data entity is an object of data in a business process which is stored in a database that can be classified and have stated relationships to other entities.

We distinguish between two main types of data dependencies: a mandatory dependency and a conditional dependency. The mandatory dependency is a dependency among data values, where a data value of a data item B is affected by a data value of the data item A. If the data value of the data item A in the representation is unknown, then the process will not be properly executed. For example, if we want to calculate the insurance premium (data item B) for shipping cargo in an export service, we need the cargo volume value (data item A) as a mandatory value. Without this value (i.e. cargo volume) the process is expected to be in a deadlock situation. Conditional dependency concerns a dependency among data values in data items along process representation, where the value of a data item B is affected by value of data item A and uses it under some conditions, i.e. conditionally depends on. The process may be executed without using this value; hence, data item A in representation can be unknown under some conditions. For example, approving customer order (data item B) conditionally depends on receiving a down payment from the customer (data item A), conditioned by the customer's risk level. If the customer's risk level (another data item) is low and there is no down payment received, i.e. the down payment value (data item A) in representation is unknown yet or null, the process is still in progress since the customer risk level is low.

Based on the idea of dependencies we built a matrix which summarizes all possible dependencies that exist between various data items and their values in a selected process. We then collect dependencies based on a study of possible process paths and assessment whether an activity depends on a certain value or not. The size of the matrix depends on the number of data items along the process. This matrix can also help us identify the type of potential failure dependencies between all data items with respect to various data quality dimensions generated by Wang and Strong [52], such as accuracy, completeness, timeliness etc. We name these potential failures 'data quality deficiencies'. A data quality deficiency is an inconformity between the view of the real-world system that can be inferred from a process representation and the view that can be obtained by directly observing a real-world system. Such an analysis at the design stage can help business process analysts and practitioners to predict potential failures in the process earlier, fix them and prevent further failures of information system design. Failures in the design process due to poor data quality can result, for example, in outputs not in the process goals set, or can lead the process to be in deadlock situation.

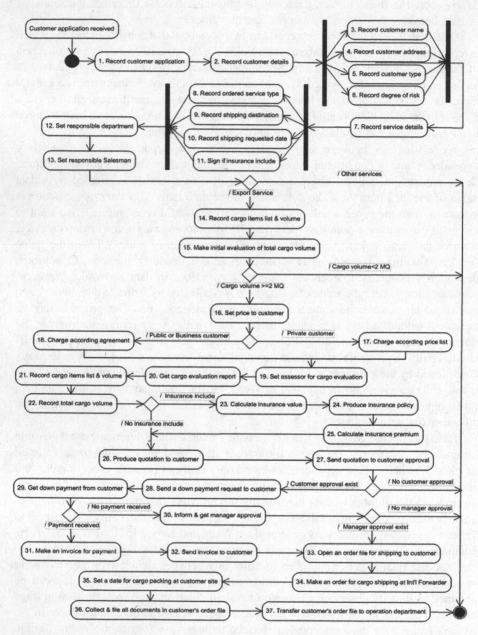

Fig. 2. The case study UML Activity diagram - sales process of sea export service. Source: own study

4   The Case Study

The case study which validated the model is based on process networks of the international forwarding and moving industry. The global freight forwarding and moving industry is vast, both in terms of market size and vast numbers of employees, and is considered one of the most important industries today [28]. According to the European Freight Forwarders Association (EFFA) [47], the term "freight forwarding industry" refers to the set of global logistics services for the exporter and importer in moving cargo to an overseas destination. An international freight forwarder is an agent for the exporter and importer in moving cargo to an overseas destination. These agents are familiar with the export and import rules and regulations of foreign countries, the methods of shipping, and the documents related to foreign trade. The global service includes sub services e.g. carriage and inland moving, storage, warehousing, freight consolidation, cargo insurance etc. Once the order is ready for shipment, freight forwarders should be reviewing all documents to ensure that everything is in order. This is of particular importance with regards to letter of credit payment terms. They may also prepare the bill of lading and any special required documentation. After shipment, they can route the documents to the seller, the buyer, or to a paying bank. Freight forwarders can also make arrangements with customs brokers overseas to ensure that the goods comply with customs export documentation regulations. A customs broker is an individual or company that is licensed to transact customs business on behalf of others. Our case study focuses on sales process of the import service. Figure 2 presents the process as the UML Activity diagram.

5   Conclusions and Summary

The existing literature on business process design and validation lacks methods and models for dealing with quality of information flow in business processes. Existing design methods in business process management remain manual and result in inefficiency in design tasks and in potential errors in workflow models [45]. The focus of research (e.g. [38, 46, 48]) has been on combining data flow with activity flow, i.e. data-aware process design, and it has been investigated already to some extent, but avoids design time errors [6, 40]. Since the research is concerned with the process design and validation activities, meant to reflect the requirements from information systems, a framework is required to describe the process with regards to information quality.

The most significant theoretical contribution expected from this research is the creation of a linkage between information quality and business process modeling, combined to generate a framework for understanding the importance of information quality on the success of the business process; later on it will be a basis for IS requirements definition. As mentioned above, there is a remarkable lack of research, methods and models in the business processes modeling and IS domains literature, especially regarding theoretical frameworks that might help us deal with information flow quality in terms of process design and validation.

The practical contribution of the research is to provide process designers, practitioners and IS workers a usable and friendly framework, intended to validate the information quality requirements in the IS development process at the analysis and design stages. The expected outcomes from application of the model and method (encompassing quality checking rules) based on our case study analysis are as follows: the ability to identify potential failures at an earlier stage in the process with regards to the dimensions of data quality, and identification of potential failures in the general level of process, e.g. wrong decision(s) making, waste of valuable time, and unnecessary expenses or work as part of the process.

References

1. van der Aalst W.M.P.: Discovering coordination patterns using process mining. In: Bocchi, L., Ciancarini, P. (eds.) First International Workshop on Coordination and Petri Nets (PNC 2004), CNR Pisa, Italy, pp. 49–64 (2004)
2. van der Aalst, W.M.P.: Business alignment: using process mining as a tool for Delta analysis and conformance testing. Requir. Eng. **10**, 198–211 (2005)
3. Aalst, W.M.P.: Challenges in business process analysis. In: Filipe, J., Cordeiro, J., Cardoso, J. (eds.) ICEIS 2007. LNBIP, vol. 12, pp. 27–42. Springer, Heidelberg (2008). doi:10.1007/978-3-540-88710-2_3
4. Blake, R., Mangiameli, P.: The effects and interactions of data quality and problem complexity on classification. J. Data Inf. Qual. (JDIQ), **2**(2) (2011)
5. Cao, L., Zhu, H.: Normal accident: data quality problems in ERP-enabled manufacturing. ACM J. Data Inf. Qual. **4**(3) (2013). Article 11
6. Cappiello, C., Caro, A., Rodríguez, A., Caballero, I.: An approach to design business processes addressing data quality issues. In: Proceedings of the 21st European Conference on Information Systems (ECIS 2013), Utrecht, 5–8 June 2013, pp. 1–12 (2013)
7. Caro, A., Rodríguez, A., Cappiello, C., Caballero, I.: Designing business processes able to satisfy data quality requirements. In: Proceedings of the 17th International Conference on Information Quality (ICIQ). Paris (2012)
8. Chandrasekaran, S., Gudlavalleti, S., Kaniyar, S.: Achieving success in large complex software projects. McKinsey & Company, pp. 1–5, July 2014
9. Daoudi, F., Nurcan, S.: A benchmarking framework for methods to design flexible business processes. Softw. Process Improv. Pract. **12**(1), 51–63 (2007)
10. DeLone, W.H., McLean, E.R.: Information systems success: the quest for the dependent variable. Inf. Syst. Res. **3**(1), 60–95 (1992)
11. DeLone, W.H., McLean, E.R.: The DeLone and McLean Model of information systems success: a ten-year update. J. Manag. Inf. Syst. **19**(4), 9–30 (2003)
12. English, L.P.: Information quality management: the next frontier. In: ASQ - Annual Quality Congress, Charlotte, vol. 55, pp. 529–533, May 2001
13. Fisher, C., Chengular-Smith, I., Ballou, D.: The impact of experience and time on the use of data quality information in decision making. J. Inf. Syst. Res. **14**(2), 170–188 (2003)
14. Fisher, C., Kingma, B.: Criticality of data quality as exemplified in two disasters. J. Inf. Manag. **39**, 109–116 (2001)
15. Frank, A.U.: Analysis of dependence of decision quality on data quality. J. Geogr. Syst. **10**, 71–88 (2008)

16. Gartner Group: Measuring the Business Value of Data Quality. Gartner Inc., Stamford (2011)
17. Glowalla, P., Sunyaev, A.: Process-driven data quality management – integration of data quality into existing process models. Bus. Inf. Syst. Eng. (BISE) **5**(6), 433–448 (2013)
18. Govil, J., Govil, J.: Data management: issues and solutions for workflow efficiency. In: SpringSim, 2008, pp. 307–312 (2008)
19. Ibrahim, R., Ayazi, E., Nasrmalek, S., Nakha, S.: An investigation of critical failure factors in information technology projects. J. Bus. Manag. **10**(3), 87–92 (2013)
20. Kahn, B.K., Strong, D.M., Wang, R.Y.: Information quality benchmarks: product and service performance. Commun. ACM **45**(4), 184–192 (2002)
21. Kappelman, L., McKeeman, R., Zhang, L.: Early warning signs of IT project failure: the dangerous dozen. EDPACS (EDP Audit, Control, and Security) **40**(6), 17–25 (2009)
22. Kaur, R., Sengupta, J.: Software process models and analysis on failure of software development projects. Int. J. Sci. Eng. Res. **2**(2), 1–4 (2011)
23. Kleiner, N.: Delta analysis with workflow logs: aligning business process prescriptions and their reality. Requir. Eng. **10**, 212–222 (2005)
24. Laranjeiro, L., Soydemir, S.N., Bernardino, J.: A survey on data quality: classifying poor data. In: Conference: The 21st IEEE Pacific Rim International Symposium on Dependable Computing (PRDC 2015), at Zhangjiajie, pp. 179–188 (2015)
25. Lee, Y.W., Pipino, L., Strong, D., Wang, R.: Process embedded data integrity. J. Database Manag. **15**(1), 87–103 (2004)
26. Iivari, J., Parsons, J., Wand, Y.: Research in information systems analysis and design: introduction to the special issue. J. Assoc. Inf. Syst. **7**(8), 509–513 (2006). Atlanta
27. Madnick, S.E., Wang, R.Y., Lee, Y.W., Zhu, H.: Overview and framework for data and information quality research. ACM J. Data Inf. Qual. **1**(1), 1–22 (2009). Article 2
28. Manners-Bell, J.: Global Logistics Strategies: Delivering the Goods. Kogan Page Publishers, New York (2014)
29. Mondragón, M., Mora, M., Garza, L., Álvarez, F., Rodríguez, L., Duran-Limon, H.A.: Toward a well-structured development methodology for business process-oriented software systems based on services. Procedia Technol. **9**(2013), 351–360 (2013)
30. Moody, D.L., Sindre, G., Brasethvik, T.: Evaluating the quality of information models: empirical testing of a conceptual model quality framework. IEEE, pp. 295–305 (2003)
31. Nasir, M.H.N., Sahibuddin, S.: Critical success factors for software projects: a comparative study. Sci. Res. Essays **6**(10), 2174–2186 (2011)
32. Nwakanma, C.I., Asiegbu, B.C., Ogbonna, C.A., Njoku Peter-Paul, C.: Factors affecting successful implementation of information technology projects: experts' perception. Eur. Sci. J. **9**(27), 128–137 (2013). September 2013 edition
33. Ofner, M., Otto, B., Österle, H.: Integrating a data quality perspective into business process management. Bus. Process Manag. J. **18**(6), 1036–1067 (2012)
34. Pierce, E.M.: Assessing data quality with control matrices. Commun. ACM **47**(2), 82–86 (2004)
35. Rajkumar, G., Alagarsamy, K.: Failure of software development projects. Int. J. Comput. Sci. Appl. (TIJCSA) **1**(11), 74–77 (2013)
36. Redman, T.C.: Data: an unfolding quality disaster. DM Rev. Mag. (2004). http://www.dmreview.com. Accessed 4 June 2014
37. Sadiq, S.: Handbook of Data Quality: Research and Practice, p. 2013. Springer, Heidelberg (2013)
38. Sadiq, S.W., Orlowska, M.E., Sadiq, W., Foulger, C.: Data flow and validation in workflow modelling. In: Fifteenth Australasian Database Conference (ADC), Dunedin. CRPIT, vol. 27, pp. 207–214 (2004)

39. Slone, J.P.: Information quality strategy: an empirical investigation of the relationship between information quality improvements and organizational outcomes. Ph.D. dissertation, Capella University (2006)
40. Soffer, P.: Mirror, mirror on the wall, can i count on you at all? Exploring data inaccuracy in business processes. Enterprise, business-process and information systems modeling. In: Proceedings of 11th International Workshop, BPMDS 2010, vol. 50, pp. 14–25 (2010)
41. Soffer, P., Wand, Y.: Goal-driven multi-process analysis. J. Assoc. Inf. Syst. 8(3), 175–203 (2007)
42. Stalk, G., Evans, P., Shulman, L.E.: Competing on capabilities: the new rules of corporate strategy. Harvard Bus. Rev. 70, 57–68 (1992)
43. Standish Group: The CHAOS report – project smart. The Standish Group International Inc. (2014). https://www.projectsmart.co.uk/white-papers/chaos-report.pdf. Accessed 12 June 2016
44. Strong, D.M., Lee, Y.W., Wang, R.Y.: Data quality in context. Commun. ACM 40(5), 103–110 (1997)
45. Sun, S.X., Zhao, J.L.: Formal workflow design analytics using data flow modeling. J. Dec. Support Syst. 55(1), 270–283 (2013)
46. Sun, S.X., Zhao, J.L., Nunamaker, J.F., Liu Sheng, O.R.: Formulating the data-flow perspective for business process management. Inf. Syst. Res. 17(4), 374–391 (2006)
47. The European Freight Forwarders Association (EFFA). https://www.effa.com. Accessed 24 Nov 2015
48. Trčka, N., Aalst, W.M.P., Sidorova, N.: Data-flow anti-patterns: discovering data-flow errors in workflows. In: Eck, P., Gordijn, J., Wieringa, R. (eds.) CAiSE 2009. LNCS, vol. 5565, pp. 425–439. Springer, Heidelberg (2009). doi:10.1007/978-3-642-02144-2_34
49. Ullah, A., Lai, R.: Modeling business goal for business-it alignment using requirements engineering. J. Comput. Inf. Syst. 51(3), 21–28 (2011)
50. Wand, Y., Wang, R.Y.: Anchoring data quality dimensions in ontological foundations. Commun. ACM 39(11), 86–95 (1996). New York
51. Wang, R.Y.: A product perspective on total data quality management. Commun. ACM 41(2), 58–65 (1998)
52. Wang, R.Y., Strong, D.M.: Beyond accuracy: what data quality means to data consumer. J. Manag. Inf. Syst. 12(4), 5–34 (1996)
53. Weske, M.: Business Process Management – Concepts, Languages, Architectures, 2nd edn. Springer, Heidelberg (2012)
54. Woodall, P., Borek, A., Parlikad, A.K.: Data quality assessment: the hybrid approach. Inf. Manag. 50(7), 369–382 (2013)
55. Xingsen, L., Lingling, Z., Peng, Z., Yong, S.: Problems and systematic solutions in data quality. Int. J. Serv. Sci. 2(1), 53–69 (2009)
56. Xu, H., Nord, J.H., Brown, N., Nord, G.G.: Data quality issues in implementing an ERP. Ind. Manag. Data Syst. 102(1), 47–58 (2002)
57. Zhu, H., Madnick, S.E., Lee, Y.W., Wang, R.Y.: Data and information quality research: its evolution and future. In: Topi, H., Tucker A. (eds.) Computing Handbook: Information Systems and Information Technology, 3rd edn. Chapman & Hall/CRC, pp. 16.1–16.20. MIT-CDO-WP-01 (2014)

DeBASE Workshop

Do You Write What You Are in Business Communications? Deriving Psychometrics from Enterprise Social Networks

Janine Viol Hacker[1]([⊠]), Alexander Piazza[1], and Trevor Kelley[2]

[1] Institute of Information Systems, University of Erlangen-Nürnberg,
Lange Gasse 20, 90403 Nürnberg, Germany
{janine.hacker,alexander.piazza}@fau.de
[2] Deloitte Touche Tohmatsu, 225 George Street, Sydney, NSW 2000, Australia
trkelley@deloitte.com.au

Abstract. In this paper, we explore the discriminability of psychometrics derived from an automated linguistic analysis within a business setting. To this end, a commercial natural language processing application is used to analyse messages posted to the Enterprise Social Network (ESN) of an Australian professional services firm. Comparing the psychometrics derived for individual users with those of other users, we find that the text posted to the ESN facilitates the detection of distinguishable personality profiles. Also, our analysis indicates the derived psychometrics to remain stable from year to year.

Keywords: Enterprise Social Network · Personality · Big Five · Natural language processing · IBM Watson Personality Insights

1 Introduction

The personality of organisational members is considered as an important criterion for decision-making at the intersection between human resources management and knowledge management. For instance, personality traits of an organisation's CEO and top management team have been related to organisational performance [8]. Also, the personality composition of teams has been found to influence their job performance [18,27]. Thus, personality traits should be taken into account when making promotion and staffing decisions. With regard to knowledge management, personality traits have been related to individuals' knowledge sharing behaviour [22] and their preference regarding e-learning tools [6]. While insights about personality traits of employees could benefit organisational decision-making, the collection and analysis of personality data, for instance, using questionnaires, involves a high manual effort and is thus, difficult to apply to whole organisations.

Social media platforms, such as social networking sites and blogs, enable users to the disclose personal information by presenting themselves in an online space [17].

© Springer International Publishing AG 2017
W. Abramowicz et al. (Eds.): BIS 2016 Workshops, LNBIP 263, pp. 171–182, 2017.
DOI: 10.1007/978-3-319-52464-1_16

Utilising natural language processing (NLP), prior research has successfully derived psychometrics from the content generated on such platforms, e.g. analysing data from the microblogging platform Twitter [10]. The analysis of the big data accumulated in public online social spaces enables companies to gain better customer insights. For instance, social media analytics can be used to generate personalised promotions or improve customer retention and loyalty [23]. With the advent of Enterprise Social Networks (ESN) large amounts of text are generated by employees on these internally used social media platforms, too. While ESN data could be used to extract psychometrics – as done with data collected from public online social spaces – it is questionable if the messages posted to an ESN are sufficiently discriminable to distinguish users. Being used in a business context, ESN users might be too constrained when posting, and hence, create posts that are very similar in terms of their linguistic and stylistic features.

The objective of this paper is to explore the discriminability of psychometrics derived through the automated linguistic analysis of messages generated in a business setting. To this end, the IBM Watson Personality Insights service [14] is used to analyse the messages posted to the ESN of an Australian professional services firm in the years 2012 to 2015. We compare the psychometrics derived for individual users with those of other users and analyse whether the derived psychometrics of the individuals remain stable over time.

With this research, we contribute to the emerging field of big data analytics in the context of ESN. As such, the application of machine learning techniques enables the analysis of larger data sets, and thus, more detailed insights about the ESN users and their activities.

2   Background and Related Work

2.1   Enterprise Social Network Analytics

ESN are web-based platforms that are implemented behind an organisation's firewall [21]. Relying on Web 2.0 technologies, they bear a lot of similarity to public social networking sites, such as Facebook. ESN enable users to present information about themselves [3], to broadcast messages to everyone in the organisation, to contribute to groups as well as to send private messages [21]. Users can explicitly connect with other users via features like "Following" as well as respond to the content posted by other users [3,21]. The communicative actions of users on the ESN lead to visible traces that persist over time [21]. As such, these so-called digital traces include data regarding user activities (usage data), content (user-generated data), and relations (structural data) [3]. Exported from the application's back end, ESN data can be analysed using qualitative methods, quantitative methods, or a mix of both. Based on usage data, Holtzblatt et al. [13], for instance, classify ESN user roles along two dimensions, i.e. based on their level of contributions and regularity of logging in to the platform. Using data characterising message content and user activities, Viol et al. [32] develop a set of metrics to identify dimensions of ESN user behaviour. Combining qualitative text analysis and social network analysis, Berger et al. [4] focus on the characterization of value-adding users in ESN. Further, a number of studies investigate the purposes of users to engage in ESN and identify different modes of use based on a content analysis of the posted messages [29]. Apart from purely qualitative analysis of the message content, some studies support the process of identifying specific types of posts, e.g. to distinguish questions from non-questions, by detecting question marks and question words in the text body [5, 31].

2.2 Personality Traits and Author Profiling

The Five Factor Model ("Big Five") is a standard taxonomy to describe and measure personality traits [33]. As such, the Big Five model comprises five dimensions [11, 25]:

- **Openness (to experience):** This dimension reflects the degree to which individuals are interested in engaging in a variety of activities.
- **Extraversion:** This dimension indicates the extent to which an individual is sociable, talkative, and outgoing.
- **Neuroticism:** Also referred to as *emotional range*, this dimension indicates the degree of emotional stability. It expresses the extent to which individuals easily experience unpleasant emotions and are sensitive to their environment.
- **Conscientiousness:** This dimension describes the tendency of acting in a thoughtful and organised way.
- **Agreeableness:** This dimension determines the extent to which an individual is compassionate and cooperative towards others. It includes attributes such as altruism, trust, and kindness.

Different survey instruments, such as the International Personality Item Pool (IPIP) [12], enable the measurement of the Big Five personality traits. In this regard, the survey participants are confronted with statements describing different facets of the five dimensions. Using such questionnaires, personality traits and different items related to social media usage have been investigated in prior work. According to Wehrli [33], for instance, conscientiousness negatively effects activity in a social networking site while neuroticism positively influences activity. Other researchers found a positive relationship between extraversion and the number of friends in the online social network [1, 26].

Compared to the traditional approach of using survey instruments, author profiling enables the prediction of different author traits, such as gender or personality [9], based on textual data. In this regard, Estival et al. [9] derive psychometric traits from email data combining different machine learning algorithms. Argamon et al. [2] predict an author's gender, age, native language, and personality based on blog data. Using data obtained from Twitter, Golbeck et al. [10] predict personality traits utilising metrics characterising user activity, such as number of followers, and by performing linguistic analyses. Furthermore, Kosinski et al. [19] infer psychometrics of Facebook users by analysing "Facebook Likes".

The cited exemplary studies indicate personality traits to be a relevant topic in social media research. The application of NLP to analyse ESN messages, e.g. in order to derive personality traits, is not addressed in prior work.

In this regard, the analysis of ESN messages might pose an even greater challenge for deriving psychometrics than doing such analyses in public online social spaces since interactions on ESN take place in a business context. Hence, the generated posts may turn out to be similar in terms of content and style and thus, might be unsuitable for the distinguishing different users.

3   Methodology

3.1   Overview of the Case and Natural Language Processing Service

This study is carried out in cooperation with the Australian partnership of Deloitte Touche Tohmatsu. Deloitte Australia has 6,000 employees located in 14 offices in Australia and provides audit, economics, financial advisory, human capital, tax, and technology services. Deloitte has used an ESN since 2008. The ESN is a browser-based platform that offers a company-wide newsfeed, allows users to create a profile, features public and private groups, the sharing of updates and files as well as communicating with others by commenting on their updates or the writing of private messages.

In this study, we used IBM's Watson Personality Insights service [14] to perform linguistic analyses on text corpuses derived from Deloitte's ESN. The Personality Insights service includes three models, i.e. the *Big Five* personality characteristics, as well as the *Needs* and *Values* of an individual [15]. Focusing on the extraction of psychometrics from ESN messages, only the results obtained for the Big Five personality characteristics are of interest for our analysis. In this regard, the service uses the coefficients reported by Yarkoni [34], who inferred personality characteristics, i.e. Big Five scores, from blogs. The coefficients in Yarkoni [34] were derived by comparing personality scores obtained from survey data with the category scores of the Linguistic Inquiry and Word Count (LIWC) that were determined by analysing text written by more than 500 individuals. According to IBM [15], the Personality Insights service requires at least 3,500 words that are written by an individual to produce a portrait with meaningful results.

3.2   Preprocessing and Dataset

Having exported the data from the ESN back end for the years 2012 to 2015, the corresponding .csv file was imported into a database. We then identified the number of messages posted to the ESN by each user and selected those users who had written at least 30,000 characters, i.e. 4,000 to 5,000 words, per year. The only years with enough users with a sufficient number of words were 2013, 2014, and 2015. Since our data analysis includes a comparison of a user's psychometrics *over time* (cf. Sect. 4.2), a user was further required to have written a sufficient number of words in at least two subsequent years. While 40 users meet this requirement for the comparison of the psychometrics obtained in the years 2013 and 2014, 54 users can be identified for our comparison of the psychometrics between the years 2014 and 2015. 26 users had written enough words in 2013, 2014, and 2015 which facilitates the analysis of the obtained psychometrics over a period of three subsequent years.

For the three years, we identified 168 texts corpuses that belong to 72 unique users.

For users who had written more than 9,000 words in a year, we randomly selected posts to limit the text analysed to around 9,000 words. We then called the IBM Bluemix Personality Insights API using a C# program to analyse the 168 individual ESN text corpuses created in the years under consideration. The IBM Personality Insights service returns the psychometrics in JSON format.

4 Data Analysis and Findings

4.1 Discriminability of Psychometrics

As a first step, we determine whether the text posted to the ESN provides enough psychometric differentiation to distinguish users. Assuming that the users in our sample show different personality traits to different extents, the psychometrics derived from the ESN should be discriminable, too.

The analyses were performed using the statistical tool R [28]. For the visual inspection of the distribution of the resulting psychometrics, box plots for each year were created (see Fig. 1).

Each personality metric p is scaled in an interval $p \in [0; 1]$. As shown in the box plots, the traits *extraversion* (Ex) and *agreeableness* (A) are well distributed within this possible value range. Values for the dimension *openness* (O) only range between 0.5 and 1. The reason for that might be due to our sampling criteria, i.e. the users being required to have written a relatively high number of words, and thus, a relatively high number of ESN messages. A tendency to post messages frequently might be connected with a higher score for *openness*. Table 1 illustrates the descriptive statistics of each psychometric dimension.

The standard deviations of the individual dimensions range between 0.11 and 0.25. Considering the box plots, the distributions for *openness, emotional range*

Table 1. Descriptive statistics of predicted psychometrics

Year	2013				2014				2015			
	∅	SD	MIN	MAX	∅	SD	MIN	MAX	∅	SD	MIN	MAX
Agreeableness	0.44	0.24	0.02	0.93	0.43	0.25	0.01	0.92	0.51	0.25	0.02	0.97
Conscientiousness	0.65	0.15	0.30	0.93	0.65	0.15	0.24	0.97	0.69	0.15	0.31	0.96
Emotional range	0.31	0.14	0.05	0.63	0.31	0.14	0.05	0.66	0.26	0.14	0.02	0.65
Extraversion	0.39	0.20	0.03	0.92	0.39	0.21	0.02	0.91	0.46	0.21	0.05	0.92
Openness	0.82	0.11	0.48	1.00	0.85	0.11	0.58	1.00	0.80	0.11	0.47	1.00

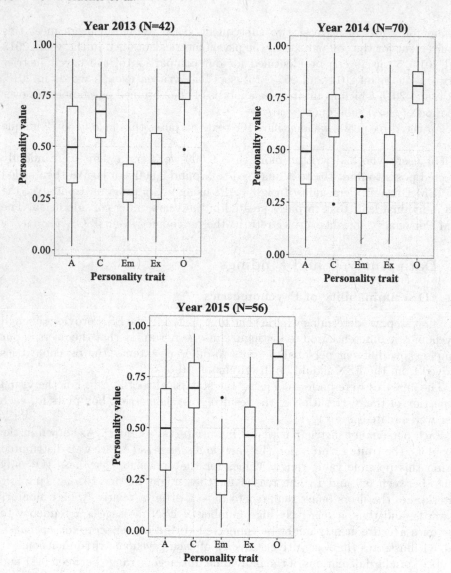

Fig. 1. Box plots showing the distribution of psychometric features per year

(Em), and *conscientiousness* (C) are skewed. Based on the descriptive statistics in Table 1, especially *agreeableness* and *extraversion* would be expected to be good differentiators as both show large standard deviations.

Apart from the analysis of the distributions of the psychometric values, the distances between the users were calculated and the resulting standard deviations

Table 2. Mean and standard deviation of the distances between all users per year

Distance metric	2013	2014	2015
Agreeableness	0.29 ± 0.20	0.27 ± 0.19	0.30 ± 0.22
Conscientiousness	0.16 ± 0.12	0.18 ± 0.13	0.17 ± 0.12
Emotional range	0.16 ± 0.12	0.15 ± 0.12	0.14 ± 0.11
Extraversion	0.25 ± 0.18	0.23 ± 0.17	0.26 ± 0.18
Openness	0.12 ± 0.09	0.12 ± 0.09	0.14 ± 0.11
All psychometrics	0.51 ± 0.25	0.49 ± 0.24	0.53 ± 0.26

were examined. To this end, the distances between one user u_i and all other users u_j were calculated by utilising the Euclidean distance d_2:

$$d_2(u_i, u_j) = \sqrt{\sum_{p=k}^{l} (u_{i,p} - u_{j,p})^2} \tag{1}$$

The distances were calculated per user and per year for the individual psychometric dimensions ($k = l$, $k \in [1; 5]$), as well as considering all five dimensions ($k = 1, l = 5$) (Table 2).

The standard deviations of the individual dimensions range between a minimum value of 0.09 and a maximum of 0.22, and the standard deviation of the combined psychometric dimensions ranges between 0.24 and 0.26. The standard deviations of the distances indicate the combined dimensions to have a stronger discriminative power than the individual five dimensions. In line with the information depicted in Fig. 1 and Table 1, *agreeableness* and *extraversion* show large standard deviations. Hence, besides the combined personality dimensions, these dimensions might be particularly useful for differentiating ESN users.

4.2 Stability of Psychometrics

As a second step, we analyse the stability of the psychometrics derived for the 72 users over time. For 46 of those 72 users, we were able to obtain the birth year from Deloitte's HR system. According to the provided information, the average year of birth of those users is 1975. Since the users in the sample are older than 30 years, their psychometrics can be expected to remain stable over time [7, 24]. Thus, a high degree of similarity between the predicted personality traits of individual users in the different years could be considered as an indicator of the correctness of the classification.

To determine the similarity of the derived psychometrics over time, a distance matrix D for all users u_i to all other users u_j considering all five personality dimensions p was calculated using the Euclidean distance d_2 as well as the following Cosine distance d_{cosine}:

$$d_{cosine}(u_i, u_j) = 1 - cos(\theta) = \frac{\sum_{p=1}^{5} u_{i,p} u_{j,p}}{\sqrt{\sum_{p=1}^{5} u_{i,p}^2} \sqrt{\sum_{p=1}^{5} u_{j,p}^2}} \tag{2}$$

The distance matrices were calculated for the time spans of 2013 to 2014, 2014 to 2015, and 2013 to 2015, using all five personality dimensions. Based on the distance matrices, distance rankings R were derived for each user $u_{i,t}$ in a year t to all users $u_{i,t+\delta t}$ in a following year $t+\delta t$. The rankings R_i were calculated using the formula $R_i = u_{i,t+\delta t} - u_{i,t}$. Based on the assumption that personality traits remain stable in the considered years, the psychometrics should be invariant over time and therefore a user u_i at a time t should be the closest one to himself at a following point in time $t + \delta t$. To determine the rank difference of a user to himself between two points in time, we calculated the self-rank difference RD_i for a user u_i by the formula: $RD_i = R_{i,t+\delta t} - R_{i,t} - 1$. Rank charts illustrate the stability of the users' personalities based on the rank differences (Fig. 2).

On the horizontal axis of the lift chart, all possible self-rank differences are indicated within a range of $[0, max(users)]$. The vertical axis indicates the cumulative number of differences per self-rank difference. In case of a perfect classification, all users have a self-rank difference of 1 resulting in a vertical line at point 0. In the worst case, all users have a maximum distance to each other resulting in a vertical line at the maximum distance step. In case of a random psychometrics generation, we expect the result being close to the diagonal line. The area between the random line and the cumulative rank count line provides a quantitative metric that aggregates the self-rank distances of all users for the years being compared. The greater the value of this metric, the better the stability of the psychometric profile. The lift l is calculated by:

$$l = \frac{v_{distance} - v_{Random} * 100\%}{\sum v_{Rlength} v_R} \tag{3}$$

v_R being the vector representing a random selection having the values from $[0, max(users)]$, and $v_{Rlength}$ being the vector comprising the number of users ($=max(users)$).

The results for two distance metrics are illustrated in Table 3. Overall, the uplift can be interpreted as high, which implicates the personality dimensions to show a stable behaviour. Regarding the distance metrics, the Euclidean distance shows a slightly better performance.

Table 3. Uplift per year and distance metric

Distance metric	2013–14	2014–15	2013–15
d_2	83.28%	80.32%	73.02%
d_{cosine}	81.88%	80.58%	71.69%

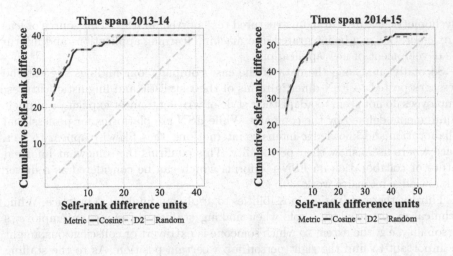

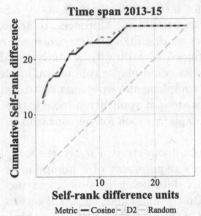

Fig. 2. Lift charts indicating the stability of the intra-person psychometrics

5 Discussion and Conclusion

In this paper, we explored the discriminability of psychometrics derived from messages posted to the ESN of an Australian professional services firm. We employed the IBM Personality Insights service, a professional NLP application, to derive psychometrics according to the Big Five personality characteristics. To our best knowledge, this is the first study investigating psychometrics in ESN using the Personality Insights service [16]. Comparing the psychometrics derived for individual users with those of other users, we found that the text posted to an ESN facilitates the detection of distinguishable personality profiles. Also, our analysis indicates these profiles to remain stable from year to year.

Our study has implications for theory and practice. Firstly, the IBM Personality Insights service allows researchers and practitioners to easily extract psychometric features from unstructured text posted on ESN. This source of feature generation can be integrated into machine learning applications and inform the development of new applications.

Secondly, analysing the data of the case company, our findings suggest the messages posted to ESN differ in terms of their stylistic and linguistic features. Employees do not seem to adapt their style of writing to meet explicit or implicit requirements defined by the company. While ESN are platforms for professional collaboration and knowledge-intensive interactions, they likewise appear to be a space where users show their personality. This confirms the somewhat informal nature of collaboration on ESN platforms which can be considered as a driver of knowledge-intensive work [30].

Thirdly, there are various possibilities to apply our findings in practice. While technical expertise plays a role when making staffing decisions, an employee's personality, e.g. the extent to which someone is extravert or conscientious, might be important to find the right person for a certain position. As to the staffing of top management teams, for instance, Colbert et al. [8] advise to select individuals who are high in conscientiousness. Moreover, to advance organisational knowledge sharing, employees scoring high on agreeableness, openness and conscientiousness should be retained according to a study by Matzler et al. [22]. Also, personality characteristics could play a role in staffing teams, for instance to select team members with complementary personality traits in order to achieve a balanced team [20]. Further areas of application include talent management or mentoring, where one might explicitly look for persons who score high on certain dimensions.

We acknowledge limitations in our study. Firstly, the sample size is relatively small due to the NLP service's requirement of a minimum of 3,500 words. Secondly, our conclusion of ESN data being feasible to extract psychometrics is based on only two aspects. On the one hand, the NLP service is able to extract diverse personality profiles. On the other hand, these profiles remain stable over time. Yet, the IBM Personality Insights service has not yet been tested with data obtained from ESN. Thus, we currently lack a benchmark to test the validity of the extracted psychometrics and are not able to estimate the fit of the generated personality profiles.

We will address these limitations in the continuation of this research project. As a first step, we will ask the employees for whom we were able to derive psychometrics based on their contributions to the ESN to participate in a Big Five questionnaire. We will then be able to compare the results obtained from the questionnaire with the automatically extracted psychometrics. Beyond the exploratory analyses and descriptive statistics presented in this paper, such analyses facilitate evaluating the discriminative power of psychometrics derived from ESN. We also plan to investigate relationships between a user's personality profile and their usage patterns on the ESN, e.g. the extent to which users start new conversations or reply to existing ones. If we find significant relationships, it might be possible to infer personality traits based on information that is easier to obtain and to analyse than the textual content created by a user.

References

1. Amichai-Hamburger, Y., Vinitzky, G.: Social network use and personality. Comput. Human Behav. **26**, 1289–1295 (2010)
2. Argamon, S., Koppel, M., Pennebaker, J.W., Schler, J.: Automatically profiling the author of an anonymous text. Commun. ACM **52**, 119–123 (2009)
3. Behrendt, S., Richter, A., Trier, M.: Mixed methods analysis of enterprise social networks. Comput. Netw. **75**, 560–577 (2014)
4. Berger, K., Klier, J., Klier, M., Richter, A.: "Who is Key..?" - Characterizing value adding users in enterprise social networks. In: Proceedings of the European Conference on Information Systems, Tel Aviv, Israel (2014)
5. Burns, M.J., Kotval, X.P.: Questions about questions: investigating how knowledge workers ask and answer questions. Bell Labs Tech. J. **17**, 43–61 (2013)
6. Calmbach, L., Bodendorf, F.: The impact of personality traits on the individual preference of e-learning tools. In: 2014 Annual SRII Global Conference, pp. 139–143. IEEE (2014)
7. Cobb-Clark, D.A., Schurer, S.: The stability of big-five personality traits. Econ. Lett. **115**, 11–15 (2012)
8. Colbert, A.E., Barrick, M.R., Bradley, B.H.: Personality and leadership composition in top management teams: implications for organizational effectiveness. Pers. Psychol. **67**, 351–387 (2014)
9. Estival, D., Gaustad, T., Hutchinson, B., Pham, S.B., Radford, W.: Author profiling for English emails. In: Proceedings of the 10th Conference of the Pacific Association for Computational Linguistics, pp. 263–272 (2007)
10. Golbeck, J., Robles, C., Edmondson, M., Turner, K.: Predicting personality from Twitter. In: 2011 IEEE Third International Conference on Privacy, Security, Risk and Trust and 2011 IEEE Third International Conference on Social Computing. IEEE (2011)
11. Goldberg, L.R.: The structure of phenotypic personality traits. Am. Psychol. **48**, 26–34 (1993)
12. Goldberg, L.R., Johnson, J.A., Eber, H.W., Hogan, R., Ashton, M.C., Cloninger, C.R., Gough, H.G.: The international personality item pool and the future of public-domain personality measures. J. Res. Pers. **40**, 84–96 (2006)
13. Holtzblatt, L., Drury, J., Weiss, D.: Evaluating the uses and benefits of an enterprise social media platform. J. Soc. Media. Organ. **1**, 1–2 (2013)
14. IBM: Personality Insights (2015). http://www.ibm.com/smarterplanet/us/en/ibmwatson/developercloud/personality-insights.html
15. IBM: Personality Insights - Overview (2016). https://www.ibm.com/smarter planet/us/en/ibmwatson/developercloud/doc/personality-insights/overview.shtml
16. IBM: Personality Insights - The science behind the service (2016). http://www.ibm.com/smarterplanet/us/en/ibmwatson/developercloud/doc/personality-insights/science.shtml
17. Kaplan, A.M., Haenlein, M.: Users of the world, unite! the challenges and opportunities of social media. Bus. Horiz. **53**, 59–68 (2010)
18. Kichuk, S.L., Wiesner, W.H.: The big five personality factors and team performance: implications for selecting successful product design teams. J. Eng. Technol. Manage. **14**, 195–221 (1997)
19. Kosinski, M., Stillwell, D., Graepel, T.: Private traits and attributes are predictable from digital records of human behavior. In: Proceedings of the National Academy of Sciences, pp. 5802–5805 (2013)

20. LePine, J.A., Buckman, B.R., Crawford, E.R., Methot, J.R.: A review of research on personality in teams: accounting for pathways spanning levels of theory and analysis. Hum. Resour. Manage. Rev. **21**, 311–330 (2011)

21. Leonardi, P.M., Huysman, M., Steinfield, C.W.: Enterprise social media: definition, history, and prospects for the study of social technologies in organizations. J. Comput. Commun. **19**, 1–19 (2013)

22. Matzler, K., Renzl, B., Müller, J., Herting, S., Mooradian, T.A.: Personality traits and knowledge sharing. J. Econ. Psychol. **29**, 301–313 (2008)

23. McAfee, A., Brynjolfsson, E.: Big data: the management revolution. Harv. Bus. Rev. **90**, 60–68 (2012)

24. McCrae, R.R., Costa, P.T.: Personality in Adulthood. Guilford Press, New York (1990)

25. McCrae, R.R., John, O.P.: An introduction to the five-factor model and its applications. J. Pers. **60**, 175–215 (1992)

26. Moore, K., McElroy, J.C.: The influence of personality on Facebook usage, wall postings, and regret. Comput. Human Behav. **28**, 267–274 (2012)

27. Neuman, G.A., Wagner, S.H., Christiansen, N.D.: The relationship between work-team personality composition and the job performance of teams. Gr. Organ. Manage. **24**, 28–45 (1999)

28. R Core Team. R: A language and environment for statistical computing. R Foundation for Statistical Computing, Vienna (2015)

29. Richter, A., Riemer, K.: The contextual nature of enterprise social networking: a multi case study comparison. In: Proceedings of the European Conference on Information Systems, Utrecht, Netherlands (2013)

30. Riemer, K., Scifleet, P.: Enterprise social networking in knowledge-intensive work practices: a case study in a professional service firm. In: 23rd Australasian Conference on Information Systems (2012)

31. Thom, J., Helsley, S.Y., Matthews, T.L., Daly, E., Millen, D.: What are you working on? Status message Q&A in an enterprise SNS. In: Bødker, S., Bouvin, N.O., Wulf, V., Ciolfi, L., Lutters, W. (eds.) ECSCW 2011: Proceedings of the 12th European Conference on Computer Supported Cooperative Work, pp 313–332. Springer, London (2011). doi:10.1007/978-0-85729-913-0_17

32. Viol, J., Bernsmann, R., Riemer, K.: Behavioural dimensions for discovering knowledge actor roles utilising enterprise social network metrics. In: 26th Australasian Conference on Information Systems (2015)

33. Wehrli, S.: Personality on Social Network Sites: An Application of the Five Factor Model. ETH Zurich Sociology Working Paper. ETH Zurich, Zurich (2008)

34. Yarkoni, Y.: Personality in 100,000 words: a large-scale analysis of personality and word use among bloggers. J. Res. Pers. **44**, 363–373 (2010)

A Framework for Describing Big Data Projects

Jeffrey Saltz[⊠], Ivan Shamshurin, and Colin Connors

Syracuse University, Syracuse, NY, USA
{jsaltz, ishamshu, cpconnor}@syr.edu

Abstract. With the ability to collect, store and analyze an ever-growing diversity of data generated with ever-increasing frequency, Big Data is a rapidly growing field. While tremendous strides have been made in the algorithms and technologies that are used to perform the analytics, much less has been done to determine how the team should work together to do a Big Data project. Our research reports on a set of case studies, where researchers were embedded within Big Data teams. Since project methodologies will likely depend on the attributes of a Big Data effort, we focus our analysis on defining a framework to describe a Big Data project. We then use this framework to describe the organizations we studied and some of the socio-technical challenges linked to these newly defined project characteristics.

Keywords: Big data · Data science · Project management · Process methodology

1 Introduction

Big Data is an emerging field that combines expertise across a range of domains, including software development, data management and statistics. A Big Data project is one that typically uses statistical and machine-learning techniques on large volumes of unstructured and/or structured data generated by systems, people, sensors or digital traces of information from people. This work is done in a distributed computing environment with a goal to identify correlations and causal relationships, classify and predict events, identify patterns and anomalies, and infer probabilities, interest and sentiment [1].

As a new field, much has been written about the use of Big Data algorithms that can generate useful results. In fact, many in the field, such as Chen [2], believe that Big Data research needs to continue to develop advanced analytics, and hence, not surprisingly, Big Data research typically has focused on improving data models and algorithms, but not on using a standard approach to execute projects [3].

However, leveraging Big Data within a business organizational context involves additional challenges beyond the analytical challenges noted by Chen. These challenges include items such as understanding what data might be available, what might be the goals of the effort, engaging the proper extended team, coordinating that extended team and establishing realistic project timelines [4]. Demonstrating the difficulty in executing big data projects, Kelly and Kaskade [5] surveyed 300 companies, and reported that "55% of data projects don't get completed, and many others fall short

© Springer International Publishing AG 2017
W. Abramowicz et al. (Eds.): BIS 2016 Workshops, LNBIP 263, pp. 183–195, 2017.
DOI: 10.1007/978-3-319-52464-1_17

of their objectives". While there are many reasons a project might not get completed, with a robust team-based process methodology, one would expect many of those reasons to be identified prior to the start of the project, or to be mitigated via some aspect of the project execution and/or coordination methodology.

In other words, organizations doing Big Data need more than just the knowledge of how to do the analytics. An additional key component required for a company to be able to optimally deploy and exploit big data as part of their overall competitive strategy is the ability for an organization to be able to project manage the big data effort. As briefly mentioned above, and discussed in more depth in the literature review, not much has been written on this topic (i.e., how organizations should manage a Big Data project). Hence the goal of this research is to improve an organization's ability to execute Big Data projects.

Since it has been proposed that multiple process methodologies are needed, based on the project's attributes [3], our initial focus is to better understand how to describe Big Data projects from a sociotechnical team-focused perspective (i.e., beyond just a data perspective). It is hoped that this categorization framework will enable a better understanding of how to manage different types of Big Data efforts. Specifically, we focused on the following research questions:

RQ1: What are the key characteristics that can best describe Big Data projects?
RQ2: Does a Big Data project framework help inform how organizations should manage Big Data projects and leverage Big Data analytics?

To address our research questions, we conducted a series of case studies on teams doing Big Data projects and then generalized our observations into a Big Data project categorization framework.

This rest of this paper first provides a review of literature related to these questions. Next, our study of eight Big Data teams is described, as are the methods used for collecting and analyzing the data. This is followed our findings, which answers our research questions. The final section synthesizes our findings by using the framework to discuss how the identified big data project characteristics can help identify likely project challenges as well as by using the framework to compare big data projects with software development projects, whose project management methods have been well documented in the literature.

2 Literature Review

As previously noted, there has not been much research on the characteristics of Big Data projects nor on the project management of a Big Data team. However, there has been some research, which is described below.

2.1 The Need for a Big Data Project Management Process

We know very little about how Big Data efforts can be most effectively coordinated to ensure organizational success [6]. Of the articles that do focus on the process organizations have used to perform Big Data projects, most report a low level of process maturity [1, 7]. Perhaps not surprisingly, it has been reported that an improved process model would result in higher quality outcomes [8] and at least some managers are open to improving their process methodology, but might not think of doing it unless prompted [7].

Furthermore, studies have shown that there has been a biased emphasis on the technical issues, such as the tools and systems used, which has limited the ability an organization to realize the full potential of analytic efforts [9]. In addition, it has been observed that most Big Data projects are managed in an ad hoc fashion, that is, at a low level of process maturity [10]. Indeed, it has been argued that Big Data projects need to focus on people, process and technology [11, 12] and that task coordination is the main challenge for data projects [6]. Perhaps because of this, researchers have begun to address the need for a team-based data science process methodology via case studies to understand effective practices and success criteria [1, 7, 11]. However, the need for more guidance is recognized; e.g., a recent Gartner Consulting report advocates for more careful management of analysis processes, though a specific methodology is not identified [13].

2.2   Characteristics of Data Projects

Big Data projects have typically been described via the '4 Vs' [14, 15]. Specifically, the components of the data context include *volume* (size of data to be analyzed - does the team need to use 'big data' techniques), *variety* (number of sources and type of data - structured, unstructured or both), *velocity* (speed of data collected/generated that needs to be analyzed) and v*eracity* (the trustworthiness of the data).

However, beyond the '4 Vs' of Big Data, there has been little work exploring the appropriate dimensions that could be used to categorize Big Data projects. Two recent case studies [1, 7] have pointed out that one way to characterize a project might be via the type of problem that a Big Data team is trying to solve. Beyond that, one might try to apply Bystron and Jarvelin's [16] classification (clarity and difficulty of the project), but one could argue that most Big Data projects are complex (i.e. more difficult) an ambiguous (i.e. less clear). So complexity and ambiguity do not cover the diversity of Big Data projects.

Understanding how to describe Big Data projects is important because there likely needs to be multiple process methodologies based on the project attributes [3]. Hence, a key goal of this research is to provide a structured way to describe the key dimensions/attributes of a Big Data project, so that future efforts can use this structured framework to determine what type of project methodology works best for the different types of Big Data projects or what type of challenges might be encountered with different types of Big Data projects.

2.3   Comparison with Other Technical Project Domains

While there are certainly parallels to other types of technical projects such as software development, Saltz [4] noted that there are differences as compared to these other types of projects (such as software development), and that this suggests that the desired organizational processes could be different than existing process methodologies used in domains such as software development. For example, these projects often have highly uncertain inputs into the project (e.g., what data might be relevant) as well as highly uncertain outcomes (i.e., will there be insight derived from analyzing the data). Furthermore, there is often the challenge of trying to determine that the data to be analyzed has no issues (such as a mismatching of timing or data cleaning issues) or determining what is the acceptable level of data quality, which is often dependent on the use of the data [17]. This challenge and ambiguity has no parallel in a software project.

In a different example, when comparing the challenges encountered by Big Data teams to more traditional quantitative research efforts (such as an individual researcher analyzing data generated from an experiment), one can see that while both types of projects have uncertainty in generating useful results, the efforts also have differences such as the big data project requiring a larger team (ex. the IT requirements needed to do the analysis, the larger number of distributed people that need to be coordinated) and that the big data project typical has the challenge of validating/describing the results to a broader, more diverse audience.

Taken together, this suggests that the process used to manage a Big Data project might be different from the process used to manage other projects, such as software development efforts. In any event, even if one argued that Big Data projects were similar to other information systems projects, there is currently a clear lack of adoption of mature team process methodology for Big Data projects.

2.4   Executing Big Data Projects

Current descriptions of how to do a Big Data project generally adopt a task-focused approach, conveying the techniques required to analyze data. For example, Jagadish et al. [18] describe a process that includes acquisition, information extraction and cleaning, data integration, modeling, analysis, interpretation and deployment. Guo [19] approaches the problem from a slightly different perspective and provides a Big Data Workflow framework. Guo's workflow defines several high-level phases such as Preparation, Analysis, Reflection, and Dissemination, with each phase having a specific series of steps that can be repeated within that phase in an iterative analysis. These views on how to do Big Data have not materially evolved in the past twenty years. For example, the *CRISP-DM* (*Cross Industry Standard Process for Data Mining*) standard, established in the 1990s, is a data mining process model for data mining experts and provides a similar step-by-step process description [20]. The model mentions six high-level phases: business understanding, data understanding, data preparation, modeling, evaluation, and deployment. While these various models differ in details, at a high level they are broadly similar.

In terms of the team context, a limitation of prior discussions of the step-by-step process for doing data projects is that the processes have been defined with the implicit assumption that one person (or at most a compact group) are doing the work. Specifically, a common way to describe the skills needed for data analysis is based on Conway's [21] three key skillsets: coding/hacking (data transformation, data storage, data visualization), statistics (machine learning, traditional statistics, data analysis techniques) and domain knowledge. These roles are consistent with a narrowly focused step-by-step single person approach.

While the use of a step-by-step description of Big Data provides some understanding of the tasks involved, it does not provide much guidance about the roles required within a Big Data team [4]. For example, a big part of the challenge to the data scientist lies in integrating the data from various systems, adding additional data from other sources, and coordinating with other teams within the organization [22]. Similarly, while Espinosa and Armour [6] agree with the typical Big Data steps, as previously mentioned, they note that the main challenge is task coordination. Unfortunately, beyond the skills needed to execute the 'step by step' process, not much has been written with respect to how to execute a Big Data project and coordinate a Big Data team.

3 Methods

To better understand the characteristics of Big Data projects, we studied eight Big Data teams, all doing Big Data within an organizational context (as opposed to a research context). Rather than focus on the analytics used by each of the teams, the observations and interviews focused on how to characterize the projects. We also focused on how the project characteristics related to the challenges the teams encountered in executing their projects.

The organizations were selected to ensure diversity across a number of theoretically salient factors [23]. First, since the 4 V's is the current approach to describe data projects, we selected organizations across a range of Volume, Velocity, Variety and Veracity. We then added the size of the organization as the final factor, in that organizational culture and team processes can vary based on the size of the organization. Table 1 provides an overview of the teams in our study, and shows the diversity across the salient factors. Note that organizations 2 & 5 were not-for-profit (the others were for-profit companies). Hence, while this study was limited to eight organizations, by getting a cross sampling across the salient factors, the results serve as a foundation upon which one can gain an understanding of the characteristics of Big Data projects and provides enough information to generate interesting and useful analysis [24].

Consistent with Eisenhardt [23], multiple data collections methods were employed. For all eight organizations, an initial semi-structured interview was performed, with either a manager or senior data scientist within that organization. For five of the organizations, a researcher was then embedded within the team, for a minimum of 10 weeks. This enabled further data to be collected via in-depth field observations. For the five organizations that had an embedded researcher, the researcher only directly observed the team members within that geographical location (many of the organizations had

Table 1. Overview of organizations participating in the study.

	Organization ID							
	1	2	3	4	5	6	7	8
Variety (Structured, Unstructured, Both)	B	S	S	S	S	B	U	S
Volume (TB/GB)	T	G	T	G	G	T	G	G
Velocity (High, Medium, Low)	M	L	H	M	L	H	L	H
Veracity (Clean, Messy)	M	C	M	M	C	M	M	C
Size of org (Small, Med, Large)	M	M	L	L	M	L	S	S
Participated in 10-week field study	Y	Y	Y	N	N	Y	N	Y

distributed virtual teams). Hence, the number of people directly observed ranged from 2 to 10, even though the full teams were larger in size. The information analyzed included researcher observations, informal discussions, semi-structured interviews and project artifacts (emails, documents, etc.). These artifacts provided the researchers a view across the team, beyond the members located in their embedded location.

To analyze the data, a within-case analysis was first performed for each organization and then cross-case patterns were then investigated (Eisenhardt 1989). The data was collected and analyzed in an iterative fashion. That is to say, to refine our understanding of each of the teams, additional semi-structured interviews occurred during the within-case analysis. This was especially true for the three teams that did not have an embedded researcher. In addition, after the fact researcher reflection (from their time within the embedded team) was also leveraged.

4   Findings

As previously mentioned in our literary review, one common approach to describe a project is with respect to the data to be analyzed (i.e. the '4 Vs' of data). However, in addition to describing the project in terms of the data to be analyzed, we identified three additional dimensions (analytical, team and organizational) that help to describe a project. Based on our within-case and then cross-case analysis, these four categorizations of a Big Data project are described below and then, as shown in Table 2, used to describe the organizations within our study.

4.1   Data Context Project Characterization

In categorizing the data of a project, we continued to use the '4 Vs' of data. Specifically, the components of the data context include *volume* (size of data to be analyzed - does the team need to use 'big data' techniques), *variety* (number of sources and type of data - structured, unstructured or both), *velocity* (speed of data collected/generated that needs to be analyzed) and v*eracity* (the messiness and trustworthiness of the data). From a data perspective, these '4 Vs' seem to have accurately categorized our projects.

The data context (especially volume) had a direct impact on the project, such as the tools and technologies that were used for the project. This impact was seen for all the

Table 2. Applying the framework to the organizations in the study.

	Organization ID							
	1	2	3	4	5	6	7	8
Data context								
Variety (Structured, Unstructured, Both)	B	S	S	S	S	B	U	S
Volume (TB/GB)	T	G	T	G	G	T	G	G
Velocity (High, Medium, Low)	M	L	H	M	L	H	L	H
Veracity (Clean, Messy)	M	C	M	M	C	M	M	C
Analytical context								
Type of analysis (Testing, Generation, Both)	B	G	B	T	T	B	G	G
Compute intensity (Preprocess, Model, Both, Neither)	P	B	B	M	N	P	N	N
Criticality of timeliness (Yes, No)	Y	N	Y	N	N	Y	N	Y
Team context								
Size of team observed (# of people)	11	8	25	8	5	25	2	4
Virtuality of team (Is part of team virtual)	Y	Y	Y	Y	N	Y	N	N
Manager experience (Scientist, Manager, Developer)	S	S	M	M	M	M	D	M
Organizational context								
Size of org (Small, Med, Large)	M	M	L	L	M	L	S	S
Org culture - Process (Strong, Medium, Weak)	W	W	S	M	W	S	W	W
Org culture - ROI (Strong, Medium, Weak)	S	W	S	M	M	S	S	W
Total number of big data teams in org	3	5	15	5	1	12	1	1

organizations (note that while all groups considered themselves to be Big Data teams, not all of the projects leveraged 'Big Data' technologies). In a different example related to the data context, organization 3 had high velocity data sources. Because of this, they developed a specific Quality Assurance test suite that leveraged the fact that the data did not change substantially from day-to-day.

4.2 Analytical Context Project Characterization

The analytical context covers the analytics that are to be performed by the team, and includes the *type of analysis* (is the focus hypothesis generation – data generated research, or hypothesis testing – the analysis focuses on answering an already known question), the *computational intensity* (is the data preparation or model execution computational intensive) and the *criticality of timeliness* (do the analytics need to be executed within a specified timeframe).

For example, organization 1 was a smaller company that typically did two types of projects – more routine hypothesis testing and more exploratory hypothesis generation. However, the organization treated both types of efforts as exploratory, with a process based on the 'team getting together and doing the work'. After our field study, the team leader agreed with the suggestion to establish two different project management processes – one for the more routine hypothesis testing efforts and one for the more exploratory hypothesis generation data driven research efforts. On the other hand, organization 4 had several Big Data teams with most of their focus on hypothesis testing (where specific questions raised by their management team needed to be addressed). This significantly simplified their project management tasks (ex. task estimation).

4.3 Team Context Project Characterization

The characteristics of the team are another important component of how we can describe the project. These include the *project team size* (number of people on the project team), *virtuality of team* (how distributed and virtual is the composition of the team, including if the core/extended teams are part of the same organizational unit within organization) and *manager experience* (the manager will typically use a process that they had previously used – even if that is 'no process').

For example, in organization 4, the manager of the team was used to working in a strong project management environment. So, even though there was not an organizational culture to execute projects with any specific project management approach, this team followed their manager's project management methodology – a waterfall-like approach for the data collection and an iterative process for the data analysis. In a different example, organization 2 was focused on hypothesis generation, where the team leader's background as a researcher encouraged an open-ended data driven research environment. In yet a different situation, the virtual nature of a team, combined with a "just do it" approach often led to challenges, such as the challenge in obtaining IT resources (organizations 1 and 2).

4.4 Organizational Context Project Characterization

Finally, the organizational context had an influence on the teams. For example, a large organization can influence or dictate the process that the team can/should/needs to use. In addition, it can impact the challenges to be encountered (ex. getting the extended team involved was often a function of the organizational context). Specifically, the organizational characteristics include the *organization size* (the number of people working within the organization), the *total number of project teams* (are there many data project teams that can share best practices, or is it just one 'isolated' team), and *organizational culture – Process* (is there a focus on process within the organization). Note that the organizational culture also includes if the organization is business case driven via *organizational culture – ROI* (does the organization prioritize efforts based on return on investment - a 'business case').

For example, organization 3 was a large company that had a strong culture (ex. project management was done in a waterfall-like manner with all projects needing a proper business case) and many groups doing Big Data projects. Because of this strong culture, the team had a challenge in knowing, at the start of a project, what data was needed for the analysis (and then being able to justify that within a business case). Organization 7 also had a strong culture. Of particular relevance was their strong focus on ensuring all efforts were properly prioritized (not just Big Data projects, but all spending across the firm). In this case, the organizational context severely limited the Big Data analysis that was done, since it was impossible for the team to realistically document the value of the Big Data effort (since the effort was more of a data driven exploratory effort). In a related example, organization 5 knew the specific patterns of interest, but had a challenge justifying the allocation of resources (time and money) for the effort, since impact was hard to estimate prior to the launch of the project. As a result, the team's manager often felt understaffed with the value of the data not being fully appreciated (or leveraged).

In a very different example of organizational context, organization 6 had a strong culture supporting agile project management. So, the group, almost by default, started using an agile scrum-like process. However, after struggling with task estimation, the team started to use other project management approaches that did not require accurate task estimation.

Finally, organization 8 was focused on generating insight from the significant amount of data that was readily available. The culture of the organization was not strong with respect to project management or project justification. In fact, the culture allowed the team to do significant data driven research since there was a belief that there was "value in the data".

5   Discussion

In this section, we test the framework to understand it's potential usefulness. Specifically, the framework is leveraged to examine the linkage between big data project challenges and big data project characteristics. We then use the framework to compare and contrast Big Data projects with software development efforts. Finally, we close with current limitations, potential next steps and a summary of our findings.

5.1   Using the Framework to Identify Potential Project Challenges

In reviewing the framework, certain project characteristics seem to more greatly influence the challenges a team experiences when executing their Big Data project. Based on our field studies, the following is an initial view of some project challenges that might be found in some projects but not others.

Analytical Context - Type of Analysis: Teams doing more open-ended analysis (i.e., hypothesis generation) typically had challenges in estimating how long projects would take to complete, as compared to the more focused hypothesis testing type of efforts.

Team Context - Team Size and Virtuality: The larger the team, and more virtual it was, the greater the perceived need for a project methodology. Similarly, a team might not experience difficulties when the team is small, but as soon as it starts to grow, the perceived need for a methodology increases.

Organizational Context - Organizational Culture: There seems to be a clear impact on the project from the organization's culture. Specifically, only teams with a strong organizational culture on process typically had a repeatable methodology to execute their projects. The manager's background, especially for organizations without a strong culture, also seemed to highly influence how the team was organized.

Data Context - Volume of Data: As one would expect, the larger the volume of data, the greater the project depended on IT resources.

5.2   Project Attributes not Found to Predict Project Challenges

The results also suggest that some project attributes are not important in characterizing the project's process or identifying potential challenges. One such project characteristic is the project's domain. While this certainly could have an impact on the type of algorithms used within the project, it did not appear to be an important characteristic in terms of how the team worked together or of the potential project challenges. Another example of a characteristic was that was not important was if the project was a not-for-profit effort or a for-profit industry effort (the type of analysis was a better way to capture the type of effort required for the project).

5.3   Comparing Big Data Projects with Software Development Projects

Below, we use our newly developed framework of Big Data characteristics to compare software development projects to Big Data projects. This comparison shows the value of the framework, as it provides a way to easily compare these different domains. One can note that while there are many similarities, there are also many differences between software projects and Big Data projects.

Data Context: There is typically less ambiguity of the data needed for a software project. Furthermore, since there is often a large amount of data (volume and/or velocity) in Big Data efforts, storing, retrieving, cleaning and validating the cleansed data is non-trivial. While part of this can be thought of as the data architecture for a software project, the "4 Vs" are much more important for Big Data projects, as is the additional challenge of identifying appropriate data sources, evaluating those sources (e.g., quality, timeliness), capturing those data sources and trying to determine a methodology to ensure the data has no issues, such as mismatching of timing or data issues after cleaning.

Analytical Context: Compared to software projects, Big Data projects, especially big data projects that have a goal of hypothesis generation, are more experimental, in that the goals (insights to be generated) are not known in advance. Therefore, it is difficult for these projects to estimate potential value and also difficult to estimate task duration. Within software projects there might be questions about what is most useful or what is most user-friendly, it is, however, typically possible to conceptualize the software that will be built. Data projects, on the other hand, are often very different in that it is often unknown what relationship will exist in the data. In fact, it is often unknown if there are meaningful patterns in a specific data set.

Team Context: While software efforts typically do have IT Operational roles, Big Data projects typically have the added complexity with the division of accountability across data engineering, IT Operations, data scientists and software developers. This increase in the number of roles demonstrates a different set of skills that must be incorporated into the project, and likely increasing coordination challenges.

Organizational Context: Within a software development context, understanding the drivers in an ROI discussion have become readily available (ex. expected cost to implement a feature). However, within a Big Data project, the cost is sometimes hard to quantify, due to the exploratory nature of the activity.

5.4 Limitations and Next Steps

One key limitation of this effort was the small number of teams observed. Hence, one next step will be to observe (or survey) additional organizations to ensure that this framework is robust across Big Data teams. We will also explore the possibility of using the framework to cluster Big Data projects, in that perhaps there are only a couple kinds projects, which could be defined using our framework.

A different potential next step could be to evaluate and document different team process methodologies (i.e. project management methodologies) used by different Big Data teams, with a goal of determining which project attributes might best drive the selection of an appropriate Big Data process methodology.

5.5 Conclusion

In this paper, a set of key characteristics that can be used to describe Big Data projects was proposed (which addresses RQ1). This framework provides a consistent vocabulary to describe different Big Data projects and can help put context around some issues big data teams encounter (which addresses RQ2). Thus, this research advances the field's understanding of the different types of big data efforts and will thus aid organizations trying to leverage big data for competitive advantage. Specifically, using this framework will enable data scientists and project leaders (the data "practitioners") to more easily identify potential project challenges and factors that impact the effectiveness of big data projects.

Finally, it is interesting to note that a couple of managers that were observed during this research felt that one could not define a process for projects that are trying to find "value in the data". However, the fact that the process is open ended does not contradict the value of a process that improves coordination of team members and prioritizes work efforts. Thus future work efforts can leverage this framework to establish appropriate process methodologies, based in part, on the type of big data project being executed.

References

1. Das, M., Cui, R., Campbell, D., Agrawal, G., Ramnath, R.: Towards methods for systematic research on big data. In: IEEE International Conference on Big Data (2015)
2. Chen, H., Chiang, R.H., Storey, V.C.: Business intelligence and analytics: from big data to big impact. MIS Q. **36**(4), 1165–1188 (2012)
3. Ahangama, S., Poo, D.: Improving health analytic process through project, communication and knowledge management. In: The International Conference on Information Systems (2015)
4. Saltz, J.: The need for new processes, methodologies and tools to support big data teams and improve big data project effectiveness. In: 3rd IEEE International Conference on Big Data (2015)
5. Kelly, J., Kaskade, J.: CIOs & BIG DATA what your IT team wants you to know (2013). www.infochimps.com/resources/report-cios-big-data-what-your-it-team-wants-you-to-know-6/
6. Espinosa, J., Armour, F.: The big data analytics gold rush: a research framework for coordination and governance. In: Proceedings of Hawaii International Conference on System Sciences (2016)
7. Saltz, J., Shamshurin, I.: Exploring the process of doing big data via an ethnographic study of a media advertising company. In: 3rd IEEE International Conference on Big Data (2015)
8. Mariscal, G., Marban, O., Fernandez, C.: A survey of data mining and knowledge discovery process models and methodologies. Knowl. Eng. Rev. (2010)
9. Ransbotham, S., Kiron, D., Prentice, P.K.: Minding the analytics gap. MIT Sloan Manage. Rev. **56**(3), 62–68 (2015)
10. Bhardwaj, A., Bhattacherjee, S., Chavan, A., Deshpande, A., Elmore, A., Madden, S., Parameswaran, A.: DataHub: collaborative data science & dataset version management at scale. In: Biennial Conference on Innovative Data Systems Research (2015)
11. Gao, J., Koronios, A., Selle, S.: Towards a process view on critical success factors in big data analytics projects. In: 21st Americas' Conference on Information Systems (2015)
12. Grady, N., Underwood, M., Roy, A., Chang, W.: Big data: challenges, practices and technologies: NIST big data public working group workshop. In: IEEE International Conference on Big Data (2014)
13. Chandler, N., Oestreich, T.W.: Use analytic business processes to drive business performance (2015). https://www.gartner.com/doc/2994617
14. Beyer, M.: Gartner says solving 'big data' challenge involves more than just managing volumes of data (2011). http://www.gartner.com/newsroom/id/1731916. Accessed 28 Feb 2016
15. IBM: the four V's of big data (2013). http://www.ibmbigdatahub.com/infographic/four-vs-big-data. Accessed 22 Feb 2016
16. Bystrom, K., Jarvelin, K.: Task complexity affects information seeking and use. Inf. Process. Manage. **31**(2), 191–213 (1995)
17. Kaisler, S., Armour, F., Espinosa, J.A., Money, W.: Big data: issues and challenges moving forward. In: System Sciences (HICSS), 2013 44th Hawaii International Conference on System Sciences, pp. 995–1004 (2013)
18. Jagadish, H., Gehrke, J., Labrinidis, A., Papakonstantinou, Y., Patel, J.M., Ramakrishnan, R., Shahabi, C.: Big data and its technical challenges. Commun. ACM **57**(7), 86–94 (2014)
19. Guo, P.: Big data workflow: overview and challenges. BLOG@CACM (2013). http://cacm.acm.org/blogs/blog-cacm/169199-data-science-workflow-overview-and-challenges/fulltext

20. Shearer, C.: The CRISP-DM model: the new blueprint for data mining. J. Data Warehouse. **5**(4), 13–22 (2000)
21. Conway, D.: The big data venn diagram (2013). http://drewconway.com/zia/2013/3/26/the-data-science-venn-diagram
22. Stanton, J.M.: Introduction to data science (2013). https://ischool.syr.edu/media/documents/2012/3/DataScienceBook1_1.pdf. Accessed
23. Eisenhardt, K.: Building theories from case study research. Acad. Manag. Rev. **14**(4), 532–550 (1989)
24. Britos, P., Dieste, O., García-Martínez, R.: Requirements elicitation in data mining for business intelligence projects. In: Avison, D., Kasper, G.M., Pernici, B., Ramos, I., Roode, D. (eds.). ITIFIP, vol. 274, pp. 139–150Springer, Heidelberg (2008). doi:10.1007/978-0-387-09682-7-9_12

Sequential Anomaly Detection Techniques in Business Processes

Christian Linn$^{(\boxtimes)}$ and Dirk Werth

AWS-Institute for Digitized Products and Processes, Saarbrücken, Germany
{christian.linn,dirk.werth}@aws-institut.de

Abstract. Many companies use information systems to manage their business processes and thereby collect large amounts of transactional data. The analysis of this data offers the possibility of automated detection of anomalies, i.e. flaws and faults, in the execution of the process. The anomalies can be related not only to the sequence of executed activities but also to other dimensions like the organization or the person performing the respective activity. This paper discusses two approaches of detecting the different anomalies types using basic sequential analysis techniques. Besides the classical one-dimensional approach, a simple approach to use multiple dimensions of the process information in the sequential analysis is discussed and evaluated on a simulated artificial business process.

Keywords: Anomaly detection · Business process · Business analytics

1 Introduction

Nowadays many companies use software systems, so called Process Aware Information Systems (PAIS), to manage their internal business processes [1]. As a consequence, transactional data from each individual execution of a process can be logged and documented. The process data is recorded in event logs which typically contain information about the executed activities such as the type of the activity, the time at which an activity was executed and the organization or person who performed the task [2]. The availability of such event logs offers the opportunity for data driven analyses of business processes. A related research field using this data resource is process mining which adopted data mining techniques to extract process-related information and discover, verify or improve a process model [3]. Of increasing interest is the use of process data for the detection of anomalies, i.e. flaws and faults that happen during the process execution [4]. Especially in cases where the process is not strictly predefined by an existing model but allows some flexibility or exceptions in execution, anomaly detection can be helpful to identify or avoid situations which are potentially harmful for a company [5]. These anomalies can be of various types and appear in different parts of the process, e.g. in the sequence of the executed activities or in the organization unit that performs a certain task. Most of the existing anomaly detection techniques for business processes concentrates on the detection of anomalies in the sequence of the executed activities (e.g. in [6, 7]).

© Springer International Publishing AG 2017
W. Abramowicz et al. (Eds.): BIS 2016 Workshops, LNBIP 263, pp. 196–208, 2017.
DOI: 10.1007/978-3-319-52464-1_18

The following paper investigates basic sequential analysis techniques to detect anomalies in other dimensions of the process data. In addition a simple approach to use multiple dimensions of process information is presented and discussed. To demonstrate the concepts, an artificial process data set is simulated containing anomalies in the activity sequence as well as in the assignment of the acting persons that perform the activities. The performance of three sequential analysis techniques are compared to gain insights in the pros and cons of using the one- and multidimensional approaches.

The structure of the paper is as follows: First some special characteristics of anomalies in business processes are discussed followed by a summary of existing research relevant to this topic. Then the strategy of the presented research is outlined. The simulation of the artificial business process data set and the details of the detection techniques are presented in the next chapters. Then the results of the comparison between the different analysis approaches are discussed followed by an interpretation and a final conclusion.

2 Anomalies in Business Processes

Anomalies can be seen in the most general way as deviations from a defined normal behavior [8]. For business processes, the main characteristics of the anomaly detection problem is the sequential nature of the data. The transactional data that is saved in the event logs usually contains information about many executions of the same process. Throughout this paper a process execution is referred to as instance of a business process. Each process instance again consists of a set of activities, i.e. events or tasks that were performed during the execution. Each activity is usually related to a moment in time at which the activity was executed. Therefore each instance of a business process can be seen as a sequence of activities [9]. Typically, each activity can in addition be related to several dimensions of data, for example information about the person who performed the activity, the organization unit or the financial budget for an activity. Therefore, several types of anomalies are possible in business processes (e.g. in [5]):

- Anomalies can occur in the sequence of activities in a process instance. Thereby, either the full process instance or subparts of the sequence can be anomalous with respect to the rest of the data. In this context, anomalous instances are often executions that happen infrequent compared to the rest of the process executions.
- Anomalies could also be present in the time dimension of a process. Either the duration of a single activity or the time behavior of the activity sequence may be anomalous.
- Anomalies can occur in the organizations or persons that perform the activities. This can for example include cases where an activity is executed by the wrong person or where the sequence of involved organizations does not correspond to the normal case. Similar to the organization and persons, other data dimension of a business process could be anomalous, for example the financial budget related to an activity.

- In many cases, a business process is accompanied with some sort of data transfer, e.g. documents, products or any other information. Anomalies can also be irregularities in this data transfer.
- Finally, there can also be cases of multidimensional anomalies, where irregularities only occur in the combination of different dimensions. An example would be when a sequence is in principle allowed but must be accounted as anomaly in case it is executed by a certain person at a certain time.

3 Previous Work

Anomaly detection is a topic with high attention and research interest in various domains. Especially in areas like financial fraud detection [10], fraud detection in healthcare [11] and network intrusion detection [12], automated anomaly detection plays an important role.

For anomaly detection in business processes, most of the literature concentrates on the development of new detection techniques for sequential anomalies. The existing detection techniques can be divided into two categories: Methods using process mining techniques to discover an underlying process model and check its conformance with the data and methods that do not require a description of a process model but instead use generic data-mining techniques to investigate the anomalies.

A general concept of using process mining for anomaly detection was discussed in [2] where only normal process instances were used to discover a process model. Anomalies are detected by determining the conformance between this model and new test instances. In [6, 13, 14] the authors overcome the need for a training set with only normal instances and propose three algorithms that can dynamically detect anomalies, based on the assumption that anomalies happen only rarely compared to normal instances. Sarno et al. use an ontology-based process model discovered from a training sample and define multi-level association rules based on this to identify anomalies in the test sample [15].

In the second major approach for detecting business process anomalies, data mining techniques are used to detect anomalies without constructing a descriptive model. In [16] the authors train a local outlier factor (LOF) algorithm to predict anomalies in future process instances. Cabanillas et al. use a Support Vector Machine trained on classified input data for real-time monitoring of processes [17]. In [7] the authors propose an approach to use Variable Order Markov Models to detect sequential anomalies. A sequence is defined as anomalous if at least one activity of the sequence is predicted with a probability value lower than a certain threshold. Finally, the authors of [18] compare a windows based and a Markovian based detection technique to identify anomalous sequences.

Only few approaches exist which also address anomalies that are not solely related to the activity sequence. In [19] the authors propose a genetic based algorithm to discover a process model and combine this with a set of rules to characterize attacks on an organization performing the activities in a process. The authors of [20] discuss an approach to detect temporal anomalies by first constructing a process model that contains statistical information about the execution times of activities and second using a hypothesis test to identify anomalies in the activity durations. Quan et al. propose to transform process data in a multidimensional feature space and construct a hyper-sphere, similar to the concept of support vector classifiers [21]. The hyper-sphere is determined from a training set where they assume that normal behaving data is much more frequent than outliers. Each test data instance lying outside this hyper-sphere is then classified as anomaly. Accorsi et al. [22] present an approach for a forensic analysis of business process logs against data flow policies. It uses propagation graphs (directly labeled graphs extracted from event log) to capture data flow in process executions and verifies with external data flow rules whether a process executions is acceptable or not.

4 Research Strategy

The existing research on anomaly detection in business processes mainly concentrates on the development of new detection techniques for anomalies in the activity sequence. One possible way for this is to use sequential data mining techniques, as for example discussed in [23], to determine the anomalous sequences or subsequences. Anomalies in other data dimension like the execution time or the responsible organization are only rarely addressed. The aim of this paper is to discuss and compare different approaches of sequential anomaly detection to identify anomalies not only in the activity sequence but also in other dimensions of business process data. Two different approaches are investigated:

- A classical one-dimensional method where the sequence of a single process data dimension is used. The standard approach is to consider the activity sequence in order to identify anomalies in the process execution. But also with other data dimension, such as the involved organization unit or the responsible person, this approach can be useful and might even be sensitive to more types of anomalies. Anomalies in the one-dimensional sequence of the responsible persons could for example be related to either a wrong person executing an activity in a normal activity sequence, or to a wrong sequence of activities resulting in a wrong sequence of acting persons.
- A multidimensional approach that combines information from two or more data dimension of a process execution and is then used in a sequential analysis. An example would be to combine the activity information with the information of the related acting person. In this case, an activity performed by *"Person A"* would be treated as a different element in the sequential analysis than the same activity performed by *"Person B"*.

In order to demonstrate the different concepts and to obtain quantitative and comparable results for the different approaches, three basic sequential anomaly detection techniques are used and applied to a simulated artificial business process data. The simulated data represents a typical sales process and contains information about the process activities as well as the involved persons. Anomalies are included in the activity sequence, in the way persons are assigned to activities and in the combination of both.

5   Simulation of Business Process Data

In order to get a reliable understanding on how the anomaly detection techniques perform for business process data with the different type of anomalies, an artificial data set is simulated. This allows a quantitative evaluation of the methods, as the normal and anomalous instances are generated in a controlled way. Special techniques for simulating business process data, have for example been used in [7, 19]. These techniques allow the generation of random business process data based on user-defined input parameters [24]. Details on the characteristics of the simulated process and the incorporation of anomalies were however not discussed but can have a significant impact on the performance of the chosen detection technique.

For this paper a slightly different simulation approach was implemented to provide a maximum transparency in the way anomalies are generated. It is a simple probabilistic approach that allows a detailed definition of transitions between process activities and the type and frequency of the generated anomalies. As an example, a typical sales process in a company was simulated, including a low frequency of anomalous instances. Figure 1 shows a sketch of the simulated process. It consists of 13 different activities (boxes). The arrows in the diagram show the transitions between the activities that are allowed in a normal process execution, together with the chosen transition probabilities. Each instance starts with activity *"Create Order"*. The next activity in the instance is randomly chosen, respecting the allowed transition probabilities. This is repeated until the instance reaches the activity *"Close Order"*. For example, if the instance after the second step consists of the sequence *"Create Order"* - *"Check customer account"* then the next activity is at 20% probability *"Create new account"* and at 80% probability *"Send order confirmation"*. For each activity a set of responsible persons is defined who can execute the respective activity. A sketch of the relation between persons and activities is given in Fig. 2. The assignment of a specific person to an activity is done randomly for each process instance, following the defined probabilities given in Fig. 2. For example the activity *"Send Order Confirmation"* is in 80% of the cases performed by person *"Sales/B"* and in 20% of the cases by person *"Sales/C"*. Finally, when the state *"Close order"* is reached the instance is completed and the simulation of the individual process execution terminates.

In addition to the normal and allowed process instances, a low probability of anomalous executions is included. Three types of anomalies are simulated: anomalous transitions in the activity sequence, anomalies in the assignment of persons to a specific activity and combinations of both cases. Each step in the simulation of a process instance is with a probability of $p_{fail} = 0.1\%$ declared as anomaly. If a step is labeled as anomalous, in 50% of the cases an anomaly in the activity sequence is generated. The respective activity is randomly chosen from all but the allowed activities. As an example this would mean that after the sequence *"Create Order"* - *"Check customer account"* any activity could follow, except *"Create new account"* and *"Send order confirmation"*. A possible next activity could be *"Order goods"*. In 40% of the

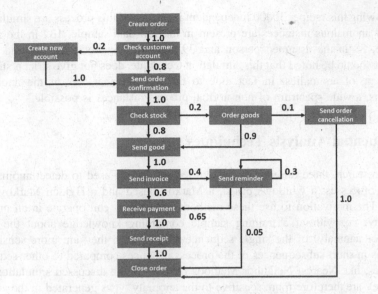

Fig. 1. Model of the simulated business process

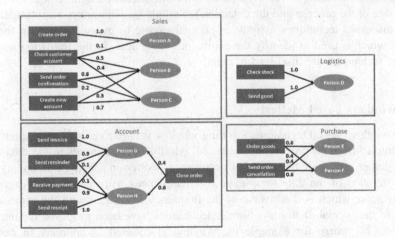

Fig. 2. Assignment of responsible persons to the process activities

anomalous process steps, an anomaly in the acting person is simulated by randomly choosing a person from all but the allowed persons for this activity. An example would be to assign person *"Sales/C"* to activity *"Check stock"*. Finally, in 10% of the anomalous process steps, both the activity as well as the acting person are chosen in the described non-normal way.

As the anomaly probability p_{fail} is included in each step of the sequence, it can happen that more than one anomalies appear in a single process execution. A completed process instance is labeled as an anomaly if at least one anomalous transition occurred during the simulation.

Following this recipe, 30000 independent instances of this process are simulated. In total 259 anomalous instances are present in the full data sample, 132 in the activity sequence, 88 in the assigned person and 39 anomalies in both, activity and related person. It should be noted that this simulation technique, does not give strict restrictions to the type of anomalies. In fact, due to the random character of the anomalous transitions, a wide spectrum of non-normal process instances is possible.

6 Sequential Analysis Techniques

For this research, three different sequential techniques are used to detect anomalies in business processes: a windows based, a Markov based and a Hidden Markov based method. The motivation to use these methods is that they can operate in an unsupervised way, i.e. without a training sample containing knowledge about the nature (normal or anomaly) of the single sequences. In addition they are more sensitive to anomalies in short subsequences of the process instances compared to other sequential techniques, like Nearest Neighbor Methods [23]. With the discussed simulation technique, they are therefore more sensitive to the anomaly types generated in the artificial process sample. Finally they are relatively simple methods, which require only limited user-input for the tuning of involved parameters and therefore might require less expert knowledge of the process and the detection technique in a future practical usage. Each of the discussed techniques assigns an anomaly score to every instance in the data sample, which is used to identify the anomalous sequences. In the following sections, the used techniques are discussed in detail.

6.1   Windows Based Method

For the windows based technique, a sliding window is used to extract subsequences of fixed length l from all process instances. All possible subsequences in the dataset are then, together with their frequency of occurrence, written in a normal dictionary. In a second iteration of the data sample, each subsequences with length l is assigned an anomaly score which is the inverse of the frequency associated with the same subsequence in the normal dictionary. Similar techniques have been proposed for intrusion detection [25] where for example the window is counted as anomaly in case the frequency is above a certain threshold (t-STIDE). The disadvantage of this method is that the threshold is another parameter in addition to the windows length l that needs to be defined. By using the inverse frequency as anomaly score for all possible subsequences this problem is avoided. In a last step, the anomaly score of the full sequence A_s is calculated as the sum of the anomaly scores of the subsequences a_s divided by the number of l length windows n_{win} in the sequence [26]:

$$A_s = \frac{\sum a_s}{n_{win}}. \tag{1}$$

6.2 Markovian Based Method

The Markovian based method estimates the conditional probability of an activity s_i in a sequence $S = (s_1, \ldots, s_n)$ based on the previous activities in the sequence. It basically relies on a higher order Markov condition, assuming that the probability for an activity s_i only depends on the previous l activities [27], i.e.:

$$P(s_i|s_1\ldots s_{i-1}) = P(s_i|s_{i-l}\ldots s_{i-1}) \text{ for } l > 1. \tag{2}$$

Technically, a sliding window is used to extract all subsequences of length l and $l-1$ from the data set. Their frequency of occurrence is stored in a normal dictionary. In a second iteration, the conditional probability of each activity in a sequence is calculated as the ratio between the frequency of the subsequences $(s_{i-l}, .., s_i)$ and $(s_{i-l}, \ldots, s_{i-1})$:

$$P(s_i|s_1\ldots s_{i-1}) = \frac{f(s_{i-l}, \ldots, s_i)}{f(s_{i-l}, \ldots, s_{i-1})}. \tag{3}$$

The conditional probabilities of the single activities s_i are combined to a total probability [23]:

$$P(S) = \prod P(s_i|s_1\ldots s_{i-1}). \tag{4}$$

To consider the different length of the full sequences, the total probability is normalized to the number of l length windows n_{win} in a sequence and the anomaly score is set to

$$A_s = \frac{1 - P(S)}{n_{win}}. \tag{5}$$

A higher anomaly score then represents a higher probability for a sequence to be anomalous. A similar approach was proposed in [18].

6.3 Hidden Markov Model

In this method a Hidden Markov Model [28] is constructed which allows to transform the observed activity sequences in the data sample in sequences of n_s hidden states. The Expectation Maximization algorithm is used to perform a maximum likelihood fit to the data sample and determine the parameters of the Hidden Markov Model for the given set of hidden states. These parameters are the transition matrix, containing the transition probabilities between the hidden states, and the emission matrix with the output probabilities of the hidden to the observed activity states. After constructing the Hidden Markov Model, the Viterbi algorithm [29] is used to determine the most probable sequence of hidden states for each individual sequence in the data sample. Finally the windows based method as discussed previously is applied to the hidden sequences and a corresponding anomaly score is assigned to each sequence. Similar approaches have been used in other research domains for anomaly detection [23].

7 Results

The windows based, Markov based and HMM based techniques are applied to the artificial process data sample. Each technique is applied four times, following the different sequential approaches discussed previously: First, only the activity sequence is analyzed in a one-dimensional way, i.e. sequences of the type *"Create Order"* - *"Check Customer Account"* -... (1d activity). Secondly, the person dimension is investigated, i.e. sequences like *"Sales/PersonA"* - *"Sales/PersonB"* -*"Sales/PersonB"* - *"Sales/PersonC"* -... (1d person). In a third approach, the one-dimensional person sequence is transformed such that consecutive identical persons are grouped together, i.e. *"Sales/PersonA"* - *"Sales/PersonB"* -*"Sales/PersonB"* -*"Sales/PersonC"* becomes *"Sales/PersonA"* - *"Sales/PersonB"* -*"Sales/PersonC"* (1d person merged). This approach tries to reflect possible situations in which the business process of a company is not split up in single activities but only contains information about the order of involved persons. Finally, in a multidimensional approach the activity and person information is combined. In this case a process event *"Create Order"* performed by *"Sales/PersonA"* is treated as different sequence element than the event *"Create Order"* performed by *"Sales/PersonB"* (2d activity-person), e.g. as *"Create Order | Sales/PersonA"* and *"Create Order | Sales/PersonB"*. Consequently, two otherwise identical process instances starting with these different elements would be counted as different.

In order to compare the performance of the different approaches, the process instances are ranked for each sequential detection technique in decreasing order according to the calculated anomaly score. With an optimal detection algorithm, all of the 259 anomalies in the sample would be at the top ranks of the anomaly score. In reality there are likely to be inaccuracies. As a performance measure to compare the different techniques, the number of detected true anomalies in the top ranked 259 instances is used. Table 1 shows the resulting number of detected anomalies for the different analysis approaches and detection techniques.

Table 1. Detected Anomalies with different analysis approaches

	1d activity	1d person	1d person merged	2d activity-person
Windows	171	221	184	253
Markovian	134	130	72	129
HMM	141	138	134	149

As discussed previously, the total number of anomalies in the sample is split up into 50% anomalies in the sequence, 40% anomalies in the person assignment and 10% in the overlap of both. The windows based method performs best for all the four approaches. Unsurprisingly, in the 1d activity case, the methods are only sensitive to the anomalies in the activity sequence and hence the number of detected anomalies is limited to this type. For the 1d person approach the situation is a bit different. Especially the windows based method detects significantly more anomalies than only the ones affecting the person assignment. This can be explained by the fact that both a wrong assignment of a person, as well as a wrong activity sequence can change the person sequence. Interestingly, the other detection techniques are not able to gain in performance by picking up the different anomaly types with this approach. Also in the 1d person merged approach the windows based method detects a reasonable fraction of the anomalies but loses accuracy compared to the 1d person approach. This could be explained by the loss of information that comes with the merging of the consecutive identical person assignments. The two-dimensional approach gives by far the best performance for the windows based method. Almost all anomalies in the sample are detected. The other techniques again seem not to profit from the two-dimensional information view.

8 Interpretation of Results

The results obtained with the different analysis approaches on the artificial data sample show that the usability of sequential detection techniques is not only restricted to the activity sequence. In fact, performing the anomaly detection analysis on other dimensions, in the presented example the acting persons, can give additional insights. In case of correlations between different dimensions, performing a one-dimensional sequential analysis might even be sensitive to anomalies occurring in the sequence of another data dimension. In the presented example, the correlation between executed activities and responsible persons allowed to also detect anomalies in the activity sequence when analyzing solely the sequence of acting persons.

Furthermore, a simple combination of the information from two dimensions offers the possibility to use sequential techniques and detect anomalies appearing in both dimensions. In the presented example, it was differentiated between activities that are performed by different persons. Technically this can be achieved by a simple relabeling of the sequence element. A practical example where the two dimensional approach would be beneficial, is the case when one person (e.g. *"Logistics/PersonD"*) is in vacation and another employee (*"Purchase/PersonE"*) with less knowledge in this domain takes over the tasks but performs either the wrong activity or the correct activity in a wrong way (e.g. sending the wrong goods). Both cases would be recognized by the two-dimensional approach as the appearance of an employee in the wrong place of the process instance would be detected as anomaly.

This concept is of course not restricted to two dimension but can be applied to multiple dimension. In this case the sequential analysis becomes in principle sensitive to anomalies present in all involved data dimensions. For processes with high complexity in the data structure, e.g. many different activities that can be performed by multiple persons in various organization units, this concept however might not be practical. In this case, many differentiations would be necessary in the sequential analysis which would lead to a significant increase of the variety of normal sequences and therefore to a reduction of the separation power between normal and anomalous sequences.

The results from the example show as well that the sensitivity of the different analysis approaches can depend heavily on the chosen detection technique. The windows based method detects the most anomalies in all four analysis approaches. In fact this is the only method which is able to use the information from the person dimension to detect also anomalies in the sequence of executed activities (1d person and 1d person merged approaches). In addition it is also the method which profits most from the two-dimensional analysis approach in the presented example. The Markov and HMM methods on the other hand do not seem to profit from the additional information available. At least when considering the total number of detected anomalies both techniques do not perform much different in the two approaches. The presented results however show only the total number of detected anomalies, not separated according to their appearance in the activity or person sequence. To understand the qualitative difference between the windows based method and the Markov an HMM based methods, a performance study separated for the anomaly types must be performed as a next step in this research.

In this context, it is also important to note that the presented results correspond only to the specific choice of parameter settings for the different techniques, i.e. windows size, number of previous activities and number of hidden states. Although a few parameter settings were investigated and showed no significant difference in the final results, it might be possible that when carefully tuning the techniques, a better performance can be reached in some of the analysis approaches. In addition, the simulated business process is rather simple and real-world processes can be much more complex, in terms of possible process executions and also in the types of the anomalies. Therefore the presented comparison cannot be seen as universally valid but must only be interpreted as first insights in the usability of sequential techniques for one- and multidimensional analysis of business process data.

9 Summary and Conclusion

The availability of transactional data from information system allows for data-driven analyses and detection of anomalies in the business processes of a company. Anomalies can occur in different dimensions of the business process. Most of the existing research concentrates on the detection of anomalies in the sequence of the executed activities. In the presented paper, different approaches were investigated to use sequential techniques also for the detection of anomalies in other dimensions of the process data. In addition a simple concept of using multiple dimensions of process information was presented. The approaches were tested with three basic sequential detection techniques, a windows based, a Markov based and a Hidden Markov Model based method. On a simulated process sample, it was shown that by performing the anomaly detection analysis on other dimensions one can gain additional insights in a wider set of anomaly types. The combination of multiple data dimensions in a sequential analysis offers the possibility to improve the total detection accuracy. From the used detection techniques, the windows based method provided the best performance on the artificial sample.

In the next steps of this research, it is necessary to understand the performance of the discussed sequential detection approaches separately for different types of anomalies and the dependence of the detection techniques on the parameter tuning as well as on the type and complexity of the business process. Especially for more complex processes, future research could investigate the usability of more advanced multi-dimensional detection approaches such as artificial neural networks.

References

1. van der Aalst, W.M.P.: Process-aware information systems: lessons to be learned from process mining. Trans. Petri Nets Models Concurr. **II**, 1–26 (2009)
2. Van Der Aalst, W.M.P., De Medeiros, A.K.A.: Process mining and security: detecting anomalous process executions and checking process conformance. Electron. Notes Theor. Comput. Sci. **121**, 3–21 (2005)
3. van der Aalst, W.M.P.: Process Mining. Springer, Heidelberg (2011)
4. Bezerra, F., Wainer, J., Van Der Aalst, W.M.P.: Anomaly detection using process mining. Management **29**, 149–161 (2009)
5. Bezerra, F., Wainer, J.: Algorithms for anomaly detection of traces in logs of process aware information systems. Inf. Syst. **38**, 33–44 (2013)
6. Bezerra, F., Wainer, J.: A dynamic threshold algorithm for anomaly detection in logs of process aware systems. J. Inf. Data **3**, 316–331 (2012)
7. Armentano, M.G., Amandi, A.A.: Detection of sequences with anomalous behavior in a workflow process. In: Chen, Q., Hameurlain, A., Toumani, F., Wagner, R., Decker, H. (eds.) DEXA 2015. LNCS, vol. 9261, pp. 111–118. Springer, Heidelberg (2015). doi:10.1007/978-3-319-22849-5_8
8. Chandola, V., Banerjee, A., Kumar, V.: Anomaly detection: a survey. ACM Comput. Surv. **41**, 1–58 (2009)
9. Jagadeesh Chandra Bose, R.P., van der Aalst, W.M.P.: Process diagnostics using trace alignment: opportunities, issues, and challenges. Inf. Syst. **37**, 117–141 (2012)
10. West, J., Bhattacharya, M.: Intelligent financial fraud detection: a comprehensive review. Comput. Secur. **57**, 47–66 (2016)
11. Joudaki, H., Rashidian, A., Minaei-Bidgoli, B., Mahmoodi, M., Geraili, B., Nasiri, M., Arab, M.: Using data mining to detect health care fraud and abuse: a review of literature. Glob. J. Health Sci. **7**, 194–202 (2014)
12. Ahmed, M., Naser Mahmood, A., Hu, J.: A survey of network anomaly detection techniques. J. Netw. Comput. Appl. **60**, 19–31 (2016)
13. Bezerra, F., Wainer, J.: Anomaly detection algorithms in business process logs. In: ICEIS 2008 – Proceedings of 10th International Conference on Enterprise Information Systems, AIDSS, pp. 11–18 (2008)
14. Bezerra, F., Wainer, J.: Fraud detection in process aware systems. Int. J. Bus. Process Integr. Manag. **5**, 121 (2011)
15. Sarno, R., Sinaga, F.P.: Business process anomaly detection using ontology-based process modelling and multi-level class association rule learning. In: 2015 International Conference on Computer, Control, Informatics and its Applications (IC3INA), pp. 12–17. IEEE (2015)
16. Kang, B., Kim, D., Kang, S.H.: Real-time business process monitoring method for prediction of abnormal termination using KNNI-based LOF prediction. Expert Syst. Appl. **39**, 6061–6068 (2012)

17. Cabanillas, C., Ciccio, C., Mendling, J., Baumgrass, A.: Predictive task monitoring for business processes. In: Sadiq, S., Soffer, P., Völzer, H. (eds.) BPM 2014. LNCS, vol. 8659, pp. 424–432. Springer, Heidelberg (2014). doi:10.1007/978-3-319-10172-9_31
18. Gupta, N., Anand, K., Sureka, A.: Pariket: mining business process logs for root cause analysis of anomalous incidents. Databases Networked Inf. Syst. **8999**, 244–263 (2015)
19. Jalali, H., Baraani, A.: Process aware host-based intrusion detection model. Int. J. Commun. Networks Inf. Secur. **4**, 117–124 (2012)
20. Rogge-Solti, A.: Temporal anomaly detection in business processes, vol. 16, pp. 35–42 (2010)
21. Quan, L., Tian, G.: Outlier detection of business process based on support vector data description. In: Computing, Communication, Control, and Management, 2009, CCCM 2009. ISECS International Colloquium, vol. 2, pp. 571–574 (2009)
22. Accorsi, R., Wonnemann, C., Stocker, T.: Towards forensic data flow analysis of business process logs. In: 2011 Sixth International Conference on IT Security Incident Management and IT Forensics, pp. 3–20 (2011)
23. Chandola, V., Banerjee, A., Kumar, V.: Anomaly detection for discrete sequences - a survey. IEEE Trans. Knowl. Data Eng. **24**, 1–16 (2012)
24. Burattin, A., Sperduti, A.: PLG: a framework for the generation of business process models and their execution logs. In: Muehlen, M., Su, J. (eds.) BPM 2010. LNBIP, vol. 66, pp. 214–219. Springer, Heidelberg (2011). doi:10.1007/978-3-642-20511-8_20
25. Warrender, C., Forrest, S., Pearlmutter, B.: Detecting intrusions using system calls: alternative data models. In: 1999 IEEE Symposium on Security and Privacy, pp. 133–145 (1999)
26. Hofmeyr, S.A., Forrest, S., Somayaji, A.: Intrusion detection using sequences of system calls. J. Comput. Secur. **6**, 151–180 (1998)
27. Ron, D., Singer, Y., Tishby, N.: The power of amnesia: learning probabilistic automata with variable memory length. Mach. Learn. **25**, 117–149 (1997)
28. Rabiner, L., Juang, B.H.: An introduction to hidden Markov models. IEEE ASSP Mag. **3**, 4–16 (1986)
29. Forney, G.D.: The viterbi algorithm. Proc. IEEE **61**, 268–278 (1973)

Social Media and Analytics for Competitive Performance: A Conceptual Research Framework

Ilias O. Pappas[1]([⊠]), Patrick Mikalef[1], Michail N. Giannakos[1], John Krogstie[1], and George Lekakos[2]

[1] Norwegian University of Science and Technology (NTNU), Trondheim, Norway
{ilpappas,patrick.mikalef,
michailg,john.krogstie}@idi.ntnu.no
[2] Athens University of Economics and Business, Athens, Greece
glekakos@aueb.gr

Abstract. Social media websites have managed in a very short period of time to attract and maintain a massive user. Recognizing their potential, the vast majority of companies are deploying strategies in order to harness their potential in various ways, and ultimately, to establish their competitive position. Nonetheless, being relevantly novel, it still remains unclear as to how it is possible to make the most out of social media, especially in competitive and highly dynamic environments. As with any new technology, it is important to understand the mechanisms and processes through which social media can be of business value for companies in order to incorporate them into their competitive strategies. To this end, the present paper aims to provide a theoretical discussion leading up to a conceptual research framework that can help explain the mechanisms through which social media and analytics lead to competitive performance gains. The conceptual research framework builds on the resource-based view (RBV) and dynamic capabilities view (DCV) of the firm, and provides a synthesis of the two theoretical perspectives.

Keywords: Business social media analytics · Dynamic capabilities · Competitive performance · Resource-based view · Environmental dynamism · IT strategy

1 Introduction

Social media have become increasingly popular over the years by connecting a wide variety of users worldwide. They have also become very important for companies, since they have the potential to provide a competitive advantage with a proper strategic implementation on various facets of a firms activities [1]. Their penetration is very high, offering various opportunities for companies (especially low cost innovators and start-ups) to reach end user and access new, untapped markets. As such, it is of high interest for executives and academics to understand the mean through which these tools can be leveraged appropriately. To do so, it is important to build on past research of

© Springer International Publishing AG 2017
W. Abramowicz et al. (Eds.): BIS 2016 Workshops, LNBIP 263, pp. 209–218, 2017.
DOI: 10.1007/978-3-319-52464-1_19

business-IT value, as well as on theoretical perspectives of management. Researchers should help practitioners by offering insight on how to make better use of the available technologies and tools, how to better engage with their customers, and how to optimally employ social media to strengthen their competitive position.

Social media literature is rather nascent, and mainly focuses on how firms behave on social media and how they use such platforms for marketing and commerce purposes. Through social media firms are able to market new products or services, build new avenues for commerce activities (e.g. social commerce), and interact directly with their customers. Similarly, social media may help firms built trust with their customers and increase their loyalty. Furthermore, they can be used to enable firms to rethink their current means of operation and adjust their business resources and strategy. Nonetheless, there is little research on how firms should adopt social media and specifically what factors will help them achieve this [2].

The most compelling effects of social media in business have not yet been documented, because the requirements and conditions for their proper implementation in business strategies remain understudied. This paper aims to identify how managers and decision makers in companies can make better use of social media, take advantage of the vast content that is available publicly, filter it, and proceed to decisions that affect the whole company both externally and internally. Our main objective is to propose a theoretical framework including innovative practices that will help in designing social media for businesses, such as social media functionality, its technical infrastructure that enables the creation of user generated content, and creative consumers that use social media to interact with the companies. Based on our aims and objectives we pose the following research questions:

RQ1: What are the core building blocks that should be taken into account when considering social media and analytics? What leveraging mechanisms need to be put in place in order to constitute them as a source of a competitive advantage?

RQ2: What conditions moderate the effectiveness of social media and analytics tools? In what areas and under what contingency aspects do social media analytics enable firms to achieve a competitive edge?

The rest of the paper is organized as follows. In the next section we present a literature review on the area of social media analytics in the business context. In Sect. 3 a theoretical discussion is presented introducing the main perspectives employed. Section 4 describes the proposed research framework and how the theories are contextualized for social media and analytics purposes. Finally, Sect. 5 concludes the paper with a brief summary and suggestions for future work.

2   Literature Review

Social media are a great example of the impact of information technology on business, both within and outside company boundaries, and both at a corporate and an operational level [3]. They transform the way that companies relate to both their customers and employees [4]. Through appropriate implementation social media platforms have the potential of renewed business value creation along with increased productivity and innovativeness[1]. The importance of business analytics is evident throughout the literature, and as they evolve they have various applications creating multiple emerging research areas [5]. In addition, the critical role of social media analytics has already been identified and there are numerous studies in various contexts on the impact of analytics from social media [6–9]. Yet, existing studies fail to connect social media analytics with business needs and strategic management, a connection that would offer companies' significant ways to evolve and gain competitive advantage.

A research framework has been recently proposed to help researchers into studying social media [10]. In detail, social media are divided into four fairly broad categories of activities, namely; design and features, strategy and tactics, management and organisation, measurement and value. Further, each activity can be analysed on a different level based on who uses social media (i.e., consumers and society, platforms and intermediaries, firms and industries). To this end, the functionality designed into social media has been identified as a very important factor because of its role on all types of social media users.

An alternative perspective that is equally important is the functionality that social media enable, with a recent framework documenting the main affordances [11]. The objective of the abovementioned framework is to explain how social media operate and how businesses should engage with them. The functionality of social media consists of seven blocks, and the proposed framework may be used to examine and explain both users' experience with social media and firms' implications from them. Such implications include suggestions for business strategies that will help them monitor, explain and act depending on the various social media activities.

The aforementioned frameworks offer valuable insight to researchers and practitioners, however a theoretical framework would be more robust if it also examined social media from a strategic management point of view. To do so howeyer, requires a hands-on approach with the companies in order to identify their needs and expectations from social media, as well as clarify how their managers and decision makers view social media. Towards this end, a very recent study aims to identify challenges and opportunities in social media for business by interviewing professionals from large organisations [12]. The interviews reveal different challenges and opportunities, which can be categorised in six different areas (e.g., social media analytics) for further research and analysis. Nonetheless, various challenges remain for organisations and managers to tackle in order to use social media for their business in the most efficient manner.

Recent studies suggest that businesses are not able to properly manage the opportunities or threats that arise from social media and analytics, because their decision makers do not fully comprehend what they are and how they function, thus they cannot visualise their potential benefits. Extant research in the area of social media and analytics (SMA) for businesses [13] proposes innovative approaches to aid companies' in collecting, monitoring, and analysing user-generated content. Their goal is to

---

[1] Business opportunities: Social Media. (2013). https://ec.europa.eu/growth/tools-databases/dem/sites/default/files/page-files/social_media_v1.1.pdf.

obtain valuable insights from these data and to acquire a competitive advantage in the market. Further, many challenges have been identified in the literature of SMA, and are based on problems that occur with the gathering and analysis of data obtained from social media [14]. However, focusing on user generating content is only a small part of the possibilities incorporated in social media. In order companies to make the most out of social media and analytics, they should incorporate them in their overall business strategy.

3 Theoretical Discussion

The growing interest in social media analytics requires a focused discussion on how it can be examined and what theoretical prisms can be employed in order to understand the critical success factors as well as its business value. Information systems literature has used various theoretical perspectives to explore these issues, with recent attempts building on the convergence of theories. When examining the impact of IT investments at the firm level of analysis, the Resource Based View (RBV) of the firm has been the primary theoretical perspective applied over the past two decades [15]. The main of the RBV is that IT resources that are valuable, rare, in-imitable, and non-substitutable are the building blocks of a competitive advantage [16]. IT resources have been distinguished into tangible (IT infrastructure), human (IT human skills & knowledge), and intangible (culture and relationships) [16]. This has enabled researchers and practitioners to identify the different types of IT resources their firms should aim to acquire and strengthen. However, although the RBV provides a basis for the raw material that are necessary to build a competitive advantage, it fails to explain how these resources are leveraged [17]. In addition, the RBV provides little explanation as to how companies react in the face of external changes [17]. These shortcomings of the RBV have also been documented in the IT literature, and have caused academics to rethink the theoretical perspectives that could complement this gap.

A growing body of literature is emphasizing on the role of dynamic capabilities as a source of sustained competitive advantage, especially in turbulent and uncertain environments. The dynamic capabilities view (DCV) of the firm posits that the ability to purposefully adapt an organizations resource and capabilities in the face of external pressures is ultimately the source of sustained competitive advantage [18]. While the DCV has only recently begun to attract the interest of IS scholars in terms of helping determine how an IT-based competitive advantage can be achieved, there have been several papers that employ the theory empirically [19]. The rationale developed in these studies is that IT that is embedded in specific capabilities can provide a competitive edge. As such, the value of IT does not lie in IT resources *per se*, although their availability is a prerequisite, but rather, on the process of integrating them into the organizational fabric. The DCV has seen a maturing in terms of its theoretical grounding over the past few years, and has been tested in empirically in several different contexts, providing a clear understanding on how to conceptualize and measure the firms' capacity to do so. The general consensus in these empirical studies is to identify between the routines or capabilities of which dynamic capabilities comprise [18]. While there are some differences in terms of the routines used, the underlying philosophy remains the same in most of these studies.

While the RBV and DCV build on different ideas to support how a company can achieve of competitive advantage, there is a growing body in literature which identifies their complementarities [20]. Despite the DCV being more appropriate in explaining competitive advantage in turbulent and unpredictable business environments, it is noted in literature that the types of resources that a firm possesses will ultimately have an effect on the responses they can initiate. The types of resources and their influence on responsive actions have also been noted in IT literature, thus reinforcing the theoretical linkages [21].

4 Research Framework

A vast amount of data is inherent in social media and most companies are already trying to process this data in order to extract specific information that will increase their value. In order to achieve their goals various tools, methods and analytical concepts are applied such as text mining or sentiment analysis. However, the amount of data is huge thus leading to information overload for company managers, decision makers and executives. Decision makers do not have the proper guidance on how to adopt and implement SMA procedures and outcomes on their business strategies. To this end, we propose a theoretical framework that will aid the integration of social media strategy with the overall strategy of the company.

The theoretical discussion of the previous section provides a basis for understanding how to approach social media analytics for business purposes and develop a research framework for future reference. The proposed research framework can therefore be used in order to avoid common pitfalls of IT research, especially in terms of novel solutions in which it is important to understand the boundaries of their business value and under what circumstances it can be attained. To do so, we demonstrate how the theoretical perspectives are associated, what core notions and aspects are relevant, as well as what contingency factors shape these relationships. Already there are several studies that attempt to define the business value of social media analytics, yet, there is no coherent theoretical framework, or an underlying unifying framework to provide a clear view of the overall business potential.

We start this discussion by isolating the different levels and dimensions pertinent to each theoretical perspective, identify how they are relevant to the context of social media business analytics, and finally attempt to describe their interdependencies. The initiating point is to demarcate the RBV in the IT context. Over the past decade there have been several studies that define the levels at which the RBV can be decomposed as aforementioned in the previous section. Building on the distinction between IT infrastructure, IT human skills and knowledge, and relational IT resources, we overview some of the work that could be used to guide researchers in the social media analytics area. In terms of IT infrastructure and the different types that exist several papers have proposed aspects that should be considered [16]. In the context of social media analytics there have been some attempts to describe the necessary infrastructure which span hardware, software, and mathematical and analytical tools [5]. Employees working in this area should have analytical thinking, ability to handle large amounts of data, knowledge of analytics techniques and statistical modeling, as well as the capacity to tackle problems with a data-driven approach [22]. In terms of relational IT resources, in the context of social media analytics it is important that companies establish a virtual presence on such mediums and clearly articulate communications and interactions strategies with their existing or potential customers [23]. Although the three afore-mentioned aspects of social media analytics are critical to establish in order to gain a competitive edge, they are of limited value if not leveraged appropriately. This means that the infrastructure, human skills and knowledge, and relational resources must be put into action and into specifically directed initiatives. To do so, a firm must have the IT competencies, i.e. the collective capacity to coordinate activities and transform and bring together individual IT resources into IT-enabled dynamic capabilities.

While the ability to effectively orchestrate IT resources may also result in opera-tional capabilities, the focus of our research framework will be on dynamic capabilities due to their importance in contemporary businesses. Therefore, we seek to explain the routines of which IT-enabled dynamic capabilities comprise, and how social media analytics can be infused into them with the purpose of augmenting them. Researchers have sought to quantify the notion of dynamic capabilities by identifying distinct and measurable dimensions, or else, capabilities [19, 24–26]. These capabilities include sensing, learning, coordinating, integrating, and reconfiguring [25]. A sensing capa-bility concerns the capacity of a firm to spot, interpret, and make sense of opportunities and threats in the business environment [24]. Social media analytics can be leveraged to enhance a firms sensing capability by helping identify customer requirements, gaining feedback on existing products or services, or even monitoring competitor moves and their customers' responses [27, 28]. A learning capability is defined as the capacity to acquire, assimilate, transform, and exploit new knowledge that enables informed decision making [29]. While this capacity closely resembles a sensing capability, it differs in that it doesn't solely rely on spotting trends, but creates distilled information that can be used in competitive actions. A coordinating capability is defined as the ability to orchestrate and deploy tasks and resources, and synchronize activities with involved stakeholders [30]. Through feedback iterations with customers over social media and developing meaningful analytics, firms can coordinate their efforts with various departments and at different stages of development, and come up with products or services that are tailored to their likings. An integrating capability includes the capacity to evaluate external resources and competences, and embed and exploit them in new or revamped ways [31]. Social media analytics can be employed towards strengthening this capability by gathering information from multiple sources and utilize them in combination, or else, through the process of bisociation. Finally, a reconfiguring capability is defined as the ability of a firm to effectuate strategic moves and demonstrate agility when there is a need to change existing modes of operation [32]. For this particular capability social media analytics are particularly relevant since by generating information at a constant flow, or else nowcasting, decision makers are equipped with knowledge that allows them to respond instantaneously, thus increasing operational agility (Fig. 1).

Building on the main theoretical arguments presented and their underlying concepts and notions, the research framework presented above and the main associations can

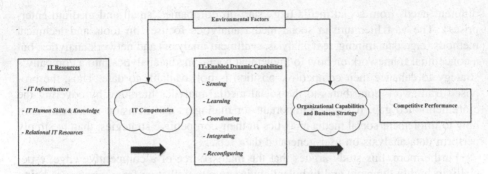

Fig. 1. Research framework for social media analytics

help guide future studies in determining the business value of social media analytics. By separating IT resources from IT-enabled dynamic capabilities, it is possible to discern the nexus of relationships through which competitive performance gains can be realized. While IT resources related to social media analytics are necessary, they are of very limited value if they are not transformed into IT-enabled dynamic capabilities through effective orchestration and management (i.e. to develop the necessary IT competencies at the group or business unit level). IT-enabled dynamic capabilities have been shown to be an important part of gaining a competitive edge, especially in turbulent and highly dynamic markets. Nevertheless, their effect on competitive performance has empirically been proven to be and indirect one, mediated by other organizational capabilities and contingent upon business strategy [33]. It is therefore important to examine how IT-enabled dynamic capabilities relevant to social media analytics operate, in terms of changing the existing modes of operation and decision making.

5 Discussion

Companies and their customers are increasingly using social media to interact with each other in various ways, thus leading to the creation of a vast amount of data on a real-time basis. For companies to gain a competitive advantage in the market and differentiate from their competitors it is important to exploit these data which will offer them valuable insights. Companies that use analytics have increased performance, and towards this direction business social media analytics may help companies identify strengths, weaknesses, transform their strategies and gain competitive performance. This work identifies the need for a paradigm shift on firms' business models and focuses at the same time on the yet underserved but highly need and requested area, that of social media and analytics for business.

　　To this end, this study proposes a conceptual framework that is based on concepts from social media and analytics literature based on theoretical arguments developed in strategic management literature. Therefore, it will provide a sound basis for the wider implementation of social media in businesses. Additionally, the framework may be accompanied by multi-modal content targeting different types of companies with different needs from social media (e.g., start-up companies, small and medium enterprises). The vast literature in social media analytics focuses on tools and technical methods (e.g., data mining, text analysis, sentiment analysis) and network analytics, but a conceptual framework on how to implement social media analytics into a company's strategy to enhance their competitive position is not available to date. Thus, the proposed framework contributes to the social media analytics literature by covering the aforementioned gap. It is more important for managers and decision makers to learn how to implement social media analytics in their competitive strategies, than to simply perform data analysis on user-generated data sets.

Furthermore, this study argues that the main source of a competitive edge, especially in highly dynamic and turbulent environments will stem from companies being able to reinforce their dynamic capabilities through targeted use of social media and analytics. This of course does not lessen the importance of IT resources, since their availability and VRIN characteristics can determine the strength of the associated IT-enabled dynamic capabilities developed [34]. The concepts used in the proposed framework may help managers better understand, plan and organize the process of implementing social media analytics within a business strategy.

This paper offers a theoretical framework on how to increase business value and competitive performance with social media analytics. Future studies should empirically test and evaluate this framework by using surveys, interviews, observation, focus groups with experts (e.g., managers, decision makers) and with customers', as well as case studies from the industry. Also, both qualitative and quantitative methods of data collection should be employed. For each different type of data, more than one ways of analysis should be used (e.g., structural equation modelling, qualitative comparative analysis).

Acknowledgments. This work was carried out during the tenure of an ERCIM 'Alain Bensoussan' Fellowship Programme.

 This project has received funding from the European Union's Horizon 2020 research and innovation programme under the Marie Sklodowska-Curie grant agreement No 704110.

References

1. European Commission. Business Innovation Observatory: Innovative Business Models for Competitiveness: Social Media for Internationalisation (2014)
2. Braojos-Gomez, J., Benitez-Amado, J., Llorens-Montes, F.J.: How do small firms learn to develop a social media competence? Int. J. Inf. Manage. **35**, 443–458 (2015)
3. European Commission: Business opportunities: Social Media (2013)
4. Chui, M.: The social economy: unlocking value and productivity through social technologies. McKinsey (2013)
5. Chen, H., Chiang, R.H., Storey, V.C.: Business intelligence and analytics: from big data to big impact. MIS Q. **36**, 1165–1188 (2012)
6. Davenport, T.H., Barth, P., Bean, R.: How big data is different. MIT Sloan Manage. Rev. **54**, 43 (2012)

7. Fan, W., Gordon, M.D.: The power of social media analytics. Commun. ACM **57**, 74–81 (2014)
8. Stieglitz, S., Dang-Xuan, L.: Social media and political communication: a social media analytics framework. Soc. Network Anal. Min. **3**, 1277–1291 (2013)
9. Zeng, D., Chen, H., Lusch, R., Li, S.-H.: Social media analytics and intelligence. IEEE Intell. Syst. **25**, 13–16 (2010)
10. Aral, S., Dellarocas, C., Godes, D.: Introduction to the special issue-social media and business transformation: a framework for research. Inf. Syst. Res. **24**, 3–13 (2013)
11. Kietzmann, J.H., Hermkens, K., McCarthy, I.P., Silvestre, B.S.: Social media? Get serious! Understanding the functional building blocks of social media. Bus. Horiz. **54**, 241–251 (2011)
12. Van Osch, W., Steinfield, C.W., Balogh, B.A.: Enterprise social media: challenges and opportunities for organizational communication and collaboration. In: 48th Hawaii International Conference on System Sciences (HICSS), pp. 763–772. IEEE (2015)
13. He, W., Wu, H., Yan, G., Akula, V., Shen, J.: A novel social media competitive analytics framework with sentiment benchmarks. Inf. Manag. **52**, 801–812 (2015)
14. Holsapple, C., Hsiao, S.-H., Pakath, R.: Business Social Media Analytics: Definition, Benefits, and Challenges (2014)
15. Wade, M., Hulland, J.: Review: The resource-based view and information systems research: review, extension, and suggestions for future research. MIS Q. **28**, 107–142 (2004)
16. Bharadwaj, A.S.: A resource-based perspective on information technology capability and firm performance: an empirical investigation. MIS Q. **24**, 169–196 (2000)
17. Kraaijenbrink, J., Spender, J.-C., Groen, A.J.: The resource-based view: a review and assessment of its critiques. J. Manag. **36**, 349–372 (2010)
18. Eisenhardt, K.M., Martin, J.A.: Dynamic capabilities: what are they? Strateg. Manage. J. **21**, 1105–1121 (2000)
19. Pavlou, P.A., El Sawy, O.A.: The "third hand": IT-enabled competitive advantage in turbulence through improvisational capabilities. Inf. Syst. Res. **21**, 443–471 (2010)
20. Helfat, C.E., Peteraf, M.A.: The dynamic resource-based view: capability lifecycles. Strateg. Manaeg. J. **24**, 997–1010 (2003)
21. Wang, N., Liang, H., Zhong, W., Xue, Y., Xiao, J.: Resource structuring or capability building? An empirical study of the business value of information technology. J. Manag. Inf. Syst. **29**, 325–367 (2012)
22. Davenport, T.H., Patil, D.: Data scientist. Harvard Bus. Rev. **90**, 70–76 (2012)
23. Grégoire, Y., Salle, A., Tripp, T.M.: Managing social media crises with your customers: the good, the bad, and the ugly. Bus. Horiz. **58**, 173–182 (2015)
24. Teece, D.J.: Explicating dynamic capabilities: the nature and microfoundations of (sustainable) enterprise performance. Strateg. Manag. J. **28**, 1319–1350 (2007)
25. Mikalef, P., Pateli, A. Wetering, R.V.D.: IT flexbility and competitive performance: the mediating role of IT-enabled dynamic capabilities. In: European Conference on Information Systems (ECIS) (2016)
26. Mikalef, P., Pateli, A.: Developing and validating a measurement instrument of IT-enabled dynamic capabilities. In: European Conference on Information Systems (2016)
27. He, W., Zha, S., Li, L.: Social media competitive analysis and text mining: a case study in the pizza industry. Int. J. Inf. Manag. **33**, 464–472 (2013)
28. Risius, M., Beck, R.: Effectiveness of corporate social media activities in increasing relational outcomes. Inf. Manag. **52**, 824–839 (2015)
29. Zahra, S.A., George, G.: Absorptive capacity: a review, reconceptualization, and extension. Acad. Manag. Rev. **27**, 185–203 (2002)

30. Pavlou, P.A., El Sawy, O.A.: Understanding the elusive black box of dynamic capabilities. Decis. Sci. **42**, 239–273 (2011)
31. Woldesenbet, K., Ram, M., Jones, T.: Supplying large firms: the role of entrepreneurial and dynamic capabilities in small businesses. Int. Small Bus. J. **30**, 493–512 (2012)
32. Lin, Y., Wu, L.-Y.: Exploring the role of dynamic capabilities in firm performance under the resource-based view framework. J. Bus. Res. **67**, 407–413 (2014)
33. Barreto, I.: Dynamic capabilities: a review of past research and an agenda for the future. J. Manag. **36**, 256–280 (2010)
34. Bowman, C., Ambrosini, V.: How the resource-based and the dynamic capability views of the firm inform corporate-level strategy. British J. Manag. **14**, 289–303 (2003)

iCRM Workshop

Social CRM: Biggest Challenges to Make it Work in the Real World

Fábio Lobato[1,2(✉)], Márcia Pinheiro[1], Antonio Jacob Jr.[1,3],
Olaf Reinhold[4], and Ádamo Santana[1]

[1] Institute of Technology, Federal University of Pará, Belém, Brazil
{lobato.fabio, jacobjr, adamo}@ufpa.br,
marcia.pinheiro@itec.ufpa.br
[2] Federal University of Western Pará, Santarém, Brazil
[3] Technological Sciences Center, State University of Maranhão, São Luís, Brazil
[4] Information Systems Institute, University of Leipzig, Leipzig, Germany
reinhold@wifa.uni-leipzig.de

Abstract. The ways of communication and social interactions are changing and web users are becoming increasingly engaged with Online Social Networks (OSN). This fact has significantly impact in the relationship mechanisms between companies and customers. Thus, a new approach to perform Customer Relationship Management (CRM) is arising, the Social CRM (SCRM). Aiming to identify state of art, a literature review was conducted to demonstrate the current state of knowledge about the topic. In addition, expert interviews and events organized by researchers involved in this project, helped in challenges validation. As main contributions, it is possible to highlight: (i) identification, categorization and discussion of SCRM most prominent challenges; and (ii) construction of a SCRM service portfolio; (iii) estimation of the distance between state of art and state of practice. Therefore, the results obtained point out a number of future research directions, demonstrating that Social Customer Relationship Management is an emerging and promising research topic.

Keywords: Social media · Customer relationship management · On-line social networks

1 Introduction

It is unquestionable the importance to establish a good relationship between enterprises and customers [1]. For this reason, there are a plenty of strategies to perform Customer Relationship Management, in order to gain new clients, induce customer fidelity/loyalty and, consequently, increase the company profits [2, 3]. Nowadays, the pervasive and ubiquitous computing technologies are changing the ways of communication and social interactions, the users are becoming increasingly engaged with On-line Social Networks and On-line collaborative media [1].

Analyzing the social media through the customers point of view, these platforms represent a channel to collect information about brands and services, as well as to give opinions about them [1]. At the enterprises perspective, OSN are powerful data sources

© Springer International Publishing AG 2017
W. Abramowicz et al. (Eds.): BIS 2016 Workshops, LNBIP 263, pp. 221–232, 2017.
DOI: 10.1007/978-3-319-52464-1_20

about the customers' behavior, besides to be a new and cheap communication channel [4]. This scenario imposes a pressure for companies to follow the OSN tendency [5]. As consequence, a new way to perform the customer relationship management is emerging, the Social Customer Relationship Management [1, 6, 7].

The SCRM aims to use and integrate information from social media and the traditional CRM systems, and to enhance the results reliability as well as to provide new sort of analysis. As consequence, SCRM systems are provoking considerable changes in the market. Thus, it can be considered a new and promising research topic. For this reason, there are countless open issues to be addressed by academia in order to fulfill the market needs [4].

Given this gap, a literature review was performed aiming to identify, categorize and discuss some of most prominent challenges to make SCRM work in the real world. In addition to the literature review mentioned, expert interviews and events organized/attended by the researchers involved in the project helped in the challenges identification and categorization, as well as to present the trends into SCRM.

The main contribution of these two additional instruments, the expert interviews and the events attendance, was to help in the validation of challenges identified in the literature review. Moreover, it was also possible to estimate the state of art and state of practice distance, which represents the impedance between industry and academia. The relevance of this work relies on the use of these multiple instruments, once each challenge identified was discussed and validated through the interviews and discussions in the mentioned events.

Considering the traditional knowledge discovery in databases process and social data analysis characteristics, the following research questions were raised:

RQ1: What questions need to be answered (analyses to be done)?
RQ2: What are your data sources?
RQ3: What are the constraints?

To answer the research questions, this paper is organized as follows: Sect. 2 presents the Materials and methods; a briefly Social CRM overview, including a service portfolio, is given in Sects. 3, 4 and 5 present results and final remarks, respectively.

2 Materials and Methods

The challenges addressed in this paper were obtained through:

i. Literature review on SCRM and related areas such as Natural Language Processing (NLP), applied computational intelligence, frontiers in massive data analysis, OSN and business model;
ii. Interviews with experts and case studies analysis;
iii. Presentations, discussion and audience feedback from some events organized/ attended by SCRM Research Center of University of Leipzig (DE) members and Laboratory of Computational Intelligence research group of Federal University of Pará (BR).

The events cited previously consisted in workshops, panels and conferences focused on SCRM, which covered basic concepts, trends, open issues, recent development and a wide range of applications described through case studies. The presenters/panelists come from both academia and industry. The knowledge obtained in these events allowed the construction of a first list of challenges and its categories.

Parallel to the events, the literature review was conducted, which is better described shortly after. The literature review, among other things, allowed the challenges list refinement. For instance, challenges previously identified were removed because they were already surpassed; or neglected challenges were included.

Then, the interview with experts and case studies analyses were conducted. The very first goal was to validate the obtained challenges list. Moreover, it was possible to contrast them against the state of practice, helping to perceive their relevance and also to categorize them. The categories used in this work were adapted from [8], as follows: process, infrastructure and data mining. These categories reflect the multidisciplinary essence of SCRM; the process category is related to information systems and marketing; infrastructure involves management, operational aspects and finance; finally, data mining category is proposed in this work aiming to encompass computer science aspects, most of them, related to knowledge discovery.

The literature review conducted aimed to identify the state of art and to demonstrate the current state of knowledge about SCRM. The literature review methodology adopted in this paper follows the structure proposed by [9]: (1) definition of review scope; (2) conceptualization of topic; and (3) literature search. The structure is better described as follows.

2.1 Definition of the Review Scope

The review scope definition of this research follows the taxonomy proposed by [10], which is qualified by six characteristics - each one having a different number of categories [10, 11] - and it is inspired by the researches of [11–13]. The research literature review characteristics are shown in Table 1.

Table 1. Scope of literature review based in taxonomy proposed by [10].

Characteristic	Categories		
(a) Focus	*Research outcomes*	Research methods	Theories
Applications			
(b) Goal	Integration	Criticism	*Central issues*
(c) Organization	Historical	*Conceptual*	Methodological
(d) Perspective	*Neutral representation*		Espousal of position
(e) Audience	*Specialized scholars*	General scholar	*Practitioners*
General Public			
(f) Coverage	Exhaustive	*Exhaustive and selective*	Representative
Central /Pivotal			

The focus (a) of this research is on identifying *research outcomes* in Social CRM challenges. The goal (b) is to discover *central issue*s in SCRM considering the research questions on a *conceptual* level (c). The perspective (d) is *neutral* because it allows an unbiased position as well as the identification of central issues from multiple research disciplines [10, 12, 13]. The target audience (e) are *specialized scholars* and *practitioners;* and the coverage (f) is *exhaustive and selective.*

2.2   Topic Conceptualization and Literature Search

According to [14], the concept of the topic (2) needs "to provide a working definition of key variable(s)". The key variables of this research seek to identify the challenges in Social CRM and lead to literature search (3). The literature search adopts the following steps: (I) a journal search, (II) a database search, (III) a keyword search and (IV) a forward and backward search. The literature search of this paper has limitations because it does not perform a rigorous (I) journal search, due to the goal of identifying central issues from multiple research areas.

The (II) database search is performed in the databases of Science Direct, Web of Knowledge and IEEE. The (III) keyword search is an approach to the querying of high quality scholar databases by the use of a specific word or phrase [15], and these keywords and related abbreviations are derived from the key variables [11]. The key variables defined for this research are "Social CRM", "Challenge", "Obstacle", "Barrier" and "Effectiveness", and the combination of these keywords defines the search phrases that are searched in the databases: ("Social CRM" OR "Social Customer Relationship Management") AND ("challenge" OR "obstacle" OR "barrier" OR "effectiveness") in the title, topic, abstract, keyword and full text. The obtained keyword search results are shown in the Table 2.

Table 2. Keyword search results.

Database	Keyword search		Forward search		Backward search
	Search phrase	Net hits	Hits	Net hits	Net hits
Web of knowledge	163	21	51	4	–
Science direct	45	6	109	1	
IEEE	32	7	1	0	
Google scholar	–		362	3	
Sum[a]		**31**	–	**8**	**7**
Total net hits		**46**			

[a] The total number is not equal to the column sum because duplicates have been counted only once.

Finally, in the step IV, the forward search is performed only for articles that contain reference to one of the 31 net hit articles which were obtained from the keyword search, using the four databases and Google Scholar [11, 16]. In this forward search, 8 additional papers are obtained. The backward search of first-level is performed only in the references of 31 net hits articles. In this backward search, 7 additional papers are obtained. As result, 46 articles are found for literature analysis.

The evaluation of the articles has been performed by analyzing title, abstract and introduction, aiming to eliminate duplicate articles. In order to keep the focus on recent work, this literature review considered only recent work from the last five years. Web of Knowledge is the data source with the highest number of results for the searched query. The journals and conferences with the highest number of net hits articles are Computers in Human Behavior, Business Horizons, Journal of Research in Interactive Marketing, Online Information Review with 4, 2, 2 and 2 articles, respectively.

3   SCRM Overview

The challenges were obtained from (i) and (ii), a simplistic point of view, in which SCRM consists in the addition of Social Media analysis to the traditional customer relationship management [1, 6, 7]. However, due to data analysis exploitation, SCRM brings up news services and market requirements. In this section, a non-exhaustive list of potential services that can be provided by SCRM is addressed, as well the technical requirements are detailed for further state of art methods discussion. Almost all sectors of an enterprise are involved with customers. Figure 1 shows the most prominent areas related to customer relationship management, which are discussed later.

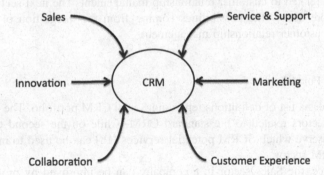

Fig. 1. Areas related to CRM. Adapted from [17].

3.1   Context

Sales are the most transparent sector for CRM, followed by services & support and marketing. These areas represent the basis of a traditional CRM system and take into account: social media campaigns, market analysis, brand management, Social Media FAQ and community support. OSN do not represent just a new communication channel, they also are important data source of customer wishes, behavior, influence network (identify influencers and influenced friends of a certain customer) *etc.* [18]. Mining on-line social network data can yield potential useful and new knowledge to be used in CRM, improving the accuracy and exploiting the analysis. Figure 2 shows some prominent tasks in social data mining.

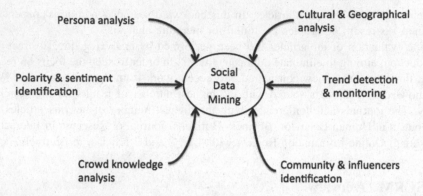

Fig. 2. Main groups of social data mining.

Figure 2 presents six main tasks; two of them are related to individual's behaviors - polarity & sentiment identification, persona analysis – while the others are related to groups of individuals. Basically, persona analysis consists in identifying clusters of users as well to characterize these clusters/individual. In the individual group analysis, it is possible to identify cultural differences enriched with geographical information. Through the correlation of the previous analysis it is possible to perform a crowd knowledge extraction. Of course, there are so many other analyses, but the ones cited here are more related to customer relationship management. The next section lists and discussess more deeply the possibilities coming from the integration of Social data analysis and customer relationship management.

3.2 SCRM Portfolio

Table 3 provides a list of definitions regarding Social CRM portfolio. The first column presents the sectors related to the standard CRM, while on the second column it is possible to observe which SCRM potential services [18] can be used to improve each traditional CRM sector.

For instance, the Sales sector in a company can be improved by product recommendations for its customers, which can increase purchases and revenue. In addition, purchase prediction can help a company to avoid missing products that people will by often in a given season.

Moreover, dissemination of a company deals can help on sales, which can easily happen sending the right information to the leads of a community, which is possible through lead identification. Similarly, the other SCRM portfolio services can help CRM in different ways.

Table 3. Definitions of social CRM portfolio.

Sectors related with CRM	Social CRM portfolio services
Sales	Product recommendation
	Purchase prediction
	Lead identification
Marketing	Market analysis
	Social media campaigns
	Adaptive brand management
	Advertising impact assessment
Service and support	Social media FAQ
	Automatic post assignment and prioritization
	Community support forums
Innovation	Private enterprise social network
	Customer wishes/needs identification
	Trends identification
Collaboration	Digital influencers identification
	Collaborators recruitment
Customer experience	Recruit brand ambassador's
	Mini-network influencers

4   Trends and Challenges Identified

Eleven challenges have been identified from the literature review. The main challenge noticed is "Integrate CRM with Social Media – Social CRM", which is cited in 20 articles. The second most cited challenge is "Tools of Social CRM" with 16 citations. The third is "Data Structure", which appears in 11 articles. Big Data (9 articles), Privacy (9 articles), Investment (8 articles), Data Security (7 articles), Operational Excellence (6 articles), Data Types (6 articles) and Velocity (6 articles) were also identified as challenges to make Social CRM work in the real world. The definition of the challenges is shown in Table 4.

The analysis of 46 net hits paper was conducted in two phases. In the first step, challenges in SCRM are selected from each paper. In the second step, each paper is re-examined with the aim to validate the results. The service portfolio described previously can answer the first question RQ1 proposed in our methodology - "What questions need to be answered (analyses to be done)?", since it provided a list of possible analyses which encompass major sectors of a company.

Thus, deciding what kind of analyses are required, it is important to evaluate the other questions RQ2 - "What are your data sources?" And RQ3 - "What are the constraints?". Basically, to perform Social CRM analyses, at least two data sources are needed: OSN and ERP. Regarding the constraints, they are interconnected with the challenges. For instance, the current obstacles to make Social CRM work in the real world are Social Data Mining challenges, CRM issues, the integration of OSN with CRM data and other relevant aspects – the latter comprises challenges that are not as technical as the previous ones.

Table 4. Definitions of social CRM challenges.

Categories	Social CRM challenges	Description
Process	Integrate CRM with social media	Many companies do not know how to integrate CRM with Social Media [2, 5, 12, 18–32]
	Metrics	Specifics Key Performance Indicators (KPIs) must be used by companies to measure the performance of Social CRM [5, 18, 20, 25, 33, 34]
Infrastructure	Operational excellence	There is a need to adequate training and culture [18] in employees in the use of Social CRM for fully living a social media culture [3, 5, 18, 25, 29, 30]
	Investment	For Small and Medium-sized Companies (SMEs) the lack or resources means maximizing use of budgets in Social CRM and see the Return on Investment (ROI) [34, 35]
	Tools	The current systems are often limited to a particular type of social media content and do not aggregate and mine such big social data [12, 20–22, 26, 28, 29, 33, 36–42]
Data Mining	Big Data	The big social data is very challenging for its inherent characteristics, such as volume, velocity and variety of contents (e.g., pictures, video, and text written in different languages, sometimes with particular idioms) [12, 21, 36, 40–44]
	Data types	The data type heterogeneity on Social Networks represents a big challenge for SCRM, as well as multimedia content for knowledge extraction techniques, which is also computationally intensive [5, 12, 18, 40, 41, 44–46]
	Data structure	Approximately 90% of social network data is unstructured, which is challenging for data mining methods, usually applied to structured data. However, the processing of unstructured data can improve SCRM significantly [5, 12, 18, 21, 36, 40–42, 44–49]
	Data security	Mechanisms for tracking and managing the reliability, authenticity and security of user-generated content can improve the performance of Social CRM techniques, but they are not considered in many SCRM techniques [5, 25, 26, 34, 41, 50, 51]
	Privacy	Ethical to collect, to process, to use and report on social media data is necessary to do not violate the customer privacy [5, 26, 40, 41, 48, 50–53]
	Velocity	There is a need for systems and processes that enable faster monitoring and data analysis [5, 11, 24–26, 36, 40, 41]

5 Final Remarks

The ways of relationship between companies and customers have changed dramatically due to web-users engagement with On-line Social Networks. Those platforms do not only represent a new communication channel, but are also a very rich data source about customer's behaviors and desires. Through the OSN data analysis, a new approach to perform Customer Relationship Management has emerged, the Social CRM, which brings up news services and market requirements.

In this paper, some challenges to make Social CRM work in real world have been addressed. Aiming to identify the state of practice and state of art in Social CRM, as well as to provide more reliability to the results obtained, three approaches were adopted. First, a literature review was conducted to demonstrate the current state of knowledge about the topic. Then, the findings were contrasted/validated through interviews with experts and case studies analysis. Moreover, presentations, discussion and audience feedback from some events organized/attended by Social CRM research center and Laboratory of Computational Intelligence members, from the University of Leipzig (DE) and Federal University of Pará (BR) respectively, were used to enrich the study.

As the major contributions of this article, the definition of Social CRM service portfolio, as well the identification and categorization of the main challenges in Social CRM context, should be highlighted. A list of potential Social CRM services was given considering the following CRM sectors: Sales, Marketing, Service and Support, Innovation, Collaboration and Customer Experience. For the implementation and delivery of the services listed, some challenges should be surpassed, for instance, the data volume produced is incompatible with some algorithms processing time, requiring optimization, as well as data reduction methods; different data types and structures demand a data fusion process in order to ensure data integrity, and, therefore, the analysis reliability. It is also important to consider the data security in order to guarantee the validity and to avoid legal and ethical issues.

Therefore, the results obtained point out a number of future research directions. This demonstrates that Social CRM is an emerging and promising research topic, involving many computer science fields such as machine learning, data fusion, information security and software development. In addition, this topic encompasses other disciplines, for instance marketing, operational research and information systems.

Acknowledgments. The research is partly supported by the German Academic Exchange Service (DAAD); National Council for the Improvement of Higher Education (CAPES); National Council for Scientific and Technological Development (CNPq); and Amazon Foundation for Studies and Research (Fapespa).

References

1. Greenberg, P.: CRM at the Speed of Light: Social CRM 2.0 Strategies, Tools, and Techniques for Engaging Your Customers, 4th edn. McGraw Hill Professional, New York (2008)
2. Chen, T.-Y., Liu, Y.-C., Chen, Y.-M.: A method of potential customer searching from opinions of network villagers in virtual communities. Online Inf. Rev. **40**, 146–167 (2016)
3. Reinhold, O., Alt, R.: Social customer relationship management: state of the art and learnings from current projects. In: 25th Bled eConference eDependability Reliab. Trust. eStructures, eProcesses, eOperations, pp. 155–169 (2012)
4. Baird, C.H., Parasnis, G.: From social media to social CRM: reinventing the customer relationship. Strateg. Leadersh. **39**, 27–34 (2011)
5. Malthouse, E.C., Haenlein, M., Skiera, B., Wege, E., Zhang, M.: Managing customer relationships in the social media era: introducing the social CRM house. J. Interact. Mark. **27**, 270–280 (2013)
6. Faase, R., Helms, R., Spruit, M.: Web 2.0 in the CRM domain: defining social CRM. Int. J. Electron. Cust. Relat. Manag. **5**(1), 1–22 (2011)
7. Van Looy, A.: Social Media Management. Springer, Cham (2016)
8. Kim, H.S., Kim, Y.G.: A CRM performance measurement framework: Its development process and application. Ind. Mark. Manag. **38**, 477–489 (2009)
9. von Brocke, J., Simons, A., Niehaves, B., Riemer, K., Plattfaut, R., Cleven, A., Brocke, J. Von, Reimer, K.: Reconstructing the giant: on the importance of rigour in documenting the literature search process. In: 17th European Conference on Information System, pp. 2206–2217 (2009)
10. Cooper, H.M.: Organizing knowledge synthesis: a taxonomy of literature reviews. Knowl. Soc. **1**, 104–126 (1988)
11. Küpper, T., Jung, R., Lehmkuhl, T., Walther, S.: Performance measures for social CRM: a literature review, pp. 125–139 (2014)
12. Rosenberger, M., Lehmkuhl, T., Jung, R.: Conceptualising and exploring user activities in social media. In: Janssen, M., Mäntymäki, M., Hidders, J., Klievink, B., Lamersdorf, W., Loenen, B., Zuiderwijk, A. (eds.) I3E 2015. LNCS, vol. 9373, pp. 107–118. Springer, Heidelberg (2015). doi:10.1007/978-3-319-25013-7_9
13. Lehmkuhl, T., Jung, R.: Towards social CRM - scoping the concept and guiding research. In: eInnovations: Challenges and Impacts for Individuals. Organizations and Society, pp. 190–205 (2013)
14. Webster, J., Watson, R.T.: Analyzing the past to prepare for the future writing a literature review. MIS Q. **26**, xiii–xxiii (2002)
15. Levy, Y., Ellis, T.J.: A systems approach to conduct an effective literature review in support of information systems research. Inf. Sci. **9**, 181–211 (2006)
16. Chen, X.: Google scholar's dramatic coverage improvement five years after debut. Ser. Rev. **36**, 221–226 (2010)
17. Alt, R., Reinhold, O.: How companies are implementing social customer relationship management: insights from two case studies. In: 26th Bled eConference, pp. 206–221 (2013)
18. Liberona, D., Ruiz, M., Fuenzalida, D.: Customer knowledge management in the age of social networks. In: Uden, L., Herrera, F., Bajo Pérez, J., Corchado Rodríguez, J. (eds.) 7th International Conference on Knowledge Management in Organizations: Service and Cloud Computing, vol. 172. Springer, Heidelberg (2013)
19. Harrigan, P.: From e-CRM to SCRM. Critical factors underpinning the social CRM activities of SMEs. Small Enterp. Res, **21**, 99–116 (2014)

20. Dey, S.S., Thommana, J., Dock, S.: Public agency performance management for improved service delivery in the digital age: case study. J. Manag. Eng. **31**, 1–11 (2015)
21. Tiruwa, A., Yadav, R.: Social CRM : An Emerging Medium. Adv. Comput. Sci. Inf. Technol. (ACSIT) **2**, 48–52 (2015)
22. Khobzi, H., Teimourpour, B.: LCP segmentation: a framework for evaluation of user engagement in online social networks. Comput. Hum. Behav. **50**, 101–107 (2015)
23. Kirakosyan, K.: The managerial view of social media usage in banking industry. In: Proceedings of the International Management Conference, pp. 225–241, Bucharest, Romania (2014)
24. Hanna, R., Rohm, A., Crittenden, V.L.: We're all connected: the power of the social media ecosystem. Bus. Horiz. **54**, 265–273 (2011)
25. Sigala, M.: eCRM 2.0 applications and trends: the use and perceptions of Greek tourism firms of social networks and intelligence. Comput. Hum. Behav. **27**, 655–661 (2011)
26. Soltani, Z., Navimipour, N.J.: Customer relationship management mechanisms: a systematic review of the state of the art literature and recommendations for future research. Comput. Hum. Behav. **61**, 667–688 (2016)
27. Killian, G., McManus, K.: A marketing communications approach for the digital era: managerial guidelines for social media integration. Bus. Horiz. **58**, 539–549 (2015)
28. Trainor, K.J., Andzulis, J., Rapp, A., Agnihotri, R.: Social media technology usage and customer relationship performance: a capabilities-based examination of social CRM. J. Bus. Res. **67**, 1201–1208 (2014)
29. Costello, T.: 2011 IT tech and strategy trends. IT Prof. **13**, 61–65 (2011)
30. Abedin, B.: Diffusion of adoption of facebook for customer relationship management in Australia: an exploratory study. J. Organ. End User Comput. **28**, 72 (2016)
31. Dănăiață, D., Margea, C., Kirakosyan, K., Negovan, A.M.: Social media in banking. a managerial perception from Mexico. Timisoara J. Econ. Bus. **7**, 147–174 (2015)
32. Jafari Navimipour, N., Soltani, Z.: The impact of cost, technology acceptance and employees' satisfaction on the effectiveness of the electronic customer relationship management systems. Comput. Hum. Behav. **55**, 1052–1066 (2016)
33. Alamsyah, A., Peranginangin, Y.: Network market analysis using large scale social network conversation of Indonesia's fast food industry, pp. 327–331 (2015)
34. Küpper, T., Wieneke, A., Lehmkuhl, T., Jung, R., Walther, S., Eymann, T.: Measuring social CRM performance. In: 12th International Conference on Wirtschaftsinformatik, pp. 887–901 (2015)
35. Wongsansukcharoen, J., Trimetsoontorn, J., Fongsuwan, W.: Social CRM, RMO and business strategies affecting banking performance effectiveness in B2B context. J. Bus. Ind. Mark. **30**, 742–760 (2015)
36. Courtney, M.: Puzzling out big data [information technology analytics]. Eng. Technol. **7** (12), 56–60 (2013)
37. Kirakosyan, K.: A Managerial view of social media usage in banking: comparative study for Armenian and Romanian banking systems. In: 24th International-Business-Information-Management-Association Conference, pp. 1152–1171, Milan, Italy (2014)
38. Li, L., Sun, T., Peng, W., Li, T.: Measuring engagement effectiveness in social media. In: Proceedings of SPIE, 83020F–83020F-9, vol. 8302 (2012)
39. Martin, C.L.: Retrospective: compatibility management: customer-to-customer relationships in service environments. J. Serv. Mark. **30**, 11–15 (2016)
40. Stieglitz, S., Dang-Xuan, L., Bruns, A., Neuberger, C.: Social media analytics. Bus. Inf. Syst. Eng. **6**, 89–96 (2014)

41. Su, W.C.: Integrating and mining virtual communities across multiple online social networks: concepts, approaches and challenges integrating and mining virtual communities across multiple online social networks: In: 2014 Fourth International Conference on Digital Information and Communication Technology and it's Applications (DICTAP) Technology and it's Applications, pp. 199–204 (2015)
42. Philip Chen, C.L., Zhang, C.Y.: Data-intensive applications, challenges, techniques and technologies: a survey on big data. Inf. Sci. (Ny) **275**, 314–347 (2014)
43. Laney, D.: 3D data management: controlling data volume, velocity and variety. META Gr. Res. Note. **6**, 70 (2001)
44. Wan, S., Paris, C., Georgakopoulos, D.: Social media data aggregation and mining for internet-scale customer relationship management. In: 2015 IEEE International Conference on Information Reuse and Integration, pp. 39–48 (2015)
45. Ma, Y., Xu, J., Peng, D., Zhang, T., Jin, C., Qu, H., Chen, W., Peng, Q.: A visual analysis approach for community detection of multi-context mobile social networks. J. Comput. Sci. Technol. **28**, 797–809 (2013)
46. Scheib, C., Lugmayr, A.: Information systems and management in media industries a first problem evaluation from a business perspective. In: 2014 IEEE International Conference on Multimedia and Expo Workshops (ICMEW), pp. 1–5. IEEE (2014)
47. Liberati, C., Camillo, F.: Discovering hidden concepts in predictive models for texts' polarization. Int. J. Data Warehous. Min. **11**, 29–48 (2015)
48. Zubcsek, P.P., Sarvary, M.: Advertising to a social network. Quant. Mark. Econ. **9**, 71–107 (2011)
49. Chan, H.K., Wang, X., Lacka, E., Zhang, M.: A mixed-method approach to extracting the value of social media data. Prod. Oper. Manag. **25**, 568–583 (2016)
50. Kizza, J.M.: Ethical and Social Issues in the Information Age: Texts in Computer Science, pp. 1–335. Springer, London (2010)
51. Sutikno, T., Stiawan, D., Subroto, I.M.I.: Fortifying big data infrastructures to face security and privacy issues. Telkomnika (Telecommun. Comput. Electron. Control **12**, 751–752 (2014)
52. Harrigan, P., Soutar, G., Choudhury, M.M., Lowe, M.: Modelling CRM in a social media age. Australas. Mark. J. **23**, 27–37 (2015)
53. Hseih, P.L.A.-Y.: Speech or silence. Online Inf. Rev. **38**, 881–895 (2014)

Emotions in Online Reviews to Better Understand Customers' Brand Perception

Armin Felbermayr[✉]

Katholische Universität Eichstätt-Ingolstadt, Auf der Schanz 49,
85049 Ingolstadt, Germany
armin.felbermayr@ku.de

Abstract. Measuring customers' opinions based on online customer reviews pose an integral part of Social CRM. However, polarity analysis, i.e., positive vs. negative opinion, fails to map the emotional mindset of customers. To complement existing Social CRM tools with a comprehensible, yet efficient way of measuring emotions towards brands, a model is presented to differentiate eight basic human emotions. Emotion terms get extracted and categorized review-wise by an eight dimensional emotion lexicon into eight dimensional feature vectors. These vectors train the random forest classifier to distinguish positive helpful from negative helpful reviews. The classifiers inherent ability to display single feature importance enables marketers to infer the importance of each basic emotion. The ability to measure the interrelationship of emotions towards brands equips marketers with a powerful tool to better understand consumers and to adapt CRM campaigns accordingly. Along with the technicalities of the model a way of interpreting results is presented.

Keywords: Brands · Emotions · Online customer reviews · Helpfulness · Text mining · Social CRM

1 Introduction

Customers use social web sites, such as social networks (e.g., Facebook) and e-commerce platforms (e.g., Amazon) to express their opinions about brands. According to Reinhold and Alt [10] five different resources from social media web sites can be differentiated: posting body (actual conveyed posting), posting envelope (meta data of postings), profile body (data of profiles), profile envelope (meta data of profiles), and links (interrelatedness between postings and profiles).

The helpfulness voting represents a very valuable instance of the posting envelope of online customer reviews in many online webshops. Although classified as meta data, helpfulness votes are directly dependent to a review's posting body, because customers vote on the helpfulness of reviews based on the textual content of a review. In a sense, the helpfulness votes may indicate the influencing power of reviews, as they represent the readers opportunity to vote for good (bad) quality reviews, which in turn will be listed higher (lower) and therefore pose a higher (lower) influence on other consumers.

W. Abramowicz et al. (Eds.): BIS 2016 Workshops, LNBIP 263, pp. 233–244, 2017.
DOI: 10.1007/978-3-319-52464-1_21

The analysis of the posting body represents another complex task to Social CRM, especially since the need for more than just a polarity (positive vs. negative) oriented analysis perspective has arisen. Albeit bipolar opinions about brands are hidden in the unstructured datasets of social web sites, such as social networks (e.g., Facebook) and e-commerce platforms (e.g., Amazon), they do not fulfil the demand for a multidimensional analysis perspective. Emotional content, however, is multidimensional and enables brand managers to better understand the way customers feel about their brands.

It has been shown that emotions which customers feel concerning a brand, have a direct effect on their perception of a brand's image, i.e., marketers can use the emotional bond between a customer and a brand for a superior brand performance. However, the task of mining emotions from large amounts of unstructured data requires very innovative Social CRM tools, because disciplines such as psychology, linguistics and informatics are involved.

As far as we know, the triangle among emotions, brands and online reviews, has not been studied at all. Therefore, we want to shed more light onto the connection between emotions and their role for brands as expressed through customers in online reviews.

In our study we ask and answer the following research questions:

- What effective, yet comprehensible methodology can be used to measure the importance of various emotions for different brands within and across several product categories?
- In what way can obtained results be analyzed by marketers to gain more insight into their or competitors' brands?

Our approach is valuable to both, practice and theory, because on the one hand it equips practitioners with a methodology to determine the emotional appeal of customers towards brands throughout and within product categories, and on the other hand it provides academia with new insight on the interplay between emotions, brands and reviews.

The remainder of this article is structured as follows: In Sect. 2 we will introduce readers into most related research results about emotions in reviews and brands. A method to extract and measure customers emotions towards brands from reviews is explained in Sect. 3. In Sect. 4 we discuss attained results of our model based on brand management literature, before we conclude our study in Sect. 5 by pointing out further related research questions in the Social CRM domain.

2   Related Work

Only very recently scholars from academia and marketing strategists from practice have realized the necessity for more investigation into the multidimensionalities of customers' opinions.

The study of [6] underscores the importance of emotional content in Social CRM. An intercept survey with more than one million US consumers across

30 industries and 400+ brands has been conducted to identify most important "emotional motivators" such as "feel a sense of belonging" and "feel a sense of freedom". In a next step the "emotional motivators" were used by multivariate regression and structural equation modelling to derive the buying behavior of customers based on sales data. The latter revealed the most important customers based on "emotional motivators" for different product categories and brands. In a final step the investments into key functions of the monitored retailer (e.g. the store location strategy) could be improved. The key findings of that study are: (i) The most important "emotional motivators" vary category-wise and brand-wise for the group of best customers. (ii) Customers' most important "emotional motivators" may change during the customer journey. (iii) The optimization of investments across companies' functions, based on "emotional motivators" improves Social CRM. (iv) In terms of emotional connectedness it is better to transition customers from highly satisfied to fully connected than from unconnected to highly satisfied.

To our knowledge, the study of [4], was the first to prove that emotion dimensions really represent a valuable feature set for *online customer reviews*. For this reason they created a model to classify reviews as "helpful" or "not helpful" by the help of term extraction, based on an emotion dictionary. Our approach varies from their study in the following main aspects: First, their study was very broad, in the sense that they aimed at enriching the list of functional feature sets with emotion dimensions. On the contrary, we close a more specific research gap by applying a classification model based on emotion vocabulary with a focus towards brands. Second, their study relies on the emotion paradigm of Scherer [11], while we rely on Plutchik's theory of emotion dimensionalities [9]. Their lexicon comprises of 267 stem words distributed across Scherer's 36 emotion dimensions, while we make use of the NRC dictionary [8], which consists of 8,202 terms distributed across Plutchik's eight emotion dimensions. For this study we rely on Plutchik's theory and the underlying NRC dictionary, however, in future work NRC's dictionary may be merged together with Scherer's dictionary (dictionary ensemble schemes).

The well-known and established theory on emotion dimensionalities of Plutchik argues that joy, trust, fear and surprise are the most basic emotions with sadness, disgust, anger and anticipation as their neutralizing counterparts [9].

In summary, the two perspectives 'emotions in reviews' and 'emotions for brands' have been well-examined in the literature separately. However, we aim at joining these two dimensions to the more specific view of 'emotions for brands in reviews.' So far, according to our knowledge, there is no study that has considered brands' emotions in reviews by using a text-mining tool. Therefore, we propose a method to close this research gap with the following study.

3   Proposed Method

The procedural order of our method is as follows: (i) Emotions are extracted from reviews, based on an emotion lexicon. (ii) Reviews are categorized into helpful or not helpful, based on their helpfulness ratings. Finally, (i) and (ii) are combined to learn which emotion dimensions influence the helpfulness of reviews for a certain product brand.

This section explains the technicalities of our classification model, which learns to categorize by the help of a feature vector and a target function. To ensure reproducibility of our approach, we introduce into the creation of the feature vector based on an example and explain the target function accordingly. Finally, the underlying classifier will be briefly described.

3.1   Problem Formulation

We aim at identifying the impact of emotion dimensions when used as features that predict the helpfulness-rating of online customer reviews. Therefore we formally define the studied problem as a classification problem, which involves the learning of a classifier γ as follows:

$$\gamma : R \longrightarrow C, \tag{1}$$

where $R = \{r_1, ..., r_n\}$ is the set of reviews and $C = \{c_1, ..., c_J\}$ is an ordered set representing discrete levels (expressed as ranges) of helpfulness-ratings. In our study we focus on two levels, namely of helpful and not helpful reviews. Each review $r_i \in R$ is assigned a helpfulness level $c_j \in C$ and a classifier learns from emotion features, represented by the classification feature vector, to determine the level of helpfulness, represented by the classification target function.

Classification Feature Vector. *The classification feature vector represents the proportional distribution of Plutchik's eight emotion dimensions, i.e., the classification feature vector is a 8×1 vector, each row representing an emotion dimension.*

In particular we define the feature vector as follows:

$$V_r = \sum_{t \in T_r} \left(\sqrt{f_t^r} \times e_t \right), \tag{2}$$

where T_r is the set of distinct terms in review r and f_t^r is the frequency of term $t \in T_r$ in review r, and the eight-dimensional vector e_t represents Plutchik's eight emotion dimensions "anger", "anticipation", "disgust", "fear", "joy", "sadness", "surprise" and "trust" for each term t. After all, V_r is the sum over the square root of the frequency of emotion terms in a review multiplied by all emotion dimensions for each word, and repeats until all terms of a review are checked.

By taking the square root of the frequency of detected review emotion terms f_t^r the impact of single overused emotion words is regularized. Please note that we choose the square root for simplicity reasons, but any other relativation means may be used.

Please refer to Fig. 1, where a fictitious example for the online review text "Perfect! This shirt is perfect! I love it! [...]" is depicted. In a first step, the review

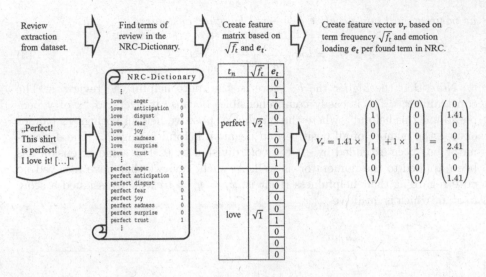

Fig. 1. An example of an unnormalized feature vector creation - the conversion from a review text through the NRC lexicon to a vectorial interpretation.

is extracted and simplified by the deletion of any punctuation and capitalization. In a second step, only terms which occur in the NRC remain for further processing. In a third step, the frequency is determined together with the emotional loading assigned by the NRC dictionary for each detected term. In a fourth step the feature vector V_r is calculated, based on the feature matrix created in step three.

The adjusted frequencies of the two terms for the example review are $\sqrt{2} = 1.41$ and $\sqrt{1} = 1$. The feature vector V_r incorporates the frequencies and the emotion weights according to Plutchik's eight dimensions as already mentioned above, so that the first item of a vector represents the first dimension ("anger"), the second item the second dimension ("anticipation"), etc. For the given example this yet unnormalized feature vector would contribute to three emotion dimensions ("anticipation","joy" and "trust").

Finally, the normalized feature vector $V_r' = (0, 0.27, 0, 0, 0.46, 0, 0, 0.27)$ is calculated, which cancels the length as a feature, by dividing V_r by its column sum. In other words the underlying review text is represented with 0.27 for anticipation, 0.46 for joy and 0.27 for trust, while anger, disgust, fear, sadness and surprise remain unused in the review example. These normalized feature vectors are calculated for all reviews and follow the intuition "the higher a feature dimension is valued, the more present is its corresponding proportional emotion intensity in the review."

Helpfulness Score. *The helpfulness score h_r of each review is defined as the logarithm of the ratio between the number of times that the review has been voted* *as positive (x_r) and negative ($y_r - x_r$) by other customers.*[1]

$$h_r = log_{10} \frac{x_r + 1}{y_r - x_r + 1} \text{ for } x_r \leqq y_r \tag{3}$$

Note that the higher the h_r score is, the more helpful the review is. The constraint $x_r \leqq y_r$ is easily comprehensible, because it refers to "x of y people found this helpful", where the number of positive helpful votings x_r cannot exceed the number of all positive *and* negative helpful votings y_r. The denominator has been extended by +1 to avoid division by 0. The same extension has been applied to the numerator as well. As such, reviews that have received no vote regarding their helpfulness (that is, $x_r = y_r = 0$) will be assigned a score $h_r = 0$, which is intuitive.

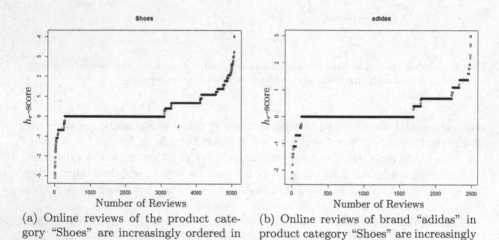

(a) Online reviews of the product category "Shoes" are increasingly ordered in terms of their h_r-score.

(b) Online reviews of brand "adidas" in product category "Shoes" are increasingly ordered in terms of their h_r-score.

Fig. 2. We use thresholds to differentiate helpful from not helpful reviews according to our helpfulness-rating h_r. The threshold achieves a balanced separation of not helpful reviews ($h_r < 0$) from helpful reviews ($h_r \geqq 0$) to improve the classifying power.

Based on the h_r scores, that we compute on Amazon's "x of y people found this helpful"-representation, we want to identify two target classes, namely the helpful and not helpful reviews. These two classes comprise the typical 'positive' and 'negative' classes in a binary classification problem. Using the real data from our empirical evaluation (see Sect. 4), all reviews can be ordered increasingly according to their h_r score. Figure 2 illustrates such a case in the left figure (a) for a product category over all brands and in the right figure (b) for only one brand within the same product category. Please note, that all other product categories and brands, that we examined in our discussion, have a similar distribution of h_r.

---

[1] We follow the assumption that, as is typical in many e-commerce sites, customers can vote a review as helpful or not helpful.

We distinguish two classes by a threshold at $h_r = 0$ for all product categories and brands based on the logic that for all discussed cases, this threshold effectively balances the amount of helpful $(h_r \geqq 0)$ and not helpful reviews $(h_r < 0)$ in a way which enables the classifier to learn the two classes.

With this possibility to discriminate the positive (helpful reviews) from the negative (not helpful reviews) class, we turn our attention to the classifier, which learns the pictured classes based on the emotion features extracted from the reviews.

3.2   Classifier

We use the popular classification algorithm Random Forest [1] to classify real-world-reviews as helpful or not helpful according to their emotion content. When comparing this method with other state-of-the-art supervised algorithms, Random Forest resides among the top approaches in terms of different performance metrics [2]. Thus, we believe that machine learning methods, such as Random Forests, enable marketers to efficiently analyze challenging data, such as text of online reviews. Random forests combine a large collection of decorrelated decision trees in order to reduce the variance of noisy and unbiased models (so called "bagging"). In contrast to standard decision trees, where all variables are taken into account to determine the best split, random forest finds its best split among a subset of randomly chosen predictors. By this inherent randomness of random forests the major problem of overfitting can be addressed. Moreover, the construction of random forests helps with the differentiation of important from not important variables, by the calculation of errors per permutation. In a sense the error per each step can be probabilistically measured and thus, the variable importance can be determined. This is a great advantage over other popular methods (such as support vector machines), since their decision finding and the interpretation of their variables are not that intuitive and self-explanatory. This is an important characteristic in our study, which focuses on identifying the importance of emotion dimensions. Thus, based on an accurate classification model (measured based on 10-fold cross validation), we can measure the importance of the used features, which reflect the importance of the examined emotion dimensions.

4   Empirical Evaluation

This Section shows which data we used to apply our approach. Additionally, in Subsect. 4.1 the F_1-score is introduced as our measure of the classification power of our model. The F_1-score measures precision and recall in a combined and strict manner.

Subsection 4.2 displays results, which we slice into different analytical perspectives in order to get a whole picture of the performance of our approach. For each of these perspectives we discuss the emotion perception by customers according to brand research literature.

4.1   Data and Performance Measure

Our method is used on the Amazon review dataset from [7], where 6.6 Million users wrote 34.6 Million reviews between June 1995 and March 2013. By applying a dataset-inherent list of brand keys, almost 70,000 products with all their corresponding reviews could be extracted from the dataset to ensure the necessary brand-relatedness of analyzed product reviews. We chose this dataset, because it contains all necessary input (review texts and helpfulness-ratings), it is publicly available, and Amazon is a representative online retailer. Amazon provides the reviewing channel openly to improve customers' decision making. There, reviews present the social interaction from customer to customer (C2C) to help each other to sort out the right reviews.

The validity and quality of review texts of this dataset has been proven by classification experiments, which showed that review texts are in accordance with their product rating (number of "stars"). However, in the process of analyzing emotions expressed for brands, we discovered that reviews in some cases duplicate in the sense that reviews from product category 'Shoes' can be found in 'Sports_Outdoors' and vice versa.

We use the calculation of precision and recall as established measures to evaluate the classification power of our model. In line with this, we use the F_1 score,

$$F_1^{\pm} = 2 \times \frac{Precision \times Recall}{Precision + Recall}, \tag{4}$$

which is a strict measure from the information retrieval domain and computes F_1 scores separately for the positive $(+)$ class $(h_r \geqq 0)$ and negative $(-)$ class $(h_r < 0)$ per product category and brand. The harmonic mean within the F_1-score in Eq. 4 accounts for the inherent strictness, because both precision and recall need to be high at the same time to yield an overall high F_1-score. Therefore, this score enables to evenly take into account both precision and recall of the positive and negative helpfulness classes in a strict manner.

In order to take into account both values equally and to have a full picture, we calculated a final combined F_1-score, as follows:

$$F_1 = \frac{F_1^+ + F_1^-}{2}, \tag{5}$$

which takes into account skewness in the available dataset. The average F_1-score of 0.76 for all considered brands, underscores that we attained a classification model which adequately discriminates reviews based on their helpfulness rating for the various examined brands.

4.2   Results

Due to the inherent methodological characteristic of a classification, the importance of each of the dependent variables (emotion dimensions) can be determined to explain the independent variable (helpfulness score). Attained results, i.e., the

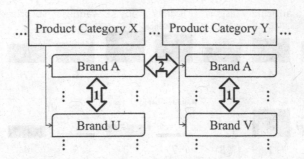

Fig. 3. Two main perspectives for a brand related analysis: within (vertical arrow "1") and across (horizontal arrow "2") product categories.

relative importance of each emotion dimension per brand, can be analyzed from various perspectives. Two basic analytical perspectives are indicated by the numbered arrows in Fig. 3. Please note that the numbered arrows are in accordance with the enumeration of the following two marketing applications:

(1) *Within one product category different brands are compared to each other:* For the *first* perspective we compare the distribution of emotion terms of two different brands (Guide Gear and Earth) with all other brands (i.e. the average across all brands) in the product category 'Shoes'. Our goal is to determine the differences of single brands to the average of all shoe brands. Any deviation from the average can imply necessary measures from the brand manager to improve the brand's emotional perception by customers. The results of our mentioned sample are depicted in Fig. 4.

When orienting to the average across all shoe-brands, then trust, joy and fear are the dominantly used emotion terms. While trust and joy seem rather intuitive, a brand manager can relate the expressions of emotion dimension fear to blisters or to diabetic feet problems.

Interestingly, Guide Gear successfully replaced fear with anticipation as one of their main three emotions in customer reviews (Fig. 4). It seems that Guide Gear's customers really anticipate this brand's shoes and express a lot of trust towards this brand. When looking more closely at Guide Gears' products it shows that their aiming is at outdoor enthusiasts, because they are specialized in heavy weight and waterproof hunting boots, which might explain the reduced 'fear' dimension, because of the strong solidity in terms of their material and massive style.

In contrast to the average shoe brand, customers of Earth seem to express much less trust (rank six) in their reviews (Fig. 4). According to brand literature the need for trust developing is crucial for customers' loyalty which should lead the respective brand manager to initiate counter measures to improve the brands' trustworthiness. Another issue is the great amount of sadness which is linked to this brands' reviews. However, one must not forget that Earth sells "health and wellness-oriented footwear" (www.earthbrands.com), which leads customers very

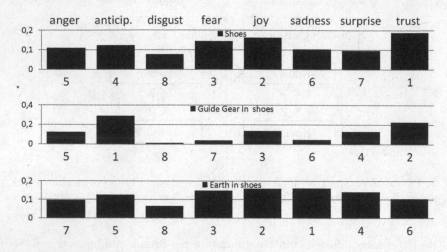

Fig. 4. Relative distribution of emotion terms for all brands in product category Shoes vs. the individual brands 'Guide Gear' and 'Earth' in product category Shoes. Numbers below each bar indicate the ranking of an emotion dimension per brand and product category.

frequently to report about their foot health issues in a very sad mood, where pain-related vocabulary adds to the respective sadness emotion dimension. For this very brand instance, even well placed measures may not be sufficient to prevent the model from detecting naturally high sadness-levels.

Our examples show, that a careful investigation of the brand, its goal, products and customer types will not be negligible when interpreting the results individually. In further research a more product category related dictionary can be created to improve the picture across all emotions.

(2) *One brand is compared across product categories:* Brands may offer various products in order to diversify their product range and to reduce their overall risk by investing into several product segments. Research has shown that an authentic perception of a brand is highly recommended, as with the existing competition in developed markets "it is no longer sufficient to be known. Therefore, brands must consistently evoke a set of values and stimulate emotional resonance" [3], which is not facilitated by contradicting perceived brands' emotions.

In the case of the brand adidas Originals, where online customer reviews are compared across the product categories 'Shoes' and 'Sports_Outdoors' (see Fig. 5), trust and anticipation are the only emotion dimensions which are almost equally ranked (rank three for shoes and rank two for Sports_Outdoors). Thus, brand management has not yet succeeded in establishing a similar emotional appeal of adidas Originals to customers throughout all product categories.

Fig. 5. Relative distribution of emotion terms of the brand adidas Originals across the product categories Shoes and Sports_Outdoors. Numbers below each bar indicate the ranking of an emotion dimension per brand and product category.

5   Conclusions

Managers can use advanced Social CRM methodologies to exploit the constantly growing amount of unstructured data of social websites. While several opinion mining techniques such as polarity analysis are already applied by many marketers, an emotion-driven approach can yield a new competitive advantage [6].

The proposed method enables marketers to learn the importance of Plutchik's eight emotion dimensions ("anger", "anticipation", "disgust", "fear", "joy", "sadness", "surprise" and "trust") for each brand within and across product categories. Knowing customers emotional perception of brands, enables marketers to anticipate actual trends and to improve their targeted advertising campaigns [5].

According to [6] emotions change with a customer's position in the customer journey. Therefore, possible future work could investigate the dynamics of emotions subject to time. While random forest presents an efficient and comprehensible method for classification, another method such as regression (and different underlying algorithms) can be compared using several descriptive statistics to find the method with the best cost-benefit-ratio. Although, the utilized dictionary contains more than 8,000 emotional terms, its enhancement by a dictionary ensemble scheme could improve the dictionary based approach. Lastly, other social media channels can be used to enhance the dataset and to test the model on other textual content than product reviews.

References

1. Breiman, L.: Random forests. Mach. Learn. **45**(1), 5–32 (2001)
2. Caruana, R., Niculescu-Mizil, A.: An empirical comparison of supervised learning algorithms. In: Proceedings of the 23rd International Conference on Machine Learning, pp. 161–168. ACM (2006)
3. Kapferer, J.-N.: The New Strategic Brand Management: Advanced Insights and Strategic Thinking. Kogan Page Publishers (2012)

4. Martin, L., Sintsova, V., Pearl, P.: Are influential writers more objective? An analysis of emotionality in review comments. In: Proceedings of the Companion Publication of the 23rd International Conference on World Wide Web Companion, pp. 799–804. International World Wide Web Conferences Steering Committee (2014)
5. Maynard, D., Bontcheva, K., Rout, D.: Challenges in developing opinion mining tools for social media. In: Proceedings of the@ NLP can u tag# usergeneratedcontent, pp. 15–22 (2012)
6. Scott, M., Alan, Z., Daniel, L.: The New Science of Customer Emotions. Harvard Business School Publishing Corporation (2015)
7. McAuley, J., Leskovec, J.: Hidden factors and hidden topics: understanding rating dimensions with review text. In: Proceedings of the 7th ACM Conference on Recommender Systems, pp. 165–172. ACM (2013)
8. Mohammad, S.M., Turney, P.D.: Crowdsourcing a word-emotion association lexicon. Comput. Intell. 29(3), 436–465 (2013)
9. Plutchik, R.: A General Psychoevolutionary Theory of Emotion. In: Theories of Emotion, vol. 1 (1980)
10. Olaf, R., Rainer, A.: Social Customer Relationship Management: State of the Art and Learnings from Current Projects (2012)
11. Scherer, K.R.: What are emotions? And how can they be measured? Soc. Sci. Inf. 44(4), 695–729 (2005)

Performance Evaluation of Sentiment Analysis Methods for Brazilian Portuguese

Douglas Cirqueira[1], Antonio Jacob Jr.[2(✉)], Fábio Lobato[3],
Adamo Lima de Santana[1], and Márcia Pinheiro[1]

[1] Electrical and Computer Engineering Department, ITEC,
Federal University of Pará, Belém 66075110, Brazil
{douglas.cirqueira, marcia.pinheiro}@itec.ufpa.br,
adamo@ufpa.br
[2] Technological Sciences Center, State University of Maranhão,
São Luís 65950000, Brazil
jacobjr@ufpa.br
[3] Federal University of Western Pará, Santarém 68035110, Brazil
fabio.lobato@ufopa.edu.br

Abstract. Daily, a big data of media, thoughts and opinions can be noticed on Online Social Networks (OSN), resulting from their user's interaction and sharing of information. In Brazil, this is strongly observed, as Brazilians are often active on the Internet. The business and academic communities around the world are aware of these events, due their possibilities to improve social customer relationship management. Therefore, this work aims to show a performance comparison between algorithms for Sentiment Analysis (SA), in their Portuguese and English versions, with datasets composed of Brazilian Portuguese comments from OSN, and their translations. The results highlight the need for proposals in specific language and Social Media context, given the performance presented by Portuguese version methods.

Keywords: Natural language processing · Text mining · Sentiment analysis · Opinion mining · Data mining

1 Introduction

Users, companies and institutions have used sites and blogs as channels for sharing information and interacting with their audience. More than this, those entities have used OSN as communication channels, another phenomenon that is born from the Web 2.0 era [1].

Daily, millions of active users are online on Facebook and Twitter, posting many sorts of contents, such as videos, photos and personal information, with relatives and friends [2, 3]. In this scenario, it is also noticeable a trending to use OSN for sharing opinions regarding other users, famous people and events. Moreover, people are also using those platforms to express their thoughts and analysis on companies and their products as well [4]. Consequently, those facts can result in influencing of other people opinions. The research and industry communities from social customer relationship

© Springer International Publishing AG 2017
W. Abramowicz et al. (Eds.): BIS 2016 Workshops, LNBIP 263, pp. 245–251, 2017.
DOI: 10.1007/978-3-319-52464-1_22

management and marketing have observed all these events [5]. One reason for this is the fact that, after launching a campaign on their social channels, brands can adapt their products and business strategy accordingly with the feedback received from their audience [6]. Although, for this to happen, it is necessary a deeper analysis regarding what people have commented on their social profiles.

In order to deal with those situations, the area of automatic sentiment detection has born, commonly known as Sentiment Analysis (SA). This field of study aims to classify text data by the polarity present on it, towards a positive, negative, and sometimes, neutral sentiment [7]. Among the previous work in Opinion Mining (OM) or SA, the English language is often found, since it was one of the first languages in which this analysis was performed [8].

In this context, Brazil is a great example of a scenario where all those facts can be observed. The Brazilian population is one of the most active on OSN in the world. This could be justified because Brazilians are very communicative and spend so much time sharing media and information [9].

Given this scenario, this work aims to present a research in progress regarding a performance evaluation of different techniques for SA, using Brazilian Portuguese text data coming from OSN. In order to achieve this, a group of algorithms and resources for OM, in their English and Portuguese versions, will be compared against a dataset composed of labels given by human evaluation. The idea is to evaluate the hypothesis that, methods specifically developed for Portuguese perform better in SA than English approaches, with translated datasets. The results have shown two methods with higher performance against others in the scenario proposed, although their results are not considered as good as necessary for real-world applications. In addition, Portuguese techniques have shown an unexpected performance, accordingly with the previous mentioned hypothesis.

2 Related Work

Some previous work in SA reveals performance evaluations from a variety of methods to perform OM in different sorts of data and using different methodologies. In Cambria et al. [11], four main approaches for performing OM are presented: keyword spotting, lexical affinity, statistical and concept-based approaches.

In Ribeiro et al. [12], the authors have done a benchmark with 22 sentence-level SA methods in order to exploit their performance on 18 gold standard datasets, composed of Social Networks, blog comments and reviews contexts. The target language was English. In addition, they have made public available a tool called iFeel, which is a web system composed of 19 SA methods ready to use. This system allows a user to perform OM in different languages, but with the aid of a translation step to English language. This can be a problem, since translation may cause loss of meaning in some expressions in another language.

The work of Balage et al. [13] provides a comparative study and analysis regarding three dictionaries for OM in the Portuguese language. The authors use LIWC [14], Opinion Lexicon [15] and SentiLex [10], in order to evaluate their performances in a corpus composed of reviews from 13 different books. Moreover, they apply an adaptation of the algorithm SO-CAL [16] to compute the polarities of documents using those dictionaries. Since the accuracy level of all methods in this work was lower than 58%, it would be interesting to try another algorithm to manipulate those sentiment dictionaries. Therefore, Ribeiro et al. [12] exploits the performance of different approaches for SA [11] only for English language or with translation-based methodology for other languages. Moreover, Balage et al. [13] considers only Portuguese language using reviews dataset, with only the SO-CAL algorithm. Given this scenario, this work aims to evaluate different methods that work for both English and Portuguese languages, using Social Networks context data in Portuguese and translated to English language.

3   Methodology

The methodological steps followed in this work are composed of: data gathering, data preparation, translation and the sentiment classification.

3.1   Data Gathering

Two main topics were selected to build the datasets for this work: public institutions management and Web bullying. The reason was the larger number of comments and presence of polarity in discussions about those themes.

The datasets were composed of Facebook comments and Twitter posts (tweets), in Brazilian Portuguese language. From Facebook, four Brazilian fanpages were selected: Municipal Government of Belém and Curitiba, Federal University of Pará Oficial (UFPA) and Humaniza Redes, which is a fanpage from the Brazilian federal government to combat violence against the Human Rights, on the Internet. The total of comments collected was 455,819, for the year of 2015, through the Facebook Graph API. Moreover, from the Twitter Rest API, 8,264 tweets were collected, containing keywords regarding the topics chosen, such as "ufpa", "prefeituradebelem" and "prefeituradecuritiba".

3.2   Data Preparation

The next step was to retrieve a random sample of 10,000 comments from all Facebook fanpages. Given the number of tweets available was already 8,264, this number of instances was kept.

Data Cleaning. From Facebook data, people's names tagged in comments were removed. Those represent mentions for other users, so they receive notifications regarding a post they were tagged in, which is a characteristic that does not have sentiment or opinion. The same is valid for retweets and check-in tweets, from Twitter data, which represent redundant documents and user location indicators, respectively. Thus, those were removed as well. Finally, comments from Facebook and tweets from the sources of data, such as UFPA and the Municipal Governments, were removed because of their probable bias towards a given sentiment. In the end, the data available was composed of 7,767 Facebook comments and 4,044 tweets.

Data Labeling. A system named OpinionLabel (http://linc.ufpa.br/opinionlabel - only available in Portuguese) was created for collecting sentiment labels from Brazilian volunteers. Those were specialists in Computer Science/Engineering and Communications from UFPA. In this system, the users were able to tag comments from the datasets as Positive, Negative or Neutral, so those contributions could be used in this work. The idea of cross-validation was used, so there were three evaluators per comment and tweet, to increase the labels confidence level.

Translation. The translation API from Yandex, a Web search platform, was used to translate all the Portuguese comments and tweets to English, for the SA algorithms in their English versions. This API was used because it is the same tool applied for translation-based SA in [12], from where the English version algorithms, used in this work, have been selected, which makes the performance analysis fair.

3.3   Sentiment Classification

The metrics of Precision, Recall, F-Measure (F1), Macro F1, Accuracy, and Coverage were selected [12] for this performance evaluation. In addition, the Agreement level was used to ensure the datasets manually labeled were reliable, regarding the labels given by the volunteers on the OpinionLabel system.

Since the idea was to compare approaches in their English and Portuguese versions, only approaches available for both languages were chosen, such as Opinion Lexicon dictionary [15], SentiStrength algorithm [17] and the method SO-CAL from [12, 13]. Vader [18] was only available for English. Then, an adaptation of this algorithm was implemented in order to work with it in the Portuguese language. This step includes the translation from English to Portuguese of Vader inner elements, such as negation terms, intensifiers, degree adverbs, contrast conjunctions and some special case idioms, such as "the bomb" in English, which can represent "o cara" in Portuguese.

4   Tests and Results

The first approach, called OpLexicon_EN and OpLexicon_PT, is a simple algorithm that counts the number of positive and negative words found in the Opinion Lexicon dictionary [15], in its English and Portuguese versions, respectively. Then, it takes the difference to retrieve the polarity. The V_OpLexicon_EN and V_OpLexicon_PT are using Vader [18] heuristics with the Opinion Lexicon [15] dictionary in both languages. In third, the SentiStrength algorithm has an English version and a multi-language implementation available at Ribeiro et al. [12], which was used. Finally, the method SO-CAL [13] was used with the Opinion Lexicon dictionary in English and Portuguese.

From the OpinionLabel system, it was possible to have contributions from 111 volunteers, which resulted in 792 positive and 544 negative comments from Facebook, while 184 positive and 227 negative tweets were obtained. In addition, for each class, 500 comments from Facebook and 150 tweets were randomly sampled.

Table 1 shows the results for the Facebook dataset, while Table 2 for Twitter data, considering the metrics previously mentioned.

Table 1. Algorithms performance for Facebook data.

Algorithm	Accuracy	P Pos	P Neg	R Pos	R Neg	F1 Pos	F1 Neg	Macro F1	Coverage
OpLexicon_EN	29.10	62.20	88.08	**31.60**	26.60	41.91	40.86	41.39	**40.50**
OpLexicon PT	**27.70**	51.96	77.12	31.80	**23.60**	**39.45**	**36.14**	**37.80**	45.90
V_OpLexicon_EN	47.40	72.37	**88.83**	56.60	38.20	63.52	53.43	58.48	60.60
V_OpLexicon_PT	37.70	55.42	72.45	45.00	28.40	49.67	40.80	45.24	60.20
SentiStrength_EN	**60.00**	**77.65**	84.29	**67.40**	52.60	**72.16**	64.78	**68.47**	**74.60**
SentiStrength_PT	50.60	70.45	78.75	43.40	**57.80**	53.71	**66.67**	60.19	67.50
SO-CAL OpLexicon_EN	47.40	73.90	87.04	57.20	37.60	64.49	52.51	58.50	60.30
SO-CAL OpLexicon_PT	34.60	56.46	**71.74**	42.80	26.40	48.69	38.60	43.64	56.30

Table 2. Algorithms performance for Twitter data.

Algorithm	Accuracy	P Pos	P Neg	R Pos	R Neg	F1 Pos	F1 Neg	Macro F1	Coverage
OpLexicon_EN	34.67	65.00	**78.79**	34.67	34.67	45.22	48.15	46.68	48.67
OpLexicon PT	**26.00**	**53.75**	61.40	**28.67**	23.34	37.39	33.82	35.60	**45.67**
V_OpLexicon_EN	46.67	71.30	77.78	**51.33**	42.00	**59.69**	54.55	**57.12**	63.00
V_OpLexicon_PT	34.33	57.00	58.33	40.67	28.00	47.47	37.84	42.65	59.67
SentiStrength_EN	45.00	70.83	69.07	45.33	44.67	55.28	54.25	54.77	**64.33**
SentiStrength_PT	38.67	70.97	64.29	29.34	**48.00**	41.51	**54.96**	48.24	58.00
SO-CAL OpLexicon_EN	45.67	68.52	77.78	49.34	42.00	57.36	54.55	55.95	63.00
SO-CAL OpLexicon_PT	32.33	58.82	**55.22**	40.00	24.67	47.62	34.10	40.86	56.33

Moreover, an evaluation of the translation quality was performed. Therefore, a set of 100 instances from the dataset was randomly sampled, composed of 25 comments or tweets per class, spliced into 50 instances from Facebook and 50 from Twitter data. After a manual evaluation for all the 100 translations from the Yandex translate, its translation output was correct 55% of the cases. For comparison purposes, this level using Google Translator was 57%, for the same random sample. In addition, a new round with the SA algorithms was performed, for this sample. Regarding the results for mean accuracy, from all the English methods using both translation tools, the results were 0.36 for Yandex and 0.37 for Google.

5 Discussion

First, the averages for levels of agreement obtained from the manual evaluation by volunteers in the OpinionLabel system was higher than 77.85, for Facebook and Twitter, for all labeled classes. This result shows that most of the time, two evaluators have analyzed a comment with the same label, against one evaluator with another conclusion. This means the labeled datasets had a good confidence level, regarding labels, to use in this performance evaluation.

From Tables 1 and 2, SentiStrength_EN for Facebook, and V_OpLexicon_EN for Twitter had the highest performances. For instance, those methods have presented the best averages in Macro F1 for both datasets, where SentiStrenth_EN had 61.62 and V_OpLexicon_EN had 57.80.

SentiStrength [17] aims to deal with informalities on the Internet language, using heuristics such as negation, repeated letters, and emoticons lists. Meanwhile, Vader [18] was built specifically for Twitter OM, also incorporating some heuristics such as capital letters, intensifiers ("really") for increasing the strength of sentiments, and polarity shift conjunctions ("but"). Those are possible reasons these methods have beaten the others in this evaluation.

Although those methods had a better performance than others, the overall results can not be considered good, regarding needs for real-world applications for industries and companies. For instance, the accuracy from SentiStrength_EN and V_OpLexi-con_EN, for Facebook and Twitter respectively, do not surpass 60%. This is a low level for this metric, which is important for identifying how the methods are precise in their classification in general. Moreover, the recall level for both algorithms is lower than 68%, which means a considerable number of false positives and negatives in their classification results.

Finally given the low precision level for translations from Yandex, which was 55% as mentioned before, the overall low performance from all SA methods can also be a consequence of the poor translation quality for the datasets. Moreover, the difference of 0.01 in mean accuracy for the SA algorithms using data translated from Yandex and Google, shows that the challenges imposed by the informalities in the OSN language context are independent of a translation tool used for translation-based SA algorithms.

6   Conclusions and Future Work

It was observed that the initial hypothesis considered was discarded, since OM methods that work with Portuguese had lower performance than English versions. One possible reason is that Portuguese version algorithms and tools for SA are still not ready to deal with OSN context data. Thus, given the maturity level of the implementations for English language, they had better performance, even with translated data. Moreover, the translation quality can be a key factor in the performance of the SA algorithms, given that wrong translations present on the datasets used in this work can cause mistakes on the classification of the SA methods.

Those facts highlight the need for proposals that work specifically for Social Media context and Brazilian Portuguese, given the fact that a translation process can generate losses of information from one language to another, and even with that, the Portuguese versions have lost.

As future work, a survey regarding the main challenges for SA in the language present on OSN context, such as informalities and grammar mistakes, could be performed. Moreover, it would be interesting to evaluate Portuguese OM tools with translated data from English to Portuguese, in order to analyze all the possibilities regarding the tools real performance for SA. Finally, new proposals for OM for Brazilian Portuguese and Social Networks could be suggested, in order to overcome the challenges faced in this scenario.

References

1. Lai, L.S., Turban, E.: Groups formation and operations in the Web 2.0 environment and social networks. Group Decis. Negot. **17**(5), 387–402 (2008)
2. Zephoria. https://zephoria.com/top-15-valuable-facebookstatistics/
3. Internet Live Stats. http://www.internetlivestats.com/twitter-statistics/
4. Mostafa, M.M.: More than words: social networks' text mining for consumer brand sentiments. Expert Syst. Appl. **40**(10), 4241–4251 (2013)
5. Heller Baird, C., Gautam, P.: From social media to social customer relationship management. Strategy Leadersh. **39**(5), 30–37 (2011)
6. Garrigos, F., Gil, I., Narangajavana, Y.: The impact of social networks in the competitiveness of the firms. In: Beckford, A.M., Larsen, J.P. (eds.) Competitiveness: Psychology, Production, Impact and Global Trends. Nova Science Publishers, Hauppauge (2011)
7. Pang, B., Lee, L.: Opinion mining and sentiment analysis. Found. Trends Inf. Retrieval **2**(1–2), 1–35 (2008)
8. Hearst, M.A.: Direction-based text interpretation as an information access refinement. In: Text-based Intelligent Systems: Current Research and Practice in Information Extraction and Retrieval, pp. 257–274 (1992)
9. We Are Social. http://wearesocial.com/sg/special-reports/digital-2016
10. Silva, Mário, J., Carvalho, P., Sarmento, L.: Building a sentiment lexicon for social judgement mining. In: Caseli, H., Villavicencio, A., Teixeira, A., Perdigão, F. (eds.) PROPOR 2012. LNCS, vol. 7243, pp. 218–228. Springer, Heidelberg (2012). doi:10.1007/978-3-642-28885-2_25
11. Cambria, E., Speer, R., Havasi, C., Hussain, A.: SenticNet: a publicly available semantic resource for opinion mining. In: AAAI Fall Symposium: Common Sense Knowledge, vol. 10 (2010)
12. Ribeiro, F.N., Araújo, M., Gonçalves, P., Benevenuto, F., Gonçalves, M.A.: A benchmark comparison of state-of-the-practice sentiment analysis methods. arXiv preprint arXiv:1512.01818 (2015)
13. Balage, P.P.F., Pardo, T.A., Aluısio, S.M.: An evaluation of the Brazilian Portuguese LIWC dictionary for sentiment analysis. In: Proceedings of the 9th Brazilian Symposium in Information and Human Language Technology (STIL), pp. 215–219 (2013)
14. Pennebaker, J.W., Francis, M.E., Booth, R.J.: Linguistic inquiry and word count: LIWC 2001, vol. 71. Lawrence Erlbaum Associates, Mahway (2001)
15. Hu, M., Liu, B.: Mining opinion features in customer reviews. AAAI **4**(4), 755–760 (2004)
16. Taboada, M., Brooke, J., Tofiloski, M., Voll, K., Stede, M.: Lexicon-based methods for sentiment analysis. Comput. Linguist. **37**(2), 267–307 (2011)
17. Thelwall, M.: Heart and soul: sentiment strength detection in the social web with sentistrength. In: Proceedings of the CyberEmotions, pp. 1–14 (2013)
18. Hutto, C.J., Gilbert, E.: Vader: a parsimonious rule-based model for sentiment analysis of social media text. In: 8th International AAAI Conference on Weblogs and Social Media (2014)

Social Media Analytics Using Business Intelligence and Social Media Tools – Differences and Implications

Matthias Wittwer[(⊠)], Olaf Reinhold, Rainer Alt, Finn Jessen,
and Richard Stüber

Leipzig University, Grimmaische Str. 12, Leipzig, Germany
{wittwer,reinhold,jessen,
stueber}@wifa.uni-leipzig.de,
rainer.alt@uni-leipzig.de

Abstract. The increasing amount of content created in Social Media platforms is calling for sophisticated filters that separate relevant from non-relevant content. Social Media Analytics (SMA) is a field that addresses this challenge by the development of strategies, methods and technologies to automate this filtering process. This work in progress paper presents an experiment, which examined two Social Media (SM) applications as well as two Business Intelligence (BI) applications for the analysis of tweets. The overall goal is to identify differences of these tool categories with regard to the analytics process itself as well as the obtained results. Using the scenario of a fitness tracking application for smartphones, data from Twitter was collected and analyzed with applications of both categories. The findings show (1) differences between BI and SM application, (2) challenges resulting from the different analytics processes, and (3) hints for decision makers as well as data analysts when to use which category for analyzing social content.

Keywords: Social media analytics · Social media · Business intelligence

1 Introduction

The diffusion of Social Media platforms within the last years is increasingly recognized as an additional resource for customer interaction by many companies [1–4]. Since social platforms, such as Twitter and Facebook, are connecting millions of social web users worldwide [5, 6], businesses face a big data problem of potentially relevant User Generated Content (UGC), which drives the demand towards automated analytical approaches, such as Social Media Analytics (SMA). The term "social analytics" is "an umbrella term that includes a number of specialized techniques, such as social filtering, social network analysis, social conversation quantification, engagement tracking, social channel analysis, sentiment analysis and paid social media measurement" [7]. Its main purpose is the qualitative description and analysis of available social content.

Specific applications, so-called Social Media Monitoring (SMM) or SMA tools, have developed over the past few years and are in co-existence with classical tools, such as Business Intelligence (BI) applications. This leads to the question to what

© Springer International Publishing AG 2017
W. Abramowicz et al. (Eds.): BIS 2016 Workshops, LNBIP 263, pp. 252–259, 2017.
DOI: 10.1007/978-3-319-52464-1_23

extent these applications actually differ in the analysis of unstructured content and the subsequent generation of insights. The present research investigates in a first step the differences and capabilities of both applications for the analyzing social content. In a second step, possible reasons for differing results are discussed and in a third step, the configuration effort of a complete analysis process is assessed for both tool categories. In a final step, first guidance for end-users is derived from the findings as a basis for further research. This leads to two research questions. RQ1: Which differences exist in analyzing social content using SM and BI applications and what are possible explanations for these differences? RQ2: Which are the strengths of each application category for SMA?

The paper is structured as follows: First, Sect. 2 explains the research methodology and Sect. 3 introduces the used applications and application categories. The respective infrastructure and analytics process to extract, prepare and analyze data is described for each category. A comparison of both categories completes the chapter. Section 4 presents differences among the application categories and aims at identifying possible reasons. Finally, Sect. 5 answers the research questions, formulates first implications for decision makers when to use each application category, and offers some guidance for further research.

2 Methodology

The research was conducted using four applications of two tool categories (BI and SMA), which are suited to the task of SMA. It is assumed that applications in the field of BI require a higher level of experience and expert knowledge for conducting an analysis of UGC than specific SM applications. Regarding the search term for the extraction of social content, these applications were configured equally to ensure comparability of results. The scenario involved the analysis of tweets on the topic "@runtastic", which refers to the official Social Media presence of an eponymous company, offering a fitness tracking application for smartphones. The topic was chosen since fitness tracking is regarded a relevant topic, which involves a large community (e.g. more than 55,600 followers in the case of Runtastic) and therefore contains many postings within Social Media. With regard to the time span and language, each application was configured to collect data from the first quarter of 2016 (1st January 2016 until 31st March 2016) in English language. To structure the analysis and to answer RQ1, the following process steps were derived from existing literature [8–10]:

- The extraction of data from relevant sources via application programming interfaces (API) and the use of user-defined keywords
- The transformation of data from different sources into one data scheme
- A data load into a database (e.g. social data warehouse) to store the data for later analysis purposes
- The actual analysis (e.g. sentiment analysis, influencer identification, word frequencies) with different approaches

In the following, each tool category is described using a defined analytics process (see Sects. 3.1 and 3.2).

3 SMA Using BI and SM Tools

3.1 SMA Using BI Tools

This research exemplarily uses. two BI tools (Microstrategy Desktop and the
SAP HANA platform), which were selected from a list of leading BI applications [11].

Data Extraction. Both tools allow to extract data from Twitter via an integrated
Twitter "Search API". Since tweets encompass over 60 different attributes, which
include e.g. the posting itself, user information, as well as some geographic data,
comprehensive demographic data are not delivered through the integrated API. Two
constraints using this interface are (1) the volume of tweets that can be extracted with
one API call is limited to 5,000 tweets per day and (2) the time span of tweets is also
limited to the last ten days. The SAP HANA platform makes use of Twitters' "Stream
API". Using this API, it is possible to extract a stream of tweets related to a specified
topic. However, it is not possible to gather past data. Furthermore, there is a restriction
to the number of available API calls per time unit. The limit is divided into 15 min
intervals.

Data Transformation and Data Load. With regard to the Microstrategy solution,
three process steps had to be performed during the transformation process. First, the
complexity and size of the data set had to be reduced as 20 attributes did not contain
any information or no useful information (e.g. longitude/latitude, playce.id, place.-
name, or user.city). Second, the data type of several attributes (e.g. "Created at") had to
be transformed into a format that is compatible with the BI tool. Subsequently, the
postings were sorted by the time they were sent. Finally, the tweets had to be transformed into "attributes" and "metrics" (e.g. the "Text" attribute was used as a metric for
an easier processing by R). The same attributes were left out in SAP HANA as well as
MicroStrategy and the automatically created data types did not require any changes for
further processing.

Data Analysis. Since both BI applications did not use predefined dashboards, which
could be used in combination with the extracted data, visualizations had to be created
manually. The analysis itself could be divided into two process steps, starting with the
structured data (e.g. attributes such as time, location, posting language, number of
friends) and continuing with the unstructured data (posting text and country name).
With regard to the structured data, both BI applications offer comprehensive analytical
functionalities. For example, there are functionalities to automatically generate geographic data from "country" or "city" attributes so that users and their respective
follower count could have been displayed on a world map. For analyzing tweets, a text
mining framework had to be integrated as mentioned above. Both tools could mine
automatically with a standard library of tagged words indicating each words' sentiment
or by manually adjusting the predefined library. Afterwards, with the numeric sentiment value of each tweet, a concealed processing could be performed through the
standard BI functionalities.

3.2   SMA Using Social Media Tools

In the SM field, Microsoft Social Engagement and Synthesio were also named as leaders in analyzing UGC [7, 12].

Data Extraction. First of all, both tools cover the entire data extraction process. During the configuration the user may determine the range of the extracted data with two basic options. The first option is the definition of the search query. Most SM tools support simple searches as well as complex Boolean searches. Simple searches only include a collection of keywords, whereas complex searches encompass the definition of logical operators (AND, OR, as well as apostrophe) together with keywords and the definition of keywords to be included in or excluded from the search. The second option is the definition of sources and channels, which are subject to the analysis (e.g. Social Media, blogs, news sites, discussion boards). Furthermore, the tools offer the selection of specific languages and geolocations.

Data Transformation and Data Load. Similar to the data extraction, the transformation of raw data (e.g. tweets) is not transparent to the user and executed automatically. The same applies to the data load and storage process. After the transformation, an analyst has the opportunity to combine several filters (e.g. time and language) to restrict the raw data equivalent to the configuration step before.

Data Analysis. Both SM tools use predefined algorithms for the analysis of social content. For example, different methods are applied to compute sentiments, which reflect whether a posting or an aggregate of postings are positive, negative, or neutral in tonality. By providing an influencer list, the tools indicate some methods for the computation of influencers. For example, a simple scoring method might include the overall sentiment of used words, whereas a more complex algorithm might also encompass the number of followers, the number of retweets, the reach of tweets among those followers, the relevance of a tweets' content, or a users' activity level. With regard to websites, page ranks (e.g. from Alexa) might be used to assess influencers' like news websites and blogs. Demographic data is used to categorize the detected Social Media user in target groups. Finally, tag clouds show the most mentioned topics, which are associated with the given search query.

4   Differences Between BI and SM Tools

As one of the BI tools required an integration with the R environment for text analytics, it is assumed that available BI applications, for the analysis of unstructured data, differ at least in their text analytics capabilities and their ability to integrate those environments. This requires different levels of expert knowledge, already before conducting the actual analysis. In consequence, this also affects a companies' structure, as knowledgeable employees are required.

With regard to both SM tools, setting up the analysis process is conceived comparatively simple as the configuration process requires less efforts: predefined query operators as well as included and excluded search terms ease the configuration process, filters help restricting data to the respective relevant aspect, and the automated data preparation establishes an overview on unstructured data. Overall only a few configurative steps were necessary to start the complete analysis process. Both analyzed SM applications appear as an integrated software suite, but, as their architecture is not transparent to the user, it is assumed that their analytical functionality and the respective results differ. In the following, a detailed description of the differences is given in terms of quantitative measures of the analyzed results and the defined analytics process.

Some differences between the tools are (see Table 1): First, the number of collected and analyzed tweets varies widely between 2,053 and 74,486 for the given period of three months. A possible reason might be each tools' individual access to historical data of each Social Media channel. As mentioned before and in the case of Twitters' database, some tools only support the last few days, whereas others deliver several month or years of retrospective data. Second, the number of identified topics differs between all tools and especially between the tool categories. A main reason is the configurability of the length of list entries, which, in the case of BI tools, is completely user-defined. On the contrary, the derivation of topics within SM applications is only little transparent. Furthermore, the tools identified almost completely different topics. Therefore, it is assumed that functionalities for text analytics are configured differently in respect of word lists for the recognition of known entities and the exclusion of irrelevant entities as well as implemented algorithms. Third, similar to the topics, influencers were identified and no overlap was observed. This supports the above mentioned assumption that influencers are defined and identified differently, either by using their amount of followers, tweets, or retweets, or by computing more complex metrics involving meta-data, such as tweet frequency. Fourth, the share of positive, negative, and neutral tweets also varies widely and leads to diverging insights. The configuration of word lists (including positive and negative words) and the computation method (e.g. word-by-word or on

Table 1. Differences of BI and SM tools

Analytics process	Business intelligence tools	Social media tools
Data extraction	- A Social Media account is required for the use of APIs	- No Social Media account is needed for the extraction
	- Fewer Social Media are supported natively	- Many different Social Media channels are supported
	- Social content of the last few days is delivered	- Up to a few years of historical data available
Data transformation and load	- Requires comprehensive data editing (e.g. data types)	- Data management is covered through the SMA application
	- User-defined data load	- Database schema is predefined
	- No automated monitoring	
Data analysis	- Analytics are set up manually, no predefined Social Media dashboards	- Predefined and non-adjustable algorithms for the analysis of social content (e.g. sentiment detection, influencer scoring, target group analysis, topic identification)
	- Manual definition and configuration of analysis algorithms	

sentence-level) are regarded as the main reasons in this context. Finally, it was found that the SM applications lacked predictive analytics features, which may easily be used within BI tools.

5 Conclusions and Research Agenda

This research in progress analyzed BI and SM tools for SMA. It focused on differences and their respective reasons between both tool categories as well as on the analytics processes. Based on this analysis, it formulates first points that might help in deciding when to use which application category.

Regarding RQ1, this research collects identifies specifics for BI and SM application (see Table 1). The second research question (RQ2) is answered through five points that derive from the first findings. Five recommendations may can be derived. First, the use of BI applications for the analysis of social content is recommended for more sophisticated analytics as this requires more resources. This leads to the suggestion to start SMA by using dedicated SM tools for obtaining first insights and broadening analytics depending on business goals and questions by adding a BI application. Second, the role of resources as well as a business strategy and a possible integration of analytics results with further applications (e.g. CRM) should be considered. Current literature discusses how firms might develop strategies [1, 13] or develop Social Media strategies [14]. Further research calls for frameworks for integrating SMA and the respective results with CRM applications [15, 16]. Third, the extent of available social data on the one hand and the number of available channels for the analysis on the other hand, need to be considered. In addition, the reliability of results is a major aspect of analytics and might be stronger with a higher scope of influence. The tool analysis shows differences in the temporal availability of tweets, which is an additional qualitative assessment criterion. Fourth, it has to be noted that ease of use is an important aspect when using SM or BI applications. For example, this encompasses the availability of predefined dashboards and relates to the temporal and personal resources of an analysis. Finally, the selection of software for the analysis of social content should be considered [9].

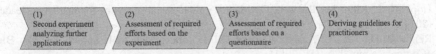

Fig. 1. Approach for further research

To answer the overall research question, the following next steps are suggested (Fig. 1). First, a comprehensive experiment including a broader selection of software from both categories could help to substantiate the first results. Second, from this experiment an assessment of efforts in terms of required time, costs as well as knowledge on the one hand and the analysis procedure on the other hand is needed in order to operationalize the impacts of existing differences. Third, potential use cases and a company's preparedness for the use of BI applications for SMA should be assessed among other aspects within a questionnaire. Fourth, a more detailed guideline for end-users and service providers could secure the applicability of research results for practitioners.

By explaining differences between SMA and BI applications for the analysis of social content, this paper contributes to the research field of SMA and SMM. Obviously it also has limitations. First of all, this research in progress focuses on four applications from two categories, which needs to be extended by future research on the topic. It cannot be excluded that specific SM tools provide predictive and integration features, for example, as the market comprises several hundred applications. Second, further experiments are required to prove existing deficits and reveal further differences of SMA and BI applications with respect to social analytics. These experiments could also serve to prove required efforts (e.g. time and knowledge) and to clarify further benefits of each application category for SMA. Finally, suitable applications architectures are necessary to make use of the potential of the two application categories analyzed in this research.

References

1. Kaplan, A.M., Haenlein, M.: Users of the world, unite! the challenges and opportunities of social media. Bus. Horiz. **53**, 59–68 (2010)
2. Band, W., Petouhoff, N.: Social CRM goes Mainstream (2010)
3. McHaney, R.W.: Web 2.0 and Social Media for Business. Ventus Publishing ApS (2012)
4. Rosenberger, M.: Social customer relationship management: an architectural exploration of the components. In: Janssen, M., Mäntymäki, M., Hidders, J., Klievink, B., Lamersdorf, W., Loenen, B., Zuiderwijk, A. (eds.) I3E 2015. LNCS, vol. 9373, pp. 372–385. Springer, Heidelberg (2015). doi:10.1007/978-3-319-25013-7_30
5. Facebook: Facebook Q2 2015 Earnings. http://files.shareholder.com/downloads/AMDA-NJ5DZ/751446228x0x842064/619A417E-5E3E-496C-B125-987FA25A0570/FB_Q215EarningsSlides.pdf
6. Twitter: Twitter Second Quarter 2015 Results. http://files.shareholder.com/downloads/AMDA-2F526X/751374626x0x841608/0DC29153-1788-4E20-B3A2-274058770AD8/2015_Q2_Earnings_Slides.pdf
7. Hopkins, J., Kihn, M., Rozwell, C.: Market guide: social analytics for marketing leaders (2014)
8. Reinhold, O., Alt, R.: Analytical social CRM: concept and tool support. In: 24th Bled eConference, pp. 226–241 (2011)
9. Stavrakantonakis, I., Gagiu, A.-E., Kasper, H., Toma, I., Thalhammer, A.: An approach for evaluation of social media monitoring tools. In: 1st International Workshop on Common Value Management, pp. 52–64 (2012)
10. Ruggiero, A., Vos, M.: Social media monitoring for crisis communication: process, methods and trends in the scientific literature. Online J. Commun. Media Technol. **4**, 105–130 (2014)
11. Parenteau, J., Sallam, R., Howson, C., Tapadinhas, J., Schlegel, K., Oestreich, T.: Magic quadrant for business intelligence and analytics platforms (2016)
12. Fan, W., Gordon, M.D.: The power of social media analytics. Commun. ACM **57**, 74–81 (2014)

13. Kietzmann, J.H., Hermkens, K., McCarthy, I.P., Silvestre, B.S.: Social media? get serious! understanding the functional building blocks of social media. Bus. Horiz. **54**, 241–251 (2011)
14. Lardi, K., Fuchs, R.: Social Media Strategy. A step-by-step Guide to Building your Social Business. vdf Hochschulverlag AG, Zürich (2013)
15. Alt, R., Wittwer, M.: Towards an Ontology-based approach for social media analysis. In: Proceedings 22nd European Conference on Information Systems, pp. 1–10 (2014)
16. Alt, R., Reinhold, O.: Social Customer Relationship Management (Social CRM). Bus. Inf. Syst. Eng. **4**, 287–291 (2012)

Assessment of Business Benefits for the Operation of a Smart City Energy Management Platform

Stefan Reichert[1(✉)] and Jens Strüker[2]

[1] Institut für Informatik und Gesellschaft, Albert-Ludwigs-Universität Freiburg,
Friedrichstr. 50, 79098 Freiburg, Germany
stefan.reichert@iig.uni-freiburg.de
[2] Institute of Energy Economics (INEWI),
Limburger Str. 2, 65510 Idstein, Germany
jens.strueker@hs-fresenius.de

Abstract. Managing energy production and consumption on a city level is an important, yet challenging task, since an increasing number of volatile renewable energies are being connected to the grid. Smart city energy management platforms could constitute a powerful tool for the involved market actors to effectively integrate renewable energies and thereby to refine existing business models. However, the implementation of such energy management tools is often hindered by privacy concerns or the lack of awareness about connected business benefits. In this paper, we present the concept for a decision support system that is tested in two pilot cities in Croatia and Bulgaria. Furthermore, we present a framework for the identification of the business benefits that are connected with the implementation of such a tool.

Keywords: Business processes · Smart city energy management · Decision support system · Benefit evaluation framework

1 Introduction

The increasing digitization in most aspects of today's society is one of the fundamental changes for the daily lives of all involved individuals. The so-called Internet of Things (IoT) allows people and devices to connect with each other at any given time independent from their current location. This opens up a wide array of opportunities of how and when we can access information. These developments are mainly targeted to increase customers' comfort, flexibility and the potential to save money, as transaction and information costs are reduced notably. However, in some other cases, the increasing digitalization is becoming also a necessity. This becomes evident in energy sectors that are aiming to reach a high share of renewable energy. Many countries around the world have set ambitious targets to reduce greenhouse gas emissions and subsequently aim to replace fossil energy sources with renewable energies, such as wind and solar power. Besides the reduction of greenhouse gases, the transition of the energy sector is oftentimes linked to broader sustainability goals, such as supporting electric mobility or raising energy efficiency. By extending energy generation from

W. Abramowicz et al. (Eds.): BIS 2016 Workshops, LNBIP 263, pp. 260–270, 2017.
DOI: 10.1007/978-3-319-52464-1_24

renewable sources, countries can replace existing non-renewable energy sources, such as coal and nuclear power. For instance, Germany strives for a two-fold change consisting of nuclear phase-out and a concurrent abolishment of most fossil fuels [1]. Local generation and the inclusion of new actors such as prosumers are key to achieve the energy efficiency targets for the next years.

However, rising shares of volatile renewable energies are also posing many challenges for the energy supply. A successful transformation of the energy sector is often seen as inseparably linked with a smarter grid, as the old paradigm that supply follows demand can no longer hold. Information Systems (IS) may constitute a key element of a smarter grid, as they provide the tools for more accurate measurements and predictions. The installation of smart meters in buildings is one of the main parts of required infrastructure. In order to provide these benefits and meet EU targets, the smart grid must be able to seamlessly integrate various existing and/or new technologies – meters, sensors, data processing systems, etc. – with the physical infrastructure required to generate, transmit and distribute electric power [2].

Utilities and city authorities have long been using network systems such as SCADA to optimize resources and monitor assets to carry out preventative maintenance. However, the rich data sets generated and stored in these "silo" systems are found in a variety of formats and are not easily accessed by third parties, thus preventing the optimal management, control and efficiency of many city services (i.e. utilities, security, health, transportation, street lighting and local government administration). Therefore, new systems are required that are fully functional within a smart grid and allow different market actors to access required data without violating the privacy of connected consumers and prosumers.

In this paper, we outline an energy management system that is deployed in two pilot cities in Croatia and Bulgaria and integrates different IoT components. In order to identify the full potential for the refinement of business processes, we present a framework that allows capturing related business benefits from the implementation of such systems.

2   The Role of Information Systems in the Energy Sector

Finding ways to increase efficiency in the energy sector by the use of information systems is a contribution to energy informatics, as the call for action by [3] describes. Energy efficiency, in this context, can be enhanced by implementing systems that promote decision making, e.g. for the balance between demand and supply.

The possibility of new services is facilitated by the bi-directional flow of energy-related data from the consumer to the supplier and vice versa. Decision support systems play a crucial role here, as they can process the data, offer analytical functionalities and allow the direct communication between market actors. This enables a new dimension of the energy market where smart energy services can offer significant energy-efficiency potentials. While general conclusions about most appropriate features are hard to derive, some of the most valued features are found to be the presentation of costs over a period of time, an appliance-specific breakdown, historical comparison, computerized and interactive tools, and in-home displays due to its visibility [4].

Recent findings from energy efficiency projects with the installation of smart meters have shown reductions in annual household consumption by 1–15% for electricity [5]. Better results are generally obtained with the provision of specific services, such as the comparison with peers or the participation in demand response programs. Although the results vary significantly between different studies, this gives an indication that developing ICT services might represent a new area for business expansion in the energy and ICT sector where data acquisition might become the most valuable commodity to energy stakeholders and potentially offering new market opportunities.

Furthermore, with an increasing share of intermittent renewable energy, information systems will be vital to optimally utilize periods with high production levels and to counteract times of low production. A literature review of existing IS research contributions to demand response is given by [6], where they identify the quantification of the economic value of shiftable loads as an important research question that needs to be addressed. To be able to shift or orchestrate myriads of loads, an advanced metering infrastructure (AMI) is expedient that can measure, collect, transmit and analyze information flows. As the individual consumption on the low-voltage level is historically intransparent, AMI – and alternative metering and communication solutions such as revenue-grade metering and communication chips embedded in smart devices - is an important element of a smarter energy system.

3   A Smart City Energy Management Platform

To efficiently manage the production, consumption and storage of energy in cities, in this paper we propose an energy management solution based on IoT for smart cities [7], which is built-up by a *Smart City Database* (SCDB) and a *smart Decision Support System* (smartDSS) divided in two-level decision approach:

- *Local Decision Support System* (LDSS). It engages consumers and prosumers by capturing near real-time data related to their energy consumption, as well as energy production from their installed Distributed Energy Resources (DER), displaying it on a user-friendly interface via smart phones, tablets, PCs, etc., and provides support for decision making.
- *Centralized Decision Support System* (CDSS). It aggregates data from all LDSSs to provide city-level decision support to authorities and energy service providers. The CDSS generates a number of parameters, including city-wide energy production and consumption forecasts (Fig. 1).

3.1   Centralized Decision Support System

The CDSS (Centralized Decision Support System) component of the proposed platform is responsible to aggregate and manage data at city and district level. That component delivers a set of functions to end-users as authorities, energy provider services, ESCO and municipalities, by collecting data that comes from other components of the system.

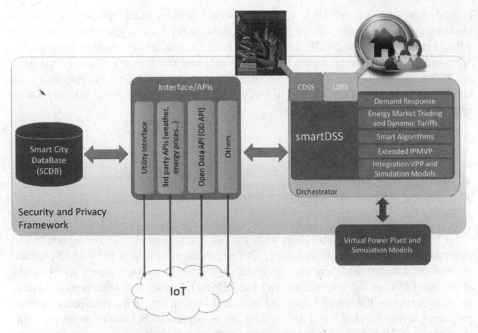

Fig. 1. The main components of the energy management platform, consisting of a local and centralized decision support system

Moreover, the CDSS provides an interface specialized for the user typologies. Thus, each user accesses only the tools useful to perform its activities. For instance, it can be considered the different approach in the data management of an analyst and a decision maker. The aim of the CDSS is to integrate measurement data, simulation data and forecasting data in a view that allows the user to manage the different aspects with a unique tool. This enables the forecast and planning renewable power generation available in the city, a real-time optimization and scalability (meaning its ability to be enlarged to accommodate that growth of data).

The CDSS allows the following activities:

- Get a continuous snapshot of city energy consumption and production
- Manage energy consumption and production data
- Forecasting of energy consumption data
- Planning of new energy "producers" for the future needs of the city
- Visualize, analyse and take decisions about the information provided by all the connected end points that are consuming or producing energy.

It is composed by a back-end and front-end. In this task, the HMI or Graphical User Interface (GUI) for CDSS is developed with a novel framework employing web technologies (HTML5, CSS3, JScript, Websocket) to provide a web 3.0 user interface. The CDSS provides the communication between the Virtual Power Plant component (VPP), smartDSS and LDSS and this makes it fundamental for the orchestration of the activities. The VPP in this context constitutes an external design tool based upon load aggregation of near real-time metered energy demand and generation data at building/apartment levels, allowing specific applications such as grouping schemes or what-if simulations. The SCDB, on the other hand, acts as an intermediate between the VPP and CDSS and grants access to common data and storage of VPP computed data.

Moreover, the CDSS provides functionalities to aggregate data in order to create the demand curves that can be used to analyse possible peaks and produce offers. Other important features of the CDSS are:

- Dynamic tariffs support
- Offers Demand Response flow
- Forecasting data management
- Near real time data visualization
- Technical losses management
- Historical data visualization

It works in strict collaboration with the VPP component that is responsible to aggregate data at city and district level. This aggregation of data is the base to produce simulation, forecast and near real time data. Another important aspect to highlight about the CDSS is the connection with the LDSS, allowing a bi-directional communication between the energy provider and end-consumers. This connection allows preparing dynamic tariffs and stimulating an engagement behaviour with the consumers. The CDSS moreover communicates with the smartDSS component in order to activate the forecast processes (Table 1).

Table 1. Open Data API services that allows 3rd parties to offer external services to the users of the platform

Component	Description
Energy data	This component exposes the energy data stored in SCDB. Provides access to current and historical data, from meter level up to city level
User data	This component provides information from users following the privacy policy
Access control	This module controls which information can be access through the open API based on the request and the type of external service accessing the data. It logs all requests and all data access from external services
Privacy policy	This module is used to set privacy policies for data access

The API service component is responsible to grant access to the energy information collected and computed within IoT NRG Manager following the security and privacy policy. It provides an open API that allows 3rd parties to offer external services to the users of the platform.

3.2   Local Decision Support System

The main goal of the Local Decision Support System (LDSS) is to engage consumers and prosumers on the efficient use of energy. The engagement is based on data, captured in near real-time, related to their energy consumption, as well as energy production from their installed Distributed Energy Resources (DER). The engagement is targeted through a user-friendly interface using every-day-use devices; smart phones, tablets and PCs.

Simplified interfaces show the users energy usage, as well as energy produced. Comparison with previous periods, as well as other consumers/prosumers, in combination with recommendations on the optimal use of energy is expected to stimulate end users on the efficient management of their energy. Additionally, the LDSS provides support for decision making, for instance, it advises how to achieve a demand response action, which dynamic tariff is more convenient and how the relation with other environment parameters (like weather) might affect the users' consumption & comfort. The users' comfort is guaranteed with the Smart Heating system of the LDSS. It provides to end users a tool, to modify at any time the target temperature of their homes. The control is composed by a main thermostat and individual thermostats. While the main thermostat is a logic device, each individual thermostat matches a physical one located at home. Key Performance Indicators (KPI) for users' behaviour and satisfaction with the LDSS are also considered. The measured data is collected for each user separately on an hourly basis. Some of the KPIs considered are: active users/month, logins/month/user, how long people stay being logged in, features (clicks)/month, advices page clicks/month. The LDSS is the link between the energy provider and the end user, which thereby also serves as a tool for customer loyalty and support.

4 Benefit Framework for the Operation of an Energy Management Platform

4.1 Evaluation Framework

As with all information systems and technologies, the benefits of the implementation of an energy management system, such as the proposed smartDSS, need to be determined ex-ante. For this, we will focus on the potential commercial operators of the system, i.e. utilities or municipalities. A business benefit can be understood as an outcome of an action or decision that contributes towards meeting one or more business objectives. We use a framework consisting of several benefit types for the identification of all potential business uses.

There are a number of existing methodologies for the quantification of benefits connected with the implementation of new technologies, such as decision support systems. For the smartDSS, there are a number of potential operators, which can yield different individual benefits. One common methodology suggests following a path similar to that applied to most other technological innovations [8]. This approach proposes the adjustment and application of well-established methods from the fields of capital budgeting and performance measurement. Mostly this method above addresses the problem of how to achieve overall quantification with the aim of establishing a basis for decisions regarding the initiation or postponement of an investment in a new technology (or, for that matter, decisions in respect of any investment accompanied by cost–benefit consequences that are insufficiently understood).

While some studies indirectly address ex ante benefit evaluation (namely field studies and live tests that require an actual implementation of the new technology), the remainder focus on only one or two of the three main aspects of benefit evaluation: classification frameworks, such as [9], help in identifying potential benefits of new applications without addressing quantification issues. Forecast models, such as the one presented by [10], address the forecast problem of investments, which is, on predicting the extent to which the number of processes and activities and/or resource consumption change, while largely neglecting the financial side. Finally, assessment models, such as [11] focus on the assessment problem, that is, on attaching a monetary value to multiple process improvements, while using 'expert estimations' to bypass the forecast problem.

Based on the work from [12], the mentioned results can be adjusted in an ex ante evaluation framework that splits up potential benefits from the implementation of a decision support system into 3 benefit types:

Information: The measurement, collection and visualization of production & consumption levels. As the smartDSS collects and displays detailed near real-time consumption and production data, it allows to create an overview of the current status of the grid and local areas. These information benefits do not require modified structures and processes. They might however include additional data gathering, which is not economically feasible without a smartDSS.

Optimization: Active balancing of production & consumption levels. As the smartDSS comprises both a centralized (CDSS) and local component (LDSS), it also allows to activate additional capacities, e.g. through demand side management. This can happen both through immediate action (direct load control) and through long-term based changes in the pricing structure (e.g. the creation of new real time tariffs). Equivalently, potential optimization benefits can comprise the optimal activation or deactivation of additional production and storage units.

Transformation: Re-engineering of existing business processes and investment decisions. Based on information and analytics functionalities of the smartDSS, decisions about investments into new infrastructure can be made, e.g. new solar panels in areas with high solar power potential or about the enhancement and reinforcement of the grid. Detailed information about consumption and production at all times allows an optimal market behavior and restructuring of the supply chain management.

4.2   Assessment of Benefits for Energy Providers

By sub-categorizing information, optimization and transformation benefits further into direct/indirect and operational/managerial benefits, we derive in total eight benefit types for the operator of a Smart City Energy Management Platform, as visualized in Fig. 2. As an operator, we thereby assume an energy provider or a utility that manages the delivery of energy to the end consumer.

Type 1 - *Automated notifications of unusual consumption and production levels*: This benefit type can be directly generated from displaying information within the smartDSS and setting thresholds for which the system automatically gives a signal when

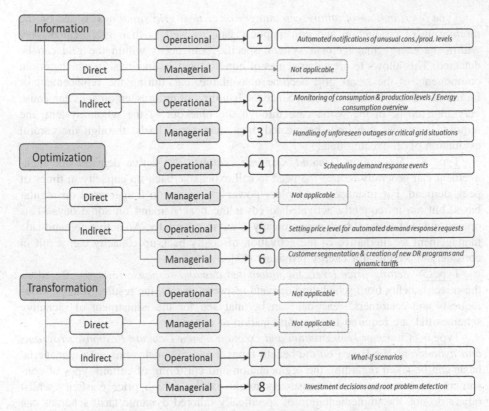

Information	Direct	Operational → **1**	*Automated notifications of unusual cons./prod. levels*
		Managerial →	*Not applicable*
	Indirect	Operational → **2**	*Monitoring of consumption & production levels / Energy consumption overview*
		Managerial → **3**	*Handling of unforeseen outages or critical grid situations*
Optimization	Direct	Operational → **4**	*Scheduling demand response events*
		Managerial →	*Not applicable*
	Indirect	Operational → **5**	*Setting price level for automated demand response requests*
		Managerial → **6**	*Customer segmentation & creation of new DR programs and dynamic tariffs*
Transformation	Direct	Operational →	*Not applicable*
		Managerial →	*Not applicable*
	Indirect	Operational → **7**	*What-if scenarios*
		Managerial → **8**	*Investment decisions and root problem detection*

Fig. 2. Segmentation of eight benefit types connected with the implementation of a Smart City Energy Management Platform

it is reached. Unforeseen fluctuations in the energy production levels of solar and wind power installations can seriously jeopardize grid stability or cause significant costs to the energy provider by the activation of expensive balancing energy. Simultaneously, aggregated consumption levels can change unexpectedly, oftentimes in response to weather conditions as well. Automated notifications thereby help to anticipate critical grid situations. They lay the basis for further actions, e.g. optimization through sending out demand response requests.

Type 2 - *Monitoring of consumption and production levels/Energy Consumption Overview*: The smart meter data captures continuous consumption data, which enables the identification of inefficient consumption behaviours, especially for public buildings, since energy consumers here have little incentives to use energy efficiently, as they do not have to pay for the costs. For instance, public buildings may be kept heated on weekends, even though they are not used. The analysis of smart meter data helps to detect those inefficiencies in consumption patterns and significantly reduce energy costs. In contrast to benefit type 1, this benefit type is generated indirectly, through the manual analysis of data.

Type 3 - *Handling of unforeseen outages or critical grid situations*: Based on the monitoring of production and consumption data, as well as their graphical display within the energy management system, specific bottlenecks within the grid can be detected. This allows to create strategies of how to handle situations, in which certain components of the smart grid become unavailable, e.g. during the replacement or failure of existing battery storages. Since the handling of unforeseen outages can cause very high costs, in the worst case through the blackout of the whole system, the required strategies can only be created on a managerial basis, through the careful evaluation of all existing data.

Type 4 - *Scheduling Demand Response requests*: An active demand-side management can generally reduce the need to call expensive back-up capacity in times of peak demand. For instance, some older power plants are no longer used on regular basis, but are infrequently activated to cover the peak demand on some days. This operation is not efficient both economically & environmentally. An active demand-side management as alternative to the activation of costly back-up capacity can result in considerable savings for energy providers [13].

Type 5 - *Setting price levels for automated demand response requests*: Based on the direct benefits from scheduling demand response events, the results from previous requests and customers' reactions can be analysed for the adjustment of incentive schemes that are required for the participation of consumers.

Type 6 - *Customer segmentation and creation of new Demand Response programs and dynamic tariffs*: Based on the benefit types 4 and 5, conclusions on a managerial basis can be taken regarding the segmentation and clustering of certain types of consumers. As some groups of consumers might exhibit a high price elasticity whilst others do not, the implementation of specifically tailored dynamic tariff schemes can help to ensure customer retention, while at the same time influencing aggregated demand in a beneficial way for the energy provider.

Type 7 - *What-if scenarios*: A powerful functionality within the energy management system is a planning tool that allows to calculate the effects of adjustments or new installations in the grid. For instance, large amounts of additional PV-panels, wind turbines or battery storages might cause large effects on a certain part of the grid or even to the whole system. The tool allows estimating these effects prior to the installation. The connected benefits therefore arise indirectly through the transformation of existing business processes.

Type 8 - *Investment decisions and root problem detection*: Lastly, the energy management platform can yield benefits that are only realized in the long-run on an indirect and managerial basis from restructuring whole business processes. For instance, an active demand-side management reduces dependencies on suppliers of back-up capacities. This can prove beneficial for the negotiation of future long-term contracts or the portfolio management at wholesale markets. Additionally, benefits arise from the detection of root problems in the infrastructure or existing business processes.

5 Discussion and Outlook

For this evaluation, we assumed an energy provider to be the operator of the smart city energy management tool. However, also other market actors can be considered here. For instance, municipalities as the urban administrative divisions are also in a good position, as they can have an interest in fostering the development of a smart city [14]. Alternatively, third-party operators as new market entrants can specialize in innovative business models, such as a provider of demand response. Being a ubiquitous energy management tool, the smartDSS can be adapted according to the different needs. Not all functionalities and benefit types are applicable to each situation. While energy providers can draw benefits from the types information, optimization and transformation, municipalities typically do not interfere in the grid system and therefore the functionalities and benefit types of optimization do not apply for them. Third-party operators, on the other hand, might draw benefits from information and optimization, but not from transformation, as they do offer only specific services.

Although the importance of innovative energy management solutions for the transition of the energy sector is generally understood, the employment of such systems is oftentimes hindered by privacy concerns or a lack of understanding about the specific connected business benefits. As [15] point out, the instalment of information systems and technologies even exhibit further positive externalities for the different market actors in the energy system, which are not even considered at this point. With our future research, we therefore plan to take also societal parameters into account for the evaluation of the outlined smart city tool.

In this paper, we outlined a smart city energy management platform that integrates several components from the Internet of Things, most importantly offering decision support systems for different involved market actors in the energy system. Open data API services and privacy protection mechanisms enable the accurate distribution of required data that can allow third party operators to offer valuable services within a smart grid. As with most new information systems and technologies, not all potential business benefits from implementation are quite self-evident. By following our proposed benefit evaluation framework, we identify and categorize several benefit types on different levels.

As the energy management tool is implemented in two pilot cities in Croatia and Rijeka, we expect further valuable insights about the created value of the system. Extensive tests will be carried out that determine the effectiveness of the developed tool. Especially, more insights are expected regarding the communication between different systems and market actors, as well as about the specific monetary value that the tool can yield based on the identified benefit types.

Acknowledgments. The research presented in this article is funded by the FP7 framework's ICT-2013.6.4 Optimising Energy Systems in Smart Cities, project iURBAN (www.iurban-project.eu), under grant agreement number 608712.

References

1. Scholz, R., Beckmann, M., Pieper, C., Muster, M., Weber, R.: Considerations on providing the energy needs using exclusively renewable sources. energiewende in Germany. In: Renewable and Sustainable Energy Reviews, vol. 35, pp. 109–125 (2014)
2. Cities, Towns and Renewable Energy: Yes in My Front Yard. International Energy Agents (IEA) (2009)
3. Watson, R.T., Boudreau, M.-C., Chen, A., Huber, M.H.: Green is: building sustainable business practices. Information Systems (2008)
4. Stromback, J., Dromacque, C., Yassin, M.H.: The potential of smart meter enabled programs to increase energy and systems efficiency: a mass pilot comparison. A Report for the European Smart Metering Industry Group (2011)
5. McHenry, M.P.: Technical and governance considerations for advanced metering infrastructure/smart meters: technology, security, uncertainty, costs, benefits, and risks. Energy Policy **59**, 834–842 (2013)
6. Strüker, J., van Dinther, C.: Demand response in smart grids: research opportunities for the IS discipline. In: 18th Americas Conference on Information Systems (AMCIS) Proceedings, Seattle, Washington, 9–11 August 2012
7. Jurado, S., Fernandez, A., Avellana, N., Oates, M., Müller, G., Perse, T.: Tailoring the next generation energy management tool for smart cities. Sustainable Built Environment (2016)
8. Boer, P.F.: The Valuation of Technology: Business and Financial Issues in R&D. Wiley, New York (1999)
9. Curtin, J.P.. Gaffney, R.L., Riggins, F.J.: The RFID e-valuation framework – determining the business value from radio frequency identification. In: Proceedings of the 42nd Hawaii International Conference on System Sciences (2009)
10. Lee, H., Özer, Ö.: Unlocking the value of RFID. Prod. Oper. Manage. **16**(1), 40–64 (2007)
11. Laubacher, R., Kothari, S.P., Malone T.W., Subirana, B.: What is RFID worth to your company? MIT Sloan School Paper #224, Cambridge, USA (2006)
12. Baars, H., Gille, D., Strüker, J.: Evaluation of RFID applications for logistics: a framework for identifying, forecasting and assessing benefits. Eur. J. Inf. Syst. **18**(6), 578–591 (2009)
13. Feuerriegel, S., Neumann, D.: Measuring the financial impact of demand response for electricity retailers. Energy Policy **65**, 359–368 (2014)
14. Scholl, H.J., AlAwadhi, S.: Smart governance as key to multi-jurisdictional smart city initiatives: the case of the eCityGov Alliance. Social Science Information (2016)
15. Römer, B., Reichhardt, P., Kranz, J., Picot, A.: The role of smart metering and decentralized electricity storage for smart grids: the importance of positive externalities. Energy Policy **50**, 486–495 (2012)

IDEA Workshop

A Meta-Framework for Efficacious Adaptive Enterprise Architectures

Rogier van de Wetering[✉] and Rik Bos

Open University of the Netherlands, Valkenburgerweg 177,
6419 AT Heerlen, The Netherlands
rogier.vandewetering@ou.nl

Abstract. Tuning enterprise architectures to stay competitive and fit is an enduring challenge for organizations. This study postulates a meta-framework for Efficacious Adaptive Enterprise Architectures (EA), the 2EA framework. We use fundamental long-standing principles found in complex adaptive systems. These principles explain adaptive success. Also, we set forward managerial implications about the dynamics of EA to function effectively on four architectural levels, i.e. enterprise environment, enterprise, enterprise systems and infrastructure. Principles of efficacious adaptation have not been incorporated into current EA frameworks and methods underlining an improvement area. Subsequently, we extend baseline work into a meta-framework and evaluate it accordingly following the design science method. Our meta-framework supports organizations to assess and adapt EA capabilities – modular units of functionality within the organization – to the continuously changing environment, stakeholder interests and internal organizational dynamics. Our research contributes to foundational work on EA and can be used for strategic EA development and maturation.

Keywords: Enterprise architecture · Efficacious adaptation · Complex adaptive systems · Meta-framework

1 Introduction

Organizations that want to be more competitive need to align their business operations and information technology (IT) resources [1] and take into account the dynamics of the changing environment [2–4]. Complementary to this they need to lever intangible resources to build competences [5]. Effective use of flexibility and adaptability of IT is one way in which large organizations can maintain a competitive edge [6, 7]. It is however, not Information systems and Information Technology (IS/IT), nor business models or any organizational arrangement that 'separately' create competitive advantage. Organizations can be viewed as complex adaptive socio-technical systems. Competitive advantage is therefore the result of an integrated, consistent and coherent business, organizational, informational and technological design [8].

Over the past decade or so, IS/IT research and management practice increased attention towards the adaptive and co-evolutionary nature of IS/IT [9, 10] and dynamic, multi-faceted, and non-deterministic processes to align IS/IT and the business in

W. Abramowicz et al. (Eds.): BIS 2016 Workshops, LNBIP 263, pp. 273–288, 2017.
DOI: 10.1007/978-3-319-52464-1_25

constantly-changing business environments [11]. This evolutionistic and dynamic approach[1] has its roots in nonlinear science such as physics, biology, bio-chemistry and economy and has a profound impact on management, strategy, organization and IS/IT studies. Merali et al. [12] even argue that such an approach should frame the future IS/IT research in terms of the development of the field.

1.1 Enterprise Architecture Research Practice

Enterprise Architecture (EA) practices enable organizations to achieve strategies through orchestrated and aligned organizational processes, governance and organizational structures, from holistic perspectives, models and views [13, 14]. In this process EA provides insights, enables communication among stakeholders and guides complicated change processes [15]. While EA capability deployment is not homogenous and universal for organizations, EA's enable organizations to get value across all business units, operations, technology, and human resources and align this with the use of resources [13]. EA's models and frameworks generally guide design decisions across the enterprise, specify how information technology is related to the overall business processes and outcomes of an organization and ensure that the relationships and dependencies among architectural components are managed [16].

EAs are commonly represented in different layers in order to describe a set of cohesive or related elements in order to create structure in a chaotic environment [16, 17]. This is also recognized by service oriented approaches, e.g. Service-Oriented Architecture (SOA) developments [18].

Since its conception in the late eighties [Cf. 19] the EA domain has received substantial interest both from theorist, government EA initiatives, consultants and IT-practitioners. However, academic and theoretical discussions remain modest [20] and extant literature stumbles upon fundamental problems. These problems include lack of uniformity in definitions and dimension [21] and lack of explanatory theory and publications delivering only modest views on how EA yields benefits. Also the focus is rather from a technical baseline [22]. Another important issue is the lack of empirical findings on how EA delivers benefits [1, 23].

To date, very little research has been done on fitness and efficacious adaptation in the context of EA. The need for an integral understanding of dynamic architectural complexity, adaption and enterprise transformation is also stressed by [24]. Although there are various studies dealing with complexity science in the domain of EA [E.g. 25] convincing attempts with proper theoretical framing are scarce. A first attempt to design a theory-based conceptual framework that helps to analyze, identify improvement areas and drive adaption of EA within organizations is valuable.

---

[1] The authors in the current article refer to the field of Complexity Science. Complexity science will be addressed in Subsect. 1.2 and Sect. 2 more extensively.

1.2   Research Premises and Objectives

This article is based on the premise that long standing first principles of efficacious adaptation – Proper et al. [26] call these scientific principles – from natural, biological, social and economical sciences explain adaptive success. These principles have a direct impact on organizations' ability to adapt and co-evolve their IS/IT capabilities to the rapidly changing environment [9, 10]. Doing so, we built upon ideas and principles from complexity science and Complex Adaptive Systems theory, CAS [27], serving as a theoretical frame of reference in the construction of a meta-framework. CAS are typically concerned with the study of nonlinear dynamical systems, and has recently become a major focus of interdisciplinary research.

EA's – or Enterprise systems architectures, as it is sometimes called [28] – come with many definitions [13, 14]. For the purpose of this paper, we define an enterprise architecture as 'an abstract representation – or blueprint – of the entire enterprise, see also Urbaczewski and Mrdalj [29] representing the high-level structure (or organization logic) of an enterprise, its business processes, IT-infrastructure capabilities and the relationships among the various capabilities across the hierarchical layers and the external environment'. We see EA capabilities, in this respect, as modular units of functionality within the organization, including processes, people, technology and assets. We consider them as loosely coupled, modular building blocks of the enterprise and its architecture. They describe *'what'* is required to meet strategic enterprise objectives, demands and be competitive irrespective of *'how'* they are managed on a lower level of design and implementation. Capabilities are thus abstractions of complex behavior and architectural structure. See Azavedo et al. for a comprehensive foundational ontological discussion [30].

Our main objective – and contribution of this current paper – is to propose a theory driven conceptual meta-framework for efficacious EA adaptation. This framework can be used to leverage current and future EA capabilities and support the process of adapting EA capabilities.

We describe our conceptual meta-framework on a generic level, so that it is both compatible with existing familiar methodologies and (reference) frameworks (like Zachman, TOGAF, Four-Domain, DODAF, FEAF, ESARC, DYA, etc.). We focus on both key challenges at I) different architectural layers and II) the position of EA in relation to an organization's effort to continuously adapt to changes in the environment and stay fit. Hence, in this paper we address the following main research question: *"How can a meta-framework for efficacious EA adaptation be designed using complexity science as a frame of reference and principles of adaptive success?"*

The remainder of the article is structured as follows. We begin with a brief review on theories in complexity science research. Section 3 introduces the framework development process, while section four describes the dynamics at various architectural layers of our meta-framework. Section five outlines and discusses eight principles of efficacious adaptive success of EA. We end with the discussion and conclusions.

2   Theories in Complexity Science Research

Complexity science and complex adaptive systems (CAS) research includes studies on themes as co-evolution, adaptation, interacting agents, decentralized control, self-organized emergent behavior, and hierarchical structure. It has a rich history having its scientific roots in physics, mathematics, and evolutionary biology [9, 27, 31–34] and builds upon open systems theory[2] [35] and also on often forgotten Cellular Automata (CA) [36].

CAS theories are based on the fundamental logical properties of the behavior of non-linear and network feedback systems, no matter where they are found [32]. CAS are considered as collections of individual agents with the freedom to act in ways that are not always totally predictable, linear, and whose actions are interconnected so that one agent's actions changes the contexts for other agents. Commonly cited examples include financial markets, weather systems, human immune system, colonies of termites and organizations [27, 31, 37, 38]. Complexity science challenges traditional (linear, or Newtonian) science and management routines on organizational behavior, and the key principle of this perspective is the notion that "at any level of analysis, order within a system is an emergent property of individual interactions at a lower level of aggregation" [32].

Complexity science is not a single theory or proposition. We recognize three phases (not necessarily time dependent) of its development and accumulating knowledge. Phase 1 is based in mathematics and can be traced down to adaptive tension and first critical values of imposed energy in physical systems [39]. The second phase is due to scholars from the Sante Fe Institute and focus on CAS and dynamic, non-linear behavior and interacting agents [27, 34, 40]. Recent complexity endeavors also focus on scalability and power laws that govern natural and social phenomena. This can be considered a third phase [41, 42].

A number of authors have stated that the science of complexity can be considered a valuable instrument to cope with organizational and IS/IT changes in non-linear turbulent environments [31–33, 37]. As whole entities and with respect to their mutually interdependent parts, they go through a series of adaptations/re-adaptation cycles [9]. This idea applies particularly well to the development, continuous adaptation and alignment of EA in organizations operating in turbulent environments. EA can be considered as a hierarchical, multilevel system, comprising aggregation hierarchies, architecture layers and views [17] and resembles common elements and behaviors [31, 37] of CAS: (1) transformative and coevolving [27], (2) massively entangled [43], (3) emergent and self-organizing due to aggregate behavior from the interaction of the systems components or agents [27, 43] defined at various scales and layers and respond to environmental changes using internalized rule sets that drive action [44].

We employ the basic thought that EA adaptation needs a 'holistic' and 'complex' theoretical framework that fits the diversity of organizational components and interactions among the many agents that are involved in the practice using EA.

---

[2] Complexity science and CAS thinking search for generative simple rules in nature that underpin complexity and do not embrace the radical holism of systems theory.

3   Framework Development Process

Our approach is exploratory of nature and follows Simon's view of a 'science of design' and hence the initial stages of the design science method [45, 46]. As such, we employ an incremental development process whereby knowledge is produced by constructing and evaluating (EA) artifacts which are subsequently used as input for a better awareness of the problem [47] and hence to serve human purposes [48].

This research focusses on 'building activities' within the general design science methodology in a first attempt to design a conceptual meta-framework for efficacious EA adaptation. Therefore, this study pays considerable attention to link the articulation of the theoretical position and existing baseline work. In their conceptual analysis, the authors ensured quality and validity through the use of complementary validation methods, i.e. extensive literature review (as a first step in the development process), re-usage of baseline work and incremental reviews as the final steps of this research. That is to say that evaluation (Peffers et al. divide what others call evaluation into two activities, demonstration and evaluation [45, 46]) and communication are currently out of scope.

As baseline work, we build on prior research from McKelvey and Benbya [9, 10] and 1st principles of efficacious adaptation drawn from natural, social systems, i.e. *applying tension, improvement of requisite variety/complexity, change rate, modular (nearly decomposable) design, positive feedback/fostering coevolution, causal intricacy, complementarity*[3] *and coordination rhythm.* Any of these interdependent principles gives an organism, species, or organization adaptive advantage [9]. These principles are discussed in more detail in Sect. 5. Having none of them is a disaster; having all particularly feeds adaptive and synergetic success [10]. Synergetic success particularly suits the notion of strategic alignment, i.e. equilibrium of different organizational dimensions, and external fit as strategy development that is based on environmental trends and changes [49–52]. This can be considered a *first pillar* of our meta-framework.

A *second pillar* of our meta-framework for EA efficacious adaptation, builds upon an integration among common architecture frameworks [53]. This pillar identifies some well-known characteristics and commonalities from previous architectural frameworks, i.e. (a) hierarchical components (thus architectural levels) and (b) the type of information (sometimes referred to as domains). Within this integrated framework each architectural layer serves as a container of capabilities that is not fixed, but flexible. Therefore, any capability can be added on each of the architectural layers. Even so, capabilities can span several architectural layers. The complexity science lens extends this second pillar and adds new concepts such as co-evolution, self-organization, edge of chaos and historicity and time dependence, which enrich old systems thinking concepts [54].

---

[3] This complementarity principle does not occur in the original work of McKelvey. We add this principle based on its longstanding tradition and its impact on modern economics and business management.

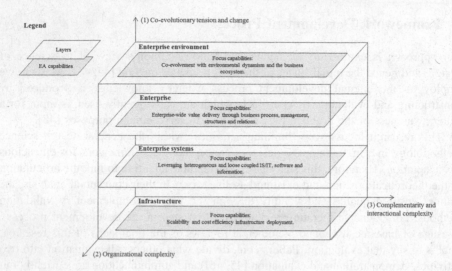

Fig. 1. 2EA framework.

As part of the design methodology, our first endeavor was to extensively review literature on complexity science, EA and adaptation creating common ground on existing architectural frameworks and gaps/voids in current literature. Building concepts – as an objective for a solution – based on the above pillars is part of this. Subsequently, initial concepts and building blocks of our framework, i.e. an initial design artifact, where then critically reviewed. These critical reviews concerning the artifact's desired purpose, functionality and its layered architecture were taken into consideration within the first iterations of the framework design and development step.

Figure 1 displays our high-level conceptual 2EA framework. It consists of (I) four architectural layers, contains (II) EA capabilities distributed among the various architectural layers and (III) three clusters, or dimensions, containing the eight principles of efficacious adaptation. The latter will be addressed in Sect. 5. Capabilities at each layer provide services to higher-level capabilities. Other relevant architectural elements, such as governance, strategy and requirements, the EA development process and business value monitoring are omitted form this framework for scope and the purpose of the current paper.

The following two sections describe the four architectural layers in more detail and applies the 1st principles of our meta-framework.

4   Dynamics at Architectural Layers of 2EA Framework

Co-evolutionistic 'lenses' are valuable for integrating both micro and macro-level evolution within a unifying framework, incorporating multiple (hierarchical) levels of analyses and contingent effects [55, 56]. Our meta-framework consists of four architectural, connected and interrelated layers with capabilities. We discuss the four layers briefly and highlight main challenges.

Enterprise environment level

At the highest level of our meta-framework, enterprise actors (e.g. supply chain partners and customers) interact as part of independent businesses (or business units), and co-evolve with the organizations ecosystem. Since many organizations need to deal with the dynamics of stakeholders and environmental uncertainties, this level is especially interesting for what Zarvic and Wieringa [53] call 'networked business constellations'. From an EA capability perspective this level typically deals with managing customers, suppliers, governmental institutions, i.e. the enterprise ecosystem. Key challenges for organizations are to deal with the dynamics of ecosystem management concerns, i.e. collaboration with partners, legislation concerns, new developments in technology, variance in requirements, competitors in the ecosystem etc.

Enterprise

The 'Enterprise' level defines how an organization operates in terms of organizational structure (and relationships among various units and divisions), its operating model (i.e. level of process integration and standardization) and business processes. All with the objective of delivering value (i.e. product, services or both) to a designated client, partner or market. Some challenges are encapsulating functionality, alignment of business processes with IT-functionality, plug-and-play components and services (e.g. business processes, end-2-end value chains) that enterprises can use to instantly response to meet specific customer and environmental demands.

Enterprise system

The 'system level' contains capabilities related to data and applications. The focus is on leveraging heterogeneous and loosely coupled IT containing different interrelated information and data applications. This layer also covers the data and information ecosystem; the infrastructure that encompasses data sources, transformation & integration and reporting & analysis. Main challenges include standardizing interfaces, API's and enterprise-wide service levels (not necessarily SLA's), loosely coupled IS/IT components offered to the 'Enterprise level'. Managing data consistency (i.e. dealing with authentic sources for each data and information object), plug-and-play software packages and managing IT-flexibility of the enterprise application landscape.

Infrastructure

This bottom layer, Infrastructure, consists of all capabilities dealing with the technical network, operating systems, hardware and (middleware-)service elements needed to facilitate the higher architectural layers [53]. Infrastructure architecture capabilities govern the way in which the infrastructure is designed and efficacious deployed in practice. Challenges at this layer include continuous security management, networking, virtualization, scalability, usage of open standards, connectivity, portability and allowing end-users with the organization to use the (self-)services wherever they are in physical space.

The above multi-level challenges can be dealt with using principles of co-evolutionary dynamics – set forward by McKelvey [9, 10]. We will discuss these principles next.

5   Applied Principles of Efficacious Adaptation

Principles of efficacious adaptation are generative forces driving adaptation in organisms and organizations. These principles are elementary drivers for efficacious adaptation of EA in organizations, in the same vain as they are drivers for Information System development [9], IS-alignment [10], technology based new ventures [57], among other applications.

The authors combined these eight principles of the 1st pillar into three main clusters, dimensions, i.e. (1) Co-evolutionary tension and change, (2) Organizational complexity and (3) Complementarity and interactional complexity. This classification is based on extensive literature study, conceptual analysis and design. In practice however, these clusters might not be exclusive. The authors had to balance between recognizing the details of practice and complying the need for overview and limitation. Based on the existing body of knowledge and a profound theoretical approach, three clusters is adequate from both a scientific and practical perspective.

The clusters are:

(1) **Co-evolutionary tension and change**
  I. *Prigogine's Adaptive Tension*: theory set forward by Prigogine and Stengers [39, 58], among others, – the cornerstone of the European School of Complexity Science – and concerns environmentally imposed tensions (energy differentials) that stimulate adaptive order creating for the system as a whole. This is also known as the dissipative structures theory.
  II. *Maruyama's Deviation Amplification Theory*: concerns the principle of coevolution via positive feedback initiated by Maruyama [59]. Mutually causal relationships can amplify an insignificant or accidental start, that may lead to order creation among agents or modules depending on different (insignificant) initial conditions.
  III. *Fisher's Change Rate*: the third principle concerns the relationship between variation and adaptation set forward by Fisher [60]. Fisher postulated that the process of adapting to a changing environment speeds up the rate that usable genetic variation becomes available. Higher internal rates of change offer adaptive advantage in changing environments.

(2) **Organizational complexity**
  IV. *Ashby's Law of Requisite Variety*: foundational law of system complexity stating that external variety can be managed by matching it with a similar degree of internal complexity [61].
  V. *Simon's Modular Design*: this fifth principle is set forward by Simon [62]. It means that complex systems consisting of nearly decomposable subunits tend to evolve faster, increase the rate of adaptive response and tune towards stable, self-generating configurations.

(3) **Complementarity and interactional complexity**
  VI. *Lindblom's Causal Intricacy*: concerns the processes of parallel interaction and mutual adjustment among heterogeneous interconnected groups (each having their own agenda) facing complex and uncertain choice and action situations [63].

VII. *Edgeworth's Complementarity Theory*: complementarity theory assumes that the individual elements of a strategic planning process cannot be individually optimized to achieve a better performance [64, 65]. Consequently, the impact of a system of complementary practices will be greater than the sum of its parts because of synergistic effects.

VIII. *Dumont's Coordination Rhythm*: the dynamic rhythm principle stems from Dumont's [66] initiating study of Hindu society. Dominance oscillates between Brahmin and Rajah (i.e. religion vs. secular forces) as the need for warfare comes and goes. In organizations, this manifests itself as entangled dualities such as centralization-decentralization, exploitation-exploration [67] and implicit vs explicit knowledge [68].

The next section discusses the above principles of our meta-framework.

5.1   Co-evolutionary Tension and Change

Adaptive Tension. The tension concept is particularly relevant to the practice of EA since energy disparities may cause a phase transition; new order creation and thus efficacious enterprise capabilities. This perspective facilitates organizations with a dynamic interplay of coevolving capabilities, mechanisms and effects across all layers of our meta-framework. In the EA context this means fostering tension between EA capabilities along the four defined architectural levels as a drive for adaptation. Tension drivers include e.g. the continuous adoption of new (modular) capabilities, competition between capabilities (i.e. survival of the fittest), enterprise-wide cost cutting etc. This co-evolutionary perspective, set in motion by tension, could spin-off into new product and service offerings based as a result of new order.

Deviation Amplification. Our main aim to apply this principle is, that deviation amplification via positive feedback mechanisms pushes the idea that self-organizing agents (or heterogenic) capabilities can create significant new structures to create a better overall functioning and thus adaptation, see also [9]. Mutual cause and effect relationships allow for small instigating events (sometimes accidents) to spiral into complex new adaptive structures that efficacious deal with turbulence in the environment. This principle can be applied to all the layers of our EA meta-framework. This principle should be governed as a mechanism for incremental EA design that fosters emergence of new architectural capabilities and generate new innovative beneficial relations among capabilities.

Change Rate. Adaptation is enhanced by the rate of internal change. We know this by Fisher [60] who found a link between variation and adaptation. This principle is particularly applicable to high velocity practices and environments. When translated to the practice of EA, it comes down to enabling continuous change of the EA spanning processes, people, technology and assets and thus increasing its absorptive capacity. Adaptation cannot proceed faster than the rate that usable and innovative variation becomes available, e.g. new knowledge, services, innovation. Therefore, organization need to propagate a continuous interaction process [69] and maintain short-term focus relations between capabilities assuring tension, disequilibrium, phase transition and new order [Cf. 57].

5.2   Organizational Complexity

Requisite Variety. For systems to remain viable, it needs to generate the same degree of internal variety as the external variety it faces in the environment [10, 61]. This requirement appears in EA literature as the capacity to integrate and connect dissimilar data and information structures, IS/IT and business capabilities as well as the ability of the EA to generate technical variety sufficient to fit changing environmental conditions, see also Benbya and McKelvey [10]. As such, it requires a technical infrastructure that enabled the foundation of capabilities upon which the enterprise business depends [70] a characteristic referred to by Duncan as flexibility [6]. For organizations to efficiously adapt to the environment and remain viable, a moderate amount of 'epistatic' relations are most suitable [Cf. 34, 71].

Modular Design. Modular design dates back to Simon's theory of near decomposability, i.e. his design principles for modular systems and 'loose coupling' [62, 72]. As a defacto standard [7], modularity within the EA infrastructure layer allows organizations to integrate disparate and geographically distributed systems across various hierarchical layers. Modular design in terms of our meta-framework refers to the extent to which it is possible to add, modify, and remove any capability with ease and with no major overall effect for practice. This approach enables organizations to decompose its enterprise architecture into atomic capabilities with very few strong with most relations among the EA capabilities being short-term. Reducing interdependencies among capabilities leads to robust designs that result in relatively stable and predictable behaviors [73]. Following this principle and recent research on the nature of modularity [74], organization should continuously decompose their EA into modular capabilities.

5.3   Complementarity and Interactional Complexity

Causal Intricacy. In hierarchical systematics, based on Lindblom [63] 'means and ends', causal influences may be multidirectional and have multilevel effects, i.e. downward, upward, horizontal, diagonal and intermittent [9]. In the context of our meta-framework, following this principle means that the interaction among the capabilities is not a static and deterministic process. Instead, it should foster co-evolution and dynamic interaction across the layers, focusing on both technical (functionality, interoperability, interfaces etc.), business and organization requirements that continuously change and are in motion [9]. Moreover, EA – from a complex adaptive systems perspective – cannot be perceived and deployed as a 'static' artifact. Expected and unexpected changes need to be made because of continuous adaptation to environmental turbulence. Strategic planning for EA can be interpreted as a combination of intended, unintended and unrealized strategic routes. This reminds of the classic, but still highly cited, vision of Henry Mintzberg on strategic planning [75].

Complementarity. The theory of complementarity that was initially introduced by Edgeworth [76]. Milgrom and Roberts [64, 65] proposed that some organizational activities, practices are mutually complementary and so tend to be adopted together. Following this logic, complementary practice results will be greater than the sum of its parts because of the synergistic effects of bundling practices together. Black and Lynch [77] argue that work practice need to be implemented in conjunction with other complementary (best-)practices. For EA this translates into the adoption and usage of complementary best-practices models, principles and guidelines on each layer. For instance, the usage of open standards (on infrastructure level) and modular plug-and-play software components (on enterprise system level), or data models (on enterprise system level) and loose coupled business processes and services (on enterprise level) as part of the EA capabilities.

Coordination Rhythm. In business management literature and other disciplines (from biology to sociology), 'dynamic rhythm' manifests itself as entangled dualities such as fast-flow, centralization-decentralization and exploitation-exploration [67], implicit vs explicit knowledge [68], offensive vs defensive strategies [78], incremental vs. revolutionary IS/IT development steps [79] and planning vs emergence [75]. We argue that for organizations to be adaptive, they should support both interaction and entangled 'top-down development' versus 'bottom-up autonomy' of EA capabilities development and deployment in practice. In fact, these poles 'complement' each other to bring about an irregular basis for adaptation of EA. Han and McKelvey [57] argue in fact that when organizations manage the duality of a moderate number and short-term ties, they are in essence managing: "..the process of parallel interaction and mutual adjustment, and coordinating a collection of diverse attributes of ties carrying different rhythms".

6 Conclusion and Outlook

Using a complexity science 'lens', we postulate that EA's and its development should not be regarded as 'static' and 'homogeneous' blueprints of organizations. Accordingly, a theorized framework for Efficacious Adaptive Enterprise Architectures, the 2EA framework, is proposed. The framework ties eight long standing principles of adaptation across three clusters to EA. Our main contribution, is the application of these principles and the dynamics across the various architectural layers of our framework. Organizations that embrace these principles in EA practice are better equipped to deal with both the internal and external dynamics. This extends the current EA body of knowledge.

In practice, the framework guides organizations to adapt their EA in alignment with the turbulent environment, organizational dynamics and constantly changing stakeholder interests. To make this possible, we suggest that organizations should explicitly identify and execute improvement activities in alignment with each of the eight principles of the 2EA framework. The meta-framework can then I. be used to leverage current, the 'as-is' EA of the organization (i.e. descriptive perspective), and future EA capabilities within the enterprise, the new EA (i.e. prescriptive perspective), IIa. be used as a grounded checklist and analysis tool to systematically identify improvement areas dealing with EA challenges and IIb. assist EA decision makers to make better investments and deployment decisions (i.e. explanatory perspective). This can systematically be done by incrementally assessing the current situation, a 'to-be' state and determining the fit-gap and thus improvement activities. Therefore, an effective EA development strategy should be complemented by a process for continuous development of EA, since strategic enterprise objectives, goals and demands continuously change within organizations.

Despite its comprehensiveness, our theorized framework has of course some limitations. First, the 2EA needs to be applied to a number of cases in order to evaluate it and to allow for critical reflection. This is in accordance with the design science method [46]. The current framework does have a plausible theoretical foundation and provides various opportunities for further research. Furthermore, the question 'how organizations can truly apply these adaptive principles in practice and benefit from them' is currently omitted and beyond the scope of this work. This is also a topic for further research. This can be done for instance using expert sessions, interviews and focus groups. Also, our 2EA framework currently does not explain how it facilitates – or is related to – the Dynamic Capabilities View (DCV) [3, 4]. DCV emerged as an influential perspective in strategic management and IS literature. It explains how firms differentiate and compete, while simultaneously evolving and reconfiguring their operations in order to remain competitive. A recent study in fact empirically demonstrated that characteristics of a firms IT architecture can facilitate (IT-enabled) dynamic capabilities [80].

This study is the first of its kind that applies principles of efficacious adaptation, to the multi-layered EA practice. Outcomes of this study support and guide enterprise architects, IT-managers and CIO's with day-to-day environmental, organizational and stakeholder challenges. It positions their work and efforts into a holistic perspective and through a complexity lens. Future research can benefit from our work to understand the nature of efficacious adaptation of enterprise architectures. This paper lays a foundation for further research in this imperative domain that can focus on validating the framework's premises using empirical data and potentially agent based, modeling, NK fitness landscape modeling and other simulation techniques to generalize outcomes [34, 71, 81]. It is our ambition to extend the application of the 2EA framework and also focus on qualitative and co-evolutionary aspects in a networked business ecosystem setting, modeling efficacious adaptive EA's, define architectural complexity measures (e.g. modularity, agility), and synthesize EA strategies following the concepts of EA fitness landscapes. These matters, among others, are currently under investigation.

References

1. Wegmann, A.: The Systemic Enterprise Architecture Methodology (SEAM). Business and IT Alignment for Competitiveness (2002)
2. Brown, S., Eisenhardt, K.: The art of continuous change: linking complexity theory and time-paced evolution in relentlessly shifting organizations. Adm. Sci. Q. **42**(1), 1–34 (1997)

3. Eisenhardt, K.M., Martin, J.A.: Dynamic capabilities: what are they? Strateg. Manag. J. **21**(10–11), 1105–1121 (2000)
4. Teece, D.J., Pisano, G., Shuen, A.: Dynamic capabilities and strategic management. Strateg. Manag. J. **18**(7), 509–533 (1997)
5. Wernerfelt, B.: A resource-based view of the firm. Strateg. Manag. J. **5**(2), 171–180 (1984)
6. Duncan, N.B.: Capturing flexibility of information technology infrastructure: a study of resource characteristics and their measure. J. Manag. Inf. Syst. **12**, 37–57 (1995)
7. Wilkinson, M.: Designing an 'adaptive' enterprise architecture. BT Technol. J. **24**(4), 81–92 (2006)
8. Hoogervorst, J.: Enterprise architecture: Enabling integration, agility and change. Int. J. Coop. Inf. Syst. **13**(03), 213–233 (2004)
9. Benbya, H., McKelvey, B.: Toward a complexity theory of information systems development. Inf. Technol. People **19**(1), 12–34 (2006)
10. Benbya, H., McKelvey, B.: Using coevolutionary and complexity theories to improve IS alignment: a multi-level approach. J. Inf. Technol. **21**(4), 284–298 (2006)
11. Vessey, I., Ward, K.: The dynamics of sustainable IS alignment: The case for IS adaptivity. J. Assoc. Inf. Syst. **14**(6), 283–311 (2013)
12. Merali, Y., Papadopoulos, T., Nadkarni, T.: Information systems strategy: Past, present, future? J. Strateg. Inf. Syst. **21**(2), 125–153 (2012)
13. Bernard, S.A.: An Introduction to Enterprise Architecture, 3rd edn. AuthorHouse, Bloomington (2012)
14. Ross, J.W., Weill, P., Robertson, D.: Enterprise Architecture as Strategy: Creating a Foundation for Business Execution. Harvard Business Press, Boston (2006)
15. Jonkers, H., et al.: Concepts for modeling enterprise architectures. Int. J. Coop. Inf. Syst. **13**(03), 257–287 (2004)
16. Janssen, M.: Framing enterprise architecture: a metaframework for analyzing architectural efforts in organizations. In: Coherency Management: Architecting the Enterprise for Alignment, Agility and Assurance. Authorhouse, Bloomington (2009)
17. Winter, R., Fischer, R.: Essential layers, artifacts, and dependencies of enterprise architecture. In: 10th IEEE International Enterprise Distributed Object Computing Conference Workshops. IEEE (2006)
18. Bell, M.: SOA Modeling patterns for service-oriented discovery and analysis. Wiley Online Library (2010)
19. Zachman, J.: A framework for information systems architecture. IBM Syst. J. **26**(3), 276–292 (1987)
20. Tamm, T., et al.: How does enterprise architecture add value to organisations. Commun. Assoc. Inf. Syst. **28**(1), 141–168 (2011)
21. Greefhorst, D., Koning, H., Van Vliet, H.: The many faces of architectural descriptions. Inf. Syst. Front. **8**(2), 103–113 (2006)
22. Ren, M., Lyytinen, K.J.: Building enterprise architecture agility and sustenance with SOA. Commun. Assoc. Inf. Syst. **22**(1), 4 (2008)
23. Foorthuis, R., et al.: A theory building study of enterprise architecture practices and benefits. Inf. Syst. Front. 1–24 (2015)
24. Zimmermann, A., et al.: Collaborative Decision Support for Adaptive Digital Enterprise Architecture (2015)
25. Janssen, M., Kuk. G.: A complex adaptive system perspective of enterprise architecture in electronic government. In: Proceedings of the 39th Annual Hawaii International Conference on System Sciences. IEEE, Hawaii (2006)
26. Proper, E., Greefhorst, D.: The Roles of Principles in Enterprise Architecture. Springer, Heidelberg (2010)

27. Holland, J.: Complex adaptive systems. Daedalus **121**(1), 17–30 (1992)
28. Nightingale, D.J., Rhodes, D.H.: Enterprise systems architecting: Emerging art and science within engineering systems. In: MIT Engineering Systems Symposium. MIT (2004)
29. Urbaczewski, L., Mrdalj, S.: A comparison of enterprise architecture frameworks. Issues Inf. Syst. **7**(2), 18–23 (2006)
30. Azevedo, C.L., et al.: Modeling resources and capabilities in enterprise architecture: a well-founded ontology-based proposal for ArchiMate. Inf. Syst. **54**, 235–262 (2015)
31. Dooley, K.: A complex adaptive systems model of organization change. Nonlinear Dyn. Psychol. Life Sci. **1**(1), 69–97 (1997)
32. Stacey, R.: The science of complexity: an alternative perspective for strategic change processes. Strateg. Manag. J. **16**(6), 477–495 (1995)
33. Anderson, P.: Complexity theory and organization science. Organ. Sci. **10**(3), 216–232 (1999)
34. Kauffman, S.A.: The Origins of Order: Self Organization and Selection in Evolution. Oxford University Press, New York (1993)
35. Boulding, K.: General systems theory-the skeleton of science. Manag. Sci. **2**(3), 197–208 (1956)
36. Wolfram, S.: A New Kind of Science, vol. 5. Wolfram Media, Champaign (2002)
37. Holden, L.: Complex adaptive systems: concept analysis. J. Adv. Nurs. **52**(6), 651–657 (2005)
38. Burnes, B.: Kurt Lewin and complexity theories: back to the future? J. Change Manag. **4**(4), 309–325 (2004)
39. Prigogine, I., Stengers, I.: The End of Certainty. Simon and Schuster, New York (1997)
40. Gell-Mann, M.: What is complexity? In: Complexity and Industrial Clusters, pp. 13–24. Springer, Heidelberg (2002)
41. Andriani, P., McKelvey, B.: Perspective-from Gaussian to Paretian thinking: causes and implications of power laws in organizations. Organ. Sci. **20**(6), 1053–1071 (2009)
42. Newman, M.E.: Power laws, Pareto distributions and Zipf's law. Contemp. Phys. **46**(5), 323–351 (2005)
43. Morel, B., Ramanujam, R.: Through the looking glass of complexity: the dynamics of organizations as adaptive and evolving systems. Organ. Sci. **10**(3), 278–293 (1999)
44. Plsek, P.: Redesigning health care with insights from the science of complex adaptive systems. In: Crossing the Quality Chasm: A New Health System for the 21st Century, pp. 309–322 (2001)
45. Peffers, K., et al.: A design science research methodology for information systems research. J. Manag. Inf. Syst. **24**(3), 45–77 (2007)
46. Venable, J., Pries-Heje, J., Baskerville, R.: A comprehensive framework for evaluation in design science research. In: Peffers, K., Rothenberger, M., Kuechler, B. (eds.) DESRIST 2012. LNCS, vol. 7286, pp. 423–438. Springer, Heidelberg (2012). doi:10.1007/978-3-642-29863-9_31
47. Hevner, A.R., et al.: Design science in information systems research. MIS Q. **28**(1), 75–105 (2004)
48. March, S.T., Smith, G.F.: Design and natural science research on information technology. Decis. Support Syst. **15**(4), 251–266 (1995)
49. Chan, Y.E., Reich, B.H.: IT alignment: an annotated bibliography. J. Inf. Technol. **22**, 316–396 (2008)
50. Van de Wetering, R., Batenburg, R.: Towards a theory of PACS deployment: an integrative PACS maturity framework. J. Digit. Imaging **27**(3), 337–350 (2014)

51. Van de Wetering, R.: Modeling alignment as a higher order nomological framework. In: Abramowicz, W., Rainer, A., Bogdan, F. (eds.) BIS 2016 Workshops. LNBIP, vol. 263, pp. 111–122. Springer, Heidelberg

52. Mikalef, P., et al.: Business alignment in the procurement domain: a study of antecedents and determinants of supply chain performance. Int. J. Inf. Syst. Proj. Manag. 2(1), 43–59 (2014)

53. Zarvić, N., Wieringa, R.: An integrated enterprise architecture framework for business-IT alignment. In: Proceedings of the CAISE 2006 Workshop on Business/IT Alignment and Interoperability (BUSITAL 2006). CEUR (2014)

54. Mitleton-Kelly, E.: Complex Systems and Evolutionary Perspectives on Organisations: The Application of Complexity Theory to Organisations. Elsevier Science Ltd. (2003)

55. Van Den Bosch, F.A., Volberda, H.W., De Boer, M.: Coevolution of firm absorptive capacity and knowledge environment: Organizational forms and combinative capabilities. Organ. Sci. 10(5), 551–568 (1999)

56. Lewin, A.Y., Volberda, H.W.: Prolegomena on coevolution: A framework for research on strategy and new organizational forms. Organ. Sci. 10(5), 519–534 (1999)

57. Han, M., McKelvey, B.: Toward a social capital theory of technology-based new ventures as complex adaptive systems. Int. J. Account. & Inf. Manag. 16(1), 36–61 (2008)

58. Prigogine, I.: Thermodynamics of irreversible processes. Thomas (1955)

59. Maruyama, M.: The second cybernetics: deviation-amplifying mutual causal processes. Am. Sci. 51, 164–179 (1963)

60. Fisher, R.A.: The Genetical Theory of Natural Selection: A Complete Variorum Edition. Oxford University Press (1930)

61. Ashby, W.: Principles of the self-organizing system. In: Principles of Self-organization, pp. 255–278 (1962)

62. Simon, H.A.: The architecture of complexity. Gen. Syst. 1965(10), 63–76 (1965)

63. Lindblom, C.E.: The science of "muddling through". Public Adm. Rev. 19(2), 79–88 (1959)

64. Milgrom, P., Roberts, J.: The economics of modern manufacturing: technology, strategy, and organization. Am. Econ. Rev. 80(3), 511–528 (1990)

65. Milgrom, P., Roberts, J.: Complementarities and fit strategy, structure, and organizational change in manufacturing. J. Account. Econ. 19(2–3), 179–208 (1995)

66. Dumont, L.: Homo Hierarchicus: The Caste System and Its Implications (trans. M. Sainsbury, L. Dumont, and B. Gulati). University of Chicago Press, Chicago (1966)

67. March, J.G.: Exploration and exploitation in organizational learning. Organ. Sci. 2(1), 71–87 (1991)

68. Nonaka, I.: A dynamic theory of organizational knowledge creation. Organ. Sci. 5(1), 14–37 (1994)

69. Davis, G.B.: Strategies for information requirements determination. IBM Syst. J. 21(1), 4–30 (1982)

70. McKay, D., Brockway, D.: Building IT infrastructure for the 1990s. Stage by Stage 9(3), 1–11 (1989)

71. Frenken, K.: A fitness landscape approach to technological complexity, modularity, and vertical disintegration. Struct. Change Econ. Dyn. 17(3), 288–305 (2006)

72. Weick, K.E.: Educational organizations as loosely coupled systems. Adm. Sci. Q. 21, 1–19 (1976)

73. Levinthal, D.A., Warglien, M.: Landscape Design: Designing for Local Action in Complex Worlds. Organ. Sci. 10(3), 342–357 (1999)

74. Clune, J., Mouret, J.-B., Lipson, H.: The evolutionary origins of modularity. In: Proc. R. Soc. Lond. B Biol. Sci. (2013)

75. Mintzberg, H.: Patterns in strategy formation. Manag. Sci. 24(9), 934–948 (1978)

76. Edgeworth, F.: Mathematical Physics: An Essay on the Application of Mathematics to the Moral Sciences. C. Kegan Paul & Co., London (1881)
77. Black, S.E., Lynch, L.M.: How to compete: the impact of workplace practices and information technology on productivity. Rev. Econ. Stat. **83**(3), 434–445 (2001)
78. Wagter, R., et al.: Dynamic enterprise architecture: how to make it work. John Wiley & Sons (2005)
79. Van de Wetering, R., Batenburg, R., Lederman, R.: Evolutionistic or revolutionary paths? A PACS maturity model for strategic situational planning. Int. J. Comput. Assist. Radiol. Surg. **5**(4), 401–409 (2010)
80. Mikalef, P., Pateli, A., Van de Wetering, R.: IT flexibility and competitive performance: the mediating role of IT-enabled dynamic capabilities. In: Proceedings of the 24th European Conference on Information Systems (ECIS) (2016)
81. Davis, J.P., Eisenhardt, K.M., Bingham, C.B.: Developing theory through simulation methods. Acad. Manag. Rev. **32**(2), 480–499 (2007)

Multi-perspective Digitization Architecture for the Internet of Things

Alfred Zimmermann[1(✉)], Rainer Schmidt[2], Kurt Sandkuhl[3],
Dierk Jugel[1,3], Justus Bogner[1,4], and Michael Möhring[2]

[1] Herman Hollerith Center, Reutlingen University, Reutlingen, Germany
alfred.zimmermann@reutlingen-university.de
[2] Munich University, Munich, Germany
[3] University of Rostock, Rostock, Germany
[4] Hewlett Packard Enterprise, Böblingen, Germany

Abstract. Social networks, smart portable devices, Internet of Things (IoT) on base of technologies like analytics for big data and cloud services are emerging to support flexible connected products and agile services as the new wave of digital transformation. Biological metaphors of living and adaptable ecosystems with service-oriented enterprise architectures provide the foundation for self-optimizing and resilient run-time environments for intelligent business services and related distributed information systems. We are extending Enterprise Architecture (EA) with mechanisms for flexible adaptation and evolution of information systems having distributed IoT and other micro-granular digital architecture to support next digitization products, services, and processes. Our aim is to support flexibility and agile transformation for both IT and business capabilities through adaptive digital enterprise architectures. The present research paper investigates additionally decision mechanisms in the context of multi-perspective explorations of enterprise services and Internet of Things architectures by extending original enterprise architecture reference models with state of art elements for architectural engineering and digitization.

Keywords: Digital transformation · Internet of Things · Digitization architecture · Multi-perspective adaptable enterprise architecture · Decision support

1 Introduction

Social networks, smart portable devices, and intelligent cars, represent only a few instances of a pervasive, information-driven vision [1, 19, 29] for the next wave of the digital economy and the digital transformation. Digitization, as in [23], is the collaboration of human beings and autonomous objects beyond their local context using digital technologies. Digitization further increases the importance of information, data and knowledge as fundamental concepts of our everyday activities.

The technological and business architectural impact of digitization has multiple aspects, which directly affect adaptable digital enterprise architectures and their related systems. Enterprise Architecture Management [4, 13] for Services Computing is the

© Springer International Publishing AG 2017
W. Abramowicz et al. (Eds.): BIS 2016 Workshops, LNBIP 263, pp. 289–298, 2017.
DOI: 10.1007/978-3-319-52464-1_26

approach of choice to organize, build and utilize distributed capabilities for Digital Transformation [1, 29]. They provide flexibility and agility in business and IT systems. The development of such applications integrates the Internet of Things, Web and REST Services, Cloud Computing and Big Data management [21], among other frameworks and methods, like software architecture [3] and architectural semantic support.

Our paper focuses on the following research questions:

RQ1: What is the architectural composition context from the Internet of Things to support the digitization of products, services, and enterprise processes?

RQ2: How should digital enterprise architecture management be holistically tailored to include Internet of Things architectures and set a decisional context for architecture analytics and optimization efforts?

RQ3: How can collaborative decision support for multi-perspective digital enterprise architectures be specifically managed?

The following Sect. 2 sets the fundamental architectural context for Digital Transformation with the Internet of Things approach. Section 3 describes our research platform for digital enterprise architecture, which was extended by concepts from adaptive case management, architectural adaptation mechanisms and a specific developed model integration method for micro-granular architectural elements. Section 4 presents our collaborative architectural engineering and transformation approach and links it with specific decision management mechanisms. Finally, in Sect. 5, we summarize our research findings and limitations, our ongoing work in academic and practical environments as well as our future research plans.

2 Digitization with the Internet of Things

The Internet of Things (IoT) [2, 17] enables a large number of physical devices to connect each other to perform wireless data communication and interaction using the Internet as a global communication environment. The Internet of Things maps and integrates real world objects into the virtual world and extends the interaction with mobility systems, collaboration support systems, and systems and services for big data and cloud environments. Sensors, actuators, devices as well as humans and software agents interact and communicate data to implement specific tasks or more sophisticated business or technical processes.

Smart connected products and services expand physical components from their traditional core by adding information and connectivity services though the Internet. Internet of Things covers often-small and micro-granular intelligent physical components, which are connected. Smart products and services amplify the basic value and capabilities and offer exponentially expanding opportunities [2]. Smart connected products combine three fundamental elements: physical components, smart components, and connectivity components. Challenging examples of digital transformation for smart products [18] results from the capabilities of the Internet of Things [29]. Major trends for the digital transformation of digitized products and services are investigated in [23]. The Internet of Things is the result of a convergence of visions [2, 10] specifically, a Things-oriented vision, an Internet-oriented vision, and a Semantic-oriented vision.

A cloud centric vision for architectural thinking of a ubiquitous sensing environment is provided by [18]. Smart products as well as their production are supported by the Internet of Things and can help enterprises to create more customer-oriented digital products and services. Furthermore, the Internet of Things is an important influence factor of the potential use of Industry 4.0 [22].

A layered Reference Architecture for the Internet of Things is proposed in [31] and (Fig. 1). Layers are instantiated by suitable technologies for the Internet of Things. The typical configuration of the Internet of Things includes besides many communicating devices a cloud-based server architecture, which is required to interact and perform remote data management and calculations. A main question of current and further research is, how the Internet of Things architecture fits into a context of a services-based enterprise-computing environment. A service-oriented integration approach for the Internet of Things was elaborated in [25].

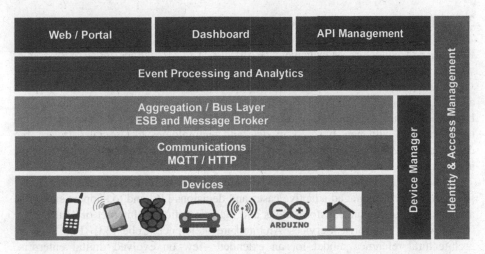

Fig. 1. Internet of Things reference architecture [31]

The Internet of Things architecture has to support a set of generic as well as some specific requirements. Generic requirements result from the inherent connection of a magnitude of devices via the Internet, often having to cross firewalls and other obstacles. Having to consider such a large and dynamically growing number of devices we need an architecture for scalability. Because these devices should be active in a 24 × 7 timeframe we need a high-availability approach [9], with deployment and auto-switching across cooperating datacenters in case of disasters and high scalable processing demands. Additionally, an Internet of Thing architecture [2] has to support automatic managed updates and remotely managed devices. Often connected devices collect and analyze personal or security relevant data. Therefore, it is mandatory to support identity management, access control and security management on different levels: from the connected devices through the holistically controlled environment.

An inspiring approach for the development for the Internet of Things environments is presented in [17]. This research has a close link to our work about leveraging the integration of the Internet of Things into a decision framework for digital enterprise architectures. The main contribution considers a role-specific development methodology and a development framework for the Internet of Things. The development framework contains a set of modeling languages for a vocabulary language to describe domain-specific features of an IoT application, an architecture language for describing application-specific functionality, and a deployment language for deployment features. Associated with this language set are suitable automation techniques for code generation and linking to reduce the effort for developing and operating device-specific code. The metamodel for Internet of Things applications [17] defines elements of an Internet of Things architectural reference model, like IoT resources of type: sensor, actuator, storage, and user interface.

3　Digital Enterprise Architecture

Enterprise Architecture Management (EAM) [4, 13, 24] defines today with frameworks, standards [15, 16], tools and practical expertise a quite large set of different views and perspectives. We argue in this paper that a new refocused digital enterprise architecture approach should support digitization of products and services, and should be both holistic [32] and easily adaptable [33] to support IoT [30] and the digital transformation with new business models and technologies like social software, big data, services & cloud computing, mobility platforms and systems, security systems, and semantics support.

In this paper we extend our service-oriented enterprise architecture reference model for the context of managed adaptive cases and decisions [26] and to support enterprise architectures for digital transformations and the integration of Internet of Things.

ESARC – Enterprise Services Architecture Reference Cube [33] (Fig. 2) is an architectural reference model for an extended view on evolved digital enterprise architectures. ESARC is more specific than existing architectural standards of EAM – Enterprise Architecture Management [15, 16] and extends these architectural standards for digital enterprise architectures with services and cloud computing. ESARC provides a holistic classification model with eight integral architectural domains. These architectural domains cover specific architectural viewpoint descriptions [7] in accordance to the orthogonal dimensions of both architectural layers and architectural aspects [32, 33]. ESARC abstracts from a concrete business scenario or technologies, but it is applicable for concrete architectural instantiations to support digital transformations. The Open Group Architecture Framework [15] provides the basic blueprint and structure for our extended service-oriented enterprise architecture domains.

Metamodels and their architectural data are the core part of the Digitization Architecture. Architecture metamodels [8, 16] should support decisions [11, 12] and the strategic and IT/Business [19] alignment. Three quality perspectives are important for an adequate IT/Business alignment and are differentiated as: (I) IT system qualities: performance, interoperability, availability, usability, accuracy, maintainability, and suitability; (II) business qualities: flexibility, efficiency, effectiveness, integration and

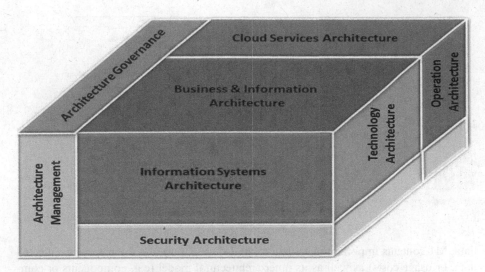

Fig. 2. Enterprise Services Architecture Reference Cube [32, 33]

coordination, decision support, control and follow up, and organizational culture; and finally (III) governance qualities: plan and organize, acquire and implement deliver and support, monitor and evaluate.

We are currently refining our previous architecture evolution approach to integrate and adapt valuable parts of existing EA frameworks, their metamodels from theory and practice [30], and extend them for small micro-granular architectural elements, like IoT and microservices. Our Enterprise Services Architecture Model Integration (ESAMI) method is based on correlation analysis, having a systematic integration process. We have linearized the complexity of these architectural mappings by introducing a neutral and dynamically extendable architectural reference model, which is supplied and dynamically extended from previous mapping iterations. We have adopted modeling concepts from ISO/IEC 42010 [7], like Architecture Description, Viewpoint, View, and Model. Architectural metamodels are composed of their elements and relationships.

In addition to a new building mechanism for dynamically extending core meta-models we are integrating with our approach small-decentralized mini-metamodels, models and data of architectural descriptions, which arise e.g. from Internet of Things devices and other micro-granular and highly distributed architectural elements, like microservices, which are not covered by classical enterprise architecture frameworks.

To integrate a huge amount of dynamically growing Internet of Things (IoT) architectural descriptions into a consistent enterprise architecture is a considerable challenge. Currently, we are working on the idea of integrating small architectural descriptions (Fig. 3) for each relevant IoT object, and similarly for other types of micro-granular architectural elements, like microservices or mobility devices.

For handling EA-Mini-Descriptions, we applied the four layers of Meta Object Facility (MOF) [14] to provide sufficient information structures for an EA integration scenario with microservices. M0 and M1 are local layers to a single IoT device/ component (*cell* metaphor). While M0 consists of operational run-time or monitoring

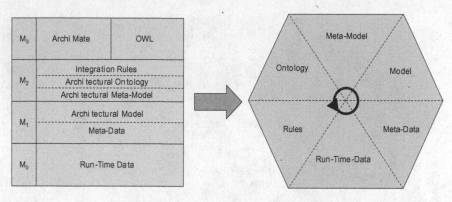

Fig. 3. Structure of EA-Mini-Description

data, M1 contains important meta-data of the IoT (e.g. purpose, the nature of collected data, or usage costs) as well as its inner architectural model (e.g. components or communication channels). On top of these, the layer M3 acts as a global meta-model layer that holds necessary information for several collaborating IoT devices/components (*body* metaphor, combining several *cells*). It incorporates architectural IoT-specific meta-models and ontologies while also providing integration rules for the semi-automatic integration of specific metamodels to the overall integrated and dynamically growing EA metamodel from the composition of EA-Mini-Descriptions. On top of that, M3 specifies the languages and semantic representations that we are using for modeling and representing these adaptable enterprise architecture metamodels.

EA-Mini-Descriptions consist of partial EA-Mini-Data, partial EA-Mini-Models, and partial EA-Metamodels associated with main IoT objects like IoT-Resource, IoT-Device, and IoT-Software-Component. Our main research question asks, how we can federate these EA-Mini-Descriptions to a global EA model and information base by promoting a mixed automatic and collaborative decision process [11, 12]. For the automatic part we currently extend model federation [20] and transformation approaches [28] by introducing semantic-supported architectural representations, e.g. by using partial and federated ontologies and associated mapping rules as universal architectural knowledge representation, which are combined with special inference mechanisms.

The flexible configuration of an integrated set of EA-Mini-Descriptions leads in this way to an adaptive digital enterprise architecture. We are introducing a new principle for an adaptable architecture by postulating: the micro-granular architectural element is fix, while the configuration of those elements leads to a flexible and adaptable architecture. Our approach extends previous research about federated enterprise architectures [20] and living architectural models [28]. Adaptation drives the survival [27] of digital enterprise architectures [33], platforms and application ecosystems. Volatile technologies and markets typically drive the evolution of ecosystems. The alignment of Architecture-Governance [19, 30] shapes resiliency, scalability and composability of components and services for distributed information systems.

4   Multi-perspective Architecture Decision Environment

A Decision Support System (DSS) is a system for improving the effectiveness of managerial decision making [12]. In particular, knowledge intensive management activities, like Enterprise Architecture Management (EAM), can benefit from a DSS to improve architectural decision-making. We are exploring in our current research, how an enterprise architecture cockpit [11, 12] can be extended to a DSS for a multi-perspective architecture environment. A cockpit presents a facility or device via which multiple viewpoints on the system under consideration can be consulted simultaneously. Each stakeholder who takes place in a cockpit meeting can utilize a viewpoint that displays the relevant information. Thereby, the stakeholders can leverage views that fit the particular role like Application Architect, Business Process Owner or Infrastructure Architect. The viewpoints are applied simultaneously and are linked to each other showing multi-perspective architectural dependencies and the impact of a change. Changes in one view are pointing to updates and dependencies in other views as well. Figure 4 gives the idea of multi-perspectives of a collaborative enterprise architecture cockpit [11].

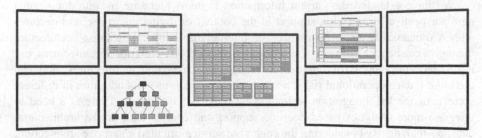

Fig. 4. Example: enterprise architecture cockpit [11, 12]

Jugel et al. [12] present a collaborative approach for decision-making for EA management. They identify decision making in such complex environment as a knowledge-intensive process strongly depends on the participating stakeholders. Therefore, the collaborative approach presented is built based on the methods and techniques of adaptive case management (ACM), as defined in [26].

The decision-making step [12] is the central activity of a decision-making case. This step can involve different optional activities in which different kinds of quantitative and qualitative analysis techniques [5, 6] are applied: expert-based analysis techniques, rule-based analysis techniques, indicator-based analysis techniques.

The decision-making step is based on case data consisting of an EA model and additional insights elicited in previous steps. Consequently, the insights gained during each step contribute to the case file of the decision-making case. Derived values, like the values of KPIs are thereby not considered additional information, but only a different way of representing and aggregating existing information. Stakeholder decisions represent new information, which is added to the case file.

5 Conclusion

According to our research questions, we have leveraged a new model of extended digital enterprise architecture, which is well suited for adaptive models and next transformation mechanisms. We have included in our work the new architectural composition context from the Internet of Things to support the digital transformation of products, services, and enterprise processes. Related to our second research question, we have presented how digital enterprise architecture management should be holistically tailored to include a lot of small Internet of Things architectures and set a decisional context for architecture analytics and optimization efforts for a new set of bottom-up and dynamically integrated small metamodels, which are originating from micro-granular architectures, like the Internet of Things. To provide our answer for the third research question, we have finally merged architectural viewpoints with user decision-making processes within a cooperative distributed environment for multi-perspective enterprise architecture management. We have introduced suitable analytics and individual decision support models and embedded them into cooperative analysis and engineering environments. We are currently working on extended decision support mechanisms for an architectural cockpit for digital enterprise architectures and related engineering processes.

We have extended the current information systems literature by introducing this new perspective for decision support in the context of digital enterprise architectures with a dynamically growing number of Internet of Things. Enterprise architecture managers can benefit from new knowledge about adaptable enterprise architectures, use it for decision support of Internet of Things use cases and architectures, and can therefore reduce operational risks. Some limitations (e.g. use and adoption in different sectors, or the IoT integration technologies) must be considered. There is a need to integrate more analytics based decision support and context-data driven architectural decision-making. By considering the context of service-oriented enterprise architecture, we have set the foundation for dynamically integrating metamodels and related ontologies for orthogonal architecture domains of our integrated Digital Enterprise Architecture approach with Internet of Things. Our results can help practical users to understand the integration of architectural models with the Internet of Things and to support architectural decisions. Limitations can be found today e.g. in the field of multi-level evaluations of our approach as well as in adoptions for practice.

Future research will extend both mechanisms for adaptation and flexible integration of digital enterprise architectures as well as decisional processes by rationales and explanations. Future work will also include conceptual work to federate EA-IoT-Mini-Descriptions to a global EA model and enterprise architecture repository by promoting a semi-automatic and collaborative decision process. We are currently extending our architectural model federation and transformation approaches with basic research for ontology-based model transformations and elements from related work. We are researching about semantic-supported architectural representations, as universal enterprise architectural knowledge representations, which are combined with special inference mechanisms. Additional improvement opportunities will focus on methods for visualization of architecture artifacts and control information to be operable in a multi-perspective architecture management cockpit.

References

1. Aier, S., Buckl, S., Gleichauf, B., Matthes, F., Winter, R.: Towards a more integrated EA planning: linking transformation planning with evolutionary change. In: Proceedings of EMISA 2011, Hamburg, Germany, pp. 23–36 (2011)
2. Atzori, L., Iera, A., Morabito, G.: The internet of things: a survey. J. Comput. Netw. **54**, 2787–2805 (2010)
3. Bass, C., Clements, P., Kazman, R.: Software Architecture in Practice. Addison Wesley, Massachusetts (2013)
4. Bente, S., Bombosch, U., Langade, S.: Collaborative Enterprise Architecture. Morgan Kaufmann (2012)
5. Buckl, S., Matthes, F., Schweda, C.M.: Classifying enterprise architecture analysis approaches. In: The 2nd IFIP WG5.8 Workshop on Enterprise Interoperability (IWEI 2009), Valencia, Spain, pp. 66–79 (2009)
6. Buckl, S., Gehlert, A., Matthes, F., Schulz, C., Schweda, C. M.: Modeling the supply and demand of architectural information on enterprise level. In: 15th IEEE International EDOC Conference 2011, Helsinki, Finland, pp. 44–51 (2011)
7. Emery, D., Hilliard, R.: Every architecture description needs a framework: expressing architecture frameworks using ISO/IEC 42010. In: IEEE/IFIP WICSA/ECSA, pp. 31–39 (2009)
8. Farwick, M., Pasquazzo, W., Breu, R., Schweda, C. M., Voges, K., Hanschke, I.: A meta-model for automated enterprise architecture model maintenance. In: EDOC 2012, pp. 1–10 (2012)
9. Ganz, F., Li, R., Barunaghi, P., Harai, H.: A resource mobility scheme for service-continuity in the internet of things. In: GreenCom 2012, pp. 261–264 (2012)
10. Gubbi, J., Buyya, R., Marusic, S., Palaniswami, M.: Internet of Things (IoT): a vision, architectural elements, and future directions. Future Gener. Comp. Syst. **29**(7), 1645–1660 (2013)
11. Jugel, D., Schweda, C.M.: Interactive functions of a cockpit for enterprise architecture planning. In: International Enterprise Distributed Object Computing Conference Workshops and Demonstrations (EDOCW), Ulm, Germany, 33–40. IEEE (2014)
12. Jugel, D., Schweda, C.M., Zimmermann, A.: Modeling decisions for collaborative enterprise architecture engineering. In: Persson, A., Stirna, J. (eds.) CAiSE 2015. LNBIP, vol. 215, pp. 351–362. Springer, Heidelberg (2015). doi:10.1007/978-3-319-19243-7_33
13. Lankhorst, M.: Enterprise Architecture at Work: Modelling, Communication and Analysis. Springer, Heidelberg (2013)
14. OMG, Meta Object Facility (MOF) Core Specification, Version 2.5 (2011)
15. Open Group: TOGAF Version 9.1. Van Haren Publishing (2011)
16. Open Group: ArchiMate 2.0 Specification. Van Haren Publishing (2012)
17. Patel, P., Cassou, D.: Enabling high-level application development for the Internet of Things. CoRR abs/1501.05080, Submitted to Journal of Systems and Software (2015)
18. Porter, M.E., Heppelmann, J.E.: How smart connected products are transforming competition. Harvard Bus. Rev. **3**, 1–23 (2014)
19. Ross, J.W., Weill, P., Robertson, D.: Enterprise Architecture as Strategy – Creating a Foundation for Business Execution. Harvard Business School Press, Boston (2006)
20. Roth, S.: Federated Enterprise Architecture Model Management – Conceptual Foundations, Collaborative Model Integration, and Software Support. PhD Dissertation TU Munich (2014)

21. Schmidt, R., Möhring, M.: Strategic alignment of cloud-based architecture for big data. In: Business Process Management Workshops, pp. 452–462. Springer (2014)
22. Schmidt, R., Möhring, M., Härting, R.-C., Reichstein, C., Neumaier, P., Jozinović, P.: Industry 4.0 - potentials for creating smart products: empirical research results. In: Abramowicz, W. (ed.) BIS 2015. LNBIP, vol. 208, pp. 16–27. Springer, Heidelberg (2015). doi:10.1007/978-3-319-19027-3_2
23. Schmidt, R., Zimmermann, A., Möhring, M., Nurcan, S., Keller, B., Bär, F.: Digitization – perspectives for conceptualization. In: Celesti, A., Leitner, P. (eds.) ESOCC Workshops 2015. CCIS, vol. 567, pp. 263–275. Springer, Heidelberg (2016). doi:10.1007/978-3-319-33313-7_20
24. Schmidt, R., Möhring, M., Härting, R.-C., Reichstein, C., Zimmermann, A., Luceri, S.: Benefits of enterprise architecture management – insights from european experts. In: Ralyté, J., España, S., Pastor, Ó. (eds.) PoEM 2015. LNBIP, vol. 235, pp. 223–236. Springer, Heidelberg (2015). doi:10.1007/978-3-319-25897-3_15
25. Spiess, P., Karnouskos, S., Guinard, D., Savio, D., Baecker, O., Sádes Souza, L. M., Trifa, V.: SOA-based integration of the internet of things in enterprise services. In: ICWS 2009, pp. 968–975 (2009)
26. Swenson, K.D.: Mastering the Unpredictable: How Adaptive Case Management Will Revolutionize the Way that Knowledge Workers Get Things Done. Meghan-Kiffer Press, Tampa (2010)
27. Tiwana, A.: Platform Ecosystems: Aligning Architecture, Governance, and Strategy. Morgan Kaufmann, San Francisco (2013)
28. Trojer, T., Farwick, M., Häusler, M., Breu, R.: Living modeling of IT architectures: challenges and solutions. In: Nicola, R., Hennicker, R. (eds.) Software, Services, and Systems 2015. LNCS, vol. 8950, pp. 458–474. Springer, Heidelberg (2015). doi:10.1007/978-3-319-15545-6_26
29. Walker, M.J.: leveraging enterprise architecture to enable business value with IoT innovations today. Gartner Research (2014). http://www.gartner.com/analyst/49943
30. Weill, P., Ross, J.W.: IT Governance: How Top Performers Manage It Decision Rights for Superior Results. Harvard Business School Press, Boston (2004)
31. WSO2 White Paper: Reference Architecture for the Internet of Things. Version 0.8.0 (2015). http://wso2.com
32. Zimmermann, A., Buckow, H., Groß, H.-J., Nandico, F. O., Piller, G., Prott, K.: Capability diagnostics of enterprise service architectures using a dedicated software architecture reference model. In: IEEE International Conference on Services Computing (SCC 2011), Washington DC, USA, pp. 592–599 (2011)
33. Zimmermann, A., Gonen, B., Schmidt, R., El-Sheikh, E., Bagui, S., Wilde, N.: Adaptable enterprise architectures for software evolution of smartlife ecosystems. In: Proceedings of the 18th IEEE International Enterprise Distributed Object Computing Conference Workshops (EDOCW), Ulm/Germany, pp. 316–323 (2014)
34. Zimmermann, A., Schmidt, R., Sandkuhl, K., Wißotzki, M., Jugel, D., Möhring, M.: Digital enterprise architecture – transformation for the internet of things. In Kolb, J., Weber, B., Hall, S., Mayer, W., Ghose, A.K., Grossmann, G. (eds.) IEEE Proceedings of the EDOC 2015 with SoEA4EE, Adelaide, Australia, 21–25 September 2015, pp. 130–138 (2015)

Data-Centered Platforms in Tourism: Advantages and Challenges for Digital Enterprise Architecture

Barbara Keller[3], Michael Möhring[2(✉)], Martina Toni[1],
Laura Di Pietro[1], and Rainer Schmidt[2]

[1] University of Roma Tre, Via Silvio D'Amico 77, 00145 Rome, Italy
{Martina.Toni,Laura.Dipietro}@uniroma3.it
[2] Munich University of Applied Sciences,
Lothstrasse 64, 80335 Munich, Germany
{michael.moehring,Rainer.Schmidt,
barbara.keller}@hm.edu
[3] Aalen University, Beethovenstr. 1, 73430 Aalen, Germany

Abstract. Digitization changes business processes and enterprise architectures in many sectors. In the Tourism sector more and more data must be analyzed and integrated into business processes. Therefore, the current architecture must be changed to a more flexible, data-driven one. Besides the basements of current Tourism application, we investigate which scenarios are possible via data-centered platforms in Tourism and how this transformation can be done.

Keywords: Tourism · Big data · Data-centered · Digital enterprise architecture

1 Introduction

There is an ongoing discussion on the basic principles of digitization [1] and how it does foster enterprises and the economy. One of the effects of digitization is the acquisition of hitherto inaccessible resources and making them available for business [2]. The mechanism to integrate these formerly inaccessible resources are often two-sides markets [3], also called platforms [4]. Network effects exist both: on one side (cis) and across the two sides (trans) of platforms [5].

A resource difficult to acquire, but eagerly demanded for are data in tourism. Marketing and management efforts in tourism have been hampered by the difficulty to collect real data. Tourists are a group of customers, which are less consulted for data collection via questionnaires, for example. They do not like to be bothered by activities that resemble to work and remember them to their daily obligations. Technically, all the data needed for marketing in tourism are available by the smartphones and other intelligent gadgets tourists taken with them. These devices collect a dense set of data points. By analyzing the movements of the customer, both his interests and his appreciation for tourist sites can be investigated.

However, the tourist has to be persuaded to provide his data. Without a clear value proposition, they will not be inclined to provide their own data. Unfortunately, up to

W. Abramowicz et al. (Eds.): BIS 2016 Workshops, LNBIP 263, pp. 299–310, 2017.
DOI: 10.1007/978-3-319-52464-1_27

now, there is no appropriate incentive that pushes tourists to share their data with companies. Existing social software [6] platforms in the tourism branch such as Tripadvisor.com collect data, but this happens often in an offline, sketchy manner. The tourists provide only data on events, places that are either clearly positive or negative. However, the data on the touristic objects in between, that are perceive neither positively nor negatively are not entered into the social media sites.

Incentives convincing tourists to share their data could be of different kind, such as money or vouchers. However, there is a huge danger, that such incentives distort the behavior of the tourist. For instance, by increasing their financial capabilities or by changing their plans due to the vouchers received.

Another kind of incentive is represented by the possibility to support the tourist in doing things he wants to do, engaging them in co-creation activities and guiding service innovation. Therefore, in this paper the creation of platform for tourists shall be envisioned, that facilitates holiday making by enabling cis- and trans-based network effects.

There exists a lack of architectural research in the field of the use and possibilities of data-driven architectures for tourism application. Therefore, this conceptual research paper address this research gap by providing insights to the state of the art of Tourism applications and data-intensive processes via the use of Big Data. According to this basements, we develop main scenarios of the use of data-driven architectures in tourism and how information system architecture must change to support this.

We will introduce a platform architecture which is providing services to the customer founding on customer data and furthermore enabling a win-win situation for the involved entities. The services provide important hints to the tourist for optimizing his holidays. By recording the behavior of the tourist, a feed-back loop is created that enables value-co-creation. The data collected can be used to optimize marketing in tourism.

The paper proceeds as follows. First the fundamentals of tourism are introduced, followed by the fundamentals of Big Data Analytics. Second, an overview on the current architecture of tourism application is presented. Then, a platform architecture for tourism is proposed. At last, related work and conclusion are provided.

2 Fundamentals of Tourism

The relevance of tourism is due to its impact on the economy [7, 8] and its ability to be an income generator [9], thus it is necessary to improve the attractiveness of a country improving the overall experience at a tourism destination. The "tourism comprises the activities of people travelling to and staying in places outside their usual environment for not more than one consecutive year, for leisure, business and other purposes" [10]. Hence the Tourism Supply Chain (TSC) is composed of a network of actors that interact with each other in a horizontal, vertical and diagonal mode [11] on the basis of the sector to which they belong: the attraction, accommodation, transport, travel organizers, destination organizations. It is a complex system where each actor can directly influence the whole network [12, 13] and no longer is able to successfully compete as independent units without the support of TSC partners [13–17]. Therefore, the whole Tourism Supply Chain (TSC) should be holistically managed, considering every actors involved throughout the tourist journey (such as transportation, lodging, cultural heritage).

Indeed, the tourist product is composed by varies services, which correspond to different actors that actively participate in tourism services' production and consumption from the supply to the delivery of all the tourism products [18]: so it involves many components such as accommodation, transport, food and beverage service providers, handicrafts, environmental cultural and heritage, tour guides and local activities, waste disposal and other supportive infrastructure [7, 19].

Certainly the composition of actor involved within the travel experience is different in relation to the type of tourist and the reason for travelling – and as consequence of the type of travel planned.

Nowadays the success of a TSC and the importance of managing it in the best way, is highlighted by the increasing competition in the global tourism market due to the fast ICT development [19]. Technologies and in particular social media are useful in order to provide a more engaging tourists and travellers experience and to make the information more accessible to the users. Hence, social media can be used to strengthen the experience enhancing also the image and attractiveness of a destination.

By now, social media – and the large amount of information that it makes available online – might represent a tool that enable collaboration between supply chain partners that are geographically separated from each other [20]; therefore, the data available online about tourists' behavior is a valuable source that need to be well-managed in order to improve the services provided by each actors engaged within the TSC. Indeed, as some authors state [21–23] the performance of supply chain is strongly linked to an accurate and timely information sharing, incentive alignment and decision synchronisation.

3   Current Architecture of Tourism Application

According to the recent literature [29] in information systems and (tourism) management, we describe the current architecture of tourism application in the following. The architecture of tourism application consist of many different information systems [30–32]. For instance, different information systems for sales & marketing, hospitality, food & beverages, accounting & finance and human resource management are needed [33]. Furthermore, most of the systems are integrated with systems of suppliers, partners and customers [33]. The goal of these information systems is to support information, material as well as the monetary flow from the view point of the supply chain management [33, 34]. These traditional applications are good for processing transactional data, but not for analytics processes [35].

Besides traditional applications, more and more mobile applications in the Tourism sector arise, because of the easy use during all phases of a trip [36]. Mobile tourism application be used for different applications like navigation, social, mobile marketing, security etc. [37]. Therefore, more possibilities of end-user applications and display increase the complexity of the architecture.

Furthermore, guest services based on Web 2.0 applications and social networks arise [18, 38] and must be integrated in the current information systems architecture. For the analysis of this huge amount of unstructured data, Big Data technologies are needed. Besides, data from "Internet of Things" will arise in the future and should be processed by information systems to be more customer-oriented [39–41]. These kind of analytics are not addressed so far by current tourism application in practice.

Furthermore, general systems for e-Security, e-commerce for booking and search engine optimization and marketing systems exist [38]. New data-intensive applications for dynamic pricing are more and more needed and must be adapted [42]. Furthermore, different electronically knowledge representations forms like ontologies can be used in Tourism [43].

In summary, the current architecture of tourism applications are built on different information systems. The complexity is high and most of the systems are not able to process a huge volume of different kind of data (like unstructured one from social networks) in a short time period. Therefore, a transformation to a more data-centric digital enterprise architecture is needed for future tourism applications.

4 Data-Centered Architectures

Nowadays, new data processing approaches such as Big Data enable the creation of data-centered architectures [24, 25]. Zikopoulos and Eaton [26] define Big Data as architectures providing a significant increase in the volume, velocity and variety of the data processed. Huge volumes of data can be processed in a short time period. Furthermore, the data to be processed can be semi- and unstructured (e.g. social media posts, customer hotel reviews).

Data-centered architectures generate new opportunities for business in different functional parts of the enterprise [27]. According to Schmidt et al. [27] Marketing, technology development and IT are the major parts of the enterprise, which benefit most of all. For instance, marketing applications can be improved by implementing recommender systems or social media monitoring and analysis [24]. Therefore, new trends in social media as well as better personal product or service recommendations can be provided.

Big Data can use concepts as predictive analytics for making better forecasts of customer as well as system behavior. In general, predictive analytics "include statistical models and other empirical methods that are aimed at creating empirical predictions, as well as methods for assessing the quality of those predictions in practice, i.e., predictive power." according to Shmueli and Koppius [28, p. 554]. In the following, we use this concepts in the Tourism sector.

5 Data-Centered Platform Architecture for Tourism

The key to implement data-centered platforms for tourism is to convince the tourists to share their data. This can be achieved by enabling cis- and trans-network effects. The platform for tourism implements a two-sided market (Fig. 1) [3], as shown below.

There are both effects between the sides (trans-effects) and with a side (cis-effects). Within the tourists, the collection of data augments the quality of services provided due to the increased set of data available. A trans-effect is created by the increasing number of tourists. This also makes the platform more attractive for tourism service vendors.

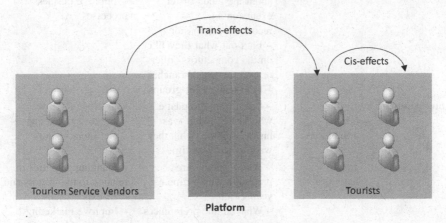

Fig. 1. Platforms as two-sided markets

Big Data enables interesting data-centric as well as customer-oriented processes in the Tourism sector. For the identification of the possibilities of Big Data support in this interesting sector, we combine basements of Tourism (Sect. 2) and Big Data (Sect. 3) based on the recent literature [29]. The results are summarized in the following table:

Table 1. Possibilities of Big Data

Tourism sector		Possibilities of big data	Examples
Attractions			
Cultural	Museum	– Help to recognize peak time – Find interesting topics for e.g. special exhibition	– Improve business processes e.g. more staff available at peak times – Improve customer service e.g. abbreviate wait or integrating customers' actual preferences and interest
	Cultural site, religious monuments	– Help to identify the peer-group	– Advices such as dress code can be given – Customizations can be implemented or even improved e.g. sign board in different languages

(continued)

Table 1. (*continued*)

Tourism sector		Possibilities of big data	Examples
	Tour guides, excursions	– Information what people think and tell about the guide or an excursion e.g. recommendation side – Find out what they like on the competitors' offers or even in other branches – Find new target groups	– Improve service and offers – Improve business processes
Entertainment	Events, special exhibitions	– Learn from the past e.g. who visited, what was his/her opinion, what they want to see next time	– Improve the offer – Improve marketing – Get more visitors
	Local activities	– Which people are present to which time e.g. year/season – What are the preferences or expectations	– Planning activities in relation to the visitors and their expectations – Improve marketing
Natural	Landscapes, seas, mountains	– Information about popular places – Information about weather – Information about water quality or experienced beauty of the landscape	– Improve services in relation to the weather forecast – Promote the quality and the beauty of the nature – Stimulate tourist to visit and after to help to protect
Sports activities		– Find out when there is the best weather forecast for your activities – Make sure that the infrastructure is due to the planned event or activity	– Improve planning
Accommodation			
	Hotel, B&B, apartment as rental	– What are the preferences of the customers – Identification of new target groups – Information about the competitors	– Improve service and business processes - Start to develop a new target group e.g. seniors with special needs (e.g. lifts available, doctor available) - Stay competitive in offer and price
	Wellness center, SPA	– Catching new and up-coming trends and vice versa	– Be one of the first who offers a new trend – Enabled to implemented higher prices

(*continued*)

Table 1. (*continued*)

Tourism sector		Possibilities of big data	Examples
Food and Beverage Service Providers			
	Restaurant, coffee/bar, fast food	– Catching new and up-coming trends and vice versa e.g. vegan food – Help to recognize peak time	– Be one of the first who offers a new trend – Be more competitive – Improve service and business processes
Transport			
Long-distance transport	Airport, airline	– Find out which destinations are popular with regard to the time of travel and to the customers who travel	– Improve price and offer – Improve flight plans
	Train	– Find out to what purpose people use the train instead of their car, the plane or the bus – What are the thoughts travelers say about the train (e.g. delays)	– Focus on the opinions and improve business processes and services – Find new purposes and light them out – Give special offers for existing purposes to improve CRM
	Coaches, private bus	– Information about the target group and their reasons for using a coach or bus	– Improve service and offers along the needs of the target group – Implement business processes and services fitting to the business and the customers (e.g. mobile reservation, insurances)
Local transport	Bus, tram, metro/subway	– Information about peak-time – Information about peoples preferences	– Higher frequency of busses (trams, metro, subway) at peak time – Longer services at the weekend
	Car sharing, pooling, bike sharing	– Information about popular pick-up places	– Ensure the avail- ability
	Taxi	– Information about popular places and times for using a taxi – Traffic information	– Ensure the availability – Find the best road
	Rented car, rented motorcycle	– Information about preferred models – Information about duration of rent	– Improve the models in the fleet – Improve the business processes

(*continued*)

Table 1. (*continued*)

Tourism sector		Possibilities of big data	Examples
	Private car	– Information about actual traffic situation (e.g. google) – Information about traffic laws and speed traps (e.g. tom tom)	– Improved trip planning – Less stress and less risk for doing a mistake
Travel Organizers			
Offline	Travel agency, tour operator	– Integration into new media (e.g. AR glasses) – Find the best offer for the customer – Information about competitors	– Improve customers' decision-making – Improve service and offers – Staying competitive
Online	Online travel agents (OTAs)	– When do people look and book holidays online – Who is the peer-group – What is their opinion about the offers and the service	– Implement strategic and dynamic pricing – Improve offer and services with regards to the peer-group (e.g. mobile booking, reservation)
Secondary Services			
	Souvenirs	– Find out the bestseller – Information about popular themes or topics of the tourists with regards to their visit	– Improve the assortment e.g. availability of the bestseller, find new interesting ideas for souvenirs
	Shopping	– Find out the bestseller – Information about customers' preferences (e.g. what kind of bread they like at home) – Find out what people think of typical products	– Improve the assortment – Making tourist feel at home – Integrate typical products into the assortment

The usage of Big Data brings along many benefits for suppliers as well as customers [27]. Many sectors already profit from the implementation of this technology [27]. The advantage the Tourism sector could gain can also not denied. In Table 1 a detailed overview is given on how Big Data can support the Tourism industry. In summary it can be said, that according to the given examples above, almost every single part of the sector can be supported and further developed, if Big Data is implemented and used. From the supplier's point of view the largest advantages could be seen in the increased knowledge about the customers, the market situation and the possibilities to predict the effectiveness of planned actions. From the customer's point of view the main advantages can be seen in the improved offers, which are highly adjusted on their preferences. However, besides of the named advantages, both parties have to cope with some challenges as well. On the one hand customers have critically to reflect and subsequently to decide, whether they share personal data and which type of data they want to share. On the other hand suppliers have to take into account that the implementation of Big Data at first stands in relation with costly investments.

To implement such data-driven processes in Tourism, some changes of the current architecture must be done. According to Sect. 4, the architecture of tourism architecture based on many different information systems integrated by different approaches (e.g. hard-coding interfaces, SOA /web services, manual, etc.). Furthermore, the current architecture has often a lack of providing the capability to analyze a huge volume of data with a different structure (structured and unstructured) in a very short time period.

The envisioned architecture can be implemented using a number of technologies. Cloud-Computing [44] provides the means to easily integrate data from a multitude of (mobile) devices. It also provides scalable computing resources to process the incoming data even in case of high demand. The analytical functions can be implemented using computing approaches based on a shared-nothing approach such as Hadoop [45] or Spark [46].

6 Related Work

There is some research in the field of management as well as information systems close to ours. First of all, generals discussions of enterprise architecture management, architectural principles and the benefits of using it can be found in [47–49].

Basements of Tourism applications are defined in [30–32]. Research of Big Data [24, 25] and predictive analytics in an architectural context are discussed by some authors. For instance, Keller et al. discuss the implementation of data-intensive business processes based on data from social media in [50]. Chen and Zhang [51] describe current opportunities, challenges and technologies of Big Data.

The theoretical aspects of using data mining for travel analysis are investigated in [52]. The analysis of user-generated content for tourism analysis is in scrutinized in [53]. Contrary to our approach, geo-data are not taken into consideration. In [54] the use of big data for gaining new knowledge from tourism web-sites is investigated.

7 Conclusion

A customer centric approach together with the development of data-driven processes are key factors for the companies that operate in the Tourism sector, fostering a higher level of competitiveness and enabling new business models as well as service innovation. New data sources such as social media arise in the past. To use this new kind of information source, a huge volume of data (mostly unstructured) must be processed in a very short time period. Therefore, a change in the current architecture of many tourism providers is needed.

Our research contribute to the current information systems research by adding new knowledge about the use of Big Data and Business Intelligence solutions in the

Tourism sector. Essential concepts of architectural transformation in this sector were described. Furthermore, practical readers can benefit from a better base of the current and future possibilities of data-driven architectures for tourism application. Our findings can be used to prepare decisions related to the implementation of this solutions.

Limitations can be found in the missing empirical validation as well as providing matured data-intensive architectural design patterns. There are good opportunities for future research in this interesting area. Future research should fill this gaps, by empirical evaluate our conceptual work and provide more detailed architectural patterns or designs.

References

1. Schmidt, R., Zimmermann, A., Möhring, M., Nurcan, S., Keller, B., Bär, F.: Digitization – perspectives for conceptualization. In: Celesti, A., Leitner, P. (eds.) ESOCC Workshops 2015. CCIS, vol. 567, pp. 263–275. Springer, Heidelberg (2016). doi:10.1007/978-3-319-33313-7_20
2. Dawson, A., Hirt, M., Scanlan, J.: The economic essentials of digital strategy | McKinsey & Company. http://www.mckinsey.com/business-functions/strategy-and-corporate-finance/our-insights/the-economic-essentials-of-digital-strategy
3. Eisenmann, T., Parker, G., Van Alstyne, M.W.: Strategies for two-sided markets. Harvard Bus. Rev. **84**, 92 (2006)
4. Parker, G., van Alstyne, M.W., Choudary, S.P.: Platform Revolution: How Networked Markets are Transforming the Economy–and How to Make Them Work for You. Norton & Company, New York (2016)
5. Parker, G., Van Alstyne, M.W., Bulkley, N., Van Alstyne, M.: Two-sided network effects: A theory of information product design. Manage. Sci. **51**(10), 1494–1504 (2005)
6. Schmidt, R., Nurcan, S.: BPM and social software. In: Ardagna, D., Mecella, M., Yang, J., Aalst, W., Mylopoulos, J., Rosemann, M., Shaw, M.J., Szyperski, C. (eds.) Business Process Management Workshops, pp. 649–658. Springer, Heidelberg (2009)
7. Tapper, R., Font, X.: Additional Research (2004)
8. Rebollo, J.F.V., Baidal, J.A.I.: Measuring sustainability in a mass tourist destination: pressures, perceptions and policy responses in Torrevieja, Spain. J. Sustain. Tourism **11**, 181–203 (2003)
9. Binkhorst, E., Den Dekker, T.: Agenda for co-creation tourism experience research. J. Hospitality Mark. Manage. **18**, 311–327 (2009)
10. Nationen, V. (ed.): Tourism satellite account: recommended methodological framework 2008. Commission of the European Communities, Eurostat [u.a.], Luxembourg (2010)
11. Michael, E.J.: Micro-clusters: Antiques, retailing and business practice. In: Micro-Clusters and Networks, vol. 63 (2006)
12. Murphy, J., Smith, S.: Chefs and suppliers: An exploratory look at supply chain issues in an upscale restaurant alliance. Int. J. Hospitality Manage. **28**, 212–220 (2009)
13. Chen, I.J., Paulraj, A.: Towards a theory of supply chain management: the constructs and measurements. J. Oper. Manage. **22**, 119–150 (2004)
14. Crotts, J.C., Aziz, A., Raschid, A.: Antecedents of supplier's commitment to wholesale buyers in the international travel trade. Tour. Manage. **19**, 127–134 (1998)
15. Lippmann, S.: Supply chain environmental management: elements for success. Corp. Environ. Strategy **6**, 175–182 (1999)

16. Lysons, K.: Purchasing. Macdonald & Evans (1996)
17. National Environmental Education & Training Foundation: Going Green... Upstream The Promise of Supplier Environmental Management. Green Business Network The National Environmental Education & Training Foundation (2001)
18. Sigala, M., Christou, E., Gretzel, U.: Social Media in Travel, Tourism and Hospitality: Theory, Practice and Cases. Ashgate Publishing Ltd., Farnham (2012)
19. Xinyue, H., Yongli, T.: Integrated tourism service supply chain management: Concept and operations processes. In: 2008 International Conference on Neural Networks and Signal Processing, pp. 644–647. IEEE (2008)
20. Piboonrungroj, P., Disney, S.M.: Supply chain collaboration, inter-firm trust and logistics performance: Evidence from the tourism sector. Available at SSRN 2050703 (2012)
21. Spekman, R.E., Kamauff Jr., J.W., Myhr, N.: An empirical investigation into supply chain management: a perspective on partnerships. Supply Chain Manage. Int. J. **3**, 53–67 (1998)
22. Akintoye, A., McIntosh, G., Fitzgerald, E.: A survey of supply chain collaboration and management in the UK construction industry. Eur. J. Purchasing Supply Manage. **6**, 159–168 (2000)
23. Kohli, A.S., Jensen, J.B.: Assessing effectiveness of supply chain collaboration: an empirical study. Supply Chain Forum Int. J. **11**(2), 2–16 (2010). Taylor & Francis
24. Chen, H., Chiang, R.H.L., Storey, V.C.: Business intelligence and analytics: From big data to big impact. MIS Q. **36**, 1165–1188 (2012)
25. Pospiech, M., Felden, C.: Big Data – A State-of-the-Art. In: Proceedings of AMCIS 2012 (2012)
26. Zikopoulos, P., Eaton, C.: Understanding Big Data: Analytics for Enterprise Class Hadoop and Streaming Data. McGraw-Hill Osborne Media, New York (2011)
27. Schmidt, R., Möhring, M., Maier, S., Pietsch, J., Härting, R.-C.: Big data as strategic enabler - insights from central european enterprises. In: Abramowicz, W., Kokkinaki, A. (eds.) BIS 2014. LNBIP, vol. 176, pp. 50–60. Springer, Heidelberg (2014). doi:10.1007/978-3-319-06695-0_5
28. Shmueli, G., Koppius, O.: Predictive analytics in information systems research. MIS Q. **35**(3), 553–572 (2010)
29. Cooper, H.M.: Synthesizing Research: A Guide for Literature Reviews. Sage, Thousand Oaks (1998)
30. Pröll, B., Retschitzegger, W.: Discovering next generation tourism information systems: a tour on TIScover. J. Travel Res. **39**, 182–191 (2000)
31. Buhalis, D.: eTourism Information Technology for Strategic Tourism Management. Pearson Education, London (2003)
32. Buhalis, D., O'Connor, P.: Information communication technology revolutionizing tourism. Tourism Recreation Res. **30**, 7–16 (2005)
33. Ünalan, D., Kaya, E., Azaltun, M.: Role of information systems in supply chain management and its application on five-star hotels in Istanbul. J. Hospitality Tourism Technol. **3**, 138–146 (2012)
34. Lee, H.L.: Creating value through supply chain integration. Supply Chain Manage. Rev. **4**, 30–36 (2000)
35. Laudon, K.C.: Managing Information Systems Managing the Digital Firm. Prentice Hall, Upper Saddle River (2013)
36. Höpken, W., Fuchs, M., Zanker, M., Beer, T.: Context-based adaptation of mobile applications in tourism. Inf. Technol. Tourism **12**, 175–195 (2010)
37. Kennedy-Eden, H., Gretzel, U.: A taxonomy of mobile applications in tourism. E-rev. Tourism Res. **10**(2), 47–50 (2012)

38. Law, R., Buhalis, D., Cobanoglu, C.: Progress on information and communication technologies in hospitality and tourism. Int. J. Contemp. Hospitality Manage. **26**, 727–750 (2014)

39. Zimmermann, A., Schmidt, R., Sandkuhl, K., Wissotzki, M., Jugel, D., Möhring, M.: Digital enterprise architecture - transformation for the internet of things. In: IEEE International Enterprise Distributed Object Computing Conference Workshops. IEEE Computer Society, Adelaide (2015)

40. Guo, Y., Liu, H., Chai, Y.: The embedding convergence of smart cities and tourism internet of things in China: An advance perspective. Adv. Hospitality Tourism Res. **2**, 54–69 (2014)

41. Lamsfus, C., Alzua-Sorzabal, A.: Theoretical framework for a tourism internet of things: smart destinations. TourGUNE J. Tourism Hum. Mobility **2013**(2), 15–21 (2013)

42. Otero, D.F., Akhavan-Tabatabaei, R.: A stochastic dynamic pricing model for the multiclass problems in the airline industry. Eur. J. Oper. Res. **242**, 188–200 (2015)

43. Ruiz-Martınez, J.M., Minarro-Giménez, J.A., Castellanos-Nieves, D., Garcıa-Sánchez, F., Valencia-Garcia, R.: Ontology population: an application for the e-tourism domain. Int. J. Innovative Comput. Inf. Control (IJICIC) 7(11), 6115–6134 (2011)

44. Mell, P., Grance, T.: The NIST Definition of Cloud Computing. http://csrc.nist.gov/groups/SNS/cloud-computing/

45. White, T.: Hadoop: The Definitive Guide. O'Reilly & Associates, Sebastopol (2015)

46. Zaharia, M., Chowdhury, M., Franklin, M.J., Shenker, S., Stoica, I.: Spark: cluster computing with working sets. In: Proceedings of the 2nd USENIX Conference on Hot Topics in Cloud Computing, p. 10 (2010)

47. Schmidt, R., Möhring, M., Härting, R.-C., Reichstein, C., Zimmermann, A., Luceri, S.: Benefits of enterprise architecture management – insights from European experts. In: Ralyté, J., España, S., Pastor, Ó. (eds.) PoEM 2015. LNBIP, vol. 235, pp. 223–236. Springer, Heidelberg (2015). doi:10.1007/978-3-319-25897-3_15

48. Winter, K., Buckl, S., Matthes, F., Schweda, C.M.: Investigating the state-of-the-art in enterprise architecture management methods in literature and practice. In: MCIS 2010 Paper, vol. 90 (2010)

49. Stelzer, D.: Enterprise architecture principles: literature review and research directions. In: Dan, A., Gittler, F., Toumani, F. (eds.) ICSOC/ServiceWave -2009. LNCS, vol. 6275, pp. 12–21. Springer, Heidelberg (2010). doi:10.1007/978-3-642-16132-2_2

50. Keller, B., Schmidt, R., Möhring, M., Härting, R.-C., Zimmermann, A.: Social-data driven sales processes in local clothing retail stores. In: Reichert, M., Reijers, Hajo, A. (eds.) BPM 2015. LNBIP, vol. 256, pp. 305–315. Springer, Heidelberg (2016). doi:10.1007/978-3-319-42887-1_25

51. Chen, C.P., Zhang, C.-Y.: Data-intensive applications, challenges, techniques and technologies: a survey on big data. Inf. Sci. **275**, 314–347 (2014)

52. Mahanta, P., Sudheendra, S.: The impact of data mining for insights in travel and tourism industry. Int. J. Comput. Electr. Eng. **6**, 114 (2014)

53. Marine-Roig, E., Clavé, S.A.: Tourism analytics with massive user-generated content: a case study of Barcelona. J. Destination Mark. Manage. **4**, 162–172 (2015)

54. Fuchs, M., Höpken, W., Lexhagen, M.: Big data analytics for knowledge generation in tourism destinations–a case from Sweden. J. Destination Mark. Manage. **3**, 198–209 (2014)

Applying the Research on Product-Service Systems to Smart and Connected Products

Lars Brehm[(⊠)] and Barbara Klein

Munich University of Applied Sciences,
Am Stadtpark 20, 81243 Munich, Germany
{lars.brehm, bklein}@hm.edu

Abstract. Digitalization has changed media and retail industry in the last decades dramatically. Currently the focus switched to physical products enhanced or completely re-thought by digitalization. These products are called smart and connected products by Porter and Heppelmann, as they have smart components (i.e. computing power) in the product and are connected to a product cloud. By that, the products are enhanced with a strong service component. Since the late 90's, there was a substantial amount of research on product-service systems (PSS). In this position paper we analyze the research on PSS and apply it to smart and connected products.

Keywords: Digital enterprises · Digitalization · Digital transformation · Product-Service system (PSS) · Smart and connected products · Servitization

1 Introduction

Digitalization has changed several industries in the last decades dramatically. After the media and the retail industry the focus switched now to physical products, which are enhanced or completely re-thought by digitalization.

These products are called smart and connected products (SCP) by Porter and Heppelmann and contain three core elements: the physical components (like mechanical or electrical parts), "smart" components (sensors, microprocessors, data storage, controls, software, embedded operating system and user interface) and the connectivity to the so-called product cloud (with the product data database, an application platform, an rules/analytics engine and the smart product applications) [1].

With that, the products are enhanced with a strong service component. This follows the trend of "servitization". Since the late 90's, there is a substantial amount of research on product-service systems (PSS) – the predecessor of SCPs. In this position paper we analyze the research on PSS and apply it to smart and connected products in a set of hypothesis. The underlying research question is "What of the results of research on PPS can be utilized for future research on SCPs and in which way?"

The paper proceeds as follows, first the content of the definitions of PSS are discussed. Then the benefits and risks of PSS based on the literature are presented. The next chapter shows how the insights of the PSS research can be applied to SCP. After that a conclusion and outlook are given.

W. Abramowicz et al. (Eds.): BIS 2016 Workshops, LNBIP 263, pp. 311–319, 2017.
DOI: 10.1007/978-3-319-52464-1_28

2 Definition of Product-Service Systems (PSS)

Many companies are undergoing the transformation from a pure manufacturer offering products towards a provider of services and hybrid products. According to Baines et al. [2], this process is referred to as servitization: "Servitization is the innovation of an organisation's capabilities and processes to shift from selling products to selling integrated products and services that deliver value in use". This term is in particular influenced by Vandermerwe and Rada [3] who describe it as "'bundles' consisting of customer-focused combinations of goods, services, support, self-service, and knowledge" [3].

As this paper does not address the transformational process of servitization but its results, it focuses on the term of product-service system (PSS). A literature review shows that several more terms, such as 'bundling'/'bundle', 'compack' (complex package), 'integrated product and service offering' (IPSO) or 'industrial product-service system' (IPS) within the business-to-business (B2B) context [4] are used. The term 'product-service system' is first mentioned in the work of Goedkoop et al. [5]. This definition is still used by many authors, for instance by [4, 6–8]. Table 1 shows this and further established definitions.

The definitions listed in Table 1 show that there are different perceptions of PSS. Whereas some authors use rather vague terms such as 'offering' [14, 16], 'marketable set' [5] or 'concept' [17], others define it as a 'business model' [9], an 'innovation strategy' [11, 15], a 'social construction' [12] or a 'value proposition' [13]. But they all (except Morelli, 2006) have in common that PSS integrate products and services, usually with the aim to satisfy customers' needs [5, 9–11, 13, 15]. Besides product and service components, Mont (2001) sees a supporting network and the infrastructure as crucial elements of the system. Baines et al. (2007), Neely (2008) and Tan et al. (2007) state that PSS provide 'value in use' which means that the customer's need is satisfied by using the PSS instead of by possessing it. Some definitions focus on further aspects, such as sustainability as a major aim of PSS [9, 10, 14], the involvement of partners [9, 10, 14] or the consideration of the entire product life cycle (PLC) [15, 17].

Furthermore, the literature distinguishes between different types of PSS. A common categorization is developed by Tukker [19] who differentiates between three main categories (product-oriented services, use-oriented services, and result-oriented services) with a total of eight subcategories. This classification is referred to by many authors, for instance: [4, 6, 7, 14, 20–24].

Table 1. Definitions of PSS, own table

Source	Definition PSS
[5]	"A Product Service system (PS system) is a **marketable set of products and services** capable of **jointly fulfilling a user's need**. The PS system is provided by either a single company or by an alliance of companies. It can enclose products (or just one) plus additional services. It can enclose a service plus an additional product. And product and service can be equally important for the function fulfilment. The researcher's need and aim determine the level of hierarchy, system boundaries and the system element's relations."

(*continued*)

Table 1. (*continued*)

Source	Definition PSS
[9]	"[…] a product-service system is defined as a **system of products, services, supporting networks and infrastructure** that is designed to be: competitive, satisfy customer needs and have a **lower environmental impact** than traditional business models."
[10]	"A Product Service System consists of **tangible products and intangible services**, designed and combined so that they **jointly are capable of fulfilling specific customer needs**. Additionally, PSS ties to reach the **goals of a sustainable development**, which means improved economic, environmental and social aspects."
[11]	"A product service system (PSS) can be defined as an **innovation strategy**, shifting the business focus from designing (and selling) physical products only, to designing (and selling) a system of products and services which are **jointly capable of fulfilling specific client demands**."
[12]	"A PSS is a **social construction**, based on "attraction forces" (such as goals, expected results and problem-solving criteria) which catalyse the participation of several partners. A PSS is the **result of a value co-production process** within such a partnership."
[13]	"Product-service systems (PSS) are a specific type of **value proposition** that a business (network) offers to (or co-produces with) its clients. PSS consist of a mix of **tangible products and intangible services** designed and combined so that they **jointly are capable of fulfilling final customer needs**."
[14]	"A PSS is an **integrated product and service offering** that delivers **value in use**. A PSS offers the opportunity to decouple economic success from material consumption and hence **reduce the environmental impact** of economic activity. The PSS logic is premised on utilizing the knowledge of the designermanufacturer [sic] to both increase value as an output and decrease material and other costs as an input to a system."
[15]	"Product/service-system (PSS) approaches are **innovation strategies** where companies provide value to their customers by supporting and enhancing the utility of their **products throughout their life cycle**. The principle behind PSS is a **shift in business perspective from product-orientation to service-orientation**, where instead of the product itself, the actual activity associated with the use of the product is considered to be of more value to the customer."
[16]	"A Product-Service System is an **integrated product and service offering** that delivers **value in use**."
[17]	"Product-Service Systems (PSS) is a **concept to integrate products and services** in one scope for planning, development, delivery, use, and EOL (end of life) treatment, thus for the **whole lifecycle**."
[18]	"A Product-Service System (PSS) **integrates product and service components**, whereby the product components may consist of mechanics, electrics/electronics and software [..]. In the context of cycle management for innovation processes, the dynamics and complexity involved in understanding, planning, and managing Product-Service Systems are of particular interest."

3 Benefits and Risks of PSS

Not only companies benefit from including PSS in the portfolio. It also has positive effects for the consumers, as well as for the society, and for the environment. The opportunities are presented in the following.

Benefits of PSS

Companies that offer PSS benefit from several financial advantages. Firstly, they may enhance their value added potential by generating further revenues during the product life cycle instead of conducting one-time transactions when the product is sold [25–27]. Secondly, a higher profit margin is often mentioned in the literature as another benefit [2, 25, 28]). Schultz and Tietze [27] additionally state that services are knowledge- and technology-intensive and therefore increase the value of a product. At least in the long run, companies may increase their revenues and become less dependent on economic cycles.

Achieving competitive advantages is another important benefit of PSS for companies. One reason for this is the creation of stronger and longer customer relationships. This is due to a more frequent contact between provider and customer during the lifecycle of a product which allows companies to gain more information about their customers and their needs and thus to provide more valuable offers. This applies especially when customers are integrated in the development of products/PSS to ensure that their needs are satisfied by the company. [26]. PSS often cause lock-in effects which may even increase customer loyalty [27]. Another reason why PSS may strengthen a company's competitiveness is that it is more difficult to imitate the service components [14, 26].

Customers however benefit from PSS especially because they provide higher value through customized offers and better quality. Service components increase the flexibility and the range of possible product-service combinations. This leads to an additional variety of possibilities (e.g. different payment schemes, sharing of products) of which the customer may choose the most suitable to his special requirements [14, 26]. As the provider of PSS often remains the owner, customers usually have less responsibility and reduced administrative effort. They may therefore focus on their core business and its related tasks [14, 26].

The positive impact on the environment is a further advantage often stated in literature, for example in [6, 14, 20, 26–28]. Sustainability is even part of many definitions. In case of PSS, producers often have more responsibility for their products during the entire life cycle. This incentivizes them to develop long-lasting products and increases their interest in maintaining, refurbishing and, due to take-back agreements, in recycling them at the end of the products' lives [14, 27]. PSS often come along with different potential users which may reduce the total amount of products [26]. All those aspects have the potential to reduce resources and waste and increase the sustainability of a PSS.

Finally, PSS support the creation of new jobs especially in the field of sales and for service activities [6, 14, 26]. As the offered services such as take-back or refurbishment are labor-intensive, the whole economy may become more labor-intensive compared to economies based on mass consumption [26].

Risks of PSS

Implementing PSS can mean financial challenges for a company. The change from offering products to offering PSS requires costly measures such as the adaption of organizational structures or the training of employees, and the involvement of all stakeholders [9, 28]. It changes the system and the source of profits from short-term profit realization at the point-of-sale to medium-and long-term amortization periods at the point-of-service [26]. Moreover, PSS lead to an increased complexity of product developing and designing which cause higher development and management costs. The integration of networks and collaborations increases the transaction costs for PSS [28] and service activities are supposed to have more limited returns [27]. Also Beuren et al. [6] state that all stakeholders involved have to cope with a higher financial risk. Besides those increased financial risks, companies might, due to the remaining ownership of PSS, absorb risks that were previously taken by their customers [14]. Furthermore, the implementation of PSS comes along with business activities in new fields. This brings further competition with new rivals such as suppliers, distributors or customers [2].

Another negative aspect of PSS is the loss of jobs in traditional manufacturing [6, 14]. Many of the new jobs related to PSS may be replaced by automatization as soon as these service components have become large-scale operations [26].

One of the main barriers mentioned in the literature is that PSS require major organizational changes. Product-oriented methods and tools have to be adapted or replaced to respond to the new service-specific particularities intangibility, heterogeneity, inseparability, perishability, and the lack of ownership. The marketing concept has to be modified [26]. The communication strategy has to focus on clearly describing the PSS's value propositions [2]. The pricing as well as the distribution channels have to be reconfigured [9, 14, 28]. According to Mont [9], internal accounting systems and financial functions might need to be restructured. For example, due to pay-per-use business models, product unit sales will become less relevant. Furthermore, many producer-owned PSS companies need product support services and systems for monitoring the products even when they are at the customers' sites [9].

Beyond the organizational changes described above, the stakeholders of PSS also face significant shifts in culture. Customers have to get used to ownerless consumption, a business concept which might be regarded skeptically in the beginning [14, 26]. They have to learn the value of having needs met through services instead of buying and owning products [6, 14]. It is therefore necessary for companies to switch from a product-centric to a customer-centric perspective [2] and particularly invest in durable customer relationships for the whole product life cycle [28]. Moreover, networks-through a closer cooperation with other stakeholders such as customers, suppliers or service producers are important for providing integrated solutions, especially during the phase of product design [2, 14, 26, 28]. As all changes, those shifts in organizational structure and culture usually cause resistance within the company and among further stakeholders. It is regarded as a major barrier to implementing PSS and a more service and customer focused strategy [2, 26].

To conclude, the main positive and negative aspects of PSS are summarized in Table 2.

Table 2. Benefits and risks of PSS, own table

Benefits	Risks
Additional revenue sources	Financial challenges
Competitive advantage	Adaption of established structures
Stronger customer relationships	New competitors
Broader variety of possibilities	Shift of culture
Increased customization	Loss of jobs in manufacturing
Focus on core competencies	
Increased sustainability	
Increase of labor-intensive jobs	

4 Impacts of PSS Research on Smart and Connected Products

Based on the above described results of the research on PSS, we apply these by drawing analogies to the new category of SCPs and develop a set of hypotheses. This set of hypotheses can be utilized for the future research on SCPs:

Even more than PSS, the SCP generates a substantial amount of detailed product and service usage data and can provide additional value to customers (e.g. by the analytics apps in the product cloud). Typical examples are the usage data of aircraft engines or combine harvesters in agriculture which enables better productivity and predictive maintenance. This is a source of stronger customer relationships and additional revenues.

H1: SCP enables stronger customer relationships and provides a source of competitive advantage.
H2: SCP provides a source of additional revenues.

With the smart components of the SCP, several functionalities can be realized in software instead of hardware. This allows to deliver additional features through software updates like semi-autonomous driving in a car or a tractor and helps to better customize resp. personalize the SCP to a specific customer just like a regular smart phone.

H3: Customers profit from SCP by a wider range of product and service features and a better customized (resp. personalized) version for them.

Based on the product and service ecosystem (incl. the software part), a company can focus on its core competency and rely on partners for parts of marketing, production, delivery and/or service. Especially for the software part a global cooperation can be realized at virtually no additional cost. This also improves scalability and favors specialization.

H4: With SCP companies can focus stronger on their core competencies.
H5: SCP leads to increased sustainability.

For the workforce, the impact regarding changes to job requirements is driven by two effects. On the one hand it will require more skilled employees, but on the other hand several knowledge intensive jobs will be replaced by algorithms utilizing the product and service usage data from SCPs. This is at the core of the current discussion on the "second machine age" by Brynjolfsson and McAfee [29].

H6: *With SCP the companies' workforce will shift to more knowledge intensive jobs.*

The digital transformation to SCP will require besides adjustments in the employees' skillset also adaption in the companies' structure (e.g. establishment of DevOps) and changes of the corporate culture. A shift towards more agile product development methods as well as cross-departmental cooperation for product development and service operations is already emerging.

H7: *Established companies need to adjust their existing structures and their corporate culture during the transition to SCP.*

The required major changes represent for the incumbents significant challenges, especially in the area of investments in new skillsets, machinery, markets, etc. and the uncertainty about new competitors, which can arise from completely different fields (like software companies for automotive manufacturers) and geographies.

H8: *The transition to SCP can lead to financial challenges for established companies.*
H9: *New competitor for SCP can arise from unexpected sectors or geographies.*

5   Conclusion and Outlook

Digitalization has changed several industries in the last years dramatically. We have summarized the relevant research on PSS and applied it to SCP. The stated set of hypotheses can provide future research on this new phenomenon of smart and connected products with a jump start.

All or a subset of the hypotheses can be used by researchers for doing research on SCP. The reference to PPS supports easier determination of relevant literature and details from the research on PPS. Especially it helps to ground new research on the existing results of earlier research work, but also adjust the findings to the new context of SCPs.

The hypotheses are generated by drawing analogies from PPSs to SCPs. This has, of course, its limitations, e.g. by selecting characteristics and facts about SCPs in an unbalanced way. More detailed research with an empirical focus is therefore required.

References

1. Porter, M.E., Heppelmann, J.E.: How smart, connected products are transforming competition. Harvard Bus. Rev. **92**, 64–88 (2014)
2. Baines, T.S., Lightfoot, H.W., Benedettini, O., Kay, J.M.: The servitization of manufacturing: a review of literature and reflection on future challenges. J. Manuf. Technol. Manage. **20**, 547–567 (2009)
3. Vandermerwe, S., Rada, J.: Servitization of business: adding value by adding services. Eur. Manage. J. **6**, 314–324 (1988)
4. Boehm, M., Thomas, O.: Looking beyond the rim of one's teacup: a multidisciplinary literature review of product-service systems in information systems, business management, and engineering & design. J. Cleaner Prod. **51**, 245–260 (2013)
5. Goedkoop, M.J., van Halen, C.J.G., te Riele, H.R.M., Rommens, P.J.M.: Product Service Systems, Ecological and Economic Basics. Report for Dutch Ministries of Environment (VROM) and Economic Affairs (EZ) (1999). http://teclim.ufba.br/jsf/indicadores/holan%20Product%20Service%20Systems%20main%20report.pdf
6. Beuren, F.H., Ferreira, M.G.G., Miguel, P.A.C.: Product-service systems: a literature review on integrated products and services. J. Cleaner Prod. **47**, 222–231 (2013)
7. Yang, X., Moore, P., Pu, J.-S., Wong, C.-B.: A practical methodology for realizing product service systems for consumer products. Comput. Ind. Eng. **56**, 224–235 (2009)
8. Yip, M.H., Phaal, R., Probert, D.R.: Value co-creation in early stage new product-service system development. In: Proceedings of the 3rd Service Design and Innovation Conference (ServDes 2012) (2012)
9. Mont, O.: Introducing and developing a Product-Service System (PSS) concept in Sweden (2001)
10. Brandstötter, M., Haberl, M., Knoth, R., Kopacek, B., Kopacek, P.: IT on demand-towards an environmental conscious service system for Vienna (AT). In: 2003 3rd International Symposium on Environmentally Conscious Design and Inverse Manufacturing, EcoDesign 2003, pp. 799–802. IEEE (2003)
11. Manzini, E., Vezzoli, C.: A strategic design approach to develop sustainable product service systems: examples taken from the "environmentally friendly innovation" Italian prize. J. Cleaner Prod. **11**, 851–857 (2003)
12. Morelli, N.: Developing new product service systems (PSS): methodologies and operational tools. J. Cleaner Prod. **14**, 1495–1501 (2006)
13. Tukker, A., Tischner, U.: Product-services as a research field: past, present and future. Reflections from a decade of research. J. Cleaner Prod. **14**, 1552–1556 (2006)
14. Baines, T.S., Lightfoot, H.W., Evans, S., Neely, A., Greenough, R., Peppard, J., Roy, R., Shehab, E., Braganza, A., Tiwari, A., Alcock, J.R., Angus, J.P., Bastl, M., Cousens, A., Irving, P., Johnson, M., Kingston, J., Lockett, H., Martinez, V., Michele, P., Tranfield, D., Walton, I.M., Wilson, H.: State-of-the-art in product-service systems. Proc. Inst. Mech. Eng. Part B: J. Eng. Manuf. **221**, 1543–1552 (2007)
15. Tan, A.R., McAloone, T.C., Gall, C.: Product/Service-system development – an explorative case study in a manufacturing company. In: Guidelines for a Decision Support Method Adapted to NPD Processes, Paris (2007)
16. Neely, A.: Exploring the financial consequences of the servitization of manufacturing. Oper. Manag. Res. **1**, 103–118 (2008)
17. Müller, P., Sakao, T.: Toward consolidation on product/service-systems design. In: CIRP IPS2 Conference 2010, April 14–15, Linköping, Sweden, pp. 219–225. Lilnköping University Press (2010)

18. Schenkl, S.A., Behncke, F.G.H., Hepperle, C., Langer, S., Lindemann, U.: Managing Cycles of Innovation Processes of Product-Service Systems. Presented at the October (2013)
19. Tukker, A.: Eight types of product–service system: eight ways to sustainability? Experiences from SusProNet. Bus. Strategy Environ. **13**, 246–260 (2004)
20. Barquet, A.P.B., de Oliveira, M.G., Amigo, C.R., Cunha, V.P., Rozenfeld, H.: Employing the business model concept to support the adoption of product–service systems (PSS). Ind. Mark. Manage. **42**, 693–704 (2013)
21. Gräßle, M., Thomas, O., Dollman, T.: Vorgehensmodelle des product-service systems engineering. In: Thomas, O., Loos, P., Nüttgens, M. (eds.) Hybride Wertschöpfung: Mobile Anwendungssysteme für effiziente Dienstleistungsprozesse im technischen Kundendienst, pp. 82–129. Springer, Heidelberg (2010)
22. Haubold, T., Möhrle, M.G.: Produkt-service-systeme – ansätze, aktuelle formen, potenziale und gestaltungshinweise. In: Kliewe, T., Kesting, T. (eds.) Moderne Konzepte des organisationalen Marketing, pp. 303–320. Springer, Wiesbaden (2014)
23. Williams, A.: Product service systems in the automobile industry: contribution to system innovation? J. Cleaner Prod. **15**, 1093–1103 (2007)
24. Yoon, B., Kim, S., Rhee, J.: An evaluation method for designing a new product-service system. Expert Syst. Appl. **39**, 3100–3108 (2012)
25. Lockett, H., Johnson, M., Evans, S., Bastl, M.: Product service systems and supply network relationships: an exploratory case study. J. Manuf. Technol. Manage. **22**, 293–313 (2011)
26. Mont, O.K.: Clarifying the concept of product–service system. J. Cleaner Prod. **10**, 237–245 (2002)
27. Schultz, C., Tietze, F.: Produkt-service-systeme als Gegenstand der betriebswirtschaftlichen innovationsforschung. In: Schultz, C., Hölzle, K. (eds.) Motoren der Innovation, pp. 57–79. Springer, Wiesbaden (2014)
28. Laurischkat, K.: Wandel des traditionellen dienstleistungsverständnisses im Kontext von product-service systems. In: Thomas, O., Nüttgens, M. (eds.) Dienstleistungsmodellierung 2012, pp. 74–95. Springer, Wiesbaden (2013)
29. Brynjolfsson, E., McAfee, A.: Second Machine Age: Work, Progress, and Prosperity in a Time of Brilliant Technologies. Norton & Company, New York (2014)

INCLuDE Workshop

An Architectural Model for High Performance Pattern Matching in Linked Historical Data

Michael Aleithe[1], Ulrich Hegerl[2], and Galina Ivanova[1,3(✉)]

[1] Institut für Wirtschaftsinformatik, Universität Leipzig, Grimmaische Straße 12,
04109 Leipzig, Germany
aleithe@wifa.uni-leipzig.de,
[2] Stiftung Deutsche Depressionshilfe, Semmelweisstraße 10,
04103 Leipzig, Germany
Ulrich.Hegerl@medizin.uni-leipzig.de
[3] Institut für Angewandte Informatik (InfAI) e.V., Universität Leipzig,
Hainstraße 11, 04109 Leipzig, Germany
galina.ivanova@uni-leipzig.de

Abstract. In times of global digitalization and interconnectedness the virtual Cyber Physical Systems (CPS) are getting more and more on importance. These CPS and their relations among themselves can be investigated using appropriate data acquired by the inherent sensors. The multivariate, multiscale, multimodal sensor data can be modeled and analyzed as a dynamically evolving spatio-temporal complex network. These graphs as well as the patterns estimated in historical data can then be used for real time comparison with momentary computed patterns. Therefore providing linked data from memory is an important need to accomplish real time constraints especially in case of CPS in critical medical systems. Since the handling of graphs in the traditional relational database systems is problematic an encouraging approach is the storage of these data in graph databases which are appropriate for the handling of linked data. Therefore we propose the graph database Neo4J and demonstrate first applications of the approach within medical use-cases.

Keywords: Cyber physical systems · Sensor networks · Body area networks · Spatio-temporal sensor graph · Graph databases

1 Introduction

The data flood in the modern digital characterized life is enormous and increasing rapidly. Main data generators are diverse sensors placed stationary or integrated in different wearables. These sensors are measuring a high number of different spatially distributed and timely evolving processes, which can be in dependent relations from each other. Therefore it is intuitive and at the same time a logical way to model and to analyze the sensor data and the inherent relations using networks respectively the complex network theory (see Fig. 1). Furthermore it is essential to extract interpretable information e.g. in form of representative values for the different state patterns or to derive reliable prediction results concerning the process behavior. Although this methodologies can be applied universally in order to be able to explain our approach in

W. Abramowicz et al. (Eds.): BIS 2016 Workshops, LNBIP 263, pp. 323–331, 2017.
DOI: 10.1007/978-3-319-52464-1_29

a sufficient detail, in this paper we focus on one highly actual biomedical use-case, the body area network.

The body area network can be considered as a special case of a Cyber-Physical System (CPS), which monitors biophysiological processes and real life situations e.g. in context of medical applications. Nevertheless the challenge of modeling can increase enormously under the requirements to represent the spatio-temporal dynamics of the underlying process in real time. Whereby the importance of complex real time computations in the medical sphere, starting from deliveries up to triggering of lifesaving measures has to be stressed additionally. Such kind of triggering can be done for instance based on the data acquired by an appropriate body area network equipped with specific biosensors and computing the outputs of specific estimation algorithms as well as predictive models. Here the models derived from historical data as well as the pattern found in this data could also play an important role.

The aim of this paper is to provide an architectural model for high-performance pattern matching in linked historical data. As a use case we consider a psycho-physiological complex network and discuss its application in a *biomedical context in particularly for the recognition, monitoring and prediction of depressive phases*. For depressive disorders no clinically useful diagnostic biomarkers are available due to disease inherent reasons self-reports tend to be unreliable. Therefore, objective approaches to detect and monitor the severity of depressive symptoms including sui-cidality are especially valuable. Furthermore changes in psychopathology might be related to certain proceeding patterns of recorded biomedical data, e.g. changes in sleep quality and motoric activity allowing the prediction of changes in disease state. Such relationships can finally be analyzed with the aim to detect causal relationships, e.g. between sleep pattern and mood changes, which then can be used for improving the individual self-management strategy of the patient. This multivariate, multimodal and multiscale relations varying in dependence of time and space can be sufficiently ana-lyzed by the complex networks methodology. The estimated information will then build the basis for reliable patterns and biomarker definition to be integrated in the self-management approach.

This scenario is very timely because increasing amount of patient generated data based on sensors are becoming available nowadays to monitor the patient's behavior. Starting on 2018, patients will have the possibility to claim for their personal medical

Fig. 1. Randomly generated complex networks with real or abstract visualization of the node and edge position.

data according to the German E-health law [1]. These personal medical data consists of information concerning the electronic health card and additional information of personal health condition. Consequently there is a further task for physicians and health insurance funds to support prevention, self-management and medical decision making by encouraging the collection and interpretation of these personal data.

2 Data

The digitalized sensor data could be considered as data packages consisting of two main components – the sensor identification (number, label, spatial assignment) and a time sampled stream of sensor values. The sensor values can be uni- and multivariate depending on the complexity of the sensor. Furthermore other characteristics estimated by analysis algorithms can be included in the time stream or a new stream with a different time resolution can be taken into consideration. Taking into account the available information we can then define the nodes of the network, whereby we can use the real sensor location or construct a sensor network with abstract node positions, however with real node assignment relation. In this case there is the demand of depicting such relations among the particular sensors as discussed in Chap. 1. Furthermore we need to define the relations between the processes acquired at the different sensors, which will be defined as network edges. These relations are usually organized in a two or n- dimensional adjacency matrix. The easiest option is to calculate the absolute values of the correlations coefficients as edges in an undirected network. However there is a number of other methods, such as coherences or phase relation indexes, mutual information and others, applicable in dependence of the problem to be treated. By estimating different univariate measures for the nodes and different bivariate characteristics for the edges it is possible to redefine the complex network. The consideration of the time and the time resolution in the construction of networks or sequences of networks depends on the methods chosen for the computation of the univariate measures for the nodes and bivariate measure for the edges. It is possible to work with aggregated measures losing the time aspect and with time dimension. However the challenge is to work with high temporal resolution e.g. with the sampling resolution or the resolution of interval/window based methods at least.

3 State of the Art and Motivation

Modelling a sensor network with space and time related data has been investigated in [2] whereby this approach is referred to as spatio-temporal sensor graph. Two main tasks can be identified concerning the storing of this kind of graphs: the storage of the at each sensor measured information and the storage of the time dependent adjacency matrix.

The data storage is usually in relational database systems (RDBMS) which are based on a table scheme. The process of loading data resp. the adjacency matrix from the memory is shown in Fig. 2. There is an extra table for the connection itself. This procedure is also explained in [3, 4]. The drawback on this approach is the fact that there is an extra table that has to be passed through if the connection between to nodes is invoked within the query. The whole operation is named a JOIN operation and costs a lot of performance. Consequently RDBMS embodies a performance bottleneck in case of accomplishing real time when linked patterns have to be invoked within linked data.

As an alternative option graph databases are suited for the challenges mentioned before [3–6] e.g. by traversing the linked data for the invoking. There are two different member types to be distinguished: native and non-native members [7]. In case of a non-native member only the representation is a graph and the data are stored as tables. In the native approach the graph structure is stored directly on the memory layer to avoid the potential bottleneck occurring by JOIN operations. This approach is also called index-free adjacency and described by Rodriguez et al. [7] in detail. Another important point is the usage of the in-memory concept, which has been discussed in [8]. Invoking linked data from in-memory will be faster executed than from main-memory. A disadvantage of in-memory is the limited capacity. The performance behavior of graph databases has been examined elaborately in [9], however only for other categories of graphs and not for the sensory graphs to be used under the already mentioned requirements.

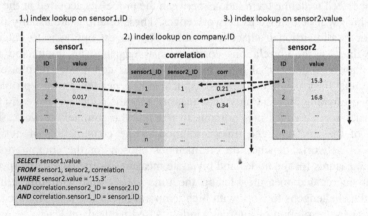

Fig. 2. The procedure of a JOIN operation in RDBMS (based on [3]) is demonstrated. The key fact is the usage of tables in case of invoking a connection of linked data. These extra table causes a performance bottleneck.

4   Approach for Modeling the Sensor Network

The target by modelling the data is to accomplish the requirements discussed in detail before. However, in fact we cannot investigate any real time behavior at this point because some implementation effects have to be observed in advance. First of all an overview of all data which we have is essential for the modelling. We have to model a network of sensor nodes which is time related and has to depict connections between each other to describe the relations e.g. the covariations and correlations among the nodes. Therefore we chose the option to model the network as a graph. Generally a graph consists of nodes and edges. The nodes represent the sensors and the edges between them represent the connections that depict the data relation at a certain time. The next point of investigation is the time dynamic. At every time point t_n respectively at every interval T_n we have a new graph. An example is demonstrated in Fig. 3. A sensor network consisting of three sensor nodes (sensor_1, sensor_2, sensor_3) with its corresponding time series per node is shown. All sensors generate values for each time except sensor_3 for t_3 so that only a subgraph of sensor_1 and sensor_2 is existing for the interval T_3. This graph is in result (see Fig. 4) an undirected one. Because all nodes are connected it is also one complete graph. The time value pairs at t_n are modeled as vector attributes on a self-directed edge per sensor node. In the same way the covariation and correlation at t_n/T_n is modeled as attribute vector on the edges between the sensor nodes.

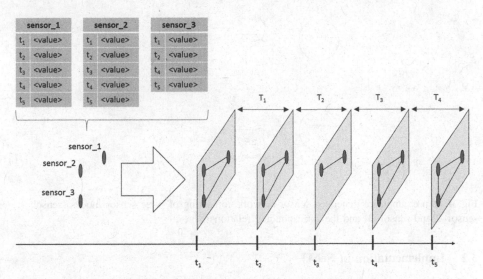

Fig. 3. An example of sensor network consisting of three sensors (sensor_1, sensor_2 and sensor_3). The values in the time intervals T_n are used in this case for a window based computation of the correlations resp. covariations represented by the edges at the time points t_n.

5 Implementation in a Graph Database

In this chapter we describe the selection of the appropriate graph database with regard to the requirements to provide patterns from memory in real time. Furthermore we are explaining the possible implementation in the database.

5.1   Selection of the Appropriate Graph Database

As explained in [3, 5, 6] there are several types of graph databases whereby the selection is determined by the respective use case. For the current use-case we have to persist the data model explained in Chap. 4. The main requirement is to invoke connected data (pattern) from memory with high performance. In respect to these main requirement and the information from [3, 5, 6] about the strategies to select an appropriate graph database two properties for the case treated can be derived: firstly it has to be a native database which stores the graph structure directly on memory layer as described in [7]; secondly the graph database has to be from type in-memory. Based on these two main specifications Neo4J was selected as the fitting graph database. A sufficient description of Neo4J can be found under [10].

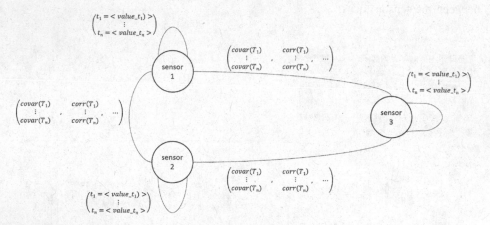

Fig. 4. An example of generated sensor network consisting of three sensors/nodes (sensor_1, sensor_2 and sensor_3) and the corresponding relations/edges.

5.2   Implementation in Neo4J

In this chapter we explain how the sensor graph model from Chap. 4 is implemented on Neo4J graph database using a property graph model (see Fig. 5). The property graph model itself is described in [11]. The available datatypes are nodes and relationships whereby both have the possibility to store properties additionally. A property is a name value pair, in which the name is represented as string and the value can be either a primitive or an array of one primitive type. The nodes represent the sensors. The label of a sensor (e.g. sensor_n) is designated by a property name with the appropriate denotation as value. The discrete timestamps of a sensor are realized by a self-directed relationship on the appropriate sensor node per each timestamp. The implementation of the time intervals between the sensor nodes is also realized as a relationship per time. The values of the specific relations are modeled as properties.

complete sensor graph   specific correlation

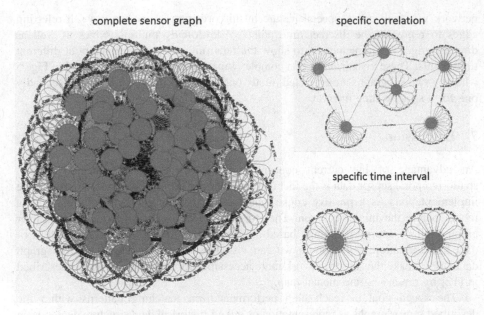

specific time interval

Fig. 5. This picture demonstrates the visualization of a sensor network. The sensor data was generated by the implemented sensor data generator. This generator was parameterized by 50 sensor nodes in sum and three sensor nodes which randomly generated values at current time steps, wherein each self-referential loop represents one discrete sampling point. Furthermore the subgraphs for a specific correlation and a specific time interval as possible pattern candidate are visualized.

6 Preliminary Results and Application

Modern sensor systems deliver a high-amount of multivariate, multiscale and multi-modal time and spatially dependent data. Based on this data we model the sensor networks as spatio-temporal sensor graphs. Furthermore due to the necessity to extract patterns e.g. representative network motifs and to compare this motifs with resulting at the moment patterns we define strong requirements regarding a potential real time application. For the storage and handling of spatio-temporal graphs we decided to use a Neo4J graph database.

Based on real data from biomedical sensor networks e.g. electroencephalogram and polygraphic (electromyogram, electrooculogram, respiration, eletrocardiogram, gala-vanic skin response) sensors as well from data acquired using wearables (Microsoft Band 2 and Intel Basis Peak) we simulated test data sets for the first implementation and validation of the proposed approach. The used test data which was used for the test was generated by a self-coded sensor data generator. This data generator creates sensor values randomly for a predefined number of time steps and a predefined number of sensor nodes. Also it can parametrize the number of current sensor nodes which should generate a random value at the current time step. The simulated test data is in the form <time step>, <sensor node>, <sensor value> and in csv-format and was imported via REST into Neo4J. Furthermore a program for the visualization of the spatio-temporal network was realized. A special feature in this program is that we use self-referring edges to represent the discreet time points. Additionally multiple edges as well as directed edges are implemented to show the relations or the directionality at different time points. These visualization of a complex sensor network is demonstrated in Fig. 5 whereby two subgraphs are extracted: firstly one for a specific correlation and secondly one for a specific time interval.

7 Discussion

An advantage of the current concept and the modelling approach to persist spatio-temporal sensor data is the fact that we have the same model for the data and the implementation. As a positive consequence there is no need to transform the data model before the implementation. Therefore it will be easier to optimize the sensor graph itself by appropriate graph based optimizations without the additional effort of data transformation. Furthermore we can visualize the graph directly on the graph database to make the sensor network more accessible for beneficiaries as it is described in [12] by preserving the mental map.

The stated goal to reach high performance on matching patterns within the described sensor graphs as representation of linked historical data structure demands an investigation of runtime behavior. During the analysis the process itself has to observe the recommendations of [13] on benchmarking such graph database systems like Neo4J. Furthermore detailed performance and impact analysis need to be done. On the basis of these results there is the possibility to survey such performance behavior of storing these linked historical data on a native graph database (Neo4J). As a result the performance compliance in case of real time requirements could be estimated and optimized before the final implementation. We need to investigate the number of nodes and complexity of networks which can be controlled in real time and the IT-resources necessary to realize the reliable operation of the solution proposed. Not least the graph based approach presupposes that all other steps e.g. data preprocessing, computation of the adjacency matrix and others must be done taking into account the respective for the use-case definition of real time.

The proposed approach will enable new options to compare a priori estimated pattern with new computed at real resp. quasi real time pattern and thus to detect critical states in the supervised system as well as to estimate a critical system trigger. In this sense critical trigger can be estimated during the monitoring of biophysical sensor data in patients suffering from depression and used as signal for intervention or for starting of selected self-management procedures.

8 Conclusion and Outlook

In this paper we discussed the modelling of sensor networks, e.g. biomedical sensor networks evolving as spatio-temporal complex networks respectively spatio-temporal graphs. Furthermore we demonstrated first implementation results in Neo4J graph database for the purposes of pattern comparison at real time and discussed the achieved first results.

We are planning to investigate the combination of a graph database and a relational database. In this case we will separate graph and data information in both types of storage concepts. We expect a significant increase of performance and thus new application possibilities. In this sense we are investigating the storage of context information and later integration of this information and the pattern matched from historical and current data. This method will help to improve the interpretability of the patterns. Furthermore the generation of critical trigger in real time will be possible. In consequence a high number of monitoring and controlling applications can be developed whereby one of the first application would be a multivariate sensor based monitoring to control and predict patterns of depressive or manic behavior.

References

1. BGBl. Teil I Nr. 54: Gesetz für sichere digitale Kommunikation und Anwendungen im Gesundheitswesen sowie zur Änderung weiterer Gesetze (21 December 2015)
2. George, B., Kang, J.M., Shekhar, S.: Spatio-temporal sensor graphs (STSG): a data model for the discovery of spatio-temporal patterns. Intell. Data Anal. Knowl. Disc. Data Streams **13**(3), 457–475 (2009). IOS Press, Amsterdam
3. Patil, S., Vaswani, G., Bhatia, A.: Graph databases - an overview. Int. J. Comput. Sci. Inf. Technol. **5**(1), 657–660 (2012)
4. Batra, S., Tyagi, C.: Comparative analysis of relational and graph databases. Int. J. Soft Comput. Eng. (IJSCE) **2**(2), 509–512 (2012)
5. Park, Y., Shankar, M., Park, B., Ghosh, J.: Graph Databases for large-scale healthcare systems: a framework for efficient data management and data services. In: IEEE 30th International Conference on Data Engineering Workshops (ICDEW), Chicago, IL, USA, pp. 12–19 (2014)
6. Ciglan, M. Averbuch, A., Hluchy, L.: Benchmarking traversal operations over graph databases. In: IEEE International Conference on Data Engineering Workshops (ICDEW), Arlington, VA, USA, pp. 186–189 (2012)
7. Rodriguez, M.A., Neubauer, P.: The Graph Traversal Pattern (2010)
8. McColl, R., Ediger, D., Poove, J., Campbel, D., Bader, D.A.: A performance evaluation of open source graph databases. In: Proceedings of the 2014 Workshop on Parallel Programming for Analytics Applications, PPAA 2014, Orlando, Florida, USA, pp. 11–18. Association for Computing Machinery, New York (2014)
9. Macko, P., Margo, D., Seltzer, M.: Performance introspection of graph databases. In: The 6th International Systems and Storage Conference, Haifa, Israel (2013)
10. The Neo4J Manual. http://neo4j.com/docs/stable/
11. The Property Graph Model. http://neo4j.com/developer/graph-database/#property-graph
12. Archambault, D., Purchase, H.C.: The "Map" in the mental map. Experimental results in dynamic graph drawing. Int. J. Hum Comput Stud. **71**(11), 1044–1055 (2013)
13. Dominguez-Sal, D., Martinez-Bazan, N., Muntes-Mulero, V., Baleta, P., Larriba-Pey, J.L.: A discussion on the design of graph database benchmarks. In: Nambiar, R., Poess, M. (eds.) TPCTC 2010. LNCS, vol. 6417, pp. 25–40. Springer, Heidelberg (2011). doi:10.1007/978-3-642-18206-8_3

Research in Progress: Implementation of an Integrated Data Model for an Improved Monitoring of Environmental Processes

Robert Schima[1]([⊠]), Tobias Goblirsch[2], Christoph Salbach[3], Bogdan Franczyk[2], Michael Aleithe[2], Jan Bumberger[1], and Peter Dietrich[1]

[1] Department Monitoring and Exploration Technologies,
UFZ-Helmholtz Centre for Environmental Research, Leipzig, Germany
robert.schima@ufz.de
[2] Chair of Information Management, Faculty of Economics and Management Science,
University of Leipzig, Leipzig, Germany
[3] Department Landscape Ecology,
UFZ-Helmholtz Centre for Environmental Research, Leipzig, Germany

Abstract. How can we benefit from innovative open-source technologies such as mobile sensors and open data platforms in the field of environmental monitoring? Due to the fact that we are facing challenging problems in terms of climate change, urbanization and a growing world population, new strategies for a more comprehensive environmental monitoring have to be developed. Here, we need to create user-specific and easy to use infrastructures as assistance tools for a comprehensive and mobile data acquisition, data processing and data provision. With regard to the variety of existing data sources, data acquisition tools and scales, this paper is focused on strategies and methods for an service oriented monitoring approach based on an integrated data model. To this end, a formal connection was defined by combining spatial, temporal and contextual information of sensor readings into one measure called the individual specific exposure (ISE), which will be later extended to a predictive individual exposure by using historical data.

Keywords: Environmental monitoring · Mobile data acquisition · Individual Specific Exposure · Data integration · Fusion of data

1 Introduction

The impact of global change, urbanization and complex interactions between humans and the environment shows different effects on different scales. Therefore, the observation and modeling of environmental processes require an extensive knowledge of a wide range of bio-geophysical and socio-demographic indicators and their mutual dependencies [1,2]. Due to the process dynamics and heterogeneity of natural systems, a comprehensive monitoring of these effects

---

R. Schima and T. Goblirsch—Contributed equally to this work.

© Springer International Publishing AG 2017
W. Abramowicz et al. (Eds.): BIS 2016 Workshops, LNBIP 263, pp. 332–339, 2017.
DOI: 10.1007/978-3-319-52464-1_30

Fig. 1. Urban areas and anthropogenically affected systems are characterized by heterogeneous structures and dynamic processes. A comprehensive monitoring of these processes would require the collection and integration of all related data sets with an increased resolution in space and time.

remains to be a challenging issue since all related data and process parameters should be considered (see Fig. 1). Especially with regard to urban areas and anthropogenically affected systems, a better understanding and the improvement of characterizing these interactions is subject of current research.

To ensure the balance between social development and the long-term protection of our livelihood, new strategies and systems are needed for the assessment of our everyday individual risks and impacts due to changing environmental conditions. This accentuates the importance to investigate alternative approaches for an individual multi-scale data acquisition, paying special attention to the user-specific exposure on a local scale. Here, exposure should be understood as the sum of all environmental impacts that act on an human being [3]. Especially with regard to urban areas, the exposure of each individual due to urban heat islands or fine dust is highly dependent on the place, the time [4–7] and circumstancing conditions, which are referred here as context. All of these aspects can be summarized as the individual specific exposure (ISE) as shown in Fig. 2. However, recent developments in microelectronics, innovative web-enabled sensor systems, the widespread use of mobile technologies and the availability of remote sensing data allow new perspectives and entirely new insights into environmental effects and processes [8]. Based on this, it is possible to derive more precise information about environmental impacts and human exposure with unprecedented spatial and temporal resolution, even on an individual scale.

Fig. 2. The individual specific exposure (ISE) can be described as the sum of all environmental impacts that act on an human being within a certain amount of time, at a specific place and under certain circumstances (context). As an example, the individual thermal load (heat stress) varies due to different conditions like land use forms, especially in urban areas (green spaces or densely built-up areas). (Color figure online)

2   Goal

Besides the continuous determination of the ISE as described above, the overarching goal of our approach is to generate not only recommendations but also predictions based on the acquired data in form of a predictive individual specific exposure ($PISE$). To this end, our attempt includes the integration and detailed declaration of each integral part on the sensor level (location, time, exposure, context) accomplished with a particular process knowledge to correlate the characteristic values and key features within a given data set and to check the plausibility of decisions and statements, and vise versa (see Fig. 3).

Fig. 3. Here, the individual specific exposure (ISE) is accomplished with particular process knowledge to allow decision making and situational prediction in form of a predictive individual specific exposure ($PISE$).

3   Integrated Monitoring - A Hands-on Practical Approach

As stated above, a variety of data must be recorded in order to be able to analyze and respond to dynamic processes in large scaled and heterogeneous structures like urban areas [3]. Current monitoring strategies from the EU and the federal state are driven by experience where limits are likely to occur [9,10]. Today, environmental measurements and urban area monitoring are typically performed by public organizations and national agencies. However, in most cases measurement stations are static, rather big and configured with professional and established equipment, which is why the methodological and financial effort is high. Based on this infrastructure it is very difficult to derive comprehensive and reliable statements about spatial distributed concentrations along roads, housing estates or indicators regarding the individual exposure of human beings [11]. Therefore, it is necessary to combine different monitoring systems to maximize the advantage of each. Our approach is focused on three different types of monitoring systems: stationary sensors, mobile sensors and remote sensing. The table below gives an overview about the values, time and spatial resolution of each system (see Table 1). The data from each system vary in spatial resolution ranging from local point information from stationary sensors to surface data derived by remote sensing, which is also true for the temporal and value resolution. The main goal in our approach is to integrate these technologies into a single homogeneous framework leading to an improvement of the overall accuracy. Therefore, the key challenge is to find a suitable and appropriate method for the fusion of these different data sets and the extraction of information from multi-scale and variable data sources.

Table 1. Properties of different types of environmental observation technologies regarding the value, time and spatial resolution.

	Stationary sensors	Mobile sensors	Remote sensing	Integrated monitoring
Value resolution	High	Medium	Low	High
Time resolution	High	High	Low	Medium
Spatial resolution	Low	Medium	High	Medium/High

3.1 Multi-scale Data Integration for an Applied Environmental Process Monitoring

Stationary sensors are very common in the field of environmental research and meteorology. In most cases they deliver data with a high resolution in time and are highly accurate. However, data derived by stationary sensors represent only single point measurements without any information about the heterogeneity of a system (see Fig. 4a).

Mobile sensors are specially designed to run autonomously for a specified period of time. Therefore, they can be deployed even on moving vehicles such as cars, busses or bicycles. Moreover, they can be carried by hand or attached to the body, which offers the opportunity to use mobile sensors as personal sensing devices, e.g. for measuring the individual exposure. For our research, we have developed an open source sensor platform (OSP) to easily include different sensor modules such as temperature sensors, a peripheral GPS receiver or a cellular modem for data transmission. Based on this platform it is possible to acquire mobile sensor readings from several devices in parallel, which allows us to immediately generate spatial exposure maps (see Fig. 4b).

Remote sensing provides comprehensive information about the surface of the earth in its spatial differentiations and physical characteristics. A traditional application is the estimation of land cover to describe the heterogeneity (e.g. vegetation, water bodies and impervious surface) of landscapes. In addition to that, some satellite sensors, e.g. Landsat 8, are able to cover the thermal infrared region, which is related to the land surface temperature [12]. Especially for large scaled and heterogeneous areas like urban regions, remote sensing represents a very helpful tool to identify spatial differences, e.g. urban heat islands, and to gather information for various applications like vegetation cover or land use. Most remote sensing data can be accessed via web repositories as well as from provided application programming interfaces, which offers the opportunity to include these data directly into data processing services (see Fig. 4c).

Starting from this generalist data based approach, the definition of the available data sources and their characteristics allows the integration of these data sets into a single information system. To illustrate the advantages offered by the aforementioned concept, the results of a sampling campaign is briefly outlined here. Figure 5 shows a set of stationary, mobile and satellite-based temperature measurements of the city center of Leipzig acquired in September 2015.

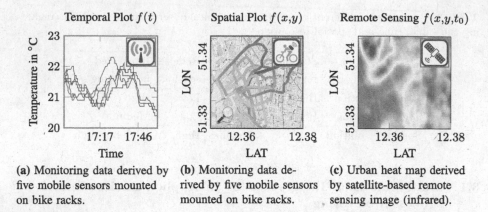

(a) Monitoring data derived by five mobile sensors mounted on bike racks.

(b) Monitoring data derived by five mobile sensors mounted on bike racks.

(c) Urban heat map derived by satellite-based remote sensing image (infrared).

Fig. 4. Illustration of the three different data sources used in this study.

By considering the data, scales and resolution in an integrated manner, it is clearly evident that the underlying systems theory approach is following a functional relationship between space and time. The measured value itself is also dependent on the situational circumstances like parks or densely built-up areas, which corresponds to *context* information mentioned in the previous section. Therefore, it becomes apparent that the overall informative value has increased by combining the benefits of each system into a single data framework.

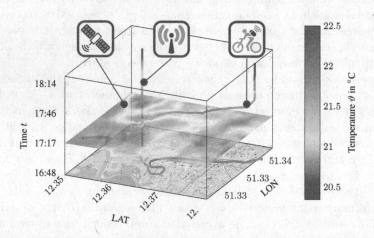

Fig. 5. By combining different data from different scales and data sources, an increased informative value about environmental processes and impacts can be achieved. Here, stationary, mobile and satellite-based temperature measurements are represented in dependence on space, time and the situational circumstances illustrating the advantages and drawbacks of each system.

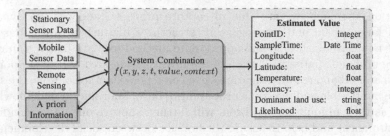

Fig. 6. Schematic drawing for an integrated environmental data model for temperature

3.2 Data Model

In order to derive maximum benefit from this approach, our research aims the development of a generic and efficient framework for an automated integration of different data sources and inhomogeneous data sets. The main intention is to define a minimum set of parameters to ensure the interoperability of the data and to assure a sufficient and reasonable data basis for the decision making and forwarding of the predictive analysis. In this connection, we are following a holistic approach starting on the sensor level. By using a predefined data acquisition routine the surveyed data enables the interoperability between different data scales and sources. Based on the above example of temperature measurement in the city center of Leipzig Fig. 6 shows the formal data model we are using. The input data can be seen on the left, separated into three different data sources (stationary sensor data, mobile sensor data and data from remote sensing). In addition, it is also possible to make use of data sources from third party providers in order to gather a priori information. In our specific application we need information about land use (maps) or meteorological conditions (wind direction and wind intensity). The system combination process is responsible for the integration of all data sources. The main challenge ahead is to find from a wide range of data processing methods (e.g. statistical methods, data fusion or data mining algorithms) a particular solution for our use case. As a result of the system combination estimated temperature values are generated for spatial-temporal data points. Additional information about the accuracy and the likelihood are also necessary for subsequent analysis and interpretations. It should be mentioned that the integration of additional information (e.g. surface models or 3D city models) are also possible but yet not implemented.

4 Conclusion

In this research in progress paper, we proposed a data model framework to derive a predictive individual specific exposure (PISE) for the use case of urban heat island detection. Therefore, we use and integrate diverse data sources from different sensors and technologies, e.g. stationary sensors, mobile sensors and remote sensing, into a single framework. With the presented multi-scale data integration approach, we are able to capture processes and process dynamics even in large scaled and heterogeneous structures like urban areas. Based on this, we now have a suitable and appropriate method for data fusion to improve the temporal and spatial resolution of the investigation area and to support our research and urban area investigations, even on a personnel scale. It can be stated that the multi-scale and real-time processing of data, information and knowledge, as well as their ubiquitous provision, will further improve our understanding of our environment and help to ensure the balance between social development and the long-term protection of our livelihood.

Finally, the generated value of this process can provide significant information for health science and can help to decrease the health risk due to extreme events (e.g. heat stress, air quality) or other related use cases, even third parties business models.

References

1. Banzhaf, E., de la Barrera, F., Kindler, A., Reyes-Paecke, S., Schlink, U., Welz, J., Kabisch, S.: A conceptual framework for integrated analysis of environmental quality and quality of life. Ecol. Ind. **45**, 664–668 (2014)
2. Paasche, H., Eberle, D., Das, S., Cooper, A., Debba, P., Dietrich, P., Dudeni-Thlone, N., Gläßer, C., Kijko, A., Knobloch, A., Lausch, A., Meyer, U., Smit, A., Stettler, E., Werban, U.: Are earth sciences lagging behind in data integration methodologies? Environ. Earth Sci. **71**(4), 1997–2003 (2014)
3. Reis, S., Seto, E., Northcross, A., Quinn, N.W., Convertino, M., Jones, R.L., Maier, H.R., Schlink, U., Steinle, S., Vieno, M., Wimberly, M.C.: Integrating modelling and smart sensors for environmental and human health. Environ. Model. Softw. **74**, 238–246 (2015)
4. Wu, H., Reis, S., Lin, C., Beverland, I.J., Heal, M.R.: Identifying drivers for the intra-urban spatial variability of airborne particulate matter components and their interrelationships. Atmos. Environ. **112**, 306–316 (2015)
5. Steinle, S., Reis, S., Sabel, C.E., Semple, S., Twigg, M.M., Braban, C.F., Leeson, S.R., Heal, M.R., Harrison, D., Lin, C., Wu, H.: Personal exposure monitoring of pm 2.5 in indoor and outdoor microenvironments. Sci. Total Environ. **508**, 383–394 (2015)
6. Weber, S., Sadoff, N., Zell, E., de Sherbinin, A.: Policy-relevant indicators for mapping the vulnerability of urban populations to extreme heat events: a case study of philadelphia. Appl. Geogr. **63**, 231–243 (2015)
7. Ho, H.C., Knudby, A., Xu, Y., Hodul, M., Aminipouri, M.: A comparison of urban heat islands mapped using skin temperature, air temperature, and apparent temperature (humidex), for the greater vancouver area. Sci. Total Environ. **544**, 929–938 (2016)
8. Hart, J.K., Martinez, K.: Toward an environmental internet of things. Earth Space Sci. **2**(5), 194–200 (2015). 2014EA000044
9. Kuhlbusch, T.A., Quincey, P., Fuller, G.W., Kelly, F., Mudway, I., Viana, M., Querol, X., Alastúey, A., Katsouyanni, K., Weijers, E., Borowiak, A., Gehrig, R., Hueglin, C., Bruckmann, P., Favez, O., Sciare, J., Hoffmann, B., EspenYttri, K., Torseth, K., Sager, U., Asbach, C., Quass, U.: New directions: the future of European urban air quality monitoring. Atmos. Environ. **87**, 258–260 (2014)

10. Hester, R., Harrison, R.M.: Air Quality in Urban Environments. Issues in Environmental Science and Technology. RSC Publishing, London (2009)
11. Weijers, E., Khlystov, A., Kos, G., Erisman, J.: Variability of particulate matter concentrations along roads and motorways determined by a moving measurement unit. Atmos. Environ. **38**(19), 2993–3002 (2004)
12. Jimnez-Muoz, J.C., Sobrino, J.A., Skokovic, A., Mattar, C., Cristbal, J.: Land surface temperature retrieval methods from landsat-8 thermal infrared sensor data. IEEE Geosci. Remote Sens. Lett. **11**(10), 1840–1843 (2014)

Exploring Context from the Consumer Perspective: Insights from eBusiness and Health Care

Olaf Reinhold[(✉)], Matthias Wittwer, Rainer Alt, Toralf Kirsten,
and Wieland Kiess

Leipzig University, Grimmaische Str. 12, 04109 Leipzig, Germany
{reinhold,wittwer}@wifa.uni-leipzig.de,
rainer.alt@uni-leipzig.de,
tkirsten@izbi.uni-leipzig.de,
wieland.kiess@medizin.uni-leipzig.de

Abstract. Many electronic services are not used in isolation, but in the context of a specific user. This user, customer or patient perspective is different from the perspective of service providers since customer processes usually involve multiple service providers. Information on the context helps to understand these user needs and to improve the coordination among services. This research in progress paper examines existing contributions as a basis towards an understanding of the concept and modeling of "context" from a context provider's perspective and proposes a preliminary model, which also serves to analyze four use cases. The paper summarizes challenges observed in these cases and presents an agenda for further research.

Keywords: Context · Context models · Context-aware systems

1 Introduction

Context is relevant to many interaction scenarios, may it be between buyers and sellers or doctors and patients [1, 2]. A well-known example is Amazon.com, where recommendations on products are given based on the transaction history of the user and other buyers. Other domains provide similar scenarios, for example in health care when a doctors define a treatment based on the patients' medical history and assessments from other specialists, or in the field of trip planning, when information on the entire journey and preferences regarding timing and pricing are used for individualized offerings. The underlying assumption is that information about the context (context information) can be used to improve the value of services to users, customers or patients [21].

Customer Relationship Management (CRM) is one of the domains where businesses have started to collect information on customers in customer profiles ([3, 4]). In this context Service Dominant Logic (SDL) postulates that value is created when companies achieve to "co-create" services based on these customer needs [5–7]. However, SDL is still regarded as a provider-driven approach, which fails to grasp the entire needs from the customer's perspective. In addition to that, smartphones,

© Springer International Publishing AG 2017
W. Abramowicz et al. (Eds.): BIS 2016 Workshops, LNBIP 263, pp. 340–346, 2017.
DOI: 10.1007/978-3-319-52464-1_31

wearables, social networks, third party data sources and other sources offer new means to obtain a more accurate understanding of the context of interactions. This perspective has led to a new understanding of the consumer, who actively influences and orchestrates the configuration of services across multiple providers (Customer Dominant Logic, CDL) [8, 9]. Context in the CDL may be understood as a relevant factor that consumers control and may provide intentionally.

However, when context is used for the provision of services in different domains, we often face the problem that context cannot be provided adequately, that it is not clear which context is relevant, how context can be measured or it is represented in context-aware systems. The planned research aims to investigate how contexts can be modelled and processed in scenarios where users control the provision of context information. As a first step of this research, this paper explores how context is defined in literature and what elements are relevant for context modelling and for building context-aware services. The findings are used for formulating a preliminary model and reviewing four real world cases. In the last section, a research agenda is proposed.

2 Literature Review About the Definition and Role of Context

To develop an understanding of the term "context" and its basic elements, an exploratory literature search in EBSCO, Science Direct, Springer Link and OECD iLibrary was conducted. In general, context may be associated with the user (e.g. [1, 10]) or with application systems (e.g. [11, 12]). According to [13], context is a multifaceted concept that has been studied within different research disciplines, for example computer science, cognitive science, linguistics, philosophy, psychology, and organizational sciences. As a result, different notions of context and customer context are discussed in literature (e.g. [14, 15]). For example, context describes "any piece of information that is known about the end user – location, customer type, products owned, open cases etc." [16] or "(...) an amalgamation of customer history (e.g., usage patterns, buying behaviors, contact preferences) combined with certain attributes" [17]. Based on the analysis of 150 definitions of context, [19] conclude that context refers to either a user, item or environment and suggest that an observer (e.g. a person or an application system) is able to gather the related contextual information. Another approach distinguishes "consumer circumstance" and "business circumstance". The former is specified via a consumer's disposition (e.g. demographic, behavioral, psychographic, affinities) and specific situation (e.g. states, needs, sentiments, events) [18]. The latter [14] explores relevant context information from the perspective of a business and differentiates in contextual information about a customer and his environment as well as the respective attributes and states.

In the literature on context-aware systems, context was initially defined as the location of the user, the identity of people near the user, the objects around and the changes in these elements [20]. In particular, a primary context (e.g. location, identity, time and activity) and a secondary context (e.g. e-mail address) are distinguished [1, 21]. A system is regarded as context-aware if it uses context to provide relevant information and/or services to the user, where relevance depends on the user's task [1].

Often, it is unknown which contextual information is relevant, useful, or even how to use them.

The literature review shows a gap between the conceptualization of context, the modelling of context and the provision of context for context-aware systems. While the conceptualization of context delivers information on the relevance and influence of context that can be applied for SDL and CDL, the modelling of context itself is often associated only with SDL and provides approaches how context can be integrated in context-aware systems. For example, context information of process instances may be used in Case Management Model and Notation (CMMN) to allow runtime flexibility during execution as an example from the health care domain [22] illustrates. However, the CDL perspective on modelling context where a user controls the provision and the use of context information seems rarely discussed.

3 Towards a Context Model from the CDL Perspective

Following the results from the literature review, context from a CDL perspective is associated with a **user/person/consumer** or a **system/service** and relates to other **persons**, **entities** (e.g. persons, places, objects) and/or their **environment**. The providing systems are in control of the person (e.g. smartphone, wearable, interface) or third party systems to which the person provides context information (e.g. social network, loyalty program). Consuming systems use context data to influence their provided results (e.g. context-aware systems, recommendations for a user). In CDL, relevant context information for a service is the overlap between a set of context information a person is willing to provide and the information that is used by the service. These settings depend on and are influenced by different factors:

- **Transfer of context information** leads to be a differentiation of automatically ("sensed") tracked data (e.g. data gained from sensors or GPS devices) and derived data (e.g. buying interests derived by viewed articles) [23].
- **Method of data collection** describes whether data is directly (e.g. through input from a user) or indirectly (e.g. user data from existing databases) collected [23].
- **Structure of context information** influences the degree of automation. Structured data can be accessed from existing databases but often also unstructured data from interactions e.g. in social networks contain relevant information and need to be considered.
- **Access and usage rights** help to prevent the misuse of context information. The applicable rights associated with context information have to be transparent to and respected at every processing stage.
- **Dynamics of context information** influences the accessibility and use of context information. Static context information can be captured once or from third party sources, whereas dynamic context information needs to be captured and integrated constantly in the service provision processes.

The literature on context-aware systems suggests relevant elements of the **application system architecture** used to exchange context information:

- *Collection* of context information refers to different sources with different data formats. Systems for analyzing structured and unstructured data are required to collect information and to enrich existing databases, e.g. from social content or document databases.
- *Integration* of heterogeneous, incomplete and dynamic context information within context models. Ontologies are a common approach for integrating context information from different resources, for example in pervasive computing environments, as described by [24] and enable a distinction of different locations a service consumer visited or medical devices a patient uses.
- *Representation* of context in an exchangeable data format so that a user can understand the exchanged data, its privacy implications and that he can use context from third parties. Specific modeling approaches, such as key-value models, markup scheme models enable the definition and graphical representations of contextual information [25].
- *Control* over context information through adding and to extracting context information for the use in other systems or results replication.

Table 1. Analysis of four cases

Domain	Case	Case Description	Observed elements	Scenario and influencing factors	Relevant elements of the application system architecture
eBusiness	o2 More Local	"o2 More Local" [27] offers an option to spread promotions through text or multimedia messages depending on (1) the user's current location, (2) additional information from the CRM (e.g. gender and age) and the (3) environment (e.g. season, weather). The goal is the selection of offers that get recognized by customers.	Person (age, gender), Environment (location by radio cell positioning, time)	Direct transfer of dynamic data (current location), smartphone app as providing entity, user as central entity	Collection (e.g. mobile phone, radio cell), Control (e.g. active/inactive GPS)
eBusiness	Outfittery	Outfittery [30] offers a clothing selection service based on customer preferences that are derived from (1) cookies that collect information (e.g. dwell time, viewed and purchased products), (2) analysis for previous requests, (3) information such as date, time, IP address as well as the referrer URL, (4) information from the CRM such as demography, addresses, payment information, clothing sizes, favorite color. The goal is the selection of an individual fitting set of cloths.	Entity (purchased products), Person (demography, address, clothing sizes, favorite color, ID provided by cookies), Environment (date, time, IP address, referrer URL, dwell time)	Direct data transfer of dynamic data (current preferences), multi-dimensional and structured attributes (e.g. colors, sizes, price-sensitivity), user as the context providing entity	Collection (e.g. cookies, user input, CRM), Representation (Profile), Control (e.g. provision of certain information)
eBusiness	Mtel Customer care	Mtel [31] provides a B2B solutions for faultless, efficient, and effective handling of customer contacts by interactive voice response (IVR) or a customer service representative (CSR) based on (1) callers identity and the call reason and enriches that information with (2) data from the companies' CRM system. The goal is the prediction of call reasons and the dynamic change of the workflow.	Person (phone number, caller identity, URL and IP address, historical CRM data, call reason), Entity (IVR menu options, order or ticket number)	User provides only little context information by its own. Direct and indirect data transfer as well as static and dynamic user data (IVR menu options, CRM data), structured data (CRM and IVR menu options)	Collection (e.g. CRM, user input), Integration (e.g. IVR menu options)
Health Care	Vital Services	Vital Services [28] provides a service for the management of treatment processes by more than one doctor based on a comprehensive database about (1) relevant features of the disease, (2) environmental factors, (3) and personal values based on a biopsychosocial concept. The goal is the provision of a multi-faceted description of the disease for the various specialists involved during a treatment.	Person (name, age, gender, health assessments, physical condition), Entity (diseases, treatment history, previous medication, discharge information, ICD coding)	Direct data collection from multiple sources (doctors, treatment database and patient), dynamic data (current condition), multi-dimensional attributes, User provides only little context information by its own	Collection (e.g. health record, patient input), Integration (e.g. health record, current constitution), Control (e.g. additional information)

These elements, influencing factors and elements of an application architecture provide a preliminary model for a structured literature analysis and case examination on context from the CDL perspective and development of a modelling approach. In a first test, this preliminary model was used for an examination of four scenarios (see Table 1). The underlying case studies were conducted by [26] in an earlier research and their results were used as raw data for this research. The selection criteria of these cases were: (1) The use of context has to be embedded in a practical application, (2) the case needs to describe an exchange between a service provider and a service consumer, and (3) several sources should be used to collect contextual information. Each case was analyzed by available white papers and information from the website of the respective companies.

4 Conclusion and Research Agenda

This research in progress paper aimed to investigate the elements, influencing factors and application architecture of "context" from the CDL perspective through an initial literature review and four use cases. It is a first step to highlight that context affects the definition and delivery of services in different domains but that methods for the description, modelling and transfer of context from the context provider perspective require further research. The findings show that a CDL based approach can build upon existing modelling approaches, but needs to incorporate the specific characteristics of CDL scenarios. Based on this initial research the following research agenda for the development of a context model from the CDL perspective is planned:

- Development of a working definition for the term and concept of "context" from the perspective of the customer based on a structured literature analysis and the preliminary model. It calls for interdisciplinary research that links social, IT and legal aspects.
- Analysis and examination of scenarios in different domains from the CDL perspective and development of an architecture for the exchange of context information. In parallel the advantages and costs of using context information in services need to be further exemplified.
- Identification of methods for collecting and merging of contextual information from different sources and for using context information in service scenarios (e.g. recommendation, search, configuration). Methods should include data fusion approaches for the integration of structured and unstructured data, for the handling of incomplete (e.g. sources may provide context in irregular intervals, different time intervals of context), and for heterogeneous contextual information (e.g. data from sensors, social networks).
- Development of a modelling approach for context on the formal and system level. For this purpose, the dynamic of context (e.g. context factors may influence each other, context may change during the service provision) and context provider perspective should be incorporated with existing models.
- The exploration of privacy issues and the development of rules and methods for privacy preserving exchange and use of context information. The context provider should be able to monitor, to control and to be informed about the use of context information that is related with him.

Further research on context models will help to better understand the available context information and enable the development of new services in different domains. Existing systems such as recommender systems [29], CRM systems or self-services will be valuable in providing contextual information for more individualized services (e.g. for a patients' treatment or for curated shopping). As this paper presents only a first step to investigate context, it is limited by several factors. First, the literature review was exploratory with the aim of identifying possible domains and concepts with relevance for the development of context models. The case analysis provides a first insight into the current role of context and is only the basis for a structured multi-case analysis. Third, the definition of required models and methods needs to be reflected with the existing knowledge base.

References

1. Dey, A.: understanding and using context. Pers. Ubiquit. Comput. **5**, 4–7 (2001)
2. Adomavicius, G., Mobasher, B., Ricci, F., Tuzhilin, A.: Context-aware recommender systems. AI Mag. **32**, 67–80 (2011)
3. Grönroos, C.: Relationship marketing: strategic and tactical implications. Manag. Decis. **34**, 5–14 (1996)
4. Paulissen, K., Milis, K., Brengman, M., Fjermestad, J., Romano, N.C.: Voids in the current CRM literature. In: Proceedings of the 40th HICSS (2007)
5. Bueren, A., Schierholz, R., Kolbe, L., Brenner, W.: Customer knowledge management - improving performance of customer relationship management with knowledge management. In: Proceedings of the 37th HICSS, pp. 1–10 (2004)
6. Akaka, M.A., Vargo, S.L., Schau, H.H.: The context of experience. J. Serv. Manag. **26**, 206–223 (2015)
7. Alt, R., Militzer-Horstmann, C., Zimmermann, H.D.: Electronic markets on customer-orientation. Electron. Mark. **26**, 1–5 (2016)
8. Heinonen, K., Strandvik, T., Mickelsson, K., Edvardsson, B., Sundström, E., Andersson, P.: A customer dominant logic of service. J. Serv. Manag. **21**, 531–548 (2010)
9. Heinonen, K., Strandvik, T.: Customer-dominant logic: foundations and implications. J. Serv. Mark. **29**, 472–484 (2015)
10. Franklin, D., Flachsbart, J.: All gadget and no representation makes jack a dull environment sensing. In: Proceedings of AAAI 1998 Spring Symposium on Intelligent Environments, pp. 155–160 (1998)
11. Rodden, T., Cheverst, K., Davies, N., Dix, A.: Exploiting context in HCI design for mobile systems. In: Workshop on Human Computer Interaction with Mobile Devices, pp. 21–22 (1998)
12. Ward, A., Jones, A., Hopper, A.: A new location technique for the active office. IEEE Pers. Commun. **4**, 42–47 (1997)
13. Adomavicius, G., Tuzhilin, A.: Context-aware recommender systems. In: Ricci, F., Rokach, L., Shapira, B., Kantor, P. (eds.) Recommender Systems Handbook, pp. 217–253. Springer, New York (2011)
14. Nemoto, Y., Uei, K., Sato, K., Shimomura, Y.: A context-based requirements analysis method for PSS design. Procedia CIRP **30**, 42–47 (2015)
15. Steel, M., Dubelaar, C., Ewing, M.: Developing customised CRM projects: the role of industry norms, organisational context and customer expectations on CRM implementation. Ind. Mark. Manag. **42**, 1328–1344 (2013)
16. Koelliker, K.: The Knowledgebase of the Future. KM World. 07–08 (2013)
17. International Data Corporation (IDC): Data Augmented with Context Provides Richer Customer Experiences, Framingham (2013)
18. Frankland, D., Brosnan, R.: Context Changes Everything, Redwood City (2015)

19. Bazire, M., Brézillon, P.: Understanding context before using it. In: Dey, A., Kokinov, B., Leake, D., Turner, R. (eds.) CONTEXT 2005. LNCS (LNAI), vol. 3554, pp. 29–40. Springer, Heidelberg (2005). doi:10.1007/11508373_3
20. Palmisano, C., Tuzhilin, A., Gorgoglione, M.: Using context to improve predictive modeling of customers in personalization applications. IEEE Trans. Knowl. Data Eng. **20**, 1535–1549 (2008)
21. Dey, A.K., Abowd, G.D.: Towards a better understanding of context and context- awareness. In: Proceedings of the CHI 2000 Workshop, The Hague, pp. 1–6 (2000)
22. Neskovic, S., Kirchner, K.: Using context information and CMMN to model knowledge-intensive business processes. In: 6th ICIST 2016, Kopaonik (2015)
23. Henricksen, K., Indulska, J.: Modelling and using imperfect context information. In: Proceedings of the 2nd IEEE annual Conference on Pervasive Computing and Communications Workshops, pp. 33–37 (2004)
24. Wang, X.H., Qing Zhang, D., Gu, T., Pung, H.K.: Ontology based context modeling and reasoning using OWL. In: IEEE Annual Conference Pervasive Computing, pp. 18–22 (2004)
25. Strang, T., Linnhoff-Popien, C.: A context modeling survey. In: 1st International Workshop on Advanced Context Modelling, Reasoning and Management, UbiComp, pp. 31–41 (2004)
26. Kleinschmidt, F., Lehrmann, N.: The importance of customer context. Unpublished Service Science Seminar Thesis, Leipzig University (2016)
27. O2 Germany: O2 More Local. https://www.o2online.de/more/local/
28. Winter, A., Alt, R., Ehmke, J., Haux, R., Ludwig, W., Mattfeld, D., Oberweis, A., Paech, B.: Manifest kundeninduzierte orchestrierung komplexer dienstleistungen. Informatik-Spektrum **35**, 399–408 (2012)
29. Desrosiers, C., Karypis, G.: A comprehensive survey of neighborhood-based recommendation methods. In: Ricci, F., Rokach, L., Shapira, B., Kantor, P.B. (eds.) Recommender Systems Handbook, pp. 107–144. Springer, New York (2011)
30. Outfittery: Shopping for men. https://www.o2online.de/more/local/
31. mtel: Mtel, the Experts in Customer Contact. http://www.mtel.eu

Research in Progress on Integrating Health and Environmental Data in Epidemiological Studies

Toralf Kirsten[1]([⊠]), Jan Bumberger[2]([⊠]), Galina Ivanova[3,4], Peter Dietrich[2],
Christoph Engel[1,6], Markus Loeffler[1,6], and Wieland Kiess[1,5]

[1] LIFE Research Centre for Civilization Diseases,
University of Leipzig, Leipzig, Germany
toralf.kirsten@life.uni-leipzig.de
[2] Department Monitoring and Exploration Technologies,
UFZ - Helmholtz Centre for Environmental Research, Leipzig, Germany
jan.bumberger@ufz.de
[3] Institute for Applied Informatics, University of Leipzig, Leipzig, Germany
[4] Information Systems Institute, University of Leipzig, Leipzig, Germany
[5] Hospital for Children and Adolescent, Centre for Pediatric Research,
University of Leipzig, Leipzig, Germany
[6] Institute for Medical Informatics, Statistics,
and Epidemiology, University of Leipzig, Leipzig, Germany

Abstract. Epidemiological studies analyze and monitor the health state
of a population. They typically use different methods and techniques to
capture and to integrate data of interest before they can be analyzed.
As new technologies and, thus, devices are available for data capturing,
such as wearables, new requirements arise for current data integration
approaches. In this paper, we review current techniques and approaches
as well as new trends in data capturing and the resulting requirement
for its integration.

Keywords: Data integration · Spatial-temporal data · Environmental
data · Epidemiological studies

1 Introduction

Epidemiological studies and other health related surveys typically determine the
health state of a population living in a geographical region of interest. Their
goal is often to recognize imbalances in health or to mirror disease trends. Such
imbalances are, for example, increasing prevalences of obesity and allergies in
modern civilization populations. These imbalances are related with diseases.
In case of obesity, they include cardiovascular diseases and diabetes which are
at least partially caused by unhealthy nutrition and missing sports activity.
Environmental factors including air pollution according to industry density and
traffic or the increasing spreading out of non-domestic plants are potential risk

---

T. Kirsten and J. Bumberger—Contributed equally to this work.

© Springer International Publishing AG 2017
W. Abramowicz et al. (Eds.): BIS 2016 Workshops, LNBIP 263, pp. 347–354, 2017.
DOI: 10.1007/978-3-319-52464-1_32

factors for allergies. Therefore, there are non-genetic causes of diseases related to endogenous and exogenous environmental conditions (Exposome) [1]. So the immediate environment of every human being is a major determinant factor for their susceptibility to illness and clearly impacts upon their well-being.　－

Typically, data capturing in epidemiological studies and health surveys is rather static. Inhabitants of a specific region are selected and invited for participation. In participation case, data are captured by input forms at the day when the participant visits the study centre. In longitudinal studies, participants are reinvited on a regular basis, e.g., annually, in order to track health developments over a longer period of time for the same individuals. Since epidemiological studies and health surveys are interested in discovering common trends or risk factors (and not that of a single individual) many participants need to be included in such studies who's data are then analyzed all together. This makes a very deep phenotyping, in which each participant is continuously monitored over a longer period, very expensive. However, recent developments in sensor and communication technologies resulting, e.g., in wearables and smartphones, which are widely and increasingly used (mostly already on a private basis) can break the cost barrier and opens new possibilities for research.

In this research in progress paper, we review traditional data capturing methods in epidemiological studies and health surveys as well as recent advances with the use of smartphones and wearables. For the first part, we refer to LIFE [2,3] as an example for epidemiological studies, while, for the second part, we include our experiences about sensor technologies we are using in environmental research at the UFZ Leipzig. In particular, we show perspectives to combine traditional and new technologies for data capturing. At the end, we will sketch their impact on data integration as indispensable step before a data analysis can start.

2　The Classic Way of Capturing Health-Related Data

In epidemiological studies, interviews, questionnaires and physical examinations are usually used to collect data about a population of interest. Data are generated by asking and examining selected and invited participants at the day they visit the study centre. Interviews are utilized to acquire data in a face-to-face interaction or by phone, i.e., in a controlled scenario in which an interviewer asks predefined questions and takes the answer given by the participant. Conversely, questionnaires are input forms which are filled by participants themselves without any interaction to the staff of the study centre. Moreover, there is a wide spectrum of physical examinations, without or by using electronic devices ranging from measuring anthropometry and blood pressure to more complex examinations, such as EEG and MRI. Latter examinations produce complex data types, such as pictures and video sequences, which necessitates an additional reading process to measure and extract relevant data for later analysis steps. In some cases, such reading processes can be automated, but often this process need manual interaction, e.g., when parameters of a sonography is measured.

Health data are usually represented in data tables; in the simplest way such a table contains the data of a selected examination for all participants.

Columns of the data table correspond to the study items, i.e., questions of an interview and questionnaire or to a measurement parameter of a single physical examination. Lines of the table represent captured scientific data, each line for a single participant. The participant and, thus, each line is identified by a participant pseudonym to clearly separate participant's identification data, such as name and address data, from the captured scientific data according to privacy requirements. Further administrative data include the study event, the time point when the data has been captured and a geographical location. The study event disambiguates lines of the data table regarding to the same participant, e.g., when data of the same participant has been captured in succeeding invitation waves (multiple visits within a longitudinal study) or in different contexts (e.g., pilot phase vs. main study). The geographical location is often represented by the participant's private address. Due to privacy reasons, address data are often represented by blurred GPS-coordinates or on a aggregated level by city districts. Both, GPS-coordinates and city districts, become important when further data to participant's health data need to be associated, such as urban data of the city and environmental data.

Complementary to data capturing processes, bio-samples, such as blood, urine, and hairs, taken from the participants are typically collected. In LIFE, one part is frozen and stored in a biobank whereas the other part is directly analyzed by a dedicated laboratory. The laboratory analysis of bio-samples follows specific profiles for defined sub-populations, including adults, pregnant women, children, and obese children. The stored bio-samples are used for special laboratory analyses, mostly focused on determining a specific hypothesis or for genetic examinations, such as gene expression, SNP analysis, and sequencing. In contrast to data captured by interviews, questionnaires etc., laboratory and genetic data are not directly associated with the participant pseudonym but with a sample identifier. Therefore, the mapping associating each sampling identifier to the participant is required to combine health-related data from interviews with corresponding lab data.

3   Advanced Methods and Technologies for Monitoring Health and Environmental Data

The crosslinking of the processes in multiple spatio-temporal scales and their interaction results in complex behavior. In this case, classical monitoring strategies to determine environmental and personalized biophysical data are not sufficient. Also a priori information of urban dynamics as well as the identification of hot moments and hot spots is insufficient. There is a need in the field of data collection for novel spatio-temporal measurement setups and an adaptive observation methodology. The metrological detection of local and personalized environmental and biophysical data related to persons who move in complex areas, requires new strategies and approaches. By information technology in recent years stationary and mobile data can be used for epidemiology studies on various scales in space and time. The potential application using new information technologies in epidemiology studies is discussed in the field of the future of the epidemiology and public health [4,5]. Furthermore, the possibly of eCohorts are discussed and one of the first study in this field are the Health eHeart Study (University of California, San Francisco, US). Following various possible data sources are briefly described.

Use publicly available map material provides a possible data source. An example would be the closeness of the probands to the next schools, kindergartens, supermarkets, green and blue infrastructures and other user-generated Points-of-Interest (POI) by using, e.g., Open Street Map. In addition to this, statistical surveys of governmental institutions can be used. Furthermore, the use of remote sensing data for the qualification of infrastructures, hyperspectral or thermal measurements as well as the future possibilities of pollutions measurements are suitable. Related to data for the determination of climate relevant parameters exists also a few off stationary measurement stations (e.g., Deutscher Wetterdienst DWD or environmental agencies of the cities). A relatively new approach is the collaborative monitoring (e.g., citizen science or volunteered geographic information) with local data interpretation and assessment by people located in the study area. This approach is a potential way such information could be rapidly captured and analyzed [6]. Examples for this are the determination of the species distribution of certain allergenic plants.

Table 1. Selected wearables in different application fields

Application field	Manufacturer	Device	Price	Parameter
Medicine	Empatica	E4 wristband	1700 $	Steps, calories, activity, heart rate, galvanic skin responses, skin temperature
	Monicahealthcare	Monica AN 24	N/A	Monitors fetal heart rate (FHR), maternal heart rate (MHR) and uterine activity (UA)
Environmental	TZOA	TZOA EnviroTracker	140 $	Particles (2.5 and 10 µm), UV intensity, temperature, humidity
	Sensorcon	Sensordrone	200 $	Temperature, gas sensors, humidity, pressure, proximity
Lifestyle	Intel	Basis peak	250 $	Steps, calories, activity, sleep, heart rate, GSR, skin temperature
	Microsoft	Band2	250 $	Steps, calories, activity, sleep, heart rate, GSR, skin temperature
	Empatica	Embrace watch	200 $	Steps, calories, activity, galvanic skin responses, skin temperature
	Jawbone	UP3	200 $	Steps, calories, activity, sleep, heart rate

For the personalized collection of relevant proband data in epidemiological studies is the use of smartphone apps and external sensors for mobile data collection under certain conditions (e.g., with extensive calibration of the sensors and use of analysis tools) similar accuracies for various environmental and biophysical variables can be achieved. Related to standard mapping approaches, this application of smartphone-based apps and sensors (for the specific collection of relevant environmental and/or biophysical data) often results in a higher spatio-temporal resolution. For example, studies of noise indicators and their impact on humans were carried out successfully in Antwerp using such methods. Other examples include the use of smartphone-based sensors for autism intervention via multimedia applications or in epilepsy using an electrodermal activity and accelerometer biosensor. The use of wearables allow collecting geo-referenced traces, which every person leave while using smart phones and smart sensors (examples see Table 1). The collection of personalized longitudinal data, describing sufficiently the subject behavior now is possible. The continuous acquirement of bio-physiological data, e.g., heart rate, blood pressure, skin conductance, speech characteristics, sleep parameters, activities level, even portable EEG-data is conceivable nowadays [7,8]. Therefore, one of the big challenges for research and industry is to develop methods, algorithms and platforms able to analyze, integrate and fuse this data in order to extract interpretable for the individual and for specific cohort behavioral patterns.

4   Challenges for Data Integration

Comprehensive analyses using environmental data as explanation for health data as captured by interviews, questionnaires etc. necessitate their integration and linking. GPS-coordinates are usually appropriate on the technical level to interrelate health and environment data. However, spatial-temporal data integration [9] become challenging when data heterogeneity, in particular, on the semantical level increase. Such challenges are earlier discussed, e.g., for all kind of spatio-temporal data [10]. We refer in the following to common problems corresponding, in particular, with new mobile devices.

Data volume: In contrast to classic data capturing techniques used in epidemiological studies reflecting the health at a specific point of participant's life, new wearables are used to monitor biophysical and environment parameters. With more and more participants are included into this continuous data collection, large data volumes are generated from numerous data sources - each sensor is a data source - which need to be managed and fused to enable comprehensive analyses.

Data privacy and data access: Biophysical parameters, such as heart rate, skin conductance etc. represent private data and, therefore, underly data privacy. Wearables often send the captured data (over a smartphone app) to a dedicated web server which is managed by the wearable vendor or a service provider. There, data can be accessed using the private account data, i.e., the user's login and password. Hence, data access is usually limited, in particular, when participants utilize private devices.

Overlapping data: While biophysical monitor data are directly associated with participants, environment data captured by mobile sensors belong to geographical positions which can be indicated by, e.g., GPS-coordinates, and a specific time. Multiple measurements, e.g., by two participants, at the same time for the same geographical location result in overlapping data. This is also true when the geographical position of one measurement is very nearby another one. Multiple measurements confirm values, e.g., outside temperature, when measurement values are nearly the same but can also result in conflicts when the measured values contradict.

Data quality and verification: Data quality is a common issue in every data integration project influencing the result of comprehensive data analyses. In particular, mobile sensors built in private wearables are usually checked and calibrated once by the vendor in production pipeline and, thus, before they are sold but later never again. Therefore, measurements (e.g. air pollution) can be different for the same location and time. Multiple measurements for the same location and time (overlapping data) can help to stabilize measured results and to identify imprecise sensors, e.g., to exclude measurements of such sensor devices.

Spatial resolution: Points, lines and regions (i.e., polygons) are different geographical space types for which data can be captured. In analyses, data often need to be merged or at least associated, e.g., to compute correlations or regressions, to find out their impact on a predefined outcome. For example, while health data are associated with GPS-coordinates (blurred addresses of study participants), population statistics are only available on city districts, i.e., a region. In another case, data are available for two distinct GPS-coordinates. Therefore, algorithms are necessary to decide how data according to different space types can be merged, on the one hand, and to merge different points, lines, and (distinct or overlapping) regions and their respective data with respect to the time they have been captured, on the other hand.

Time resolution: Health-related data which are directly generated by the study participant are typically associated with an exact point in time at which data has been captured. Contrary, other data resources, such as yearbooks provided by cities or countries comprising data and facts about a population or region of interest (e.g., population density, unemployment rate but also urban data) are often available on lower time granularity, e.g., annually. Moreover, there is typically a time lack before such data become available. For example, the statistical yearbook of 2014 is often published during the first two quarters of 2015. Hence, data and facts of the predecessor yearbook are usually used until the new yearbook is published. Therefore, an integration and data analysis need to consider different time resolutions and time shifts.

Existing classical data integration approaches don't contribute towards the described challenges. Relatively new methods are under development in the research domain 'Internet of Things'. A recent survey [11] overviews current approaches in this domain. The domain independent semantic web approach allows to uniformly access and query data but necessities data in a specific format (RDF schema) and doesn't solve the quality and resolution challenges. Other approaches and solutions aim at very specific goals; in some cases they combine data integration and analysis [12].

5   Conclusion

In this paper, we described methods for data capturing as they are currently used in epidemiological studies and health surveys. Additionally, we gave an overview over data sources collecting environmental data as well as recent developments capturing health and environmental data using mobile sensors. Such sensors can be used by study participants generating data during a dedicated time interval and, thus, can be utilized to continuously monitor biophysical parameters (according the health state) of persons together with environmental data from their surroundings. However, the integration requirements increase (with respect to privacy and data access but also data quality) when inhabitants living in a region of interest (e.g., citizen science approach) use mobile devices, in particular, life style products. Next steps are the development of suitable data model and integration approaches for the utilization of this data types. Therefore, we reviewed current challenges occurring when health and environmental data need to be integrated from such sources.

Acknowledgment. This publication is supported by LIFE (Leipzig Research Center for Civilization Diseases, University of Leipzig). LIFE is funded by means of the European Union, by the European Regional Development Fund (ERFD) and by means of the Free State of Saxony within the framework of the excellence initiative.

References

1. Wild, P.W.: Complementing the genome with an "exposome": the outstanding challenge of environmental exposure measurement in molecular epidemiology. Cancer Epidemiol. Biomark. Prev. **14**, 1847 (2005)
2. Quante, M., Hesse, M., Döhnert, M., et al.: The life child study: a life course approach to disease and health. BMC Pub. Health **12**(1), 1021 (2012)
3. Loeffler, M., Engel, C., Ahnert, P., et al.: The LIFE-Adult-Study: objectives and design of a population-based cohort study with 10,000 deeply phenotyped adults in Germany. BMC Pub. Health **15** (2015)
4. Richardson, D.B., Volkow, N.D., Kwan, M.P., et al.: Spatial turn in health research. Science **339**(6126), 1390–1392 (2013)
5. Kostkova, P., Brewer, H., de Lusignan, S., et al.: Who owns the data? Open data for healthcare. Fronties Pub. Health **4**(7), February 2016
6. Danielsen, F., et al.: Local participation in natural resource monitoring: a characterization of approaches. Conserv. Biol. **23**(1), 31 (2009)
7. Chan, M., Estève, D., Fourniols, J.Y., Escriba, C., Campo, E.: Smart wearable systems: current status and future challenges. Artif. Intell. Med. **56**(3), 137–156 (2012)

8. Soh, P.J., Vandenbosh, G.A.E., Mercuri, M., Schreurs, D.: Wearable wireless health monitoring: current developments, challenges, and future trends. IEEE Microwave Mag. **16**(4), 55 (2015)
9. Ma, H., Zhao, D., Yuan, P.: Opportunities in mobile crowd sensing. IEEE Commun. Mag. **52**(8), 29–35 (2014)
10. Pitts, R.: Geospatial data integration challenges and considerations, 12 November 2013. http://sensorsandsystems.com/geospatial-data-integration-challenges-and-considerations/
11. Ganti, R.K., Ye, F., Lei, H.: Mobile crowdsensing: current state and future challenges. IEEE Commun. Mag. **49**(11), 32–39 (2011)
12. Sagl, G., Resch, B., Hawelka, B., Beinat, E.: From social sensor data to collective human behaviour patterns: analysing and visualising spatio-temporal dynamics in urban environments. In: Proceedings of the GI-Forum, pp. 54–63 (2012)

Doctoral Consortium

Decision Support Enhancement
for Player Substitution in Football:
A Design Science Approach

Pavlina Kröckel[(✉)]

Institute of Information Systems, Friedrich-Alexander University
of Erlangen-Nuremberg, Nuremberg, Germany
pavlina.kroeckel@fau.de

Abstract. Football players are constantly being tracked during the live games
by means of automated tracking technologies. Every event that happens on the
field is recorded in a who-what-where-when fashion. These data are used in pre-
and post-match analyses to improve strategies and tactics. To date such data
have not yet been used for in-game decision making. Considering the impact of
the substitute players on the final outcome of the game, this paper proposes an
approach for enhancing the substitution decision. The goal is to support the
coach and his staff during live matches by developing an algorithm or using an
existing analytic method which will evaluate and rate the players' performance
and recommend a player that should leave the game.

Keywords: Football · Soccer · Substitution · Decision support · Design
science

1 Research Background

Analytics in sports became popular with the book "Moneyball: The Art of Winning an
Unfair Game" by author Michael Lewis, published in 2003. The book demonstrates
how a relatively unpopular baseball team successfully used analytics to ensure a win.
Perhaps this was a major drive for baseball to be one of the first sports to truly embrace
and believe that analytics can help improve the performance of the team and support
coaches and trainers in their decision making. Other sports have also gradually introduced analytics – tennis, cricket, American football.

Football, or soccer is one of the sports that although has already embarked on the
analytics journey, has not fully grasped the advantages that data might offer to decision
makers. From a research perspective, there are several issues with the academic field of
sports analytics, including football. First, research remains fragmented – most of the
articles are published by authors who do not further pursue this field [1]. Specifically
for football, it is noticeable that only few authors' names appear constantly in publications related to analytics from a specifics group of schools – mainly in the UK and
Portugal. Second, due to the competitive nature of sports there is a tendency to keep the
results secret and therefore a large number of the efforts are not published [2]. Finally,

© Springer International Publishing AG 2017
W. Abramowicz et al. (Eds.): BIS 2016 Workshops, LNBIP 263, pp. 357–366, 2017.
DOI: 10.1007/978-3-319-52464-1_33

the academic field of sports analytics has no natural target and thus, authors may be unsure of the most appropriate place to publish their research [2].

Despite of the above-mentioned issues, research in sports science and specifically football has advanced considerably in recent years, driven by the availability of technology for *notational analysis* (analysis of movement patterns, strategies and tactics in team sports [3]). The ultimate goal of such analysis is optimizing the performance of sports teams, their strategies and training programs.

Notational analysis is part of **performance analysis** (PA), which [4] described as an emerging discipline within sports science. Since then, there has been an increase in published papers on PA, mainly due to the availability of tracking technologies, as seen in [5]. In a nutshell, the goal of PA is to describe behaviors of performers (the players) in a "who (did)-what-where-and-when" fashion [6].

For football, and other sports, this is done by using **performance indicators.** A performance indicator (PI) is a demonstrated valid measure of important aspects of performance [4], like, shots, shots on goal, tackles, passes, dribbles, ball possession etc. There are quite a few companies offering solutions for gathering these data based on camera or sensor systems - Prozone and Opta Sports are some good examples. There is a rich body of research on PI in various sports, including football. From research perspective, the analyses are normally done ex post facto and is rather descriptive in nature [7]. In the last few years several authors are also requesting more research on alternative theory and methods for PA based on the notion that a football team acts as a horde of fish – players are constantly interacting and dynamically adjusting to each other's movements and actions [8–12]. An exhaustive review of the PA research in football is out of the scope of this paper. However, it should be briefly pointed out that in football, the performance indicators used in PA are generally classified in several categories [13]:

- Match classification: shots on/off target, corners, crosses etc.
- Biomechanical: kicking, ball projection velocity, throw-in etc.
- Technical: passes to opposition, tackles won and lost, dribbles etc.
- Tactical: passes/possession, shots, pace of attack etc.

Indicators as the above mentioned are used by sports analysts in practice who work with coaches and analyze the various data sources primarily pre-match and post-match. Until this moment, such data have not been extensively analyzed and used for in-game decision making in football. While club analysts are increasingly present during the game, it is not clear to which extent they support the coaches in this 90 min time-frame. In the future, football, similarly to other sports like basketball, cricket and baseball, will increasingly take advantage of the opportunities data analytics offers for improvement of decision making. The main drivers for adopting analytics are:

- The technology for tracking the players and the ball is constantly improving.
- Data storage and real-time processing becomes cheaper and more feasible.
- Benefits from data analysis are already clear both from other sports and from football itself. Major clubs like Liverpool and Chelsea are using data analysis for training purposes, signing contracts etc. [14].

2   Literature Review

Undoubtedly, the most important decision a football coach has to make during the live game is to decide when and which player should leave the game, and who he should be replaced with. This could have an important impact on the outcome of the match (latest popular example was Robert Lewandowski scoring five goals for Bayern Munich after he came in as a halftime substitute into a game which Bayern was losing 1–0 [15]).

There is a long list of factors that need to be considered to make this decision – physiological, psychological and fitness characteristics of the players, the quality and level of the opponent, match status and location, strategy, tactics [5, 16, 17]. In the past football coaches have mostly based their decisions on intuition and experience and were reluctant to use statistics because "that's the way it's always been done" [18]. This has brought them a lot of wins, but also losses. It used to be the norm since there were no cameras and sensors that could provide them with additional information on which to make an informative decision (some may argue that is not necessary today either). There are examples of coaches with excellent sense and intuition in football at times when such systems were something no one could think to be of any use in football (e.g., Sir Alex Ferguson). And yet, today the technology is available and the way football was perceived is over. Major football clubs are increasingly relying on tracking systems to improve the performance of their players. In addition, science has demonstrated that coaches can recall at most 40% of what happens during the game [19–21]. The proposed research project therefore, aims to explore possibilities to assist coaches in avoiding making decisions that can cost them to lose the game.

Based on the above, the **motivation** for this dissertation project is based on the following: the abundance of PA research in football, the availability of modern technologies for player tracking, and the impact of the substitution decision on the final outcome of the game. The **objective** is to develop a framework which will give the necessary process steps and method to be implemented for such system to be applied in practice.

A systematic literature review was conducted to extract papers related to substitution in football, or in-game decision support systems for coaches. Following the advice of [4], first, two highly relevant journals in Sports Science were searched through for review papers on substitution. These journals are *Sports Medicine* and *Exercise and Sport Sciences Reviews*, known for publishing only research reviews. The search ended without finding any review papers on substitution. I therefore continued to search for primary sources, which in sports science, according to [4], are papers in which data are analyzed and findings presented. The databases used were: Google Scholar, PubMed, Scopus, Sport Discus, Web of Science, and Springer. The keywords used were the following: substitution, tactics, strategy, "soccer AND substitution", "football AND substitution", "substitution AND basketball", "substitution AND rugby", "substitution AND hockey", "substitution AND volleyball", "substitution AND handball", "substitution AND sport". In total 33 papers on substitution in team sports were found, 15 of which were addressing football or soccer. In the following, only papers related to football substitution are discussed. Papers that directly investigated the substitution aspect in football were selected for deeper analyses. Each paper was then analyzed based on the guidelines for reviewing previous literature provided by [4]. An overview of the papers is presented in Table 1.

Results in Table 1 demonstrate that what [1, 2] mentioned as issues in sports science research, is still valid today. Most of the papers are from different authors with the exception of Hirotsu and Wright publishing occasionally between 2002 and 2009. There is a variety in the publication outlets as well. The focus of the review were peer reviewed journal articles but a few papers published in sports/football relevant magazines and discussion papers, were also considered [22–24].

Researchers so far have investigated which factors lead to substitution (e.g., home or away, current score, time left), the optimal timing for making substitution decision, including [25] who suggested a rule for optimal timing based on decision tree approach; optimal substitution strategy for changing formation and tactics [26–29]. Only one study has directly attempted to evaluate the match performances of substitute players – the authors, however, suggest that more work is needed to understand exactly what the impact of the substitute players are on the final outcome of the match [30].

The main issues identified from the reviewed papers have been reported previously in review papers such as the one by [5]. Some authors use a single match data [28]; others like [29, 31] use one season data from the English and the Spanish premier leagues respectively, while [22] uses match data from several seasons from the Bundesliga, and [25] use 485 observations of substitution patterns from three major leagues in Europe. Indication on number of matches from each team and season, however, are missing. Most of the authors do not describe in detail the data sets they used in their analysis, and specifically, valid contextual information about the matches analyzed, is missing. There is rarely an explanation of the data quality insurance or even how the data was collected. Finally, considering the different dataset, leagues, and analytical methods it would be unwise to make general conclusions or assumptions of when a substitution is best made taking into account factors like home or away, current game score, level of the opponent, among others.

Considering the above, the proposed research project seeks to answer the following **research question**: How can the substitution decision of the coach be enhanced in real-time by using live player tracking data? What would the requirements be? Which steps must be undertaken? Which data points are necessary/available and which analytical methods for real-time analytics would give the best results?

To answer the above question, there are a few additional points that need to be investigated as well:

- How has substitution affected the final outcome of football matches so far i.e. how important is substitution as a "tool" for coaches to influence the game?
- Which factors are most relevant for coaches when making substitutions? E.g., which performance indicators, contextual information?
- What type of analytics systems do coaches use during live games?
- How do coaches perceive the use of a decision support system for player substitution?
- How could coaches take advantage of the substitution system? E.g., formulate recommendations for usability and/or design principles which can be used by

Table 1. Literature review results

Author	Title	Year	Journal
Hirotsu and Wright	Using a Markov process model of an association football match to determine the optimal timing of substitution and tactical decisions	2002	The Journal of the Operational Research Society
Lenahan and Solari	The right players, right system: choosing lineups, changing systems, making substitutions in Real Madrid's title run	2002	Soccer Journal
Hirotsu and Wright	Determining the best strategy for changing the configuration of a football team	2003	The Journal of the Operational Research Society
Hirotsu and Wright	Modeling tactical changes of formation in association football as a zero-sum game	2006	Journal of Quantitative Analysis in Sports
Janković and Leontijević	Substitution of players in function of efficiency increase of tactic play plan in football	2006	Fizička kultura
del Corral et al.	The determinants of soccer player substitutions: a survival analysis of the Spanish soccer league	2008	Journal of Sports Economics
Geyer	Auswechselverhalten im Fußball - eine theoretische und empirische Analyse	2008	Sport und Gesellschaft – Sport and Society
Hirotsu et al.	Modeling tactical changes of formation in association football as a non-zero-sum game	2009	Journal of Quantitative Analysis in Sports
Woods and Thatcher	A qualitative exploration of substitutes' experiences in soccer	2009	Human Kinetics
Myers	A proposed decision rule for the timing of soccer substitutions	2012	Journal of Quantitative Analysis in Sports
Coelho et al.	Effect of player substitutions on the intensity of second-half soccer match play	2012	Revista Brasileira de Cineantr. & Desem. Humano
Bartling et al.	Expectations as Reference Points: Field Evidence from Experienced Subjects in a Competitive, High-Stakes Environment	2012	SSRN Journal
Bradley et al.	Evaluation of the match performances of substitution players in elite soccer	2014	International Journal of Sports Physiology and Performance
Rey et al.	Timing and tactical analysis of player substitutions in the UEFA champions league	2015	International Journal of Performance Analysis in Sport
Hindriyanto et al.	Soccer game optimization with substitute players	2015	Journal of Computational and Applied Mathematics

tracking system companies or club analysts to develop such system or use the method to analyze the player data.

In order to answer the above questions and be able to make general conclusions, three main steps will be undertaken

- A detailed literature review on performance analysis and substitution in football;
- Qualitative study with coaches and their staff – since none was identified from the literature so far;
- An extensive quantitative data analysis of publicly available match data from approx. ten seasons back from three major leagues in Europe – to address the issues with existing quantitative studies as described previously.

[4] mentions the challenges that original research can bring to the researcher in that previous research in the field will be scarce or non-existent. In such cases the author suggests that students should rely on work in related areas. For this research project a major challenge is that similar systems for football have not been developed, and information on substitution systems for other team sports is also rather scarce. There is an abundance of performance analysis research however, as well as previous, albeit non-conclusive research on substitution in football. Finally, conducting an original research is not unusual in the field of sports science as a relatively young research area [4].

3   Research Design

To answer the research questions presented in the previous section, the proposed project will use design science as research framework. According to [32] design is both a product (the innovative artifact) and a process (the steps necessary to create that product). The evaluation phase will then provide feedback to improve both the process and the product [32].

There are three research cycles in the DSR process [33]. The **relevance cycle** provides the problem or opportunity to be addressed in the chosen application *environment*. For the present research project, the opportunity was recognized by means of a preliminary literature review in the area of football analytics, and a consequent study with 22 coaches [34] (refer to Sect. 4 for more information). These two steps in the beginning revealed the opportunity for using the existing tracking systems and the fact that football is opening up to the world of analytics, to design a method/solution that would support the coach and his stuff during the live game. The **design cycle** builds on the findings in the *knowledge base*, which consists of review of existing tracking systems in football, performance analysis research, and a quantitative and qualitative studies that will be or are currently running (see Sect. 5). This part of the research is a constant feedback between the *build* and *evaluate* phases. Different alternatives for the algorithm will be tested and evaluated until satisfactory results are obtained. The **rigor cycle** should ensure that the knowledge base has been thoroughly referenced, that chosen design processes and methods for building and evaluating the artifact(s) are such that ensure their originality [33]. It must also provide the new *additions to the knowledge* - the artifacts and the experiences gained from the design science process. The research project will have three artifacts:

The **data model** will be based on the results of the quantitative and qualitative study, and the exhaustive review of PA research, as well as available tracking systems and the data types they collect. It will provide the *input* for the substitution recommendation to the coach. These will basically be the necessary data points that need to be collected in order for the recommendation/substitution suggestion to be generated. Examples include the previously mentioned performance indicators: tackles, passes, fouls, ball possession etc.

The **analytical method** will explain how the identified data points will be processed for the recommendation (the *output*) to be provided to the coach.

Design principles – presenting the guidelines for the chosen process steps for constructing the above artifacts and implementing them in practice based on the experiences from this research project.

The design science research methodology requires that the final artifact is **evaluated**. For this research project, the algorithm is the artifact that needs to be rigorously evaluated for accuracy and performance. The data schema will be primarily based on which data are available in general via reliable sources (e.g., OPTA Sports). Therefore, I will primarily focus on the algorithm evaluation and conclude with suggestions of how the data schema can be further extended in the future, when more data are available from the live game (e.g., fitness data). Determining whether a substitution recommendation made any difference for the match outcome, is a non-trivial task. If the coach follows the algorithms suggestion, how can we be certain that even in case of a win, it was the substitute player that contributed to it (unless this player is the one who scored the goal)? If the coach does not follow the recommendation, it is similarly hard to argument that it would have made an impact if he did. Therefore, the algorithm will be evaluated in retrospect. This means that it will be tested on games that have a known outcome and known substitute players.

4 Expected Contribution

The findings of this study should provide basis for a fruitful discussion on the advantages and disadvantages of using such system in football. When the technology is available and improving constantly, and the fact that analytics are being used increasingly in football, there is no reason to suggest that the system would not be useful for coaches. In fact, we conducted a preliminary study with 22 coaches from different leagues in Germany [34]. On a scale from 1 to 5 (with 1 meaning you would never use such a system and 5 that you always use it) none of the coaches said they would always use it, and only 4 said they would never use it. Most of the coaches stated that they would just use it as a support system as giving some hints but not without bringing in their own opinion and knowledge. And this is precisely the goal of the system [4] states that for a research in PA to be relevant, it should have some application in practice. The schema and the method developed by this study will probably not lead to immediate/instant application of the system in practice. The knowledge provided by this research project could be used in initial design and implementation of experimental DSS for player substitution in football.

5   Next Steps

The next steps include two major studies necessary for the data model to be determined. These are explained below.

Quantitative Study – analysis of substitution patterns and reasons, including starting formation and how this changes consequently following the substitution(s). Match data from seasons 2005 to 2015 from three major leagues in Europe will be analyzed in detail (the English Premier League, the German Bundesliga and the Spanish La Liga). The main objective is to remove the bias from the small sample sizes in previous studies and to consider tactical information as well as other contextual data, as explained previously. The expected insights are to understand better how, when and why substitutions are made and how this has affected the final outcome of the match.

Qualitative Study – interviews with coaches or co-coaches from professional leagues. The objective is to gain firsthand information on factors coaches consider when substituting a player, the analytical systems they are using during the live game (if any) and whether they would consider using a substitution system to support them in real-time in making a decision. From the reviewed papers, only [35] did a qualitative study, and this was exploring mainly the perceptions of the players being substitutes. A combination of both qualitative and quantitative study would therefore avoid the disadvantages of both types of research methods. Currently, ten interviews have been conducted with football experts like Christoph Daum and Stefan Effenberg among others.

In addition to the above steps, an in-depth literature review on performance analysis and available tracking systems that could be used to gather the data points necessary for the decision support system, is currently also being conducted and the preliminary results are available.

References

1. Wright, M.B.: 50 years of OR in sport. J. Oper. Res. Soc. **60**, S161–S168 (2009). doi:10.1057/jors.2008.170
2. Coleman, B.J.: Identifying the "players" in sports analytics research. Interfaces **42**(2), 109–118 (2012). doi:10.1287/inte.1110.0606
3. Carling, C., Williams, A.M., Reilly, T.: Handbook of Soccer Match Analysis. A Systematic Approach to Improving Performance. Routledge, London (2005)
4. O'Donoghue, P.: Research Methods for Sports Performance Analysis. Routledge, Milton Park (2009)
5. Castellano, J., Alvarez-Pastor, D., Bradley, P.S.: Evaluation of research using computerised tracking systems (Amisco and Prozone) to analyse physical performance in elite soccer: a systematic review. Sports Med. (Auckland, N.Z.) **44**(5), 701–712 (2014). doi:10.1007/s40279-014-0144-3
6. Vilar, L., Araújo, D., Davids, K., Button, C.: The role of ecological dynamics in analysing performance in team sports. Sports Med. (Auckland, N.Z.) **42**(1), 1–10 (2012). doi:10.2165/11596520-000000000-00000

7. Atkinson, G., Nevill, A.M.: Selected issues in the design and analysis of sport performance research. J. Sports Sci. **19**(10), 811–827 (2001). doi:10.1080/026404101317015447
8. Reed, D., Hughes, M.: An exploration of team sport as a dynamical system. Int. J. Perform. Anal. Sport **6**(2), 114–125 (2006)
9. Lames, M., McGarry, T.: On the search for reliable performance indicators in game sports. Int. J. Perform. Anal. Sport **7**(1), 62–79 (2007)
10. McGarry, T.: Applied and theoretical perspectives of performance analysis in sport: scientific issues and challenges. Int. J. Perform. Anal. Sport **9**(1), 128–140 (2009)
11. Travassos, B., Araújo, D., Correia, V., Esteves, P.: Eco-dynamics approach to the study of team sports performance. Open Sports Sci. J. **3**, 56–57 (2010)
12. Travassos, B., Davids, K., Araújo, D., Esteves, P.T.: Performance analysis in team sports: advances from an ecological dynamics approach. Int. J. Perform. Anal. Sport **13**(1), 83–95 (2013)
13. Hughes, M.D., Bartlett, R.M.: The use of performance indicators in performance analysis. J. Sports Sci. **20**(10), 739–754 (2002). doi:10.1080/026404102320675602
14. Lewis, T.: How computer analysts took over at Britain's top football clubs. The Guardian, 9 March 2014. http://www.theguardian.com/football/2014/mar/09/premier-league-football-clubs-computer-analysts-managers-data-winning. Accessed 22 Feb 2016
15. Das, A.: Robert Lewandowski Scores Five Goals in Nine Minutes for Bayern Munich. The New York Times, 22 September 2015. http://www.nytimes.com/2015/09/23/sports/soccer/robert-lewandowski-bayern-munich-five-goals.html. Accessed 22 Feb 2016
16. Castellano, J., Blanco-Villaseñor, A., Álvarez, D.: Contextual variables and time-motion analysis in soccer. Int. J. Sports Med. **32**(06), 415–421 (2011). doi:10.1055/s-0031-1271771
17. Taylor, J.B., Mellalieu, S.D., James, N., Shearer, D.A.: The influence of match location, quality of opposition, and match status on technical performance in professional association football. J. Sports Sci. **26**(9), 885–895 (2008). doi:10.1080/02640410701836887
18. Anderson, C., Sally, D.: The Numbers Game. Why Everything You Know About Football is Wrong. Penguin Books, London (2014)
19. Hughes, M., Franks, I.M.: Notational Analysis of Sport. Systems for Better Coaching and Performance in sport, 2nd edn. Routledge, London (2004)
20. Hughes, M., Franks, I.M.: The Essentials of Performance Analysis. An Introduction. Routledge, London (2008)
21. Franks, I.M., Miller, G.: Training coaches to observe and remember. J. Sports Sci. **9**(3), 285–297 (1991). doi:10.1080/02640419108729890
22. Geyer, H.: Auswechselverhalten im Fußball: Eine theoretische und empirische Analyse. IÖB-Diskussionspapiere 5/08, University of Münster, Institute for Economic Education (2008). https://ideas.repec.org/p/zbw/ioebdp/508.html
23. Bartling, B., Brandes, L., Schunk, D.: Expectations as reference points. Field evidence from experienced subjects in a competitive, high-stakes environment. SSRN J. (2012). doi:10.2139/ssrn.2053180
24. Coelho, D.B., Coelho, L.G.M., Morandi, R.F., Ferreira Junior, J.B., Marins, J.C.B., Prado, L.S., Soares, D.D., Silami-Garcia, E.: Effect of player substitutions on the intensity of second-half soccer match play. Rev. Bras. de Cineantropometria Desempenho Humano **14**(2), 183–191 (2012)
25. Myers, B.R.: A proposed decision rule for the timing of soccer substitutions. J. Quant. Anal. Sports **8**(1) (2012). doi:10.1515/1559-0410.1349
26. Hirotsu, N., Wright, M.B.: Modeling tactical changes of formation in association football as a zero-sum game. J. Quant. Anal. Sports **2**(2) (2006). doi:10.2202/1559-0410.1017

27. Hirotsu, N., Ito, M., Miyaji, C., Hamano, K., Taguchi, A.: Modeling tactical changes of formation in association football as a non-zero-sum game. J. Quant. Anal. Sports **5**(3) (2009). doi:10.2202/1559-0410.1138
28. Hirotsu, N., Wright, M.: Using a Markov process model of an association football match to determine the optimal timing of substitution and tactical decisions. J. Oper. Res. Soc. **53**(1), 88–96 (2002)
29. Hirotsu, N., Wright, M.: Determining the best strategy for changing the configuration of a football team. J. Oper. Res. Soc. **54**(8), 878–887 (2003). doi:10.1057/palgrave.jors.2601591
30. Bradley, P.S., Lago-Peñas, C., Rey, E.: Evaluation of the match performances of substitution players in elite soccer. IJSPP **9**(3), 415–424 (2014). doi:10.1123/ijspp.2013-0304
31. Del Corral, J., Barros, C.P., Prieto-Rodriguez, J.: The determinants of soccer player substitutions. A survival analysis of the Spanish soccer league. J. Sports Econ. **9**(2), 160–172 (2007). doi:10.1177/1527002507308309
32. Hevner, A.R., March, S.T., Park, J., Ram, S.: Design science in information systems research. MIS Q. **28**(1), 75–105 (2004)
33. Hevner, A.R., Chatterjee, S.: Design Research in Information Systems. Theory and Practice. Integrated Series in Information Systems, vol. 22. Springer, New York (2010)
34. Davcheva, P., Schuster, B., Hille, M., Götz, R., Zhang, J.: Decision support system for player substitution in football - prototypical implementation Nürnberg: Lehrstuhl Wirtschaftsinformatik, insbes. im Dienstleistungsbereich, Universität Erlangen-Nürnberg (2016)
35. Woods, B., Thatcher, J.: A qualitative exploration of substitutes' experiences in soccer. Sport Psychol. **23**(4), 451–469 (2009)

A Bayesian Network Approach to Assessing the Risk and Reliability of Maritime Transport

Milena Stróżyna[✉]

Poznań University of Economics and Business, Poznań, Poland
milena.strozyna@kie.ue.poznan.pl

Abstract. The paper presents a conception of a doctoral dissertation, which concerns the problem of estimation of maritime risk and reliability of maritime transport services. In the dissertation a method for dynamic risk assessment based on the Bayesian Network approach is presented. The method concern the risk of an individual ship and its aim is to identify ships, which pose a potential threat due to their individual behaviour and characteristics. Within the article, the following aspects of the dissertation are presented: motivation standing behind the research, main assumptions for the proposed method, its novelty in comparison to existing solutions as well as preliminary results.

1 Introduction

Along with the development of technology, shipping has become an increasingly efficient and swift mode of transport. Nowadays, around 90% of the global trade by volume and 70% by value is carried by sea. As a result, the maritime transport plays nowadays a key role in transporting goods and supply chain management, being the backbone of the international trade and the leader in terms of transport economics. In this context, provision of high reliability of maritime transport is key. The reliability means successful performance of shipment under operating conditions, at a given time and with no damage to a cargo. This, in turn, requires ensuring supply security and risk management.

Taking into account the variety of maritime threats and anomalies, like involvement of ships in illegal activities, maritime accidents, pollution, piracy and terrorism, estimation of the maritime risk and the transport reliability is a crucial aspect. However, there is still a need for appropriate methods and systems, which would allow to assess the risk for an individual ship, taking into account a wide range of possible threats and which would allow to assess risk dynamically and on a continual basis. The existing approaches to the maritime risk assessment do not include all these aspects and focus mainly on a single type of threat and the estimation of risk in the long term.

This paper presents a method for assessment of the maritime risk, by estimating dynamically the risk posed by an individual ship. The method is based on the Bayesian Network and allows to evaluate the reliability of the maritime transport in the short-term horizon. The proposed approach is addressed to various entities from the maritime domain, such as logistics providers and receivers

© Springer International Publishing AG 2017
W. Abramowicz et al. (Eds.): BIS 2016 Workshops, LNBIP 263, pp. 367–378, 2017.
DOI: 10.1007/978-3-319-52464-1_34

of transported cargo, since it is about facilitating the automatic comparison of ships from the point of view of the risk they pose and the reliability of supply.

The structure of the paper includes the motivation for the research (Sect. 2), literature review (Sect. 3), indication of identified gaps, followed by presentation of research objectives and the method (Sect. 4) as well as preliminary research results (Sect. 5). The article concludes with indication of future work.

2   Importance of the Research

With the growing seaborne trade increases the usage of maritime areas. This in turn leads to the rising number of various maritime threats and anomalies, despite existence of a number of maritime codes and conventions, which regulate the security and performance of the maritime transport. The threats encompass a behaviour, deviating from what is usual, normal, expected, or that is not conforming to rules and laws in force, such as illegal activities at sea, pollution, piracy and terrorism as well as a trend to register merchant vessels under the "flag of convenience" and dangerous behaviour of ships (grounding, sudden change of speed, deviation from standard route, close proximity to other objects) [1,2]. As a result, the issues of controlling the maritime traffic, providing security and safety of ships and cargo and ensuring the reliability of maritime transport gain nowadays in importance.

The maritime security is the status of conditions under which a threat to life, health, property and environment does not exceed the acceptable level of risk [3]. The maritime security can be also considered from the point of view of the supply reliability. It is defined as the level of guarantee that the cargo shipped by a vessel will be successfully delivered to a customer (recipient of cargo).

The measure of the supply reliability is a risk (probability of occurrence) of an undesired event (threat), negatively influencing the delivery. This event can be related to human life, ship or environment. This means that the higher risk posed by a ship, the lower reliability of supply. Thus, assessment of the maritime risk is required in order to determine the reliability of maritime transport.

According to the SOLAS convention, ships and ports are obliged to develop individual plans of protection and defence against threats. The plan should include analysis and assessment of risk for various categories of threats and mitigations measures. However, such a plan is developed by the shipowner and is confidential. It means that other entities do not have access to the results of the risk assessment of a particular ship and are forced to assess the risk level on their own.

Taking into account the above-mentioned challenges, the dissertation concerns development of a novel approach to dynamic assessment of risk posed by an individual ship. The proposed method may be helpful for various entities from the maritime domain in conducting a risk analysis and determination of reliability of supply of goods by sea.

3 Literature Review

The research on risk assessment has a long history in other domains, like health, finance, insurance or project management as well as in transport industries (air, rail and military). In various applications different approaches, analytic methods and systems are used, starting from the statistical analysis, through simulation based on historical data, artificial intelligence methods to rule-based systems. Depending on the specific features of the domain, different methods, variables and data are used. In this context, also the risk assessment of the maritime transport requires taking into consideration domain-specific features, such as dynamic changes of sea conditions, types of data (e.g. localization and routes) and the variety of maritime threats.

There exist diverse approaches to the maritime risk analyses (see e.g. [4]). In 2010, shipping companies agreed to use standardized procedures in order to assess risk in key shipboard operations, proposed by the International Maritime Organisation. It is called the Formal Safety Assessment (FSA) [5,6]. FSA process consists of five steps [7]:

1. Identification of all hazards related to an activity or a ship,
2. Risk assessment, consisting in building a risk model and determining probabilities and consequences for all branches of the risk model,
3. Identification of risk control options, which can mitigate the most important risk,
4. Costs/benefits assessment for each option of risk mitigation and preparing a ranking of risk control options,
5. Recommendations for decision making and development of a plan of the activities, if viable.

There are many different analysis techniques and models that have been developed to aid in conducting different FSA steps. Since FSA is relatively new standard, these methods are still under development and testing. Some examples are presented in the following paragraphs[1].

With regard to hazard identification, popular methods are: literature review, brainstorming, interviews with experts, or more formalized methods like HAZOP, FMEA, HAZID [7,8]

The risk assessment concerns mainly building a risk model. From the point of view of information systems, the risk models are developed based on various artificial intelligence and machine learning methods. They focus mainly on modelling a "normal behaviour" of a ships by using supervised and unsupervised techniques, such as classification, SVM, clustering, neural networks, rule-based systems [9–11].

The existing methods can be also divided into qualitative and quantitative. The first includes statistic analysis based on historical data [12], Fault and Event Tree Analysis [6], Bayesian Networks [5], correlation analysis and fuzzy

---

[1] Since the research focuses only on the first two steps of FSA, only methods for risk identification and assessment are presented.

logic [13,14]. The quantitative methods encompass risk matrices, risk profiles or risk indexes/rankings [8]. The last one can be used to make relative comparison of various objects of the same type when it comes to their attributes (e.g. ship's characteristics).

In this research, utilization of Bayesian Network (BN) is assumed. This approach has some advantages in comparison to other methods, which are important from the point of view og the risk analysis. These are: ability to model cause-effect and casual relations between variables and their probability distribution (inclusion of uncertainty), tolerance for missing data, possibility to include a prior information (expert knowledge) and ability to model changes in time (by using the dynamic BNs). BNs are also easier to validate and evaluate [15]. Moreover, the literature shows that BNs were successfully used in other domains for the risk assessment: ecology [16], natural hazards [17,18], project and enterprise risk management [11] and health [19]. Finally, BN models are more and more used in dependability analyses to support aspects such as reliability, availability and maintainability [20].

4   Research Objectives and Method

The problem of detection of high risk ships, which do not provide high reliability of transport services, is one of the key aspects of international supply chains management. It is crucial for various entities working in the maritime domain (e.g. logistic providers, maritime operators) to effectively assure high quality of logistic services.

The conducted literature review allowed to reveal some shortcomings or disadvantages of the existing methods. Firstly, they focus on estimating risk of either a specified hazard (e.g. collision, oil spill) or an undesired event in relation to ship's technical attributes (e.g. problem with engine) or a human error. As a result, they take into account only selected factors, strictly connected with a given type of hazard. Besides, the estimated risk concerns a particular group of ships (e.g. tankers with the same or similar characteristics) instead of an individual ship.

Secondly, the analysed methods use limited set of factors, like technical characteristics of a ship, experience of the crew, history of accidents. They do not include aspects which may change in time (e.g. flag, owner, classification status), current and historical anomalies in ship's behaviour, past routes and current localization.

Finally, they provide information about the long- or mid-term risk level (especially, when it comes to reliability of supply performed by merchant ships) [21]. The short-term risk, which may change dynamically in time is not included (with exception of the method proposed by Balmat et al. [13]).

Behind the background discussed in the previous sections as well as identified gaps in the area of maritime risk assessment, the author propose a novel Maritime Risk Assessment Method (MRAM) for merchant ships, allowing to dynamically assess level of risk and reliability of supply of an individual ship.

In the following sections the research objectives and main assumptions of the proposed method are presented.

4.1 Research Objectives

The objectives of the research are as follows:

1. To develop a Maritime Risk Assessment Method (MRAM), based on Bayesian Network approach, used for dynamic analysis of risk and reliability of an individual ship.
2. To evaluate the efficiency of the proposed method through set of experiments performed using the real data.

The overall methodology used within the dissertation follows principles devised by the design science [22]. The research is structured into the following steps: state of the art analysis, identification of shortcoming and gaps (problem definition), artifact design in order to fulfil the requirements identified during the problem definition and finally evaluation based on a set of experiments. The research assumes adoption of solutions known in other fields (Bayesian Networks) to new problems (maritime risk analysis). The artifact to be developed and evaluated is MRAM method.

The posed research questions and detailed research goals encompass:

- How to indicate which ships are the most risky with regard to realization of the transport service? Which ships guarantee the highest reliability of goods' supply?
  Goals: determination of quality attributes of transport services realized by sea, definition of the maritime risk and its relation with security of the maritime transport and the reliability of goods' supply.
- How to estimate individual risk level for a ship? What factors and variables determine this risk level?
  Goal: review and selection of quantitative and qualitative methods for the risk assessment and creation of risk classifiers based on real maritime-related data.
- Which factors and variables are significant for the risk assessment?
  Goal: determination of weights for given variables, according to various business scenarios.
- How to estimate risk dynamically (short-term risk) and individually for each ship?
  Goal: proposal of a method for dynamic processing and analysing of maritime-related.
- How to evaluate the proposed method?
  Goals: conduct set of experiments based on real maritime-related data, which would allow to determine the efficiency of MRAM and compare it to other maritime risk assessment approaches.

We hypothesise that utilization of MRAM, which dynamically evaluates individual risk of a ship, will allow to improve the process of discovering and ranking ships from the point of view of the risk they pose and the reliability of goods' supply.

4.2 Research Method

MRAM dynamically calculates the individual risk of a given ship and thus allows to assess the quality and the reliability of the transport service realised by the ship. The method is based on the risk index approach, which consists of four types of risk factors (classifiers): static, dynamic, voyage-related and history-related.

The individual risk index means that the risk is being estimated separately for each ship based on its individual features. The dynamic risk assessment means that the level of risk for each ship may change in time and depends not only on static variables (e.g. age, size), but also dynamic ones (e.g. actual route, position, navigational status). The index is an one-dimensional measure, which indicates the level of reliability of the transport service being realised by a particular ship.

Moreover, MRAM assumes differentiation of critical factors, which more heavily may influence the overall risk. These factors are distinguished by assigning weights to them. This allows to take into account different context and business scenarios in which the method can be used (e.g. the importance of a given factor can be different for different actors/stakeholders).

In MRAM, we limit our discussion to the risk of an undesirable event and define the maritime risk as the probability of occurrence of an undesirable event, or the chance of a loss, which in turn may negatively influence the reliability of supply. This undesirable event may be caused by a ship, due to its individual features and/or behaviour.

In the research we focus only on transport performed by merchant cargo vessels. It includes only ships, which transport cargo for hire, such as general cargo, tankers, bulk carriers, containers.

In comparison to the existing methods for the maritime risk assessment, MRAM provides some advantages. Firstly, it focuses on estimation of the overall risk for a ship, not the risk of an undesirable event or threat related to human error or technical matters. Moreover, it takes into account 4 different types of risk and includes variables, which have not been yet used to estimate the maritime risk, such as past anomalies, classification status, detentions and bans, etc. Finally, the proposed method calculates the risk dynamically, what allows to determine the reliability of supply in the short-term horizon and individually for each ship.

The proposed approach is a flexible solution, which may be utilized by various entities from the maritime domain. Firstly, MRAM can provide information about the ships with the low supply reliability. Here interested entities are logistic companies, senders and recipients of goods, ship owners/managers, etc. Besides, the results may indicate ships which require special attention due to safety and security reasons. Here potential users are port authorities (maritime offices, custom services, SAR, etc.) and state authorities (in order to control the supply of key resources like gas or oil). The aim of MRAM is to support users in making decisions and may be incorporated into the existing maritime and logistic systems for monitoring fleet or maritime traffic as well as in intelligent navigational systems.

5   Preliminary Results

In this section the results of the already conducted work on the proposed method is presented. It encompasses identification of risk factors, selection of data sources, determination of statical variables significant for the risk estimation and proposal of models for the static risk classifier.

5.1   Risk Factors and Risk Assessment

The risk for a ship may depend on various factors and variables, which altogether determine the overall risk level (risk index). In the proposed method these variables were divided into 4 risk factors (Table 1).

Table 1. Risk factors

Name	Description	Variables
Static	Static attributes of a ship, which do not change at all or change very rare	Size, flag, age, type, classification society, classification status
Voyage-related	Variables connected with a current voyage of a ship	Crew, type of cargo, departure and destination port/country
Dynamic	Variables that change during the voyage as well as anomalies in ship's behaviour	Weather conditions, incomplete AIS messages, deviations from standard routes, change of static parameters, ambiguous identification, loitering at high sea
History-related	Historical information about a ship and detected past anomalies	Past detentions, accidents, visited ports, port state controls

Moreover it is assumed that each risk factor and each variable has a different weight assigned. The weights may change for different maritime scenarios/contexts and reflect the significance of a given factor for a given stakeholder in a given context.

Table 1 and Fig. 1 presents examples of variables, which may be taken into account in MRAM for calculation of the overall risk. Each of these variables can have a positive or a negative influence on the risk level. This influence may be estimated based on analytical methods (quantitative approach) or opinion and knowledge of experts (qualitative approach). The quantitative approach encompasses such analyses methods as correlation, regression, building classifiers or rankings [23], which provide information about significance of a given variable in the further reasoning and the assessment of risk. The qualitative approach includes a fuzzy logic and if-then rules techniques [14]. In order to connect results of both approaches, Bayesian Networks (BN) are used, which allows to include both deterministic and probabilistic information.

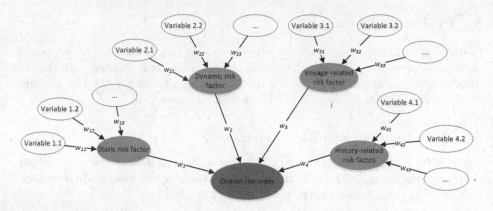

Fig. 1. The risk factors and the overall risk index

In the proposed method, BN allows to model the structure of variables which influence a given risk factor and based on that estimate the risk level. Knowing the value of the overall risk index it is then possible to rank the ships according the risk they pose (the reliability of supply).

5.2 Data Sources

In order to assess the maritime risk, various data may be used. The author has already analysed and selected data sources, which are going to be used to perform the evaluation of MRAM and to determine variables which should be taken into account in the risk calculation.

The first data source is Automatic Identification System (AIS). AIS is an automatic tracking system used for identifying and locating vessels in real time. It is based on automatic exchange of data about a ship and its movement with other nearby ships, AIS base stations and satellites. It includes navigational data (location, course, speed, navigational status), static data (identification numbers, type, name, callsign) and voyage data (destination port, estimated time of arrival). Nowadays, AIS is used as one of the main data source in the maritime surveillance.

Another group of data sources are open Internet databases (open data published in various maritime-related Internet sources). They encompass data about ship's accidents (GISIS database[2]), detentions and inspections of ships (databases of Tokyo[3], Indian Ocean[4], Mediterranean[5] and Black Sea[6] MoU's and US

---

[2] https://gisis.imo.org.
[3] http://www.tokyo-mou.org/.
[4] http://www.iomou.org/.
[5] http://www.medmou.org/.
[6] http://www.bsmou.org/.

Coast Guard[7]), ships characteristics (data available at MarineTraffic[8], Maritime-Connector[9] and ITU MARS[10]) and classification of ships (IACS database and reports[11]).

The data from the selected sources has already been retrieved during the work on the related project SIMMO.

5.3   Selection of Variables for Static Classifier

After definition of MRAM's assumptions and selection of data sources, the further work concerned assessment and selection of variables for the proposed risk classifiers. In the first instance, the analyses were focused on variables for the static factor. The analysed variables included: ship's age, size, type, flag, classification society and classification status.

In order to determine, which of the static variables are significant for the risk determination, three types of analyses were conducted: correlation, logistic regression and finally building of BN.

In the conducted analyses, apart from the data about ships retrieved from the data sources listed in the previous paragraph, also data on maritime accidents from the GISIS database was used. It was assumed that if a ship took part in an accident, the risk level for this ship is higher than for ships that never caused any accident. The size of the sample was 466 accidents, including 533 ships (accidental ships), which have happened in the period 01.01.2014-15.03.2016. Besides, for some of the conducted analyses also the data about non-accidental ships was included.

Firstly, it was analysed what is the relation between the static attributes (flag, classification society, classification status, type, size and age) and the accident rate. Based on that the following results were obtained:

– *flag* - a list of flags with the highest accident rate and weights for different flags, saying how risky the ships flying a given flag are, taking into account the accident rate,
– *classification society* - selection of unreliable classification societies (with regard to the accident rate),
– *classification status* - selection of classification statuses, which may influence the accident rate; almost one third of the ships with accident history had *suspended* or *withdrawn* status, when accident happened; both statuses indicate that the accidental ships did not meet all safety-related requirements and standards, what may have contributed to the accident,
– *type* - a list of the most dangerous ship types,

---

[7] http://cgmix.uscg.mil/PSIX/PSIXSearch.aspx.
[8] https://www.marinetraffic.com.
[9] http://maritime-connector.com.
[10] http://www.itu.int/en/ITU-R/terrestrial/mars/Pages/MARS.aspx.
[11] http://www.iacs.org.uk/shipdata.

– *size* - a distribution of ship's size among the accidental ships; result: mostly small ships (below 500GT) cause the accidents,
– *age* - a distribution of ship's age among the accidental ships; result: mostly young ships (below 5 years) cause the accidents;

Then, the correlation analysis between the accident rate and the ship's age and flag using 3 correlation coefficients was performed[12]. The obtained results show that there is a moderate positive relation between flag and accident rate. It means that along with the increase of the number of ships flying a given flag, increases the accident rate. Correlation between the accident rate and the age is moderate and negative, which means that with the age, the number of accidents decreases. The calculated coefficients can be used as a weights for particular variables.

In the next step, the regression analysis was performed and two logistic regression models were developed (using the Bayesian generalized linear model). The models allow to determine the probability of an accident based on the static attributes of a ship. The main difference between the models is that the first takes the original distribution of all variables, while the second takes the linearised quantitative variables (age, size)[13]. Nevertheless, evaluation of the models showed that both can be used as the static risk classifiers, however only two variables (age and type) are significant.

Finally, in order to determine relations between all the analysed static variables, a model of Bayesian Network was developed. The model shows the cause-effect relationships between variables and provides probability distribution of the static attributes. It can be used to estimate the probability of making an accident by a particular ship, knowing its static attributes.

The structure of the BN was learnt, based on the real data about ships and accidents, using the method proposed by [24]. To determine the best version of the BN, a set of experiments were performed, in which various versions of BN were analysed and compared. In this process also results and constraints from the previous analyses (correlation and regression) were taken into account. Based on the log marginal likelihood measure, the model of BN best fitted to the empirical data was then selected (Fig. 2). The model shows that the significant variables for assessment of risk for the static classifier are: age, type, classification status (suspended and withdrawn).

To sum up, the paper presents the assumptions and results of work conducted on the Maritime Risk Assessment Method. The research so far concerned the definition of the maritime factors and variables, the selection of data sources as well as the analyses of variables for the estimation of the static risk factor. Future

---

[12] Correlation analysis was limited to quantitative variables only (age and number of ships flying a given flag). It results from the assumptions to use the following coefficients: Pearson, Kendall and Spearman. Besides, the existence of correlation between ship's size and accident rate was confirmed using the nCochran-Mantek-Haenschel and Fisher tests.

[13] The distribution of original quantitative variables (age and size) is not linear what may influence the results of model's calculations.

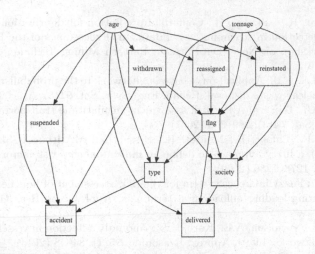

Fig. 2. Model of Bayesian Network for static risk factor

work on will concern further verification of the developed models for the static risk estimation, determination of models for the three remaining risk factors and the overall risk index, and finally evaluation of the whole method. Moreover, consultation with the maritime experts is envisioned in order to ensure that results of MRAM meet their requirements and needs.

References

1. Krzysztof, F., Sokołowski, W.: Środki transportu morskiego w zapewnieniu bezpieczeństwa dostaw gazu ziemnego. Logistyka **401** (2012)
2. el Pozo, F., Dymock, A., Feldt, L., Hebrard, P., di Monteforte, F.S.: Maritime surveillance in support of CSDP. Technical report, European Defence Agency (2010)
3. Urbański, J., Morgaś, W., Specht, C.: Bezpieczeństwo morskie – ocena i kontrola ryzyka. Zeszyty Naukowe Akademii Marynarki Wojennej **2**(173), 53–68 (2008)
4. Goerlandt, F., Montewka, J.: Maritime transportation risk analysis: review and analysis in light of some foundational issues. Reliab. Eng. Syst. Saf. **138**, 115–134 (2015)
5. Trucco, P., Cagno, E., Ruggeri, F., Grande, O.: A Bayesian belief network modelling of organisational factors in risk analysis: a case study in maritime transportation. Reliab. Eng. Syst. Saf. **93**(6), 823–834 (2008)
6. Berle, O.Y., Asbjørnslett, B.R.E., Rice, J.B.: Formal vulnerability assessment of a maritime transportation system. Reliab. Eng. Syst. Saf. **96**(6), 696–705 (2011)
7. Ellis, J., Forsman, B., Gehl, S., Langbecker, U., Riedel, K., Sames, P.C.: A risk model for the operation of container vessels. WMU J. Marit. Aff. **7**(1), 133–149 (2008)
8. ABS: Guidance notes on Risk Assessement Applications for the Marine and Offshore Oil and Gas Industries. Technical report, American Bureau of Shipping (2000)
9. Chandola, V., Banerjee, A., Kumar, V.: Anomaly detection: a survey. ACM Comput. Surv. **41**(3), 15:1–15:58 (2009)

10. Laxhammar, R., Falkman, G.: Conformal prediction for distribution-independent anomaly detection in streaming vessel data. In: Proceedings of the First International Workshop on Novel Data Stream Pattern Mining Techniques, pp. 47–55. ACM (2010)

11. Lee, C.J., Lee, K.J.: Application of bayesian network to the probabilistic risk assessment of nuclear waste disposal. Reliab. Eng. Syst. Saf. **91**(5), 515–532 (2006)

12. Soares, C.G., Teixeira, A.P.: Risk assessment in maritime transportation. Reliab. Eng. Syst. Saf. **74**(3), 299–309 (2001)

13. Balmat, J.F., Lafont, F., Maifret, R., Pessel, N.: MAritime RISk Assessment (MARISA), a fuzzy approach to define an individual ship risk factor. Ocean Eng. **36**(15–16), 1278–1286 (2009)

14. Elsayed, T.: Fuzzy inference system for the risk assessment of liquefied natural gas carriers during loading/offloading at terminals. Appl. Ocean Res. **31**(3), 179–185 (2009)

15. Mascaro, S., Nicholson, A.E., Korb, K.B.: Anomaly detection in vessel tracks using bayesian networks. Int. J. Approx. Reasoning **55**(1), 84–98 (2014)

16. Pollino, C.A., Woodberry, O., Nicholson, A., Korb, K., Hart, B.T.: Parameterisation and evaluation of a bayesian network for use in an ecological risk assessment. Environ. Model. Softw. **22**(8), 1140–1152 (2007)

17. Grêt-Regamey, A., Straub, D.: Spatially explicit avalanche risk assessment linking bayesian networks to a GIS. Nat. Hazards Earth Syst. Sci. **6**(6), 911–926 (2006)

18. Straub, D., et al.: Natural hazards risk assessment using bayesian networks. Saf. Reliab. Eng. Systems Struct., 2535–2542 (2005)

19. Liu, K.F.R., Lu, C.F., Chen, C.W., Shen, Y.S.: Applying Bayesian belief networks to health risk assessment. Stoch. Env. Res. Risk Assess. **26**(3), 451–465 (2012)

20. Weber, P., Medina-Oliva, G., Simon, C., Iung, B.: Overview on bayesian networks applications for dependability, risk analysis and maintenance areas. Eng. Appl. Artif. Intell. **25**(4), 671–682 (2012)

21. Kowalski, J., Kozera, J.: Mapa zagrożeń bezpieczeństwa energetycznego RP w sektorach ropy naftowej i gazu ziemnego. In: Bezpieczeństwo Narodowe, pp. 301–324. BBN, Warszawa (2009)

22. Alan, H., March, S.T., Park, J., Ram, S.: Design science in information systems research. MIS Q. **28**(1), 75–105 (2004)

23. Eleye-Datubo, A.G., Wall, A., Wang, J.: Marine and offshore safety assessment by incorporative risk modeling in a fuzzy-Bayesian network of an induced mass assignment paradigm. Risk Anal. **28**(1), 95–112 (2008)

24. Friedman, N., Koller, D.: Being Bayesian about network structure. In: Proceedings of the Sixteenth Conference on Uncertainty in Artificial Intelligence, pp. 201–210. Morgan Kaufmann Publishers Inc. (2000)

Development of an Information System Architecture for Online Surgery Scheduling

Norman Spangenberg[✉]

Information Systems Institute, Leipzig University,
Grimmaische Straße 12, 04109 Leipzig, Germany
spangenberg@wifa.uni-leipzig.de

Abstract. This work presents the current state of a PhD thesis about optimizing decision-making in operating room management with an integrated information systems architecture for a decision support system. A design-science research approach is used to develop an architecture that fills the gap for operational decision support by integrating data sources, decision support models and real-time information. After identifying the current state-of-the-art in operational decision support systems, a requirements analysis was started. The first results lead to an architecture in development status. Future work will complete requirements and architecture model and further in a prototypical implementation for evaluation.

Keywords: Online surgery scheduling · Information systems architecture · Decision support systems

1 Introduction and Importance of the Research

Many kinds of business activities need support for decision making, e.g. for the strategic, tactical or operational planning of service operations or production plans. While there are many research contributions and business solutions for the strategic and tactical level of business planning, the support for operational business execution gained less attention. Most of these systems just support the tasks before the execution of the schedule starts. Within execution of the schedules, production managers or dispatchers are on their own. They have to observe the environment, detect deviations and handle unpredictable events to reschedule the execution plan for further optimizations just in seconds without support of information systems (IS) [1, 2]. A main reason for this lack of support is a lack of fine-grained and up-to-date information about the status of resources or process progress. So the decisions were resolved by intuition and experience but humans are not able to control or optimize such complex production environments [3]. Such situations can be described as dynamic decision tasks. They occur in many business use cases like maintaining ships [4] or aircrafts [5], but also in manufacturing environments with labour-intensive work [6]. Another very important area with uncertainties, unexpected events, urgency and time pressure [7] in operational decision making is in disaster and emergency management, e.g. for flood-warnings [8] or emergency response [9].

© Springer International Publishing AG 2017
W. Abramowicz et al. (Eds.): BIS 2016 Workshops, LNBIP 263, pp. 379–388, 2017.
DOI: 10.1007/978-3-319-52464-1_35

One facility to treat such emergencies are hospitals. Inside the hospital with the intensive care unit and the operating theatre area are facilities with many uncertainties and time pressure. Further, in healthcare there is an ever-increasing cost pressure too. Studies in Germany reveal that only operating theatre unit have cost rates about 3000€ [10, 11] per hour and operating room. For an efficient operating room area various planning and scheduling decisions about hospital facilities, patients and medical staff have to be done. Additionally emergency cases and possible delays have to be considered in real-time by the operating room manager, who is the leading decision maker in operational operating room management (OPM). The tasks for online surgery scheduling are embedded in the area of responsibilities of the operating room management. OPM is defined as the coordination of all surgical-related processes in a hospital. The overall goal is to provide surgical treatment in a high quality and secondary to achieve a high productivity and efficiency [12–14]. In detail there is also a distinction for the strategic and tactical tasks of OPM and operational tasks in OPM, which are labelled operating room or surgery scheduling [15–17]:

- Strategic level: Means the scaling and determining of core resources for business operations, e.g. number of operating rooms, medical staff and devices. The planning horizon is long-termed, usually one year or more.
- Tactical level: Defines a coarse-grained surgery plan with specific time blocks for medical departments and allocates limited resources, but has no fixed sequences for cases. The time horizon is mid-termed, e.g. 2–6 weeks.
- Operational level: Consists of an offline scheduling phase for specifying surgery orders and detailing resource allocation with a one-week time horizon. In an online-scheduling phase the management and monitoring of a surgery day, as well as the handling of emergency patients and delays is done.

The key feature of the scheduling process at operational level is the coordination of several and multiple activities in an uncertain environment. It is characterized by various uncertainties like duration of single cases, complications and interruptions, recovery processes, emergency patients, patient no-shows or staff availability [17].

This dynamics and uncertainties make it challenging to coordinate the surgical processes in an efficient and patient-safe manner. Much communicative effort is needed to collect all information about the current status and timely progress of surgical interventions, because there is no or just inaccurate and outdated data provided by the hospital information system (HIS) [13, 17]. Further the operating room manager needs a lot of experience and expert knowledge to handle uncertainties and events, or to estimate remaining surgery durations. Although some guidelines for such decisions exist, the manager can vary in their decisions [18]. And lastly, there is no software support for the online surgery planning. Despite there are tools for offline planning included in the HIS, there is no support for gathering and visualizing data for online surgery scheduling, even less for a decision support. In academia much effort is expended to develop new models and algorithms for surgical planning and scheduling problems [17, 19]. But the focus of this work is on offline planning, not on online scheduling. In addition the applicability of research effort according to [19] is small and even more so the integration of this models in HIS or other software applications in the surgery management.

The rest of this work is structured as follows. In Sect. 2 some theoretical foundations concerning the topic are introduced. Section 3 provides the considered research questions and Sect. 4 first results. Section 5 describes the research methodology, followed by the conclusion and outlook.

2 Literature Review

This section discuss basic literature about the organizational structure and decision tasks in surgery planning and scheduling. In addition there is an overview about fundamentals of DSS.

2.1 Online Surgery Scheduling Problem

According to the categorization of scheduling problems by [2] surgery scheduling can be seen as predictive-reactive scheduling [20]. This type of scheduling is characterized by a two-step process consisting of a predictive scheduling phase and a rescheduling phase. Related to the tasks of an operating room manager, the initial planning of a surgery day describes the desired behaviour, e.g. patient arrivals or operating room occupancy. In case of unexpected disruptions mentioned above the rescheduling phase modifies the current schedule concerning e.g. integrating emergency cases, just as start time or overall time of running and future procedures.

The problem of coordinating human activities can also be seen from an organizational perspective [21]. From this point of view the online surgery scheduling problem is a hierarchical coordination problem with a higher instance (surgery manager) which decides which resources have to be used in case of rescheduling. In particular it's a functional hierarchy where the executive manager decides about strategic and tactical aspects, the functional manager about operational tasks.

In scientific literature exist a lot of work for operational level of surgery scheduling, but few for online scheduling that modifies an existing schedule since urgent or emergency arrivals occur. [17] presents an overview of approaches for models and algorithms for rescheduling surgery plans with manifold target variables like optimizing OR utilization or reduce waiting times. They argue that they are few papers that address online scheduling of urgent cases and rescheduling elective surgeries. Latest research approaches only support long- and mid-term scheduling and provide just a component for manual changes in short-term plans but without decision support. But in case of daily planning horizons, the possibility of rescheduling is not considered [22, 23]. In contrast the approach of [24] is based on rescheduling and uses latest information for surgery due times.

2.2 Operational Decision Support Systems

Scheduling problems are similar to decision-making problems with a set of resources, constraints and explicit and tacit knowledge [2]. Decision support systems (DSS) have a long history in companies for supporting decision making and problem-solving.

By definition they have to facilitate decision processes, respond quickly and should support rather than automate the decision-making process [25]. In the past many DSS were designed to support long-term managerial decisions on strategical and tactical business layers. With the rise of real-time data of RFID, other sensors and smart devices new opportunities for supporting short-term decision making [26]. Especially complex dynamic business situations with incomplete information and uncertainties can benefit by such operational decision support system.

Due to the advanced capabilities accompanied by the Internet of Things, smart devices and sensor systems, there are new ways to support operational decision tasks. As well in healthcare sector this data providers collect information about patients, medical devices or facilities [27, 28]. In use cases like manufacturing [3, 6], disaster response [9] or fleet management [1] these possibilities are used for operational decision support systems, also referred to as RFID-based intelligent decision support systems [6] or dynamic decision-making support systems [9].

In clinical decision making DSS are used for diagnostic processes to support physicians to find correct results and procedures for patients and their diseases. As well DSS assist in different administrative and management tasks in hospitals e.g. in operating room management. [19, 22] include surveys about the latest approaches on this topic.

3 Research Questions and Methodology

Up to now there has been no approaches for a decision support architecture in online surgery scheduling. Indeed there are many approaches for surgery planning and scheduling models, but with small practical utility due to few integrated approaches for the online surgery management and scheduling [17, 29].

Based on the outlined gaps and challenges in research and practice, the main goal of the research is to provide a solution to support operational decision tasks in online surgery scheduling. So the overall research question of the dissertation is:

How can operational decision tasks with uncertainties in online surgery scheduling *be adequately supported by information technology?*

This question is divided into four research steps:

- How do existing approaches support online surgery scheduling?
- How should a decision support model for operational decision support in online surgery scheduling be designed?
- How should an information system architecture be designed to support operational decision tasks in online surgery scheduling?
- Which optimizations can be achieved by the usage of advanced business analytics concepts in online surgery scheduling?

The first question is intended to describe the current research issues. The second question investigates an approach in form of an application system for online scheduling approaches including real-time data. The latter questions focus on explanatory aspects, especially the links between the designed solution and the addressed research gaps.

To answer the research questions a design-oriented research approach according to [30] is used. It is particularly characterized by the focus on constructing artefacts, rather than analysing and describing system behaviour like in the behaviourism-based information systems research approach. This design-oriented research framework is composed of four phases namely Analysis, Design, Evaluation and Diffusion. In the analysis phase, the foundations for the upcoming research are laid. The aim of this phase is to identify research problems and gaps for example via literature analysis of existing approaches. In design phase, the artefacts that target the research goals and questions are constructed. Common artefacts in design-oriented IS research are e.g. prototypes, models and methods, that are achieved by research methods like prototype construction, (reference) modelling and method engineering [30]. The third phase evaluates the constructed artefacts to provide scientific rigor against the specified goals and the applied research methods. The review process of scientific publications is the validation for the scientific audience, while workshops and case studies help to evaluate intermediate results of the research. The final step is the diffusion of the research outcome to the target groups like researchers and practitioners. Publications in journals and conference proceedings, practitioner papers or oral presentations are instruments in this phase that finally leads to the diffusion in a dissertation theses (Fig. 1).

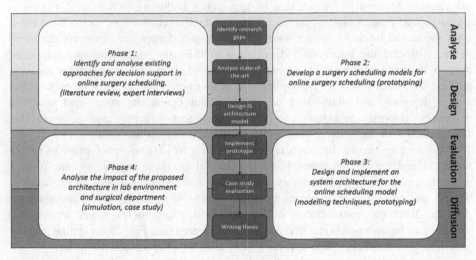

Fig. 1. Anticipated research design including research methods based on the research framework by [30].

The research framework will be passed several times, at least one time per research question. So the goal of the SQ1 is to get an overview about the research topic and to identify relevant research gaps concerning operational decision support systems. For this purpose, a systematic literature review already was performed according to the method of [31]. As a result a description of the state-of-the-art and a research agenda was formulated, which was evaluated and diffused in internal seminars and oral presentations in front of researchers and practitioners.

Phase 2 will result in a new approach for an operational decision support model in online surgery scheduling. This guidelines will be based on requirements collected in literature reviews and field studies. The evaluation of this artefact will be in expert interviews. Phase 3 and SQ3 lead to an architecture model for an operational decision support system, which is designed with modelling technologies like UML. The evaluation of this artefact will be an instantiation of the architecture in the form of a prototype. Lastly, in order to answer SQ4 a field experiment will be performed to measure the impact and performance of the instantiated architecture for decision processes in online surgery scheduling.

4 Preliminary Findings

The research process started with the identification of research gaps in the considered field of research. In a literature review 62 paper of eclectic journals and conference proceedings were analysed how they address problems with operational decision support systems. The synthesis of the analysis yields that there are many mathematical models for operational decision support. Many of them have small practical use because of unrealistic boundary conditions and poor integration in existing or future information systems. In the rare case of approaches including architectural, organisational or user-related aspects, the focus was on data layer and how to integrate them with the model layer. Moreover none of the considered approaches targets the interaction with and the information distribution to the user which both are important aspects in operational business processes because of short time horizons for decision making. A critical aspect for the applicability of an operational decision support system is the detection and notification of deviations in operations status and involved resources. Information system components to detect, interpret and integrate this information with the above mentioned mathematical models are scarce.

Further a systematic literature review according to [31] was performed to gather technical and design requirements on operational decision support system from a scientific perspective. Contemporary case studies and IS analysis will be executed to extend this collection with functional requirements of operating room management domain. With the consolidation of the collected requirements a first conceptual architecture for an operational decision support system (see Fig. 2) for online surgery scheduling in hospitals. Table 1 gives a brief abstract of requirements so far.

An integration layer was modelled due to R1. This part of the architecture ties different applications and data producers. Examples are ERP systems like the HIS or medical department-specific systems e.g. from anaesthesia. Further this layer integrates real-time information from data producers with high generation rates, e.g. RFIDs, mobile devices, medical devices or smart building sensors. This layer forwards the data to a persistent storage and to a context engine.

The need for a context engine derives from requirements R2 and R3. Foremost it uses the data sources to measure and visualise the operational status of the running instances (surgeries) as well as available resources (rooms, staff, equipment). With this functionality the operating room manager is able to get an overview about incoming real-time data and use this with expert knowledge to derive context and situation

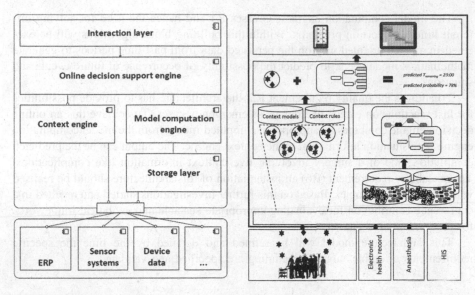

Fig. 2. Architecture model from a conceptual perspective (left) and a surgery scheduling perspective (right)

Table 1. Abstract of the requirements catalogue.

	Type	Requirement	Description
R1	Functional requirements	Data source integration	The system must integrate different kinds of data sources and granularities, e.g. RFID or ERP
R2	Functional requirements	Monitoring of operating status	The system must measure and visualise the actual situation
R3	Functional requirements	Automatic context recognition	The system must recognize deviations from planned status and trigger alarms under certain conditions
R4	Functional requirements	Solve multiple decision problems	The system must supply different solution procedures to given problem instance (algorithm library)
R5	Quality requirements	Online and real-time capability	The system must be operated in real-time and provide prompt responses
R6	Quality requirements	Scalability	The system must be able to handle large & increasing amounts of data and compute them in a fast way

information, as well about running surgical or business process tasks. To simplify this step, the context engine will allow to recognize critical deviations or important tasks automatically. This reduces the human-factor to recognize situations in stressful and complex environments.

The model computation engine addresses R4 and hence the need for solving different kinds of decision problems. Within this building block algorithms will be executed in a batch-oriented way on the persisted data from past time periods to generate mathematical models, e.g. to predict the possibility of occurrence of future events and situations.

To address the quality requirement R5, the architecture has to provide possibilities for fast reactions on events like delays or emergency cases. To achieve this an online decision engine combines an appropriate computed model from the model computation engine with situation information of the context engine. The output can be the predicted completion time of a surgery involving live context information like complications. The scalability requirement (R6) an instantiation of this architecture should be realised with scalable technologies. Based on this further investigations started and resulted in a conference contribution for evaluating appropriate scalable and analytical frameworks for processing large datasets [32].

This architecture model will be refined and detailed by the time the specific requirements of online surgery scheduling are specified and validated.

5   Summary and Outlook

Until now there are a lot of mathematical models concerning decision tasks like planning and scheduling in operating room management but a lack of approaches for an integrated information system to support this tasks on operational level. This work presents a research approach for an information system architecture that should remedy the issues related to operational decision tasks in surgery scheduling. So far the presented approach consists of a multi-tier architecture referred to the design requirements for operational decision support systems and functional requirements of the corresponding application domain. To answer the formulated research questions a design-oriented research methodology is used and adjusted for the planned research goals. In future work the functional requirements of surgery scheduling will be extended and integrated in the proposed architecture. Simultaneously a prototype to evaluate suggested architecture will be implemented.

Acknowledgement. This work was funded by the German Federal Ministry of Education and Research within the project Competence Center for Scalable Data Services and Solutions (ScaDS) Dresden/Leipzig (BMBF 01IS14014B) and by the German Federal Ministry of Economic Affairs and Energy within the project InnOPlan (BMWI 01MD15002E).

References

1. Ngai, E.W.T., Leung, T.K.P., Wong, Y.H.M., Lee, C.M., Chai, P.Y.F., Choi, Y.S.: Design and development of a context-aware decision support system for real-time accident handling in logistics. Decis. Support Syst. **52**, 816–827 (2012)
2. Aytug, H., Lawley, M.A., McKay, K., Mohan, S., Uzsoy, R.: Executing production schedules in the face of uncertainties. a review and some future directions. Euro. J. Oper. Res. **161**, 86–110 (2005)

3. Zhang, Y., Huang, G.Q., Sun, S., Yang, T.: Multi-agent based real-time production scheduling method for radio frequency identification enabled ubiquitous shopfloor environment. Comput. Ind. Eng. **76**, 89–97 (2014)
4. Ahluwalia, R., Pinha, D.: Decision support system for production planning in the ship repair industry. Ind. Syst. Eng. Rev. **2**, 52–61 (2014)
5. Bajestani, M.A., Beck, J.C.: Scheduling a dynamic aircraft repair shop with limited repair resources. J. Art. Int. Res. **47**, 35–70 (2013)
6. Guo, Z.X., Ngai, E., Yang, C., Liang, X.: An RFID-based intelligent decision support system architecture for production monitoring and scheduling in a distributed manufacturing environment. Int. J. Prod. Econ. **159**, 16–28 (2015)
7. Chen, R., Sharman, R., Rao, H.R., Upadhyaya, S.J.: Coordination in emergency response management. Commun. ACM **51**, 66–73 (2008)
8. Fang, S., Xu, L., Zhu, Y., Liu, Y., Liu, Z., Pei, H., Yan, J., Zhang, H.: An integrated information system for snowmelt flood early-warning based on internet of things. Inf. Syst. Front. **17**, 321–335 (2015)
9. Way, S., Yuan, Y.: Transitioning from dynamic decision support to context-aware multi-party coordination: a case for emergency response. Group Decis. Negot. **23**, 649–672 (2013)
10. Fleischer, W.: OP-organisation - erste hilfe für das herzstück. Deutsches Ärzteblatt **109**, 2555–2556 (2012)
11. Macario, A.: What does one minute of operating room time cost? J. Clin. Anesth. **22**, 233–236 (2010)
12. Dexter, F., Epstein, R.H., Traub, R.D., Xiao, Y.: Making management decisions on the day of surgery based on operating room efficiency and patient waiting times. Anesthesiology **101**, 1444–1453 (2004)
13. Kindscher, J., Rockford, M.: Operating room management. In: Miller, R.D. (ed.) Miller's Anesthesia, pp. 3023–3040. Churchill Livingstone Elsevier, Philadelphia (2009)
14. Marjamaa, R., Vakkuri, A., Kirvelä, O.: Operating room management: why, how and by whom? Acta Anaesthesiol. Scand. **52**, 596–600 (2008)
15. Hans, E.W., Vanberkel, P.T.: Operating theatre planning and scheduling. In: Hall, R. (ed.) Handbook of Healthcare System Scheduling. International Series in Operations Research & Management Science, vol. 168, pp. 105–130. Springer, Heidelberg (2012)
16. Stepaniak, P.S., van der Velden, R.A.C., van de Klundert, J., Wagelmans, A.P.M.: Human and artificial scheduling system for operating rooms. In: Hall, R. (ed.) Handbook of Healthcare System Scheduling. International Series in Operations Research & Management Science, vol. 168, pp. 155–175. Springer, Heidelberg (2012)
17. Guerriero, F., Guido, R.: Operational research in the management of the operating theatre: a survey. Health Care Manage. Sci. **14**, 89–114 (2011)
18. Dexter, F., Lee, J.D., Dow, A.J., Lubarsky, D.A.: A psychological basis for anesthesiologists' operating room managerial decision-making on the day of surgery. Anesth. Analg. **105**, 430–434 (2007)
19. Demeulemeester, E., Belién, J., Cardoen, B., Samudra, M.: Operating room planning and scheduling. In: Denton, B.T. (ed.) Handbook of Healthcare Operations Management. International Series in Operations Research & Management Science, vol. 184, pp. 121–152. Springer, Heidelberg (2013)
20. May, J.H., Spangler, W.E., Strum, D.P., Vargas, L.G.: The surgical scheduling problem: current research and future opportunities. Prod. Oper. Manag. **20**, 392–405 (2011)
21. Malone, T.W.: Modeling coordination in organizations and markets. Manag. Sci. **33**, 1317–1332 (1987)

22. Dios, M., Molina-Pariente, J.M., Fernandez-Viagas, V., Andrade-Pineda, J.L., Framinan, J. M.: A decision support system for operating room scheduling. Comput. Ind. Eng. **88**, 430–443 (2015)
23. Riise, A., Mannino, C., Burke, E.K.: Modelling and solving generalised operational surgery scheduling problems. Comput. Oper. Res. **66**, 1–11 (2016)
24. Samudra, M., Demeulemeester, E., Cardoen, B., Vansteenkiste, N., Rademakers, F.E.: Due time driven surgery scheduling. Health Care Manage. Sci., pp. 1–27 (2016)
25. Shim, J.P., Warkentin, M., Courtney, J.F., Power, D.J., Sharda, R., Carlsson, C.: Past, present, and future of decision support technology. Decis. Support Syst. **33**, 111–126 (2002)
26. Power, D.J., Burstein, F., Sharda, R.: Reflections on the Past and Future of Decision Support Systems. Springer, New York (2002)
27. Islam, S.M.R., Kwak, D., Kabir, M.D.H., Hossain, M., Kwak, K.S.: The internet of things for health care: a comprehensive survey. IEEE Access **3**, 678–708 (2015)
28. Niederlag, W., Lemke, H.U., Strauß, G., Feußner, H.: Der digitale Operationssaal. Health Academy 2. De Gruyter, Berlin (2014)
29. Cardoen, B., Demeulemeester, E., Beliën, J.: Operating room planning and scheduling: a literature review. Euro. J. Oper. Res. **201**, 921–932 (2010)
30. Österle, H., Becker, J., Frank, U., Hess, T., Karagiannis, D., Krcmar, H., Loos, P., Mertens, P., Oberweis, A., Sinz, E.J.: Memorandum on design-oriented information systems research. Euro. J. Inf. Syst. **20**, 7–10 (2011)
31. Vom Brocke, J., Simons, A., Riemer, K., Niehaves, B., Plattfaut, R., Cleven, A.: Standing on the shoulders of giants: challenges and recommendations of literature search in information systems research. Comput. Ind. Eng. **37**, 205–224 (2015)
32. Spangenberg, N., Roth, M., Franczyk, B.: Evaluating new approaches of big data analytics frameworks. In: Abramowicz, W. (ed.) BIS 2015. LNBIP, vol. 208, pp. 28–37. Springer, Heidelberg (2015). doi:10.1007/978-3-319-19027-3_3

Towards Automatic Business Networks Identification

Elżbieta Lewańska(✉)

Department of Information Systems,
Faculty of Informatics and Electronic Economy, Poznan University
of Economics and Business, al. Niepodleglosci 10, 61-875 Poznan, Poland
e.lewanska@kie.ue.poznan.pl

Abstract. Dynamic changes on of the business environment force business experts to continuously monitor and analyze situation and relations on the market. Due to the volume of available data and huge number of entities that operates on most markets, it is very time and cost consuming to perform the analysis manually. The paper presents an outline of analysis method that focus on identification on business networks and analysis of business environment of the specific business entity. The method operates on a set of semantically described profiles that are automatically processed and analyzed according the to user's criteria.

Keywords: Business networks · Ontology · Reasoning · Business environment

1 Motivation

According to the research, currently business experts face the problem of information overload rather than shortage of available data for analysis [1]. On the other hand, information and communication technologies (ICT) have been proven to reduce information overload. With the spread of ICT and increasing volume of data indexed by search engines, it is believed that currently information retrieving is less problematic than information processing: analysis and interpretation [2].

In modern enterprises, efficient, ongoing analysis of its business environment is crucial for gaining competitive advantage. Research results suggest that companies that actively use information about its business network are performing better on global markets [3].

A business network is defined as a set of business entities and relations between them [3–6]. Relations might be formal (i.e., defined by the contracts between business entities) and informal (i.e., based on interaction between entities rather than contracts). Relation might also occur between business entities and their offerings (products and services, i.e., market subjects) and between offerings. What is important, all entities on the market are a part of some business networks but some do not realize it.

© Springer International Publishing AG 2017
W. Abramowicz et al. (Eds.): BIS 2016 Workshops, LNBIP 263, pp. 389–398, 2017.
DOI: 10.1007/978-3-319-52464-1_36

There are a number of problems while acquiring and processing information for the purpose of analyzing business environment of a company. First, business expert usually requires information about a huge number of business entities (companies, organizations, etc.), as well as offerings related to them. Second, while formal relations are relatively easy to define, it is not clear how to find and name informal relations, which are sometimes even more important. Finally, the process of acquiring information about a business network from the Web is usually complicated, especially if performed automatically. The last problem is caused by several factors. The number of subjects that manifest themselves on the Web is enormous and getting bigger and bigger. There is too much data to process it manually (even with the search engines' support), finally there is a lack of tools to automatically monitor web resources. Moreover, data about business networks changes frequently.

2   Research Method

The research have been conducteed according to the Design Science approach [7,8]. The objectives of this research are to: (1) develop a model and method for automated analysis of business environment based on semantically annotated data, and (2) evaluate these artifacts in a set of experiments using real data.

There are four specific research goals:

- To identify elements of company's business environment and relations between them.
- To develop a metamodel of a semantically enriched profile of a business entity as well as procedure for its specialization.
- To identify online sources of semantically enhanced data, that will feed the business entities profiles.
- To develop a method for analysis of business entities profiles that will allow for automatic identification of relations between entities.

The main goal of this paper is to provide an outline of the proposed business environment analysis method as well as to share the findings from the carried out research. The paper is structured as follows. First the related work is discussed. Section 4 describes developed artifacts, an outline of the proposed method for business networks identification is presented in Sect. 5. Finally, results of the evaluation process are briefly discussed.

3   Literature Review

A business environment may be analyzed as a static model distinguishing between a proximal and distant environment [9], or as a 'dynamic' model focusing on relations between business entities. Within the latter approach, the concept of "business network" is used (e.g., [5,10]). A business network is defined as a set of relations – either formal or informal ones – connecting two or more business entities, characterized by a continuous interaction, interdependence (of resources, objects and actions), and a lack of clear boundaries and structures [4]. Although organizations are well aware of their formal relations, an awareness problem might arise regarding the informal ones [4]. The informal relations are not defined by contracts but are the result of long-term dependencies between entities on the market. They may for instance take a form of competition between organizations, informal cooperation when two organizations offer complementary products, or competition when two organizations share the same supplier. Those kinds of relations are difficult to keep track of, however, the knowledge about them is of great importance in the decision-making process, and thus, the identification of informal relations is a crucial element of every market or business environment analysis [3, 4].

Common tools to overcome information overload are information technologies [2]. Especially with the use of semantic technologies, such tools supports (semi)automatic data analysis. The contribution of the Semantic Web paradigm to the enterprises description is twofold. First, it provides ontologies that act like shared knowledge bases across the Web [11,12]. Second, it provides a logic to infer how such terms may be combined to create more complex artifacts.

At the moment, semantically described data is just a small part of web resources, but initiatives like Linked Open Data are gaining more and more attention [13].

In order to represent a business entity for the needs of processing data about it by information system, it is usually represented in the form of profile. A number of enterprise profiles have been developed [14–17] however authors focused on a very specific purpose and those profiles did not include enough information to be used for business networks identification.

Finally, a number of analysis methods have been compared against business networks identification and analysis requirements. [18] defines five main areas of data exploration: estimation, classification, prediction, clustering, and pattern discovering. Clustering methods turned out to be the best fit for the business environment analysis, as they are widely used for data segmentation (including customers segmentation) [19].

4   Research Results

There are several challenges that need to be addressed in order to develop the envisioned solution. Firstly, a method operates on profiles of business entities, thus its effectiveness depends on data availability and quality. It is assumed that the content provided by the semantic data sources is rich, reliable and up to date. Secondly, reasoning rules and methods must include knowledge from the area of economics. The mapping between relations from the existing semantic data sources and relations from real-world business networks must be defined. The analysis must consider hierarchical and non-hierarchical dependencies.

Business entity metamodel. Business entities and their offerings are the main objects occurring in the business environment. The method operates on the set of business entities profiles that are instances of the (meta)model, extracted from several semantic data sources (e.g., DBpedia[1], CrunchBase[2], for more details, cf. [9]). Metamodel has been developed based on the analysis of business experts information needs (described in [9,20]). Metamodel is domain-independent and includes only those attributes that are independent of the specific line of business. Metamodel consists of five so-called "layers" (Fig. 1):

- Distinctive attributes – unique attributes that allow for business entity identification. This layer is used for reasoning but only for object identification.
- Structured attributes – elements that have formal structure but there is no need to describe them semantically (using ontologies). Used for reasoning.
- Semantically described attributes – elements most important for reasoning. Describes as concepts from domain ontologies.
- Unstructured attributes – free-text elements that are not used by the method by might be useful for the business user (provide more information).
- Relations – defined based on the closed dictionary. Used for reasoning and analysis.

Moreover, each business entity might be related to its offerings. Offerings do not influence business environment analysis directly but are used for reasoning about relations.

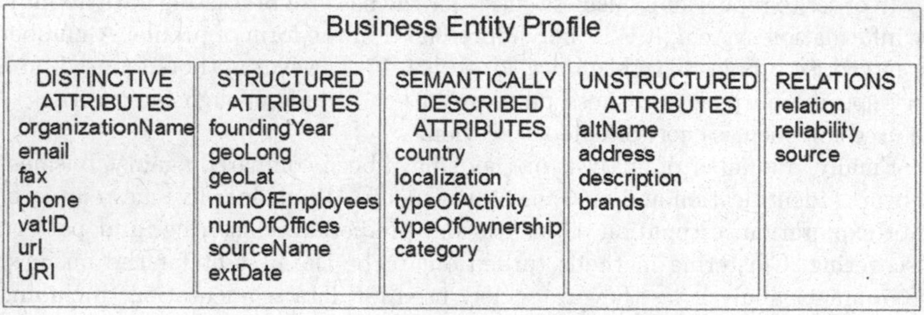

Business Entity Profile				
DISTINCTIVE ATTRIBUTES	STRUCTURED ATTRIBUTES	SEMANTICALLY DESCRIBED ATTRIBUTES	UNSTRUCTURED ATTRIBUTES	RELATIONS
organizationName	foundingYear	country	altName	relation
email	geoLong	localization	address	reliability
fax	geoLat	typeOfActivity	description	source
phone	numOfEmployees	typeOfOwnership	brands	
vatID	numOfOffices	category		
url	sourceName			
URI	extDate			

Fig. 1. Metamodel of business entity.

A domain-dependent specialization of metamodel is called "business entity model". Specialized model has additional attributes that are specific for the certain domain. Moreover, the specialization process might include defining a set of wages for model attributes.

Set of ontologies. Since the semantic representation of business entities was required in order to provide information on the business entity and its environment, the set of domain ontologies has been developed. The ontology stack includes (Fig. 2):

---

[1] dbpedia.org.
[2] crunchbase.com.

Fig. 2. Profiles (ellipses) and related ontologies (squares).

- ontology for classification of lines of business (categories),
- ontology for classification of activity types,
- offering types ontology,
- location ontology,
- type of ownership ontology.

The ontology stack has been further described in [21]. One of the goals while developing the ontology stack was to allow for integration of existing domain ontologies. Thus it is possible to extend or replace current domain ontologies with other, more suitable to the information needs of the user.

Reasoning rules. The goal of reasoning is to fulfill profiles with additional information that are not directly stated in the data source. Reasoning process in the method focuses mostly on finding informal relations between business entities. Most sources have very limited data about relations and usually it includes only formal relations (e.g., investments, acquisition). However, research on the information needs related to the process of business environment analysis and business networks identification [9,22] shown that informal relations are as important as formal ones.

Each relation added to the business entity profile has also a defined strength. The more evidences about the specific relation, the stronger it is. Also, the stronger relation is, the more influence have business entities on each other. The relation is very strong if it was defined directly in data source (selected data sources are considered as very reliable). The relation is strong if it was reasoned based on several rules. Moderate strength is defined for relations that are reasoned based on a single rule but for direct mapping between ontology concept (e.g., based on the information that two products belong to the same offering type). Finally, relation is considered as weak if it is reasoned based on the single, indirect rule (e.g., two products belong to the related types).

During the method development, the following relations have been identified and added to the business entity metamodel [22]:

- acquisition, succession – formal, very strong relation, defined based on the source data;
- competition – informal, strong if extracted from data source, weak, moderate or strong if reasoned;
- cooperation – usually formal but is specific cases might be also informal (e.g., if two entities offer complementary products); strong if extracted from data source, weak, moderate or strong if reasoned;
- investment – formal, very strong relation, defined based on the source data;
- supplier-customer – rather formal but sometimes based on very short-term contracts; strong if extracted from data source, weak, moderate or strong if reasoned;

The reasoning rules were defined based on literature review and with experts from the field of economics. All rules are formally implemented in the method prototype but for the clarity needs, are described in the natural language in the paper. Exemplary reasoning rules are as follows:

- If business entities offer products or services belonging to the same offering type on the same localization, they might be competitors.
- If business entities offers substitute products, they might be competitors.
- If business entities offers complementary products, they might be cooperators.
- If one business entity invested in the other, they might be connected through "investment" relation.
- If one business entity acquired another, they might be connected through "successor" relation and they should not be competitors.

The more reasoning rules results with the specific relation, the more reliable it is considered during the analysis.

5   Business Networks Identification Method

The developed method realizes three main scenarios. First, it allows to identify business entity, that is the most similar to the given one. This is especially important for benchmark analysis. Secondly, it identify a business network of the given entity (i.e., *central business entity*). Network is identified based on the relations between entities and according to the depth of analysis[3] defined by the user. Finally, method analyzes business environment by conducting a clustering algorithm and grouping entities into several groups. Clustering algorithm has been chosen for this purpose because it allows to identify sub-groups of business entities.

---

[3] Depth indicates the maximum path length between central business entity and any other entity in the network.

The designed method is in fact an expert system as it constitutes a computing system capable of representing and reasoning about some knowledge-rich domain and provides information [23,24].

The method operates on a set of business entity profiles, offerings profiles and a set of domain ontologies. It is divided into two subsequent steps: pre-reasoning and business analysis.

The pre-reasoning stage belongs to the back-end and encompasses several steps. First, profiles that describe the same entity but were extracted from different sources, are integrated into one normalized profile. At the same time, all semantically described attributes are mapped to the appropriate domain ontologies. Then, based on the defined rules, the system reasons about relations between entities. All pre-reasoned information is stored in the profile database.

The second stage is an actual use of the method by a business user. User defines tone out of three usage scenario, choose the base business entity (the one that he would like to analyze) and analysis context. Context allows to defined a sub-set of business entities profiles that are a subject of analysis. E.g., context might limit the analysis to the specific geographic location and a certain offering type. Markets and companies significantly varies thus defining context is crucial for the analysis. Moreover, there might me thousands of profiles in the data base and without limiting the scope of the analysis, the results might be too general for business expert needs.

The method (in all scenarios) operates on semantic profiles and analyzes not only similarities among entities, but also relations between market subjects and objects by taking advantage of the rules formalizing economic knowledge defined in the form of axioms. Such an analysis might help to identify niches, groups of similar competitors or ways to segment the market.

Depending on the scenario, the results might be presented in as a graph (business network identification), ranking list of similar entities (most similar object) or list of clusters (business environment analysis). An identified business network might be a subject of further analysis.

6   Evaluation

The implementation of the proposed method is an example of an expert system. Thus evaluation has been conducted with the use of the apropriate methods. Evaluation included verification of the developed artifacts and validation of the results. Verification confirmed the correctness of the built ontologies and fulfilement of the formulated requirements.

During the validation step, each of the usage scenario have been evaluated. The same analysis tasks have been solved by the method and human experts. The results have been evaluated using a Turing-like tests by a third-party expert who was not aware which results were produced by human and which by the method. Expert classified each element from the results as one of the following: *correct, partially correct, incorrect*. For example, for the third scenario, business environment analysis, 80–90% of results returned by human, and 60–85% of results returned by the method were classified as correct.

For the business network identification scenario, expert evaluated each of the relations returned by the method. Experts classified the relations as correct results however they pointed out that some of them are too specific. Than, business network models returned by the expert and by the method have been compared. Method was able to identify much more relations than a human (447 relations between 35 entities). Of course, data visualization techniques should be applied to such a complicated model in order to use it efficiently in business analysis.

The initial experiments confirmed that the method provides results of the similar quality to the business expert's manual work, but in much shorter time (for 100 profiles analysis phase takes 5–20 s while human classified the same set in 30–60 min).

The method has been evaluated on a set of profiles that describe personal computers and mobile devices providers. Adding resources for other lines of business is planned as future work. However, the characteristics of those two domains suggests that the method will be applicable to other business areas as well.

7   Conclusions

The main results of the research is the method for business networks identification and business environment analysis.

Conducted experiments confirmed that the developed method might be used by business experts in their day-to-day work as a support tool for analysis of business environment and business networks identification. The results returned by the method have similar or slightly lower quality but are produced in much shorter time.

The conducted research allows to use the existing semantic web artifacts for business needs. Those artifacts includes semantically described data sources, models and profiles, ontologies as well as data analysis algorithms.

Future work includes development of domain specialization for metamodel as well as further development of artifacts.

Acknowledgments. The work published in this article was supported by the project titled: "Clustering Method to Support Strategic Decision-Making Process in the Semantic Web" financed by the National Science Centre (NCN) (decision no. DEC-2012/05/N/HS4/01875).

References

1. Edmunds, A., Morris, A.: The problem of information overload in business organisations: a review of the literature. Int. J. Inf. Manag. **20**(1), 17–28 (2000)
2. Citroen, C.L.: The role of information in strategic decision-making. Int. J. Inf. Manage. **31**, 493–501 (2011)
3. Håkansson, H., Snehota, I.: No business is an island: the network concept of business strategy. Scand. J. Manag. **22**(3), 256–270 (2006)

4. Ratajczak-Mrozek, M.: Sieci biznesowe a przewaga konkurencyjna przesiębiorstw zaawansowanych technologii na rynkach zagranicznych. Wydawnictwo Uniwersytetu Ekonomicznego w Poznaniu, Poznań (2010)

5. Ford, D., Gadde, L., Hakansson, H., Snehota, I.: Managing Business Relationships. Wiley (2011)

6. Ritter, D.: From network mining to large scale business networks. In: WWW 2012 - LSNA 2012 Workshop, Lyon, France (2012)

7. Hevner, A.R., March, S.T., Park, J., Ram, S.: Design science in information system research. MIS Q. **28**(1), 75–105 (2004)

8. Hevner, A., Chatterjee, S.: Design Research in Information Systems. In: Integrated Series in Information Systems, vol. 22. Springer Science+Business Media, LLC (2010)

9. Bukowska, E.: Semantically enhanced analysis of enterprise environment for the needs of business networks identification. In: Abramowicz, W. (ed.) BIS 2013. LNBIP, vol. 160, pp. 232–243. Springer, Heidelberg (2013). doi:10.1007/978-3-642-41687-3_22

10. Campbell, A., Wilson, D.: Managed networks. In: Iacobucci, E. (ed.) Networks in Marketing. Sage Publications, USA (1996)

11. Gruber, T.R.: A translation approach to portable ontology specifications. Knowl. Acquis. **5**(2), 199–220 (1993)

12. Fensel, D., Horrocks, I., Harmelen, F.V., McGuinness, D., Patel-Schneider, P.F.: Oil: ontology infrastructure to enable the semantic web. IEEE Intell. Syst. **16**, 38–45 (2001)

13. Heath, T., Hepp, M., Bizer, C.: Linked data - the story so far. Special Issue on Linked Data, Int. J. Semant. Web Inf. Syst. (IJSWIS) (2009)

14. Nado, R.A., Huffman, S.B.: Extracting entity profiles from semistructured information spaces. SIGMOD Rec. **26**(4), 32–38 (1997)

15. Lee, T., Chams, M., Nado, R., Siegel, M., Madnick, S.: Information integration with attribution support for corporate profiles. In: Proceedings of the Eighth International Conference on Information and Knowledge Management, CIKM 1999, pp. 423–429. ACM, New York (1999)

16. Li, W., Srihari, R., Niu, C., Li, X.: Entity profile extraction from large corpora. In: Proceedings of Pacific Association for Computational Linguistics 2003 (PACLING 2003), Halifax, Nova Scotia, Canada, pp. 295–304 (2003)

17. Wieloch, K.: Rozprawa doktorska: Budowanie profili przedsiębiorstw z wykorzystaniem utożsamiania odwołań semantycznych do przedsiębiorstw w polskich tekstach ekonomicznych. Uniwersytet Ekonomiczny w Poznaniu (2011)

18. Larose, D.T.: Discovering Knowledge in Data: An Introduction to Data Mining. Wiley, Warszawa (2014)

19. Algergawy, A., Mesiti, M., Nayak, R., Saake, G.: Xml data clustering: an overview. ACM Comput. Surv. **43**(4), 25:1–25:41 (2011)

20. Bukowska, E.: Semantyczne źródła informacji w procesie podejmowania decyzji strategicznych przez przedsiębiorstwa funkcjonujące w gospodarce elektronicznej. In: Matematyka i informatyka na usługach ekonomii: teoria i zastosowania. Wydawnictwo Uniwersytetu Ekonomicznego w Poznaniu (UEP), pp. 169–182 (2014)

21. Lewańska, E., Kaczmarek, M.: Ontologies for business networks identification. In: Cuel, R., Young, R. (eds.) FOMI 2015. LNBIP, vol. 225, pp. 13–24. Springer, Heidelberg (2015). doi:10.1007/978-3-319-21545-7_2

22. Lewańska, E.: Zastosowanie technologii semantycznych na potrzeby analizy relacji pomiędzy podmiotami gospodarczymi. In: Systemy wspomagania organizacji SWO 2015. Wydawnictwo Uniwersytetu Ekonomicznego w Katowicach, pp. 121–132 (2015)

23. Jackson, P.: Introduction to Expert Systems. Addison-Wesley Longman Publishing Co. Inc., Boston (1986)

24. Weiss, S.M., Kulikowski, C.A.: A Practical Guide to Designing Expert Systems. Rowman & Allanheld Publishers (1984)

Classification of Data Analysis Tasks
for Production Environments

Sebastian Eckert[(✉)] and Jan Fabian Ehmke

Department Information Systems, FU Berlin,
Garystr. 21, 14195 Berlin, Germany
{Sebastian.Eckert,JanFabian.Ehmke}@fu-berlin.de

Abstract. In the age of "Industry 4.0", the rising amount of data from production environments is primarily used to control the operational production
environment. However, companies frequently do not exploit the data's potential
for strategic and tactical decision making. A possible reason is that many data
analysis tools follow a method-centric perspective, which is not compatible with
the problem-centric view of the tasks of a particular department. This dissertation project investigates the theoretical and practical improvement of data
analysis processes in industrial corporations. To overcome these often distinct
perspectives and foster the implementation of state-of-the-art methods of data
analysis such as data mining, we propose the standardization of data analysis
tasks in industrial corporations by construction of a reference model that can
help building data analysis tools. As a first step, we survey different types of
analysis tasks arising in the environment of the automotive industry, namely the
AUDI AG.

Keywords: Data analysis tasks · Reference modeling · Business analytics

1 Introduction

In the age of "Industry 4.0", industrial corporations face increasing competitive pressure through higher product variance and shorter product life cycles [1]. Thus, the
ability to make fast, but yet substantiated business decisions has become a competitive
advantage. Highly automated production processes generate large amounts of operational data, which could improve the quality of decision making not only on the
operational level, but also for taking tactical and strategic decisions. However, the
aggregation of operational data and its analysis with data-driven methods remain a
significant challenge.

Business Intelligence (BI) approaches proved effective for the collection, aggregation and processing of extensive sets of business data. BI has been successfully
implemented for the support of operational decision-making [2]. However, the collected data is rarely used for more complex analyses, though. In contrast, the number of
data analysis methods and systems grows along the plethora of questions raised from
operational decision support, the amount of data available and the IT resources at one's
disposal. As a result, comprehensive and growing classes of methods and algorithms
for descriptive and predictive data analysis tasks have been developed for different

© Springer International Publishing AG 2017
W. Abramowicz et al. (Eds.): BIS 2016 Workshops, LNBIP 263, pp. 399–407, 2017.
DOI: 10.1007/978-3-319-52464-1_37

purposes from OLAP over planning and prediction to simulation and data mining [3]. Especially the latter are rarely applied to practical questions, though.

Data analysis tasks in industry production are mostly subject to restrictions regarding available personnel, material and time resources. Specifications of data analysis tasks, the potential of state-of-the-art descriptive and predictive analysis methods as well as knowledge of auxiliary software are not wide spread in practice. Thus, strategic and tactical decisions of planning and control are often inadequately backed with appropriate information. Standard office software such as Microsoft Excel is commonly used as an "all-purpose" tool, while more sophisticated products such as SAS, SPSS, KNIME or RapidMiner are either unknown or not accepted by many analysts. Although these software tools offer a comprehensive range of descriptive and predictive algorithms, they are not adopted to the requirements of planning and control tasks, i.e., the mapping of suitable data analysis algorithms to specific data analysis tasks has to be done by the analyst. While the number of analysis software tools and methods constantly rises, efforts to merge the problem-specific view stemming from domain experts as end users with the method-specific view of data analysts are scarce. Only a few software providers offer wizards for the choice of certain groups of methods or parametrization, and some vendors already aim to automate the entire analysis process based on the input data provided. Both attempts still leave out domain-specific knowledge or are restricted to certain products or functions. In practice, domain experts differ from data scientists in their analysis knowledge and time constrains often do not allow for extensive data mining projects. In order to bridge this gap, we want to examine the data analysis processes found in practice and investigate them with regard to standardization.

2 Research Question

This dissertation project focuses on the improvement of data analysis processes in industry practice. Models of business processes and information systems have been constructed, analyzed and synthesized utilizing general or domain-specific modeling languages such as ARIS or BPMN for decades. Especially reference modeling as method of abstraction and reuse of tasks, processes and data has been studied thoroughly [4]. Generalized process models such as Knowledge Discovery in Databases (KDD, [5]) and Cross Industry Standard Process for Data Mining (CRISP-DM, [6]) have been developed and used to organize complex data analysis tasks. These process models inherently treat the provision of information for analytic decision making as non-recurring projects, which facilitated acceptance among consultants and data analysis experts. However, this cannot be said for their acceptance in special departments.

Research Question. How can information systems help closing the gap between the problem-specific view of analysis tasks in practice and the method-specific view of data analysis tools?

As depicted in Fig. 1, these two views can be described by their differences which need to be overcome: user groups, usage of language, tools and tasks. Furthermore, the dynamic development of new tools and methods on one hand and the flexibility and

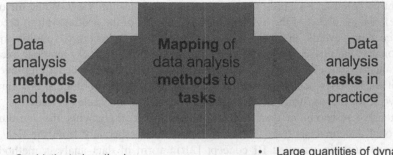

- Sophisticated methods
  - Complex tools
- Analysis language
- Project-oriented processes

- Large quantities of dynamic tasks
- Simple tools
- Heterogeneity of users
- Domain language

Fig. 1. Research question concept.

diversity of analysis tasks on the other hand add to the difficulty of spanning the gap between the two views.

We propose the construction of a reference model in order to bridge problem- and data-centric perspectives on data analysis tasks. The core idea is to standardize data analysis tasks in industry practice. We expect this to increase the quality of data processing and the efficiency of production while reducing costs for ad-hoc and non-recurring data analysis tasks. We exemplify and evaluate our approach based on planning and control tasks from the automobile manufacturer AUDI.

In the following, we give an overview of related and relevant research findings from the field of business processes and task modeling as well as BI. This leads to the main approach we pursue in this research project following the constructivist methodology of design science. Subsequently, we exemplarily show classification of data analysis tasks within the automotive industry as prerequisite for the reference modeling step. We conclude with a project plan.

3 Theoretical Background

In this section, we summarize the theoretical foundation of modeling operational data analysis tasks, BI methods of data analysis and the corresponding process. We examine concepts from business information systems engineering focusing on the structure of business tasks and data analysis methods, respectively. Finally, we explain our choice of methodology.

From a business information systems point of view, business tasks can be modeled and analyzed with regard to the appropriate level of automation. Ferstl and Sinz [9] provide a general structure to model business tasks. They propose different classifications for business tasks and classify them by model type, implemented solution method, class of language used to describe the task and the flexibility regarding task planning and execution. They present an object-oriented task structure and distinguish different perspectives on a task, namely "outside" and "inside" view. While the outside view reflects the object of the business task, the targets of the task as well as preceding and succeeding events, the inside view describes the implemented solution method. Additionally, the phase concept of tasks includes a procedure of planning, execution and evaluating the choice of the solution method. Dangelmeier et al. employed this concept for the construction of a reference model [8]. A morphological box serves as framework for the construction of a reference model of after-sale services.

Extensive research on data analysis algorithms complements the multitude of operational data analysis tasks. Relevant IS literature especially from the field of BI follows an analytics-oriented BI concept [2] in form of data analysis methods and systems (e.g. [2, 10]) as well as sorting patterns of analysis systems [2] e.g. according to management levels (MIS, DSS, OLAP, EIS) or functional views (generic systems, concept-oriented systems). Lenz and Müller [3] point out the interdisciplinary character of BI methods and integrate a set of operational decision support functions into a BI tool set. The fact that some of the support functions represent subsets of others (e.g. prediction and decision support) or depend on each other (e.g. data mining and fraud detection) impedes the applicability of this concept.

Some general proposals for process models for data analysis have been made [2], yet most of which show method-specific biases. Here, the field of Data Mining in particular is to be highlighted for its popularity and complexity. Process models such as *Cross Industry Standard Process for Data Mining* (CRISP-DM, Berthold and Hand op. 2003) and *Sample, Explore, Modify, Model, Assess* (SEMMA) are major contributions enabling a structured approach of data analysis. These models describe data analysis as sequence of steps, including task understanding, data preparation, modeling as well as evaluation and deployment. How to choose a suitable algorithm during the process has not been elaborated, though [11]. Despite its publicity, CRISP-DM is one process model for operational data analysis tasks among several used in practice [12]. Although Provost and Fawcett [13] presented a general data analysis approach based on CRISP-DM, tangible modeling rules regarding the choice of analysis methods are still an open question.

New approaches to method selection in data analysis are needed, as growing numbers of users of different analytical backgrounds carrying out data analysis tasks [10] in practice have to choose from more data analysis methods and algorithms being developed. Potential benefits and requirements of broader and easier access to data analysis methods and systems are discussed as "*Business Intelligence for the masses*" (e.g. [14]). This approach can help to enabling access to more complex methods of data analysis, but faces the risk of oversimplification of complex statistical methods. The standardization of data analysis processes can make a contribution to achieving the quantitative and qualitative goals of business practice within given resource constraints.

Broad research contributions have been made to task and process modeling as well as to information systems and solution methods for data analysis. Since the applicability of the former often relies on domain knowledge and time-consuming manual modeling activity and the latter results in technical software implementations with little connection to the specific operational task at hand, linking tasks and methods can only be realized at higher levels of abstraction.

4 Research Method

Our approach to examine information systems and construct a reference model as artifact led us to choose the constructivist concept of design science research [8, 15] as scientific method. While the cooperation with AUDI as our industry partner allows for the application and evaluation of the artifact in a relevant business environment, the use of reference models is backed by a substantial scientific knowledge base, as argued in the methodology section.

Following the paradigm of design science research, we build an artifact while complying to the concepts of practical relevance and theoretical rigor. Our design artifact is a reference model for data analysis tasks. Reference models in IS have been studied and built for years. As reference points, they are intended to be reused for building application models. Construction techniques were proposed to facilitate that process [8]. Furthermore, modeling principles were developed to assess model quality. Complying with these procedures ensures theoretical rigor for our approach. The same procedures apply for application models. Thus, the construction of application models and their implementation and assessment in practice serves as evaluation process for our approach (Fig. 2) as applicability is a key factor for successful reference modeling [16]. The left upright pyramid represents the aggregation of analysis tasks and the reference modeling. The right downwards pyramid depicts the disaggregation and application process for the models. Both pyramids are connected by the classification arrow at the top and the evaluation arrow at the bottom. Components in italics are direct links to elements of design science research.

Our approach to standardize data analysis tasks is the construction of a reference model for data analysis tasks. Reference models are developed in order to provide a reference for the construction of company-specific models of information systems [7]. Using a reference model for data analysis tasks allows for the construction of more

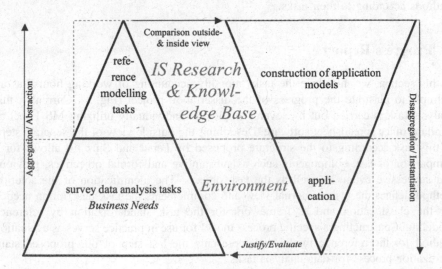

Fig. 2. Methodology.

transparent, complete and comparable task models. Rules developed in academia for the construction of models such as the GOM [8] ensure modeling quality while the evaluation of models in practice justifies their practical relevance.

Prior to the construction of the reference model, we need to understand the use of tools and data analysis tasks in practice. A representative survey is currently prepared with different departments at AUDI AG in Neckarsulm, Germany. At their production plant, over 272,000 cars were produced in 2015 by 16,300 employees. Among the departments surveyed are operations management, production controlling, workforce demand planning as well as productivity control and industrial engineering. These departments share a common focus on supporting the operation of production by conducting analysis tasks on operational data. With a questionnaire, we cover task related issues, the choice of analysis methods, process models and data analysis tools.

In the following, the department of operations management may serve as an example for the wide range of analysis tasks arising in practice. Providing the production management with tailored input data for decision making such as expected costs and availability of personnel, the tasks range from cost analysis and productivity prediction to budget allocation and resource planning. In our survey, these tasks will be structured according to Ferstl and Sinz' inside and outside task views [9]. Additionally, the process models of these tasks will be acquired for the construction of the reference model.

After having studied data analysis in practice at AUDI, we then strive to generalize the surveyed tasks. In doing so, we might be able to provide a solution suitable for other automotive companies or industry production corporations in general. Our intended approach is to classify operational data analysis tasks into task categories that allow for their assignment to specific descriptive or predictive methods from BI and DM. The objective is to establish a linkage between classes of business tasks and classes of data analysis methods. This will not only help building tools using domain-specific tasks and language. It will also support analysts to choose solution methods according to their tasks.

5   Progress Report

In this section, we introduce the task "monthly accounting of working hours" as an example to illustrate the progress of the dissertation project (Fig. 3). Currently, this analysis task is carried out by several employees individually utilizing MS Excel as standard office spreadsheet software. Describing the outside view of the separate steps of this task according to the structure proposed by Ferstl and Sinz [9] allows for a comparison of task components such as substantive and formal objectives, previous and successive events as well as the task objects. The identification of the solution method defines the task's internal view and complements the task description needed for the classification and as framework for the task standardization by reference modeling. Constructing a specific process model for use in practice serves as evaluation method for the reference model and represents the last step of our proposed standardization process for data analysis tasks.

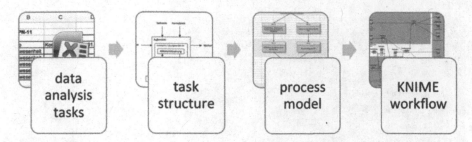

Fig. 3. Research approach for example task "monthly accounting of working hours".

As support tool for data analysis, we chose the popular graphical data mining application *Konstanz Information Miner* (KNIME). The KNIME workflow of the example task depicted in Fig. 4 maps the data flow from left to right. The nodes represent separate processing steps transforming the input on the left into the output on the left. Meta nodes are gray-colored, constitute sub workflows and consist of nodes and edges themselves.

The task comprises three different phases (highlighted by three colored shades in Fig. 4). The blue phase contains the core activity and transforms input data from Enterprise Resource Planning (ERP) systems and manual input into transaction data. The applied analysis method can be assigned to the group of "exact methods" as defined by Ferstl and Sinz. It generates an output readable by ERP systems while satisfying substantive and formal objectives. Within the "red phase", a set of productivity KPIs for the different production segments are computed from the output of the previous blue phase as well as manual input. Eventually, the "green phase " converts the results of both preceding phases into reports and machine-readable outputs for ERP systems. Nodes that are not placed in either of the colored phases represent metadata or phase-independent transformation activities.

The KNIME workflow, compared to the highly individual task execution in Microsoft Excel spreadsheets (Fig. 3), represents a facility-wide standardization of the example task. As a result, transparency, execution time and process stability are expected to be improved. By using advanced analysis methods provided in KNIME, result quality improved over the conventional process. However, the replacement of analysis methods for a large number of data analysis tasks is time-consuming and requires both substantial domain and methodological knowledge. Constructing KNIME workflows implies composing technical nodes such as data transformation as well as statistical and analytical methods. The use of meta nodes and text notes to add domain- and task-specific terms gains acceptance with the domain experts.

In Table 1, we outline the project progress in a dissertation schedule. We defined our research objective and our approach in 2015. The cooperation with AUDI started in 2015 and we held two out five workshops to date. We organized these first two workshops to introduce the entire team to our project approach and stage an exchange of state-of-the-art data analysis methods and analysis tasks in business practice. The upcoming two workshops in 2016 are planned to cover the empirical topics of task survey, questionnaire

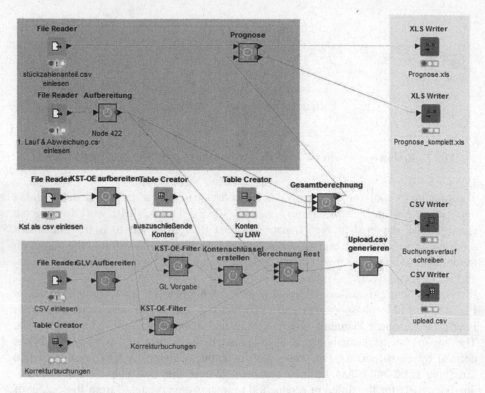

Fig. 4. KNIME workflow of example task "monthly accounting of working hours".

Table 1. Dissertation schedule.

Year	Quarter	Content	Empirical project phase
2015	II	Definition of research objective	Workshops 1 & 2 State of the art data analysis of operational data
	III & IV	Development of hypotheses	
2016	I & II	Empirical studies	Workshops 3 & 4
2016/2017	III & IV I	Reference modeling	Survey and classification of data analysis tasks
2017	II	Evaluation	Workshop 5 Tools for data analysis
	III & IV	Finishing dissertation	

and task classification. In the first quarter of 2017, we expect the classification and reference modeling to be finished so we can evaluate the resulting model in practice. The entire dissertation is intended to be finished by end of 2017.

References

1. Lasi, H., Fettke, P., Kemper, H.-G., Feld, T., Hoffmann, M.: Industrie 4.0. WI **56**, 261–264 (2014)
2. Kemper, H.-G., Mehanna, W., Baars, H.: Business Intelligence - Grundlagen und praktische Anwendungen. Eine Einführung in die IT-basierte Managementunterstützung. Vieweg +Teubner, Wiesbaden (2010)
3. Lenz, H.J., Müller, R.M.: Business Intelligence. Springer, Heidelberg (2012)
4. Scheer, A.-W.: Wirtschaftsinformatik. Referenzmodelle für industrielle Geschäftsprozesse. Springer, Heidelberg (1997)
5. Fayyad, U.M.: Advances in Knowledge Discovery and Data Mining. MIT Press, Menlo Park (1996)
6. Chapman, P.: The CRISP-DM User Guide. http://lyle.smu.edu/~mhd/8331f03/crisp.pdf
7. Schütte, R.: Grundsätze ordnungsmäßiger Referenzmodellierung. Gabler, Wiesbaden (1998)
8. Becker, J. (ed.): Referenzmodellierung: Grundlagen, Techniken und domänenbezogene Anwendung. Physica-Verlag, Heidelberg (2004)
9. Ferstl, O.K., Sinz, E.J.: Grundlagen der Wirtschaftsinformatik. Oldenbourg, R, München (2013)
10. Gluchowski, P., Gabriel, R., Dittmar, C.: Management-Support-Systeme und Business Intelligence: Computergestützte Informationssysteme für Fach- und Führungskräfte. Springer, Heidelberg (2008)
11. Berthold, M., Hand, D.J.: Intelligent Data Analysis: An Introduction. Springer, Heidelberg (2003)
12. Mariscal, G., Marbán, Ó., Fernández, C.: A survey of data mining and knowledge discovery process models and methodologies. Knowl. Eng. Rev. **25**, 137–166 (2010)
13. Provost, F., Fawcett, T.: Data Science for Business: What You Need to Know About Data Mining and Data-Analytic Thinking. O'Reilly & Associates, Sebastopol (2013)
14. Schildhauer, T.: Business Intelligence: Durch E-Business Strategien und Prozesse verbessern. BusinessVillage, Göttingen (2004)
15. Hevner, A.R., March, S.T., Park, J., Ram, S.: Design science in information systems research. MIS Q. **28**, 75–105 (2004)
16. Frank, U., Strecker, S., Fettke, P., Brocke, J., Becker, J., Sinz, E.: Das Forschungsfeld „Modellierung betrieblicher Informationssysteme". WI **56**, 49–54 (2014)

Toward a Configuration Model
for User-Oriented Representations
of Analytical Services

Christian Hrach[(✉)]

Information Systems Institute, University Leipzig,
Grimmaische Str. 12, 04109 Leipzig, Germany
hrach@wifa.uni-leipzig.de

Abstract. Currently there is insufficient support regarding the user-oriented modeling of analytical information systems. More precisely, there is a lack of semiformal and detailed conceptual models, which could represent the functional and nonfunctional requirements of analytical users. Addressing this issue, this article motivates the development of a conceptual analytical service configuration model, gives a short insight into previous research and describes the range of necessary modeling content, which contains functional and nonfunctional requirements of the user context. Then, this article presents first ideas concerning the model structures and discusses potential application areas.

Keywords: Analytical service · Configuration model · Conceptual analytical service model

1 Motivation

1.1 Deficits Concerning the User-Oriented Specification of Analytical Information Systems

Analytical information systems, also known as business intelligence (BI) systems [1], are technical components, which provide analytically prepared information to operating departments and the management. These systems provide functionality to extract, transform and load data from operational information systems, store and analyze the data, and provide access to the resulting analytical information [2]. Considering the paradigm of service-oriented architectures, analytical services contain and provide functional analytical components and the corresponding analytical content/information [3].

The technical design of analytical information systems can be deduced from the business respectively functional requirements of the analytic-supported processes (e.g. calculation of mean values), from the special requirements of the process users (e.g. to display the results on a smart phone) as well as from the organizational and technical surrounding conditions (e.g. daily data backup). All these aspects constitute the functional and nonfunctional user-oriented requirements, which are the foundation of the subsequent steps in information system development.

In practice it is often a challenge until different users/user groups within an organization get a common vision concerning their requirements of an analytical information

W. Abramowicz et al. (Eds.): BIS 2016 Workshops, LNBIP 263, pp. 408–417, 2017.
DOI: 10.1007/978-3-319-52464-1_38

system. A lot of past research already made a contribution to this topic (compare [4]), e.g. using techniques like interviews or workshops. However, in practice there are still huge problems in executing analytical software projects: Goodwin [5] numbers the failure rate of BI projects with 70–80% based on the experience of Gartner Inc. Practice-oriented literature (e.g. [6, 7]) often mention the following reasons:

- Unclear requirements respectively expected project results
- Missing detailed specifications respectively insufficient documentation

Therefore, the structured modeling of user requirements in the context of analytical information systems seem to be a research topic which needs closer attention. This dissertation project marks out the evolution of a common vision within the user group and assumes, that prospective users of an analytical information system have a half-decent clear idea concerning their corporate informational, functional and pre-sentational requirements. This user vision could be stated more precisely and be documented with the special support of an analytical service configuration model during discussions with analytical software developers (see Sects. 1.3 and 5.1).

In literature there are a lot of requirements documentation approaches (e.g. [8]), but most of them are domain-unspecific and not precisely adapted to the context of ana-lytical information systems. But also previous analytical-oriented requirements man-agement approaches provide only a limited capability for detailed requirements documentation (compare [4]). Conceptual information system modeling notations (e.g. information system diagram in ARIS [9]) are another visual aids to represent the (prospective) structure of an analytical information system, but again these models contain no analytical-specific model objects.

Analytical information systems and their information provision are embedded in user processes. In the age of digital (process) transformation and the dispersal of big data use cases the enrichment of operational processes with analytical information (e.g. status overviews, alerts, simulations) becomes more important. For example the col-laboration diagram of the Business Process Model and Notation (BPMN) displays process-relevant information with the model object *data object,* and the support of information systems with the model object *lane* [10]. Besides the pure use case-specific naming of these model objects, the BPMN standard provide neither detailed specifi-cations nor additional meta information (compare [10]). But this additional content about the source and the creation of analytical process information could be a valuable benefit for process users and system developers.

In contrast to these approaches, user requirements are often documented in written form using running text or bullet points in real software development projects. Despite the easy usage and common understandability of natural language, this form of doc-umentation has significant disadvantages: On the one hand it is a less formal specifi-cation with a higher risk of misunderstandings and ambiguity, and on the other hand there is a higher risk to achieve incomplete, less detailed and less structured specifi-cations. That can lead to a situation, that subsequent technical-oriented models of information systems (e.g. modeled with UML or using the Zachman framework) or even program code/prototypes created by software developers do not fit the real demands in user context.

1.2   Service-Oriented Analytical Information Systems

Service-orientation in terms of service-oriented architectures (SOA) is an established paradigm in the domain of operational information systems and operational processing. Here functions are encapsulated as so called services with standardized interfaces. These services can be orchestrated dynamically and support the reusability of business-/process-oriented and IT-related components. Services combine business-oriented tasks with their supporting technical infrastructure [11]. For this reason (the business-oriented parts of) services are suitable to specify user-oriented requirements concerning analytical information/analytical information systems.

Since several years the integrated examination of SOA and BI as well as the accompanied chances (e.g. [12]) and limitations (e.g. [13]) has been discussed. On the one hand there are numerous practice-oriented publications provided by business consultancies and software companies which promote the idea of service-oriented analytic and describe the expected benefits (e.g. [14]), but in most cases they contain no detailed conceptual descriptions of analytical services. In addition there are several analytical software products (e.g. from SAS, MicroStrategy or Oracle) which allow a service-oriented access to analytical functionality (see Sect. 2). But on the other hand researchers find fault with the small amount of scientific articles about this topic (e.g. [13, 15]). The few previous scientific publications examine design-factors (e.g. [15]), coarse-granular analytical service architectures (e.g. [16]) and the technical implementation of analytical services (e.g. [17]), but so far the field of detailed conceptual description of analytical services is explored insufficiently (see Sect. 3).

At the same time approaches like *cloud BI* or *BI software as a service* (e.g. [18]) become real in the form of innovative service offers which provide external analytical functionality. Out there companies like Oracle[1] or IBM[2] sell their own cloud-based analytical information systems, and there are also first analytical offers on common service marketplaces (e.g. Yellowfin[3] on Amazon Web Services Marketplace). Usually these offers contain only short textual service descriptions, which impede users to find the appropriate services for their specific requirements. Based on the ongoing trend to combine analytical information systems with service-orientation and the emerge of cloud-based analytical applications, models in the area of user-oriented analytical information system modeling should be service-oriented, too.

1.3   Conceptual Analytical Service Configuration Model as a Research Goal

According to the explanations in the previous sections it lacks in a detailed, service-based modeling approach for the user-oriented description of analytical information systems. For this reason this dissertation project aims at the conception of an

---

[1] https://cloud.oracle.com/business_intelligence.

[2] http://www.ibm.com/cloud-computing/us/en/cloud-solutions/cloud-analytics/.

[3] https://aws.amazon.com/marketplace/pp/B00OSDNMIW/ref=srh_res_product_title?ie=UTF8&sr=0-2&qid=1416228352295.

analytical service configuration model. This model should specify the functional range, the informational content and the look and feel of analytical user interfaces from a user perspective. The configuration model should be used in a broad range of application scenarios, e.g. to specify analytical dashboards as well as document-oriented report-generating applications.

Thereby this research belongs to the topic of domain-specific modeling, because the prospected configuration model has to support the specific domain of analytical information systems and should have a high degree of problem specificity (compare [19]). In addition the configuration model supports conceptual modeling, because the model has to represent a user-oriented view on the structure and functionality of analytical information systems (compare [20]).

This article contains first insights in the projected research proceeding (Sect. 2) and gives an overview about approaches of service structuring in the context of analytical information systems (Sect. 3). Section 4 provides first insights in the prospected configuration model including the projected content and structure, whereas Sect. 5 gives a short prospect in future application scenarios. A summary completes the article in Sect. 6.

2 Research Method

This research follows design-oriented information systems research with its four phases analysis, design, evaluation and diffusion [21]. The analysis started with the examination of the problem space. Interviews with BI developers and a literature review of practice-oriented publications revealed deficits in the area of requirements documentation within analytical development projects. Subsequent a literature review of scientific publications showed a research gap in the area of detailed conceptual as well as service-oriented modeling of analytical information systems. A first appraisal of two service-oriented analytical information systems (*MicroStrategy 10* and *Oracle Business Intelligence Enterprise 11g*) revealed, that *MicroStrategy* uses single services with attributes, and *Oracle* more complex service structures with attributes and integrated methods as well as hierarchical sub-services. Unfortunately in both tools the analytical services are used for technical implementation only (e.g. specifying the status of an analytical service) and not for conceptual specification. The analysis continues with the examination of modeling approaches from different areas to get hints regarding the single model elements and their relations within the projected configuration model. This comprises models for analytical (e.g. presented in [4]) and generic requirements documentation, service modeling notations which describe the structure of single services (e.g. web ontology language for web services (OWL-S) [22]) and the relations between services (e.g. service-oriented modeling framework (SOMF) [23]) as well as conceptual models which specify the organizational structure of information systems (e.g. [9]). Finally the literature-based analysis and compilation of the functional range of contemporary analytical information systems as well as the identification of user-relevant influencing factors (e.g. information latency) are the main basis for the domain-specific content of the projected configuration model.

Within the design phase it is the goal to develop the conceptual analytical service configuration model based on the results of the previous analysis. The first draft of the configuration model should be tested and evaluated by a set of students. Based on given text-based analytical user requirements one group should specify them with the new configuration model, and another group should use a hitherto modeling approach. Afterwards a revised version of the configuration model should be tested in a real development project of an analytical software solution center.

3   Prior Research on Analytical Service Modeling

There are first approaches for service structuring in the analytical context delineated in scientific and practice-oriented literature. Gluchowski et al. [24] separates *basic BI services* (services for direct data access) from *analytical services* (services for the allocation of simple or complex analytical results). In contrast to that Besemer [25] distinguish *front-end BI services* (e.g. *query and reporting services, dashboard and scorecard services*) from *back-end BI services* (e.g. *transformation and integration services, movement between sources services*). Dinter [26] presents a slightly elaborated structuring which differentiates *sourcing services, transformation services, infrastructure services* and *analytical services*. Here *analytical services* includes the core functionalities of analytical information systems. A similar approach from Martin [3] separates e.g. *reporting services, analyzing services* (data visualization, data mining), *alerting services* and *dashboard services*.

The analysis of the afore mentioned approaches leads to the following insights: Previous analytical service structures (1) have different and partly contrary service clusters, (2) contain only short textual descriptions of single service types, and (3) provide no dependencies or complex relations between the service types. Therefore these approaches could give only a first advice concerning the supreme structuring levels/main service types of a analytical service configuration model.

4   Conceptual Analytical Service Configuration Model

4.1   Model Content

First of all, elements of the conceptual analytical service configuration model base upon the current technical functions of a wide range of analytical information systems. This comprehends typical analytical functions (like reporting, data mining or online analytical processing (OLAP)), associated detailed aspects (like analytical algorithms, diagram types, performance indicators) and user requirements concerning technical basic functions (like data extraction and storage). But also aspects derived from more recent BI trends (e.g. collaborative BI [27] or social media analytics [28]) have to gain consideration in the service structure (e.g. collaborative BI: provision of an *annotation service* for dashboards). On the other hand the configuration model has to consider nonfunctional requirements from the user context (compare [29]) as well (e.g. data privacy restrictions, the amount of simultaneous system users, maximum response time), because these aspects can have a significant effect on the subsequent technical implementation (e.g. a high amount of users could require distributed server facilities). Therefore the content of the conceptual analytical service configuration model is not limited to the presentation and information allocation level (compare [29]) of an analytical information system architecture (e.g. user-oriented requirements regarding the granularity of analytical information or expected graphical visualizations), but also include user experience-related elements from the data storage and data collection levels (e.g. time interval for the data update from operational information systems). In contrast the prospected configuration model excludes explicitly the area of technical data models, because one the one hand these are downstream aspects of the technical implementation, and on the other hand there are a multiplicity of established models in theory and practice (e.g. multidimensional star schema).

A domain-specific model should be balanced between a broad usability and the detailed description of domain-specific content [19]. Therefore the analytical service configuration model has to be designed strictly from the perspective of user requirements regarding the analytical information systems and the informational process support. In other words, only aspects take center stage which can be described by a user (e.g. the look and feel of an analytical screen and the necessary performance indicators), whereas derived aspects like technical details of software implementation should remain unconsidered within this configuration model. For example a modeled requirement *maximum response time = 2 s* leaves open whether a software engineer implements in-memory or column-oriented databases.

4.2   Model Structure

First of all it is necessary to create a comprehensive and coordinated set of analytical service types which have a significant importance in analytical context (e.g. *reporting service*, *diagram service*, *alerting service*) based on the spectrum of analytical model content outlined in Sect. 4.1 and on the previous structuring of analytical service types in Sect. 3. Specific attributes aligned to the particular service types should facilitate the closer description of these types (e.g. service type *diagram service* contains attributes like *diagram type* or *dimension of x-axis*). In line with the explanations in Frank [19], selectable attribute values should be predefined. The (hierarchic) interlink of different service types enables the buildup of complex analytical service systems. First examinations of analytical software applications have adduced, that e.g. the product *Oracle Business Intelligence Enterprise 11g* already uses hierarchic service interlinks for the technical specification.

Figure 1 shows the projected schematic structure of a hierarchic service configuration model. In this example the team leaders in a sales department need a dashboard with analytical information for their sales processes. The dashboard has to contain a line diagram with monthly sales figures of a product P and the results of a customer clustering. In addition an alerting has to inform the team leaders in case of a shortfall of a given monthly sales value. The particular values of the different service attributes concretize functional (e.g. *diagram type: line diagram*) and nonfunctional (e.g. *update interval of performance indicator: once a day*) user requirements.

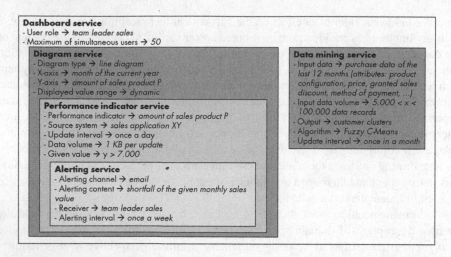

Fig. 1. Illustration of the configuration model by the example of a sales dashboard.

5 Application Areas

5.1 Requirements Documentation

The requirements management of analytical information systems is divided into different phases/areas of activity. Based on the requirements engineering framework of Pohl [30] the projected analytical service configuration model could be used as a supporting technique in the area of requirements documentation. Other central activities of requirements management, like requirements investigation (e.g. with the help of interview- or workshop-oriented approaches) and the achievement of congruent requirements within the whole user community (e.g. with the help of view-oriented requirements models [29]), are not in the application focus of an analytical service configuration model, because there are already a lot of other specialized approaches (compare [4]).

However, analytical service configuration models could assist the documentation of (consolidated and final) user requirements at the boundary point between unstructured requirements knowledge (e.g. the mental ideas of a key user) and a structured and preferably formal requirements documentation. According to statements of so far two interviewed BI developers, in most cases they document the user comments in headwords, afterwards they convert it in plain text and give the text back to the users for correction. In the future the BI developers and users could develop, detail and verify the requirements documentation together in one single step using an analytical service configuration model. The so far interview results reveal, that the developers of analytical information systems expect both a higher degree of clearness and completeness within the documented requirements and temporal/monetary savings regarding a future use of the projected configuration model.

5.2   Process Modeling

The structure of an analytical service configuration model explained in Sect. 4.2 and the application area of requirements documentation described in Sect. 5.1 represents a static view on an analytical information system. As mentioned in Sect. 1.1, the use of analytical information and related analytical information systems is usually embedded in the execution of processes. These dynamic sequence flows link separate activities with their specific analytical requirements. In process models the superficial informational objects (see Sect. 1.1) annotated to the activities could be replaced by specific analytical service configuration models (see Fig. 2).

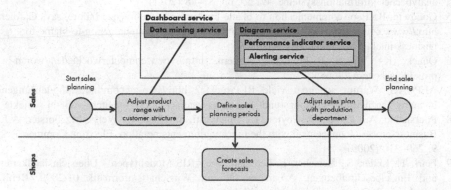

Fig. 2. Integration of the configuration model in a BPMN process model.

6   Conclusion

The presented analytical service configuration model could reduce the challenges in the development of analytical information systems which occur by reason of insufficient documentation of user requirements. To achieve a conceptual, preferably formal and comprehensive configuration model it is necessary to consider analytic-functional as well as nonfunctional requirements of the utilization context. The projected configuration model will address the current functions of analytical information systems at a specific time. Because new analytical functions, new trends and new user scenarios will evolve in the future, the configuration model has to be extensible (compare [19]).

The next steps in the dissertation project will focus on the finalization of analysis in the areas of service, requirements and information system modeling to find model structures and model objects suitable in the projected model context. Furthermore the ongoing collection of analytical functions and factors influencing the behavior and utilization of analytical information systems from a user perspective will be the foundation for the development of basic elements (e.g. service types, service attributes and relationships between service types) of the configuration model.

References

1. Schieder, C.: Historische Fragmente einer Integrationsdisziplin – Beitrag zur Konstrukt-geschichte der Business Intelligence. In: Gluchowski, P., Chamoni, P. (eds.): Analytische Informationssysteme. Business Intelligence-Technologien und -Anwendungen, pp. 13–32. Springer, Heidelberg (2016)
2. Grossmann, W., Rinderle-Ma, S.: Fundamentals of Business Intelligence. Springer, Heidelberg (2015)
3. Martin, W.: Analytics meets Enterprise SOA - Wertschöpfende Geschäftsprozesse durch Analytik. S.A.R.L. Martin (2006)
4. Stroh, F., Winter, R., Wortmann, F.: Methodenunterstützung der Informationsbedarfsanalyse analytischer Informationssysteme. WI 53, pp. 37–48 (2011)
5. Goodwin, B.: Poor communication to blame for business intelligence failure, says Gartner. http://www.computerweekly.com/news/1280094776/Poor-communication-to-blame-for-business-intelligence-failure-says-Gartner
6. Quack, K.: Woran BI-Projekte scheitern. http://www.computerwoche.de/a/woran-bi-projekte-scheitern,2366850
7. AEP AG: Warum scheitern viele BI-Projekte? http://aep-ag.com/index.php/leistungen/beratung/ganzheitliche-planungs-und-steuerungssysteme/warum-scheitern-viele-bi-projekte
8. Pourshahid, A., Amyot, D., Peyton, L., Ghanavati, S., Chen, P., Weiss, M., Forster, A.J.: Business process management with the user requirements notation. Electron. Commer. Res. **9**, 269–316 (2009)
9. Feiri, T., Keller, S., Kerscher, I., Lehmann, F.: ARIS-Modelltypen - Übersichtslandkarten und Einzelbeschreibungen. Arbeitsberichte zur Wirtschaftsinformatik 01/2009, Berufs-akademie Ravensburg, Ravensburg (2009)
10. Object Management Group: Business Process Model and Notation (BPMN) - Version 2.0 (2011)
11. Erl, T.: Service Oriented Architecture: Principles of Service Design. Prentice Hall, Upper Saddle River (2008)
12. Panian, Z.: How to make business intelligence actionable through service-oriented architectures. In: 2nd WSEAS International Conference on Computer Engineering and Applications, pp. 210–221 (2008)
13. Müller, R.M., Linders, S., Ferreira Pires, L.: Business intelligence and service-oriented architecture: a delphi study. Inf. Syst. Manage. **27**, 168–187 (2010)
14. Gordon, S., Grigg, R., Horne, M., Thurman, S.: Service-oriented business intelligence. Microsoft Architect. J. (2006). https://msdn.microsoft.com/en-us/library/bb245659.aspx
15. Dinter, B., Stroh, F.: Design factors for service-oriented architecture applied to analytical information systems: an Explorative Analysis. In: Proceedings of the 17th ECIS, Verona (2009)
16. Wu, L., Barash, G., Bartolini, C.: A service-oriented architecture for business intelligence. In: IEEE International Conference on Service-Oriented Computing and Applications (SOCA 2007), pp. 279–285 (2007)
17. Pospiech, M., Felden, C.: Service-oriented business intelligence reference architecture in face of advanced BI concepts. In: Proceedings of the AMCIS (2013)
18. Mircea, M., Ghilic, B., Stoica, M.: Combining business intelligence with cloud computing to delivery agility in actual economy. J. Econ. Comput. Econ. Cybern. Stud. **45**, 39–54 (2011)

19. Frank, U.: Domain-specific modeling languages: requirements analysis and design guidelines. In: Reinhartz-Berger, I., Sturm, A., Clark, T., Cohen, S., Bettin, J. (eds.): Domain Engineering. Product Lines, Languages, and Conceptual Models, pp. 133–157, Springer, Heidelberg (2013)
20. Becker, J., Pfeiffer, D.: Konzeptionelle Modellierung - ein wissenschaftstheoretischer Forschungsleitfaden. In: Proceedings of the MKWI 2006, vol. 2, pp. 3–19 (2006)
21. Becker, J.: Prozess der gestaltungsorientierten Wirtschaftsinformatik. In: Österle, H., Winter, R., Brenner, W. (eds.): Gestaltungsorientierte Wirtschaftsinformatik: Ein Plädoyer für Rigor und Relevanz, pp. 13–18, infowerk ag (2010)
22. Martin, D., Burstein, M., McDermott, D., McIlraith, S., Paolucci, M., Sycara, K., McGuinness, D.L., Sirin, E., Srinivasan, N.: Bringing semantics to web services with OWL-S. World Wide Web 10, 243–277 (2007)
23. Bell, M.: SOA Modeling Patterns for Service-Oriented Discovery and Analysis. John Wiley & Sons, Hoboken (2010)
24. Gluchowski, P., Dittmar, C., Gabriel, R.: Management Support Systeme und Business Intelligence. Springer, Berlin (2008)
25. Besemer, D.: Getting started now on SOA for BI. DM Rev. 17, 26–37 (2007)
26. Dinter, B.: Einsatzmöglichkeiten serviceorientierter Architekturen in der Informationslogistik. In: Töpfer, J., Winter, R. (eds.): Active Enterprise Intelligence. Unternehmensweite Informationslogistik als Basis einer wertorientierten Unternehmenssteuerung, pp. 221–242. Springer, Berlin (2008)
27. Dayal, U., Vennelakanti, R., Sharma, R., Castellanos, M., Hao, M., Patel, C.: Collaborative business intelligence: enabling collaborative decision making in enterprises. In: Meersman, R., Tari, Z. (eds.): On the Move to Meaningful Internet Systems, pp. 8–25. Springer, Berlin (2008)
28. Alt, R., Wittwer, M.: Towards an ontology-based approach for social media analysis. In: Proceedings of the 22nd ECIS (2014)
29. Goeken, M.: Anforderungsmanagement bei der Entwicklung von Data Warehouse-Systemen. In: Schelp, J., Winter, R. (eds.): Auf dem Weg zur Integration Factory. Proceedings der DW2004 - Data Warehousing und EAI, pp. 167–186. Physica Verlag, Heidelberg (2005)
30. Pohl, K.: Requirements Engineering. dpunkt Verlag, Heidelberg (2008)

Improving the Quality of Art Market Data Using Linked Open Data and Machine Learning

Dominik Filipiak[(✉)] and Agata Filipowska

Departament of Information Systems, Poznań University of Economics and Business,
Aleja Niepodległości 10, Poznań, Poland
{dominik.filipiak,agata.filipowska}@kie.ue.poznan.pl
http://kie.ue.poznan.pl

Abstract. Among numerous research studies devoted to art markets, very little attention is given to the quality of the data. Availability of a decent amount of observations is a problem in many fields; the art market is no different, especially in Poland. Therefore, it constitutes a severe obstacle in explaining the market behaviour. The use of Linked Open Data and Machine Learning can pave the way to improve the quality of data and enrich results of other art market research as a consequence, such as building indices. This paper is an outline of the method for combining such fields and summarises effort already made to achieve that.

Keywords: Art market · Data science · Machine learning · Linked open data

1 Problem, Motivation and Research Questions

Plattner has written about *a market where producers don't make work primarily for sale, where buyers often have no idea of the value of what they buy, and where middlemen routinely claim reimbursement for sales of things they've never seen to buyers they've never dealt with* [1]. One might say that this quote perfectly sums up the art market. However, for such an *irrational* market, there are *rational* tools available and it has been under investigation of researchers since several decades.

Most of the quantitative research on art market focuses on building indices to yield an easy-to-interpret outlook and compare art to other collectibles or forms of investment. Since these methods rely mostly on a variety of linear regression models, they are tightly coupled to the data. A single lot (a painting, for example) can be deconstructed to a set of features describing it, such as its author, size, style or technique. Methods used to construct art market indices usually pair the hammer price and these features using a linear model to examine their influence on the hammer price. What makes art market data useful is a large number of features to examine in such models. Therefore, the richer and better a data source is, the more accurate a model will be.

© Springer International Publishing AG 2017
W. Abramowicz et al. (Eds.): BIS 2016 Workshops, LNBIP 263, pp. 418–428, 2017.
DOI: 10.1007/978-3-319-52464-1_39

There is no common agreement among scientists on what constitutes the quality of data, since it is a subjective term. For example, Zaveri et al. have gathered and examined efforts of researchers on this subject [2]. Among numerous dimensions of data quality, they listed syntactic validity, semantic accuracy, and completeness. Other researchers also underline the importance of data completeness [3,4]. These traits are interlocked with building robust art market indices. To the best of our knowledge, there are no researchers nor publications focused on improving these features with regard to art market data.

The aforementioned motivation paves the way to enunciate the main research problem, which is: *How to improve the quality and usefulness of data for the Polish art market?* To solve this problem, the following research questions need to be addressed:

Q1: What are the primary sources of the Polish art market data? How to collect and organise these data?

Q2: Can Linked Open Data datasets enrich art market data? Which data sources and methods have the best performance in such matters?

Q3: Can computer vision methods yield useful results in terms of art market analysis? Which one has the best performance in such matters?

Q4: How can we use and evaluate such an enriched dataset?

Therefore, the underlying hypothesis of this research is as follows:

Hypothesis 1. *Data enrichment using Linked Open Data and Machine Learning methods will improve the quality (in terms of completeness) and usefulness (regarding building indices) of art market data.*

This hypothesis will be tested through developing a method satisfying aforementioned research questions, and evaluating the efficacy of the proposed artifact (i.e. method) through a set of simulation experiment with real data.

The main goal of this paper is to show an outline of the method which should tackle the aforementioned problem and answer posed questions. This paper is organised as follows. The next section is a literature review, which gives an outlook on state-of-the-art achievements in fields related to the problem. In the following section the proposed method is explained in detail. The next one discusses the guidelines of the used methodology. The preliminary results section gives a glimpse of achieved results by the date of writing this paper. Future work sums up to-be-done tasks in terms of reaching stated goals. The last section is a summary of this paper.

2 Literature Review

Art Market Research. The Polish art market was analysed in several papers using various approaches [5–7]. In general, most efforts to measure the art market focus on creating various types of indices. Their purpose is to [8]:

- outline general art market trends and provide a way to compare investment in arts with other forms of investment, such as stocks and bonds,
- measure the art market volatility in comparison with other types of investment,
- investigate how different social and economic incentives influence the art market,
- appraise the overall value of artworks.

Two main methods of art market index building may be outlined, based on their creation process. The first group considers repeated-sales regression (RSR). Intuitively, it relies on artworks sold at least twice and the ratio of the first to the second price. Though this approach may seem rational, it suffers from a lack of data. Art is a long-term investment, therefore it is hard to collect enough observations to build a reliable index. An example of this kind is the famous Mei &Moses index, which bases on Christie's and Sotheby's repeated sales [9].

The second approach employs so-called hedonic regression, which is a form of linear regression. Usually, it compares a natural logarithm of the hammer price of a given artwork to explanatory variables, consecutively measuring a lot's features during a given period. These variables may be numerical (like the size of a painting) or dummy (like the medium used or the year of a sale). Dummies are equal to 0 or 1 depending on a presence of a given attribute. This approach is widely used in art market analysis [10,11], because it can take into account all sold lots. An example of an index built based on hedonic regression is the German Art All 2-step hedonic index [12].

Linked Data. The concept of enriching data with semantic information is not an entirely new idea. Due to its wide range of possible applications, data enrichment has been used for different subjects. SPARQL language [13] gained popularity and has become a wide-recognised tool for extracting information from Linked Open Data (abbreviated as LOD) sources. Paulheim et al. investigate a more general approach for adding background knowledge in the data mining field [14]. They outline linking as the first step in combining original information with ancillary data sources. Basing on a tool presented in their paper, various types of linking may be enlisted: pattern-based linking, label-based linking, lookup linking, or SameAs linking. This framework is applicable to any dataset, so it can be used in the art market as well.

Computer Vision and Art. Being a part of Machine Learning (hereafter ML) domain, Computer Vision is a field of computer science for acquiring, processing, analysing, and understanding images. Recently, an intense effort is observed in the development of deep and convolutional neural networks (CNN). These Machine Learning concepts have been used in the art market domain, too. For example, CNN was used for large scale image recognition [15] to extract features connected to paintings' style. This work has even got commercialised as the DeepArt project[1]. In other research, paintings were analysed in terms of creativity, which was defined by two criteria: originality and influence [16].

---

[1] http://deepart.io.

3   Research Method

The methodology behind the research follows the principles of Design Science. As the method itself operates at the intersection of Quantitative Economics and Computer Science, the special guidelines for Information Systems [17] apply as well. The applied methodology consist of five phases: *Awareness of Problem, Suggestion, Development, Evaluation,* and *Conclusion.* After a broad analysis of the art market research literature review [18], the problem was formulated in Sect. 1. It was extended to a form of research questions (also Sect. 1). Suggestions to tackle this problem and answer research questions were formulated in Sect. 4. The current state of this ongoing research is described in Sect. 5. Some evaluation tools, such as completeness regarding the quality of the data were suggested in Sect. 4.

Design Science Research Guidelines are followed as presented below. An artifact in the form of a method will be produced in described research (*Design as an Artifact*). Research problem was justified in Sect. 1 (*Problem Relevance*). To test the quality and utility of the artifact, Controlled Experiment has been chosen as an evaluation method (*Design Evaluation*). To the best of our knowledge, this is the very first artifact devoted to the quality of art market data (*Research Contributions*). To ensure that the research process will yield the best results, (*Research Rigor*) is enforced and the most of this paper is devoted to describe it. *Design as a Search Process* will be followed especially when it comes to choose the best ML method based on its accuracy. Finally, results obtained thanks to the artifact will be understandable to any audience, since it can be depicted on a chart as an index (*Communication of Research*).

4   Artifact Description

This section is to give an outline of the proposed method. The proposed method consists of four stages (Fig. 1). The first one is Data Acquisition. After that, some cleansing is necessary, so the next stage is Data Refinement. The following stage is Data Enrichment, which consists of two sub-stages: the first one is related to LOD and the second one to ML methods. The final stage is Data Fusion.

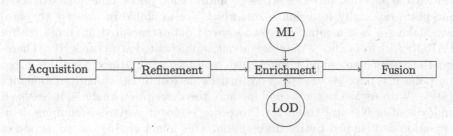

Fig. 1. The four stages of the proposed method

Data Acquisition. This stage addresses the research question Q1: *What are the primary sources of the Polish art market data? How to collect and organise these data?* Bidding results are often presented by auction houses online. Although the art market connotes mostly Christie's and Sotheby's duopoly, the research is devoted to Poland, where the market is still relatively unexplored. Therefore, four biggest Polish auction houses were taken into account: Desa Unicum, Rempex, Agra Art, Polswiss Art. To perform experiments, data have to be gathered on one's own. To overcome this problem, crawlers may be used. A crawler (sometimes called a spider) is a program written to systematically visit given Web pages and collect selected information. Popular examples of software or libraries supporting the data collection are Apache Nutch[2] or Scrapy[3].

Data Refinement. This stage addresses the research question Q1: *How to collect and organise these data?* Data refinement and cleansing is indispensable in order to obtain robust results. These actions consider re-formatting and structural transformation of data obtained in the previous step. Missing data, encoding problems or typos are common issues, to name a few. Some auction houses do not publish hammer prices directly on their pages – they are doing it in the form of PDF files. Therefore, the data extraction involves not only the crawling, but also the processing of PDF files. It may be done e.g. using software like Apache Tika[4]. For example, due to a human error, some observations have misspelled information about artists. This issue may be resolved by applying various fuzzy string matching algorithms. According to the so-called *garbage in, garbage out* principle, this step is crucial to assure the quality of the experiment's results.

Data Enrichment. This stage consists of two parts – the one related to Linked Open Data and the one to Machine Learning. The first sub-stage addresses the research questions Q2: *Can Linked Open Data datasets enrich art market data? Which data sources and methods have the best performance in such matters?* There are two ways of using LOD for enriching an art market dataset. Since a single considered observation contains information about a lot's author and (sometimes) its description, it can be analysed separately. DBpedia, tightly coupled with Wikipedia, provides access to information about numerous extracted concepts – especially from infoboxes, which are available in an easy to parse way. Making a vast amount of crowd-sourced data structured, it comes with a SPARQL API to facilitate querying about sophisticated structures [19]. Therefore, the artists' names and surnames can be linked with DBpedia entities. From that point it is possible to extract e.g. artist's date of birth or death, nationality or style. With regard to the second method, the description analysis, it needs an employment of Natural Language Processing, since it requires stemming, lemmatisation and Named Entity Recognition. This might enable the extraction of

---

[2] http://nutch.apache.org.
[3] http://scrapy.org.
[4] https://tika.apache.org.

single concepts from the description. The second sub-stage addresses the research questions Q3: *Can computer vision methods yield useful results in terms of art market analysis? Which one has the best performance in such matters?* This part is to analyse paintings' style and genre. By employing deep convolutional neural networks it is possible to classify images regarding these features. A classifier might be trained using WikiArt[5] data, a decent source of labeled artworks. This will enable to connect observations with their styles and features.

Data Fusion. This stage is to answer the research question Q4 (*How can we use and evaluate such an enriched dataset?*) It collects the results of all previous subsequent stages and examines them in terms of quality and usefulness. By quality we mean semantic validity, semantic accuracy and completeness. Semantically valid data have no syntax errors, syntactically accurate values and no malformed type literals. Semantic accuracy is connected to getting rid of outliers, inaccurate values and labels. Finally, a high completeness stands for a low ratio of missing data. With regard to usefulness, it may be proven by using the outcome of the proposed method for building a Polish art market index. A simple example of a linearised model is presented in the following equation:

$$\ln P_{it} = \alpha + \sum_{j=1}^{z} \beta_j X_{ij} + \sum_{t=0}^{\tau} \gamma_t D_{it} + \varepsilon_{it}, \tag{1}$$

where $\ln P_{it}$ represents the natural logarithm of a price of a given painting $i \in \{1, 2, ..., N\}$ at time $t \in \{1, 2, ..., \tau\}$; α, β and γ are regression coefficients for estimated characteristics. X_{ij} represents hedonic variables included in the model, whereas D_{it} stands for time dummy variables. Considered hedonic variables are, for example, the artist's name, the painting's size, year of creation and other related features describing a given painting. Indirect information, such as a time of death of the artists, may also be included. In some cases information can be missing, therefore this method is considered to be prone to the selection bias. Having a wide range of relevant data is one of the most important steps in the index calculation process. Therefore, this is the place where the approach discussed in the paper can be used for yielding more accurate indices. More complete data with extracted variables allows to build more sophisticated representation of a painting. Used in the Eq. (1), it results in more accurate coefficients representing various sales periods (γ_t). These coefficients are actually employed to construct indices:

$$Index_t = e^{\gamma_t} \tag{2}$$

5   Preliminary Results

This section summarises the results of the carried out research so far. Crawlers to collect the data from the biggest Polish auction houses were written using the

Table 1. Datasets characteristics from the crawled data

Auction house	Characteristics	Number
Desa Unicum	Observations	25837
	Unique authors	5691
Agra Art	Observations	23746
	Unique authors	2792
Polswiss Art	Observations	2599
	Unique authors	1584
Rempex	Observations	14758
	Unique authors	3846

Scrapy Python library. After performing some cleansing with OpenRefine, the data are ready for further research. Table 1 summarises the collected dataset.

Apache Spark [20] is the primary tool for doing research, since it has its interface in Python language and copes well with various Machine Learning algorithms. The usage of DBpedia and NLP were analysed in already published papers [21,22]. Birth and death dates, style and nationality are among the most commonly used hedonic variables in the art market domain. Therefore we examined artists in terms of the presence of four RDF properties: *dbpedia-owl:birthDate* for artists' birth dates, *dbpedia-owl:deathDate* for artists' death dates, *prop-pl:styl* for artists' styles, *prop-pl:narodowość* for artists' nationalities. The results of the analysis are presented in Table 2.

The detailed insight on the most popular nationalities and styles are presented in Tables 3 and 4. As it was expected, the Polish nationality dominated this ranking. Artists of Lemkos, Austrian, Lithuanian, and Jewish descent were also popular. A closer look at the results shows some inconsistency in Wikipedia/DBpedia conventions. For example – with regard to nationality – *polska*, *Polak*, *Polka* means the very same (Polish), as well as http://pl.dbpedia.org/resource/Polacy (an entity representing Poles as a nation) and http://pl.dbpedia.org/resource/Polska (an entity for Poland). Therefore, as a continuation and next step of this research it will be needed to tackle this issue by mitigating the problem of semantically similar entities and strings, with regard to grammatical and language-specific differences. This issue is a complex problem, since *Poland*, for instance, intuitively has an identical meaning as *Poles* in this context, whereas technically these words mean different things. Results on style are biased in the same way as the nationalities are. Plain strings appear to be mixed with DBpedia entities (*symbolizm* and the named entity *Symbolizm* as a symbolism). Another example of inconsistencies is related to the Realism entity representation in two ambiguous forms (*Realizm_(malarstwo)* and *Realizm*). Some initial work on using Machine Learning for processing has also been made already [23]. The Support Vector Machine as a supervised learning model yielded accurate results, but the research on this still needs to be investigated.

---

[5] http://www.wikiart.org.

Table 2. Changes in the dataset using data from DBpedia

Auction house	Attribute	Observations updated	Unique authors updated
Desa Unicum	Birth date	16.04 %	6.68 %
	Death date	13.76 %	4.87 %
	Style	7.52 %	1.02 %
	Nationality	11.03 %	0.44 %
Agra Art	Birth date	30.54 %	10.85 %
	Death date	27.34 %	8.24 %
	Style	16.04 %	1.76 %
	Nationality	25.12 %	0.93 %
Polswiss Art	Birth date	10.39 %	5.24 %
	Death date	8.58 %	4.04 %
	Style	5.54 %	1.77 %
	Nationality	7.46 %	0.44 %
Rempex	Birth date	30.94 %	9.20 %
	Death date	27.61 %	7.38 %
	Style	18.39 %	1.53 %
	Nationality	19.77 %	0.78 %
(all)	Birth date	24.25 %	4.49 %
	Death date	21.43 %	3.22 %
	Style	12.86 %	0.59 %
	Nationality	17.81 %	0.31 %

Table 3. Most popular nationalities found using DBpedia in the whole dataset

	Nationality	Count
1	Polska	5032
2	http://pl.dbpedia.org/resource/Polacy	5028
3	Polak	715
4	http://pl.dbpedia.org/resource/Łemkowie	243
5	Polka	185
6	http://pl.dbpedia.org/resource/Polska	167
7	Polska	95
8	Austriacka	81
9	Litewska	64
10	http://pl.dbpedia.org/resource/Żydzi	52

So far, both LOD- and ML-based methods for enriching art market data seem promising. DBpedia seems to be quite a rich data source, since it can update even up to 30 % of observations in one of the analysed auction houses. Seeking other

Table 4. Most popular styles found using DBpedia in the whole dataset

	Style	Count
1	http://pl.dbpedia.org/resource/Realizm_(malarstwo)	1429
2	http://pl.dbpedia.org/resource/Impresjonizm	1008
3	http://pl.dbpedia.org/resource/Symbolizm	704
4	http://pl.dbpedia.org/resource/Modernizm_(sztuka)	581
5	Symbolizm	504
6	http://pl.dbpedia.org/resource/Ekspresjonizm_(sztuka)	448
7	http://pl.dbpedia.org/resource/Realizm	301
8	http://pl.dbpedia.org/resource/Sztuka_konceptualna	250
9	Koloryzm	244
10	http://pl.dbpedia.org/resource/Prymitywizm_(malarstwo)	243

data sources and training robust models for image processing seem to be the next stages of this ongoing research. To conclude, the preliminary results show that the research hypothesis will be proved and the posed research question will be anwered.

6   Summary and Future Work

This article has presented an outline of the method for enriching art market data using Linked Open Data and Machine Learning. Experiments carried out so far indicates that the method is promising and can be examined and validated in further research.

Having annotated descriptions of artists and artworks, it is possible to conduct further research. The next stage considers a comparison of Machine Learning algorithms to select the one which will be used as the image classifier. After that, Data Fusion stage might be performed. A complementary, detailed and semantically enriched *catalogue raisonné* obtained in the previously mentioned process could be a valuable source of information for performing art market analysis itself. In addition, well-structured data may pave the way towards the usage of methods from a graph theory or topic labelling.

References

1. Plattner, S.: A most ingenious paradox: the market for contemporary fine art. Am. Anthropolog. **100**(2), 482–493 (1998)
2. Zaveri, A., Rula, A., Maurino, A., Pietrobon, R., Lehmann, J., Auer, S.: Quality assessment for linked data: a survey. Semant. Web **7**(1), 63–93 (2015)

3. Wand, Y., Wang, R.Y.: Anchoring data quality dimensions in ontological foundations. Commun. ACM **39**(11), 86–95 (1996)
4. Pipino, L.L., Lee, Y.W., Wang, R.Y.: Data quality assessment. Commun. ACM **45**(4), 211–218 (2002)
5. Borowski, K., Kosmala, W.: The contemporary art market in Poland - paintings. J. Manag. Financ. Sci. **17**(15), 63–80 (2014)
6. Witkowska, D., Kompa, K.: Constructing hedonic art price indexes for the Polish painting market using direct and indirect approaches. AESTIMO, The IEB Int. J. Financ. **10**, 2–25 (2015)
7. Witkowska, D., Lucińska, A.: Hedoniczny indeks cen obrazów sprzedanych na polskim rynku aukcyjnym w latach 2007–2013. Zeszyty Naukowe Uniwersytetu Szczecińskiego. Finanse. Rynki finansowe. Ubezpieczenia (75 Rynek kapitałowy: skuteczne inwestowanie), pp. 515–527 (2015)
8. Ginsburgh, V., Mei, J., Moses, M.: The computation of prices indices. In: Handbook of the Economics of Art and Culture, vol. 1. pp. 947–979. Elsevier (2006)
9. Mei, J., Moses, M.: Art as an Investment and the Underperformance of Masterpieces (2002)
10. Renneboog, L., Spaenjers, C.: Buying beauty: on prices and returns in the art market. Manag. Sci., 1–33, April 2012
11. Locatelli-Biey, M., Zanola, R.: The sculpture market: an adjacent year regression index. J. Cult. Econ. **26**, 65–78 (2002)
12. Kräussl, R., Wiehenkamp, C.: A call on art investments. Rev. Deriv. Res. **15**(1), 1–23 (2011)
13. Hartig, O., Bizer, C., Freytag, J.-C.: Executing SPARQL queries over the web of linked data. In: Bernstein, A., Karger, D.R., Heath, T., Feigenbaum, L., Maynard, D., Motta, E., Thirunarayan, K. (eds.) ISWC 2009. LNCS, vol. 5823, pp. 293–309. Springer, Heidelberg (2009). doi:10.1007/978-3-642-04930-9_19
14. Paulheim, H., Ristoski, P., Mitichkin, E., Bizer, C.: Data mining with background knowledge from the web (2014)
15. Simonyan, K., Zisserman, A.: Very deep convolutional networks for large-scale image recognition. CoRR abs/1409.1556 (2014)
16. Elgammal, A.M., Saleh, B.: Quantifying creativity in art networks. CoRR abs/1506.00711 (2015)
17. Hevner, A.R., March, S.T., Park, J., Ram, S.: Design science in information systems research. MIS Q. **28**(1), 75–105 (2004)
18. Filipiak, D., Filipowska, A.: Towards data-oriented analysis of the art market. Financ. Internet Q. **12**(1), 21–31 (2016)
19. Lehmann, J., Isele, R., Jakob, M., Jentzsch, A., Kontokostas, D., Mendes, P.N., Hellmann, S., Morsey, M., van Kleef, P., Auer, S., Bizer, C.: DBpedia - a large-scale, multilingual knowledge base extracted from wikipedia. Semant. Web J. **6**, 167–195 (2014)
20. Zaharia, M., Chowdhury, M., Franklin, M.J., Shenker, S., Stoica, I.: Spark: cluster computing with working sets. In: Proceedings of the 2nd USENIX Conference on Hot Topics in Cloud Computing, HotCloud 2010, p. 10. USENIX Association, Berkeley (2010)
21. Filipiak, D., Filipowska, A.: DBpedia in the art market. In: Abramowicz, W. (ed.) BIS 2015. LNBIP, vol. 228, pp. 321–331. Springer, Heidelberg (2015). doi:10.1007/978-3-319-26762-3_28

22. Filipiak, D., Węcel, K., Filipowska, A.: Semantic annotation to support description of the art market. In: 11th International Conference on Semantic Systems, SEMANTiCS 2015, vol. 1481, pp. 51–54. CEUR-WS (2015)
23. Filipiak, D., Agt-Rickauer, H., Hentschel, C., Filipowska, A., Sack, H.: Quantitative analysis of art market using ontologies, named entity recognition and machine learning: a case study. In: Abramowicz, W., Alt, R., Franczyk, B. (eds.) BIS 2016. LNBIP, vol. 255, pp. 79–90. Springer, Heidelberg (2016). doi:10.1007/978-3-319-39426-8_7

Author Index

Aleithe, Michael   323, 332
Alt, Rainer   252, 340

Babič, František   85
Bogner, Justus   289
Borchardt, Ulrike   123
Bos, Rik   273
Brehm, Lars   311
Bresfelean, Vasile Paul   44
Bumberger, Jan   332, 347

Cirqueira, Douglas   245
Connors, Colin   183

Di Pietro, Laura   299
Dietrich, Peter   332, 347
Dovydaitis, Laurynas   79

Eckert, Sebastian   399
Ehmke, Jan Fabian   399
Engel, Christoph   347

Felbermayr, Armin   233
Fellmann, Michael   23
Filipiak, Dominik   418
Filipowska, Agata   158, 418
Filzmoser, Peter   57
Franczyk, Bogdan   332

Giannakos, Michail N.   209
Goblirsch, Tobias   332
Grad-Gyenge, László   57
Gutschmidt, Anne   123

Hacker, Janine Viol   171
Hegerl, Ulrich   323
Hrach, Christian   408

Ivanova, Galina   323, 347

Jacob Jr., Antonio   221, 245
Jessen, Finn   252
Jugel, Dierk   99, 289

Keller, Barbara   299
Kelley, Trevor   171

Kiebusch, Sebastian   3
Kiess, Wieland   340, 347
Kirsten, Toralf   340, 347
Klein, Barbara   311
Krebs, Irene   13
Krebs, Thorsten   148
Kriksciuniene, Dalia   36
Krogstie, John   209
Kröckel, Pavlina   357

Lantow, Birger   23
Lekakos, George   209
Lewańska, Elżbieta   389
Linn, Christian   196
Lobato, Fábio   221, 245
Loeffler, Markus   347
Lopata, Audrius   69

Macelaru, Mara Hajdu   44
Magyar, Róbert   85
Mikalef, Patrick   209
Mocean, Loredana   44
Möhring, Michael   289, 299

Oroszi, Andreas   148

Pappas, Ilias O.   209
Paralič, Ján   85
Patalas-Maliszewska, Justyna   13
Piazza, Alexander   171
Pinheiro, Márcia   221, 245

Rasymas, Tomas   79
Reichert, Stefan   260
Reinhold, Olaf   221, 252, 340
Rudžionis, Vytautas   79

Sakalauskas, Virgilijus   36
Salbach, Christoph   332
Saltz, Jeffrey   183
Sandkuhl, Kurt   23, 99, 123, 289
Santana, Ádamo   221
Schima, Robert   332

Schmidt, Rainer   289, 299
Shamshurin, Ivan   183
Shilov, Nikolay   148
Sinko, Mario   148
Smirnov, Alexander   148
Spangenberg, Norman   379
Stróżyna, Milena   367
Strüker, Jens   260
Stüber, Richard   252

Toni, Martina   299

Vaknin, Michael   158
van de Wetering, Rogier   111, 273
Veitaite, Ilona   69

Werth, Dirk   196
Wittwer, Matthias   252, 340

Zemaityte, Neringa   69
Zikra, Iyad   136
Zimmermann, Alfred   99, 289

Printed in the United States
by Bookmasters

Printed in the United States
By Bookmasters